To the Best
in Zion.
Love
Ben & May
June 15, 1991

APPROACHING
ZION

The Collected Works of Hugh Nibley

Volumes published to date:

Old Testament and Related Studies
Enoch the Prophet
The World and the Prophets
Mormonism and Early Christianity
Lehi in the Deseret/The World of the Jaredites/There Were Jaredites
An Approach to the Book of Mormon
Since Cumorah
The Prophetic Book of Mormon
Approaching Zion

The Collected Works of Hugh Nibley: Volume 9
Education, Politics, and Society

APPROACHING ZION

Hugh Nibley

Edited by
Don E. Norton

Deseret Book Company
Salt Lake City, Utah
and
Foundation for Ancient Research and Mormon Studies
Provo, Utah

Library of Congress Cataloging-in-Publication Data

Nibley, Hugh, 1910–
    Approaching Zion / by Hugh Nibley ; edited by Don E. Norton.
      p. cm. — (The Collected works of Hugh Nibley ; v. 9)
    Includes bibliographical references.
    ISBN 0-87579-252-9
    1. Church of Jesus Christ of Latter-day Saints—Doctrines.
2. Mormon Church—Doctrines. 3. Church and social problems—
Mormon Church. I. Norton, Don E. II. Title. III. Series: Nibley,
Hugh, 1910–   Works. 1986 ; v. 9.
BX8637.N5 1989
230'.9332—dc20   89-33824
                                                      CIP

Printed in the United States of America

10   9   8   7   6   5   4

Contents

Key to Abbreviations

CWHN   *Collected Works of Hugh Nibley*

HC   Joseph Smith, *History of The Church of Jesus Christ of Latter-day Saints*, 2nd ed. rev., edited by B. H. Roberts (Salt Lake City: The Church of Jesus Christ of Latter-day Saints, 1932-51)

JD   *Journal of Discourses*, 26 vols. (London: Latter-day Saints' Book Depot, 1854-86)

PG   J.-P. Migne, *Patrologiae Cursus Compleus . . . Series Graeca*, 161 vols. (Paris: Migne, 1847–1866).

TPJS   Joseph Smith, *Teachings of the Prophet Joseph Smith*, selected by Joseph Fielding Smith (Salt Lake City: Deseret Book Company, 1938)

WJS   Joseph Smith, *The Words of Joseph Smith*, compiled and edited by Andrew F. Ehat and Lyndon W. Cook (Provo, Utah: Brigham Young University Religious Studies Center, 1980)

WPQ   *Western Political Quarterly*

Foreword

Many essays in this volume will be new to readers; most have not been published, except through the Foundation for Ancient Research and Mormon Studies (F.A.R.M.S.), and all have been written since 1971. Brother Nibley explains:

> All my life I have shied away from these disturbing and highly unpopular — even offensive — themes [the uses of money]. But I cannot do so any longer, because in my old age I have taken to reading the scriptures and there have had it forced upon my reluctant attention, that from the time of Adam to the present day, Zion has been pitted against Babylon, and the name of the game has always been money — "power and gain" (see below, page 58).

Perhaps no one in our dispensation dwelt so pointedly on this theme as Joseph Smith and Brigham Young, whom Brother Nibley cites liberally. Heber C. Kimball, Mosiah Hancock, John Taylor, Wilford Woodruff, Lorenzo Snow, Joseph F. Smith, and others had the same vision of impending doom brought about by the Saints' succumbing to Satan's materialistic ploys (Brigham Young aptly calls them "decoys").

In counseling the Saints on how to resist covetousness, President Young used, in his words, a "most plain and homely" analogy: just "keep your dish right side up." The Saints should not be "in a hurry" to obtain wealth, he cautioned; they should entertain no preoccupations with acquiring the goods of this world. Rather they should attend to their prayers, ask for forgiveness before the Lord, and seek the Lord's protection from temptation; "Guide your steps aright, that you may do something" (*JD* 15:36-37). Don't *you* try to fill your own dish; to attempt to do so is to partake of the spirit of Babylon. If the Lord wishes an individual to have more than a sufficiency for basic needs, he will so provide: "And having food and raiment let us be therewith content" (1 Timothy 6:8); the sole justification for "seeking" any surplus is to bless the poor, whose presence among us is, as it were, a test of our commitment.

In that same spirit of plainness, Brother Nibley stands on its head one of the maxims of many Saints and some politicians of our day: "There's no such thing as a free lunch." "It's pretty much all a free lunch," Nibley counters (at least "the price [of lunches] varies"). Board and room are free on this earth; everything is a gift of God, which we can obtain by preparing ourselves through constant repentance. It is Satan who exacts a price: "Sin pays its servants; the wage is death. God's gift to man is eternal life" (Romans 6:23).

Thus this volume will certainly be among the most controversial of Hugh Nibley's *Collected Works*, troubling to Latter-day Saints who think to accumulate and enjoy Satan's salient icon in this world—money. Many readers of Nibley have confessed that reading one or two of Nibley's Zion essays is stimulating. Reading and rereading all these essays is thoroughly sobering, based, as they are, in Nibley fashion, on ample reference to the scriptures and the best thinking of all ages. Job's words perhaps apply: "For God speaketh once, yea twice, yet man perceiveth it not" (Job 33:14). Study of these many essays produces an arresting cumulative impression: in no place do the scriptures, including the voices of our modern prophets, assent to the goal of amassing the goods of this earth. Such a course is to yield to Satan's Golden Question: "Do you have any money?"

Nibley's comments are not to be misconstrued as a call to reinstitute formally the law of consecration. Nibley explains that it does remain the privilege of individuals to live the law in their personal lives, as they so covenant regularly in the temple — to seek first the kingdom of God, and to share freely one's various resources with those who may have less. In time the law will be reinstituted; in the meantime, Nibley sets forth lucidly the principles that enable us to live that law in face of the feeble realities of the present. The ideal is before us, and nothing prevents us as individuals from living that law, thus enjoying its blessings and preparing ourselves for its renewal.

A parallel exists in the Word of Wisdom. The Saints realize that its principles extend far beyond abstinence from tea, coffee, liquor, and tobacco, yet it has taken many of the Saints years to appreciate the ramifications of even the basics of this inspired health code; and the education is not yet complete. How much more there is to be learned in the principles of consecration!

This volume, perhaps more than others, also reflects Nibley's characteristic style of thinking and writing. Many of the essays have a highly informal flavor, being carefully edited transcriptions of Nibley's rapid-fire, often extemporaneous remarks from notecards. And Nibley's mind is constantly at work, even in the midst of formal discourse, working and reworking ideas and resource materials, ever discovering and making new connections and drawing new inferences.

Thus the same scriptures, themes, anecdotes, arguments, and quotations frequently recur in different contexts in these essays. For example, the essays "Gifts" and "Deny Not the Gifts" contain some of the same material, though the introductions are quite different.

The editors even wondered whether all these texts warranted publication, for a few are discursive and unpolished in other ways. We decided to go ahead. Together, these essays and transcripts offer a vivid impression of the man Nibley and his most deeply felt concerns. Regular readers of Nibley will welcome them all.

Nibley also does a good deal of paraphrasing and individual translating of scriptures and foreign-language texts. The retention of his words creates a degree of coherence and individuality that, again, reflect his style of work.

In the spirit of all the prophets, Brother Nibley yearns for Zion; and his broad historical perspective enables him to define with precision why the people of the covenant, and other Utopians as well, have achieved, or failed to achieve, this goal. The scriptures speak of Zion. Joseph Smith received the principles and essential elements of the Zion order. Brigham Young and others preached them. On this theme, Nibley's voice is one of the most outspoken of our century.

Some may resist Nibley's views, considering them unjustifiably extreme, for he uncompromisingly exposes the foibles of modern society. He leaves nowhere to hide. In this regard, however, his message is basically the same as that of President Ezra Taft Benson's April 1989 Conference talk on pride, "the universal sin, the great vice." Both men define the problem of pride very broadly—it manifests itself in competition, selfishness, contention, power-seeking, backbiting, living beyond our means, coveting, climbing the ladder of worldly success at the expense of others, and in a multitude of ways that "pit our will against God's" and limit our progression. As President Benson warns, "Pride affects all of us at various times and in various degrees. . . . Pride is *the* stumbling block to Zion." This, too, is essentially Nibley's cry in *Approaching Zion*.

Hugh Nibley is more than an idealist; he practices what he preaches. His life is profound precisely because of its simple, clearsighted, often childlike vision of the priorities and stewardships of the kingdom.

So his remarks are certified by a life of careful scholarship and personal application of the principles he hopes to see in place among the Saints. Missing this point, some may question his credentials to talk on such subjects as "management" (the label universities attach to business programs nowadays). An economics professor recently asked, "If Nibley knows so much about management, then why isn't he rich?"

The essays in this volume are, with some exceptions (the two "work" essays and the two "gifts" essays), arranged chronologically, reflecting the pattern of Hugh Nibley's thinking and speaking in the past two decades, and the increasing urgency of his message.

The first article, "Our Glory or Our Condemnation" (1971), is a literalistic interpretation of the Tenth Article of Faith — which is in essence a charge to maintain the earth in as paradisiacal state as possible, and to prepare to receive the beauty and joy of Zion, when that order returns to the earth. We are not to convert the resources of our planet into cold cash, which is the driving force of Babylon.

"What Is Zion? A Distant View" (1973) is an extended definition of the Zion order, in contrast to Babylon, the order of the world. Many of the contrasts are from the contemporary scene, in which the Saints awkwardly try to straddle both orders.

One of Nibley's best-known sermons on saintly priorities is "Zeal without Knowledge" (1975). As he delivered this stinging indictment of the Saints' topsy-turvy value systems, the air in the Varsity Theater (in the Wilkinson Center on BYU campus) was electric: no one had ever said so plainly what so many present had been suspecting. "Amens" were sometimes audible. The lecture takes its title from Joseph Smith's admonition to the Saints to match their enthusiasm with intelligence. Nibley is especially dis-

tressed by presumptions (notably at BYU) that latter-day
revelations excuse us from the joyous and hard mental
work of figuring out life and building up the kingdom.

In "Gifts" (1979), Nibley argues from King Benjamin's
premise that "we are all beggars equally—100 percent is
as far as you can go." The necessities of life come as gifts
from God; by definition they cannot be earned, despite the
Saints' dogged insistence on earning their worldly keep,
and thus contradicting Moroni's final and passionate plea,
"Deny not the gifts of the Spirit."

Both "Gifts" and "Deny Not the Gifts" (1982) take issue
with the commonly held belief that "this is mine because
I earned it." "We never *should* ask the Lord whether or
not we should commit adultery, theft, murder, or fraud.
Likewise we should never ask, 'Should I seek after
riches?'" because God furnishes us all room and board on
this planet free (even eternal life is a gift of God). We can
but accept the gifts (by definition a gift cannot be earned)
and share them; and they are available but for the asking.
On this point "the Book of Mormon is fiercely emphatic; . . . no one should ever set his heart on riches." It
is Satan who exacts a price, who turns the earth's bounty
into commodities, which his disciples in turn convert into
power and ruin.

In "How Firm a Foundation! What Makes It So?" (1979),
Nibley summarizes the "secure" foundation laid by Joseph
Smith—an "arresting, original, satisfying" scenario: a
prodigality of gifts, a gospel that is not culturally conditioned, the ideas of revelation and restoration, charismatic
gifts, priesthood and authority, the ordinances, the temple
rituals, a third-dimensional gospel, individual testimony,
and the gift of prophecy. Superseding all these gifts is the
concept of Zion—the law of consecration.

In the book of Deuteronomy lies the key to "success"
in this world—"How to Get Rich" (1982). The spirit of the

law, as given to ancient Israel, as well as many of its practices, are still binding today.

Two of Nibley's speeches have particularly stirred discussion: "Work We Must, but the Lunch Is Free" (1982) and the logical sequel, "But What Kind of Work?" (1987). When many of his audience and readers for years pressed him to explain what kind of "work" he was talking about (they had difficulty conceiving of work that did not produce material benefit), he simply rehearsed what Brigham Young had so often exhorted: repent, forgive, say your prayers, study the word of God, and in general do the work of the kingdom.

Both lectures were delivered to the Cannon-Hinckley Club in Salt Lake City. The first article begins with a review of some of the latest suspicions by leading scientists that "somebody out there cares—in other words, that there is direction and purpose to what is going on" in the universe; and "that gifts sent down from above are more than childish tradition." God liberally furnishes board and room to his children; it is Satan who charges a fee.

The principle of Israel's manna holds today as firmly as it did in Moses' day: the manna was free, and it could not be accumulated or marketed. Particularly reprehensible in Nibley's view is the common practice of some employers who, in the spirit of the perverse "work ethic," withhold from laborers the necessities of life in exchange for services—"life in exchange for profits." "To make merchandise of another's necessity is an offense to human dignity." "The prevailing evil of the age" is "that men withhold God's gifts from each other in a power game."

There is a work to do, which is largely the work of the mind, and it is spelled out in the ordinances of the temple, where, if one but looks, one can find "practically nothing else but things to do."

Why are we so often decoyed? Nibley replies, "We know what Zion is, we know what Babylon is, we know that the two can never mix, and we know that Latter-day Saints, against the admonition of their leaders, have always tried to mix them. How is that done? By the use of rhetoric—"The art of making true things seem false and false things seem true by the use of words." The trick is to appear rich as the result of being good—to cultivate the virtue of respectability. The "worst sinners, according to Jesus, are . . . the religious leaders with their insistence on proper dress and grooming, their careful observance of all the rules, their precious concern for status symbols, their strict legality, their pious patriotism." Their philosophy is the survival of the fittest: "the lunch-grab as the supreme law of life and progress" versus the scriptural principle that "there is enough and to spare."

The funeral address for Donald Decker (1982) is a unique piece—a discursive sermon in which Nibley describes the Zion attributes of a model mind and pure heart, which he found in a good friend with whom he spent many stimulating hours. There are exceptional people who go a long way toward living the ideals of Zion.

"Three Degrees of Righteousness in the Old Testament" (1982) discusses three economic orders: heaven (the celestial), Eden (terrestrial), and Babylon, the world (telestial).

Then follows, in "We Will Still Weep for Zion" (1984), a historical overview of the rejection of the Zion society in the last dispensation, from its first mention by Joseph Smith in 1831 to Spencer W. Kimball's firm warnings in our present day.

The lecture entitled "Breakthroughs I Would Like to See" (1985) addresses the modern addiction to the "cult of change," the notion that change equals progress. The only change worthy of pursuit is repentance.

Nibley's most complete overview of the Zion society is "The Law of Consecration" (1986)—the lecture's tone is urgent and the commentary candid. It is a historical sum-

mary of the Lord's attempts to institute the law of consecration, and of man's attempts (including attempts by
some Church leaders) to delay or divert us temporarily
from that ideal day. The contrasts between the contemporary scene and the scriptural idea are starkly drawn.

In an excellent historical overview of the notion of Uto-
pianism (1986), Nibley addresses "the great question with
which all utopians deal . . . : Can the mere convenience
that makes money such a useful device continue to outweigh the horrendous and growing burden of evil that it
imposes on the human race and that ultimately brings its
dependents to ruin?" The lesson of 4 Nephi suggests that
it cannot; only the law of consecration will do away with
"money and private property," which are the "insuperable
obstacles to the achievement of utopia."

Nibley was disappointed with the reception of his remarks on "Goods of the First and Second Intent" (1987)
at the Retired Teachers Association. While he speculated
on the probable causes of today's classroom crises, the
seasoned educators "mostly dozed," he commented. The
address in fact sets forth a fundamental premise of his life's
work: We should set our hearts and minds on those things
that are good for their own sake, goods that are "good and
everlasting in themselves," things that satisfy the "hunger
of the mind." "Goods of the second intent" are those that
lead to goods of the first intent; hence they are of secondary
import, "good for the sake of getting something else." Our
contemporary society has reversed the priorities: "I think,
therefore I am" has become "I shop, therefore I am." "It
is not the economic man at all that keeps the culture going,
but his questions about his position in this life as well as
the next." The tragedy is that most universities now concern themselves largely with enabling students to achieve
practical success through a cult of careerism.

"The Meaning of the Atonement" (1988) will likely
become one of the great sermons of our day on the atone-

ment. "There is not a word among those translated as 'atonement' that does not plainly dictate the return to a former state or condition; one rejoins the family, returns to the father, becomes united, reconciled, embracing and sitting down with others after a sad separation." The Book of Mormon is full of such imagery, and hence is, to a greater extent than many have supposed, full of temple imagery. Becoming one with the Father means receiving the homecoming embrace, for the scriptural terms for *atonement* all imply such a literal reunion. By contrast, Satan would embrace us with worldly things, and hence gain power over us.

Literally thousands of hours have gone into the production of this volume: checking and double-checking references, typing, editing, consulting, confirming all sorts of details, and proof-reading. Contributors included Glen Cooper, James Fleugel, John Gee, Fran Clark Hafen, Daniel McKinlay, Brent McNeely, Phyllis Nibley, Georgia Norton, Shirley Ricks, Stephen Ricks, Matthew Roper, James Tredway, and John Welch; and of course the staff at Deseret Book. Not only their work, but their enthusiasm, have brought this volume about.

The title — *Approaching Zion* — is Hugh Nibley's own. He explains, "It captures the theme and suggests movement toward that all-important goal, Zion."

DON NORTON
EDITOR

1

Our Glory or Our Condemnation

If I thought this really was my last lecture, it would be to an empty hall. Because it would be at least ten hours long and I would be the only auditor, inured to boredom by a lifelong habit of talking to myself. The subject would certainly be the Tenth Article of Faith. That is why the lecture would have to be so long, because Article Ten has at least five distinct parts, and this talk will be only a brief outline of one of them.

If there's anything that sets the gospel of Jesus Christ apart from all other religions of the world (and this could be demonstrated in detail), it's the literal, matter-of-fact view it takes of realities in this life and beyond this life, the view resting on the experience of very real and vivid contacts between men upon the earth and beings from higher spheres. This sense of literal reality is most clearly set forth in our Tenth Article of Faith. The other articles have to do with our beliefs, principles, ordinances, and divine gifts: they are timeless in their application and could belong to any dispensation. But Article Ten deals explicitly with our time and our space and sets forth the steps by which God intends to consummate this great latter-day work.

There are five such steps: (1) the literal gathering of

This talk was given October 6, 1971, as part of the Last Lecture Series, and it was published in ASBYU Academics Office Presents: Last Lecture Series, 1971-72 *(Provo, UT: Brigham Young University, 1972), 1-14.*

Israel (note the word *literal*); (2) the restoration of the Ten Tribes; (3) the building of Zion (the New Jerusalem) upon the American continent (is that specific enough?); (4) Christ's personal reign upon the earth (not spiritual, in some undefined realm); and (5) the renewal of the earth in its paradisiacal glory. In each of these steps earthly time and place are implicit. The statement does not pinpoint either, but it leaves no doubt at all that things are going to happen in a definite temporal order and involve people living in definite places on this particular planet.

The Latter-day Saints have often become confused about the "game plan" of unfolding processes in these latter days by giving undue priority to one event over another or by arbitrarily shifting the order of events to suit some preconceived plans of their own. But one thing is clear: the Lord has given us here an outline of the whole plan as far as it concerns us.

It behooves us, therefore, to keep the whole plan in mind and, as in all great projects, never to lose sight of the ultimate goal while we are working toward the necessary intermediate goals or steps. Here the final step in the whole progression is that the earth will be renewed and receive its paradisiacal glory. Quite literally, "heaven is our destination." This idea is clearly brought forward in our new home evening manual with its theme "A Bit of Heaven." That is more than a sentimental Irish tag (though we in the Church today do seem to have an incurable appetite for trite and sentimental "kitsch"); it is an invitation actually to model our domestic life on the celestial order, as God commanded the Saints to do from the first: "And Zion cannot be built up unless it is by the principles of the law of the celestial kingdom; otherwise I cannot receive her unto myself" (D&C 105:5).

A bit of heaven? What is heaven like? What will Zion be like? We Mormons do not believe with Descartes that God is the self-thinking thinker who thinks only of thought.[1] We think of the mind as reacting to other minds and to its own physical surroundings. We think of its operations as affecting others and also affecting those surroundings. The spirit of man, as it were, projects itself into the surrounding world and leaves its mark. We believe that heaven is not only a state of mind but an actual environment. Brother and Sister DeHoyos have written about a "celestial culture."[2] There is most certainly a "celestial environment."

Every way of life produces its own environment and in turn is influenced by that environment. It is possible for a powerful mind to have joy amidst vile surroundings, but it can have greater joy in pleasant surroundings. There are degrees of joy, and God wants our joy to be full, that is, with every possible factor contributing. Milton's Satan declares when he is cast out of heaven, "The mind is its own place, and in itself can make a heaven of hell, a hell of heaven."[3] But that same Satan misses his heavenly home, and when he sees the glories of God's earth, he covets them, lusts after them, and yearns to possess them. The story of the Garden of Eden teaches us that environment is important. It was not a matter of indifference to Adam whether he was inside the Garden or outside, whether he was living in a world most glorious and beautiful or in a dark and dreary world. And our Article Ten assures us that God intends that the paradisiacal conditions of Eden shall be restored again to this earth. Again we repeat: "the earth will be renewed and receive its paradisiacal glory."

What, then, is heaven like? Paul tells us, "But as it is written, eye hath not seen, nor ear heard, neither have entered into the heart [that is, the imagination] of man, the things which God hath prepared for them that love him" (1 Corinthians 2:9). But paradise is its earthly counterpart, the nearest earthly approach to heaven. This state is going to be restored to earth, but in a series of steps. If it were brought all at once, right now, the "culture shock" would kill us. Indeed, we have been given the challenge, "Who may abide the day of his coming? and who shall stand when he appeareth?" (Malachi 3:2). Only those who have prepared for the new environmental change by adapting themselves to it though a rigorous course of training. First must come the "literal gathering of Israel" in which we are now engaged. Then the return of the Ten Tribes, which we hope is soon to come. Then the building up of the kingdom of God on earth preparatory to the establishment of Zion, Zion in turn preparing the earth to receive the Lord, after whose coming it will be possible to achieve the final state in which the earth is renewed and given its former glory. The midpoint and focus of the whole operation is Zion. Zion is the great moment of transition, the bridge between the world as it is and the world as God designed it and meant it to be.

We'd better say a few things about Zion here. *Zion* is a code word denoting a very real thing. Zion is any community in which the celestial order prevails. Zion is "the pure in heart" (D&C 97:21), but Zion is also a real city or any number of real cities. It is a constant; it is unchanging. There are Zions among all the worlds, and there are Zions that come and go.[4] Zion is a constant in time and place — it belongs to the order of the eternities. We're not making Zion here, but we're preparing the ground to receive it. As the Lord says, "My people must be tried in all things, that they may be prepared to receive the glory that I have for them, even the glory of Zion; and he that will not bear chastisement is not worthy of my kingdom" (D&C 136:31). We must be prepared to receive this glory; we don't produce it ourselves. We must be ready, so that we won't die of shock when we get it.

In every dispensation, we are told, there has been a Zion on the earth; first of all in the time of Adam, when "the Holy One of Zion . . . established the foundations of

Adam-ondi-Ahman" (D&C 78:15). After Adam, Enoch had his Zion when "the Lord called his people ZION" and Enoch "built a city that was called the City of Holiness, even ZION" (Moses 7:18-19). But then "it came to pass that Zion was not, for God received it up into his own bosom; and from thence went forth the saying, ZION IS FLED" (Moses 7:69).

Zion comes and goes. When the world cannot support Zion, Zion is not destroyed but taken back home. "And thou hast taken Zion to thine own bosom, from all thy creations," says Moses 7:31. And when the world is qualified to receive Zion, "there shall be mine abode, and it shall be Zion, which shall come forth out of all the creations which I have made" (Moses 7:64). Accordingly, the ancient prophets of Israel yearned for the time when Zion would be restored again. Jeremiah and Isaiah hoped to see Zion restored in their time. They certainly knew it would come in a later day. Typical of their attitude is the prophecy of the Psalmist: "My days are like a shadow that declineth; and I am withered like grass. But thou, O Lord, . . . shalt arise, and have mercy upon Zion: for the time to favour her, yea, the set time, is come. . . . When the Lord shall build up Zion, he shall appear in his glory." And then he adds, "This shall be written for the generation to come" (Psalm 102:11-18). After all the calamities, said Jeremiah, "there shall be a day, that the watchmen upon the mount Ephraim shall cry, Arise ye, and let us go up to Zion unto the Lord our God" (Jeremiah 31:6). And of course we all know the prophecy of Micah 4:1-2: "But in the last days . . . the mountain of the house of the Lord shall be established in the top of the mountains, and it shall be exalted above the hills; and people shall flow unto it. And many nations shall come. . . . For the law shall go forth of Zion, and the word of the Lord from Jerusalem." This was the hope of the prophets. It was also anticipated in the days of the ancient apostles that "ye are come unto mount Sion, and unto the city of the living God, the heavenly Jerusalem, and to an innumerable company of angels," as Paul describes the Church (Hebrews 12:22).

But it's in the last days that the fulfillment will really get underway with the restoration and the steps approaching the establishment of Zion. In every age, though, as the Doctrine and Covenants tells us, the saints are "they who are come unto Mount Zion, and unto the city of the living God, the heavenly place, the holiest of all, . . . the general assembly and church of Enoch, and of the First-born" (D&C 76:66-67). That is the eternal order of Zion, and the saints have been at work for many years, supposedly preparing to receive it.

What is this ideal Zion like? In the last days, we are told, it will be a place of refuge in a doomed world. "It shall be called the New Jerusalem, a land of peace, a city of refuge, a place of safety for the saints of the Most High God; . . . and the terror of the Lord also shall be there, . . . and it shall be called Zion" (D&C 45:66-67). At that time, "every man that will not take his sword against his neighbor must needs flee unto Zion for safety" (D&C 45:68). And the wicked shall say that Zion is terrible. Terrible because it is indestructible. Her invulnerability makes her an object of awe and terror. As Enoch said, "Surely Zion shall dwell in safety forever. But the Lord said unto Enoch: Zion have I blessed, but the residue of the people have I cursed" (Moses 7:20). So Zion was taken away and the rest destroyed. Zion itself is never in danger; on the contrary, it alone offers safety to the world, "that the gathering together upon the land of Zion, and upon her stakes, may be for a defense, and for a refuge from the storm, and from wrath when it shall be poured out without mixture upon the whole earth" (D&C 115:6). It would seem that Zion enjoys the complete security of a bit of the celestial world and that nothing can touch it as long as it retains the character. But celestial order it *must* be. As we have seen, Zion cannot be built up "unless it is by the principles of the law of the celestial kingdom" (D&C 105:5). It must at all times be holy enough to receive the Lord himself in person. "For the Lord hath chosen Zion; he hath desired it for his habitation" (Psalm 132:13); "Behold mine abode forever" (Moses 7:21). Zion is heaven. It is where God lives. A bit of heaven indeed.

The two words most commonly used to describe Zion are *beauty* and *joy,* and the same two words most often relate to heaven and paradise. Beauty comes first, for beauty is whatever gives joy. Now we approach the question of what Zion looks like: "The city of our God. . . . Beautiful for situation, the joy of the whole earth, is mount Zion. . . . Let mount Zion rejoice, let the daughters of Judah be glad. . . . Walk about Zion and go round about her" (Psalm 48:1-2, 11-12). An eminently delightful place. "Out of Zion, the perfection of beauty, God hath shined" (Psalm 50:2). "For Zion must increase in beauty, and in holiness; . . . Zion must arise and put on her beautiful garments" (D&C 82:14). "And blessed are they who shall seek to bring forth my Zion at that day; . . . and whoso shall publish peace, . . . how beautiful upon the mountains shall they be" (1 Nephi 13:37). These are more than figures of speech. As President Joseph F. Smith put it, "Things upon the earth, so far as they have not been perverted by wickedness, are typical of things in heaven. Heaven was the prototype of this beautiful creation when it came from the hand of the Creator, and was pronounced 'good.' "[5] There you have the environment of Zion; and for a foretaste of it, all we have to do is go to the canyons and look around us. For the earth comes from the hand of the Creator most glorious and beautiful, with great rivers, small streams, and mountains and hills to give variety and beauty to the scene, designed by God as a place of beauty and delight. That is the way we must keep it.

The order of Zion is such as will leave the earth as near

its primordial, paradisiacal condition as possible. The paradise of Eden is called in the scriptures "the garden of the Lord" (Genesis 13:10), and we are told that God and his holy angels delighted to come to it and commune with Adam in its delightful surroundings. This earth has been compared by many—most recently by a Latter-day Saint pharmacologist, Dr. A. B. Morrison—to "an exquisitely equipped spaceship."[6] It is enormously productive and contains an unlimited supply for all who come to live on it, as long as they use its bounty "with judgment, not to excess, neither by extortion," the Lord has said (D&C 59:20), that is, properly distributed, without waste or inequality. It contains "all things . . . made for the benefit and the use of man, both to please the eye and to gladden the heart; yea, for food and for raiment, for taste and for smell, to strengthen the body and to enliven the soul" (D&C 59:18-19). Notice here that the eye and the heart have priority over the stomach, that taste and smell have claims equal to appetite, that the enlivening of the soul is as important as the strengthening of the body. "And out of the ground made I, the Lord God, to grow every tree, naturally, that is pleasant to the sight of man; and man could behold it" (Moses 3:9). Here the value of trees as a crop is not even mentioned, and God plainly does not share the belief of another august personage that "once you've seen one redwood you've seen them all." "All the creations are His work," said Brigham Young, "and they are for His glory and for the benefit of the children of men; and all things are put into the possession of man for his comfort, improvement and consolation, and for his health, wealth, beauty and excellency."[7]

But if the earth is perfectly adapted and completely outfitted for all our physical and spiritual needs, what is there left for us to do? Won't it weaken our character to have everything handed to us ready and prepared for our use? That question, the most natural one in the world to ask in our society, shows how far removed we are from the celestial order of things. It's the same question that is asked by the small boy who comes to visit you for summer vacation: "If a guy can't break everything around the house and yard, drown kittens, shoot birds, cut down the apple tree, take the baby buggy apart, stick things in the piano, throw rocks at bottles, what can a guy do?" If we advise the little fellow to acquire more sophisticated tastes and follow our example, to seek his diversions more constructively as we do, watching westerns on TV, going hunting, playing golf, going to football games, attending X-rated movies, or driving a car, he can protest that such activities differ from his own only in being more passive and less imaginative, but really they are quite as trivial and immature and unproductive as his. We might then admonish him to hard work. Pope Gregory VII wrote a letter to the bishop of Rheims in the eleventh century in which he told how the barons of the time were literally destroying Europe in thousands of private wars and feuds and raids on each others' castles and lands and serfs, and how, when he protested what they were doing, they asked him in all seriousness, If we don't do this, what else is there for us to do? For what other purpose were gentlemen placed upon the earth? What else can a normal man possibly want to do? The activities of the modern world that go by the name of work may not have been as spectacularly destructive as those of the barons of the middle ages, yet we are beginning to find out now that they *are* destructive. And it is high time that we begin to ask ourselves, as we ask the little fellow who's spending the summer with us, whether what we are doing is really what we *ought* to be doing. There is full-time employment for all simply in exploring the world without destroying it, and by the time we begin to understand something of its marvelous richness and complexity, we'll also begin to see that it does have uses that we never suspected and that its main value is what comes to us directly from mere coexistence with living things—the impact on our minds and bodies, subtle and powerful, that goes far beyond the advantages of converting all things into cash or calories.

Now we all know that Adam could not stay in the Garden. He was expelled and told to get his living by the sweat of his brow. In return for hard physical labor, the earth would yield him of her abundance (Moses 4:23-25). It was a fair exchange—he was to put hard work into the soil, and in return the soil would sustain him. He was to live by work, though, not by plunder. I spent my mission among the fields of Europe, which had been under the plow for literally thousands of years and were still yielding their abundance. After my mission I visited a glorious redwood grove near Santa Cruz, California. Only there was no grove there; the two-thousand-year-old trees were all gone: not one of them was left standing. My own grandfather had converted them all into cash. It wasn't hard to do in those days. You looked up the right people, you got your name on some pieces of paper, and presto! you were rich for a short while and the earth was impoverished forever. I'm pleased to state that my grandfather recognized that there was something wrong with this, that he was not fulfilling the commandment given to Adam, that it was not the kind of work Adam was assigned to do. There was no proportion whatever between the amount of work and the return, between what man took from the earth and what he gave to it. Grandfather took something priceless and irreplaceable and gave in return a few miles of railroad ties. He not only broke the cycle of life so beautifully exemplified in those all but immortal groves, he destroyed it for quick wealth, which served only to corrupt his children and lead them out of the Church. In those days, we enjoyed a feeling of immense prosperity through the simple device of using up in twenty or thirty years those reserves of nature's treasury that were meant to last for a thousand years. With such prodigal waste, of course, we were living high. There's no permanency in economy that takes a hundred from nature and gives back one. There's no survival value in such an operation, which is certainly the business of systematic and organized looting—the very opposite of making a fair exchange with the earth. Above all, it ignores the ancient doctrine of man's obligation to "quicken" the earth that bears for him. The old Jewish teaching is that Adam had a right only to that portion of the earth that he "quickened," on which he labored with the sweat of his brow.[8] Let us not confuse the ethic of work with the ethic of plunder.

Granted that when Adam was turned out of the Garden, he immediately got to work, as instructed, to render the new region in which he found himself as much like his former paradise as possible. And angels came and showed him how he could work his way back to the type of paradise he had left. The order of Zion already established that Adam was to prepare the earth to resume its paradisiacal glory as soon as possible. Zion is a return to a former state of excellence. The gospel message today is that we must prepare ourselves to return to the Garden again, by the wisdom of hard experience. But he *was* to return. It is in that state and in those paradisiacal surroundings that he is to spend the eternities. The saints in every dispensation have always worked and prayed for the day when God "shall open the gates of paradise, and [he] shall remove the threatening sword against Adam, and he shall give to the saints to eat from the tree of life, . . . and all the saints shall clothe themselves with joy."[9] Zion is to be the headquarters for God's reconquest of the earth. "For the land of Zion shall be a seat and a place to receive and do all these things" (D&C 69:6).

"And again, verily I say unto you, my friends, a commandment I give unto you, that ye shall commence a work of laying out and preparing a beginning and foundation of the city of the stake of Zion, here in the land of Kirtland, beginning at my house" (D&C 94:1). Here we are dealing with the first steps only, not the culmination. The Church is a trial run for Zion, just as Zion is for paradise, and as paradise is for the heaven of God. It is a place of gathering. All things there shall be gathered together in one; they shall be "of one heart and one mind, and there are no poor among them" (Moses 7:18). In every dispensation that it has been upon the earth, Zion is described in the same terms.

The early saints took the physical appearance of Zion very seriously. "Can we preach to the world by practice?" asked Brigham Young. "Yes, we are preaching to them by setting out these shade trees. When they come here from north, south, east, or west, they say, 'Your city is a perfect paradise, with its streams of water and beautiful shade trees down every street.' "[10] The idea, according to Brigham Young, is to beautify the face of the earth until it becomes like the Garden of Eden. Again, Brigham says, "The city looks beautiful, . . . the appearance of a huge flower garden."[11] The "shade trees, fountains of water, crystal streams, and every tree, shrub, and flower that will flourish in this climate to make our mountain home a paradise and our hearts wells of gratitude to the God of Joseph."[12] Recently Thor Heyerdahl testified, before a Senate subcommittee, that "clearly, the time has passed when ocean pollution was a mere offense to human aesthetics."[13] Brigham Young knew, however, that a feeling for beauty was the surest guardian of survival. He said, "You watch your own feelings when you hear delightful sounds, for instance, or when you see anything beautiful. Are those feelings productive of misery? No, they produce happiness, peace and joy."[14] These feelings, according to Brigham, can be trusted, and without them we would soon destroy ourselves. "Man's machinery makes things alike," he says. "God's machinery gives to things which appear alike a pleasing difference."[15] "Now let us . . . prove to the heavens that our minds are set on beauty and true excellence, so that we can become worthy to enjoy the society of angels."[16]

In Paradise, as everybody knows, all creatures lived together in peace. So too, in Zion when it is restored to the earth, the lion shall lie down with the lamb. God's other creatures are an important part of the picture of heaven. A marvelous statement by Joseph Smith on this subject gives us a flash of insight into an amazing future: "John learned that God glorified Himself by saving all that His hands had made, whether beasts, fowls, fishes or men; and He will glorify Himself with them."[17] Brigham Young said: "The millennium consists in this, every heart in the Church and kingdom of God being united in one. . . . All things else will be as they are now, we shall eat, drink, and wear clothing. Let the people be holy . . . and filled with the Spirit of God, and every animal and creeping thing will be filled with peace; the soil of the earth will bring forth in its strength, and the fruits thereof will be meat for man."[18]

The Garden of Eden is not a one-crop enterprise — everything grows there. "Every living creature that moveth, . . . and every winged fowl after its kind; . . . all things which I had created were good. And I, God, blessed them, saying: Be fruitful and multiply. . . . And I, God, saw that all these things were good" (Moses 2:21-24). It is significant that in the oldest traditions and records of the human race all those men who turned against God and man are represented at the same time as making war against the animals, the birds, and the fishes, and destroying the forests and defiling the pure waters. This is told of Satan in the beginning, of Cain, of Ham, of Nimrod, of the Egyptian Seth, of the mad huntsmen of the steppes, of Nebuchadnezzar, of Esau, of Caesar, of Assurbanipal, and so on, all of whom sought dominion over others, over all others, and to achieve it in only one way—by force.[19] The code name for such an order of things and such a program is Babylon.

We can't discuss Zion very long without running into Babylon, because Babylon is, in all things, the counterpart of Zion. It is described just as fully, clearly, and vividly in the scriptures as Zion is and usually in direct relationship to it. "By the rivers of Babylon . . . we wept, when we remembered Zion" (Psalm 137:1). "They shall ask the way to Zion" when word comes to "remove out of the midst of Babylon" (Jeremiah 50:5, 8). "There will be the voice of them that flee out of the land of Babylon to declare in Zion the vengeance of the Lord," and, "Deliver thyself, O Zion, that dwellest with the daughter of Babylon" (Zechariah 2:7). So it goes on: Just as surely as Zion is to be established, Babylon is to be destroyed. "The burden of Babylon. . . . Howl ye; for the day of the Lord is at hand; it shall come as a destruction from the Almighty" (Isaiah 13:1, 6). Babylon is not to be converted, she's to be destroyed. "We would have healed Babylon, but she is not healed: forsake her" (Jeremiah 51:9). Today's world is the "substance . . . of an idol, which waxeth old and shall perish in Babylon, even Babylon the great, which shall fall" (D&C 1:16). "For after today cometh the burning . . . and I will not spare any that remain in Babylon" (D&C 64:24). I could quote a hundred scriptures to show that Babylon is nothing but the inverse image of Zion. Babylon is a state of mind, as Zion is, with its appropriate environment. Just like Zion, Babylon is a city. "Babylon the great is fallen, is fallen" (Revelation 18:2). The great world center of commerce and business, "the kings of the earth have committed fornication with her, and the merchants of the earth are waxed rich through the abundance of her delicacies" (Revelation 18:3). Indeed, "thy merchants were the great men of the earth; for by thy sorceries were all nations deceived" (Revelation 18:23). Babylon's economy is built on deceptions.

Babylon is described fully in Revelation 18: She is rich, luxurious, immoral, full of fornications, merchants, riches, delicacies, sins, merchandise, gold, silver, precious stones, pearls, fine linens, purples, silks, scarlets, thyine wood, all manner of vessels, ivory, precious wood, brass, iron, marble, and so on. She is a giant delicatessen, full of wine, oil, fine flour, wheat; a perfume counter with cinnamon, odors, ointments, and frankincense; a market with beasts and sheep. It reads like a savings stamp catalog or a guide to a modern supermarket or department store. Horses and chariots and all manner of services are available; slaves in the souls of men. These are "the fruits thy soul lusted after . . . and all things which were dainty and goodly" (Revelation 18:14). And it is all for sale. "O virgin daughter of Babylon, . . . thou hast labored . . . [with] thy merchants, from thy youth" (Isaiah 47:1, 15). In her power and affluence she is unchallenged. "For thou hast trusted in thy wickedness: thou hast said, None seeth me. Thy wisdom and thy knowledge, it hath perverted thee; and thou hast said in thine heart, I am, and none else beside me" (Isaiah 47:10). Babylon is number one. She dominates the world. Her king is equated to Lucifer, who says, "I will be like the most High" (Isaiah 14:14). And all the nations are weakened at her expense. He was the man that "made the earth to tremble, that did shake kingdoms; that made the world as a wilderness" (Isaiah 14:16-17). The "lady of kingdoms" who rules over polluted lands and says, "I shall be a lady forever" (Isaiah 47:5, 7) – she leads the world. "The nations have drunken of her wine; therefore the nations are mad" (Jeremiah (51:7). "Babylon the great, all nations have drunk of the wine of the wrath of her fornication" (Revelation 18:3). And when Babylon falls, all the world is involved: "At the noise of the taking of Babylon the earth is moved, and the cry is heard among the nations" (Jeremiah 50:46). And "at Babylon shall fall the slain of all the earth" (Jeremiah 51:49). Her clever, experienced, and unscrupulous men will be helpless. She thinks she can get away with anything, and says, "None seeth me." But "thy wisdom and thy knowledge, it hath perverted thee" (Isaiah 47:10). "And I will make drunk her men; and they shall sleep a perpetual sleep" (Jeremiah 51:57). Her military might is helpless: "A sound of battle is in the land, and of great destruction. How is the hammer of the whole earth cut asunder and broken!" (Jeremiah 50:22-23).

Babylon then, like Zion, is a type. If Zion is wherever the celestial order prevails, Babylon is the culmination of the worldly power wherever it happens. Through the ages, that power has actually culminated in just such world centers as ancient Babylon. Rome itself was entirely eligible for the name. The church of Rome called itself "the church that is at Babylon" (1 Peter 5:13). Rome was Babylon the great in every respect. And in the last days we must have a Babylon, too. For the call has gone forth, "Go ye out of Babylon. Be ye clean that bear the vessels of the Lord. Go ye out of Babylon; gather ye out from among the nations" (D&C 133:7). "Go ye out from among the nations, even from Babylon, from the midst of wickedness, which is spiritual Babylon" (D&C 133:14).

It is important in building up Zion and preparing for Paradise to keep an eye on Babylon, because the saints have always had a habit of subsiding into the ways of Babylon. Joseph Smith stood up on the framework of a new school building that was being erected in Far West, Missouri, and told the brethren, "Brethren, we are gathering to this buitiful [sic] land, to build up Zion." But instead he says, "I see signs put out Beer signs, speculative scheems are being introduced this is the ways of the world—Babylon indeed, and I tell you in the name of the God of Israel, if thare is no repentance . . . and a turning from such ungodliness, covetousness and self will, you will be Broken up and scattered from this choice land to the four winds of Heaven."[20] Saints start out building up Zion and end up building Babylon. Brigham Young said exactly the same thing in language just as strong when the Saints got to the valley: "Have we not brought Babylon with us? Are we not promoting Babylon here in our midst? Are we not fostering the spirit of Babylon that is now abroad on the face of the whole earth? I ask myself this question, and I answer, Yes, yes, . . . we have too much of Babylon in our midst."[21] It is hard for us to envisage the concept of Zion, let alone Paradise, when we have been so long accustomed to living in Babylon. We are disquieted by vague images of people wandering around in gardens apparently with nothing to do. Far more appealing to us are the vigor and give-and-take and drama of the marketplace. We are still like the little boy who likes to break the bottles. The world today is about as different from Zion as any world possibly can be. In fact, it has reached the point, the Lord has told us in emphatic terms, where he is about to remove the whole thing—sweep the slate clean, that Zion may be established.

Just as the order of Zion began with Adam in the garden, the rival system is just as old. It, too, was proposed to Adam, and he rejected it, while his son Cain accepted it. The plan Satan proposed to Adam was to put everything in this glorious and beautiful world up for sale. You could have anything in this world for money, but you had to have money. This launched a scramble that has gone on ever since Cain slew Abel, his brother, for gain; and he, says the Pearl of Great Price, "gloried in that which he had done, saying: I am free; surely the flocks of my brother falleth into my hands" (Moses 5:33). And this vigorous competition has imparted an air of dynamism and excitement to the scene that some find most attractive. What would the human drama be to us without an element of conflict and competition? We would find it insufferably dull. Who would exchange this for the pale and bloodless activities of Eden? In the Book of Mormon, the Nephites, the Jaredites, and the Jews at Jerusalem all walked straight to their certain destruction because they were helpless to conceive of acting in any other way. They were so completely captivated by one way of life that they could not conceive of any other. Laman and Lemuel saw nothing but visionary insanity in the teachings of their father and of their brother Nephi (1 Nephi 2:11). When Mormon suggested wisdom and restraint to the Nephites, they became hysterical and furious with him (Moroni 9:4-5). They were so hypnotized by the necessity of what they were doing that they didn't even let the fear of death deter them, he says. The Jaredites fought to the last man for nothing, rather than change their ways. They were reduced to the nightmare of private shelters and total insecurity, and finally total destruction. This is what the Greeks called *atē*, the point of no return, beyond which it becomes impossible to change, and only one solution to a problem remains possible. You simply have to play out the play to the end the way you've been doing it.

Whether or not this is the state of the present world, it is important before it is too late to point out that there are alternatives to Babylon. We should not be condemned because they are so different from what we've been accustomed to. There is an unbridgeable gap between Zion and Babylon. We cannot compromise on the two ways, because the two ways lead in opposite directions. In recent years, the course of the whole world has suddenly and dramatically vindicated the position taken by the early saints and largely forgotten by their descendants. We are discovering that there really *are* two worlds; that the one leads to sure destruction written in capital letters on everything we behold, as Joseph Smith put it,[22] and only the other offers salvation. This is the ancient doctrine of the "Two Ways" taught in the early church — the way of darkness and the way of light.[23] It was impossible to try to compromise between them because they led in opposite directions. Yet in the ancient church, it was the compromisers, the *dyophysites*, who won.[24] When we try to mix Zion and Babylon, Babylon has already won the game. It is amazing that any teaching so fundamental and so clearcut could be so effectively silenced today among people professing to preach and to practice the restored gospel. Here is an example from President Joseph F. Smith of what I mean:

> Our innocent little birds, natives of our country, who live upon the vermin, . . . are indeed enemies to the farmer and to mankind. It is not only wicked to destroy them, it is abominable, in my opinion. I think that this principle should extend, not only to the bird life, but to the life of all animals. . . . I never could see why a man should be imbued with a blood-thirsty desire to kill and destroy animal life. I have known men—and they still exist among us—who enjoy what is, to them, the "sport" of hunting birds. . . . I think it is wicked for men to thirst in their souls to kill almost everything which possesses animal life. It is wrong, and I have been surprised at prominent men whom I have seen whose very souls seemed to be athirst for the shedding of animal blood. They go off hunting deer, antelope, elk, anything they can find, and what for? "Just for the fun of it."[25]

Here is a practice designated by the President and Prophet of the Church as abominable, the ancient sport of the masters of Babylon—the descendants of Cain, of Ham, of Nimrod, all of whom were mighty hunters. And yet there are men today engaging in such practices who at the same time speak piously of building up Zion. How is this possible? It is the old word game of the early Christians and of others. In the newly discovered gospel of Philip, there is a wonderful passage describing how Satan rules this world by the skillful manipulation of labels. In this world we communicate through symbols, through labels,

it explains. Therefore, in this Satan possesses a powerful
tool to comfort the wicked, enabling them to discredit the
righteous and to brand the righteous with whatever epithets suit them and to unload their own guilt on others.[26]
   Today, as in the ancient church, those who embrace
Babylon in its stark reality do not renounce Zion. They
don't need to. As the Great Apostasy progressed, the
Christian world got ever more mileage out of the name of
Christianity. As the apostolic fathers and the early apolo-
gists observed, the farther they fall away from real Christianity, the more loudly they proclaim and the more enthusiastically they display the name and the banner of
Christ. Christianity became an impressive *pompa*, a military
parade rallying the righteous against the wicked. Finally,
all you had to do to be righteous was to wave the flag of
Christianity. As these early church fathers say, the word
Christian completely lost its meaning.[27] Today the beautiful
word *Zion*, with all its emotional and historical associa-
tions, is used as the name *Christian* was formerly used, to
put the stamp of sanctity on whatever men chose to do.
The Hebrew word for financial activity of any kind is *ma-
monut*, and the financier is a *mamonai*; that is, financing is,
quite frankly, in that honest language, the business of
Mammon. From the very first there were Latter-day Saints
who thought to promote the cause of Zion by using the
methods of Babylon. Indeed, once the Saints were told to
make friends with the Mammon of unrighteousness (D&C
82:22), but that was only to save their lives in an emergency.
We have the word of the Prophet Joseph that Zion is not
to be built up by using the methods of Babylon. He says,
"Here are those who begin to spread out buying up all the
land they are able to do, to the exclusion of the poorer
ones who are not so much blessed with this worlds goods,
thinking to ley foundations for themselves only, looking
to their own individual familys and those who are to follow

them. . . . Now I want to tell you that Zion cannot be built up in eny such way [sic]."[28]

What do we find today? Zion's Investment, Zion Used Cars, Zion Construction, Zion Development, Zion Bank, Zion Leasing, Zion Insurance, Zion Securities, Zion Trust, and so on. The institutions of Mammon are made respectable by the beautiful name of Zion. Zion and Babylon both have their appeal, but the voice of latter-day revelation makes one thing perfectly clear as it tells us over and over again that we cannot have them both.

Let us go back to the beginning of this latter-day work. When the youthful Joseph Smith began to think about those things, he went to his knees in the Sacred Grove. He said,

> This was a grief to my Soul thus from the age of twelve years to fifteen I pondered many things in my heart concerning the sittuation of the world of mankind the contentions and divions [divisions], the wickedness and abominations and the darkness which pervaded the minds of mankind my mind become exceedingly distressed. . . . [He found himself in a wicked world, yet the natural world surrounding him was one of heavenly beauty.] I looked upon the sun, the glorious luminary of the earth and also the moon rolling in their majesty through the heavens and also the Stars Shining in their courses and the earth also upon which I stood and the beast of the field, and the fowls of heaven and the fish of the waters and also man walking forth upon the face of the earth in majesty and in the Strength of beauty whose power and intiligence in governing the things which are so exceding great and marvelous even in the likeness of him who created them and when I considered upon these things my heart exclaimed well hath the wise man Said, it is a fool that Saith in his heart there is no God my heart exclained all all these bear testimony and bespeak an omnipotent and omnipreasant power [sic].[29]

What was young Joseph's problem when he compared

the world that God had made to the world that man had made? One is the world as it should be; the other the world as it should not be. The boy's feelings in the matter were confirmed from the mouth of the Lord himself, who spoke to him in the grove (and note well, it was in a grove of trees that the Father and the Son appeared to Joseph), saying, "Behold the world lieth in sin at this time, and none doeth good, no not one. And mine anger is kindled against the inhabitants of the earth to visit them according to their ungodliness."[30]

Well, here we have it: the world we have made and are making is not the world God meant us to have, and the world he made for us in the beginning is the world we *must* have. With our present limited knowledge we could devise a perfectly practical order of things in which there would be no need for doctors, lawyers, insurance men, dentists, auto mechanics, beauticians, generals, real estate men, prostitutes, garbage men, and used-car salesmen. Their work is justified as an unpleasant necessity, yet there have been successful human societies in which none of those professions existed, any more than dukes, earls, and kings need to exist in our society. Nature around us, such of it as has remained, admonishes us that paradise is a reality. Through modern revelations we have learned that Zion also is a reality. Paradise is the proper environment of Zion. Here we are faced with a clear-cut proposition that recent developments of world history, if nothing else, admonish us we can no longer afford to ignore. The Tenth Article of Faith contains our future: our glory or our condemnation.

Notes

1. A. Boyce Gibson, *The Philosophy of Descartes* (New York: Russell and Russell, 1969), 108-9.

2. Arturo and Genevieve DeHoyos, "The Universality of the Gospel," *Ensign* 1 (August 1971): 9-14.

3. John Milton, "Paradise Lost," *The Poetical Works of John Milton*, comp. James Montogomery, 2 vols. (London: Bohn, 1861), 1:12.

4. *JD* 23:175.

5. Ibid.

6. A. B. Morrison, "Our Deteriorating Environment," *Ensign* 1 (August 1971): 65.

7. *JD* 13:151.

8. Jacob Neusner, *Genesis Rabbah*, 3 vols. (Atlanta: Scholars Press, 1985), 1:224; Philip B. Gove, ed., *Webster's Third New International Dictionary* (Springfield, MA: Merriam, 1971), 1864, defines quickened as follows: "to come to life: become alive: become charged with life ⟨seed that [quicken]s and becomes ripe grain⟩."

9. Testament of Levi 18:10-14.

10. *JD* 12:271-72.

11. *MS* 27:415.

12. *JD* 10:4.

13. Thor Heyerdahl, Hearings before the Subcommitte on Oceans and Atmosphere of the Committee on Commerce, United States Senate, Ninety-Second Congress; Second Session on International Conference on Ocean Pollution, October 18 and November 8, 1971 (Washington: U.S. Government Printing Office, 1972), 50-51.

14. *JD* 12:314.

15. Ibid., 9:370.

16. Ibid., 11:305.

17. *TPJS* 291.

18. *JD* 1:203.

19. Regarding Nimrod, see *MS* 17:674.

20. Edward Stevenson, *The Life and History of Elder Edward Stevenson* (n.d.), 40-41.

21. *JD* 17:38.

22. *TPJS* 16.

23. Epistle of Barnabas 18-20; for English translation, see "The Epistle of Barnabas," *Ante-Nicene Fathers*, 10 vols. (Grand Rapids: Eerdmans, 1978), 1:148-49.

24. James L. Barker, *Apostasy from The Divine Church* (Salt Lake City: Deseret Book, 1960), 369-74.

25. *Gospel Doctrine, vol. 1: A Course of Study for Melchizedek Priesthood Quorums, 1971-1972*, 371-72; selections from the sermons and writings of Joseph F. Smith.

26. Gospel of Philip, 53:25–54:5; for English translation, see *Nag Hammadi Library*, tr. James M. Robinson (New York: Harper and Row, 1977).

27. Louis Duchesne, *Early History of the Christian Church*, 3 vols. (London: Murray, 1948), 3:4.

28. Stevenson, *The Life and History of Elder Edward Stevenson*, 40-41.

29. The 1832 recital of the First Vision as dictated by Joseph Smith to Frederick G. Williams. See Milton V. Backman, *Joseph Smith's First Vision* (Salt Lake City: Bookcraft, 1971), appendix A; cf. Dean C. Jessee, ed., "The Early Accounts of Joseph Smith's First Vision," *BYU Studies* 9 (1969): 280.

30. Ibid., 157.

2

What Is Zion? A Distant View

The first thing to note is that Zion is perfect, flawless, and complete—not a structure in the process of building. We work for the building up of the kingdom of God on earth and the establishment of Zion. The first step makes the second possible. Zion has been on the earth before in its perfection, as (we are told) it is to be found in other worlds. When the world has been ready to receive it at various happy times in the past, Zion has been brought down from above; and we have the joyful promise that at some future time it will again descend to earth. When men are no longer capable of supporting Zion on earth, it is bodily removed—taken up to heaven; whence go forth the sayings, "Zion is fled" and "Zion is no more." It is no more here but continues to thrive elsewhere. For it is a constant quantity, as perfect things are.

In its present state, the world is far from qualified to receive a celestial society into its midst. But if we today cannot achieve Zion, we can conceive of it. Whenever we use that resounding word, the idea of perfection is always implied, even though we may be using it only in a local and limited sense. Thus, when the Prophet Joseph says, "We will still weep for Zion,"[1] it is not an imperfect Zion he is weeping for, but the absence of true Zion; he weeps

---

This talk was originally given at Brigham Young University on February 25, 1973, as "Waiting for Zion." It was circulated by ASBYU under the title What Is Zion? Joseph Smith Lecture Series, 1972-73 *(Provo: BYU Press, 1973), 1-21 and reprinted as "What Is Zion? A Distant View" in* Sunstone 13 (April 1989):20-32.

because the Zion he has so clearly in mind has not been realized. One does not weep for paradise, a place of consummate joy, but only for our memory of paradise, for paradise lost, even as the Jews, by the waters of Babylon, wept for a Jerusalem that was no more. Brigham Young admonished the people who came to the Valley lest they "go into error when they expect to see that Zion here which they have seen in vision."[2] The Zion in the vision was the real one. It must always be kept in mind, not as a present reality, but as the goal toward which all the labor of the Church is a preparation.

"Blessed are they who shall seek to bring forth my Zion at that day" (1 Nephi 13:37). If they are obedient, "they shall have power after many days to accomplish all things pertaining to Zion" (D&C 105:37). "My people must be tried in all things, that they may be prepared to receive the glory . . . of Zion" which lies ahead (D&C 136:31).

When all the accidentals and incidentals are stripped away, what remains that is quintessentially Zion? Buildings, walls, streets, and gates—even of gold and jasper— do not make Zion; neither do throngs in shining robes. Zion is not a Cecil B. DeMille production; the properties do not make the play, no matter how splendid they may be. What makes Zion? God has given us the perfect definition: Zion is the pure in heart—the pure in heart, not merely the pure in appearance. It is not a society or religion of forms and observances, of pious gestures and precious mannerisms: it is strictly a condition of the heart. Above all, Zion is pure, which means "not mixed with any impurities, unalloyed"; it is all Zion and nothing else. It is not achieved wherever a heart is pure or where two or three are pure, because it is all pure—it is a society, a community, and an environment into which no unclean thing can enter. "Henceforth there shall no more come into thee the uncircumcised and the unclean" (3 Nephi 20:36). It is not even pure people in a dirty environment, or pure people with a few impure ones among them; it is the perfectly pure in a perfectly pure environment. "I . . . will contend with Zion . . . and chasten her until she overcomes and is clean before me" (D&C 90:36).

This makes it so different from our world that it almost begins to sound distasteful. But a moment's reflection will show that Zion cannot possibly be other than wholly pure. For Zion is the eternal order; it has existed elsewhere from the eternities and will someday be permanently established on this earth. Even the smallest impurity or flaw in anything designed to continue forever would, in the course of an infinite stretching of time, become a thing of infinite mischief. The most perfect structures men have been able to erect have been short-lived because of tiny, all-but-imperceptible flaws. Hence, any flaw, no matter how small, must be removed from a system designed to be timeless; otherwise, there will be no end of trouble. The only kind of life that can be endured forever is one completely devoid of sin, for we are told that the most calamitous thing that could befall man at present would be for him to reach forth his hand and partake of the tree of life and live forever in his sins. Jeremiah describes Zion as a comely and delicate woman who cannot live in the presence of what is vile (Jeremiah 6:2-7). "When men presume to build up Zion in their sins, they labor in vain, for the daughter of Zion withdraws from the scene entirely" (Micah 4:10).

If only to preserve its purity, Zion is set apart from all contaminating influences. For it must be holy enough to receive the Lord himself: "For the Lord hath chosen Zion; he hath desired it for his habitation. This is my rest for ever: here will I dwell; for I have desired it" (Psalm 132:13-14). Ancient writers assure us repeatedly that the temple is the earthly type of Zion, a holy place removed from contact with the outer world, set apart for ordinances from which the world is excluded; while it is in the world, the temple presents a forbidding front of high gates, formidable walls, narrow doors, and frowning battlements, dramatizing the total withdrawal of Zion from the world and its defensive position over against it. Zion itself, of course, is absolutely impregnable and unassailable, since the world has no access to it. Should the world get too close, Zion withdraws: "[God] dwelt in the midst of Zion; and it came to pass that Zion was not, for God received it up into his own bosom; and from thence went forth the saying, ZION IS FLED" (Moses 7:69). Hence, it is often described as a refuge and a place of safety: "And it shall be called the New Jerusalem, a land of peace, a city of refuge, a place of safety for the saints; . . . the terror of the Lord also shall be there, . . . and it shall be called Zion" (D&C 45:66-67). Her invulnerability makes Zion an object of awe and terror to her enemies. Hence, scripture speaks of "the gathering together upon the land of Zion, and upon her stakes, . . . for a defense, and for a refuge from the storm, and from wrath when it shall be poured out without mixture upon the whole earth" (D&C 115:6). In a hostile world, those seeking for Zion form a sort of bridgehead, a command post from which God may expand his work "for the rising generations that shall grow up on the land of Zion, to possess it from generation to generation, forever and ever" (D&C 69:8). That can be the real Zion only after the groundwork has been laid for it. It is always described as a place of unearthly beauty.

The Bible contains a fairly complete description of Zion, but there is one aspect of it that only the Latter-day Saints have taken to heart (or did formerly), and it is that doctrine that sets them off most sharply from all of the other religions, namely, the belief that Zion is possible on the earth, that men possess the capacity to receive it right here and are therefore under obligation to waste no time moving in the direction of Zion. The instant one realizes that Zion is a possibility, one has no choice but to identify himself with the program that will bring about the quickest possible realization of its perfection. The call is to awake and arise, to "push many people to Zion with songs of everlasting joy upon their heads" (D&C 66:11). If undue haste is not desirable, delay is inexcusable; a sense of urgent gravity has ever marked the latter-day work: "I am Jesus Christ, who cometh quickly, in an hour you think not" (D&C 51:20). "Wherefore, stand ye in holy places, and be not moved, until the day of the Lord come; for behold, it cometh quickly" (D&C 87:8).

"When we conclude to make a Zion," said Brigham Young, "we will make it, and this work commences in the heart of each person."[3] Zion can come only to a place that is completely ready for it, which is to say Zion must already be there. When Zion descends to earth, it must be met by a Zion that is already here: "And they shall see us; and we will fall upon their necks, and they shall fall upon our necks; . . . and there shall be mine abode, and it shall be Zion" (Moses 7:63-64). Hence, President Young must correct a misunderstanding among many of the Saints who "gather here with the spirit of Zion resting upon them, and expecting to find Zion in its glory, whereas their own doctrine should teach them that they are coming here to make Zion,"[4] that is, to make it possible. "The elements are here to produce as good a Zion as was ever made in all the eternities of the Gods."[5] Note that Zion is an eternal and a universal type and that the local Zion, while made of the substances of this earth, "shall come forth out of all the creations which I have made" (Moses 7:64). "I have Zion in my view constantly," said Brother Brigham, making it clear that Zion for this earth is still an unrealized ideal of perfection. "We are not going to wait for angels, or for Enoch and his company to come and build up Zion, but we are going to build it,"[6] so that we will be ready. If we did not have a responsibility for bringing Zion, and if we did not work constantly with that aim in view, its coming could not profit us much—for all its awesome perfection and beauty, Zion is still our business and should be our constant concern.

Throughout the scriptures, Zion is brought into the clearest focus by placing it against a dark background; and like Zion, that background world is given a code name: *Babylon*. Babylon, like Zion, is a real society—a type, place, and environment of human existence, described in the scriptures with great clarity and precision. (The word *Babylon* is not just a general term to indicate anything that is not Zion; it is the designation of a very particular and specific type of society.) Though Babylon is vividly described by the prophets, the best way to define her is as the exact opposite of Zion in all things. Babylon is just as pure in its way as is Zion; it is pure evil—for even good, when it becomes contaminated and perverted, becomes an evil. The main thing is that Babylon and Zion cannot mix in any degree; a Zion that makes concessions is no longer Zion.

One may well ask if it is necessary to choose between such absolute extremes, and wonder if there is not some more moderate approach to the problems. By the very nature of things, there is no third way—as the early Jewish and Christian writers remind us repeatedly in their doctrine of the Two Ways. According to this oldest and best-established of teachings (though quite unpopular with the conventional Christianity and Judaism of our time), there are Two Ways lying before every person in this life, the Way of Light and the Way of Darkness, the Way of Life and the Way of Death; and every mortal every day of his life is required to make a choice between them. Unfortunately for our peace of mind, any compromise between the Two Ways is out of the question, since they lead in opposite directions. As the wise Heraclitus pointed out long ago, "The up-road and the down-road are one and the same."[7] Which one you are on depends entirely on the way you are facing. To go off at an angle is to get nowhere; if you find the road to Zion, the Heavenly City, too steep, you may mitigate the climb by striking off on a more level course — but in that case you will never, never reach Zion. The only road to Zion is the shortest road, for to take any other shows a lack of faith and zeal, which will exclude you from the city.

As there is no compromise between the Two Ways, so there is no mixing of Babylon and Zion; God will not tolerate any concessions by Zion: "A scourge and judgment [is] to be poured out upon the children of Zion. For shall the children of the kingdom pollute my holy land?" (D&C 84:58-59). Zion does not make war on Babylon: "I forgive all men. I feel in my heart to forgive all men in the broad sense that God requires me to forgive all men, and I desire to love my neighbor as myself; and to this extent I bear no malice toward any of the children of my Father. . . . I leave them in the hands of the just Judge. Let him deal with them as seemeth him good. . . . I would not harm a hair of their heads."[8] We don't need to. Zion has never made war on Babylon, for when the environment has become too foul for Zion, she has simply been removed. Babylon is always reserved for the burning — she is never converted or reformed; though many may leave her for Zion, her fate is to be overthrown, violently, suddenly, unexpectedly, and completely by the direct intervention of God. "Thou shalt not know from whence it riseth: . . . thou shalt not be able to put it off, and desolation shall come upon thee suddenly, which thou shalt not know" (Isaiah 47:11). "Babylon is suddenly fallen and destroyed; howl for her. . . . We would have healed Babylon, but she is not healed: forsake her" (Jeremiah 51:8-9).

From the beginning the cry went forth to the Saints, repeating the words of the ancient prophets: "Go ye out from Babylon. Be ye clean. . . . Go ye out from among the nations, even from Babylon, from the midst of wickedness, which is spiritual Babylon" (D&C 133:5, 14). The substance of this woe "is that of an idol, which waxeth old and shall perish in Babylon, even Babylon the great, which shall fall" (D&C 1:16). Babylon's time is all but used up, and the only thing for the Saints to do is to get out of her. As we all know, they sought to do this in a very physical as well as a spiritual sense. "I will that my saints should be assembled upon the land of Zion . . . and lift a warning voice . . . by word and by flight" (D&C 63:36-37). How could they stay in the world? "We are trying to be the image of those who live in heaven; we are trying to pattern after them, . . . to walk and talk like them, to deal like them, and build up the kingdom of heaven as they have done."[9] That meant a total renunciation of the world and its ways: "It is useless for us to expect the favor of the world. We have been called out of the world, therefore the world hates us. If we were of the world, then the world would love its own, and we should have no trouble with them."[10] That was what the Lord often told his disciples. You cannot be "in the world but not of the world," "for all that is in the world . . . is not of the Father, but is of the world," and that in the most literal sense (1 John 2:16).

The world lost no time in getting the message, and if the antipathy was mutual, the ferocity of the attack on the one side matched the finality of retreat on the other. "In the first place," said Brigham, "they will not fellowship us, and in the next place we cannot fellowship them. . . . I would not give a snap of my finger for them; for as the world is I want not their fellowship."[11] Right from the beginning, the standard charge against Joseph Smith and the Mormons was treason. And why not? That was the only possible charge when the crime was simply that of rejecting a whole way of life: "They accused him [Joseph Smith] of treason, because he would not fellowship their wickedness."[12] In a way he had asked for it, for he would make no concession: "It may be considered treason," said

Brigham Young, "to say that the kingdom which that Prophet [Daniel] foretold is actually set up; *that* we cannot help, but we know it is so, and call upon the nations to believe our testimony."[13] "Do you blame the wicked for being mad?" he asks. "No. They desire to rule, to hold the reins of government on this earth; they have held them a great while. I do not blame them for being suspicious of us; men in high standing are suspicious of us, hence the frequent cry, 'Treason, treason, we are going to have trouble with the people in Utah.' "[14] So God drives a wedge between Zion and Babylon, an intense mutual antipathy that constantly forces them apart. "If the wicked come here they do not wish to stay, no matter how well they are treated, and I thank the Lord for it; and I want hard times, so that every person that does not wish to stay, for the sake of his religion, will leave."[15] Whenever the Lord prepares for Zion, there must be a division among the people. "The Lord is building up Zion, and is emptying the earth of wickedness, gathering his people, bringing again Zion, redeeming his Israel, sending forth his work, withdrawing his Spirit from the wicked world, and commencing to build up his kingdom."[16] The perennial "Mormon Problem" was not how to fellowship the Mormons but how to liquidate them;[17] but that was not surprising: "The cry has been against the Prophets of every age, against the Apostles and against Jesus himself, and against all those who have ever preached the truth, and why? Because the systems of the world are errors; while the Gospel is true."[18] "Joseph Smith, in forty-seven prosecutions, was never proven guilty of one violation of the laws of his country. They accused him of treason, because he would not fellowship with their wickedness."[19] The nature of their hatred and their charges is reported by Joseph Smith himself:

> If there were priests among them of all the different sects, they hated us, and that most cordially too. If there

were generals, they hated us; if there were colonels, they hated us; and the soldiers, and officers of every kind, hated us . . . —they all hated us, most cordially. And now what did they hate us for? . . . Was it because we have committed treason against the government in Daviess county, or burglary, or larceny, or arson, or any other unlawful act in Daviess county? We know that we have been so reported by priests, and certain lawyers, and certain judges, who . . . for a number of years have tried, by a well contemplated and premeditated scheme, to put down by physical power a system of religion that all the world . . . by any fair means whatever, were not able to resist.[20]

There is no third way: "Those who believe and obey the Gospel of the Son of God forsake all for its interests, belong to the kingdom of God, and all the rest belong to the other kingdom."[21]

And so we have Zion and Babylon, and never the twain shall meet. That is, they wouldn't if we did not take human nature into account, for how many humans have ever succeeded in renouncing the world completely? The separation of the Saints from the world was, in most cases, not a matter of choice—it was forced on them; God is constantly driving wedges between the Church and the world, or in Brigham Young's vivid terms, there are always cats coming out of the bag to put us at odds with the world, whether we want it that way or not. "The brethren and sisters came across the plains because they could not stay; that is the secret of the movement."[22]

"Do you think we came here of our own choice? No; we would have stayed in those rich valleys and prairies back yonder."[23] When the first revelation was given to prepare for Zion by the gathering of Israel, "when the people came to Jackson county, . . . they were as far from believing and obeying that revelation as the east is from the west."[24] "And so we have got to continue to labor, fight, toil, counsel, exercise faith, ask God over and over, and have been praying for thirty odd years for that which we might have received and accomplished in one year."[25] That complete break between the Saints and the world that must precede the coming of Zion has not yet taken place.

"They have not learned 'a' concerning Zion; and we have been traveling now forty-two years, and have we learned our a, b, c's? . . . I will say, scarcely. Have we seen it as a people? How long shall we travel, . . . how long shall God wait for us to sanctify ourselves and become one in the Lord, in our actions and in our ways for the building up of the kingdom of God, that he can bless us?"[26] "How long, Latter-day Saints, before you will believe the Gospel as it is? The Lord has declared it to be his will that his people will enter into covenant, even as Enoch and his people did, which of necessity, must be before we shall have the privilege of building the Center Stake of Zion."[27]

This was one of the last public addresses of the prophet Brigham, and the people were still not ready to go all the way. They still wanted to mix Babylon and Zion; or, as he put it, "Some of the Latter-day Saints had an idea that they could take the follies of the world in one hand and the Savior in the other, and expect to get into the presence of the Lord Jesus."[28] Such heaping up gold and silver would prove their destruction.[29] Again and again the Lord had to rebuke even Joseph Smith for little concessions to the world: "You have feared man and have not relied on me for strength as you ought" (D&C 30:1). "Your mind has been on the things of the earth more than on the things of me, . . . and you . . . have been persuaded by those whom I have not commanded; . . . you shall ever open your mouth in my cause, not fearing what man can do, for I am with you" (D&C 30:2, 11). "How oft you have transgressed the commandments and the laws of God, and have gone on in the persuasions of men. For behold you should not have feared man more than God" (D&C 3:6-7).

Speaking to the Mormon Battalion in 1848, President Young warned them: "If we were to go to San Francisco and dig up chunks of gold or find it here in the valley it would ruin us. Many wanted to unite Babylon and Zion; it's the love of money that hurts them."[30] In his last public address, he noted that because they are still "lusting . . . after the things of this world, [the Latter-day Saints] are . . . shaking hands with the servants of the devil, instead of sanctifying themselves. . . . When I think upon this subject, I want the tongues of seven thunders to wake up the people."[31] Even though the Lord said, "Zion cannot be built up unless it is by the principles of the law of the celestial kingdom; otherwise I cannot receive her unto myself" (D&C 105:5), the Latter-day Saints still wanted to compromise and say, "We will not go up unto Zion, and will keep our moneys"—but as long as that was their plan, there could be no Zion: "Mine elders should wait for . . . the redemption of Zion" (D&C 105:8-9). For God had made it perfectly clear: "I give not unto you that ye shall live after the manner of the world" (D&C 95:13). "For after today cometh the burning. . . . I will burn them up . . . and I will not spare any that remain in Babylon" (D&C 64:24). It had to be the one or the other.

"Shall we now seek to make ourselves wealthy in gold and silver and the possessions which the wicked love and worship, or shall we, with all of our might, mind, and strength, seek diligently first to build up the Kingdom of God? Let us decide on this, and do the one thing or the other."[32] Notice that every time the issue is raised, it is made clear that the powerful link that continues to bind the Mormons to the world and that advocates the perverse doctrine of a deal between Zion and Babylon is a deep-seated desire of the Saints to acquire personal wealth. Joseph Smith's speech at Far West is a vividly specific statement of the case:

> Brethren, we are gathering to this buitiful land to build up Zion. . . . But since I have been here I perseive the spirit of selfishness, coveteousness exists in the hearts of the saints. . . . Here are those who begin to spread out, buying up all the land they are able to do; . . . thinking to ley foundations for themselves only, looking to their own individual familys. . . . Now I want to tell you that Zion cannot be built up in eny such way. . . . I see signs put out, Beer signs, speculative scheems are being introduced. This is the ways of the world—Babylon indeed, and I tell you in the name of the God of Israel, if thare is not repentance . . . you will be Broken up and scattered from this choice land [sic].[33]

We all know that this prophecy was literally fulfilled: God would not tolerate such a mockery of Zion. We cannot compromise between the way of Babylon and the way of Zion, because they do lead in opposite directions, as Brigham Young explains: "I am sorry that this people are worldly-minded. . . . Their affections are upon . . . their farms, upon their property, their houses and possessions, and in the same ratio that this is the case, the Holy Spirit of God—the spirit of their calling—forsakes them, and they are overcome with the spirit of the evil one."[34]

Every step in the direction of increasing one's personal holdings is a step away from Zion, which is another way of saying, as the Lord has proclaimed in various ways, that one cannot serve two masters: to the degree in which he loves the one he will hate the other, and so it is with God and business, for *mammon* is simply the standard Hebrew word for any kind of financial dealing.

So money is the name of the game by which the devil cleverly decoys the minds of the Saints from God's work to his.[35] "What does the Lord want of us up here in the tops of these mountains?" Brigham asked twenty years

after the first settling of the Valley. "He wishes us to build
up Zion. What are the people doing? They are merchan-
dizing, trafficking and trading."[36] "Elders are agreed on
the way and manner necessary to obtain celestial glory,
but they quarrel about a dollar. When principles of eternal
life are brought before them—God and the things pertaining to God and godliness—they apparently care not half
so much about them as they do about five cents."[37] "Instead
of reflecting upon and searching for hidden things of the
greatest value to them, [the Latter-day Saints] rather wish
to learn how to secure their way through this world as
easily and as comfortably as possible. The reflections, what
they are here for, who produced them, and where they
are from, far too seldom enter their minds."[38] Well, what
was wrong with that? Isn't a comfortable living what we
all want? It would be all right if we did not have our choice,
but if we fail to realize that "we are engaged in a higher-
toned branch of business than any merchants or railroad
men, or any institution of an earthly nature,"[39] and give
priority to the comfortable and respectable life after we
have seen the greater light, we are in great danger. "Are
their eyes single to the building up of the Kingdom of God?
No; they are single to the building up of themselves."[40]
"Does this congregation understand what idolatry is? The
New Testament says that covetousness is idolatry; therefore, a covetous people is an idolatrous people."[41] "Man
is made in the image of God, but what do we know of him
or of ourselves, when we suffer ourselves to love and
worship the god of this world—riches?"[42] Had the Latter-
day Saints gone so far? They had, from the beginning;
when the Church was only a year old, the Prophet Joseph
observed that "God has often sealed up the heavens because of covetousness in the Church."[43] Three years later,
God revoked that "united order" by which alone Zion
could exist on earth (D&C 104:52-53)—in their desire for
wealth, the Saints had tried to embrace both Babylon and

Zion by smooth double-talk. The Mormons would have to wait for their blessings until they learned their lesson: "If the people neglect their duty, turn away from the holy commandments which God has given us, seek for their own individual wealth, and neglect the interests of the kingdom of God, we may expect to be here quite a time — perhaps a period that will be far longer than we anticipate."[44]

Satan has many arrows in his quiver: "I cannot tell you all the things whereby we may commit sin," said King Benjamin to his people, "for there are divers ways and means, even so many that I cannot number them" (Mosiah 4:29). These were the closing words, however, of a speech devoted to warning his people against the ways in which they were most likely to commit the greatest sins, namely, in the search for private gain. Of all the devil's arrows, this has ever proven the most deadly and effective. "My experience is that this people have too great a tenacity for the goods of this world, and the Enemy thinks he can get the advantage over them in this respect, and he is improving the time."[45] Did not Paul say, "Love of money is the root of all evil" (1 Timothy 6:10)? And has God not restated the proposition for our own generation through the mouth of his prophet, Mormon? "Behold, I speak unto you as if ye were present, and yet ye are not. But . . . Jesus Christ hath shown you unto me, and I know your doing. . . . For behold, ye do love money, and your substance, and your fine apparel, and the adorning of your churches, more than ye love the poor and the needy, the sick and the afflicted" (Mormon 8:35, 37). That is not Zion as described by God: "They were of one heart and one mind . . . and there was no poor among them" (Moses 7:18). The people "do not understand the power of the devil and how liable they are to be decoyed."[46] Wealth is a pleasant and heady narcotic that gives the addict an exhilarating sense of power accompanied by a growing

deadening of feeling for anything of real value. It seals up
the heavens and closes the mind to revelation;[47] it takes
possession of the heart and darkens the spirit;[48] it works
by deception, bewitching the nations (Revelation 18:23); it
becomes an obsession—"We wish the wealth or things of
the world; we think about them morning, noon, and night;
they are first in our minds when we awake in the morning,
and the last thing before we go to sleep at night";[49] it gives
a false sense of security against which the Prophet Joseph
warned: "Every man who is afraid, covetous, will be taken
in a snare," adding that the only security in the future
would be "in Zion and her stakes";[50] it paralyzes the mind's
perception of higher things: "Are not the sordid things of
this life before our eyes, and have they not thrown a mist
before them so that we can not see? . . . What do we know
of heavenly things?"[51] "When you see the Latter-day Saints
greedy, and coveteous [sic] of the things of this world, do
you think their minds are in a fit condition to be written
upon by the pen of revelation?"[52]

There are exceptions, but they are dangerously rare,
for wealth is a jealous mistress: she will not tolerate any
competition; rulers of business are openly contemptuous
of all other vocations; and all those "how-to-get-rich"
books by rich men virtuously assure us that the first and
foremost prerequisite for acquiring wealth is to think of
nothing else—the aspirant who is guilty even of a momentary lapse in his loyalty, they tell us, does not deserve
the wealth he seeks. That is why there are so few exceptions: "I know," says Brigham Young, "that there is no
man on this earth who can call around him property, be
he a merchant, tradesman, or [farmer], with his mind continually occupied with: 'How shall I get this or that; how
rich can I get?' . . . No such man ever can magnify the
priesthood nor enter the celestial kingdom."[53] The game
is almost always demoralizing: "You may take the class
called merchants, also the doctors, the priests in the various

sects, the lawyers, and every person engaged in any branch of business throughout the world, and as a general thing, they are all taught from their childhood to be more or less dishonest."[54] "In my young days I had to quit the business of painting purely because I had either to be dishonest or quit; and I quit."[55] "But the great majority of men who have amassed great wealth have done it at the expense of their fellows, on the principle that the doctors, the lawyers, and the merchants acquire theirs. Such men are impositions on the community."[56]

All this in the relatively simple and innocent nineteenth century. Brigham grieved to see how inevitably covetousness led to dishonesty among the Saints. "Their cheating and lying, their scheming in every possible way . . . [have] caused my spirit to weep and mourn."[57]

Was there no trend toward improvement? The whole tenet of the dualism of Babylon and Zion, the Two Ways, is that one does not move gradually and easily from a sinful to a righteous life. One forsakes sin completely, or one does not forsake it. That danger of covetousness did not diminish with the flight of the Saints from Babylon: "Have we separated ourselves from the nations? Yes. And what else have we done? . . . Have we not brought Babylon with us? Are we not promoting Babylon here in our midst? Are we not fostering the spirit of Babylon that is now abroad on the face of the whole earth? . . . Yes, yes, to some extent, and there is not a Latter-day Saint but what feels that we have too much of Babylon in our midst."[58] Many years before, Brigham had laid it on the line: "I am more afraid of covetousness in our Elders than I am of the hordes of hell. Have we men out now of that class? I believe so. I am afraid of such spirits; for they are more powerful and injurious to this people than all hell outside of our borders. All our enemies in the United States or in the world, and all hell with them marshalled against us, could not do us the injury that covetousness in the hearts of this people

could do us; for it is idolatry."[59] "Whether you can see it
or not, I know that this people are more or less prone to
idolatry; for I see that spirit manifested every day, and hear
it from nearly every quarter."[60]

I have a long list of quotations in which President
Brigham Young, down through the years, repeats this
warning with growing concern. Way back in Kirtland the
Lord had said, "[The saints] do not forsake their sins, and
their wicked ways, the pride of their hearts, and their
covetousness" (D&C 98:20). Thirty-five years later Brigham
says, "My experience for the best part of forty years teaches
me that they never progress—they are as they were, and
as they no doubt will be."[61] And six years after that, he
says: "The Lord . . . is sending forth his voice . . . into the
hearts of his people, crying unto them—'Stop! Stop your
course! Cease to bring in and build up Babylon in your
midst!' "[62] In his last sermon he said: "The devils in hell
[are] looking at this people, too, and trying to overthrow
us, and the people are still shaking hands with the servants
of the devil, instead of sanctifying themselves and calling
upon the Lord and doing the work which he has commanded us and put into our hands to do."[63]

If those who have been "called out of the world" still
admit its charms, we can hardly expect the world itself to
improve. The world *as such* is Babylon and always has been.
It will not change. "Evil is here," says Brigham. "The Devil
reigns on the earth, and has held dominion on it for thousands of years."[64] "The Devil has the mastery of the earth:
he has corrupted it, and has corrupted the children of men.
He has led them in evil until they are almost entirely
ruined, and are so far from God that they neither know
Him nor his influence, and have almost lost sight of everything that pertains to eternity. This darkness is more prev-
alent, more dense, among the people of Christendom than
it is among the heathen. They have lost sight of all that is
great and glorious—of all principles that pertain to life

eternal."[65] "We are here in this wicked world, a world shrouded in darkness, principally led, directed, governed, and controlled, from first to last, by the power of our common foe . . . — the devil. Lucifer has almost the entire control over the whole earth, rules and governs the children of men and leads them on to destruction."[66] "The whole world are wrapt up in the garment of corruption, confusion, and destruction; and they are fast making their way down to hell, while we have the words of eternal life."[67] "Will the inhabitants of the earth receive the truth? They will not."[68] "It never enters the hearts of the mass of mankind that they are preparing for the day of calamity and slaughter."[69] "You will see that the wisdom of the wise among the nations will perish and be taken from them. They will fall into difficulties, and they will not be able to tell the reason, nor point a way to avert them any more than they can now in this land. They can fight, quarrel, contend and destroy each other, but they do not know how to make peace. So it will be with the inhabitants of the earth."[70]

We have presented this basic historical proposition of the Latter-day Saints in little-known but powerful words of the Prophet Brigham Young to call to mind how faithfully such sayings continue the teachings of the Prophet Joseph and foreshadow the world in which we live. Almost the first words spoken by the Lord himself to the boy Joseph in his first vision were, "Behold the world lieth in sin at this time and none doeth good no not one they have turned asside [sic] from the Gospel and keep not my commandments they draw near to me with their lips while their hearts are far from me and mine anger is kindling against the inhabitants of the earth to visit them acording [sic] to this ungodliness."[71] The preface to the Doctrine and Covenants repeats this: "They seek not the Lord, . . . but every man walketh in his own way . . . in Babylon, even Babylon the great, which shall fall" (D&C 1:16). And so on down: "Behold, the world is ripening in iniquity" (D&C 18:6). "The hour is nigh and the day soon at hand when the earth is ripe; and all the proud and they that do wickedly shall be as stubble; . . . I will take vengeance upon the wicked, for they will not repent; for the cup of mine indignation is full" (D&C 29:9, 17). "All flesh is corrupted before me; and the powers of darkness prevail upon the earth, . . . and all eternity is pained, and the angels are waiting. . . . The enemy is combined" (D&C 38:11-12). (Do such words mean nothing to us?) "Behold, the day has come, when the cup of the wrath of mine indignation is full. . . . Wherefore, labor ye; . . . for the adversary spreadeth his dominions, and darkness reigneth; and the anger of God kindleth against the inhabitants of the earth; and none doeth good, for all have gone out of the way" (D&C 43:26, 28; 82:5-6). "Darkness covereth the earth, and gross darkness the minds of the people, and all flesh has become corrupt before my face. Behold, vengeance cometh speedily . . . upon all the face of the earth. . . . And upon my house shall it begin, . . . first among . . . you . . . who have professed to know my name and have not known me" (D&C 112:23-26).

So the word of the Lord is that Babylon is to remain in Babylon until the day of destruction. Things have not improved since Joseph Smith wrote of "the most damning hand of murder, tyranny, and oppressions, supported and urged on and upheld by the influence of that spirit which has so strongly riveted the creeds of the fathers, who have inherited lies, upon the hearts of the children, and filled the world with confusion, and has been growing stronger and stronger, and is now the very mainspring of all corruption, and the whole earth groans under the weight of its iniquity."[72] "Some may have cried peace," he wrote (and no man ever loved peace more than he), "but the Saints and the world will have little peace from henceforth."[73] "*Destruction*, to the eye of the spiritual beholder, seems to be written by the finger of an invisible hand, in large capitals, upon almost every thing we behold."[74] "There is a spirit that prompts the nations to prepare for war, desolation, and bloodshed—to waste each other away," said Brigham twenty years later. "Do they realize it? No. . . . Is it not a mystery?"[75] "When the nations have for years turned much of their attention to manufacturing instruments of death, they have sooner or later used those instruments. . . . [They] will be used until the people are wasted away, and there is no help for it."[76]

This, then, is how things stand: (1) We know what Zion is, (2) we know what Babylon is, (3) we know that the two can never mix, and (4) we know that the Latter-day Saints, against the admonitions of their leaders, have always tried to mix them. How is this done? (And now comes our sermon.)

In order to reconcile the ways of Babylon with the ways of Zion, it has been necessary to circumvent the inconvenient barriers of scripture and conscience by the use of the tried and true device of *rhetoric,* defined by Plato as the art of making true things seem false and false things seem true by the use of words.[77] This invaluable art has, since the time of Cain, invested the ways of Babylon with an air of high purpose, solid virtue, and impeccable respectability. "The servants of sin should appear polished and pious, . . . able to call to their assistance . . . the subtle, persuasive power of rhetoric."[78] "The devil is an orator; he is powerful; . . . he can tempt all classes."[79]

Years ago I published a number of articles in various journals dealing with the Roman world of the fourth century A.D.[80] Let us recall that early Jewish and Christian writers referred to Rome simply as Babylon; it was the true Babylon of the time, but a Babylon sustained by a high sense of virtue. For, as the Romans became ever more corrupted by wealth (the Roman satirists, shrewd and observant men, infallibly put their finger on the spot every time), they became more and more fascinated with the image of themselves as honest, hard-working, straightforward, tough-minded citizens: *Hic est Ausonia* ("Here is Ausonia"), they said: "The Western world of clean, fresh, simple, unspoiled pioneers." This fiction became the very cornerstone of the official doctrine. "Rome was great because Rome was good, giving expression to the old Roman belief in the close association between piety and success."[81] This was the rhetoric of wealth, and it was inevitable—it always follows in such a situation, because people simply can't live virtuously and viciously at the same time. Yet they want to be good and rich at the same time, and so they reach a compromise called respectability, which is nothing less than Babylon masquerading as Zion.

Any social worker or observer knows that no one can be more straitlaced, puritanical, and exquisitely respectable than a harlot. She has to reek with virtue to relieve her terrible inner tensions. There is nothing the Godfather prizes more than his respectability, and extensive surveys have shown that he has become something of a hero-figure in this country. A patriot (he loves America with such a passion that a squadron of government lawyers cannot induce him to leave it), a church-going family man, impeccably proper in dress and etiquette, he outwits all his brutal rivals and establishes his credibility by instant liquidation of all who stand in his way. It is not enough for the wicked to make excuses or explanations; in order to live with themselves and succeed in their undertakings, they must stand forth and be counted as pillars of righteousness, raising a hue and cry with practiced skill against those who would jeopardize their position, demonstrating, usually with the aid of paid rhetoricians, ministers, and lawyers, that it is not they but their opponents who are wicked. This is a *leitmotif*, a main theme, in the Book of Mormon: "We know that the people . . . in the land of Jerusalem were a righteous people; . . . and our father hath judged them, and hath led us away" (1 Nephi 17:22). Thus said the self-righteous Laman and Lemuel. "This man doth revile against our laws which are just, and our wise lawyers whom we have selected." Amulek, thus accused, answered: "Have I testified against your law? . . . I have spoken in favor of your law, to your con-demnation. . . . And . . . the people cried out against him, saying: Now we know that this man is a child of the devil, for he hath lied unto us; for he hath spoken against our law . . . and . . . reviled . . . against our lawyers, and our judges. And . . . the lawyers put it into their hearts that they should remember these things against him. . . . Now the object of these lawyers was to get gain" (Alma 10:24-32).

"Ye do not remember the Lord your God," said Samuel the Lamanite to the people of Zarahemla, "but ye do always remember your riches" (Helaman 13:22). (And how self-righteous they were about it!)

> Now when ye talk, ye say: If our days had been in the days of our fathers of old, we would not have slain the prophets. . . . Behold ye are worse than they; for . . . if a prophet . . . testifieth of your sins, . . . ye are angry with him; . . . yea, you will say that he is a false prophet, and that he is a sinner, and of the devil, because he testifieth that your deeds are evil. But behold, if a man . . . saith that all is well, then ye will not find fault with him. [On the contrary,] ye will clothe him with costly apparel . . . because . . . he saith that all is well (Helaman 13:25-28).

These people did not want to hear what was *wrong* with Zarahemla, only what was *right* with Zarahemla. Any-one who wanted their vote had only to avoid any mention of repentance and tell them that they had done no wrong, that Zarahemla was great because Zarahemla was good.

We do not have time here to examine the *loci communes*, the tried-and-true, sure-fire topics that made up the arsenal of the rhetoric of wealth. I was brought up on them and could talk on the subject all night. Suffice it here to mention a few of the most powerful and persuasive talking points.

First, of course, the work ethic, which is being so strenuously advocated in our day. This is one of those neat magician's tricks in which all our attention is focused on one hand while the other hand does the manipulating. Implicit in the work ethic are the ideas (1) that because one must work to acquire wealth, work equals wealth, and (2) that that is the whole equation. With these go the corollaries that anyone who has wealth must have earned it by hard work and is, therefore, beyond criticism; that anyone who doesn't have it deserves to suffer — thus penalizing any who do not work for money; and (since you have a right to all you earn) that the only real work is for one's self; and, finally, that any limit set to the amount of wealth an individual may acquire is a satanic device to deprive men of their free agency — thus making mockery of the Council of Heaven. These editorial syllogisms we have heard a thousand times, but you will not find them in the scriptures. Even the cornerstone of virtue, "He that is idle shall not eat the bread . . . of the laborer" (D&C 42:42), hailed as the franchise of unbridled capitalism, is rather a rebuke to that system which has allowed idlers to live in luxury and laborers in want throughout the whole course of history. The whole emphasis in the holy writ is not on whether one works or not, but what one works for: "The laborer in Zion shall labor for Zion; for if they labor for money they shall perish" (2 Nephi 26:31). "The people of the church began to wax proud, because of their exceeding riches, . . . precious things, which they had obtained by their industry" (Alma 4:6) and which proved their undoing, for all their hard work.

In Zion you labor, to be sure, but not for money, and not for yourself, which is the exact opposite of our present version of the work ethic. "The non-producer must live

on the products of those who labor. There is no other way,"
says Brigham, and he gives the solution: "If we all labor
a few hours a day, we could then spend the remainder of
our time in rest and the improvement of our minds."[82]
That is the real work we are called to do and the real wealth
we are to accumulate individually. "Work less, wear less,
eat less, and we shall be a great deal wiser, healthier, and
wealthier people than by taking the course we do now."[83]
Work does not sanctify wealth: "I know that there is no
man on this earth who can call around him property, . . . and dicker and work, and take advantage here
and there — no such man ever can magnify the priesthood
nor enter the celestial kingdom. Now, remember, they will
not enter that kingdom."[84] He gives a concrete illustration:
"When the Twelve Apostles were chosen in this dispensation, they were told not to labor with their hands, but
to preach the Gospel to the nations of the earth. Some of
them before a year had elapsed were engaged in trade;
they became merchants, and they apostatized."[85] "If we
lust . . . for the riches of the world, and spare no pains
[hard work] to obtain and retain them, and feel 'these are
mine,' then the spirit of the anti-Christ comes upon us.
This is the danger . . . [we] are in."[86] Admirable and indispensable in themselves, hard work, ingenuity, and enterprise become an evil when they are misdirected, meaning directed to personal aggrandizement: "A man says, 'I
am going to make iron, and I will have the credit of making
the first iron in the Territory. I will have the credit of
knowing how to flux the ore that is found in these regions,
and bringing out the metal in abundance, or no other man
shall.' Now, the beauty and glory of this kind of proceeding
is the blackest of darkness, and its comeliness as deformity."[87] An act, good in itself, becomes a monstrous
deformity when thus misdirected.

The first rule of economics is that everyone should
provide, as far as possible, for himself. The second, which

receives vastly more attention in the scriptures, is that
man's wants are few. "Having food and raiment," says
Paul, "let us be therewith content" (1 Timothy 6:8). "If we
have our hundreds or thousands," says Brother Brigham,
"we may foster the idea that we have nothing more than
we need; but such a notion is entirely erroneous, for our
real wants are very limited. What do we absolutely need?
I possess everything on the face of the earth that I need,
as I appear before you on this stand."[88] With our real wants
thus modest, there is plenty on earth for everyone, "for
the earth is full and there is enough and to spare" (D&C
104:17), and no excuse whatever for competitive grabbing—"wherefore the world lieth in sin" (D&C 49:20). To
take more than we need is to take what does not belong
to us.

In Zion, all are "of one heart and one mind, . . . and
there [are] no poor among them" (Moses 7:18), thus showing that equality extends into all fields, as it must also be
in the preparation for Zion: "For if ye are not equal in
earthly things ye cannot be equal in obtaining heavenly
things. For if you will that I give you a place in the celestial
world, you must prepare yourselves" (D&C 78:6-7). "And
you are to be equal, . . . to have equal claims, . . . every
man according to his wants and his needs, . . . every man
seeking the interest of his neighbor, and doing all things
with an eye single to the glory of God" (D&C 82:17, 19).
Well, there is a great deal of this. In the words of the
Prophet Joseph, "The greatest temporal and spiritual blessings which always come from faithfulness and concerted
effort, never attended individual exertion or enterprise"[89]
(a statement I do not recall having heard from the stand
for some time). This was a hard lesson to learn: to come
down to earth. "The Latter-day Saints, in their conduct
and acts with regard to financial matters, are like the rest
of the world. The course pursued by men of business in
the world has a tendency to make a few rich, and to sink

the masses of the people in poverty and degradation. Too many of the Elders of Israel take this course. No matter what comes they are for gain — for gathering around them riches; and when they get rich, how are those riches used? Spent on the lusts of the flesh."[90] As to the idler eating the bread of the laborer, "I have seen many cases . . . ," says Brigham, "when the young lady would have to take her clothing on a Saturday night and wash it, in order that she might go to meeting on the Sunday with a clean dress on. Who is she laboring for? For those who, many of them, are living in luxury. And, to serve the classes that are living on them, the poor, laboring men and women are toiling, working their lives out to earn that which will keep a little life within them. Is this equality? No! What is going to be done? The Latter-day Saints will never accomplish their mission until this inequality shall cease on the earth."[91] "The earth is here, and the fullness thereof is here. It was made for man; and one man was not made to trample his fellowman under his feet, and enjoy all his hearts desires, while the thousands suffer."[92] Regardless of who works and who doesn't, no just father is going to order one son clothed in robes and another in rags (D&C 38:26).

Of course, the man who devotes himself to the tiring routines of business should be rewarded, but should all others be penalized who do not engage in that particular line of work? "Where, then, is your great ability? In your pockets — in the god so much adored," says Brigham with contempt; there is other work to be done and far greater: "But take the men that can travel the earth over, preach the Gospel without purse or scrip, and then go to and lay their plans to gather the saints. That looks like the work of angels."[93] Granted that those who acquire wealth are sometimes people of superior talent (though for every real artist, or poet, or composer in America, there are at least ten thousand millionaires), "those who are blessed with superior abilities," even in business, "should use those

blessings . . . to administer to others less favored." Our
gifts and talents are to be put at the disposal of the human
race, not used to put the race at our disposal. "Instead of
this," Brigham notes, "man has become so perverted as
to debar his fellows as much as possible from those blessings, and constrain them by physical force or circumstances
to contribute of the proceeds of their labour to sustain the
favoured few."[94] That is not Zion, but that is what we
have. Should we settle for it?

> The doctrine of uniting together in our temporal la-
> bors, and all working for the good of all is from the
> beginning, from everlasting, and it will be for ever and
> ever. No one supposes for one moment that in heaven
> the angels are speculating, that they are building rail-
> roads and factories, taking advantage one of another,
> gathering up the substance there is in heaven to ag-
> grandize themselves, and that they live on the same
> principle that we are in the habit of doing. No Christian,
> no sectarian Christian, in the world believes this; they
> believe that the inhabitants of heaven live as a family,
> that their faith, interests and pursuits have one end in
> view — the glory of God and their own salvation, that
> they may receive more and more. . . . We all believe
> this, and suppose we go to work and imitate them as
> far as we can.[95]

"There are men in this community who, through the
force of the education they have received from their parents
and friends [i.e., this is an established ethic among us],
would cheat a poor widow out of her last cow, and then
go down upon their knees and thank God for the good
fortune he had sent them and for his kind providences
that enabled them to obtain a cow without becoming ame-
nable to *any law of the land*, though the poor widow has
been actually cheated."[96] Here, please note, the defense
of immorality is *legality*: if it is legal, all is well, even though
the law has been contrived under pressure of interest
groups.

God recognizes only one justification for seeking wealth, and that is with the express intent of helping the poor (Jacob 2:19). One of the disturbing things about Zion is that its appeal, according to the scriptures, is all to the poor: "The Lord hath founded Zion, and the poor of his people shall trust in it" (Isaiah 14:32). Of course, once in Zion, no one suffers from poverty, for they dwell in righteousness and there are no poor among them (Moses 7:18). The law of consecration is a minimal requirement, for "if my people observe not this law, . . . it shall not be a land of Zion unto you" (D&C 119:6). Here our rhetoric engages in a neat bit of sophistry that has always been popular:

> Elders of Israel are greedy after the things of this world. If you ask them if they are ready to build up the kingdom of God, their answer is prompt—"Why, to be sure we are, with our whole souls; but we want first to get so much gold, speculate and get rich, and then we can help the church considerably. We will go to California and get gold, go and buy goods and get rich, trade with the emigrants, build a mill, make a farm, get a large herd of cattle, and *then* we can do a great deal for Israel."[97]

I have heard this many times from friends and relatives, but it is hokum. What they are saying is, "If God will give me a million dollars, I will let him have a generous cut of it." And so they pray and speculate and expect the Lord to come through for them. He won't do it: "And again, I command thee that thou shalt not covet thine own property" (D&C 19:26). "Let them repent of all their sins, and of all their covetous desires, before me, saith the Lord; for what is property unto me? saith the Lord" (D&C 117:4). He does not need our property or our help.

Every rhetorician knows that his most effective weapons by far are *labels*. He can demolish the opposition with simple and devastating labels such as communism, socialism, or atheism, popery, militarism, or Mormonism, or give his clients' worst crimes a religious glow with noble labels such as integrity, old-fashioned honesty, tough-mindedness, or free competitive enterprise. "You can get away with anything if you just wave the flag," a business partner of my father once told me. He called that patriotism. But the label game reaches its all-time peak of skill and effrontery in the Madison Avenue master stroke of pasting the lovely label of Zion on all the most typical institutions of Babylon: Zion's Loans, Zion's Real Estate, Zion's Used Cars, Zion's Jewelry, Zion's Supermart, Zion's Auto Wrecking, Zion's Outdoor Advertising, Zion's Gunshop, Zion's Land and Mining, Zion's Development, Zion's Securities—all that is quintessentially Babylon now masquerades as Zion.

There is a precedent for the bit of faking—a most distinguished one. Satan, being neither stupid nor inexperienced, knows the value of a pleasing appearance—there are times when it pays to appear even as an angel of light. He goes farther than that, however, to assure that success of his masquerade (given out since the days of Adam) as a picturesquely repulsive figure—a four-star horror with claws, horns, or other obvious trimmings. With that idea firmly established, he can operate with devastating effectiveness as a very proper gentleman, a handsome and persuasive salesman. He "decoys" our minds (a favorite word with Brigham Young) with false words and appearances. A favorite trick is to put the whole blame on sex. Sex can be a pernicious appetite, but it runs a poor second to the other. For example: We are wont to think of Sodom as the original sexpot, but according to all accounts "this was the iniquity of thy sister Sodom": that great wealth made her people cruel and self-righteous.[98] The worst sinners, according to Jesus, are not the harlots and publicans, but the religious leaders with their insistence on proper dress and grooming, their careful observance of all the rules, their precious concern for status symbols, their strict legality, their pious patriotism. Longhairs, beards, necklaces, LSD and rock, Big Sur and Woodstock come and go, but Babylon is always there: rich, respectable, immovable, with its granite walls and steel vaults, its bronze gates, its onyx trimmings and marble floors (all borrowed from ancient temples, for these are our modern temples), and its bullet-proof glass — the awesome symbols of total security. Keeping her orgies decently private, she presents a front of unalterable propriety to all. As the early Christian writers observed, Babylon always wins: in every showdown throughout history, Satan has remained in possession of the field, and he still holds it. Its security and respectability exert a strong appeal: "When I see this people grow and spread and prosper," said Brigham Young, "I feel there is more danger than when they are in poverty. Being driven from city to city . . . is nothing compared to the danger of becoming rich and being hailed by outsiders as a first-class community."[99]

Brigham Young has this to say on the Puritan ethic, which shifts the burden of guilt from wealth to sex:

> When the books are opened, out of which the human family are to be judged, how disappointed the professedly sanctified, long-faced hypocrites and smooth-toned pharisees will be, when the publicans and harlots enter into the kingdom of heaven before them; people that appeared to be full of evil, but the Lord says they never designed to do wrong; the Devil had power over them, and they suffered in their mortal state a thousand times more than you poor, miserable, canting, cheating, snivelling, hypocritical pharisees; you were dressed in purple and fine linen, and bound burdens upon your weaker brethren that you would not so much as help to lift with your little fingers. Did you ever go without food, suffer with tooth-ache, sore eyes, rheumatism, or the chills and fever? You have fared sumptuously all your days and you condemned to an everlasting hell these poor harlots and publicans who never designed an evil. Are you not guilty of committing an evil with that poor

harlot? Yes, and you will be damned while she will be saved.[100]

When the Saints were shocked by growing juvenile delinquency in their midst, who were the real criminals? Brigham knows: "I have not the least hesitation in saying that the loose conduct, and calculations, and manner of doing business, which have characterized men who have had property in their hands, have laid the foundation to bring our boys into the spirit of stealing. You have caused them to do it, you have laid before them every inducement possible, to learn their hands and train their minds to take that which is not their own."[101] But the respectable appearance will nearly always win, though the Lord has said, "Judge not according to the appearance, but judge righteous judgment" (John 7:24).

Here are a few notes from Brigham on this clever campaign: "The devil appears as a gentleman when he presents himself to the children of men."[102] "The devil does not care how much religion there is on earth; he is a great preacher, and to all appearance, a great gentleman. . . . It is popular now-a-days to be religious; it has become the seasoning to a great deal of rascality, hypocrisy and crime."[103] "The adversary presents his principles and arguments in the most approved style, and in the most winning tone, attended with the most graceful attitudes; and he is very careful to ingratiate himself into the favour of the powerful and influential of mankind, uniting himself with popular parties, floating into offices of trust and emolument by pandering to popular feeling, though it should seriously wrong and oppress the innocent."[104] No atheism here! "The servants of sin should appear polished and pious, . . . able to call to their assistance . . . the subtle, persuasive power of rhetoric."[105] "The devil is an orator," said Joseph Smith. "He is powerful; . . . he can tempt all classes."[106]

It is not difficult to discover the plot of the drama of the restored gospel. But the prince of this world does not like certain aspects of the play, and so his people have undertaken to rewrite the script. What has today happened is an old story and is crassly obvious — they have switched villains on us. They have cast an obnoxious young light-weight (a very minor devil) to the role of the Evil One while the one most qualified to play it prefers to take the part of a dignified, upright, mature, and often charming gentle-man. It was clever to put a pathetic, long-haired, dirty, neurotic, mixed-up, idealistic, sex-hungry fool in the role of the heavy while an actor of infinitely greater skill and experience takes the highly respectable part of the arch-pillar of society. But no one whose knowledge of life and letters has taken him as far as a season of TV westerns or soap operas would be fooled for a minute by the shift. The well-groomed, well-dressed, well-fed, successful, respect-able man of the world (in the western, it's the banker, mineowner, or local landbaron) points a finger trembling with righteous wrath and scorn at the miserable, half-baked tramp or cowboy who gives himself away all over the place.

The sorriest thing about Babylon's masquerade and the switched villains is that there is nothing the least bit clever or subtle about it. It is all as crude, obvious, and heavy-handed as it can be, and it only gets by because everybody wants it to. We rather like the Godfather and the lively and competitive world he moves in: what would TV do without it? What other world have our children ever known? We want to be vindicated in our position and to know that the world is on our side as we all join in a chorus of righteous denunciation; the haircut becomes the test of virtue in a world where Satan deceives and rules by ap-pearance. The full-fledged citizen of Babylon is an orga-nization man: Daniel was thrown to the lions before he would give up his private devotions offensive to the administration to which he belonged; his three friends preferred being cast into a fiery furnace to the simple act of facing and saluting the image of the king of Babylon who had given them wealth, power, and position in his kingdom, to whom they owed all allegiance, when the band played in the Plain of Dura. For Brigham Young, conformity is the danger signal: "I am not a stereotyped Latter-day Saint," he said, "and do not believe in the doctrine. . . . Away with stereotyped 'Mormons'!"[107] When, as a boy, he was asked by his father to sign a temperance pledge, he resolutely refused.[108] Youth rebelling against respectability? No, honesty resisting social pressure and hypocrisy.

Why this highly unoriginal talk? Because if this is a very important and cosmic part of the gospel, it is also a much neglected one.

All my life I have shied away from these disturbing and highly unpopular — even offensive — themes. But I cannot do so any longer, because in my old age I have taken to reading the scriptures and there have had it forced upon my reluctant attention, that from the time of Adam to the present day, Zion has been pitted against Babylon, and the name of the game has always been money — "power and gain."

> It has been supposed that wealth gives power. In a depraved state of society, in a certain sense it does, if opening a wide field for unrighteous monopolies, by which the poor are robbed and oppressed and the wealthy are more enriched, is power. In a depraved state of society money can buy positions and titles, can cover up a multitude of incapabilities, can open wide the gates of fashionable society to the lowest and most depraved of human beings; it divides society into castes without any reference to goodness, virtue or truth. It is made to pander to the most brutal passions of the human soul; it is made to subvert every wholesome law of God and man, and to trample down every sacred bond that should

tie society together in a national, municipal, domestic and every other relationship.[109]

Cain slew "his brother Abel, for the sake of getting gain" (Moses 5:50). For Satan had taught him "this great secret, that I may murder and get gain" (Moses 5:31). He excused himself to God: "Satan tempted me because of my brother's flocks" (Moses 5:38), and having gotten the best of his brother in competition, Cain "gloried in that which he had done," rejoicing in the rhetoric of wealth: "I am free; surely the flocks of my brother falleth into my hands" (Moses 5:33).

He felt no guilt, since this was fair competition. Abel could take care of himself: "Am I my brother's keeper?" (Moses 5:34).

It was all free competitive enterprise where "every man prospered according to his genius, and . . . every man conquered according to his strength; and whatsoever a man did was no crime" (Alma 30:17). This is no mere red thread running through the scriptures but the broad highway of history.

Commenting on the astonishingly short time in which the Nephites turned from a righteous to a wicked nation, Nephi puts his finger on the spot: "Now the cause of this iniquity of the people was this—Satan had great power, unto the stirring up of the people to do all manner of iniquity, . . . tempting them to seek [in other words, work] for power, and authority, and riches, and the vain things of the world" (3 Nephi 6:15).

I pray that there may be some Latter-day Saints who do not succumb to the last and most determined onslaught of Babylon, which I believe may be coming.

Notes

1. *TPJS* 19.
2. *MS* 21:825.
3. *JD* 9:283.

4. Ibid., 5:4.

5. Ibid., 9:285.

6. Ibid., 9:284.

7. Fragment 60, in Hermann Diels and Walther Kranz, *Die Fragmente der Vorsokratiker*, 3 vols. (Berlin: Weidmann, 1951), 1:164.

8. Joseph F. Smith, *Gospel Doctrine* (Salt Lake City: Deseret Book, 1978), 337.

9. *JD* 9:170.

10. *MS* 29:268.

11. *JD* 14:153.

12. Ibid., 10:111.

13. Ibid., 1:203.

14. Ibid., 4:38.

15. Ibid., 4:32.

16. Ibid., 9:144.

17. *MS* 27:713, from *Deseret News*, 33:42.

18. *JD* 18:360.

19. Ibid., 10:111.

20. *TPJS* 125.

21. *MS* 20:34.

22. *JD* 4:111.

23. Ibid., 12:61.

24. Ibid., 13:148.

25. Ibid., 11:300.

26. Ibid., 15:4.

27. Ibid., 18:263.

28. *MS* 35:275.

29. *JD* 8:169-70; 16:26.

30. Journal History, LDS Church Archives (October 1, 1848).

31. *MS* 39:118-19.

32. *JD* 10:268.

33. Edward Stevenson, *Life and History of Elder Edward Stevenson* (n.d.), 40-41.

34. *JD* 11:216.

35. Ibid., 3:222.

36. Ibid., 12:154.

37. Ibid., 9:249.

38. Ibid., 7:282.

39. Ibid., 15:34.

40. Ibid., 11:324-25.

41. Ibid., 6:196.

42. Ibid., 10:267.

43. *TPJS* 9.
44. *JD* 11:102.
45. Ibid., 8:343-44.
46. Ibid., 3:222.
47. *TPJS* 9.
48. *JD* 1:335.
49. Ibid., 18:238-39.
50. *TPJS* 161.
51. *JD* 15:3.
52. Ibid., 11:241.
53. Ibid., 11:297.
54. Ibid., 6:72.
55. Ibid., 9:29.
56. Ibid., 19:97.
57. Ibid., 3:118.
58. Ibid., 17:38.
59. Ibid., 5:353.
60. Ibid., 6:197.
61. Ibid., 12:269.
62. Ibid., 17:37.
63. Ibid., 18:304.
64. Ibid., 8:285.
65. Ibid., 8:209.
66. Ibid., 3:223.
67. Ibid., 6:43.
68. Ibid., 11:255.
69. Ibid., 3:273.
70. Ibid., 10:315.
71. The 1832 recital of the First Vision as dictated by Joseph Smith to Frederick G. Williams. See Milton V. Backman, *Joseph Smith's First Vision* (Salt Lake City: Bookcraft, 1971), appendix A; cf. Dean C. Jessee, ed., "The Early Accounts of Joseph Smith's First Vision," *BYU Studies* 9 (1969): 280.
72. *TPJS* 145.
73. Ibid., 160.
74. Ibid., 16.
75. *JD* 8:174.
76. Ibid., 8:157.
77. Plato, *Apology* 18B.
78. *JD* 11:234.
79. *TPJS* 162.
80. Hugh W. Nibley, "Victoriosa Loquacitas: The Rise of Rhetoric

and the Decline of Everything Else," *Western Speech* 20 (1956): 57-82; Hugh W. Nibley, "Sparsiones," *Classical Journal* 25 (1945): 515-43; Hugh W. Nibley, "The Unsolved Loyalty Problem: Our Western Heritage," *WPQ* 6 (1953): 631-57; Hugh W. Nibley, "The Hierocentric State," *WPQ* 4 (1951): 226-53.
81. Nibley, "Unsolved Loyalty Problem," 638.
82. *JD* 19:47.
83. Ibid., 12:122.
84. Ibid., 11:297.
85. *MS* 30:626.
86. *JD* 10:300.
87. Ibid., 9:257.
88. *MS* 32:818.
89. *TPJS* 183.
90. *JD* 11:348.
91. Ibid., 19:47.
92. Ibid., 19:46.
93. Ibid., 8:353.
94. *MS* 17:673-74.
95. *JD* 17:117-18.
96. Ibid., 6:71 (emphasis added).
97. Ibid., 1:164.
98. Hugh W. Nibley, "Setting the Stage—The World of Abraham, (Part 9, continued)," *Improvement Era* (November 1969): 118, citing references.
99. *JD* 12:272.
100. Ibid., 10:176.
101. Ibid., 1:255.
102. Ibid., 11:236.
103. Ibid., 11:251.
104. Ibid., 11:238.
105. Ibid., 11:234.
106. *TPJS* 162.
107. *JD* 8:185.
108. Ibid., 14:225.
109. Ibid., 10:3.

3

Zeal Without Knowledge

In one of his fascinating scientific survey books, this time dealing with the latest discoveries about the brain, Nigel Calder notes, "Two of the most self-evident characteristics of the conscious mind [are that] . . . the mind attends to one thing at a time, [and] that, at least once a day, . . . the conscious mind is switched off."[1] Both of these operations are completely miraculous and completely mysterious. I would like to talk about the first of them. You can think of only *one* thing at a time!

If you put on a pair of glasses, one lens being green, the other being red, you will not see a grey fusion of the two when you look about you, but a flashing of red and green. One moment everything will be green, another moment everything will be red. Or you may think you are enjoying a combination of themes as you listen to a Bach fugue, with equal awareness of every voice at a time, but you are actually jumping between recognition first of one and then another. "The eye," like the ear, in the words of N. S. Sutherland, "is always flickering about; . . . the brain adds together a great variety of impressions, at high speed," and from these we select features from what we see and make a rapid succession of "models" of the world in our minds.[2] Out of what begins as what William James

This academic awareness lecture was presented June 26, 1975, and was later printed in manuscript form. It was then reprinted in Dialogue: A Journal of Mormon Thought *11/2 (Summer 1978): 101-12, as well as in* Nibley on the Timely and Timeless *(Provo, UT: Religious Studies Center, 1978), 261-77.*

calls the "big blooming, buzzing confusion"[3] of the infant's world, we structure our own meaningful combination of impressions, and all our lives select out of the vast number of impressions certain ones that fit best into that structure. As Neisser says, "The 'model' is what we see, and nothing else."[4] We hold thousands of instantaneous impressions in suspension just long enough to make our choices and drop those we don't want. As one expert puts it, "There seems to be a kind of filter inside the head [that] weaken[s] the unwanted signals, . . . [but] cannot be a complete block to background information."[5] *Why* the mind chooses to focus on one object to the seclusion of all others remains a mystery.[6] But one thing is clear: the blocked-out signals are the unwanted ones, and the ones we favor are our "deliberate choices."

This puts us in the position of the fairy-tale hero who is introduced into a cave of incredible treasures and permitted to choose from the heap whatever gem he wants— but only one. What a delightful situation! I can think of anything I want to—absolutely anything!—with this provision: that when I choose to focus my attention on one object, all other objects drop into the background. I am only permitted to think of one thing at a time; that is the one rule of the game.

An equally important rule is that I must keep thinking! Except for the daily shutoff period, I cannot evade the test. "L'âme pense toujours"[7] ("the soul is always thinking") says Malebranche: We are always thinking of *something,* selecting what will fit into the world we are making for ourselves. Schopenhauer was right: "Die Welt ist meine Vorstellung"[8] ("the world is how I perceive it"). And here is an aside I can't resist: What would it be like if I could view and focus on two or more things at once, if I could see at one and the same moment not only what is right before me but equally well what is on my left side, my right side, what is above me and below me? I have the

moral certainty that something is there, and as my eyes
flicker about, I think I can substantiate that impression.
But as to taking a calm and deliberate look at more than
one thing at a time, that is a gift denied us at present. I
cannot imagine what such a view of the world would be
like; but it would be *more* real and correct than the one we
have now. I bring up this obvious point because it is by
virtue of this one-dimensional view of things that we mag-
isterially pass judgment on God. The smart atheist and
pious schoolman alike can tell us all about God — what he
can do and what he cannot, what he must be like and what
he cannot be like — on the basis of their one-dimensional
experience of reality. Today the astronomers are harping
on the old favorite theme of the eighteenth-century en-
cyclopedists, who, upon discovering the universe to be
considerably larger than they thought or had been taught,
immediately announced that man, as a very minor creature
indeed, would have to renounce any special claim to divine
favor, since there are much bigger worlds than ours for
God to be concerned about, and in the end give up his
intimate and private God altogether. This jaunty icono-
clasm rested on the assumption that God is subject to the
same mental limitations that we are; that if he is thinking
of Peter, he can hardly be thinking of Paul at the same
time, let alone marking the fall of the sparrow. But once
we can see the possibilities that lie in being able to see
more than one thing at a time (and in theory the experts
tell us there is no reason why we should not), the universe
takes on new dimensions and God takes over again. Let
us remember that quite peculiar to the genius of Mormonism is the doctrine of a God who could preoccupy
himself with countless numbers of things: "The heavens,
they are many, and they cannot be numbered unto man;
but they are numbered unto me, for they are mine" (Moses
1:37).

Plainly, we are dealing with two orders of minds. "My

thoughts are not your thoughts, neither are your ways my
ways, saith the Lord. For as the heavens are higher than
the earth, so are . . . my thoughts than your thoughts"
(Isaiah 55:8-9).

But why this crippling limitation on our thoughts if we
are God's children? It is precisely this limitation that is the
essence of our mortal existence. If every choice I make
expresses a preference, if the world I build up is the world
I really love and want, then with every choice I am judging
myself, proclaiming all the day long to God, angels, and
my fellowmen where my real values lie, where my treasure
is, the things to which I give supreme importance. Hence,
in this life every moment provides a perfect and foolproof
test of your real character, making this life a time of testing
and probation. And hence the agonizing cry of the Prophet
Moroni, speaking to our generation: "I speak unto you as
if ye were present, and yet ye are not, but behold, Jesus
Christ hath shown you unto me, and I know your doing"
(Mormon 8:35). He calls upon us, "Be wise in the days of
your probation; . . . ask not, that ye may consume it on
your lusts" (Mormon 9:28), in other words, that you may
use up or consume your probation time just having a good
time or doing what you feel like doing—nothing could be
more terrible than that: "But *wo* unto him . . . that *wasteth*
the days of his probation, for *awful* is his state!" (2 Nephi
9:27). It is throwing our life away, to think of the wrong
things, as we are told in the next verse, that the cunning
plan of the evil one is to get us to do just that—trying, in
Brigham Young's phrase, to "decoy the minds of thy
Saints"[9] to get our minds on trivial thoughts, on the things
of this world, against which we have so often been warned.

Sin is waste. It is doing one thing when you should be
doing other and better things for which you have the capacity. Hence, there are no innocent, idle thoughts. That
is why even the righteous must repent, constantly and
progressively, since all fall short of their capacity and call-

ing. "Probably 99 per cent of human ability has been wholly wasted," writes Arthur Clarke; "even today . . . [we] operate for most of our time as automatic machines, and glimpse the profounder resources of our minds only once or twice in a lifetime."[10] "No nation can afford to divert its ablest men into such essentially non-creative, and occasionally parasitic, occupations as law, advertising, and banking."[11] Those officials whom Moroni chides for sitting "upon [their] thrones in a state of thoughtless stupor" (Alma 60:7) were not deliberately or maliciously harming anyone—but they were committing grave sin. Why do people feel guilty about TV? What is wrong with it? Just this—that it shuts out all the wonderful things of which the mind is capable, leaving it drugged in a state of thoughtless stupor. For the same reason, a mediocre school or teacher is a *bad* school or teacher. Last week it was announced in the papers that a large convention concerned with violence and disorder in our schools came to the unanimous conclusion (students and teachers alike) that the main cause of the mischief was *boredom*. Underperformance, the job that does not challenge you, can make you sick: work that puts repetition and routine in the place of real work begets a sense of guilt; merely doodling and noodling in committees can give you ulcers, skin rashes, and heart trouble. God is not pleased with us for merely sitting in meetings: "How vain and trifling have been our spirits, our conferences, our councils, our meetings, our private as well as public conversations," wrote the Prophet Joseph from Liberty Jail,—"too low, too mean, too vulgar, too condescending for the dignified characters of the called and chosen of God."[12]

This puts a serious face on things. If we try to evade the responsibility of directing our minds to the highest possible object, if we try to settle for a milder program at lower stakes and safer risks, we are immediately slapped and buffeted by a power that will not let us rest. Being here, we must play the probation game, and we pay an awful forfeit for every effort to evade it. We must think— but about what? The substance of thought is knowledge. "The human brain depends for its normal alertness, reliability and efficiency on a continuous flow of information about the world; . . . the brain craves for information as the body craves for food."[13] "What is true of individuals is also true of societies; they too can become insane without sufficient stimulus."[14] If the mind is denied functioning to capacity, it will take terrible revenge. The penalty we pay for starving our minds is a phenomenon that is only too conspicuous at Brigham Young University. Aristotle pointed out long ago that a shortage of knowledge is an intolerable state, and so the mind will do anything to escape it; in particular, it will invent knowledge if it has to. Experimenters have found that lack of information quickly breeds insecurity in a situation where any information is regarded as better than none.[15] In that atmosphere, false information flourishes; and subjects in tests are "eager to listen to and believe any sort of preposterous nonsense."[16] Why so? We repeat, because the very nature of man requires him to use his mind to capacity: "The mind or the intelligence which man possesses," says Joseph Smith, "is co-equal with God himself." What greater crime than the minimizing of such capacity? The Prophet continues, "All the minds and spirits that God ever sent into the world are susceptible of enlargement. . . . God himself, finding he was in the midst of spirits and glory, because he was more intelligent, saw proper to institute laws whereby the rest could have a privilege to advance like himself. The relationship we have with God places us in a situation to *advance* in *knowledge.*"[17] *Expansion* is the theme, and we cannot expand the boundaries unless we first reach those boundaries, which means exerting ourselves to the absolute limit.

Now we come to a subject with which the Prophet

Joseph was greatly concerned. To keep the Saints always reaching for the highest and best, the utmost of their capacity, requires enormous motivation—and the gospel supplies it. Nothing can excite men to action like the contemplation of the eternities. The quality in which the Saints have always excelled is zeal. Zeal is the engine that drives the whole vehicle: without it we would get nowhere. But without clutch, throttle, brakes, and steering wheel, our mighty engine becomes an instrument of destruction, and the more powerful the motor, the more disastrous the inevitable crack-up if the proper knowledge is lacking. There is a natural tendency to let the mighty motor carry us along, to give it its head, to open it up and see what it can do. We see this in our society today. Scientists tell us that the advancement of a civilization depends on two things: (1) the amount of energy at its disposal, and (2) the amount of information at its disposal.[18] Today we have unlimited energy—nuclear power; but we still lack the necessary information to control and utilize it. We have the zeal but not the knowledge, so to speak. And this the Prophet Joseph considered a very dangerous situation in the Church. Speaking to the new Relief Society, "[he] commended them for their *zeal*, but said sometimes their zeal was not according to *knowledge*."[19] What good is the power, he asks, without real intelligence and solid knowledge?

He gives the example of those Saints who were carried away at the thought and prospect of "a glorious manifestation from God." And he bids them ask, "a manifestation of what? Is there any intelligence communicated? . . . All the intelligence that can be obtained from them when they arise, is a shout of 'glory,' or 'hallelujah,' or some incoherent expression, but they have had the 'power.' "[20] Another time he warned the sisters against being "subject to overmuch zeal, which must ever prove *dangerous*, and cause them to be rigid in a religious capacity."[21] Zeal makes us loyal and unflinching, but God wants more than that.

In the same breath, the Prophet said that the people "were depending on the Prophet, hence were darkened in their minds, in consequence of neglecting the duties devolving upon *themselves*."[22] They must do their own thinking and discipline their minds. If not, that will happen again which happened in Kirtland: "Many, having a zeal not according to knowledge," said the Prophet, "have, no doubt in the heat of enthusiasm, taught and said things which are derogatory to the genuine character and principles of the Church."[23] Specifically, "soon after the Gospel was established in Kirtland, . . . many false spirits were introduced, many strange visions were seen, and wild, enthusiastic notions were entertained; . . . many ridiculous things were entered into, calculated to bring disgrace upon the Church of God."[24] This was the time when some of the brethren in Kirtland were out to prove that they were smarter than the Prophet and produced the so-called *Egyptian Alphabet and Grammar*, to match *his* production of the book of Abraham.

This illustrates another point, that knowledge can be heady stuff, but it easily leads to an excess of zeal!—to illusions of grandeur and a desire to impress others and achieve eminence. The university is nothing more nor less than a place to show off: if it ceased to be that, it would cease to exist. Again the Prophet Joseph is right on target when he tells us that true knowledge can never serve that end. Knowledge is individual, he observes, and if a person has it, "who would know it? . . . The greatest, the best, and the most useful gifts, would be known nothing about by an observer. . . . There are only two gifts that could be made visible—the gift of tongues and the gift of prophecy."[25]

Our search for knowledge should be ceaseless, which means that it is open-ended, never resting on laurels, degrees, or past achievements. "If we get puffed up by thinking that we have much knowledge, we are apt to get a

contentious spirit," and what is the cure? "Correct knowledge is necessary to cast out that spirit."[26] The cure for
inadequate knowledge is "ever more light and knowledge." But who is going to listen patiently to correct knowledge if he thinks he has the answers already? "There are
a great many wise men and women too in our midst who
are too wise to be taught; therefore they must die in their
ignorance."[27] "I have tried for a number of years to get the
minds of the Saints prepared to receive the things of God;
but we frequently see some of them . . . [that] will fly to
pieces like glass as soon as anything comes that is contrary
to their traditions: they cannot stand the fire at all."[28] If
"I . . . go into an investigation of anything that is not contained in the Bible, . . . I think there are so many over-
wise men here, that they would cry 'treason' and put me
to death."[29] But, he asks, "Why be so certain that you
comprehend the things of God, when all things with you
are so uncertain?"[30] True knowledge never shuts the door
on more knowledge, but zeal often does. One thinks of
the dictum, "We are not seeking for truth at the BYU, we
have the truth!" So did Adam and Abraham have the truth,
far greater and more truth than what we have, and yet the
particular genius of each was that he was constantly "seeking for *greater* light and knowledge" (cf. Abraham 1:2).

The young, with their limited knowledge, are particularly susceptible to excessive zeal. Why do it the hard
way, they ask at the BYU, when God has given us the
answer book? The answer to that is, Because if you use
the answer book for your Latin or your math, or anything
else, you will always have a false sense of power and never
learn the real thing: "The people expect to see some wonderful manifestation, some great display of power," says
Joseph Smith, "or some extraordinary miracle performed;
and it is often the case that *young* members of this Church,
for want of better information, carry along with them their
old notions of things, and sometimes fall into egregious

errors."[31] "Be careful about sending boys to preach the
Gospel to the world," said Joseph Smith. Why? Certainly
not because they lacked zeal; that's the one thing they had.
The Prophet explains: "Lest they become puffed up, and
fall under condemnation. . . . Beware of pride; . . . apply
yourselves diligently to *study*, that your minds may be
stored with all necessary *information*."[32] That is doing it the
hard way. Can't the Spirit hurry things up? No—there is
no place for the cram course or quickie, or above all the
superficial survey course or quick trips to the Holy Land,
where the gospel is concerned: "We consider that God has
created man with a mind capable of instruction, and a
faculty which may be enlarged in proportion to the heed
and diligence given to the light communicated from heaven
to the *intellect*; . . . but . . . no man ever arrived in a moment: he must have been instructed . . . by *proper degrees*."[33] "The things of God are of deep import; and time,
and experience, and careful and ponderous and solemn
thoughts can *only* find them out. Thy mind, O man! if thou
wilt lead a soul unto salvation, must stretch as high as the
utmost heavens."[34] No shortcuts or easy lessons here! Note
well that the Prophet makes no distinction between things
of the spirit and things of the intellect.

Some years ago, when it was pointed out that BYU
graduates were the lowest in the nation in all categories
of the Graduate Record Examination, the institution characteristically met the challenge by abolishing the examination. It was done on the grounds that the test did not
sufficiently measure our unique "spirituality." We talked
extensively about "the education of the whole man" and
deplored that educational imbalance that comes when students' heads are merely stuffed with facts—as if there was
any danger of that here! But actually, serious imbalance is
impossible if one plays the game honestly: true zeal feeds
on knowledge, true knowledge cannot exist without zeal.
Both are "spiritual" qualities. All knowledge is the gospel,

but there must be a priority, "proper degrees," as the Prophet says, in the timing and emphasis of our learning, lest like the doctors of the Jews, we "strain at a gnat and swallow a camel" (Matthew 23:24). Furthermore, since one person does not receive revelation for another, if we would exchange or convey knowledge, we must be willing to have our knowledge *tested*. The gifted and zealous Mr. Olney was "disfellowshiped, because he would not have his writings *tested* by the word of God," according to Joseph Smith.[35]

Not infrequently, Latter-day Saints tell me that they have translated a text or interpreted an artifact, or been led to an archaeological discovery as a direct answer to prayer, and that for me to question or test the results is to question the reality of revelation; and often I am asked to approve a theory or "discovery" that I find unconvincing, because it has been the means of bringing people to the Church — such practitioners are asking me to take their zeal as an adequate substitute for knowledge; but like Brother Olney, they refuse to have their knowledge tested. True, "it needs revelation to assist us, and give us knowledge of the things of God,"[36] but only the hard worker can expect such assistance: "It is not wisdom that we should have all knowledge at once presented before us; but that we should have a little at a time; then we can *comprehend* it."[37] We must know what we are doing, understand the problem, live with it, lay a proper foundation. How many a Latter-day Saint has told me that he can understand the scriptures by pure revelation and does not need to toil at Greek or Hebrew as the Prophet and the Brethren did in the School of the Prophets at Kirtland and Nauvoo? Even Oliver Cowdery fell into that trap and was rebuked for it (D&C 9). "The principle of knowledge is the principle of salvation. This principle can be comprehended by the faithful and diligent," says the Prophet Joseph.[38]

New converts often get the idea that having accepted

the gospel, they have arrived at adequate knowledge. Others say that to have a testimony is to have everything they have sought and that they have found thereby the kingdom of heaven; but their minds go right on working just the same, and if they don't keep on getting new and testable knowledge, they will assuredly embrace those "wild, enthusiastic notions" of the new converts in Kirtland. Note what a different procedure Joseph Smith prescribes: "This first Comforter or Holy Ghost has no other effect than pure intelligence [it is not a hot, emotional surge]. It is more powerful in expanding the mind, enlightening the understanding, and storing intellect with present knowledge, of a man who is of the literal seed of Abraham, than one that is a Gentile."[39]

> For as the Holy Ghost falls upon one of the literal seed of Abraham, it is calm and serene; and his whole soul and body are only exercised by the pure spirit of intelligence. . . . The Spirit of Revelation is in connection with these blessings. A person may profit by noticing the first intimation of the spirit of revelation; for instance, when you feel pure intelligence flowing into you, it may give you sudden strokes of ideas, . . . thus by learning the Spirit of God and understanding it, you may grow into the principle of revelation.[40]

This is remarkably like the new therapeutic discipline called "biofeedback."

The emphasis is all on the continuous, conscientious, honest acquisition of knowledge. This admonition to sobriety and diligence goes along with the Prophet's outspoken recommendation of the Jews and their peculiar esteem and diligence for things of the mind.

> If there is anything calculated to interest the mind of the Saints, to awaken in them the finest sensibilities and arouse them to enterprise and exertion, surely it is the great and precious promises made by our heavenly Father to the children of Abraham . . . and the dispersed

of Judah . . . and inasmuch as you feel interested for the
covenant people of the Lord, the God of their fathers
shall bless you . . . He will endow you with power, wisdom, might and intelligence, and every qualification necessary; while your minds will expand wider and wider,
until you can . . . contemplate the mighty acts of Jehovah in all their variety and glory.[41]

In Israel today, there are great contests in which young
people and old from all parts of the world display their
knowledge of scripture and skill at music, science, or mathematics, in grueling competitions. This sort of thing tends
to breed a race of insufferably arrogant, conceited little
show-offs—*and* magnificent performers. They tend to be
like the Jews of old, who "sought for things that they could
not understand," ever "looking beyond the mark," and
hence falling on their faces: "they must needs fall" (Jacob
4:14). Yet Joseph Smith commends their intellectual efforts
as a corrective to the Latter-day Saints, who lean too far
in the other direction, giving their young people and old
awards for zeal alone, zeal without knowledge—for sitting
in endless meetings, for dedicated conformity and unlimited capacity for suffering boredom. We think it more commendable to get up at five A.M. to write a bad book than
to get up at nine o'clock to write a good one—that is pure
zeal that tends to breed a race of insufferable, self-righteous
prigs and barren minds. One has only to consider the
present outpouring of "inspirational" books in the Church
that bring little new in the way of knowledge: truisms and
platitudes, kitsch, and clichés have become our everyday
diet. The Prophet would never settle for that. "I advise all
to go on to perfection, and search deeper and deeper into
the mysteries of Godliness. . . . It has always been my
province to dig up hidden mysteries—*new things*—for my
hearers."[42] It actually happens at the BYU, and that not
rarely, that students come to a teacher, usually at the beginning of a term, with the sincere request that he refrain

from teaching them anything new. They have no desire, they explain, to hear what they do not know already! I cannot imagine that happening at any other school, but maybe it does. Unless we go on to other new things, we are stifling our powers.

In our limited time here, what are we going to think about? That is the all-important question. We've been assured that it is not too early to start thinking about things of the eternities. In fact, Latter-day Saints should be taking rapid strides toward setting up that eternal celestial order which the Church must embody to be acceptable to God. Also, we are repeatedly instructed regarding things we should *not* think about. I would pass by this negative thing lightly, but the scriptures are explicit, outspoken, and emphatic in this matter; and whenever anyone begins to talk about serious matters at the BYU, inevitably someone says, "I would like to spend my time thinking about such things and studying them, but I cannot afford the luxury. I have to think about the really important business of life, which is making a living." This is the withering effect of the intimidating challenge thrown out to all of us from childhood: "Do you have any money?" with its absolute declaration of policy and principle: "You can have anything in this world for money!" and its paralyzing corollary: "Without it, you can have NOTHING!" I do not have to tell you where that philosophy came from. Somebody is out to "decoy . . . [our] minds," to use Brigham Young's expression, from the things we should be thinking about to those we should not care about at all.

One oft-repeated command in the scriptures, repeated verbatim in the Synoptic Gospels, the Book of Mormon, and Doctrine and Covenants 14, is: "Take ye no thought for the morrow, for what ye shall eat, or what ye shall drink, or wherewith ye shall be clothed, for consider the lilies of the field" (Matthew 6:25; Luke 12:22; 3 Nephi 13:28; D&C 84:81-82). We cannot go here into the long, scriptural catalog of commandments telling us to seek for knowledge in one direction but not in another. "Seek *not* for riches, but for wisdom," "lay up *not* treasures on earth" but in heaven, for where your treasure is, there will your heart be also. You *cannot* serve two masters; you must choose one and follow him alone: "For all that is in the world . . . *is not* of the Father, but is of the world" (1 John 2:16). We take comfort in certain parables; for example, "Which of you, intending to build a tower, sitteth not down first, and counteth the cost" (Luke 14:28-30) — as if they justified our present course. But the Lord is not instructing people to take economic foresight in such matters — they already do that: "Which of you does *not*?" says the Lord. He points out that people are only too alert and provident where the things of *this* world are concerned and says to their shame: "If you're so zealous in such matters, why can't you take your eternal future seriously?" And so he ends the parable with this admonition: "Whoever he be of you that forsaketh not all that he hath cannot be my disciple" (Luke 14:33). That is the *same* advice, you will observe, that he gave to the rich young man. The Lord really means what he says when he commands us *not* to think about these things; and because we have chosen to find this advice hopelessly impractical "for our times" (note that the rich young man found it just as impractical for his times!), the treasures of knowledge have been withheld from us: "God had often sealed up the heavens," said Joseph Smith, "because of covetousness in the Church."[43] You must choose between one route or the other. Brigham Young says if we continue "lusting after the grovelling things of this life, [we will] remain fixed with a very limited amount of knowledge, and, like a door upon its hinges, mov[ing] to and fro from one year to another without any visible advancement or improvement. . . . Man is made in the image of God, but what do we know of him or of ourselves, when we suffer

ourselves to love and worship the god of this world—
riches?"[44]

"I desire to see everybody on the track of improvement, . . . but when you so love your property . . . as
though all your affections were placed upon the changing,
fading things of earth, it is impossible to increase in the
knowledge of the truth."[45]

What things then should we think about, and how?
Here the Prophet is very helpful. In the first place, that
question itself is what we should think about. We won't
get very far on our way until we have faced up to it. But
as soon as we start seriously thinking about that, we find
ourselves covered with confusion, overwhelmed by our
feelings of guilt and inadequacy—in other words, repenting for our past delinquency. In this condition, we call
upon the Lord for aid, and he hears us. We begin to know
what the Prophet Joseph meant about the constant searching, steadily storing our minds with knowledge and information—the more we get of it, the better we are able
to judge the proper priorities as we feel our way forward,
as we become increasingly alert to the promptings of the
Spirit which become ever more clear and more frequent,
following the guidance of the Holy Ghost: and as we go
forward, we learn to cope with the hostile world with
which our way is sure to bring us into collision in time.
That calls for sacrifice, but what of that? Eternal life is not
cheaply bought.

This may sound very impractical to some, but how
often do we have to be reminded of the illusory and immoral nature of the treasures we are seeking on earth?
Even without the vast powers of destruction that are hanging over our heads at this moment, even in the most peaceful and secure of worlds, we would see them vanishing
before our eyes. Such phenomena as ephemeralization and
replication, once dreams of the science-fiction writers, are
rapidly becoming realities. Speaking of ephemeralization,

of technological obsolescence, Arthur C. Clarke writes that within the foreseeable future all the most powerful and lucrative callings in our world will exist no more. Because of new processes of synthesizing, organizing, programming basic materials of unlimited supply into the necessities of life, we shall soon see "the end of all factories, and perhaps all transportation of raw materials and all farming. The entire structure of industry and commerce . . . would cease to exist; . . . all material possessions would be literally as cheap as dirt. . . . [Then] when material objects are all intrinsically worthless, perhaps only then will a real sense of values arise."[46]

Yes, you say, but meantime "we must live in the world of the present." Must we? Most people in the past have got along without the institutions which we think, for the moment, indispensable. And we are expressly commanded to get out of that business, says Brigham Young:

> No one supposes for one moment that in heaven the angels are speculating, that they are building railroads and factories, taking advantage one of another, gathering up the substance there is in heaven to aggrandize themselves, and that they live on the same principle that we are in the habit of doing. . . . No sectarian Christian in the world believes this; they believe that the inhabitants of heaven live as a family, that their faith, interests and pursuits have one end in view—the glory of God and their own salvation, that they may receive more and more. . . . We all believe this, and suppose we go to work and imitate them as far as we can.[47]

It is not too soon to begin right now. What are the things of the eternities that we should consider even now? They are the things that no one ever tires of doing, things in themselves lovely and desirable. Surprisingly, the things of the eternities are the very things to which the university is supposed to be dedicated. In the Zion of God, in the celestial and eternal order, where there is no death, there will be no morticians; where there is no sickness, there will be no more doctors; where there is no decay, there will be no dentists; where there is no litigation, there will be no lawyers; where there is no buying and selling, there will be no merchants; where there is no insecurity, there will be no insurance; where there is no money, there will be no banks; where there is no crime, there will be no jails, no police; where there are no excess goods, there will be no advertising, no wars, no armies, and so on and so on.

But this happy condition is not limited to celestial realms of the future; it actually has been achieved by mortal men on this earth a number of times, and it represents the only state of society of which God approves. All the things that are passing away today are the very essence of "the economy," but they will be missing in Zion. They are already obsolescent; every one of them is make-work of a temporary and artificial nature for which an artificial demand must be created. Moreover, few people are really dedicated to them, for as soon as a man has acquired a superquota of power and gain, he cuts out and leaves the scene of his triumphs, getting as far away as he can from the ugly world he has helped create—preferably to Tahiti. The race has shown us often its capacity to do without these things we now find indispensable:

> The Devil has the mastery of the earth: he has corrupted it, and has corrupted the children of men. He has led them in evil until they are almost entirely ruined, and are so far from God that they neither know Him nor his influence, and have almost lost sight of everything that pertains to eternity. This darkness is more prevalent, more dense, among the people of Christendom, than it is among the heathen. They have lost sight of all that is great and glorious—of all principles that pertain to life eternal.[48]

"Suppose that our Father in heaven, our elder brother, the risen Redeemer, the Saviour of the world, or any of the Gods of eternity should act upon this principle, to love truth, knowledge, and wisdom, because they are all powerful," says Brigham Young, "they would cease to be Gods, . . . the extension of their kingdom would cease, and their God-head come to an end."[49] Are we here to seek knowledge or to seek the credits that will get us ahead in the world? One of the glorious benefits and promises for the gospel given the Saints in these latter days is that "inasmuch as they *sought* wisdom they might be instructed; . . . and inasmuch as they were humble they might be made strong, and blessed from on high, and receive *knowledge* from time to time" (D&C 1:26, 28). But they had to want it and seek for it. What is the state of things? The late President Joseph Fielding Smith wrote in the *Melchizedek Priesthood Manual*: "We are informed that many important things have been withheld from us because of the hardness of our hearts and our unwillingness, as members of the Church, to abide in the covenants or seek for divine knowledge."[50] "A faculty . . . may be enlarged," says Joseph Smith, "in proportion to the heed and diligence given to the light communicated from heaven to the intellect."[51] "If [a man] does not get knowledge he will be brought into captivity by some evil power in the other world as evil spirits will have more knowledge [and] consequently more power than many men who are on the earth. Hence [there needs to be] Revelation to assist us [and] give us knowledge of the things of God."[52] There is indeed an order of priority. The things of God come first, and the seeker ever tries to become aware of that priority. "All science," says Karl Popper, "is cosmology,"[53] concerned fundamentally with the questions of religion. The most important question of all is that of our eternal salvation.

I once acted as counselor to students in the College of Commerce for a couple of years. Most of these students were unhappy about going into business and admitted that

Satan rules this earth and rules it badly, with blood and horror, but they pointed out the intimidating circumstance that you cannot have money without playing his game, because he owns the treasures of the earth. They could see he owns them as loot, and by virtue of a legal fiction with which he has, in Joseph Smith's terms, "riveted the creeds of the fathers,"[54] but still the students would ask me in despair, "If we leave his employ, what will become of us?" The answer is simple. Don't you trust the Lord? If you do, he will give you the guidance of the Holy Spirit and you will not end up doing the things that he has expressly commanded us not to do.

May God help us all in the days of our probation to seek the knowledge *he* wants us to seek.

Notes

1. Nigel Calder, *The Mind of Man* (London: British Broadcasting, 1970), 25.

2. N. S. Sutherland, quoted in ibid., 169.

3. William James, "Precept and Concept," in *Some Problems of Philosophy* (Cambridge, MA: Harvard University Press, 1979), 32; cf. William James, *Essays, Comments and Reviews*, ed. Frederich H. Burkhardt (Cambridge, MA: Harvard University Press, 1987), 199: "Our sensible perceptions present to us nothing but an endless confusion of separate things; our reason whispers that all these things are connected and that what appears superficially confusion is at the bottom perfect order and harmony."

4. Neisser, quoted in Calder, *The Mind of Man*, 169.

5. Ibid., 29.

6. Ibid., 29, 184.

7. Nicolas Malebranche, *The Search after Truth*, tr. Thomas M. Lennon and Paul J. Olscamp (Columbus: Ohio State University Press, 1980), 198-99.

8. Arthur Schopenhauser, *Schopenhausers sämtliche Werke*, 5 vols. (Leipzig: Insel, 1922), 1:33.

9. *MS* 39:372.

10. Arthur C. Clarke, *Profiles of the Future* (New York: Holt, Rinehart and Winston, 1984), 213.

11. Ibid., 112.

12. *HC* 3:295-96.

13. Calder, *Mind of Man*, 33.
14. Clarke, *Profiles of the Future*, 95.
15. Lyall Watson, *Supernature* (New York: Anchor/Doubleday, 1973), 240: "Left without its normal barrage of stimuli, the brain embellishes and elaborates on reality, drawing on its store of unconscious paraphernalia to fill the time and space available."
16. Donald Hebb, quoted in Calder, *The Mind of Man*, 77.
17. *TPJS* 353-54 (emphasis added).
18. Carl Sagan, *The Cosmic Connection* (New York: Doubleday, 1973), ch. 34.
19. *TPJS* 201 (emphasis added).
20. Ibid., 204.
21. Ibid., 238 (emphasis added).
22. Ibid. (emphasis added).
23. Ibid., 80.
24. Ibid., 213-14.
25. Ibid., 246.
26. Ibid., 287.
27. Ibid., 309.
28. Ibid., 331.
29. Ibid., 348.
30. Ibid., 320.
31. Ibid., 242.
32. Ibid., 43 (emphasis added).
33. Ibid., 51 (emphasis added).
34. Ibid., 137 (emphasis added).
35. Ibid., 215 (emphasis added).
36. Ibid., 217.
37. Ibid., 297.
38. Ibid.
39. Ibid., 149.
40. Ibid., 149-51.
41. Ibid., 163.
42. Ibid., 364 (emphasis added).
43. Ibid., 9.
44. *JD* 10:266-67.
45. Ibid., 7:337.
46. Clarke, *Profiles of the Future*, 175-76.
47. *JD* 17:117-18.
48. Ibid., 8:209.
49. Ibid., 1:117.
50. Joseph Fielding Smith, *Melchizedek Priesthood Manual, Answers to Gospel Questions* (1972-73), 229.

51. *TPJS* 51.

52. *WJS* 114.

53. Karl Popper, *Conjecture and Refutations* (New York: Basic Books, 1962), 136.

54. *TPJS* 145; cf. D&C 123:7.

4

Gifts

There were some things I wanted to settle in my own mind, so I started asking questions and got into a heated debate with myself. Here's the debate that followed.

We begin with question number one: "What are the principal issues?" I ask myself (not knowing anything about these subjects): "What are the principal issues in political science today? The economy and defense—how to have a prosperous nation and a secure one. What can I say about that?" Nothing significant. "Why not?" Because I don't know enough. "Who does?" I don't know. "Have I made the effort to find out?" Yes, I get two newspapers and four news magazines and listen to TV panels; but the experts, especially the economists (including Nobel Laureates), can't seem to agree on anything. "Do you think the situation is hopeless?" Yes, theirs is hopeless. "But is there any hope in sight?" Indeed there is. (This becomes a very optimistic talk from now on.)

I call attention particularly to the Book of Mormon, which I consider the handbook for our times—as its author intended it to be. "Isn't the author a bit out of date?" No, he is a living prophet. "What do you mean by that?" Just what I say. The man is Moroni: He was a living, resurrected being when he gave that big dossier to Joseph Smith; he is still living, and at some future time he is going to be

This is a transcription of a talk given March 13, 1979, at Brigham Young University. Some parts of this presentation were repeated in "Deny Not the Gifts," pages 118-48.

active on the earth again (as we are told in D&C 27). "But isn't the story he tells ancient history?" Consider his visit to Joseph Smith. Joseph described Moroni's person and the manner and nature of his arrival and his departure in clinical detail—very concretely. It was a real visit. And since the angel repeated his lesson four times in one night, and then once a year, the same night (on the autumnal equinox) for the ensuing four years, Joseph was able to record the message exactly—it consisted entirely of quotations from earlier writers, earlier prophets, earlier visitors to the earth, a sort of pastiche of messages. Joseph says Moroni commenced by quoting the prophecies of the Old Testament. Then he gave a long list of passages. Moroni changed some and quoted others word for word as they are given in the King James Version of the Bible. In fact, Moroni's message was simply a long list of Bible quotations. (But so is much of the Bible itself.) He quoted all of that stuff because it was going to be relevant. The heavenly messenger updated everything that had gone before without ever losing sight of it. He put it all together—he said, in effect, that he was doing just that: "This is now about to be fulfilled; you've been looking forward to this; this has been fulfilled; this is where we stand now with reference to these things." So we'll take Moroni as our guide.

"Would you say that present-day, living prophets supersede him?" No, not any more than they compete with him. He's as alive as they are. Notice that the scriptures are never outdated. Moroni quoted prophecies thousands of years old because those prophecies were still in effect; and in some cases, in Joseph's writing (JS–H 1:40-41), they were about to be fulfilled at last. Nothing could be more pertinent than that message. Moroni was bringing Joseph up to date.

"Well, how about other angels?" Exactly the same. For the dispensation of the meridian of time was ushered in by an angel who first appeared to a priest in the temple

(Luke 1:11-20), talking to him all morning, quoting ancient scriptures. And then the same angel, from the presence of God, went to Mary at her house (Luke 1:26-38) and repeated other ancient scriptures that were about to be realized in her.

But the most significant example is that of the Lord himself, who after his resurrection came to instruct the apostles; and we are told in Luke that beginning at Moses and all the prophets, he expounded unto them from all the scriptures things concerning himself. "Then opened he their understanding, that they might understand the scriptures" (Luke 24:45). Just as he had commanded the Nephites always to search the scriptures and add their own careful records to them, he expounded to them all of the scripture they had received, and said to them, "Behold, other scriptures I would that ye should write, that ye have not" (3 Nephi 23:6), and proceeded to dictate the words of Malachi to them. Then he called them to bring forth the records, and "he cast his eyes upon them" (3 Nephi 23:8) and proceeded to point out some important omissions (among them one of the prophecies of Samuel the Lamanite).

In these important cases, notice that the heavenly messengers, including the resurrected Lord himself, do not waive the old written record. They don't say, "The *ipse dixit* [the autonomous source] is here himself; now we can forget about the old musty records." They stick right to them—though the living Lord himself is there (imagine that!). If you pray for an angel to visit you, you know what he'll do if he comes. He'll just quote the scriptures to you— so you're wasting your time waiting for what we already have. Though you are amused by my saying this, I'm quite serious about it.

"Well, does that mean we give the written records priority over the living word?" No, of course not. Heavenly visitors and the Holy Ghost must take charge. The written

88

APPROACHING ZION

record is their text, and they expound upon it. "And why do they have to have a text?" Because it is always with us. Remember that after the Lord had expounded everything concerning himself to the Nephites, he said, in essence, "I want you to write this down, because I'm not always going to be with you—you'll always have this to go by" (cf. 3 Nephi 23:4). But he's not going to leave us on the strength of the text itself—it must be read when moved upon by the Holy Ghost.

"But who's to interpret it? Do I have a right to interpret the scriptures as much as anyone else?" Of course. You may remember that the wars of the Reformation were fought on that issue: "Does the ordinary person have the right to read the scriptures?" We regard that as a definite step forward in the Lord's work on the earth, and in the Church every individual is commanded to read the scriptures for himself. Of course, the story of the last dispensation begins with the Prophet Joseph, as a young boy, reading the scriptures very much for himself, putting the most literal interpretation on them, belonging to no church at the time, without asking for anybody's permission. So we do that also. As far as official interpretation of the scriptures is concerned, the Latter-day Saints scoff at the idea that one must study special courses and get a special degree—"training for the ministry"—and thus interpret the Bible for others. Joseph Smith noted many times that interpreters of the scriptures like William W. Phelps and Frederick G. Williams read the scriptures quite differently than he, but he didn't order them to stop or to change. He said we should try to use reason and testimony, but that's all we can do. The Brethren are instructed to stick to the scriptures in all their teachings: "No man's opinion is worth a straw: advance no principle but what you can prove, for one scriptural proof is worth ten thousand opinions."[1]

"Why all the fuss about the scriptures?" Because I intend to take Moroni as my guide to the present world situation. "Why him?" Moroni and his father are the principal, definitive editors of the Book of Mormon. They not only compiled and edited; they also went through and picked out things they felt would be important for us. Then they evaluated that and applied it to us and explained everything to us. What a marvelous thing to have it all summed up for us by the principal actors in this thing. And both Moroni and his father were concerned with two things: the questions with which we began, the questions of prosperity and security—the great, inseparably related issues of wealth and war.

"Does Moroni give specific advice to us?" Most emphatically! His great closing narration is this (he repeats it again and again)—an impassioned appeal to us: Do not deny the gifts of God (Moroni 10:8).

"What gifts? Who would want to deny them? Why?" One question at a time.

The gifts are spiritual and they are temporal, but in fact they are inseparable. A temporal gift is in one dimension spiritual. Gifts are listed in the scriptures. Please recall very quickly the spiritual gifts—you know them. One is to know that Jesus Christ is the Son of God—one of the gifts given to some. To others it is given to believe on their words, to some to know the differences of administration, to some to know the diversity of operations, to others the word of wisdom, to others the word of knowledge, to some to prophesy, to some the working of miracles, to some the discernment of spirits. A long list of these spiritual gifts is given to us by the Lord (Moroni 10:8-18). We can't conjure them up for ourselves. The Lord gives them, and he says he gives them. We must ask for them with real intent and with an honest heart. We can have them—any gift. And a nice protective clause is written in there: If we're not supposed to have a gift, what we *are* worthy of, what *is* beneficial or expedient, we shall have *that* (since if we are left to our own wisdom, we may ask for very foolish things). But all these things are available—all we need to do is ask. But we must *ask* for them, and of course if we ask not we receive not. The gifts are not in evidence today, except one gift, which you notice the people *ask* for—the gift of healing. They ask for that with honest intent and with sincere hearts, and we really do have that gift. Because we are desperate and nobody else can help us, we ask with sincere hearts of our Lord. As for these other gifts, how often do we ask for them? How earnestly do we seek for them? We could have them if we did ask, but we don't. "Well, who denies them?" Anyone who doesn't ask for them. They are available to all for the asking, but one must ask with an honest heart, sincerely.

"Do people prefer temporal gifts today?" It's a strange thing, but people don't want them either. "What are the temporal gifts?" Anything you could possibly ask for in order to get along in the world. "People don't want them?" No, not as gifts—they are proud and don't want to accept a dole. "Isn't that rather admirable?" It looks that way. Their hearts are really set on these things—they want to have them, but they want to earn them fair and square and to be beholden to no one for them. They want to say, "This is mine because I earned it." No one has a *right* to a gift; no one can go to the giver and demand it as something he has earned. What is owed you, you don't receive as a present but as your due. In our Anglo-Saxon ethic we just don't like the idea of having to depend upon anyone else—we must be independent before all things. "What's wrong with that?" We think we are being realistic about it, but are we? Independent of what? Of God? Of our fellowman? Of nature?

"What is the issue here? You said the economists don't agree on anything. Do *you* expect to come up with a definitive answer?" The issue is the scriptures. This would not be *my* answer in a million years, but it keeps getting through at me and I can't get away from it. They speak out loud and clear — persistently and urgently — on the subject: "Deny not the gifts of God" (Moroni 10:8). Everything you have is a gift — everything. You have earned nothing. There is no concern for prosperity and survival where the gospel is concerned. Everything we could possibly need for survival is given us at the outset as a free gift.

"But surely God expects us to work!" Of course he does, but we keep thinking of one kind of work, and he wants us to think of another. "Please explain," says the wise guy. "Willingly," says the informant.

Let us begin our story with Adam. The antiquity of the story can be affirmed by a large number of early apocryphal Adam writings that have been unearthed in recent years[2] — just as lots of things have been turning up recently to change all our ideas about astronomy and so forth and to confirm the ideas of Einstein (whose birthday we celebrate tomorrow); many documents are pouring out to confirm things we all know. What I am saying here is not stolen from any Latter-day Saint protocol; it can be confirmed directly from sources that are now quite abundant.

Adam came down to earth. It was an earth fully equipped for his support and delight. "We have made for you this earth and have placed upon it everything you could possibly need — every type of fruit and herb you could possibly imagine growing spontaneously, of which you may partake freely. All a gift." The earth was created *for* Adam: "And we have planted a garden all ready for you — all you have to do is take note of it. And everything is for the taking." One gift, however, is withheld from Adam: the fruit of the tree of good and evil — the tree of knowledge. So long as Adam was immortal, the tree of life presented no problem.

So into this world, most glorious and beautiful, with everything supplied, come Adam and Eve. And then comes somebody else. Satan's been *lying in wait for them,*

as a matter of fact. That's one of the things the word *Satan*
actually means, the one who lies in wait, who lurks in
ambush, waiting—he was there first, waiting.[3] And so
Satan's first act is to offer to Adam and Eve the one gift
that has been forbidden them.

For acting out of order, the stranger (no longer a
stranger) is denounced and cursed. He has given the fruit
to Adam and Eve; it was not his prerogative to do so—
regardless of what had been done in other worlds. (When
the time comes for such fruit, it will be given us legitimately.) So, nettled by this rebuke and the curse, he flares
up in his pride and announces what his program for the
economic and political order of the new world is going to
be. He will take the resources of the earth, and with precious metals as a medium of exchange he will buy up
military and naval might, or rather those who control it,
and so will govern the earth—for he is the prince of this
world. He does rule: he is king. Here at the outset is the
clearest possible statement of a military-industrial complex
ruling the earth with violence and ruin. But as we are told,
this cannot lead to anything but war, because it has been
programmed to do that. It was conceived in the mind of
Satan in his determination "to destroy the world" (Moses
4:6). The whole purpose of the program is to produce blood
and horror on this earth.[4]

Adam is now cast out of the garden, consigned to a
new life. The first person he meets in the new world is
already looking him up, waiting for him; and it is the same
person that looked him up in the garden. He has come to
Adam with a deal. He announces that the earth is his
property from one end to the other, and that he rules and
stands for no nonsense. He asks twice what Adam wants:
"What is it you want?" He will supply any gifts forthcom-
ing in this world—but at a price. When Adam says that
what he really wants is more light and knowledge, Satan
offers to provide that, and after some dickering he hires a

preacher to do the instructing. When the real preachers, whom God has proposed, arrive (sometimes called the three strangers, the three visitors, sometimes the Angel Michael—it is different ones in different versions, but it is a very consistent story),[5] Satan challenges them as trespassers who have tried to take over his splendid property. They come to give Adam priceless gifts; Satan asks them if they have any money—not just pocket change, but big money; they can have anything in this world for money. Adam pointedly observes (as Peter does to Simon Magus later when Simon enters the picture) that the gifts of God are not negotiable. "Thy money perish with thee, because thou hast thought that the gift of God may be purchased with money" (Acts 8:20). You cannot buy these gifts; they are not negotiable; you cannot use them in business.

Adam refuses Satan's offer, and Satan discusses contracts with the minister. This is the false Horus, a comic character in the very early Egyptian temple ceremony.[6] Satan insists that he is true to his business agreements, which he is. He is all business. But having failed to sell Adam, he later goes to Adam's son, Cain. He offers to make a contract with him and tells him how to get possession of his brother's wealth in return for Cain's help in organizing his work in the world. Cain loves the idea; he loves Satan more than God. He then makes the famous pact with the devil (a theme that comes down through the literature) (Moses 5:29-30).[7]

Satan gives him a special course to make him prosperous in all things: the Mahan technique, the great secret of converting life into property. Later Lamech graduates with the same degree—"Master Mahan, master of that great secret" (Moses 5:49). He glories in what he has done; it becomes the normal world economy. Nearly all the posterity of Adam, we are told, entered into business, and all Adam and Eve could do about it was to mourn before the Lord (Moses 5:27). Everyone went off following the Cainites.[8] And Cain did it all, we are told, for the sake of getting gain (Moses 5:31). He was not ashamed; he "gloried in that which he had done." He said, "I am free; surely the flocks of my brother falleth into my hands" (Moses 5:33).

Moroni picks it up at this point. The order of Cain carries right over into Book of Mormon passages, in fact, like something just cut out of the paper today. Let's start out with Ether 9:11: "Now the people of Akish were desirous for gain, even as Akish was desirous for power; wherefore, the sons of Akish did offer them money, by which means they drew away the more part of the people after them." Akish got elected because he offered the people money. He wanted power and they wanted gain, and they made a bargain. The reference I have here is this: A poll shows that 85 percent of this year's contested Senate races went to the candidate who spent the most. You can indeed buy that sort of thing, as Akish did. People got their money and Akish got his power. "And it came to pass that thus they did agree with Akish. And Akish did administer unto them the oaths which were given by them of old who also sought power, which had been handed down even from Cain" (Ether 8:15).

So Moroni here picks up the story—it comes from the time of Cain, "who was a murderer from the beginning" (Ether 8:15). It carries on in Helaman, where we get an interesting discussion. It is important here because it tells us how the principle leads directly and necessarily to war:

> Now behold, it is these secret oaths and covenants which Alma commanded his son should not go forth unto the world, lest they should be a means of bringing down the people unto destruction. Now behold, those secret oaths and covenants did not come forth unto Gadianton from the records which were delivered unto Helaman; but behold, they were put into the heart of Gadianton by that same being who did entice our first parents to partake of the forbidden fruit—Yea, that same

being who did plot with Cain, that if he would murder his brother Abel it should not be known unto the world. And he did plot with Cain and his followers from that time forth. And also it is that same being who put it into the hearts of the people to build a tower sufficiently high that they might get to heaven. And it was that same being who led on the people who came from that tower into this land; who spread the works of darkness and abominations over all the face of the land, until he dragged the people down to an entire destruction, and to an everlasting hell. Yea, it is that same being who put it into the heart of Gadianton to still carry on the work of darkness, and of secret murder; and he has brought it forth from the beginning of man even down to this time. And behold, it is he who is the author of all sin. And behold, he doth carry on his works of darkness and secret murder, and doth hand down their plots, and their oaths, and their covenants, and their plans of awful wickedness, from generation to generation according as he can get hold upon the hearts of the children of men. And now behold, he had got great hold upon the hearts of the Nephites; yea, insomuch that they had become exceedingly wicked; yea, the more part of them had turned out of the way of righteousness, and did trample under their feet the commandments of God, and did turn unto their own ways, and did build up unto themselves idols of their gold and their silver (Helaman 6:25-31).

All this happened "in the space of not many years" (Helaman 6:32). And what was the result of that? In the next chapter Nephi tells us:

But behold, it is to get gain, to be praised of men, yea, and that ye might get gold and silver. And ye have set your hearts upon the riches and the vain things of this world, for the *which* ye do murder, and plunder, and steal, and bear false witness against your neighbor, and do all manner of iniquity. And for this cause wo shall come unto you except ye shall repent. For if ye will

not repent, behold, this great city, and also all those
great cities which are round about, which are in the land
of our possession, shall be taken away that ye shall have
no place in them; for behold, the Lord will not grant
unto you strength, as he has hitherto done, to withstand
against your enemies (Helaman 7:21-22).

"For this cause" directly — that they had set their hearts
on the economy. This is an interesting thing: It is not which
economy. Remember what Samuel the Lamanite said: Your
trouble is that you always think of your riches, and for
that reason you are going to lose them. They will become
slippery that you cannot hold them (Helaman 13:31). You
have no control over the stock market at all; the more
closely you watch it, the more it escapes you. We won't
follow *that* up; we'll leave it to the economists.

How this motive leads to war can be illustrated by Alma
60, the ending of the great fourteen-years' war. That episode begins with a postwar boom (very well described in
Alma 45). The next period of war ended after the phase
very well described in 3 Nephi 6:10-14: rebuilding and the
repairs of the cities, the big contracts, building of roads
between the towns, bustling intercoastal trade — it all being
extremely profitable. The result of this tremendous postwar boom is degeneration and annihilation. And then the
stroke of doom. The cause of their wickedness was this:
Satan (right back to the Garden again) had put it into their
hearts to seek after power, authority and riches. This was
their undoing.

Back to the Alma version now. After the postwar boom,
Helaman, as the head of the church, is alarmed. He sees
how the prosperity leads people to set their hearts on
riches: "Therefore, Helaman and his brethren went forth
to establish the church again in all the land, yea, in every
city throughout all the land which was possessed by the
people of Nephi. And it came to pass that they did appoint

priests and teachers throughout all the land, over all the churches" (Alma 45:22).

He tries to do something about it, and immediately the resentment of those whom he rebukes flares up against him. They propose an action program—quite a dangerous one. Being closely knit, interested families, they begin to organize an opposition party, and it is taken over by a man of considerable genius who is capable and unscrupulous: Amalickiah, who organized the coalition. The coalition consisted of these people, in this order: first, the rich; second, ambitious judges seeking for power and office (including lawyers); third, some members of the church who didn't know any better (see Alma 46:6-7—Alma knows how to put it); fourth, aspiring businessmen and officials— merchants, lawyers and officers—people distinguished by rank according to their riches and their chances for learning (the movie *Paper Chase*); fifth, important families (those judges had many friends and kinsmen, and almost all the lawyers and high priests united in the interests of those judges—the upper-crust—and stuck together); sixth, those professing the blood of nobility—snobs; seventh, those who were in the favor of kings (those of high birth). (They themselves sought to be kings, and they supported those who sought power and authority over the people; the same theme is found later in 3 Nephi.)

It is all perfectly clear: the economy we are all familiar with and the obsession with that economy. These people were determined to defend their economic interests and privileges by force, and this led them right into the great war.

Very fittingly, Amalickiah's people are now designated by the overall name of "king-men." From the first, their tendency, we are told right in the opening verse, is to violence: "And it came to pass that as many as would not hearken to the words of Helaman and his brethren were gathered together against their brethren. And now behold, they were exceedingly wroth, insomuch that they were determined to slay them" (Alma 46:1-2).

They were intemperate and self-righteous, like Laman and Lemuel—that's why Amalickiah was able to advance his interests among them by gathering together a wonderfully faithful following of all sorts of mixed interests. Time and again he threatened the peace and very existence of the Nephite state, constantly entreating the Lamanites and exploring opportunities, using their power to his advantage. Thus he went over with a host to stir up the Lamanites to anger against his own people and caused them to come to battle against them. He was a real war monger, opposed at every turn by Moroni, whose sole object was to keep peace with the Lamanites (Alma 46:31) and among his own people (Alma 46:37). Moroni was supported by the nation as a whole, not a particular party. Actually the king-men (this formal title is bestowed later) seem to have been quite a small group, merely an element of Amalickiah's coalition. The rest of the people were referred to simply as the people of liberty, who, in a free election, put the king-men to silence. When Moroni by his title of liberty calls attention to the serious threat posed to freedom by the militant opposition, who are actually in arms, "behold, the people came running together with their armor" (Alma 46:21). He compares them with the forlorn outcast remnant of Joseph rather than a mighty army. In Moroni's history, internal and external security are inseparably comingled with the conflict of economic and party interest (it's quite a picture).

The fiction has been diligently cultivated that Moroni on this occasion put all the pacifists to death. Those put to death were not those who had refused to take up arms to defend their country, but those who had taken up arms to attack it and who were on their way to join the enemy across the border, glad in their hearts when they heard that the Lamanites were coming down to battle against their country; they were dissenters to the enemy. Pacifists? They were all members of Amalickiah's army, armed to their teeth on their way to join the enemy when Moroni caught them. "And . . . whomsoever of the Amalicki-ahites that would not enter into the covenant, . . . he caused to be put to death; and there were but few" (Alma 46:35). Armed violence, not pacifism, had been their program from the beginning. We can sum up the issue by referring to Alma 51:17: "And it came to pass that Moroni commanded that his army should go against those king-men, to pull down their pride and their nobility and level them with the earth, or they should take up arms and support the cause of liberty." It was a coalition of the important people, the persons who lifted the sword to fight against Moroni; it was a pitched battle, not an execution. If you had arms in your hands and were fighting, then if you didn't lay them down, if you didn't surrender (as in any war), you had to suffer the consequences. "Insomuch that as they did lift their weapons of war to fight against the men of Moroni they were hewn down. . . . And those of their leaders who were not slain in battle were taken and cast into prison" (Alma 51:18-19). The remainder yielded to the standard of liberty.

In a later battle, "the men of Pachus received their trial, according to the law, and also those king-men; . . . whosoever would not take up arms in the defense of their country, but would fight against it, were put to death" (Alma 62:9). They were all fighting men taken with weapons in their hands, refusing to give them up.

It is interesting in all of this that the title *freemen* first appears only in the late stages of the war as defenders of Pahoran, the legitimately elected judge. They took to themselves a name and a covenant. The man they supported, the incumbent chief judge, won the election, although he was later driven from office. But in the correspondence between them, both Moroni and Pahoran refer to the freemen simply as "their people"—it could be a group of special people with them or just their side in general—the most dedicated, or more dedicated, of the Nephites. Moroni refers to his brave soldiers holding a sector of front as "part of my freemen" (Alma 60:25). Pahoran refers to part of his supporters as freemen and reports that those now in power have "daunted our freemen, that they have not come unto you" (Alma 61:4). In all these instances, the freeman may represent a more dedicated part of the Nephites or just the Nephites in general. But what they stood for—freedom, homes, country and so forth—are the cliches that both sides in every war fight for, perfectly justified and sincere. When the fighting starts, you have to defend. This is the way it is rigged. Specifically, we are told what they were against and why they were fighting against it—which could only be called a coalition of vested interests that aimed at seizing the government. Occasionally they succeeded, and when they did, they legislated for their own sweet interests, with the inevitable result, we are told, of war and contentions: "And thus they did obtain the sole management of the government, insomuch that they did trample under their feet and smite and rend and turn their backs upon the poor and the meek, and the humble followers of God" (Helaman 6:39).

The Gadiantons—this is, remember, a paramilitary group—"did obtain the sole management of the government," and doing that, they filled the judgment seats, having usurped the power and authority of the land, laying aside the commandments of God; and "they did trample under their feet . . . the humble followers of God" (Helaman 6:39). As soon as they got into power, they started legislating in their own interests. They put judges in who were doing what? "Letting the guilty and wicked go unpunished because of their money"; holding them "in office at the head of [the] government, to rule and do according to their wills, that they might get gain and glory of the world" (Helaman 7:5). They governed in the interest of one class alone.

So this is the situation: they were in office to get gain and the glory of the world, and they did everything with an eye single to *their* glory. They were politically, socially, and economically ambitious. They were opposed by the common people organized by Moroni, who made them conscious of themselves as the poor and humble afflicted outcasts of Israel, always calling upon the Lord. Here we have the two totally different, clearly defined ideologies; the one prevails throughout the world today and throughout ancient, medieval, and modern history (you know which side that is: war and economics are the two sides of the same coin, like the famous Shield of Achilles).[9]

But let us return to the question: "If everything is given to us, do we have to work?" Of course. The gifts do not excuse us from work, they leave us free to do the real work. The instrument is given to you; it is up to you to show what you can do with it. I'll give you the piano or I'll give you the violin—the real work is showing what you can do with it. The Lord provides the tools. "I'll give you the stone and the chisel—now you show that you are a Michelangelo." It is much harder to be a Michelangelo than to work enough to buy a chisel and some stone.

Here is a parable. A businessman had a young child who showed great promise in music and wanted to learn to play the piano. "Very well," said the shrewd, realistic, hard-headed businessman father, "as soon as you have manufactured a piano for yourself, going out and mining the metals and getting together all of the other materials, doing all the work necessary to make a piano, then I will consider letting you take piano lessons."

The child protests: "These are two different kinds of work."

Playing a piano and making a piano are related, but in your short time on earth you can't do both. That's just the way it is. I'm not saying that temporal things are not important—they are indispensable. We must have them at the outset free of charge. Our welfare is a very important matter to God. And God has recognized that and has taken care of it. He picks up the tab and expects us not to concern ourselves with it, certainly not as constantly and exclusively as we do, or even give it priority. He supplies us with bodies free of charge and with their upkeep, also free of charge.

"Well, isn't this idealistic immaterialism quite unrealistic?" Indeed it is, for non-Latter-day Saints; it is simply laughable in the present world. Remember, what we regard as real and what the rest of the world regards as real are by no means the same thing. For us the great reality is the visitation of heavenly beings to the world. Nothing could be further from reality or distract one's mind further from cold, factual workaday realities of life than an angel with gold plates or a gold book. The Latter-day Saints will tell you a story that to them is perfectly real, whatever the world may think about it.

"But what about the struggles of this life, the clipping and striving, the developing of strength and character?" It's very exhilarating to climb the ladder—but the question to ask is which ladder are you going to climb? "Does it matter as long as you develop your character?" It makes all the difference in the world. What are the qualities that make for success in the business world? Hard work, dependability, sobriety, firmness, imagination, patience, courage, loyalty, discrimination, intelligence, persistence, ingenuity, dedication, consecration—you can add to the list. But these are the same qualities necessary to make a successful athlete, artist, soldier, bank robber, musician, international jewel thief, scholar, hit man, spy, teacher, dancer, author, politician, minister, smuggler, con man, general, explorer, chef, physician, engineer, builder, astronaut, scientist, godfather, inventor. Again, you name it. Too often these attributes of character are represented as unique to the business world, putting a stamp of glory on the man in the executive suite.

You don't have to go into business to develop character. On the contrary, consider statistics: There are over one half million millionaires in the country—but how many first-rate composers or writers or artists or even scientists? A tiny handful. It's a commonplace in Church history that those leaders and Saints who had denied the gifts became more depraved, intemperate, and self-deceived than others (Alma 47:36; 24:30). As usual, the Book of Mormon has the explanation for that—in the Zoramites. They had many good qualities; they were wonderful people. But they misdirected their virtues, and that made them all the more vicious. Alma found them to be the wickedest people in the world. He couldn't believe that people could be so evil. "Misdirected for what?" Because with all their virtues, they set their hearts upon riches (Alma 31:24-38). Alma couldn't stand it. He couldn't look at it anymore. It hurt too much. How could people be so wicked? This is what was wrong: "Behold, O my God, their costly apparel, and their ringlets, and their bracelets, and their ornaments of gold, and all their precious things which they are ornamented with; and behold, their hearts are set upon them, and yet they cry unto thee and say—We thank thee, O God, for we are a chosen people unto thee, while others shall perish" (Alma 31:28). "O, how long, O Lord, wilt thou suffer that thy servants shall dwell here below in the flesh, to behold such gross wickedness among the children of men? Behold, O God, they cry unto thee, and yet their hearts are swallowed up in their pride. Behold, O God, they cry unto thee with their mouths" (Alma 31:26-27). Remember, they went to church once a week, and they bore their testimony, and they were very strict in dress regulations, and so forth. They were brave and courageous and enterprising and prosperous and all those other things—but this was what was wrong: the "and yet" (as Cleopatra says, I do not like "but yet"[10]). "They cry unto thee with their mouths, while they are puffed up, even to greatness, . . . [with] their ringlets; . . . and behold, their hearts are set upon them, *and yet* they cry unto thee and say [at the same time], We thank thee, O God, for we are a chosen people unto thee" (Alma 31:27-28). And that was what the great crime was. Don't try to combine the two.

Here we have a final powerful motive moving you along, and it's a wonderful thing to have, except when you are moving in the wrong direction. Like Adam, it makes a difference which ladder you are climbing. Like Adam, we are sent to this earth to go to school to learn things by our own experience, to be tried and tested and to seek ever greater light and knowledge. While we are here at school our room and board are all paid up by our kind, indulgent Father. What are we to study? Are we to spend all of our time at school studying how to get more and fancier room and board? That's a vote of low confidence in our kindly benefactor; that's a cynical sort of thing to do. But then I ask myself, "Isn't that part of the experience of life?" Why ask me? Ask the one who is paying the bills for us what he intends us to study. He is most generous and explicit in his instructions, which are the first commandment given to the Church in these last days: "Seek not for riches but for wisdom, and behold, the mysteries of God shall be unfolded unto you, and then shall you be made rich. Behold, he that hath eternal life is rich" (D&C 6:7). "Ha! Make you rich after all!" The Father explains that: He who has eternal life is rich. That is the wealth he wants us to have. "What's wrong with having both kinds?" Again, don't ask me. The scriptures are full of answers to that one. You cannot lay up treasures both on earth and in heaven; you cannot live the gospel and be concerned with the cares of the world. That's what happened to the sower: he accepted the gospel but did not give up the cares of this world. You *cannot* serve God and Mammon, you must hate the one and love the other. The rich man cannot enter heaven except by a very special dispensation. You cannot accept the Lord's invitation to his banquet without neglecting other business. Remember, the Lord said a man gave a banquet. Everything was all ready, and he wanted his friends all to come and enjoy themselves. Ah! But they had more important things to do. The business of the world was more important. One of them said, "Well, I bought some land and I have to go inspect it"; another said, "I'm looking over a few oxen and they are important"; and another said, "I have a social obligation with this wedding I have to go to." The Lord was angry with them all. "You will never get to my feast, then. You must either come to my feast or do your business" (see Matthew 22:2-14).

So many students have told me (hundreds of times), "I would like to study this. I would like to study that (music, astronomy, and so on). But after all, I have to do the important things, the real things of life—I have to go out and make money." The Lord says that if you do that, you will never get to the banquet. We are told this in each of the Gospels, in the Doctrine and Covenants, in the Book of Mormon, and in the Pearl of Great Price. We are told it again and again. "Take *no* thought for what you should eat, or what you should drink or what you should wear." We are clearly told what we should not be doing. "Well, what *should* we be doing, for heaven's sake?" I'm glad I asked that.

The Doctrine and Covenants repeatedly tells the Saints how they should spend their time.

"How's that?"

As Adam did. May I remind you that Adam was invited to work even before the fall.

"What kind of work?"

"Go to. Dress this garden and take good care of it.

Have a good time. Be happy and have joy—you and all the other creatures" (they were created especially to have joy). My, my, what a time, the existence there. Yes, and work was part of the fun—not work to make a living, I must repeat. At that time the earth brought forth spontaneously every kind of delicious food, of which Adam was invited to partake freely. He wanted Adam to work and have a good time. But then came the Fall, after which Adam was instructed to get back to that paradisiacal existence as soon as possible. Messengers were sent to him with one gift after another—while Satan tried to decoy him into a business deal.

"What are we instructed to do in our fallen state?" The shortest and most concise section of the Doctrine and Covenants puts that to us: "Let your time be devoted to the studying of the scriptures, and to preaching, and to confirming the church, . . . and to performing your labors on the land" (D&C 26:1)—farming, church work, and study. Even so, Adam was told to cultivate his garden, to do church work among his children (which was most strenuous—remember, he spent many, many years working among them, teaching the gospel to them, in sheer despair), and finally, to seek ever greater light and knowledge. This he did, and the Lord promised it to him if he asked for it.

We have enough when we have sufficient for our needs—which is very soon, we learn in 1 Timothy—"having food and raiment let us be therewith content" (1 Timothy 6:5-11). But they who would have more—"they that will be rich fall into temptation," which means desires for things which they shouldn't have. This leads many people astray. You don't need money—"Have you any money?" Sure, sufficient for our needs.

"That's all right, but we need more."

You don't; you don't need more than you need. More than enough is more than enough.

Back to the point again. Then we are ready for the real work, when we have sufficient for our needs; and that is pretty soon. If we get sidetracked on supplying our needs, then we are in real trouble, Timothy tells us. We have been decoyed exactly as Satan planned. But still we have to consider mundane things. Of course we do. Consider 3 Nephi 17 and 19. Here the Lord bestows gifts on the people of such a sacred nature that it is forbidden to discuss them; but before he bestows those gifts, he makes sure that their temporal condition is taken care of. "Have ye any that are sick among you? . . . Have ye any that are lame, or blind, or halt, or maimed, or leprous, or that are withered, or that are deaf, or that are afflicted in any manner? Bring them hither and I will heal them" (3 Nephi 17:7).

Then he commanded his disciples "that they should bring forth some bread and wine unto him" (3 Nephi 18:1). And when the multitude "had eaten and were filled" (3 Nephi 18:5), then he taught them about the sacrament. Then all people, beginning with Nephi himself, went down into the water and were baptized—cleaned up for a special meeting with the Lord on the next day, at which he wanted everybody in a perfect state so he could begin his teaching. But all of their physical needs had to be taken care of first—and they were. But that is where the gospel *begins*; that is where other activities end. Once we have taken care of that part of it, once the people are all fed and clothed and healed of any afflictions and cleaned up, the work is done. "What do we do now, sit around and be bored?" No—then the teaching begins. All this in preparation for real teachings and manifestations that follow. The gift of the mysteries is far beyond the imagination.

The Lord recognized that taking care of physical wants is the beginning of wisdom. Feeding, healing, and cleaning the people up is the first step. That leads us to the threshold of the gospel, but as I say, with most churches that is the whole story; with us it is a minimal requirement, like the Word of Wisdom. These blessings are given to the Nephites (we are told the Word of Wisdom is *given* to us) as all temporal blessings are—as a free gift. The spiritual feast to follow is also a free gift. And these are the gifts that Moroni pleads with us not to reject.

"Still, it makes me uncomfortable that everything should be just given to us," you respond.

Everything is not given unconditionally, only some gifts. How is your health, for example? My health is very good—no aches, pains, disabilities, headaches, hangups, blackouts, no chronic ills. (The doctor asks me that every year and is very disappointed when I say no, no, no, no, no. He figures I should have some of those ailments!)

"Well, doesn't that make your life very dull?" These things are taken care of without any effort on your part. Does that easy, good health make you feel uncomfortable, lazy, guilty? How dull your life must be without aches and pains!

The ancients use the same word for *work* and *toil* as for *pain* and *suffering*. Yet you don't "suffer" when you work and toil.

"You find good health boring?"

No, it is not so.

So we have the paradox: the body serves us best when we are least aware of it, and so with money. We have to have some, but to "set our hearts on riches"—that is what the scriptures keep harping away at. "The love of money is the root of all evil" (1 Timothy 6:10). That is a quotation from the Pseudepigrapha,[11] which is quoted by Paul, and it is also quoted in the Book of Mormon. To set our hearts on riches is, in the Book of Mormon, the ultimate disaster.

To return to the wonderful events of 3 Nephi: the Lord fed the people miraculously, as he did on more than one occasion in the New Testament. They were hungry and he gave them food. "Now, when the multitude had all eaten and drunk, behold, they were filled with the Spirit; and they did cry out with one voice, and gave glory to Jesus, whom they both saw and heard" (3 Nephi 20:9).

"Why this great outburst of rejoicing? Hadn't they ever eaten bread and wine before? Was eating bread and fish such a novelty to them?"

No, it wasn't the gift. It was the hand of the giver. They actually saw the hand of the giver: "They both saw and heard" (3 Nephi 20:9). They knew where the gift came from. So one gives glory upon being raised from the sickbed. Eventually, everyone is bound to get well, but the manner of the healing is the joy in it—the hand of the giver: the comfort and joy, the feeling of the power and love that is there. This is behind the whole thing.

In most passages of scripture where the gifts are specifically mentioned (I have here a list of all mentions of gifts in the scriptures), almost invariably there is a reference to the power of God and the grace of God. Grace is *charis,* it is charity. These gifts are all free gifts, and of course Moroni ends on the theme of faith, hope, and charity (Moroni 10:20). If we don't have them, we have nothing; and if we do have them, we have nothing to worry about, and we will not concern ourselves with these other things. What is a fortune, or even a few more years of life, or a good harvest, compared with the awareness of the love and power of the giver? If the giver loves me, I can leave the selection of gifts up to him.

In return for giving us everything, God asks only two things: first, to recognize his gifts for what they are, and not to take credit to ourselves and say, "This is mine": "And now I ask, can ye say aught of yourselves?" (Mosiah 2:25). "For behold, are we not all beggars? Do we not all depend upon the same Being, even God, for all the substance which we have, for both food and raiment, and for gold, and for silver, and for all the riches which we have of every kind?" (Mosiah 4:19). Notice, he is speaking here of temporal blessings, of which we actually earn nothing. None of us has so much as earned our own keep, as he says. "I say, if ye should serve him with all your whole souls yet ye would be unprofitable servants" (Mosiah 2:21) — that is, consuming more than we produce. Nobody can pay his own way here.

"What is the second thing he requires?" That we should not withhold from others his gifts to us — as if we had a special right to them. "Behold, all that he requires of you is to keep his commandments" (Mosiah 2:22). "What are they?" "Ye will not have a mind to injure one another, but to live peaceably. . . . Ye will not suffer your children that they go hungry, or naked. . . . Ye yourselves will succor those that stand in need of your succor; ye will administer of your substance, . . . ye will not suffer that the beggar putteth up his petition to you in vain," saying perhaps, "the man has brought upon himself his misery; . . . for behold, are we not all beggars?" (Mosiah 4:13-14, 16-17, 19).

"Well, perhaps, in a sense, but some more than others?"

No, equally, namely 100 percent. Back to Benjamin: "In the first place, he hath created you, and granted unto you your lives, created you, and has kept and preserved you . . . from day to day, by lending you breath, . . . even supporting you from one moment to another. . . . And ye are still indebted unto him, and are, and will be, forever and ever; therefore, of what have ye to boast?" (Mosiah 2:23, 20-21, 24). We are all beggars equally — 100 percent is as far as you can go.

That reminds us of another thing — it is all miraculous, totally beyond our power of comprehension. Before the loaves and fishes there was the manna. The manna was a gift from heaven, yet some shrewd and far-sighted Israelites tried to show their appreciation by going into business. And the manna rotted before the day was over (Exodus 16:15-21). They were not allowed to hoard it. It was not negotiable. It was a gift of God. The miracle of the loaves and fishes was also the miracle of our daily bread, for which the Lord has told us to pray to him. It was just as miraculous, following King Benjamin, as the loaves and fishes. In it we acknowledge the hand of the giver whenever we give thanks; whenever we give the blessing, we acknowledge the hand of the giver. But we still have the attitude of the old Danish man in Sanpete, whom Brother Jensen used to tell about: "That's a fine carrot patch you and the Lord have there, Brother Peterson." "Yes, and you should have seen what it looked like when the Lord was doing it alone."

As long as we turn our minds to the things of this world, which means just that, and think that we can manage things pretty well for ourselves, we are doomed—not only to frustration but to destruction. So say the prophets, and now every newspaper and magazine tells us that they are right. It's a poor time to dedicate ourselves to that philosophy.

Finally, there is no free lunch, says Korihor (Alma 30:17-18). It is all free lunch, says King Benjamin. I side with Korihor the realist—if lunch is the aim and purpose of life, then Korihor is right, as he firmly believed, when he said that "when a man dies that is the end thereof" (Alma 30:18). A Marriott lunch is the best thing you can hope for in that world, and so he's right. But since I accept the gospel, that's out of the question. Either we believe that the lunch has been taken care of, or we are in for a long, horrible contest, both internal and external, over who is going to get the most.

Should I end on a note as negative as this? This is the thing that Moroni is telling us: this may seem extreme—and it is. It is utterly fantastic. But what is the alternative? It is in the Book of Mormon. "It happened to the Jaredites, it has happened to us, and it will happen to any other people on the continent that go the way we did—if they set their hearts on the same things" is the message of Moroni.

Here's a quotation from the chairman of the Board of Governors of the Federal Reserve Board: "Our economy is a form of fraud perpetrated by everybody on everybody. It is a world in which nobody keeps his word. Even if you could adjust perfectly for it, it would be a very unpleasant world." That's your maximizing of profits. So we are given that choice. But, I say, "That is so extreme. Can't you be realistic?" This *is* being realistic—though you have to give it a try. We are seeking for the wrong things, and we are never going to find them.

Since there are no questions . . .

I asked the questions and I answered them—though not entirely to my satisfaction.

Questions and Answers

Question: Alexandr Solzhenitsyn gave a talk about a year ago and said Americans have become very imperialistic.[12] What do you think?

Answer: That is my theme all the way through. I left out his comments for fear I would get started on that theme. Yet it is the whole thing. Our plans will not work. "Take no thought what you should wear"—that will never work in this world as it is. If you don't want to get involved in the neighborhood brawl, there's only one thing you can do—move out of the neighborhood. And we refuse to do that. We stay in the neighborhood, and we're upset because we choose sides and have to get in these neighborhood brawls, for both sides are wrong.

Satan's masterpiece of counterfeiting is the doctrine that there are only two choices, and he will show us what they are. It is true that there are only two ways, but by pointing us the way he wants us to take and then showing us a fork in *that* road, he convinces us that we are making the vital choice, when actually we are choosing between branches in his road. Which one we take makes little difference to him, for both lead to destruction. This is the polarization we find in our world today. Thus we have the choice between Shiz and Coriantumr—which all Jaredites were obliged to make. We have the choice between the wicked Lamanites (and they were that) and the equally wicked (Mormon says "more wicked") Nephites. Or between the fleshpots of Egypt and the stews of Babylon, or between the land pirates and the sea pirates of World War I, or between white supremacy and black supremacy, or between Vietnam and Cambodia, or between Bushwhackers and Jayhawkers, or between China and Russia, or between Catholic and Protestant, or between fundamentalist and atheist, or between right and left—all of which are true rivals, who hate each other. A very clever move of Satan!—a subtlety that escapes us most of the time. So I ask Latter-day Saints, "What is your position frankly (I'd like to take a vote here) regarding the merits of cigarettes vs. cigars, wine vs. beer, or heroin vs. LSD?" It should be apparent that you take no sides. By its nature the issue does not concern you. It is simply meaningless as far as your life is concerned. "What, are you not willing to stand up and be counted?" No, I am not. The Saints took no sides in that most passionately partisan of wars, the Civil War, and they never regretted it.

What then of the choice between entering into divisions, schools, controversies, contentions, vanities, or avoiding them? How can you avoid them? As I say, to avoid these neighborhood fights, you must move out of the neighborhood. We of course don't do that without supernatural aid. That's where it comes in; the whole thing is supernatural. That's the part where you won't believe me, where nobody will believe me. But it is on a supernatural plane. That changes everything, of course. The argument then ceases. We are dealing in absolutes there.

That's just where the gospel comes in. Consider the stories of all the great patriarchs — Adam, Enoch, Abraham, Noah, Jared, Ether, Moses, Elijah, Isaiah, Lehi, and Alma. All are the stories of individuals who faced the problem of contending against the whole world — a world in rapid decline.

Why are these stories told to us in such harrowing detail? Do you think they don't apply? This fatal polarization is a very effective means of destruction. As the Romans knew, "divide and conquer" is the means of gaining power and leadership. So we have always been told we must *join* the action to fight against communism, or *must* accept the leadership of Moscow to fight fascism, or *must* join Persia against Rome (or Rome against Persia — that's the fourth century). Or in World War I, you must join the Allies or the Central Powers. While all the time there is only one real choice — between accepting the gifts of God for what they are on his terms and going directly to him and asking for whatever you need, or seeking the unclean gift, as it is called, of power and gain. Remember, Moroni ends by saying; "Deny not the gifts of God, . . . and touch not the evil gift, nor the unclean thing [filthy lucre and so forth]" (Moroni 10:8, 30). So that's the choice I think we have. Do you think that's a practical solution? Well, many of us have had the door banged in our face for that very reason, because "You people are nuts!" All right, so we're nuts — there's nothing to argue about in that case, is there? So let us not argue.

Question: Are we supposed to be seeking truth and light?

Answer: Yes.

Question: But I have to pay tuition to attend your lectures.

Answer: You didn't have to pay tuition to get here — I know people at BYU who didn't pay tuition (laughter). This is an earthly institution; you touched right on the point there. We *shouldn't* have to pay. At the ideal university the learning is supposed to be supplied. You are supposed to get what is called "a liberal education," because it is *not* the work of the world you are dealing with. You are dealing with types and models and concepts — things like that. The other things can be put off for now, but the liberal education is that which is *liberalis* — it is not a trade school. There are other trade schools, and there are fine ones, but this is not the trade school.

Should our whole economy be the other sort of thing? The funny thing is that there are some people in our society — I can think of some — that trust the Lord, and he never lets them down. There are some. You'd be surprised.

But of course there's the idea of paying tuition — we're into it up to our necks here. This is strictly a business institution, as you know. But you're in it. "Come out of her, my people." This is Babylon. "Come out of her, my people, that ye be not partakers of her sins, and that ye receive not of her plagues" (Revelation 18:4). We're willing to take that chance, and we pay a high price for it. Where are the gifts? "The visions and glories of old are returning, and angels are coming to visit the earth." We do have healing, and we pray earnestly for that. Nobody is much interested in other gifts. They don't particularly care about them. They'd much sooner settle for the cash. "But I'll work hard for it." We think we're so idealistic.

You don't have to wait for the Prophet to tell you everything to do. Remember, there is another commandment given us: You approach the Lord directly. The Lord says to Joseph and his followers: "Trouble me no more concerning this matter" (D&C 59:22). He says the people are to use their judgment. The people are relying too much on the Prophet, and therefore they are darkening their minds. This is one of the things that puzzles the General Authorities. They can't have people running to them with every petty personal problem. They hand it down to a lower echelon; even so, people insist they have to go right to the top of the Church, right to the head of the Church, as if the president could handle all these things personally, as if he were *supposed* to handle them all personally. How do you personally escape this? Notice the persons we are talking about, the heroes we have mentioned, the patriarchs of old, who didn't have particular authority or any particular office at the time. They were all outcasts, every blessed one of them. It was later—after they had been outcasts, after they had been tested and tried—that the Lord gave to them the power and authority over the followers as leaders of the Church, as founders of dispensations. Yet every one of them was plagued for a long time by troubles. "My father Lehi was sorely oppressed and he went forth and as he went forth he prayed to the Lord, he prayed for light" (see 1 Nephi 1:5). Adam himself prayed and prayed, and *after many days* he finally got an answer. It was the same thing with Abraham, who said, "Thy servant has sought thee earnestly, now I have found thee" (Abraham 2:12). He at last found the Lord. But you must seek first. You must ask with a sincere heart and with real intent. We don't need to go through any other channels. The Lord won't let you starve. Satan puts that fear into us, which is the opposite of faith. I can honestly say that everything that I have asked for with an honest heart, I have received. Hope leads to faith, though it doesn't happen all at once.

Notes

1. *Times and Seasons*, 11 (November 1839): 13; message signed by Brigham Young, Heber C. Kimball, John E. Page, Wilford Woodruff, John Taylor, and George A. Smith.

2. Apocryphal Adam texts—see F.A.R.M.S. bibliography [CLO-88] entitled "The Old Testament Apocrypha and Pseudepigrapha and the Dead Sea Scrolls: A Selected Bibliography of Text Edtitions and English Translations," compiled by Robert A. Cloward; Stephen E. Robinson, "The Apocalypse of Adam," *BYU Studies* 17 (Winter 77): 131-53.

3. Riukah S. Kluger, *Satan in the Old Testament* (Evanston: Northwestern University Press, 1967), 27.

4. 1 Enoch 8-9.

5. Hugh W. Nibley, "The Expanding Gospel," *BYU Studies* 7 (Autumn 1966): 12; reprinted in *CWHN* 1:201, note 61.

6. Seth is the false Horus who, in the "Contendings of Horus and Seth," seeks to take the place of Horus upon the throne of Osiris. Cf. Alan H. Gardiner, *The Library of Chester Beatty* (Oxford: Oxford University Press, 1931), 13-26.

7. See Adam and Eve 78-79, in *The Lost Books of the Bible and the Forgotten Books of Eden* (Canada: Collins World, 1974), 56-59.

8. Second Book of Adam and Eve 19:8; 20:1-38.

9. *Iliad* 18, 478-540; cf. Nibley, "The Expanding Gospel," 19.

10. William Shakespeare, *Antony and Cleopatra*, act II, scene v, lines 50-53.

11. Testament of Judah 18:1-2; 19:1.

12. Aleksandr I. Solzhenitsyn, "A World Split Apart," in *Solzhenitsyn at Harvard* (Washington, D.C.: Georgetown University, 1979), 3-20.

5

Deny Not the Gifts of God

The famous geologist Julian Huxley was a zealous preacher of anti-sermons: "In the evolutionary pattern of thought there is no longer need or room for the supernatural," he said. "The earth was not created; it evolved. So did all the animals and plants, . . . mind and soul, as well as brain and body. So did religion."[1] G. G. Simpson was fond of reminding his audiences that there is no Santa Claus, that even though it may be hard for children to give up Santa Claus, bringing his presents from the sky, mature people should abandon such wishful thinking and accept reality. The only causes at work in the universe are the random causes of blind chance. This is "that 'modern' view, still current today," writes one scientist, "that the earth with everything in it is dangling in the isolation of a universe whose cold majesty disdains it. Today we have long since become used to the thought of our humble position in the cosmos. Deep down, we are probably even proud of the detachment with which we accept our 'true' situation. . . . Much of the cynicism and nihilism characteristic of the modern psyche can be traced to this chilling conception."[2] (In my youth the in thing was to quote the Rubaiyat on the subject: "Lift not thy hands to it for help."[3]) But the scientist in question, Hoimar von Ditfurth (a researcher with an unusually broad background), continues,

---

This is a transcript of an address given in the spring of 1982. It covers several of the same points made in "Gifts," pages 85-117.

118

"Scientists are now discovering this world view to be essentially *false*."⁴

Three different approaches can illustrate the surprising trend:

1."Local physical systems are always exporting energy."⁵ "All living tissue . . . must *import* . . . energy."⁶ "Energies emanating from celestial regions remote from Planet Earth are indeed converging and accumulating in Planet Earth's biosphere . . . both as radiation and as matter."⁷ "We aboard Earth are receiving just the right amount of energy to keep biological life regenerated on board despite our manifold ignorance and . . . wastage."⁸ "Van Allen belts, . . . ionosphere, . . . atmosphere progressively refract the radiation, separating [it] . . . into a variety of life-sustaining increments."⁹ "Vegetation . . . [is] the prime energy impounder."¹⁰ Earth is measurably [retaining and] impounding the [stellar] radiation "by progressively angular refractions . . . into separately discrete frequencies; . . . [then] the biologicals are continually multiplying their beautiful cellular, molecular, and atomic structurings which . . . constitute a comprehensive pattern . . . of orderly energy concentration, . . . [resulting in] the . . . formation of the Earth's chemically regenerative topsoils [being] . . . progressively pressure buried . . . as high energy concentrate fossil fuels. . . . Energy . . . impoundment . . . in both the Earth's atmosphere and . . . hydrosphere . . . provides [for] the weather and ocean currents."¹¹

Such gifts from on high make Santa Claus look like Scrooge by comparison. (For that matter, Dr. Simpson's precious evolutionary rule of thumb that answers all our ultimate questions for us without further effort would be a far more fervidly wished-for present than anything one could ask of Santa.)

2. More recent and detailed than Buckminster Fuller's poetic exposition is a book by the above-mentioned von

Ditfurth. "A planet capable of sustaining life did not come into being independently of the rest of the universe."[12] "Our earth can be shown to be a focal point where various cosmic powers conjoin to fashion a living world. . . . Certainly the earth is not the center of the universe. . . . But this crowded earth *is* a focal point in the universe: one of those perhaps innumerable places in the cosmos where both life and consciousness could flourish. . . . What a concentration of mighty forces upon one more or less tiny point!"[13] He makes the surprising observation that "more discoveries have been made [in astronomy] . . . during the *past ten years* than in all the centuries since Copernicus."[14]

He tells us how the earth is exposed to solar winds from one direction and cosmic radiation from the other; how they check each other (as evidenced by the "Forbush Effect") and so keep us from getting too much of either, while Van Allen belts absorb excess radiation and release it in more sensible quantities; how the earth is protected from an excess of both by its magnetic field, made possible by the moon; how that field is temporarily disrupted from time to time by the jarring effect of giant meteors striking the earth; how the weakening of that protective magnetic shield allows breakthroughs of "background radiation" that affects the genes of living creatures, leading to the disappearance of some species and the sudden appearance of others,[15] and so on. He goes on to explain how comets swapping orbits effect "a constant exchange of matter . . . at the border regions of neighboring solar systems" and how "our Milky Way too contains matter . . . [that] has continually filtered down to the surface of the *earth*."[16] "The earth is the child of the universe; the matter composing our planet came out of the depths of space."[17] More gifts from heaven.

3. Most recently, the eminent and never-dull astronomer Sir Fred Hoyle, in a talk given at Caltech last November [1981], brings us up to date.[18] Beginning with the

strange fact that all space is filled with particles whose presence is only too apparent in the way in which they make all nebulas look like nebulas (hazy and foggy), he recounts how in the 1950s those grains were believed to be formed of particles of water ice, then later of graphite, then of a mixture, but each time they failed to fill the requirements for such. So the astronomers tried various metals and silicates in different combinations but finally concluded that they had to consist largely of carbon, nitrogen, and oxygen—in what form? "The grains had to be made up largely of organic material."[19] (Brigham Young said, "There is not a particle of element which is not filled with life, and all space is filled with element."[20]) But such could not survive "the heat of the solar nebula," so they must flourish far out, "especially in the regions of the distant comets." So, Hoyle concludes, life did not begin on earth but was conveyed through space by comets, "breaking up and scattering their contents all the time"[21] in a process that is still going on. Examining "the origin of the information carried by the explicit structures of biomolecules," Hoyle, as he reports it,

> was constantly plagued by the thought that the number of ways in which even a single enzyme could be *wrongly* constructed was greater than the number of all the atoms in the universe [vs. only in the right way]. *So* try as I would, I couldn't convince myself that even the whole universe would be sufficient to find life by random processes—by what are called the blind forces of nature. . . . *By far* the simplest way to arrive at the correct sequences of amino acids in the enzymes [forming those biological grains out in space] would be by *thought, not* by random processes. . . . Rather than accept the fantastically small probability of life having arisen through the blind forces of nature, it seemed better to suppose that the origin of life was a *deliberate intellectual act*.[22]

So here we are being constantly showered with gifts

from the sky as part of a great conscious plan, the greatest being the gift of life itself, planted, as we have always been taught, by visiting angels acting upon higher instructions. Thus, organizing is an open-ended process (see Moses 1:33). I have quoted some passages at length because they bring out two important facts relevant to the recently revived and long-lived debate between the Darwinists and the Fundamentalists, in which I think the gospel rejects the most basic principle of each side. The official definition of creation accepted by conventional Christianity and Judaism and by their scientific opponents alike requires a creation that Aquinas specifies must be (1) instantaneous and (2) simultaneous—*everything* was created, and that in a single flash. That idea came out of Alexandria and is *not* found in the early Christian or Jewish writers. This is the "creationism" they are arguing about—it does not concern us in the least. Neither does Darwinism concern us. Nothing could be further from the picture given by modern revelation of the long succession of phases, each preparing the ground for the next, according to the plan worked out and agreed among the intelligences existing before the world was, with much discussion, deep thought and debate, testing and inspecting. That second point, thought and discussion, rejects the very keystone of Darwinism, the one sublime contribution to thought with which Darwin's discipline credits him above all others: "In the evolutionary pattern of thought," writes Huxley, "there is no longer need or room for the supernatural."[23] Darwin hardly deserves the credit that was poured on him during the Darwin Centennial year—after all, Laplace told Napoleon the same, as Lucretius and a long line of Sophists told the ancients.

    This surprising turnabout of 180 degrees in the thinking of some renowned scientists is matched at the same time by the reversal of our moral philosophy in the *opposite* direction. Heretofore most people have believed in a kind, benevolent *providence* that cared for us and somehow watched over us—the "Santa Claus" that Professor Simpson dismissed with such withering contempt. (To that some would now recall us, without knowing how we should go about it.) The great Russian physicist Nikolai Kozyrev objects to the cold, impersonal universe in which by the law of entropy everything can only run down—it is negative, repellent; and above all, he says, it is false, for all around us we see something at work against that inevitable disruption and dissolution.[24] The famous biologist Lewis Thomas (author of *The Lives of a Cell*) puts it this way: "I cannot make my peace with the *randomness* doctrine; I cannot abide the notion of purposelessness and blind chance in nature. And yet *I do not know what to put in its place for the quieting of my mind.* . . . We talk—some of us, anyway—about the *absurdity* of the human situation, but we do this because we do not know how we fit in, or what we are for. The stories we used to make up to explain ourselves *do not make sense anymore,* and we have run out of new stories, for the moment."[25] The gospel recognizes the claims of entropy (2 Nephi 9:6-7).

We would say it is time for these people to consider the gospel—what would they lose, since they confess themselves utterly out of ideas in any other direction? But it is precisely many who have accepted the gospel today who are assuring us that *there are no gifts from heaven.* That is indeed the foundation of our economic and social life today. But just as the gospel spares us the folly of time wasted in that old debate, so it likewise delivers us from the cosmic tussle between capitalism and communism, since, as Solzhenytsin observed in a talk recently given at Harvard,[26] both rest on the same identical ground principle—*there are no gifts from heaven;* there is no Pie in the Sky, no Free Lunch. Each is a thoroughgoing dialectical materialism in which we are all ordered to work like mad or perish. The one fact of life is the *economy.* Darwin was the

Bible of both camps, and dialectical materialism of the one was matched at every point by that of the other—Ayn Rand's militant atheism is as realistic as that of any Marxist. For both, the earth is nothing but a source of raw materials, and the object of life is not joy but power and gain. In a word, *both reject the free lunch*; for both, the bottom line is survival; and for both, survival means work, work, work— everybody must work.

No free lunch? I lived on free lunches once. I never worked so hard in my life as when I was getting free lunches. I had a university fellowship; in accepting it I had to agree not to accept any gainful employment as long as the fellowship lasted. Lunch and room and clothing were provided with the understanding that I would engage in much more important and *much* harder work than it would take to earn any amount of lunch. But more emphatically I was *not* to work for lunch. Was I guilty of getting a free lunch?

Brigham Young with his usual insight applied this situation to all of us: We have been permitted to come here, he explained, to go to school, to acquire certain knowledge and take certain basic tests[27]—"wherefore," says Nephi, this "state became a state of probation" (2 Nephi 2:21). While we are at school our generous parent has provided us with all the necessities of life we will need to carry us through. ("Adam, I have created *for* you this earth and have provided it with everything you will need—go to, enjoy yourself, take care of the Garden"—that was work. But Adam was not working for lunch: that was free—"Of every tree thou mayest *freely* eat!") Now suppose toward the end of the first semester of the school year my kind patron pays a visit to the school, meets me, and asks me how I am doing—"Oh," I say, "I am doing very well, thanks to your bounty." "Are you learning a lot?" "Yes, I am making good progress." "What fields are you studying in particular just now?" "Oh, I'm studying how to get lunch." "You study *that*? All the time?" "Yes, that's the important thing in life, isn't it—how to get more lunch; there's no free lunch, you know." "But my dear boy, I'm providing you with that right now." "Yes, for the time being, and I am grateful—but my purpose in life is to get more and better lunches. Room and board is nice, but I want super room and board—and other things." "Things of this world," says the patron. "Yes, that's it." The patron is disgusted, to quote Brigham Young!

Or take another parable. A man had a very gifted child who wanted to become a pianist. A worthy goal, said his father; great pianists make lots of money. But before you can begin lessons you must earn your own piano. Pianos are very expensive. You can begin with a job in a super-market, then become perhaps a car salesman or real estate agent; you might even be able someday to start your own business. Then by the time you are thirty or so you can even have your own piano. Just a minute, says his mother. At that rate he will never become a pianist. That reminds me of my cousin Jake, she adds, who had a beautiful voice and went to work in a boiler-factory to get enough money to take singing lessons—but by the time he had earned the money he was stone deaf. Well, says the father, why can't the kid do both? Why can't he be both a business man and a musician? Because, says the boy, who has been to Sunday School, we are granted enough time on earth to serve only one master. Every day of our lives we have to make a choice, a choice that will show where our real interests and desires lie. From the very beginning of the world the choice was provided as a test for each of us during this time of probation. Satan is allowed to try and tempt us in his way, and God is allowed in his: as Moroni puts it, "The devil . . . inviteth and enticeth to sin, and to do that which is evil *continually*. But behold, that which is of God inviteth and enticeth to do good *continually*" (Moroni 7:12-13). It is going on all the time, the ancient doctrine of the Two Ways. The point is that we *cannot* choose both ways. They go in opposite directions — man simply *cannot* serve both God and mammon, the Lord said, and mammon is simply the Hebrew word (both ancient and modern) for dealing in money. So the first commandment given to the Church was "Seek not for riches but for wisdom" (D&C 6:7) — making it perfectly clear that they are mutually exclusive. This sounds to most Latter-day Saints today like an alarming doctrine, so I wish now to avoid the controversial side of it entirely (which should be easy, since there *is* no controversial side — if the world is overwhelmingly leaning to the one side, the scriptures are crushingly overloaded on the other, and I go by the scriptures). I want now to think about the delightful, happy side of the whole thing. *"Deny not the gifts of God"* (Moroni 10:8) is the impassioned plea that sums up and concludes the Book of Mormon. I put it this way: Try accepting them and see what happens.

The words *gift* and *giving* are the key words.

Adam comes into a new world in which he is given everything the heart of man could desire. He did not make the world; it was already prepared for him when he opened his eyes: "We have prepared for you this earth, and placed in it all manner of foods and delights, everything springing forth spontaneously."

"We have also planted for you a garden eastward, already planted, already blooming. Now go to, get to work, take good care of the garden — which we gave you and wanted you to have. Enjoy yourself, be happy." Adam did work before the fall, but not for money, or to accumulate anything, for the garden brought forth everything spontaneously — a free lunch all the time. Notably, the Creator himself worked for six periods and rested on the seventh. So Adam did not need to work to keep body and soul together, because he was immortal.

Cast out of the garden, Adam still must work; he and

Eve must both "labor," he to bring forth the fruits of the earth, she to bear children. Yet all is still a gift. In neither case do they produce anything: it is all given them. Adam cannot make a blade of grass grow; and as for producing children, the lowest of God's creatures can do the same! There is no credit here: as elsewhere, the work is stimulating exercise.

The solution to Adam's problem in the desert is still a gift, which he must ask for, seeking ever greater light and knowledge, which God had promised him if he would but ask. It is all *brought* to him as a *gift,* one brought down from another world by special messengers sent to instruct Adam in things he never could have discovered or made for himself, worlds without end. The instructions, laws, charges, covenants, signs, tokens, and ordinances are expressly *given* to him. "Adam," says the messenger, "we have been instructed to *give* unto you . . . "

These gifts enable Adam to return to his former blessedness in the shortest possible time. The word *give* and its synonyms occur ninety-nine times in the record.

So Adam is well on his way back when an old rival shows up, whom he does not recognize. He announces to Adam, as he does later to Abraham and Moses, that he is the God of this world. Everything in it is his private property — his greatness and glory. He rules the whole thing as a model estate, with everything under his strict control — and nobody had better make any trouble! He is not giving anything away; yet we can have anything with money, and you get the money by working for *him*: no free lunch.

When he meets others on the premises, he immediately charges them with trespassing, with trying to take his property from him. He is willing to let anyone have anything in his world — but at a price. All is for sale: there is no free lunch in his kingdom.

To Adam, the rival offers to put the gift business on a paying basis. He starts out by offering Adam his gifts,

asking him three times, "What is it you want?" assuring
Adam that he is able to give whatever is requested.

And in fact, he does rule; he is "the prince of this
world" (John 14:30), having staked a claim on all the mineral riches of the earth — gold, silver, and other treasures.
He then is able to buy up political, military, and ecclesiastical support and run the whole show.

He assures Adam that he has the supreme gift, the gift
that will get Adam anything else in the world: "At the
devil's booth are *all* things sold, each ounce of dross."[28]
But Adam turns him down, refusing to sell for money the
gifts God has given him, for they are sacred. The heavenly
gifts are *not negotiable*. Which is what Peter told Simon
Magus: "But Peter said to him, Thy money perish with
thee, because thou hast thought that the gift of God may
be purchased with money" (Acts 8:20). You "requite" his
goodness in another way.

But as the case of Simon shows, Satan was able to find
plenty of other people willing to go along with his system.
Cain and Lamech became willing partners in his deals.
Before long, almost all of Adam's posterity preferred Lucifer's lucrative contracts and "gifts": "They loved Satan
more than God" (Moses 5:13), while poor Adam and Eve
could do nothing but "[mourn] before the Lord" (Moses
5:27).

So ever since the Mahan school of economics was
founded, we have had — instead of free gifts — bargains,
earnings, percentages, options, returns, markets, investments, deals — which utterly deny the gifts of God. Necessarily — because you cannot have both. They despise the
gifts of God, gently or scornfully pushing them aside: "That
was all right for those times, but this is the 'modern
world.' " Indeed it is, and the last days of that world. As
the Lord told Joseph in the grove, "Behold, the world lieth
in sin."[29]

Help yourselves to all you need; there is no need to

take more than you need (manna for forty years)! There is plenty around this earth for men. Trust me.

The gifts of God include everything we can possibly want. All we have to do to get them is to *ask* him for them, and he will give us "whatsoever things ye shall ask" (3 Nephi 27:28). Will that spoil us, weaken our character? No more than my fellowship did—it was the most toughening experience I ever had—doing exactly what I wanted to do with the most immense exertions. We ask him for good health; that makes things easier for us. Does it weaken our character? You do not miss your health if the whole object is study; to preserve it you must eat—would you make *that* your main design? But God promises to give us anything at all—as a specific bonus: it will include, if we agree to it, only what is "expedient for us to have." And that in itself is one of the nicest gifts of all, since deciding what we really should have in the long run, in consideration of future developments of which we have not an inkling, is practically impossible for us; to solve that problem we would have to spend all of our time toiling away at computers. But God has taken care of that for us too. The law of the harvest is that God gives the increase. You reap by *design* of grain, you say, but you did not produce the seed in the first place and you expect much *more* than you sowed. That increase is a gift of God.

This granting us only what is expedient not only keeps us out of mischief and saves us a lifetime of wasted endeavor, it also lets us know all the time when we are on the right track. Like Oliver Cowdery, we are instructed to make our own decisions and then ask God whether they have been right (see D&C 9). This does not mean that we need to weigh and measure the advantages and disadvantages of breaking any of the Ten Commandments—we do not even consider such a possibility. We never *should* ask the Lord whether or not we should commit adultery, theft, murder, or fraud. That question would never arise.

Another question we should never ask is "Should I seek after riches?" For if there is any point on which the Book of Mormon is fiercely emphatic, it is that no one should ever set his heart upon riches. "Now the *cause* of this iniquity of the people was this—*Satan* had great power, unto the stirring up of the people to do all manner of iniquity, . . . *tempting* them to seek for power, and authority, and riches, and the vain things of the world" (3 Nephi 6:15). Note that Satan had the power to try man and to tempt him; he was given that power in order to put the people on this earth to a test, by placing his gifts by the side of God's, with every man free to choose between them.

The choice *is* a hard one: Would I make a living first or would I take a chance on the lunch? It was not meant to be easy. It *is* hard to give up financial security to demonstrate your faith in the good intentions of your Heavenly Father. It is a seemingly sensible and innocent concern: to get rich. Speaking on "Sixty Minutes" last Sunday, Malcolm Forbes (publisher of *Forbes*), the archapostle of the rich, was shown addressing the students at a commencement at the University of Ohio. He made a remark which I immediately wrote down, for to me it said everything: "Nothing gives freedom like a buck in the bank!" I immediately thought of Cain's cry of joy and triumph when by a conspiracy (D&C 84:16) he succeeded in putting his brother out of the way for the sake of getting gain; he was not ashamed at all, we are told, but "gloried in that which he had done, saying: *I am free*; surely the flocks of my brother falleth into my hands[!]" (Moses 5:33).

But almost all the young people I know today want to believe that we do not have to make such a drastic choice as between trusting in God entirely and working for money in the bank. Again may I remind you, the choice was deliberately designed to be a hard and searching one. But surely, I hear all the time, there must be a compromise, a

common ground between them. The favorite text to support this is "Seek ye first the kingdom of God, and his
righteousness; and all these things shall be added unto
you" (Matthew 6:33). This is commonly interpreted as
meaning that I should first go on a mission or get a testimony, thus seeking the kingdom of God, and then I will
be free to seek the other things. First wisdom, then riches.
But you *never* cease seeking wisdom, and you are forbidden
to seek riches. This is a classic case of a text out of context.
There is no thought here of *seeking* the other things—if you
need them they will be added: When are you supposed to
stop seeking the kingdom of heaven?

We Latter-day Saints are meticulously selective in pick-
ing our way among those verses of scripture that seem to
support our economic position; but this passage, like many
others to the same effect, must be taken as a whole. And
if we do not like scriptural passages on this subject, we
say: "Oh, that is out of context." Therefore let us take them
in context. What the Lord is saying here, as clearly as it
can be said, is that we are not to worry about the room
and board, because God will provide it if we, so to speak,
accept the fellowship and spend our time doing the things
he wants us to do: Listen to him as he addresses his hearers
as "O ye of little faith[!]" (Matthew 6:30).

"Lay *not* up for yourselves treasures upon earth [se-
curities, annuities, investments, and so on; as President
Kimball says: seeking security in these things is an act of
little faith, a vote of no confidence in God]. . . . *But* lay up
for yourselves treasures in heaven [note again that you
can't have both]. . . . For where your treasure is, there will
your heart be also [you must choose the one *or* the
other]. . . . No man *can* serve two masters. . . . Ye *cannot*
serve God *and* mammon [meaning in this case explicitly
business security, as the Lord continues to pour it on].
Therefore I say unto you, *Take no thought for your life*, what
ye shall eat, or what ye shall drink [your three squares a

day, no less]; nor yet for your body, what ye shall put on" (Matthew 6:19-21, 24-25).

He concludes: "Therefore *take no thought*, saying, What shall we eat? or, What shall we drink? or, Wherewithal shall we be clothed? (For after all these things do the Gentiles seek) [Of course they do! Aren't they vital to our very survival on earth? Indeed they are, and in the next sentence the Lord takes full cognizance of that fact] for your *heavenly Father knoweth that ye have need of all these things*. [And since he is fully aware of that, *he* will provide us with them if we do his work:] But seek ye first the kingdom of God, and his righteousness; *and all these things shall be added* unto you" (Matthew 6:31-33). By *him*, that is, since the Lord has just told us in the preceding verses how he provides for his other creatures that "sow not, neither do they reap, nor gather into barns; yet your heavenly Father feedeth them. Are ye not much better than they?" (Matthew 6:26). "Take therefore [he repeats in conclusion, driving the lesson home again] no thought for the morrow" (Matthew 6:34). We're being "improvident," and yet this happens to be the most repeated passage in all the scriptures!

The same discourse is contained in Luke 12, where the Lord makes it clear that he is speaking to the whole church, not just to the apostles; here, however, he explains things even more fully as yet another parable: he tells the story of a man who was very provident and who *did* gather into barns and made himself very rich and secure for the future the way we would all like to be. "The ground of a certain rich man gave forth plentifully: And he thought within himself [being very far-sighted], saying, What shall I do, because I have no room where to bestow my fruits [he was expanding—a growing economy]? . . . This I will do: I will pull down my barns, and build greater [bigger and better]. . . . And I will say to my soul, Soul, thou hast much goods laid up *for many years* [now you can retire and take things easy for a while]; take thine ease, eat, drink, and be merry. But God said unto him, Thou fool, this night thy soul shall be required of thee: then whose shall those things be, which thou hast provided?" (Luke 12:16-20). They won't be yours anymore; you take nothing with you. It is certain. You are free to choose treasures in heaven *or* treasures on earth, but you cannot have both. In this life men are free to go after what they please, just as they are free to break all the commandments of God, if they choose, which millions do every day. (Note that the sacred principle of free agency does *not* sanctify the ways men choose to use it, though this is often taken as a justification for seeking after riches.)

When a rich man felt horribly deprived in his afterlife, Abraham spoke to him from on high and said, "Son [for he *was* a son of Abraham—a member of the Church], remember that thou in thy lifetime receivedst thy good things, and likewise Lazarus evil things [he was a beggar— we do *not* like beggars in our Latter-day Saint community]: but now he is comforted, and thou art tormented. . . . There is a great gulf fixed: so that they which would pass from hence to you cannot; neither can they pass to us, that would come from thence" (Luke 16:25-26). There is no passing between you. The rich man did have feelings, however, for he begged Abraham to send the beggar to his five brothers "that he may testify unto them, lest they also come into this place of torment" (Luke 16:28). That will not be necessary, Abraham told him, since it is already laid out for them in the scriptures. Yes, said the rich man, but if someone actually came to them from the dead—that would really convince them to repent. No, Abraham replied, "If they hear not Moses and the prophets, neither will they be persuaded, though one rose from the dead" (Luke 16:31).

Note it well—on this very matter of whether to seek riches or not, the scriptures have spoken so clearly and so much that we are out of order in asking for more revelation on the subject. We are already swamped with instruction; we have to maneuver skillfully to avoid it. No doubt the five brothers would immediately protest that the scriptures are being quoted "out of context." That is what the populations think today. When we can use that argument, what do we do? When I took up the first version of the new Topical Guide to the scriptures and turned to the heading "riches," lo and behold, there was nothing on the subject—the word was not even there. I had to assume that this was a deliberate omission, since the word *riches* is a very convenient topical handle, and it occurs no less than sixty-one times in our modern scriptures. It is hardly possible that all sixty-one times could be put out of context! Why was such an important item left out? (In more recent editions, it has been included.) "Treasures" is there, an ambivalent term that can be either good or bad but is mostly spiritual—"riches" is the bottom line, and one has only to read the passages found under that label in ordinary concordances to learn that what modern revelation has to say about acquiring riches is anything but encouraging to those who do it.

There are evil gifts: "Lay hold upon every good *gift*, and touch not the *evil gift*, nor the *unclean* thing" (Moroni 10:30). What is the evil gift, the unclean thing? What first springs to mind is the powerful epithet—*filthy* lucre. That is what is unclean. This is what Satan had to offer: gold and silver, the treasures of earth.

Which claimant do we recognize? The one says: "The earth is full, and there is *enough and to spare*; yea, I prepared all things, and have *given* unto the children of men to be agents unto themselves" (D&C 104:17). Help yourself but be careful of one thing. It is all free on this condition: "If any man shall take of the *abundance* which *I have made*, and impart not his portion, according to the law of my gospel [contained in Deuteronomy, the New Testament parables, the Book of Mormon, and the Doctrine and Covenants], unto the poor and the needy, he shall, with the wicked, lift up his eyes in hell, being in torment" (D&C 104:18), which of course refers us to the story of the rich man and Lazarus.

The other tells us that "every man fared in this life according to the management of the creature; therefore every man prospered according to his genius, and . . . conquered according to his strength; and whatsoever a man did was no crime" (Alma 30:17)—there is no such thing as a rip-off. Judgment hereafter? Just remember, says Korihor, "when a man was dead, that was the end thereof" (Alma 30:18). Forget about rules "laid down by ancient priests" (Alma 30:23) to keep you from doing as you please, so that you dare "not look up with boldness, and . . . enjoy [your] rights and privileges" or even "make use of that which is [your] own" because of a lot of old teachings taken out of context (Alma 30:27-28).

If we ask not we receive not. The gifts are not in evidence today, except one gift, which you notice the people *ask* for—the gift of healing. They ask for that with honest intent and with sincere hearts, and we really do have that gift. Because we are desperate and nobody else can help us, we ask for it with sincere hearts of our Lord.

As for these other gifts—how often do we ask for them? How earnestly do we seek for them? We could have them if we did ask, but we don't. "Well, who denies them?" Anyone who doesn't ask for them. They are available to all for the asking, but one must ask with an honest heart, sincerely. The greatest gifts are those listed in Moroni 10, ten gifts.

Do people prefer temporal gifts today? That's a strange thing; people don't want them, either. "What are the temporal gifts?" we ask ourselves. Anything you could possibly ask for in order to get along in the world. "People don't *want* them?" No, *not as gifts*—they are proud and don't want to accept a dole. (I'm arguing with myself here.)

"Isn't that rather admirable?" It looks that way. Their hearts are really set on these things—they want to have them but they want to earn them fair and square and to be beholden to no one for them. They want to say, "This is mine because I earned it." No one has a right to a gift; no one can go to the giver and demand it as something he has earned. What is owed you, you don't receive as a present but as your due. That makes us all beggars. In our Anglo-Saxon ethic we just don't like the idea of having to depend upon anyone else—we must be independent before all things. Well, I say, "What's wrong with that?" I answer, we think we are being realistic about it, but are we? Independent of what? Of God? Of our fellowman? Of nature? So we actually reject the gifts of God. *As gifts* we despise them.

"Ye are cursed because of your riches," says the prophet Samuel, "and also are your riches cursed because ye have set your hearts upon them, and have not hearkened unto the words of him who *gave* them unto you. Ye do not remember the Lord your God in the things with which he hath *blessed* you, but ye *do always remember your riches,* not to thank the Lord your God for them" (Helaman 13:21-22). They simply refused to regard or treat their riches as *gifts,* but insisted that they were *earnings.*

The gifts of God are intimate and personal. You do *not* ask God for gifts for someone else, because only God knows the mind, heart, and the real needs of any individual, and only he knows what is really expedient in each case. What I ask for you might be what you neither want nor need—a sheer impertinence on my part. Gifts can embarrass. That is why we are told that in giving a gift to another you must "not let your left hand know what your right hand is doing" (cf. Matthew 6:3)—there is no bookkeeping of gifts. The manna experience and the Lord's prayer teach us that!

There is something infinitely degrading about worrying

whether others—especially those who have less than we do—are getting more than they deserve. We think of the spoiled child at the party, who jealously watches what the other children are getting, grabs everything in sight, and starts fights when the goodies are being handed out, then complains that he has not got as much as somebody else. But don't judge the little fellow—he is merely maximizing profits, like the rest of us. We see the heroes of epic literature and oriental romances jealously measuring their "portions" at the banquet table lest the "meed of honor" of one noble lord be either too far above or below that of another. That leads to nasty remarks, jealous outbreaks, savage brawls, and usually to bloodshed—all over *gifts*, of all things!

In the repeated passage, "Seek not for riches but for wisdom, and behold, the mysteries of God shall be unfolded unto you, and *then* shall you be made rich. Behold, he that hath eternal life is rich" (D&C 6:7). *That* is the wealth the Lord is speaking of, the riches he promises: "You shall have eternal life, which *gift* is the greatest of all the *gifts* of God" (D&C 14:7). It is a pure *gift*—we have no *right* to it; we have proven our helplessness to achieve it and our unworthiness to possess it. Jesus Christ bought it *for* us: he paid the ransom price, he redeemed us when we could not redeem ourselves, and he gave us eternal life as a free gift. He has taught us how to qualify for the gift, but the gift itself we could never earn by our own efforts. And what does he require of us in order to qualify, to show that we do not hold such a sacrifice cheaply or disdain it because it is a gift? In return for the gifts, without which we cannot survive an hour, God seeks of us, first of all, that "we despise not his gifts" by putting them in second place to our own "virtuous industry." "A certain man made a great supper, and bade many: And sent his servant . . . to say to them that were bidden, Come; for all things are now ready. . . . [Come and help yourselves!

But they all alike began to make excuses:] I have bought a piece of ground, and I must needs go and see it. . . . I have bought five yoke of oxen, and I go to prove them. . . . I have married a wife, and therefore I cannot come. . . . The master of the house being angry [and insulted at these people who placed business before pleasure, sent his servant to bring in the poor, maimed, halt, and blind, those so poor they must have been lazy bums]. . . . For I say unto you, That none of those men which were bidden shall taste of my supper" (Luke 14:16-21, 24).

Matthew 22 gives a shorter version: A king invites them to a marriage feast with all things prepared—a magnificent spread. "But they *made light of it* [they despised it], and went their ways, *one to his farm, another to his merchandise*" [they were all business]. Then the king said: "The wedding is ready, but they which were bidden were *not worthy.*" They thought that each of these can be worked for, each of these can be bought. But they were fools (Matthew 22:2-10).

Some accept the heavenly gift and then go back to business again, and put it in second place: Such a one "received [the] seed [and] . . . heareth the word; and the care [the word is *merimna*—concern, business] of this world, and the *deceitfulness of riches* [*apatē tou ploutou*—they promise you what they cannot deliver] choke the teaching, and he becometh unfruitful" (Matthew 13:22).

God's second requirement of us is that we share what he gives us liberally and impartially: "Let every man esteem his brother as himself. For what man among you having twelve sons . . . and they serve him obediently, and he saith unto the one: Be thou clothed in robes and sit thou here; and to the other: Be thou clothed in rags and sit thou there—and looketh upon his sons and saith I am just?" (D&C 38:25-26). On the other hand, the one who serves

Mammon most obediently can count on getting more than all his other brothers put together—for a time.

The supper is still spread: "For, behold, the beasts of the field and the fowls of the air, and that which cometh of the earth, is ordained for the use of man for food and for raiment, and that he might have *in abundance*" (D&C 49:19), with the strict understanding, "Wo be unto man that sheddeth blood or that wasteth flesh *and hath no need*" (D&C 49:21). You take all you need—it is provided in abundance—but *never* more than you need. Above all, "it is *not given* that one man should possess that which is above another, wherefore *the world lieth in sin*" (D&C 49:20). More than enough corrupts us with his gifts; he will not allow us to take more. How then can anyone who has more than his fellows claim that *God* has given it to him, when God has declared in the strongest terms that that inequality is the basic cause of evil in the world today?

All gifts come from God and are freely given. It is a risky business when men start dealing in gifts—the careful reckoning of who gives what and how much, and who gets what and how much from whom, leads to dangerous complications and bloodshed in the gift-giving of heroic literature or the legends of the gods—the gifts always lead to trouble.

First with Satan's gifts: "Thou shalt take no gift: for the gift blindeth the wise, and perverteth the words of the righteous" (Exodus 23:8). "Thou shalt not wrest judgment; thou shalt not respect persons, neither take a gift: for a gift doth blind the eyes of the *wise*, and pervert the words of the *righteous*" (Deuteronomy 16:19). Whenever we accept a gift from another we are under obligation to him.

But God *wants* us to be under obligation to *him*; he wants us to feel our dependence on him at all times: on a day-to-day basis: "Give us this day our *daily* bread" (Matthew 6:11). This is the *manna*; they could not do business with it.

But there is more: we have too often returned God's
kindness with disobedience to him and meanness to our
fellows, so the Lord continues: "And forgive us our debts,
as *we forgive* our debtors" (Matthew 6:12). We ask the maximum from him, and in return he asks us to give a little
of it to our fellowmen. He tells us the Parable of the Steward:

> [There was] a certain king, . . . [and] one was
> brought unto him, which owed him ten thousand tal-
> ents. But . . . he had not to pay, [and] his lord com-
> manded him to be sold . . . and all that he had, and
> payment to be made. The servant therefore fell
> down, . . . saying, Lord, have patience with me, and I
> will pay thee all. Then the lord of that servant was moved
> with compassion, and loosed him, and for*gave* him the
> debt. But the same servant went out, and found one of
> his fellowservants, which owed him an hundred pence:
> and he laid hands on him, and took him by the throat,
> saying, Pay me that thou owest. And his fellowservant
> fell down at his feet, and besought him, saying, Have
> patience with me, and I will pay thee all. And he would
> not: but went and cast him into prison, till he should
> pay the debt. . . . His lord . . . said unto him, O thou
> wicked servant, I forgave thee all that debt. . . .
> Shouldest not thou also have had compassion on thy
> fellowservant, even as I had pity on thee? . . . and de-
> livered him to the tormentors (Matthew 18:23-34).

Please note that the strict, no-nonsense servant was
acting within his legal rights; even as his master was acting
within *his* legal rights in cracking down on a delinquent.
The servant, freed by the compassion of his master to
exercise his own legal rights, took advantage of his refound
liberty by claiming his own legal rights on another to the
full extent of the law. Legal, to be sure, but what could be
more base or depraved than to *use* the gifts and advantages
God has given us as a club to deprive others of the lesser

gifts which God has given them! Yet we see this all the time. We hear a lot today about a certain meanness of spirit which is becoming more conspicuous in our lives. An ancient philosophy has been revived, according to which the holdings of men whose wealth increases without their knowledge and while they sleep call their increase "earnings"—as if Trimalchio or Seneca or Varro or Brutus had worked a thousand times harder or were a thousand times smarter than the rest of us (that being how much richer they are); and these huge accumulations of capital were held to be (in Rome) the ultimate source of all wealth, so that even slaves should feel grateful to these men for at least providing them with a living. Accordingly, the owners of the earth were under no obligation whatever to give anything to anybody, since their only obligation to society was to get richer, so that in the long run everybody would benefit. Indeed, anything that would diminish their holdings in any way was considered morally wrong as damaging to the well-spring of the economy. An exception was Herodes Atticus: it was the right of those who had it to *abuse* the gifts of God, even more vicious, that everyone was forced to play *the* game.[30] Such were the imperial Romans of whom we read in the great satirical literature of Rome and in the Church Fathers, who, to paraphrase Moroni, adorn themselves with that which hath no life, and yet suffer the hungry, and the needy, and the naked, and the sick and the afflicted (who *did* have life—but not a very happy one) to pass by them, and *notice them not* (cf. Mormon 8:39). "Behold, the sword of vengeance was hanging over you; and the time soon cometh that he avengeth the blood of the saints upon you" (Mormon 8:41). Because Rome ignored these principles, it fell—the best thing it ever did. According to President Kimball, those words which I just read from Moroni himself—the one who talked with Joseph Smith—were describing not only our own day but our own society.[31] (Incidentally, Seneca observed that great fortunes come *easily* or not at all—they do *not* come by hard, continual, lifelong toil, which at best lays aside a rather pitiful nest egg compared with the treasures of the earth, which are won through manipulations in the law courts.)

We may ask for some gifts, as they are given, *without measure*, without limit; with others enough is enough, as Paul tells us (see 2 Corinthians 10:13). The *unlimited* gift that God's children from Adam on have been encouraged to seek with unceasing zeal is of course light and truth: "And finding there was greater happiness and peace and rest *for me* [says Abraham], I *sought* for the blessings of the fathers, . . . desiring also to be one who possessed great knowledge . . . and to possess a *greater* knowledge, . . . desiring to receive instructions" (Abraham 1:2). Selfish? The greatest pleasure in having knowledge is to spread it around.

The other is the limited gift: "We brought nothing into this world, and it is certain we can carry nothing out. And having food and raiment let us be therewith content. But they that will be rich fall into temptation and a snare [for the *rich* person by definition is one who has more than he needs—and that is too much; the *snare* is a trap—Satan has caught them], and into many foolish and hurtful lusts, which drown men in destruction and perdition. For the *love of money* is the root of all evil; which while some coveted after, they have erred from the faith, and pierce themselves through with many sorrows" (1 Timothy 6:7-10). The word for *love* here is not sexual love—the English translation is unique in giving us that way of escape: it is *philargyria* or *cupiditas*, which simply means desire for wealth.

And so the two gifts are placed side by side before us in *the first commandment given to the Church in these latter days*: "Seek *not* for riches, but seek for wisdom" (D&C 6:7).

How is your health, my aging cronies ask me. My health is very good. No aches, pains, disabilities, headaches, blackouts, hangups, no chronic ill? No, none at all. You do not have to watch it all the time? No, it is the same as always. Then you are getting a free ride. There are many at this age who spend most of their time testing drugs and visiting specialists, toiling and suffering at being hypochondriacs. The ancients used the same words for work, toil, labor, pain, and suffering. Doesn't your good health make your life dull — nothing to talk about? Doesn't it make you feel lazy, uncomfortable, guilty? Doesn't it *weaken your character?* What I am getting at is that working for lunch all the day is just as silly as concentrating on the condition of your physical plant in other ways. *If* it is working well, you should forget it and do the more admirable things of which it is capable. Take the case of the Nephites: The Lord is about to bestow upon them *gifts* of such a nature that it is forbidden to discuss them. But *before* he bestows those gifts, he makes sure that their *temporal* wants are all taken care of: "Have ye any that are sick among you? Bring them hither. Have ye any that are lame or blind, or halt, or maimed, or leprous, or that are withered, or that are deaf, or that are afflicted in *any* manner? Bring them hither and I will heal them" (3 Nephi 17:7). Then he commanded his disciples "that they should bring forth some bread and wine unto him" (3 Nephi 18:1), and when the multitude "had eaten and were filled" (3 Nephi 18:4), he taught them about the sacrament. Then Nephi himself went down into the water, and he and all the others were baptized — cleaned up for a special meeting with the Lord the next day. Once he had taken care of all their physical wants, *then* his great teaching could *begin.* Once the people are all fed, clothed, and healed of any physical affliction, and cleansed of all impurities, *then* they can receive the gospel. With most churches that preliminary requirement is the whole story; it gives them all a worthy program, and it is an *indispensable* prerequisite in which we too should be engaged. But like the Word of Wisdom (another free gift and a temporal blessing), it is only to put us in condition for the real work, in which by now we should all be deeply engaged. Instead of which, I hear everywhere, "Wait until I can make enough money — then I can help the Church." God asks no such favors, "What is property unto me?" he asks (D&C 117:4).

We are often told that wealth is the reward of certain qualities of character — admirable qualities — and that is certainly true. Among the qualities that make for success in business are hard work, dependability, sobriety, firmness, imagination, patience, courage, loyalty, discrimination (taste), intelligence, persistence, ingenuity, dedication, courtesy, humor, sensitivity, determination, tact, and so on. Those happen to be the very same qualities necessary to make a successful athlete, musician, soldier, international jewel thief, painter, scholar, hit man, spy, teacher, dancer, bank robber, minister, politician, author, general, con man, astronomer, builder, engineer, physician, smuggler, astronaut, inventor, godfather, explorer, and so on. Too often these attributes of character are represented as the singular and unique adornments of the business world, putting a stamp of special glory on the man in the executive suite, whereas actually they are needed everywhere. Consider the statistics alone. There are over 600,000 millionaires in the country — but how many first-rate composers, or artists, or even scientists are there by comparison? Some of the largest corporations in the country wisely reject applicants whose IQs are too high.

All those professions we just named are ladders to be climbed. Each one develops character and offers rewards, but as Brother Packer reminded us, it is not only important to be climbing a ladder, the really important thing is *which* ladder we climb.[32] I once heard Stephen L Richards give a talk in which he denounced careers in making it clear that *any* career is the wrong ladder, since careers are only for the short run (we retire from them eventually), while we should be doing what is for the long run—the eternal run, and that here and now![33]

Perhaps the most pernicious aspect of today's state of things is that it permits us only a very limited choice of ladders, nay, it *forces* us to choose between business and law, the alternative being starvation. (A man must become a sharp operator, as Isaiah observes bitterly, purely in self-defense: if you do not learn to take others you will get taken; Isaiah 59:15.) Of course, the choice of ladders is actually as wide as ever, but our young people are thoroughly intimidated. Satan wants to get us in that position where we are paralyzed to oppose him: "If I leave his employ, what will become of me?" This is a terrifying thought from the chairman of the board to the one working on the assembly line. The answer is very reassuring: "Hear the teachings of the gospel along with the rest of the human race—and follow them, and you will not have to worry about Satan's hold on the economy, for then you will observe and keep the law of consecration."

What are we instructed to do, then, in our fallen state? One of the shortest and most concise sections of the Doctrine and Covenants tells us, "Let your time be devoted to the *studying* of the scriptures; and to *preaching*, and to confirming the church . . . and to performing your labors on the *land*" (D&C 26:1). The Great Triple Combination — farming, church, and study. Even so Adam was told to cultivate his garden, preach the gospel among his children (a most strenuous mission), and finally to seek ever greater light and knowledge. Let me remind you that this system has *worked* throughout the ages, whenever it has been given a try. What is the result of our industrial-military complex, which seems to be the inevitable trend of every greedy industrial society? It has never worked; not for one decade has it failed to fill the earth with blood and horror. Where has it brought us at the present moment? Hear the words of Henry C. Wallich, the Governor of the Federal

Reserve, as he describes our society in which the *economy* is all-in-all: "It's a form of fraud, perpetrated *by* everybody *on* everybody. It is a world in which *nobody keeps his word.* Even if you could adjust perfectly for it, it would be a *very unpleasant world."*

"Well, don't you think this idealistic immaterialism of yours is quite unrealistic?" (I ask myself). Indeed it is for non–Latter-day Saints; it is simply laughable in the present world. Remember—what we regard as real and what the rest of the world regards as real are by no means the same thing. For us the great reality is the visitation of heavenly beings to the world. Nothing could be further from reality or distract one's mind further from the cold, factual, work-aday realities of life than an angel with gold plates or a gold book. The Latter-day Saints will tell you a story that to them is perfectly real, whatever the world may think about it.

So the gifts of God are to be received in the same unstinting and joyful spirit in which they are given—freely, magnanimously, never counting the cost. (That was Brigham Young's motto: When the work of the Lord is to be done, *never count the cost.*[34])

"If ye then, being evil, know how to give *good gifts* unto *your* children, how much more shall your Father who is in heaven give good things to them that ask him?" (3 Nephi 14:11). God gives us temporal things, Brigham Young was fond of saying, expressly to see what we would do with them.[35] He is to be our example in all things, and he has given us one of the finest gifts of all, the privilege of practicing gift-giving exactly as he does. And don't worry. As anyone can tell you who has practiced the art even a little, *the gifts will never run out,* for they are what we would call supernatural: "Now, when the multitude had all eaten and drunk, behold, they were filled with the Spirit; and they did cry out with one voice, and gave glory to Jesus whom they both saw and heard" (3 Nephi 20:9).

What was all the excitement about—hadn't they ever had bread and wine to eat before? Was a good meal such a novelty to them? No, it was not the gift but the privilege of actually seeing and hearing the *giver*. Many a person afflicted with a sore but temporary illness, upon being healed by the ministrations of the priesthood, has shouted for joy. But if he was bound to get well anyway, where is the thrill of it? Again, it is not the gift but the hand of the giver that is everything. The momentary glimpse of the source is what is reassuring. The gift we appreciate might have come by chance. Such a thing may never happen to us again. It is the awareness in receiving the gift that it comes from the infinite and inexhaustible love that fills the immensity of space and enlivens the eternities that admonishes us to look upon *everything* good of which we are aware as the gift of God.

Notes

1. Julian Huxley, quoted in John C. Whitcomb and Henry M. Morris, *The Genesis Flood* (Philadelphia: Presbyterian and Reformed Publishing, 1964), 443.

2. Hoimar von Ditfurth, *Children of the Universe* (New York: Atheneum, 1976), 10.

3. Omar Khayyam, *Rubaiyat of Omar Khayyam,* tr. Edward Fitzgerald (New York: Avon, n.d.), LII.

4. Von Ditfurth, *Children of the Universe*, 10 (emphasis added).

5. R. Buckminster Fuller, *Intuition* (Garden City, NY: Doubleday, 1972), 81.

6. Ibid., 82 (emphasis added).

7. Ibid., 105 (emphasis added).

8. Ibid., 107.

9. Ibid., 109.

10. Ibid., 110.

11. Ibid., 111-13.

12. Ibid., 12.

13. Ibid., 13.

14. Ibid., 15 (emphasis added).

15. Ibid., 89-92.

16. Ibid., 265-66 (emphasis added).

17. Ibid., 266-67.

18. Fred Hoyle, "The Universe: Past and Present Reflections,"
20. *Engineering and Science* 45 (November 1981): 8-12.

19. Ibid., 10.

20. *JD* 3:277.

21. Hoyle, "The Universe: Past and Present Reflections," 10.

22. Ibid., 11-12 (emphasis added).

23. Julian Huxley, in Whitcomb, *The Genesis Flood*, 443.

24. Nikolai Kozyrev, "An Unexplored World," *Soviet Life* (November 1965): 27, 43-45.

25. Lewis Thomas, "On the Uncertainty of Science," *Key Reporter of Phi Beta Kappa* 46 (Autumn 1980): 2.

26. Aleksandr I. Solzhenitsyn, "A World Split Apart," in *Solzhenitsyn at Harvard* (Washington, D.C.: Georgetown University, 1979), 3-20.

27. *JD* 8:135.

28. James Russell Lowell, *The Vision of Sir Launfal* IV, lines 25-27.

29. The 1832 recital of the First Vision as dictated by Joseph Smith to Frederick G. Williams. See Milton Backman, *Joseph Smith's First Vision* (Salt Lake City: Bookcraft, 1971), appendix A; cf. Dean C. Jessee, "The Early Accounts of Joseph Smith's First Vision," *BYU Studies* 9 (Spring 1969): 275-94; cf. also D&C 49:19-20.

30. For Herodes Atticus, see Philostratus *Lives of the Sophists* II, 546-48. For an English tr., see E. H. Warmington, *Philostratus and Eunapius* (Cambridge, MA: Harvard University Press, 1968), 139-41.

31. Spencer W. Kimball, "The False Gods That We Worship," *Ensign* 6 (June 1976): 3-5.

32. Boyd K. Packer, "The Arts and the Spirit of the Lord," *Ensign* 6 (August 1976): 61.

33. Stephen L Richards, *Where Is Wisdom* (Salt Lake City: Deseret, 1955), 400.

34. *JD* 8:355.

35. Ibid., 9:255.

6

How Firm a Foundation!
What Makes It So

One hundred fifty years is not as long as you think—
the Lord has not delayed his coming. I well remember my
great-grandfather, who was twenty years old when Joseph
Smith was still leading the church—and the Prophet died
as a young man. Also I remember very well indeed attending the centennial celebrations in Salt Lake City in
1930. It was just after my mission on one of my rare visits
to Utah. I stayed at my grandfather's house on the corner
of North Temple directly across from Temple Square, and
we had some long talks together. The theme of the centennial pageant was "The Gospel through the Ages." In
the years since then, I have come to see that I had no idea
at that time how vast and solid the foundations of the
Church really are.

At that time I was going to UCLA and majoring in, of
all things, sociology. For my year's research project, I was
making a study of the churches in Glendale, California,
gathering statistics (such as, that church attendance
dropped sharply on rainy Sundays and increased propor-
tionately at the movies) and having interviews, sometimes
quite frank and revealing, with the pastors. With every
one, the strength of the Latter-day Saint position became

*This lecture was given September 20, 1979, as part of the Sesquicentennial
Lectures on Mormon Arts. It was published by* Dialogue *12/4 (1979): 29-45;
and later by the Harold B. Lee Library Forum Committee and the Friends of
the BYU Library in 1980 as a fifteen-page leaflet.*

more apparent to me. Here are some of the things on which the foundation rests secure.

1. Joseph Smith came before the world with a "scenario," arresting, original, satisfying. Because of that alone, he couldn't lose. Consider: he had *nothing* going for him, and his enemies had *everything* going for them: they moved against him with all the wealth, education, authority, prestige, complete command of the media, tradition, culture, the books, the universities, the appointments, the renown, and so on, on their side. And they ganged up against him with dedicated fury. Why was he able to survive the first onslaught? If they had had anything at all to put up against his story, he could not have lasted a week—but they had nothing. "Question them," said Brigham Young, "and they cannot answer the simplest question concerning the character of the Deity, heaven, or hell, this or that,"[1] and it had been so ever since Origen wrote his work on the *First Principles.*[2] "Outside of the religion we have embraced, there is nothing but death, hell and the grave," he said.[3] If they had anything to offer, they could have produced it any time. Those who embraced the gospel were those who had been seeking long and hard—and *not* finding. In the eloquent words of Brigham Young: "The secret feeling of my heart was that I would be willing to crawl around the earth on my hands and knees, to see such a man as was Peter, Jeremiah, Moses, or any man that could tell me anything about God and heaven. But to talk with the priests was more unsatisfactory to me then than it now is to talk with lawyers."[4]

2. It was a choice between nothing or something—and what a something! The staggering *prodigality* of the gifts brought to mankind by Joseph is just beginning to appear as the scriptures he gave us are held up for comparison with the newly discovered or rediscovered documents of the ancients purporting to come from the times and places he describes in those revelations. He has placed in our

hands fragments of writings from the leaders of all the major dispensations; and now, only in very recent times, has the world come into possession of whole libraries of ancient texts against which his purported scriptures can be tested.

3. The thing that impressed me in talking to the ministers was that our gospel is not culturally conditioned. I had just been spreading the gospel in four countries, and everywhere the reception was exactly the same. My son recently wrote an arresting comment on that phenomenon from his mission in Japan:

> One thing I've really come to be sure of is that the gospel applies to all people. East is East and West is West, but wherever the sheep are, they know the Shepherd's voice. The Japanese see Christianity in somewhat the same way Americans see Buddhism, as a strange, complex and exotic philosophy that would take years of research to understand at all. When I go into a house to teach, I always tell the people that my knowledge is very limited; and therefore I will not teach them from my knowledge, but I simply come as a witness of spiritual truths that I have myself experienced. I tell them that if they will surrender their prejudice, they will themselves have the experience of the Holy Ghost. . . . I've never had anyone say that they weren't feeling the Spirit. Of course, getting them to follow it and give up their sins is different.

If the gospel is not culturally conditioned, neither is it nationally conditioned. Which nation do you prefer as a Latter-day Saint? Answer: "Whichever gives me the inalienable right to practice my religion"; and for years there was only one nation that met that qualification, the United States under its Constitution. It was the glorious principles of the Bill of Rights that opened the door to the gospel in this dispensation; that was the indispensable implementation of the gospel, without, however, being part or portion of that plan which transcends all earthly disciplines.

4. Nothing was more offensive in the teachings of Joseph Smith than the ideas of revelation and restoration. The Protestant doctrine was *sola scriptura*; the Catholic claim was that the *only* sources of revelation were (1) scripture *and* (2) tradition. But in our own generation both revelation and restoration have ceased to be naughty words; and Catholics and Protestants are exploiting them in a way that makes us forget how recently and how vigorously they were condemned as a peculiarly wild aberration in Joseph Smith.

5. A recent newspaper headline announces that the churches are now, for the first time and in a big way, beginning to cultivate the charismatic gifts, not in the revivalist manner, but as a necessary part of the sober Christian life.[5] Years ago I wrote a series of articles called "Mixed Voices" in which I surveyed most of the available anti-Mormon writings in the Church Historian's Office since the beginning.[6] The claims to heavenly visitations and miraculous gifts, especially healing and tongues, were treated as nothing short of the most heinous crimes by Joseph Smith's critics. Today, we are apt to forget that too.

6. The ideas of priesthood and authority were revolutionary. For generations after Joseph Smith, the learned divines were to debate the tension between "Office" and "Spirit." But nothing is more wonderful than the way in which the Spirit operates through the priesthood; especially firm was its foundation in a principle by which true priesthood cannot be abused or misused: its power cannot be applied to further private or party interests, or to impose, coerce, or intimidate—the moment it is directed to such ends, it automatically becomes inoperative.

The priesthood is further more invulnerable because it is indivisible. As long as *one* true holder of the higher priesthood is on the earth, the potentiality of the church is there. It suggests the idea of cloning, that from one cell one can produce a whole organism; it also suggests present-day ideas of manifestations of energy at various levels: "And without the *ordinances* thereof, and the *authority* of the priesthood, the *power* of godliness is not *manifest* unto men *in the flesh*" (D&C 84:21). As in physics, the reality of particles and forces is apparent only after certain very specific conditions have been met.

7. Which brings us to another unshakable foundation-stone—the ordinances. Protestant authorities admit that one of the weakest parts of their position is the inadequacy of their liturgy.[7] The Reformation abolished a lot of pomp, ceremony, and ritual but put nothing in its place. And now it becomes clear that the ancient Christians made much of certain rites and ordinances that had indeed been lost. But what could the Reformation do but get rid of things that were plainly late and unauthorized intrusions from patently pagan sources? In the nineteenth century, Roman Catholic researchers, beginning with Dom Guranger, abbot of the monastery of Solesmes, began to discover from the study of old manuscripts that the rites of their mass were indeed later innovations, differing markedly from the earliest practices.[8] And today we have seen the Ecumenical movement largely devoted to correcting and *restoring* (theologians actually use the word) rites and ordinances that had been lost.

8. Ritual is in the nature of a public and social thing, but the rites of the *temple* are something else. Here again, Joseph Smith has given us something solid and substantial that invites a world of comparative study, which will show from the very outset that this was no mere theatrical gesture. The whole concept of the "hierocentric point" around which all the sacral civilizations were built is presented here in its fullness.[9] It is at the temple that all things are bound together. The ancient word for the temple was "the binding point of heaven and earth."[10] This is no time to go into the inexhaustibly rich symbolism and indispensable reality of the ordinances and the significance of the temple

in binding the human family together. The point here is that Joseph Smith gave us the whole thing, and it is a marvel beyond description.

9. With his "scenario" of protology and eschatology, the prophet has brought the indispensable *third dimension* to the gospel. This is a manner of speaking, but an instructive one. The teachings of men are two-dimensional unless they have actually experienced the third. We live in a flat, two-dimensional world with no depth or extension beyond our *present* experience either into time or space: "When the man dies, that is the end thereof" (Alma 30:18). Religion is supposed to go beyond that; it wants to, but it lacks confidence and so uses all the devices of art and eloquence to fake that third dimension — as we look up into the soaring vaults of St. Peter's, we marvel at the skill with which the architect and painters, in a setting of bells, music, and a splendid pageantry of robes, lights, and incense (not without some narcotic effect), seem to give us the *illusion* of passing into a third dimension of reality. Why bother with the devices if they have the real thing? The futility of such contrivance appears in almost any attempt of the Latter-day Saints to achieve spiritual uplift through music, poetry, painting, drama, or special effects, all of which invariably fall short; to those to whom the third dimension is real, any attempt to enhance it by two-dimensional materials is bound to appear pitifully inadequate.

10. If the Church has any first foundation, it is the unimpeachable *testimony* of the individual. Since this is nontransmissible, one might dismiss it as irrelevant, an absolute beyond discussion, criticism, or demonstration. Even for the individual, the testimony comes and goes in accordance with faith and behavior. If it is real, then it is indeed unassailable and imponderable. I cannot force my testimony on you, but there are certain indications to which I might call your attention. People who lose their testimonies and renounce the Church or drop out of it, if they

are convinced of their position, should be totally indifferent to the folly of their deluded one-time brethren and sisters: if *they* want to make fools of themselves, that is up to them, but we are intellectually and socially above all that. Well and good, that is how it is in other churches; but here it does not work that way.

Apostates usually become sometimes feverishly active, determined to prove to the world and themselves that it is a fraud after all. What is that to them? Apparently it is everything — it will not let them alone. At the other end of the scale are those who hold no rancor and even retain a sentimental affection for the Church — they just don't believe the gospel. I know quite a few of them. But how many of *them* can leave it alone? It haunts them all the days of their life. No one who has ever had a testimony ever forgets or denies that he once *did* have it — that it was something that really happened to him. Even for such people who do not have it anymore, a testimony cannot be reduced to an illusion.

11. Ten points should be enough, but we cannot pass by the word of *prophecy* without notice. It is just becoming apparent today that the scriptures that have come to us by modern revelation are replete with prophecy — there is far more prophecy in them than anyone suspected. It is the fulfillment of things that never seemed possible that is bringing this out. We rightly cite the prophecy on war (D&C 87) as clear evidence for the prophetic guidance of the Church — without ever bothering to take to heart its message for us. It still comes through loud and clear with a prophetic message: the consummation of the whole thing is to be "a *full end* of *all* nations" (D&C 87:6), not a full end of some or a partial end of all, but a *full end* of *all*; and that by *war*, not as a possibility or contingency, but as a "consumption decreed" — it *must happen*. "Wherefore" the special instructions with which it ends, "stand *ye* in *holy* places, and be not moved" (D&C 87:8). I have been re-

reading *The Life of Wilford Woodruff*. Woodruff often marvels at the vast and unshakable foundation laid by Joseph Smith, and at the same time he wonders if the Saints have continued to build on it. If he has some doubts, what about that superstructure?

I had thought to go on adding yet more building blocks and to discuss the changes in the Church that I have personally observed between the Centennial and Sesquicentennial—another of those pageants, so to speak. But that word *holy* has stopped me in my tracks. Naturally I would have talked about the *growth* of the Church. But is there a critical size or number upon reaching which a state of holiness is obtained, or is there a set period of time, a term at the completion of which one routinely rises a step in *holiness?* I remember that as the ancient church grew in numbers, it *diminished* in holiness. If it is numbers God wants, there is no problem: "God is able of these stones to raise up children unto Abraham" (Matthew 3:9), said the Lord.

To be instructed from on high, you must "sanctify yourselves and ye shall be endowed with power" (D&C 43:16), "and thus ye shall become instructed in the law of my church, and be *sanctified* by that which ye have received, and ye shall *bind* yourselves to act in *all holiness* before me" (D&C 43:9). After all, we are stuck with the title of Latter-day *Saints*—people sanctified, literally "set apart" in the last days, when "the adversary spreadeth his dominions, and darkness reigneth; and the anger of God kindleth against the inhabitants of the earth; and *none* doeth good, for *all* have gone out of the way" (D&C 82:5-6). This is the world in which Joseph Smith was "inspired of the Holy Ghost to lay the *foundation* [of the Church] . . . and to build it up unto the most *holy* faith" (D&C 21:2). This is not just another institution.

The greatest change I have noticed in the fifty years since I used to make the three-day bus trip from Los Angeles to Salt Lake is the absence of that thrill I felt when the golden words would begin to appear on the buildings of every little town: *Holiness to the Lord,* over-arching the all-seeing eye that monitors the deeds of men. That inscription was the central adornment of every important building, including each town's main store — the Co-op, as committed as any other institution of the Church to the plan of holiness. Next to that, what moved me most was the sight of the St. George Temple in its beautiful oasis. What became of "holiness"? Did it pass away with all the noble pioneer monuments all along the highway, wiped out by the relentless demands of a bottom-line economy? Those delightful old stakehouses, bishop's storehouses, schools, wardhouses, homes, and even barns have been steadily replaced by service stations, chain restaurants, shopping malls, motels, and prefabricated functional church and school buildings right from the assembly line: admittedly more practical, but must every house and tree and monument be destroyed because it does not at present pay for itself in cold cash? The St. George Temple is now lost in a neon jungle and suburban tidal-wash of brash, ticky-tacky commercialism. One can only assume that it bespeaks the spirit of our times. God has said that the Saints must build Zion with an eye to two things, holiness and beauty: "For Zion must increase in *beauty* and in *holiness*" (D&C 82:14) — with no qualifying provision, "Insofar as an adequate return on the investment will allow."

Everything in Zion is to be holy, for God has called it "My Holy Land," and that with a dire warning: "Shall the children of [Zion] . . . pollute my holy land?" (D&C 84:59). Apparently it is possible. *Holy things are not for traffic;* they are not negotiable: "Thy money perish with thee, because thou hast thought that the gift of God may be purchased with money" (Acts 8:20). Things we hold sacred we do *not* sell for money. Consequently, to become commodities of trade, the land of Zion and what is in it must be *de*-sanc-

tified. Here we meet with an interesting and ancient precedent in Israel, recorded both in the Dead Sea Scrolls and
in the Book of Mormon. When the people were in mortal
danger from their enemies, they could carry the battle to
them and wage destruction on the land; but that was only
permitted after the high priest had stood boldly between
the ranks of the armies and in a loud voice formally pronounced the enemy land to be "Desolation" — *Horma, Horeb*
(the Moslem *Dar al-Harb* and the *ager hosticus* of the Romans), while their own land under God's protection was
holy land, Bountiful, *Dar al-Islam, ager pacatus*.[11]

Even so, the land of Zion must become un-holy (what
was *con*-secrated must be *de*-secrated) before it can be used
for gain. "The soil, the air, the water are all pure and
healthy," said Brigham Young to the Saints arriving in the
Valley. "Do not suffer them to become polluted with
wickedness. Strive to preserve the elements from being
contaminated."[12] "Keep your valley pure, keep your
towns . . . pure."[13] "The Lord blesses the land, the air and
the water where the Saints are permitted to live."[14] "Our
enemies . . . would like to see society in Utah polluted,
and their civilization introduced; but it would be a woful
day for the Israel of God, if such efforts were to be successful."[15] We have shown elsewhere that they were successful in Kirtland, in Far West, in Nauvoo, and finally in
Utah. Time and again the Saints have made a bungle of
the superstructure, unwilling to conform to the foundation
laid down in the beginning.

When I first came to Utah in the 1940s, it was a fresh
new world, a joy and a delight to explore far and wide
with my boys and girls. But now my friends no longer
come on visits as they once did, to escape the grim commercialism and ugly litter of the East and the West Coast.
We can watch that now on the Wasatch Front. The Saints
no longer speak of making the land blossom as the rose,
but of making a quick buck in rapid-turnover real estate.

All the students I have talked with at the beginning of this semester intend eventually to go into law or business; Brigham Young University is no longer a liberal arts college. They are not interested in improving their talents but in trafficking in them.

Come with me to the places I used to visit in happier times, taking the four distinct zones that run north and south parallel with the Wasatch.

Zone 1. First the mountains, the impregnable retreat of God's creatures, whom he has commanded to multiply and be happy in their proper sphere and element—and this is certainly it. The loggers, miners, cattle and sheepmen have grabbed all they can get and are still on the prowl for anything left over. But now, wondrous to relate, even where the resources are skimpy, indeed the "developers" invade en masse, determined to make a marketable commodity of the only remaining value—solitude. They are selling that, and of course destroying it in the process. And we must not forget those who kill for pleasure, the hunters whose campers line the freeways bumper to bumper.

Zone 2. Come with me next down into the valley, where the Saints once converted the plain into a garden, blossoming as the rose, with the stately trees and running waters I remember so well—they had in mind preparing a place fit for Deity to visit and for angels to dwell in: fertile, bounteous, unspoiled by those who planted and dressed their gardens, taking good care of the land and being happy in it. Then a long tentacle started reaching down South State Street, which was then the main highway, with its brash commercial clutter and its vulgar procession of arrogant billboards designed to distract the eye and the mind with their insolent message: "Never mind that, look what *I'm* selling!" It was the blare and vulgarity of petty promotion and massive corporeal presence, which even then was rendering the whole land of

America a monotonous desert of regimented, uniform assembly lines and places where things were sold.

Quickly this spread out all over the valley as freeways connected one shopping center with the next, while subdivisions wiped out the only available orchard-lands within five hundred miles, and on all sides the farms and their way of life melted away before the relentless inroads of real-estate promoters from all over the land. I see Joseph Smith standing on the framework of a schoolhouse under construction in Far West, whither he had led the Saints to establish a new Zion, an advance company to prepare the ground for the great influx of immigrants to follow. What were they doing? Grabbing up everything in sight for a quick resale to the newcomers at inflationary prices. The Church was afflicted with the real-estate fever from the beginning, with tragic results. This is that the Prophet said:

> Brethren, we are gathering to this buitiful land, to build up Zion. . . . But since I have been here I perseive the spirit of selfishness, covetousness, exists in the hearts of the saints. . . . Here are those who begin to spread out, buying up all the land they are able to do, . . . thinking to ley foundations for themselves only, looking to their own individual familys. . . . Now I want to tell you that Zion can not be built up in eny such way. I see signs put out, Beer signs, speculative scheems are being introduced. This is the ways of the world—Babylon indeed, and I tell you in the name of the God of Israel, if there is not repentance, . . . you will be Broken up and scattered from this choice land [sic].[16]

But they continued to build this ambitious superstructure until presently the whole enterprise was swept away in the worst mobbings the people ever knew. This same sermon was recalled and its lesson repeated to the Saints by Brigham Young immediately after the arrival of the pioneers in the Valley, as recorded by Wilford Woodruff, who in turn repeats the lesson for our generation.

Zone 3. We move into another zone, to the highly min-
eralized mountains that line the west side of the valley.
They are called the Oquirrh, the "forest mountains," by
the Indians. Not any more! Under a canopy of deadly
smelter-fumes, the forests have long since departed. All
along their length, the mountains are being torn up on an
enormous scale — the local people once boasted of the largest open-pit mine in the world. But not the people who
lived there: as in other copper kingdoms, century-old
towns have been bulldozed away against the protest of
their inhabitants; to dig out the last morsels of metal-bear-
ing ore, no stone is left unturned that might yield a little
profit. Here, for over a century, hard-pressed and poorly
paid miners toiled away. When I was small, my father,
whose father had worked as a child in the horrible mines
of Scotland, and my mother, whose father had been a
supervisor in Park City when she was growing up, would
tell about the heroic and laborious lives of the brave miners
who transferred the treasures of the earth to the coffers of
the rich and in return received nothing but abuse. The
mining operations naturally extended down into the valley
to the smelters, refineries, and mills that still go on impudently pouring the foul industrial wastes into the limited
air space of the valleys — mostly by night — obscuring the
"mountains high and the clear blue sky" with foul, chok-
ing, miasmic fumes, and claiming immunity from all restraints on the grounds that attempts to limit the pollution
cut into profits. The ideal condition toward which promoters, developers, and senators seem to be striving is
that of the blessed state of Kuwait, where the people sit
on unlimited amounts of money in the midst of industrial
desolation, a technological wasteland of superhighways
and highrises, of a bleakness and monotony that render
all their riches futile and forlorn. What good is all the wealth
in the world if one must live in a sewer to get and keep
it?

Zone 4. As we once thought the mountains in their remote majesty to be immune to the invasion of a defiling civilization, so we thought that the desert at least would be left alone as of little cash value to anyone. One of my favorite haunts was the sand dunes near Lindel: Utter solitude and the dramatically haunting beauty of the place were wonderfully soothing, refreshing, and inspiring to body and mind. Then suddenly the recreational vehicle market was discovered, and overnight it became a Walpurgis of noise, brawling, drinking, drugs, fights, vandalism, theft, and sex, where mindless youth could run riot with their costly mechanical toys.

But this was nothing. Already, vast tracts of the desert had been set aside for the practice of various ways in which life may be taken most effectively and on the largest possible scale. First it was bombing ranges, systematically developing the most efficient and thorough ways of demolishing man and his works. But this was the age of innocence compared with the next step: the deadlier, nastier, meaner, more insidious and depraved arts of chemical warfare, where nature is drafted to war against nature. This culminates in the deadly nerve gases, including the futile and horrible wet-eye bombs which some have been eager to bring in because of the business that might come with them. But experience has shown that even these devices can miss. There must be something more absolutely destructive of life. Well, there is. Southern Utah has always been known for its peculiarly pure air and its "Kodachrome-blue" skies, which seem to prevail no matter what is going on in the rest of the world. Almost a hundred atom bombs exploded in that chaste atmosphere have converted it into a strange new element whose gift was the most dreaded of all diseases — cancer. Professor Teller was brought to the BYU, more than once, to tell us that the testing in the air was utterly harmless, salubrious in fact, and absolutely essential to our position as No. 1 nation.

And as the culminating abomination of desolation, we find that corner of "Zion," which to me always recalls that moving phrase, "Holiness to the Lord," has now been set apart, "consecrated" as it were, for the fantastic MX game, the ultimate in waste, futility, and desecration of the land. As they welcome the wet-eye bombs abhorred in Colorado, so the Saints now welcome the MX after New Mexico has spurned it with loathing. Why? Because it brings money: 50 billion spent on a trick that just *might* fool the Russians, and if it works will certainly destroy us — what life will be possible after a dozen H-bombs (the minimum that the mighty installation will attract) have done their work within our borders? And if we count on divine protection, let us recall our very limited immunity to the Nevada testing.

Such considerations admonish me to ask whether all is well in Zion, and I find the answer in myself alone. Have I taken the message seriously? No. I have been quite half-hearted about it, and much too easily drawn into what I call the *Gentile Dilemma*. That is, when I find myself called upon to stand up and be counted, to declare myself on one side or the other, which do I prefer — gin or rum, cigarettes or cigars, tea or coffee, heroin or LSD, the Red Rose or the White, Shiz or Coriantumr, wicked Nephites or wicked Lamanites, Whigs or Tories, Catholic or Protestant, Republican or Democrat, black power or white power, land pirates or sea pirates, commissars or corporations, capitalism or communism? The devilish neatness and simplicity of the thing is the easy illusion that I am choosing between good and evil, when in reality two or more evils by their rivalry distract my attention from the real issue. The oldest trick in the book for those who wish to perpetrate a great crime unnoticed is to set up a diversion, such as a fight in the street or a cry of fire in the hall, that sends everyone rushing to the spot while the criminal as an inconspicuous and highly respectable citizen quietly walks off with the loot.

It can be shown that in each of the choices just named, one of the pair may well be preferable to the other, but that is not the question. There is no point in arguing which other system comes closest to the law of consecration, since I excluded all other systems when I opted for the real thing. The relative merits of various economies is a problem for the gentiles to worry about, a devil's dilemma that does not concern me in the least. For it so happens that I have presently covenanted and promised to observe most strictly certain instructions set forth with great clarity and simplicity in the Doctrine and Covenants. These are designated as the law of consecration, which are absolutely essential for the building up of the kingdom on earth and the ultimate establishment of Zion. "Behold, this is the preparation wherewith I prepare you, and the foundation and the ensample which I give unto you, whereby you may accomplish the commandments which are given you; that through *my* providence, notwithstanding the tribulation which shall descend upon you, that the church may stand independent above all other creatures beneath the celestial world" (D&C 78:13-14). It is all there, this law of consecration, by which alone the Saints can implement God's plans for Zion in spite of the persecution it will bring on them; this is the foundation on which they must build (see D&C 48:6). The alternative is to be dependent on baser things, for "Zion cannot be built up unless it is by the principles of the law of the celestial kingdom; otherwise I cannot receive her unto myself" (D&C 105:5).

But should I ask for tribulation? I live in the real world, don't I? Yes, and I have been commanded to "come out of her, . . . that ye be not partakers of her sins" (Revelation 18:4). It is *not* given "unto you that ye shall live after the manner of the world" (D&C 95:13). Well, then, you must be "in the world but not of the world." That happens to be a convenient para-scripture (we have quite a few of them today), invented by a third-century Sophist (Diognetos), to the great satisfaction of the church members, who were rapidly becoming very worldly. The passage as it appears in the scriptures says quite the opposite: "For [whatsoever] that is *in* the world . . . is not of the Father, but *is of* the world" (1 John 2:16). The Lord has repeatedly commanded and forced his people to flee out of the world into the wilderness, quite literally; there is only one way to avoid becoming involved in the neighborhood brawls, and that is to move out of the neighborhood. There is nothing in the Constitution that forbids me doing certain things I have covenanted and promised to do; if the neighbors don't like it, they have no legal grounds against me, but there are ways of getting me to move; "the tribulation . . . shall descend upon you," said the Lord, but do things *my* way and "my providence" will see you through (D&C 78:14). This inescapable conflict is part of our human heritage, as we learn from dramatic passages of scripture.

The story begins, according to many ancient writings and unknown to the Prophet Joseph Smith, with Satan seeking to promote himself even in the premortal existence, and being cast out of heaven in his pride, and dedicating himself upon his fall to the destruction of this earth, "for he knew not the mind of God" (Moses 4:6). Lying in wait for Adam in the Garden, he fails in a direct attack, repelled from his prey by a natural enmity between the two; whereupon in a fit of rage and frustration (such as he also displayed in dealing with Moses [Moses 1:19-20]), he boasts just how he plans to put the world under his bloody and horrible misrule: He will control the world economy by claiming possession of the earth's resources; and by manipulation of its currency—gold and silver—he will buy up the political, military, and ecclesiastical complex and run everything his way. We see him putting his plan into operation when he lays legal claim to the whole earth as his estate, accusing others of trespass, but putting everything up for sale to anyone who has the money. And how will they get the money? By going to work for him. He not only offers employment but a course of instruction in how the whole thing works, teaching the ultimate secret: "That great secret" (Moses 5:49-50) of converting life into property. Cain got the degree of Master Mahan, tried the system out on his brother, and gloried in its brilliant success, declaring that at last he could be free, as only property makes free, and that Abel had been a loser in a free competition.

The discipline was handed down through Lamech and finally became the pattern of the world's economy (Moses 5:55-56). We may detect "the Mahan Principle" vigorously operative in each of the four zones we talked about: As the animals are being wiped out in Zone 1, so all forms of vegetation are yielding to asphalt in Zone 2, and human life is made short and miserable in Zone 3; while the total destruction of *every* form of life is guaranteed by the macabre exercises in the desert zone. And all for the same purpose: Cain slew "his brother Abel *for the sake of getting gain*" (Moses 5:50)—not in a fit of pique but by careful business planning, "by the conspiracy" (D&C 84:16). The great secret he learned from Satan was the art of converting life into property—all life, even eternal life! The exchange of eternal life for worldly success is in fact the essence of the classic Pact with the Devil, in which the hero (Faust, Jabez Stone, even Jesus) is offered everything that the wealth of the earth can buy in return for subjection to Satan hereafter. There is no question of having some of both— "You *cannot* serve two masters" (see Matthew 6:24), the one being Mammon; if you try to have it both ways by putting off the final settlement, says Amulek, "the Spirit of the Lord hath withdrawn from you, and has *no* place in you, and the devil hath *all* power over you" (Alma 34:35). One may see Mahan at work all around, from the Mafia, whose adherence to the principle needs no argument, down to the drug pusher, the arms dealer, the manufacturer and seller of defective products, or those who poison the air and water as a shortcut to gain and thus shorten and sicken the lives of all their fellow creatures. Is Geneva Steel Works worth emphysema?

At last we come to the lowly snail-darter. Recently, Congress pronounced the doom of that species, which stands in the way of construction of a dam. It seems like a fantastic disproportion—between a two-inch fish and a big dam—and it is, with the overwhelming weight of the argument all on the side of the fish. What is the cash value of living things who have been commanded by God to multiply in their proper sphere and element? There is none. Yet there are those who are offended, outraged, at the suggestion that some little finny, furry, or feathered species should dare to stand in the way of a mighty bulldozer and the mightier corporate interest behind it. In the snail-darter debate, the ultimate expression of contempt for life came from a senator from Utah who with heavy sarcasm asked, Why not declare the smallpox virus an endangered species? Where business interests are concerned, small living things are to be esteemed as no more than viruses. "He who has done it to the least of these" (see Matthew 25:40) applies in the bad sense as well as the good: "He who despises the least of these my creatures, despises me!" "Wo unto him who offends one of these little ones!"

But how about the law of consecration, which is the foundation of Zion? It is, as I said, contained in the Book of Doctrine and Covenants, explained there not once but many times, so that there is no excuse for not understanding it. The three basic principles are (as so plainly set forth by Wilford Woodruff): (1) *everyone* gets what he really needs, his wants being met from a common fund that belongs entirely to the Lord and is administered through the bishop of the church; (2) *nobody* keeps more than he

really needs, his surplus all going to that fund; (3) dickering
and controversy over the amounts involved is forestalled
by the clear statement of the intent and purpose of the
law, which is that all may be *equal* in temporal as in spiritual
things. One man's needs may be greater than another's —
for example, because his family is larger; but once those
needs are met for each, then all are equal, satisfied, at
peace, each free to develop his own talents and do the
Lord's work, for that is the purpose of the law. There is
plenty to do to satisfy the work ethic without a profit
motive, "but the laborer in Zion shall labor for Zion; for
if they labor for money they shall perish" (2 Nephi 26:31).
Failure to observe this law places one man above another,
abominable in the sight of the Lord, and for that reason,
we are told, "the world lieth in sin" (D&C 49:20), in Satan's
power indeed.

This law, the consummation of the laws of obedience
and sacrifice, is the threshold of the celestial kingdom, the
last and hardest requirement made of men in this life. It
is much harder to keep than the rules of chastity and sobriety, for those temptations subside with advancing age,
while desire for the security and status of wealth only
increases and grows through the years. Yet none may escape the law of consecration, none are exempt from it in
the Church (D&C 42:70-73; 70:10); none may outlive it, for
it is "a permanent and everlasting" law (D&C 78:4; 72:3),
a "covenant and a deed which cannot be broken" (D&C
42:30), even by transgression — there is no escaping it (D&C
78:10-11). It cannot be put off until more favorable circumstances offer (D&C 70:16); it was given to the Saints because
the time was ripe for them. One cannot move into it gradually to ease the shock (D&C 78:3), or observe it partially
(D&C 42:78), or even grudgingly (D&C 70:14). It is so fundamental that the early leaders of the Church (Brigham
Young, Wilford Woodruff, Parley P. Pratt, and others) declared that their first impulse after being baptized was to

give away all their property to the poor and trust the hand of God to supply their wants in the mission field, for in any case they could take no money with them. Was that a hard choice? Let us recall the case of the righteous young man who had kept every point of the law and asked to become a disciple of Christ: "Yet lackest thou one thing," the Lord told him (Luke 18:22), "if thou wilt be perfect" (Matthew 19:21). There was yet one thing—the law of consecration, which crowns all the others. But the young man could not take that one step because he was very rich, and for that the Lord turned him away sorrowing: he did not call him back to suggest easier terms but turned to his disciples and pointed out to them by this example how hard it is for a rich man to enter heaven—only a special miracle could do it, he explained; it is as impossible to enter the celestial kingdom without accepting the celestial law as it is for a camel to get through the eye of a needle (Matthew 19:24). The disciples marveled greatly at this, for *they* had never heard of that convenient postern gate, invented by an obliging nineteenth-century minister for the comfort of his well-heeled congregation—the ancient sources knew nothing of that gate, and neither did the baffled apostles. (That is another "para-scripture.") If I keep all the other commandments, says Amulek, and ease up on this one, my prayers are vain, and I am a hypocrite (see Alma 34:28). Tithing is merely a substitute—a very different thing; once we start making concessions and explanations, the whole thing becomes a farce. If business expenses and necessities are deducted from tithable income, nothing is left. God takes a serious view of any attempt to cut corners: he struck Ananias and his wife dead not for failure to pay anything, but for "holding back" part of what they should have paid (Acts 5:2, 5, 10). The free-wheeling interpretation of "stewardship" offers no way out, for example, piously announcing that the stuff is only mine during this lifetime (a generous concession indeed!), or admission that I must dispose of it in a responsible way (as if others had no such responsibility). One is "a steward over his own property," namely "that which he has received by consecration, as much as is sufficient for himself and family" (D&C 42:32). That is "his own property" to which he has exclusive right, and that is the limit of his stewardship—and it is all consecrated, whether given or received. One does not begin by holding back what he thinks he will need, but by consecrating *everything* the Lord has given him so far to the Church; then he in return receives back from the bishop by consecration whatever he needs.

To "consecrate," says the dictionary, means "to make or declare sacred or *holy*; to set apart, dedicate, devote to the service or worship of God; to deliver up or give over often with or as if with due solemnity, dedication, or devotion."[17] God is going to "organize my kingdom upon the consecrated land" (D&C 103:35), the land "which I have consecrated to be the land of Zion" (D&C 103:24), for a consecrated people. "Let the city, Far West be a *holy* and *consecrated* land unto me; and it shall be called most *holy*, for the *ground* upon which thou standest is *holy*" (D&C 115:7). The word appears more than 140 times in the Doctrine and Covenants. It was when some of the brethren began trading in this holy land that the Prophet denounced them, telling them in the name of Israel's God that Zion could never be built up in such a way. The foundation of the Holy City was to be nothing other than the law of consecration (D&C 48:6).

Is the law unrealistic, impractical? It is much too late for me to worry about that now, for I have already accepted it and repeated my acceptance at least once every month. (At a recent conference [October 1978], Elder Mark E. Petersen spoke of the importance of keeping *all* the covenants we have made—and none is more important, more specific, more sacred than this one.) What about Brother So-

and-So or President So-and So? He is free to do as he pleases; I did not covenant with him! I knew quite well what I was promising to do and when and where I was to do it, and why—now it is up to me! This is not like plural marriage, which was suspended by a formal decree because the whole of American society and government had thrown their weight against it with dedicated and unrelenting fury that disrupted the whole course of life in the Church and even the nation. When the United Order was dissolved in 1834, it was through no pressure from outside but because of greed and hypocrisy ("covetousness, and with feigned words," D&C 104:4, 52) within the Church. Brigham Young revived it again—the Brigham Young Academy at Provo was founded for the explicit purpose, in his words, of countering "the theories of Huxley, of Darwin, or of Miall and the false political economy which contends against cooperation and the United Order."[18]

But after him the old covetousness and feigned words triumphed again as rich men quietly bought up controlling shares of the cooperatives without changing the name. To quote a recent study, "astute businessmen gradually gained control of the cooperatives . . . [and] completely changed the character of the companies; though they often kept the company name the same, in order to take advantage of the local appeal that cooperatives still held. By the mideighties, most of the stock of the cooperatives had been sold to a few businessmen who now controlled the entire operation, . . . whose main concern became profit-making." Moreover, by "operating under the name of the now defunct cooperatives," these businesses enjoyed a monopoly in the land.[19] In 1882 President John Taylor sent out a letter declaring, "If people would be governed by correct principles, laying aside covetousness and eschewing chicanery and fraud, dealing honestly and conscientiously with others, . . . there would be no objection" to their free enterprise[20]—he was appealing to them to do away with covetousness and feigned words, the very things that had put them in control of the economy. But while attempts to implement it come and go, the covenant remains, and those who have entered it must live by it or be cursed (D&C 104:3-5), for in this matter God is not to be mocked (D&C 104:6). I am in a perfectly viable position at this moment to observe and keep it, as I have promised, independently of any other party. I do not have to wait for permission from any other person or group to act; I do not have to join any body of protesters who feel that others are not on the right track before I can keep the rules of chastity or sobriety, nor do I have to join a club or splinter group in order to keep the Ten Commandments. The essence of the law of consecration is charity, without which, as Paul and Moroni tell us, all the other laws and observances become null and void. Love is not selective, and charity knows no bounds—"For if ye love them which love you, what reward have ye? do not even the publicans the same?" (Matthew 5:44-47). How do you keep the most important commandments? the apostles asked, and in reply the Lord told them of a man who was neither a priest, nor a Levite nor even of Israel—a mere Samaritan, who did not wait for clearance before yielding to a generous impulse to help one in distress who was completely unknown to him: "Go, and do thou likewise!" (Luke 10:37) was the advice—you are on your own. "It is not meet that I should command in all things" (D&C 58:26). I made my covenants and promises personally with God, in the first person singular. "I want you to understand," said Heber C. Kimball, "that you make covenants with God, and not with us. We were present and committed those covenants to you, and you made them with God, and we were witnesses."[21] Paul recognizes this in his lucid statements about the law of consecration in his letters to Timothy, which should be studied carefully. And he is talking about the foundation of the Church, which rests on the personal contract between God and the individual: "Nevertheless the foundation of God standeth sure, having *this seal,* the Lord knoweth them that are his. And, Let every one that nameth the name of Christ depart from iniquity" (2 Timothy 2:19). The Lord alone knows who are the true church; he alone stands at the gate, "and he employeth no servant there" (2 Nephi 9:41), as he takes each one by the hand and speaks each name. Even the Prophet does not know who are in the covenant and who are not, "as you cannot always judge the righteous, or as you cannot always tell the wicked from the righteous, therefore I say unto you, hold your peace until I shall see fit to make all things known" (D&C 10:37).

What is there to stop *me* from observing and keeping the law of consecration at this very day as *I* have already covenanted and promised to do without reservation? Is the foundation too broad for *us* to build on? *We* are in the position of one who has inherited a number of fabulously rich and varied franchises. Only two or three of the enterprises really appeal to *him,* and so he devotes all his attention to them and neglects all the others. How often have we heard, even from outsiders—if the Latter-day Saints only realized what riches they possess! Well, there is a clause in the will stating that if the heir neglects *any* of the franchises, he will forfeit them all. What am I doing with genealogy, temple work, Sunday School, priesthood, home teaching, scripture study, and all my meetings? I simply can't do them all; I cannot begin to do justice to them. Why not? Because I am, as my grandfather used to say and not entirely in jest, too taken up with the cares of the world and the deceitfulness of riches, by which he meant business. But must you spend so much time at it? Don't you know that if you lived by the law of consecration you would have time enough for all of it? But that is out of the question; our way of life demands the other. Which is exactly why God has always commanded his people to give up that way of life, come out of the world, and follow his special instructions. The main purpose of the Doctrine and Covenants, you will find, is to implement the law of consecration.

[A question-period followed this presentation. The questions were in the nature of practical objections—very sensible and reasonable. For example: "People now moving into Utah Valley must have somewhere to live, therefore the orchards must go."

Response: What could be more sensible and to the point? In such a spirit a friend says to me, "I *must* have my two cups of coffee every morning; otherwise I cannot get through the day." Perfectly sensible; what is the answer? What do you mean by getting through the day? "Well, I have to go the office—the old rat race, you know, a real strain." Must you go to the office? Is there no other way? Who tells you there is no other way? The more completely committed you are to a prescribed way of doing things, the fewer options you enjoy, until you end up a helpless prisoner to your precious "way of life." If you are resigned or dedicated to a regime that you do not really like, or that wastes your talents, then you are a prisoner indeed—in Satan's power. In short, when you say, "There is no other way," the game is lost and he has won. The number of possible solutions to any problem is legion, limited only by our own mental resources, and God is anxious to give us all the light and guidance we are *willing* to receive in solving our problems (D&C 88:32-33). The mental paralysis of our times strongly suggests that God has withdrawn his Spirit from among men, as he said he would. Quite recently the newspapers and journals have been full of the alarming decline in mental capacity and learning among the rising generation, in which, I sorrow to say, Utah leads the parade with its appalling 26 percent drop in Scholastic Aptitude Test scores and the lowest rating in all the land in mathematics — the one subject that requires some real discipline. Can such people ever be independent? We lamely submit to atom-bomb tests, wet-eyes, and the MX maze, we inhale the dust of vitriol tailings for years on end and rally to the support of the nation's No. 1 polluter in our midst, as we surrender that last wilderness heritage on earth in the name of "unlocking" it to private land-grabbers. Satan has us where he wants us — helpless, scared to death: "If we leave his employment, what will become of us?" For he has us convinced that there is no other way, nothing to do but go along. Ah, but there *is* another way. If you and the rest of Adam's children will only listen to the gospel, you will soon learn that ample provision has been made in the providence of God through his law of consecration.]

Notes

1. *JD* 1:39.

2. Origen, *De Principiis*; for English translation, see Alexander Roberts and James Donaldsen, eds., *Ante-Nicene Fathers*, 10 vols. (Grand Rapids: Eerdmans, 1978), 4:239-82.

3. *JD* 10:352.

4. Ibid., 8:228.

5. Walter C. Klein, "The Church and Its Prophets," *Anglican Theological Review* 44 (January 1962): 17. For more on this subject, see Hugh W. Nibley, *The World and the Prophets* (Salt Lake City: Deseret Book, 1974), 264-69; reprinted in *CWHN* 3:291-95.

6. Hugh W. Nibley, "Mixed Voices," *Improvement Era* (March-November 1959); "Kangaroo Court: A Study in Book of Mormon Criticism," 62 (March 1959): 145-48, 184-87; "Kangaroo Court: Part Two," 62 (April 1959): 224-26, 300-301; "Just Another Book? Part One," 62 (May 1959): 345-47, 388-91; "Just Another Book? Part Two," 62 (June 1959): 412-13, 501-3; "Just Another Book? Part Two, Conclusion," 62 (July 1959): 530-31, 565; "The Grab Bag," 62 (July 1959): 530-33, 546-48; "What Frontier, What Camp Meeting?" 62 (August 1959): 590-92, 610, 612, 614-15; "The Comparative Method," 62 (October 1959): 744-47, 759; "The Comparative Method," 62 (November 1959): 848, 854, 856; reprinted in *CWHN* 8:127-206.

7. See Hugh W. Nibley, *Since Cumorah* (Salt Lake City: Deseret Book, 1970), 12-14; reprinted in *CWHN* 7:11-13; cf. Bayard H. Jones,

"The Quest for the Origins of the Christian Liturgies," *Anglican Theological Review* 46 (January 1964): 5-6, who states that "the subject of liturgies is the youngest field of theological studies. . . . As a science, it is certainly still in its infancy. . . . It is significant that the first publication of texts of the Eastern Rites were made in part as an answer to the radical Protestants, who were vigorous in their denunciation of the abominable idolatries of the Mass." Massey H. Shepherd, "The Dimension of Liturgical Change," *Anglican Theological Review* 51 (October 1969): 255, cites the following: "Father Thomas F. O'Meara, O.P., of the Aquinas Institute in Dubuque, Iowa, has taken up Mr. Marshall McLuhan's insights into the differing impacts of 'hot' and 'cool' media of communication, and has applied these categories in a striking way to the problem of liturgical reform. He speaks of our inherited liturgy which in Protestantism even more than in Catholicism is largely a form of words, as one that . . . 'contains a great deal of content, of information; it is low on personal involvement; it repeats itself over and over; it keeps the same structure, filling it out with different blocks of detailed information about God and saints; it dictates our responses. . . . The liturgy is a disciplined and orderly structure, and the individual can become involved with this liturgy only by first entering the structure. The liturgy remains hot in a cool generation—high in detailed content, low in creative involvement.' "

In the 1970s efforts were made to improve the liturgies in the Anglican Church. Leo Malania, "The New Rites: The Place of the Bishop," *Anglican Theological Review*, 57 (April 1975): muses: "To me, as one who has sat in on the process of revision for the past seven years, one of their most striking features is their use of vivid imagery, and not only in words, such as the great image of the Crucified in the canon of the Second Service of the Holy Eucharist or in the blessing of the font in the new rite of Holy Baptism, but imagery on a larger scale: the imagery presented by the rites themselves, taken as a whole. For the new rites present the image of the Church in its organic unity, in the unity of the faithful, the one Body of Christ. One of the major aspects of this acted-out, living image of the church is the restoration of the Bishop to a central place in its major sacramental acts."

8. Romey P. Marshall and Michael J. Taylor, *Liturgy and Christian Unity* (New Jersey: Prentice Hall, 1965), 125; cf. Nibley, *Since Cumorah*, 14; in *CWHN* 7:13; Nibley, *The World and the Prophets*, 133-39; in *CWHN* 3:146-53.

9. For articles on the hierocentric point, see Hugh W. Nibley,

"Hierocentric State," *WPQ* 4 (1951): 226-53; in "Comments," *Mormonism: A Faith for All Cultures*, F. LaMond Tullis, ed. (Provo: BYU Press, 1978), 22-28.

10. For further information, see Hugh W. Nibley, "What Is a Temple?" *The Temple in Antiquity: Ancient Records and Modern Perspectives* (Provo: Religious Studies Center, 1984), 19-20; Hugh W. Nibley, "The Idea of the Temple in History," *MS* 120 (August 1958): 228-49; reprinted in *CWHN* 4:357-58.

11. Varro, *de Lingua Latina* V, 33; for English translation, see Varro, *On the Latin Language*, tr. Roland G. Kent, 2 vols. (Cambridge, MA: Harvard University Press, 1967), 1:30-33.

12. *JD* 8:79.

13. Ibid., 8:80.

14. Ibid., 10:222.

15. *MS* 27:205-6.

16. Edward Stevenson, *Life and History of Elder Edward Stevenson* (n.d.), 40-41.

17. The word *consecrate* is found in *Webster's Third New International Dictionary* (Springfield, MA: Merriam, 1961), 482.

18. Brigham Young's letter (October 19, 1876) to Willard Young, in Dean C. Jessee, ed., *Letters of Brigham Young to His Sons* (Salt Lake City: Deseret Book, 1974), 199.

19. Michael E. Christensen, "The Making of a Leader: A Biography of Charles W. Nibley to 1890" (Ph.D. diss., University of Utah, 1978), 1:128-29.

20. Letter (May 1, 1882) from John Taylor, George Q. Cannon, and Joseph F. Smith, in James R. Clark, ed., *Messages of the First Presidency*, 6 vols. (Salt Lake City: Bookcraft, 1965), 2:334.

21. *JD* 6:127.

7

How to Get Rich

Deuteronomy is the definitive statement of the law by which Israel is supposed to live. That law was never rescinded, but only superseded by the higher law, which embraced and reinforced all its principles. The New Testament repeats it with emphasis, as do the Book of Mormon, Doctrine and Covenants, Pearl of Great Price, the *Teachings of the Prophet Joseph Smith*, the *Discourses of Brigham Young*, and so on. Like the Word of Wisdom, it "points our souls forward." It is preparation for more to come when we are ready to receive it, and its strict observance is the indispensible prerequisite to any further progress.

I have chosen the Deuteronomy version of the old law, because the reward it promises explicitly and repeatedly is success — prosperity and long life in the new land of promise. One looks in vain for direct promises of eternal life and exaltation. That is why Jacob 4:5 says that the early Nephites knew that salvation did not come by the law of Moses, but they followed it to the letter because they could not receive higher law on any other conditions; it pointed their minds forward. But Deuteronomy definitely is the plan, guide, and handbook for "success" in this world; and as such, it is accepted as no other book by Israelis today. No commentaries or comparisons are required hereafter! And the rules for them are the rules for *us!*

Chapter 5 begins with Moses announcing for the last time that in bidding farewell to the children of Israel, he

---

This address was given in March 1982 in St. George, Utah.

is summarizing for them exactly what their law is to be (Deuteronomy 5:1). They are to consider it not as something for the ancients, a mere tradition, but something meant for "those living right now and right here" (Deuteronomy 5:3). This statement is followed by the Ten Commandments. What we are given in Deuteronomy is to be received henceforward as the law by which Israel will live; not a word is to be added to it or taken from it until God sees fit to make what changes he will (Deuteronomy 4:2). Once men start "clarifying" the words of the prophets, they can rewrite the book; God will not tolerate that. If, with the passing generations, Moses tells them, they should dilute it or corrupt it, they will not be merely reprimanded but utterly destroyed — scattered among the nations and reduced to pitifully small numbers (Deuteronomy 4:25-27). They are instructed to write the law down and memorize it (Deuteronomy 31:9). Every seven years the whole nation shall gather together and the high priest "shall read this law before all Israel in their hearing." This includes women, children, *and* outsiders, that all "may *hear*, and *learn*, and *fear* the Lord, and observe to *do all* the law" (Deuteronomy 31:10-12). They are to take good care of the holy book, keeping it carefully guarded in the Ark of the Covenant "for a witness against thee," that is, it will always be there as a standard to judge them by (Deuteronomy 31:25-26). Thus they will be left without excuse, "for this commandment this day . . . is not hidden from you, nor is it something far off. Not in heaven, that you should say: Who shall go up for us to heaven and bring it unto us? . . . You don't have to send anyone over the sea to fetch it, . . . but the word is very nigh unto thee, in thy mouth, and in thy heart, that thou mayest do it" (Deuteronomy 30:11-14).

The first rule, and one never to be forgotten, is that *everything* you have or ever will have, individually and collectively, is a *gift from God*, something that he blesses

you with, has blessed you with, or will bless you with—
you owe it all to him. Throughout the book, the refrain is
repeated at the end of almost every pronouncement: You
must do this in recognition of your dependence to God,
because first and foremost he has given you your lives, he
rescued you from Egypt, and he *redeemed* you—that is, he
paid the price for you that you could not pay yourself:
"And thou shalt remember that thou wast a *bondman* in
Egypt, and Jehovah thy God *redeemed* thee [brought you
free, paid the price, for nothing], . . . and therefore I *command* thee this thing today" (Deuteronomy 5:15). You are
not to turn to any other source of life and guidance; "do
not look to the sun or the moon or the stars" to represent
me. "It is to me directly and to me only that you must
turn: The Lord who brought you out of Egypt" (Deuteronomy 4:19-20). Remember that he "is God of gods, and
Lord of lords, a great God, a mighty, and a terrible" (Deuteronomy 10:17); all persons are equal to him, and he cannot be bought. How can you make a deal with him when
you have nothing to offer? "Behold, everything in heaven
and earth belongs to him" (Deuteronomy 10:14).

The first thing the Israelites are to do when they have
settled in their new land is to fill a basket with firstfruits,
the first gifts of the land, and bring it to the priest, who
sets it before the altar; then they are to recite these verses:
"A Syrian *ready to perish* was my father, and he went down
into Egypt, and sojourned there with a few, and became
there a nation, great, mighty, and populous: and the Egyptians evil entreated us, and afflicted us, and laid upon us
hard bondage. We called upon the Lord . . . and he heard
us. . . . He brought us forth out of the land of Egypt . . .
with signs and wonders, and he brought us to this place
and *gave* us the *land*, a land flowing with milk and honey"
(Deuteronomy 26:5-9). Why a Syrian or Aramaean? Why
was he also called "Abraham the Hebrew"? All of those
words denote a displaced person, a vagabond, a starving

wanderer, a homeless outcast moving among wicked and haughty people. It was from such a condition, "ready to perish," that God raised them up. The great gathering and feasts, whose strict observance makes up such an important part of the old law, all have the same purpose, to remind the Israelites that everything they had was a free gift from God. In holding these solemn conferences, "you and yours — sons, daughters, servants, . . . strangers, orphans, widows must all come together and rejoice and be happy," as one big happy *family*. That is the spirit in which this must be done, and that is the spirit of the *law of consecration* and the United Order. "Remember that thou wast a bondman in Egypt" — if some are slaves, all are slaves. This is to show where we stand with each other and the Lord. Thus in the Feast of the Tabernacles at the harvest, *all* must share, *all* rejoice together as one family, "thou and thy son and thy daughter, and thy manservant and thy maidservant, and the Levite, and the stranger, and the fatherless, and the widow that are within thy gates," for seven days in the appointed place. Three times a year, all males come together before Jehovah at an appointed place for the feasts of (1) unleavened bread, (2) weeks, and (3) tabernacles. And they must *never come empty-handed*: "Every man shall give as he is able, [that is,] according to the blessing of the Lord thy God, which *he* hath *given thee*" (Deuteronomy 16:11-17).

Moses reminds the people that they are about to settle down *not* in the lush Nile valley, but in the hill country that depends on the rains for life, "the rain of heaven" — a free gift. "If you will keep the commandments, [and so on,] . . . I will give you the rain your land needs and that at the proper seasons and in the proper amounts for maximum harvest. . . . And I will send grass for the flocks and herds as long as you take heed to yourselves. . . . If you do not, the Lord 'will *shut up the heaven*,' and you will get no rain and no harvest" (Deuteronomy 11:11-17). What is more, God has given good things to other nations also, some of them weaker than Israel, and all of them hostile. Those gifts of God to others are to be strictly respected. Speaking of Edomites, Ammonites, and Moabites, the Lord gave stern commandments: weaker nations are greatly concerned about the Israelite threat: "Meddle (*titgaru*) not with them; not an inch of their land belongs to you, because I gave it to them. I gave it all to the children of Esau" (Deuteronomy 2:5). The same applies to the Moabites (Deuteronomy 2:9) and to the Ammonites: "When you come to the children of Ammon, distress them not nor meddle with them" (Deuteronomy 2:19). He tells them that when he has a score to settle with other nations, he will let Israel know if it concerns them. Meanwhile, let no one interfere with the gifts God chooses to bestow on others!

The second point Moses insists on is that Israel understand very clearly that they have *not earned* the good things they enjoy. Beware, he says, "lest when you have eaten and are full, . . . and your silver and gold has piled up along with everything else," you get the idea that you earned it. "Then your heart will be lifted up, and you will forget the Lord thy God. . . . And you say to yourself: My ability and hard work (*kokhi we-otzem yadhi*) has made for me this fortune (*khayil*, power, influence, success). But you must keep in mind that it is God himself who has given you the *koakh* (capacity) to make *khayil* (success), for the sake of confirming the agreement (covenant) which he made with your fathers. [It is for their sake that he has blessed you.] If after that you forget in any degree any stipulation of the covenant, you will be *destroyed*" (Deuteronomy 8:12-20). That is why Moroni ends with his impassioned plea: "Deny not the gifts of God" (Moroni 10:8). Despise not the gifts of God. Never fail to recognize the pure gifts. No one, says King Benjamin, can so much as pay his own way. If we work day and night for twenty-four hours, we are still unprofitable servants. "Can ye say aught of yourselves? . . . [He] is preserving you from day to day, by lending you breath" (Mosiah 2:25, 21).

Furthermore, the Israelites are not to get the idea that because the Lord has turned out other people to give them the land, it is because of their righteousness, or that victory in the field has come to them as a reward of virtue: "Speak not thou in thine heart saying: For my righteousness the Lord hath brought me to possess the land: but rather for the wickedness of these nations the Lord doth drive *them* out" (Deuteronomy 9:4). This is exactly the lesson of Nephi to his brothers as they pass through those same lands. Whether or not these people were more or less wicked than Israel is for the Lord alone to decide. But here he tells them that it was not because they are righteous, but because the others were wicked; he had a score to settle with them and would have smitten them whether Israel had been anywhere around or not (1 Nephi 17:33-38). "Understand therefore, that Jehovah thy God is giving you this good land, not as a reward of righteousness, because you are not righteous, you are a stiffnecked people" (Deuteronomy 9:6). There were times when he told Moses, "Let me alone that I may destroy them and blot their names out and raise up a better people," specifically from Moses' line. When God said the Israelites were no better than the others and deserved the same, Moses was terrified at what was going to happen. He begged the Lord to spare the people just once more, "and the Lord hearkened to me at that time also" (Deuteronomy 9:13-19). Even so, he was ready to spare the very wicked cities of Sodom and Gomorrah for the sake of Abraham (Genesis 18:20-33). Again and again Moses hammers home the point: Don't get the idea that you are the good people and your enemies are the bad people: "Ye have been rebellious against the Lord ever since the day I first became acquainted with you" (Deuteronomy 9:24). And his final word to them was, "I know what a stiffnecked people you are. If you are rebel-

lious while I am still alive . . . and will utterly corrupt yourselves, and turn aside from the way I commanded, . . .
you will suffer evil accordingly" (Deuteronomy 31:27-29).
"I have led you for forty years, and up to now you still
have not learned. . . . Yet the Lord hath not given you a
heart to perceive, and eyes to see, and ears to hear *unto
this day*" (Deuteronomy 29:5, 4).

The third rule is that since God is giving it all away
free to everyone, regardless of all other circumstances,
everyone has a right to whatever he needs to live on. Thus
if you have taken a man's coat for security, you *must* return
it to him by sundown, because he needs it to wear or to
sleep in. Whether he has paid up or not has nothing to
do with it. If you feel short-changed, "Jehovah your God
will give you credit," so don't worry (Deuteronomy 24:13).
Under no circumstances can you take for a pledge or security a millstone or anything else upon which a person's
livelihood depends (Deuteronomy 24:6).

In passing through anyone's vineyard, you may help
yourself to whatever you can eat, but you may not carry
off any in a container. If the owner denies you what you
need, he is greedy; if you take more than you need, then
you are greedy (Deuteronomy 23:24). In a field of grain,
take what you need then and there, but don't take a sickle
to cut or collect it. If you take it for profit or gain over and
above what you need, you are in danger (Deuteronomy
23:25). As Paul also reminds us, it was when the people
of Sodom and Gomorrah denied passing strangers and
even the birds of heaven their share of the fruit on the
trees that Abraham cursed them in the name of his God;
according to the *Midrash*, their sexual aberrations were
second in wickedness to such meanness of spirit.[1]

And what does God ask us to do to requite his goodness? He does not need anything from us to show him
and ourselves whether we have learned our lesson. The
basic rule of his economy is that he is just and equitable:

"He doth execute the judgment (*mishpaṭ*) for the orphan and the widow, and he loves the stranger and wants him to be provided with food and clothing. *Therefore, you* must do the *same*: love the stranger—remember that you too were strangers [and *were* oppressed] in the land of Egypt" (Deuteronomy 10:18-19). Yes, we are to imitate God's freedom and bounty, to be as free with the substance he has given us as he is in giving it to us. He lets his rain fall upon the just and the unjust. He was good to you though you were disobedient; so when you give to others, never ask whether they deserve it (King Benjamin taught the same text in Mosiah 4:11-24). "And now I [the priest] have brought the firstfruits of the land, which thou, O Lord, hast *given* me. . . . Set it down before the Lord and worship him and rejoice in every good thing which Jehovah thy God hath *given* unto thee *and* to thy house *and* to the Levites *and* to the *strangers* among you" (Deuteronomy 26:10-11). (You do not have to be an Israelite to qualify.) "In the third year you start tithing, giving it to the Levite, stranger, fatherless, and widow, that they may eat within thy gates and be filled. At this time you will say: 'I have brought away the things of my house which have been sanctified, and also have given them to the Levite, stranger, fatherless, widow, according to *all* thy commandments. . . . I have not transgressed thy commandments, or forgotten them' " (Deuteronomy 26:12-13).

The word *sanctified* in the King James Version means the same as consecrated, set apart; and it is the law of consecration, given as it is at the culmination of all the other laws. And in all of this, Israel is being put to the test: the Feast of the Weeks requires "a tribute of a freewill offering of thine hand." The offering is required—it is tribute, but the amount is freewill; you determine it yourself, on the basis of *how much the Lord has given you* [the Septuagint *kathoti hē cheir sou ischyei* means to the limit of your ability], what he has given you, even with what your God has blessed you (Deuteronomy 16:10; *bless* here means to give: All that with which the Lord has blessed you or with which he may bless you.) What is more, you must recognize any kindness shown you by others. Thus Israel is not to despise the Edomite or the Egyptian, though both of these had opposed and oppressed Israel, because Israel was permitted to pass through their lands in spite of everything (Deuteronomy 23:7).

But though we must be kind to each other, we are not to go into debt with each other. God wants us to be in debt to him alone and not to each other. This raises a problem to which the law of Moses provides the only possible solution. It is almost impossible in the world's economy to pay off a debt without incurring more debt. Young people optimistically expect to work off their indebtedness, naively overlooking their helplessness in the hands of creditors, who can always decide how much their work is worth to them. And so we find ourselves strapped. Get out of debt! we are told, but go into business! How do you do both? We hear both themes at the Credit Union banquets: "Don't borrow," the speakers tell us, "but please do your borrowing from us." God gives Israel the solution to the dilemma. Do not decide these things on the basis of your own self-interest; someone must draw the line and say, "Here this business of depending on each other must stop." Before all things, we are told today that Latter-day Saints must be independent. It is only by the law of "the Lord's release" that the massive logjam that paralyzes the world today can be broken: every seven years all debts are canceled (Deuteronomy 15:2). This is admittedly not a human arrangement—to us it appears laughable. But God absolutely insists upon it. Every seven years you *must* make a release (Deuteronomy 15:1). After six years of service, any and all Hebrew servants must go absolutely free no matter what you paid for them (Deuteronomy 15:12). And you can not turn them out into the world: "Thou shalt not let him go away empty" (Deuteronomy 15:13). A week's severance pay? Not at all. Again, "thou shalt furnish him *liberally* out of thy flock, out of thy winepress; out of whatsoever the Lord thy God hath blessed thee, thou shalt give unto him" (Deuteronomy 15:14). You know exactly what that means and what God wants you to do. But he is not holding you to any specific figure — that is up to you. That is the whole idea.

When men receive gifts from each other, they become dependent upon each other; and jealousy and meanness follow. The judicial order in Israel must rest on absolute fairness without respect of person. "Thou shalt not wrest judgment; thou shalt not respect persons; neither take a gift: for a gift does blind the eyes of the wise and pervert the words of the righteous" (Deuteronomy 16:19). Note well, it is not only the foolish who are blinded or the wicked who are perverted — when we start passing the gravy around, it is even the wise who are blinded and the righteous who are perverted.

The key to all this is the spirit in which it is done and which alone can make it workable. The first and most common word in every decree is, surprisingly, *love.* "And now, Israel, what doth the Lord thy God require of thee, but to fear the Lord thy God, to walk in all his ways, to love him, and to serve the Lord thy God with all thy heart and with all thy soul, to keep the commandments of the Lord, and his statutes, which I have commanded you to keep this day, all for *your good*" (Deuteronomy 10:12-13). The question is never raised, "Will this work, is it practical, is it sensible, is it realistic?" Quite the contrary, the main question always is whether people feel good about serving him: "O that there were such a heart in them, that they would really feel it that they would fear me and keep all my commandments always that it might be well with them and with their children forever!" (Deuteronomy 5:26). God feels for us and worries about us. His concern for our welfare is far greater than our own. Again and again a special command is introduced with the words of the first great commandment, and the second follows hard upon: "Thou shalt love the Lord thy God, with all thy heart, . . . soul, . . . might. And these words, which I command thee this day, shall be in thy heart" (Deuteronomy 6:5-6). This is the main theme of Deuteronomy, and it is an admonition against that very legalism which later became the obsession of the rabbis as well as our own society.

But how can a law of love be legislated or enforced? Simply by the society's becoming completely immersed in it: "Thou shalt teach them diligently unto thy children, talk of them when you are sitting at home, talk of them whenever you are on the move, about town or on a journey, talk of them going to bed and getting up. Bind them on your hand and make them like a sign between the eyes" (Deuteronomy 6:7-8). (This had mystical connotations for later Judaism — the law is not only in your heart, it is written all over your person, marked in your manner and your appearance.) "And you shall write them on the *mezuzoth* of your houses and gateways" (Deuteronomy 6:9). This shall be ingrained in the consciousness of everyone in a natural, even unconscious, manner. One is to take advantage of every opportunity to answer children's questions and take care in various ways to stimulate the asking of those questions. Your children will hear you talking about these things, and "when at any time in future a child shall ask, 'Daddy what are these *edoth* [testimonies, witnesses, ordinances, the Ten Commandments, councils, assemblies, and so on] and the *huqqim* and the *mishpatim* which Jehovah our God ordered you to keep?' you shall answer by telling him the story of the deliverance from Egypt" (Deuteronomy 6:20-21). The whole thing is kept alive on a family basis with a warm and urgent appeal to take these things to heart. "Thou shalt also consider in thy *heart*, that as a man chasteneth his son, Jehovah your God chasteneth you"—think of him in that way, as a kind Father, who would not do anything that was not for his son's good (Deuteronomy 8:5).

Now comes the most important part of the business: the reaching out beyond immediate family to all the world. "If there be a poor man of your brethren living anywhere within your knowledge, in thy land which the Lord thy God giveth thee, thou shalt not harden thy heart, nor shut thy hand from thy poor brother" (Deuteronomy 15:7). These are Benjamin and Mosiah's orders also (Mosiah 4:13-25). We have no laws requiring a man to be generous or penalizing meanness of spirit, for the obvious reason that no one can know exactly what is in another's heart. But God knows, and he does require these things in his law. You shall not only give to the poor man, but you should do it magnanimously (and this is a direct order): "But thou shalt open thy hand *wide* unto him, and shalt surely lend him sufficient for his need of whatever he is in want" (Deuteronomy 15:8). But that is not all! It is not enough to do merely what you are told, you must do it in the right spirit without any mental reservations. In this case you are not supposed to calculate how near the day of the Lord's release is. Let us say it is only ten days away, which means that if I loan him something, he won't ever have to pay it back: "Beware that there is not a thought in thy wicked heart, saying the seventh year, the year of release is at hand; if I give anything to him now he will not have to repay it, and I will never get it back, and thine eye be evil against thy poor brother, and thou givest him nought, . . . and he cry to the Lord, and *it be a sin unto thee*" (Deuteronomy 15:9). (Leave the computer and the calculating alone! Remember, a gift given grudgingly is a curse on the giver.) Speaking in general terms, "Thou shalt surely give him, and thy heart shall not be grieved when thou givest unto him" (Deuteronomy 15:10). My Scottish forebears, how it hurt them to part with a penny! "Because for that

thing the Lord thy God shall bless thee [no amount spec-
ified] in all thy works" (Deuteronomy 15:10). He guarantees full payment. It may seem severe to us to say, "Thou
shalt *not* deliver unto his master the servant which is escaped from his master unto thee" (Deuteronomy 23:15).
But the law goes further. Not only shall the refugee "dwell
with thee . . . in that place which *he* shall choose," but
while he is with you, "thou shalt not oppress [*tonennu*,
grumble about, mutter under your breath, complain about]
him" (Deuteronomy 23:16). When the time comes for your
own servant to leave you after his six years, he does not
have to leave if he has become attached to your service
(Deuteronomy 15:16-17); the important thing is that if he
does want to go, you must let him go cheerfully. "It shall
not *seem* hard unto thee when thou sendest him away
free" — you will be happy about it, because he has worked
for you all that time, because you are doing the will of the
Lord, and because you have faith in his judgment and
goodness: "If you do that," the order continues, "the Lord
thy God will bless thee" — you can't lose a thing (Deuteronomy 15:18).

If a man has two wives and loves the one and can't
stand the other, and the unloved one has a son before the
other, that son must inherit a double portion, for a man
must always deal fairly and play no favorites (Deuteronomy 21:15-17). That is the essence of the law — complete
fairness at all times.

But the fair thing is also the decent thing, the noble
thing. "If a man take a beautiful captive to wife, he must
allow her the full period of mourning for her own family,
respecting her feelings and allowing her to make the transfer" (Deuteronomy 21:11-13). If after all he decides not to
marry her, then she is free to go where she will. Though
a captive of war, she is a free woman: "Thou shalt not
make merchandise of her because thou hast humbled her"

(Deuteronomy 21:14). The respect for human dignity and the feelings of others always have priority on other claims.

This principle is clearly shown in the rules of battle. If you have the right on your side, you are not to fear the enemy (Deuteronomy 20:1). Before the battle, the priest gives an address to the people, a pep talk, telling them, "Let not your hearts be faint, . . . for Jehovah your God goes with you to fight for you . . . and to save you." The main thing is that you know perfectly well that your own hearts and hands are pure (Deuteronomy 20:2-4). But certain men are not permitted to go into battle: "anyone who has bought a house and not yet dedicated it, or who has planted a vineyard and not yet eaten of it," for life must go on, and such homely matters have priority over the claims of the military. Indeed, they are the only justification for the military anyway, whose whole purpose is supposed to be to protect the life of the society. One who has "betrothed a wife and not yet taken her" may not go to battle, "lest he die and another man take her" (a favorite theme of wartime romances) (Deuteronomy 20:5-7). But it is mostly out of consideration for the bride. The husband may not be required to go to war or indeed to engage in any distracting business for one year—"for the sake of cheering his wife" (Deuteronomy 24:5). It is her feelings that deserve first consideration. Most significant is the rule that before the battle, the fearful and faint-hearted should be allowed and even requested to go home without prejudice, "lest his brethren's heart faint as well as his heart" (Deuteronomy 20:8). This recognizes the simple fact that all men are human and have their limits of endurance. The host is not divided into higher heroes and cowards in the Patton fashion, but into those with lower and higher thresholds of resistance to fear, with the understanding that everyone has a breaking point—Peter broke when he denied the Lord because he was scared stiff. The weak-hearted are to be dismissed in recognition of the fact that

all men suffer from the same weakness – the timid soul is
dangerous because the rest of us are *almost* as susceptible
as he is and only too easily affected by his example. So we
must let him go, before *we* get cold feet too!

It is always the spirit that counts. The celebrations in
which everyone is generous and open-handed in recognition of God's bounty are joyous affairs. Sons, daughters,
servants, strangers, orphans, and widows must all come
together and rejoice and be happy as one big happy *family*.
That is the spirit in which this must be done, and that is
the spirit of the law of consecration and the United Order.
"Remember that thou wast a bondman in Egypt" – if some
are slaves, all are slaves. This is to show where we stand
with each other and the Lord (Deuteronomy 16:11-12).

From all of this it would appear that the one thing God
will not tolerate in his children is that meanness of spirit
which would take advantage of his other children and even
of him. "Thou shalt not sacrifice unto the Lord . . . any
bullock, or sheep with any blemish or fault whatever or
any evil-favoredness: for that is an abomination unto the
Lord thy God" (Deuteronomy 17:1). Why? Because it is
cheap, it is mean, the equivalent of shaving one's tithing
or underestimating one's fast offering. As Isaiah reminds
Israel, God does not need your offering, it is *you* he is
testing. He does not ask us to get rich so that we can help
him; as Brigham Young said so often, God has put these
things into our hands so that we can show him and all the
world and ourselves how we will handle them and what
we will do with them. It is meanness of spirit that will
disqualify us before everything else for a celestial assignment. No double bookkeeping, says the Lord. Do not
"carry diverse measures with you or keep such in your
house; . . . such little tricks and strategies of business to
maximize profits are an abomination" (Deuteronomy
25:13-16). Those habits of thrift that were taught me as
shining virtues by my Scottish forebears can easily lead to

meanness, and for that we have the famous law of the gleaning: "When thou cuttest down thine harvest in thy field, and hast forgotten a sheaf in the field, *thou shalt not go again to fetch it,*" It is not yours anymore: "It shall be for the stranger, for the fatherless, and for the widow" (Deuteronomy 24:19). Don't worry, the Lord will bless you for it. In beating the olive trees, "thou shalt not go over the boughs again" (Deuteronomy 24:20); granted that this is sound business practice, it is nonetheless forbidden. When you gather grapes in the vineyard, "thou shalt not glean it afterward" (Deuteronomy 24:21); it is for the disadvantaged. The usual explanation is given for all this: "Never forget that you were a bondsman in Egypt" (Deuteronomy 24:22).

Mention of processing olives and grapes brings up the word "extortion"; the literal meaning of the word "is to squeeze the last drop out of a thing." The gifts of God, we are told, which are the bounties of the earth, are to be used "with judgment, not to excess, neither by *extortion*" (D&C 59:20). How often it is that these last drops mean the extra profit we so eagerly pursue. And now comes one of the most famous passages in the Bible: "For the poor shall never cease out of the land" (Deuteronomy 15:11). We have given this a rather mean twist today, arguing that since the poor will always be there, it is a waste of time to help them, for that will only encourage them and make more of them. Thus we ignore the rest of the verse (I have never heard anyone quote it), which is: "Therefore I command thee, saying thou shalt open up thy hand wide unto thy brother, to thy poor, and to thy needy, in thy land" (Deuteronomy 15:11). Their perpetual presence is not to make us indifferent, but it is a constant reminder that God has his eye on us.

What we are warned against more than anything else is taking advantage of those who are disadvantaged—the stranger, the orphan; "nor take the widow's raiment to pledge," always remembering that you were once the disadvantaged (Deuteronomy 24:17-18). A list of things is given for which people are told they will be cursed. Of the nine specific crimes, all but one—the worship of graven images—are in the nature of taking advantage of weaker parties: holding one's aged father or mother in contempt; removing a neighbor's landmark (while he is not looking); taking advantage of a blind person, "making the blind to wander out of the way" (Deuteronomy 27:18); taking advantage of strangers, orphans, and widows with the help of lawyers; incest; striking anyone off guard, as Cain did Abel; and taking a reward to slay someone who has not offended you (the Mahan principle) (Deuteronomy 27:15-25). The one person who is held up as a monster of wickedness so evil that he should be forever forgotten by all men was Amalek, king of the Amorites, who "smote the hindmost of thee, the feeble laggards on the march; when you were faint and weary, he attacked, and he feared not God (Deuteronomy 25:17-19). The most common way of taking advantage of another's need is loaning money at interest, and this is strictly forbidden, though it is the cornerstone of our present-day economy (Deuteronomy 23:19). But even more effective is the iron law of wages, which forces a worker to accept the lowest possible pay from you because he is desperate for work—as long as his labor brings you a profit, you will continue to hire him; when it doesn't, you let him go. And in all this, you pose as his benefactor. "Thou shalt not oppress an hired servant that is poor and needy" (Deuteronomy 24:14). What is more, you must not only pay him a living wage, but you must pay him every day before sundown: "Because he is poor, and setteth his heart upon it" (Deuteronomy 24:15). Everyone has a right to his daily bread.

In a word, the right to life always supersedes the right to profit. Thus, "thou shalt *not* deliver unto his master the servant which is escaped from his master unto thee" (Deuteronomy 23:15). Here is the clear confrontation of life versus property, which played such a large role in the history of this country; apparently the pious slave owners never read this part of the Bible. And everyone knows the law that "thou shalt not muzzle the ox when he treadeth out the corn" (Deuteronomy 25:4). The beast is working for you—give him a break.

Indeed, "anyone stealing an Israelite to make merchandise of him or sell him outright must *die*" (Deuteronomy 24:7). In the ancient world, stealing and selling people into slavery was at all times one of the most profitable businesses. But in our free Anglo-Saxon tradition, it has been carried out in a more covert (and therefore more respectable) manner: press-gangs, indentured servants, slave-raids, pimping, enlistment of workers for unknown jobs that turn out to be sweatshops or labor camps, brain washing by certain cults, and so on. And here is an interesting one: criminals in the law of Israel even have human rights. When a felon is to be beaten, the judge must prescribe a set number of blows, but never one strike more than forty, regardless of the crime, "lest thy brother seem vile to thee" (Deuteronomy 25:2-3). Making those we don't like seem vile is one of the most advanced techniques of modern society.

The question arises, Are these laws realistic? Are they workable in the modern world? No! They are very special laws given to very special people. They are simply fantastic as far as the world is concerned. But that is just the point, says the Lord. The people of the world are not good enough to be my people. "I have called you out of the world. Your covenant is not with them, nor need you make any concessions to (*tekhannem*) them. Do not intermarry with them, for marriage is a covenant. You must have nothing to do with them, because you are something different from the world—holy, set apart, chosen, special—peculiar (*am segullah*; sealed, *segulloth*), not like any other people upon the face of the *adamah*. God will keep faith with you all the way; he is merciful and loving and wants to bless you for a thousand generations" (Deuteronomy 7:1-9). To reject such an offer of love is to incur resentment and disaster; disposed love turns to hate. If you hate him, you will have to pay for it. That is fair, because he intends to make you blessed above all other people. You will be a veritable Zion, of eternal increase, without sickness (Deuteronomy 7:10-15). You shall not follow their fashion. No cutting and tattooing (*titgodadu*) or shaving of eyebrows for the dead.

In his farewell prayer for his people, Moses calls upon the Lord: "Look down from thy holy habitation . . . and bless thy people Israel, and the land which thou hast given us, . . . flowing with milk and honey." The Lord has insisted that you observe and do these things with all your heart and soul, and you have promised and covenanted this day that you would do that. While he has covenanted with you and accepted you this day as his *sealed people*, the wonder of other nations is that you may be a *holy people*, as he has said. This is the conclusion of a prayer in which the whole emphasis is on the Levite, the stranger, the orphans and the widows (Deuteronomy 26:15-19). The best security, and in the end the only assurance of survival, is this: "That which is altogether just shalt thou follow, that thou mayest live, and inherit the land which Jehovah thy God giveth to thee" (Deuteronomy 16:20). "Ye shall not respect persons. . . . Ye shall hear the small as well as the great" (Deuteronomy 1:17). What makes this a practical and working scheme is that God himself guarantees the bottom line. If you observe all of these things, he says, you can't lose. You will be overwhelmed with blessings: blessed in the city and in the field, in families, crops, and herds, in your harvest and in your storage, in your going out and in your coming in; when your enemies rise up against you, they shall be smitten and scattered (Deuteronomy 28:1-7). But only if you keep his commandments and walk in his ways will he give you boundless prosperity; "he will open unto thee his good treasure, the heaven to give rain unto thy land in his season, . . . if you heed and carry out all his commandments, not deviating from them to right or to left" (Deuteronomy 28:12-14). You may look forward to times "when there shall be no poor among you; for the Lord shall greatly bless thee," but "only if you carefully hearken and strictly observe and do these commandments which you now receive" (Deuteronomy 15:4-5).

The last four chapters of Deuteronomy are devoted to the most harrowing, detailed, prophetic descriptions of what will happen to Israel if the people do not walk up to all the covenants. The Lord insists on a viable equation: the promise on the land is equal to the curse; the greater the blessing if the laws are kept, the greater the curse if they are broken. This vast land is yours, and in giving it to you, "behold, I set before you this day a *blessing* and a *curse*." For there is no contract without a penalty clause. A blessing, if ye obey, and a cursing, if ye will not obey (Deuteronomy 11:26-28). The Lord orders the heads of six tribes to pronounce the blessing on the people as they enter the land, and the heads of six others to curse the people "with a loud voice"; and after each blessing and cursing, all the people cry "Amen!" formally accepting the conditions (Deuteronomy 27:12-14). Great stones are set up and inscribed in bold, plain, legible letters so that no one can ever forget what they are committed to. Then Moses and all the priests address the people, telling them that they are formally and legally the people of the Lord, henceforward under obligation to obey his voice, observe his rules and carry out his commandments (Deuteronomy 27:2-10). After listing all the blessings in the first half of chapter 28, Moses turns to the second half, beginning, "but . . . if thou will not hearken, . . . these curses shall come upon thee" (Deuteronomy 28:15); then he lists the *same* blessings, but in *reverse.* "The curses will dog you in all your undertaking, until thou be destroyed, and until thou perish quickly" (Deuteronomy 28:20). This is the Book of Mormon situation also, which is characteristic only of Israel to this degree; other nations have sinned and suffered, and they are still in existence, still sinning and suffering, after thousands of years; but in the Old World, and the New, Israel was smashed and scattered. Epidemics, war and drought will wipe you out.

Reversal of the Blessings

1. If you do not keep the covenant you have made, "the heaven will be brass over your head and the earth will be iron under your feet" (Deuteronomy 28:23).

2. Your rain-clouds will be clouds of dust (Deuteronomy 28:24).

3. You will be destroyed like the Jaredites by the hand of the Lord, for "the Lord shall cause thee to be smitten before thine enemies: thou shalt go out one way against them, and flee seven ways before them" (Deuteronomy 28:25).

You will suffer crushing defeats:

4. You will wither away physically (Deuteronomy 28:26).

5. There will be most unsightly skin diseases, itches, scabs, hemorrhoids (Deuteronomy 28:27).

6. And also mental illness of all sorts: "madness, blindness, and astonishment of heart" (Deuteronomy 28:28).

7. You will "grope at noonday . . . and shalt not prosper in thy ways." Everything you try will fail (Deuteronomy 28:29).

8. Everything you prepare will go to someone else (Deuteronomy 28:30).

9. You will end up in the hands of your enemies (Deuteronomy 28:31).

10. Even your sons and daughters will go over to oth-

ers. It will all be more than you can stand (Deuteronomy 28:32).

11. "So that thou shalt be mad for the sight of thine eyes which thou shalt see" (Deuteronomy 28:34). (It sounds like wild poetry—not so fantastic anymore.)

And it is also history for the Jews:

12. "The Lord shall bring thee . . . to a nation your fathers never knew" (Deuteronomy 28:36).

13. "Thou shalt become an astonishment, a proverb, a byword among all nations whither the Lord shall lead thee" (Deuteronomy 28:37). (The unique history of the Jews bids us take the whole scenario seriously.)

14. The toil and desperate moves and ultimate checks and frustrations they have had to suffer in the world—still half their own fault—is described (Deuteronomy 28:38-40).

15. And all this will go on "till thou be destroyed" (Deuteronomy 28:45).

16. "Because thou servedst not Jehovah thy God with joyfulness and with gladness of heart for the abundance of all things, therefore, shalt thou serve thine enemies?" (Deuteronomy 28:47-48). (This is how he wants you to accept his blessings, to make everybody happy.)

17. "The Lord shall bring a nation against thee from afar . . . whose language you don't understand" (Deuteronomy 28:49).

18. There will be fierce, warlike people "which shall not regard the person of the old, nor show favor to the young"—hard-faced military officers, such as rule the world today (Deuteronomy 28:50).

19. They will take everything over and reduce you to nothing" (Deuteronomy 28:51).

20. Your supplies will be reduced to the point where you prey on each other without mercy, everyone turning against everyone else (Deuteronomy 28:54).

21. You will suffer from chronic epidemics (Deuteronomy 28:59).

22. Your populations will dwindle away (Deuteronomy 28:62).

23. In short, "as the Lord rejoiced . . . to do you good and to multiply you, so the Lord will rejoice . . . to destroy you, and reduce you to nothing," an endangered and homeless species (Deuteronomy 28:63).

24. Among these nations shalt thou find no peace (Deuteronomy 28:65).

25. "And shalt have none assurance of thy life" (Deuteronomy 28:66). (Absolutely no security. No matter how rich and powerful they have become in many countries and in many centuries, even the greatest of them have been subject to immediate torture and death without notice.)

26. At night you will wish for day, and all day wish for night (Deuteronomy 28:67).

The next chapter begins the windup. "Ye stand this day all of you before Jehovah your God . . . that he may establish thee today for a people unto himself. . . . Let there be no one with any mental reservations as to what he has sworn to; . . . that will be gall and wormwood" (Deuteronomy 29:10, 13, 18). Someone who thinks the words of the curse will not apply to him will say: This won't bother me—I'll just go my way! But "the Lord will not spare him. . . . All the curses written in this book will be upon him." You will be bringing the fate of Sodom and Gomorrah, Admah and Zeboim upon you. People will marvel at what a desert the land has become and wonder why. Answer: "Because they have forsaken the covenants of the Lord" (Deuteronomy 29:10-25).

And then Moses' own testimony: "See I have set before thee this day life and good, and death and evil. Your choice is to flourish or perish. . . . I call heaven and earth to record this day against you, that I have set before you life and death, blessing and cursing: therefore choose life, . . . that thou mayest love the Lord, . . . obey his voice, . . . *cleave*

unto him: for he is thy life and the length of thy days"
(Deuteronomy 30:15-20).

Notes

1. Gerald Friedlander, *Pirkê de Rabbi Eliezer* (New York: Hermon
Press, 1965), 176; cf. Louis Ginzberg, *The Legends of the Jews*, 7 vols.
(Philadelphia: Jewish Publication Society of America, 1968), 1:245-
50; and Nathan Ausubel, *A Treasury of Jewish Folklore* (New York:
Crown, 1948), 124.

8

Work We Must,
but the Lunch Is Free

Bounty from on High—All or Nothing

The famous geologist Sir Julian Huxley used to go from
school to school in the manner of a traveling revivalist,
preaching his gospel of evolution: "In the evolutionary
pattern of thought there is no longer need or room for the
supernatural. The earth was not created; it evolved. So did
all the animals and plants that inhabit it including our
human selves, mind and soul, as well as brain and body.
So did religion."[1] He was fond of reminding his audiences
that there is no Santa Claus, and that mature people should
give up wishful thinking about such things as gifts and
blessings, spiritual or material, bestowed from on high.

The high school youth of my day took great satisfaction
in reciting the words of Omar Khayyam: "And that inverted bowl we call the sky, whereunder crawling coop't
we live and die, lift not the hands to It for help, for It rolls
impotently on as Thou or I."[2] This is, as one eminent
commentator on the scientific scene, Hoimar von Ditfurth,
puts it, "that 'modern view,' still current today, that the
earth with everything in it is dangling in the isolation of
a universe whose cold majesty disdains it. . . . Deep down
we are probably even proud of the detachment with which

*This talk was given April 20, 1982, to the Cannon-Hinkley Club at the Lion
House in Salt Lake City. It was published in* BYU Today *(November 1982):
8-12.*

we accept our 'true' situation. . . . Much of the cynicism
and nihilism characteristic of the modern psyche can be
traced to this chilling conception."[3]

But within the past decade or so, leaders in scientific
research have begun to express the opposite opinion to
this, saying that they more than suspect the possibility (1)
that the somebody out there cares — that is, there is direction and purpose to what is going on; and (2) that gifts
sent down from above are more than a childish tradition.

The first of these ideas was recently expressed by the
biologist Lewis Thomas: "I cannot make peace with the
randomness doctrine; I cannot abide the notion of pur-
poselessness and blind chance in nature. And yet I do not
know what to put in its place for the quieting of my
mind. . . . We talk — some of us, anyway — about the absurdity of the human situation, but we do this because we
do not know how we fit in, or what we are for. The stories
we used to make up to explain ourselves do not make
sense anymore, and we have run out of new stories, for
the moment."[4] A grand old-timer in biology, the 1937 Nobel Prize winner, Albert Szent-Györgyi, recently wrote:

> According to present ideas, this change in the nucleic
> acid [which determines the nature of protein molecules
> formed in a cell] is accomplished through random var-
> iation. . . . If I were trying to pass a biology examination,
> I would vigorously support this theory. Yet in my mind
> I have never been able to accept fully the idea that the
> adaption and the harmonious building of those complex
> biological systems, involving simultaneous changes in
> thousands of genes, are the results of molecular acci-
> dents. . . . The probability that all of these genes should
> have changed together through random variation is prac-
> tically zero. . . . I have always been seeking some higher
> organizing principle that is leading the living system
> toward improvement and adaptation. I know this is bi-
> ological heresy, . . . e.g., I do not think that the ex-

tremely complex speech center of the human brain . . . was created by random mutations that happened to improve the chances of survival of individuals. . . . I *cannot accept* the notion that this capacity arose through random alterations, relying on the survival of the fittest. I believe that some principle must have guided the development toward the kind of speech center that was needed.[5]

More surprising is the story now unfolding as various fields of research combine to give us a picture of gifts being showered upon us from on high — the literal reading of the Santa Claus or Kachina myth. Thus Buckminster Fuller says: "Energies emanating from celestial regions remote from Planet Earth are indeed converging and accumulating in Planet Earth's biosphere . . . both as radiation and as matter."[6] "We aboard Earth are receiving gratis just the amount of prime energy wealth, to regenerate biological life on board. . . . Van Allen belts, . . . the ionosphere, stratosphere and atmosphere all refractively differentiate the radiation frequencies, . . . separating [them] into a variety of indirect life-sustaining energy transactions."[7] "Vegetation [is] . . . the prime energy impounder";[8] from stellar radiation "the biologicals are continually multiplying, their beautiful cellular, molecular, and atomic structurings" that complete the equation.[9] "Certainly the earth is not the center of the universe," writes von Ditfurth, ". . . but this crowded earth *is* a focal point in the universe; one of perhaps innumerable places in the cosmos where life and consciousness could flourish. . . . What a concentration of mighty forces upon one more or less tiny point!"[10] Is it possible that someone does have us in mind?

This is the thesis the famous astronomer Sir Fred Hoyle is now pursuing. In a talk given at Caltech last November (1981), he begins with the strange fact that there are distributed in all directions throughout the immensity of space particles whose presence is revealed by the way in which they obscure the galaxies everywhere, making them all look hazy — whence their original designation as "nebulas" or fuzzy clouds. After almost twenty years of investigation, the inescapable conclusion has been reached that "the grains had to be made up largely of organic material." Like the biologists quoted above, Hoyle too, as he puts it, "was constantly plagued by the thought that the number of ways in which even a single enzyme could be wrongly constructed was greater than the number of all the atoms in the universe [and yet these were correctly constructed], so try as I would, I couldn't convince myself that even the whole universe would be sufficient to find life by random processes — by what are called the blind forces of nature." That is where he, too, balks. "By far the simplest way to arrive at the correct sequences of amino acids in the enzymes would be by thought, *not* random processes. . . . Rather than accept the fantastically small probability of life having arisen through the blind forces of nature, it seemed better to suppose that the origin of life was a deliberate intellectual act." One of the most exciting things about the process, he finds, is that it is still going on, and always has been, and to all purposes always will be. Instead of beginning with a single cell on this one lone planet billions of years ago, life has been brought down to earth from realms above in massive installments. "It was quickly apparent that the facts pointed overwhelmingly against life being of terrestrial origin . . . [here Hoyle pursues a long line of argument and review of research]; e.g., because a few comets are breaking up and scattering their contents all the time, the process was not relegated to the remote past."[11] "Taking the view, palatable to most ordinary folk but exceedingly unpalatable to scientists, that there is an enormous intelligence abroad in the universe, it becomes necessary to write blind forces out of astronomy,"[12] as Thomas and Szent-Gyrgyi do out of biology.

As if to counteract these growing heresies, the old Darwinian view is being puffed today for all it is worth in a half dozen prestigious TV documentaries in which we are treated to endless footage of creatures ranging from amoebas to giant carnivores stalking, seizing, and with concentrated deliberation soberly crunching, munching, swallowing, and ingesting other insects, fishes, birds, and mammals. This, we are told again and again, is the real process by which all things were created. Everything is lunching on everything else, all the time, and that, children, is what makes us what we are; that is the key to progress. And note it well, all these creatures when they are not lunching are hunting for lunch—they all have to work for it: There is *no* free lunch in the world of nature, the real world. Lunch is the meaning of life, and everything lunches on something else—"Nature red in tooth and claw." Tennyson's happy phrase suited the Victorian mind to perfection. He got the idea from Darwin, as Spencer did his even happier phrase, "Survival of the fittest." Darwin gave the blessing of science to men who had been hoping and praying for holy sanction to an otherwise immoral way of life. Malthus had shown that there will never be enough lunch for everybody, and therefore people would have to fight for it; and Ricardo had shown by his Iron Law of Wages that those left behind and gobbled up in the struggle for lunch had no just cause for complaint. Darwin showed that this was an inexorable *law* of nature by which the race was actually *improved*; Miall and Spencer made it the cornerstone of the gospel of Free Enterprise— the weaker must fall by the way if the stock is to be improved. This was movingly expressed in J. D. Rockefeller's discourse on the American Beauty Rose, which, he said, "can be produced . . . only by sacrificing the early buds which grow up around it. . . . This is not an evil tendency in business. It is merely the working-out of a law of nature and a law of God."[13]

In this divinely appointed game of grabs, to share the

lunch-prize would be futile, counter-productive, nay im-moral. Since there is not enough to go around, whoever gets his fill must be taking it from others—that is the way the game is played. "In Liverpool, Manchester, Preston, or anywhere else in England," as Brigham Young reported the scene in 1856, workers knew that "their employers would make them do their work for nothing, and then compel them to live on roots and grass if their physical organization could endure it, therefore, says the mechanic, 'If I can get anything out of you I will call it a godsend,' "[14] and does what he can to rip off the boss. If he gets caught, he is punished, yet he is only playing the same game as his employer.

Three years after Brigham made his observation, the *Origin of Species* appeared, putting the unimpeachable seal of science on the lunch-grab as the Supreme Law of Life and Progress. And it was expressly to refute that philos-ophy on which Brigham Young founded Brigham Young University in 1875: "We have enough and to spare, at present in these mountains, of schools where . . . the teachers . . . dare not mention the principles of the gospel to their pupils, but have no hesitancy in introducing into the classroom the theories of Huxley, or Darwin, or of Miall and the false political economy which contends against co-operation and the United Order. This course I am resolutely and uncompromisingly opposed to. . . . As a beginning in this direction I have endowed the Brigham Young Academy at Provo and [am] now seeking to do the same thing in this city [Salt Lake City]."[15] With his usual unfailing insight, President Young saw it was the economic and political rather than the scientific and biological im-plications of natural selection that were the real danger and most counter to the gospel.

The Two Employers

But what about those goodies that actually descend from the sky, according to the New Astronomy? They take

us back to our Latter-day Saint creation story in which all
the earth's food supply is indeed brought from above, as
seeds of all kinds are carried down and planted in a special
program of preparing the earth for its great calling. "Adam,
we have created for you this earth, and have placed in it
everything you could possibly need—all finished and
ready for use. Help yourself—of every tree thou mayest
freely eat." Was Adam idle and bored, his character un-
dermined by such easy living? Hardly! He went happily
about his work of taking good care of the place; he enjoyed
frequent conversation with angels, and in the cool of the
evening he strolls with the Lord himself—what a vast expansion of mind and spirit that evokes! And to spend one's
days with a woman of infinite understanding, whom age
could not wither nor custom stale, was enough to fill the
days with endless delight. When Adam left the garden,
he went right on with his work of cultivating the earth,
himself, and his numerous posterity, engaging in the three
activities that are recommended as the proper way of life
to all who work in the vineyard: "Behold, I say unto you
that you shall let your time be devoted to [1] the studying
of the scriptures, and [2] to preaching, and to confirming
the church, . . . and [3] to performing your labors on the
land" (D&C 26:1). Study, the work of the kingdom, and
the cultivating of the soil were Adam's calling for almost
a millennium—and he never got bored. Though no longer
in Paradise, he enjoyed the visitation and instruction of
heavenly visitors, who undertook to teach him how he
was to return again to his preexistent splendor with enhanced qualifications and credentials for what lay ahead.
To merit such promotion, he was to be tried and tested
while he was here, and for that express purpose Adam
had to come to an understanding with another type of
visitor, a person of enormous ambition and cunning, who
was purposely turned loose in the place to put Adam and
Eve to the test. What he tempts them with is lunch. We

can put the situation in terms of two employers who are competing for the services of the man Adam and his posterity, who are intentionally placed in the middle between them: on the one hand, "the devil . . . inviteth and enticeth . . . continually" to work for him, while on the other, "God inviteth and enticeth . . . continually" to work for him (Moroni 7:12-13).

The first employer offers us lunch, and since lunch is something everybody must have, he is in a powerful position to bargain. He explains that this glorious earth is his private estate, that it all belongs to him to the ends thereof; in particular he owns the mineral rights and the media of exchange, by controlling which he enjoys the willing cooperation of the military, ecclesiastical, and political establishments, and rules with magnificent uproar. He keeps everything under tight control, though, for all the blood and horror – nobody makes any trouble in his world from the rivers to the ends thereof. Well can he ask Adam, "What is it you want?" for he claims to be the God of this World, and the Lord himself grants him the title of Prince of this World. All who are not working for him on his estate he charges with trespassing, including even heavenly messengers, whom he accuses of spying out his vast property with an eye to taking over the whole of it. But he is willing to make a deal if they have money. To have merely sufficient for your needs, however, is not what he has in mind – that would be the equivalent of the free lunch, lamely ignoring the endless possibilities for acquiring power and gain that the place offers; this developer has a vision of unlimited sweep and power – "You can have anything in this world for money!" Beginning, of course, with lunch. Because money is the only thing that will get you lunch – and since everybody must have lunch, that is the secret of his control.

This almost mystical identity of money with lunch we see in the reports of Brigham Young, Heber C. Kimball, and others of their missions in England, where people were literally starving to death in the streets, while many in the city were living in the greatest opulence. The trouble was that the poor people had to starve because they could get no money, and they could get no money because the factories were closed, and the factories were closed because of an unusually severe winter—an act of God. So there was plainly nothing to be done and no one to blame—one does not oppose the laws of nature and of God: There is *no* free lunch. Brother Kimball tells how his family in this fair land lived for weeks on boiled milkweed; they had worked very hard, but still there was no lunch for them, because the money they had saved up by their diligent toil was suddenly worthless—it is money alone that gets you lunch, mere work is not enough. Your prospective employer explains how that is: The money part is necessary to keep things under control. For the Kimballs, lunch was life itself, the bottom line of any economy. What would happen, then, if lunch was always provided free for them? Would they not lose their most immediate incentive to work—the need for lunch-money? And since money, as they tell you in Economics 101, is "the power to command goods and services," who would ever do any work again? How can you command somebody to work for you if he doesn't need your lunch? That, the shrewd employer explains, is why he must never cease reminding one and all in his domain that there is no free lunch. It is that great teaching which keeps his establishment going. "All I have to do to bring my people into line," he says, "is to ask them: 'If you leave my employ, what will become of you?' That scares the daylights out of them; from the man on the dreary assembly line to the chairman of the board, they are all scared stiff. And so I get things done."

So let us go across the road for an interview with the Other Employer. To our surprise, he answers our first question with an emphatic: "Forget about lunch! Don't

even give it a thought!" "Take no thought of what ye shall
eat or what ye shall drink or wherewith ye shall be
clothed!" "But what will become of me then?" you ask.
Not to worry, "We will preach the gospel to you, and then
you will find out that lunch should be the least of your
concerns." Let Brigham Young explain the situation.

We have been permitted to come here to go to school,
to acquire certain knowledge and take a number of tests
to prepare us for greater things hereafter. This whole life,
in fact, is "a state of probation" (2 Nephi 2:21). While we
are at school our generous patron has provided us with
all the necessities of living that we will need to carry us
through. Imagine, then, that at the end of the first school
year your kind benefactor pays the school a visit. He meets
you and asks you how you are doing. "Oh," you say, "I
am doing very well, thanks to your bounty." "Are you
studying a lot?" "Yes, I am making good progress." "What
subjects are you studying?" "Oh, I am studying courses
in how to get more lunch." "You study that? All the time?"
"Yes. I thought of studying some other subjects. Indeed
I would love to study them—some of them are so fascinating!—but after all it's the bread-and-butter courses that
count. This is the real world, you know. There is no free
lunch." "But my dear boy, I'm providing you with that
right now." "Yes, for the time being, and I am grateful—
but my purpose in life is to get more and better lunches;
I want to go right to the top—the executive suite, the
Marriott lunch." "But that is not the work I wanted you
to do here," says the patron. "The question in our minds
ought to be," says Brigham Young, "what will advance
the general interests . . . and increase intelligence in the
minds of the people[?] To do this should be our constant
study in preference to how shall we secure that farm or
that garden [that is, where the lunch comes from!]. . . . We
cannot worship our God in public meeting or kneel down
to pray in our families without the images of earthly pos-

sessions rising up in our minds to distract them and make our worship and our prayers unprofitable."[16] Lunch can easily become the one thing the whole office looks forward to all morning: a distraction, a decoy — like sex, it is a passing need that can only too easily become an engrossing obsession. Brigham says, "It is a folly for a man to love . . . any other kind of property and possessions. One that places his affections upon such things does not understand that they are made for the comfort of the creature, and not for his adoration. They are made to sustain and preserve the body while procuring the knowledge and wisdom that pertain to God and his kingdom [the school motif], in order that we may preserve ourselves, and live forever in his presence."[17]

And about work? I once had a university fellowship for which I had to agree *not* to accept any gainful employment for the period of a year — all living necessities were supplied: I was actually forbidden to work for lunch. Was it free lunch? I never worked so hard in my life — but I never gave lunch a thought. I wasn't supposed to. I was eating only so that I could do my work; I was not working only so that I could eat. And that is what the Lord asks us: to forget about lunch, and do his work, and the lunch will be taken care of.

Not being an economist, I must here turn to the scriptures, where I find a succinct but detailed and lucid statement of the lunch situation, that is, of God's economic precepts for Israel, in the book of Deuteronomy.

Moses Distributes the Lunch

After Moses had led the children of Israel for forty years, he summed up all the rules and regulations by which they were to live in a great farewell address, which was to be preserved in writing on stone and parchment and periodically and publicly read to all the people. All prosperity and life itself in the new promised land would depend on the strict observance of the law. Certain general principles were to govern every aspect of life among the children of the covenant:

1. This is the law by which you are to live, and the *only law* (Deuteronomy 4:1): "It is your life: and through this ye shall prolong your days in the land" (Deuteronomy 32:47).

2. However impractical and unrealistic these rules and precepts may seem to the world, you are not of the world, but wholly withdrawn from it, a people chosen, set apart, removed, "peculiar," sanctified, "above all people that are on the face of the earth," "an holy people" (Deuteronomy 7:6). Israel is under a special covenant with God that has nothing to do with the normal economy of men; they are forbidden to do some things and required to do others that may seem perfectly absurd to outsiders.

3. The legal aspects of the thing are not what counts — the business of lawyers is to get around the law, but you must have it written in your hearts (Jeremiah 31:33), to keep it "with all thine heart, and with all thy soul," because you really love the Lord and his law, which begins and ends with the love of God and each other (Deuteronomy 6:5). It must be a natural thing with you, taken for granted, your way of life as you think and talk about it all the time, so that your children grow up breathing it as naturally as air (Deuteronomy 6:7-9).

4. Remember that everything you have is a free gift from God: You had nothing and he gave you everything (Mosiah 2:23-25).

5. Never get the idea that you have *earned* what you have; beware lest "when thou hast eaten and art full, . . . then thine heart be lifted up and thou forget the Lord thy God," and you say to yourself: "My power [ability] (*koakh*) and might of mine hand [hard work: *otsem yadhi*, meaning the strength of my hand, or *etzem yadhay*, meaning my own two hands] hath gotten me this wealth [fortune]" (Deu-

teronomy 8:10, 14, 17). But you must bear in mind that God alone has given it all to you, and that it is not for any merit of yours, but for the sake of confirming promises made to your fathers that he has done it—if you forget that for a moment you will be destroyed (Deuteronomy 8:18-19). "And while our flocks and herds were increasing upon the mountains and the plains," said Brigham, "the eyes of the people seemed closed to the operations of the invisible hand of Providence, and they were prone to say, 'It is our own handi-work, it is our labor that has performed this!' "[18]

6. The gifts of God have come to you not because of your righteousness, because you are not righteous, and have in no wise deserved what you have received, nor are you worthy of it (Deuteronomy 9:4-29). It is all given to fulfill promises made to righteous men before you. Moses' parting word to the people after forty years of struggling with them was, "Behold, while I am yet alive with you this day, ye have been rebellious against the Lord; and how much more after my death?" (Deuteronomy 31:27).

As the law is laid down to Israel by Moses, each precept is accompanied by a reminder of their endless obligation to Jehovah, who took them in his charge when they were the lowest of the lowly and brought them with signs and wonders to a land where they have everything. With this in mind, God expects them to be as loving, merciful, and open-handed in dealing with down-and-outers as he has always been with them (see Deuteronomy 15:7-8). With this goes a promise, that no matter how much they give to others, he will always make it up to them many times over, "for the Lord shall greatly bless thee" (Deuteronomy 15:4).

Let us remember that Israel had been living for forty years on a free lunch—manna from heaven. They did not have to work for it; indeed, they were effectively prevented from taking any advantage of such a bonanza—it was simply their daily bread to which everyone had a right and of which no one could take more than he needed for himself on one day. If you ate more, it would make you sick; if with far-sighted business sense you stocked up on it, you would find yourself properly rebuked, for the stuff rotted and stank after twenty-four hours, except on the Sabbath. Every attempt to make the manna an object of free enterprise was ruled out — this was the ultimate free lunch. On the day the people entered the promised land, Moses told them that from then on there would be no more manna — but the free lunch would continue without a break. For in this hill country, he explained, they would be just as dependent on the rain of heaven as they ever were on manna from heaven for their sustenance, and God alone would provide it as ever (Deuteronomy 11:11-15). And what would they do to keep it coming? "If ye shall hearken diligently unto my commandments, . . . I will give you the rain of your land in his due season, . . . that thou mayest gather in thy corn, and thy wine, and thine oil. And I will send the grass . . . for thy cattle, that thou mayest eat and be full" (Deuteronomy 11:13-15).

And what were the specific commandments they are thus enjoined to keep? That is what Deuteronomy is about. A large part of the law is taken up with "forms and observances" (cf. Ezekiel 43:11); in particular, all the people are required to come together at regular intervals to celebrate, feasting and dancing together with great rejoicing, both to thank God for the abundance he had given them and to solicit a continuance of his bounty. Everybody was to have a good time and observe perfect equality in all things, seeing to it that nobody went hungry or neglected. With the first harvest in the new land, they were to bring a basket with samples of all the firstfruits in it, place it before the altar, and say: "a Syrian ready to perish was my father [Amorite, meaning "displaced homeless wanderer, vagrant"], dying of hunger; and he hath brought us into this place, and hath given this land, even a land that floweth with milk and honey. And now, behold, I have brought the firstfruits of the land, which thou, O Lord, hast given me." The starving Syrian in question was Abraham the Hebrew (which also means "a displaced vagrant"). Saying this, "thou shalt set it before the Lord thy God, and worship before the Lord thy God: and thou shalt rejoice in every good thing which the Lord [Jehovah] thy God hath given unto thee, and unto thine house, thou, and the Levite, and the stranger that is among you," to show the Lord: "I have not transgressed thy commandments, neither have I forgotten them" (Deuteronomy 26:5, 9-13). If the people ever fail to observe this joyful activity of giving and sharing, they will suffer a complete reversal of all the promised blessings, "because thou servedst not the Lord [Jehovah] thy God with joyfulness, and with gladness of heart, for the abundance of all things" (Deuteronomy 28:47). In bringing his substance to the Lord, every man shall say: "I have brought away the hallowed things out of mine house" and then "give them unto the Levite and unto the stranger, to the fatherless, and to the widow, according to all thy commandments" (Deuteronomy 26:13). What was thus *hallowed* or *consecrated* to the Lord's work could not be used for any other purpose—it was still manna and not negotiable.

In passing through any field or vineyard in Israel, anyone was free to take what he needed if he was hungry (as the Lord and the apostles did; Mark 2:23); if the owner denied him that, he was breaking the law; if the person took more than he needed for lunch, then *he* was breaking the law—it was still manna (Deuteronomy 23:24-25). When gathering harvest, said the law, never go back to make sure that you have taken all the olives, grapes, or grain of your farm to the barn or to the press. That may be sound business practice, but the Lord forbids it. Some of it must always be left for those who might need it. From the wine and olive presses we get the word "extortion," meaning to squeeze out the last drop, another way to make a margin of profit—putting the squeeze on, wringing out the last drop. The Latter-day Saints, like the ancient Israelites, are to accept God's gifts gratefully and not "by extortion" (D&C 59:20).

The "primitives" and the ancients everywhere celebrated the free gifts of heaven with seasonal rites closely resembling those of the Israelites. The ritual showering of food from heaven was an important part of the ceremonies, dramatized by the actual throwing down of food and tokens from a high platform, mobile or stationary, into the crowd of worshipers. To these rites, which we have treated at some length elsewhere,[19] Israel added a strong sense of moral obligation. Under the Mosaic Law everyone was constantly being tested for his generosity quotient; for as Brigham Young often reminded the Saints, God has placed whatever we have in our hands only to see what we will do with it—whether we will waste, hoard, or bestow it freely. Though generosity cannot be legislated, no one in Israel could get out of taking the proper test, to show how far he was willing to go, granted complete free agency, in carrying out God's express wishes regarding the distribution of his bounties. "A tribute of a freewill offering of thine hand" was required of everyone; the offering could not be evaded, but the *amount* was left entirely up to the giver, "a freewill offering . . . according as the Lord has blessed thee" or, as the Septuagint puts it, "to the limits of your ability." The amount is left up to you because it is you who are being tested (Deuteronomy 16:10).

Thus at the end of six years, a servant must be allowed to leave the master absolutely free of all obligations; and "thou shalt not let him go away empty" (Deuteronomy 15:13); no, nor with two weeks' severance pay, either: "Thou shalt furnish him liberally out of thy flock, and out of the floor, and out of thy winepress, of that wherewith the Lord thy God hath blessed thee thou shalt give unto him" (Deuteronomy 15:14). And then comes the most important part of the test: "Thou shalt surely give him, *and thine heart shall not be grieved when thou givest unto him*" (Deuteronomy 15:10). It is how you really feel about it that counts. If you hear of a poor man in the neighborhood, "thou shalt not harden thine heart, nor shut thine hand from thy poor brother" (Deuteronomy 15:7-11). It is not sound business sense, obedience to orders, compliance with custom, or recognition of duty that are being tested, but the feelings of the heart, the capacity for compassion. No one is ever to charge interest for a loan, and every seven years all debts shall be automatically canceled (Deuteronomy 15:1-2). Only by such a sweeping and uncompromising order as "the Lord's release" can men break the insidious network of indebtedness by which Satan holds all mankind in his power.

But one may not refuse a loan because the Lord's release is near, in which whatever you lent will not have to be paid back: "Beware that there be not a thought in thy wicked heart, saying, The seventh year, the year of release, is at hand; and thine eye be evil against thy poor brother [the calm, appraising stare], and thou givest him nought; and he cry unto the Lord against thee, and it be sin unto thee" (Deuteronomy 15:9). This is an example of that meanness of spirit that offends God more than anything else. We have no laws ordering men to be charitable and open-handed, or penalizing that meanness of spirit that so often means an enhanced profit, for the obvious reason that no one can know what is in the heart of another. But God knows, and meanness of spirit is the one thing he will not tolerate. If one loved God with all his heart and soul and his neighbor as himself, few if any laws would be necessary; for such love, said the Lord, comprises all the Law and the Prophets; laws against base and contemptible actions are unnecessary for people to whom such actions are themselves unthinkable.

Thus, to bring a flawed offering to the temple may be a shrewd and thrifty move, but it "is an abomination unto the Lord" because it is also a mean and petty thing (Deuteronomy 17:1), as are also double bookkeeping and different sets of weights in business (Deuteronomy 25:13). For the strong to take advantage of the weak is the standard pattern of meanness: Israel is not to pull its weight against weaker nations nor "meddle" in their affairs, even in her own interest (Deuteronomy 2:4-5). The greatest of curses was reserved for King Amalek, because he attacked the feeble ones who lagged behind when the Israelites were passing through his land (Deuteronomy 25:17-18). Israel must never forget any favor shown them by another nation, even reluctantly—ingratitude is meanness (Deuteronomy 23:7-25). To make merchandise of another's necessity is an offense to human dignity (though it is the basic principle of present-day employment practice). Thus, if one takes a captive woman to wife and then wants to get rid of her, she must go her way free and not be sold for money, for "thou shalt not make merchandise of her" (Deuteronomy 21:14). Anyone who takes advantage of a virgin must marry her and pay her father handsomely, for "he hath humbled her" (Deuteronomy 22:28-29). One who is just married is not permitted to go to war, for by law he must stay home one year and "cheer up" his bride (Deuteronomy 24:5). It is base to question the virginity of a bride (Deuteronomy 22:13-30), and one who refuses to beget issue by his brother's widow is openly held in contempt, though he cannot be punished—he has offended her human feelings (Deuteronomy 25:5-10). One is required by law not only to shelter any escaped servant who flees to one's house, but also to treat him well, living in his new home "where it liketh him best"; and what is more, the benefactor may not grumble about it—the slave's humanity outweighs all other factors (Deuteronomy 23:15-16).

Particularly reprehensible in Israel was the withholding of lunch from the helpless, the best-known rule of all being that "thou shalt not muzzle the ox when he treadeth out the corn" — that is, to keep him from eating any (Deuteronomy 25:4). We are told that the people of Sodom and Gomorrah put nets over their trees to deny the birds their lunch, and "Abraham, seeing it, cursed them in the name of his God."[20] The Ammonites and Moabites were under a special curse for having refused the Israelites, their enemies, bread and water while marching through their lands (Deuteronomy 23:4) — "aid and comfort to the enemy," indeed! The Iron Law of Wages may never be invoked in Moses' world: "Thou shalt not oppress an hired servant that is poor and needy," that is, by offering him the right to work on your terms (Deuteronomy 24:14). Some of Moses' laws would be quickly repealed by our present legislatures, such as that making it a crime to pretend not to notice when another man's ox or ass has fallen down and needs help (Deuteronomy 22:4) — even as a priest and Levite once looked away from one lying helpless and bloody by the road to Jericho. Regardless of expense, every man must put a railing around the flat roof of his house lest somebody fall and get hurt (Deuteronomy 22:8); that smacks of safety inspection — anathema to industry and especially to our Utah congressmen.

Private Property

In all the law of Moses with its perpetual concern for giving and receiving, there is never any mention whatever of who *deserves* what, whether rich or poor, or who is worthy to receive what he needs — God "maketh his sun to rise on the evil and the good, . . . the just and on the unjust" (Matthew 5:45). *Need* is the only criterion where lunch is concerned. Those who basely set themselves to scrupulously calculate the exact point at which they can open or close their hand to their brother, with meticulous definitions of "the truly needy," should consider how much of what they are giving is "truly private property," since the law of Moses deals impressively with the concept.

The words *property* and *private* have the same root (*prop* = *priv* by Grimm's Law) and emphasize the same thing — that which is the most intimate and personal part of an individual. The *Oxford English Dictionary* specifies "*privatus* — peculiar to oneself . . . that belongs to or is the property of a particular individual; belonging to oneself, one's own." And "*proprius* — own, proper, . . . property, the holding of something as one's own." Both definitions fall back on Old English *agen* (German *eigen*), "expressing tenderness or affection . . . in superlative, very own." Webster has "Latin *privatus* apart from the state . . . of or belonging to one-self, . . . single, private, set apart for himself." What is *privatum* or *proprium* is therefore peculiar to one person alone (not a corporation). It is something that I could not do without, under any social or economic system, and that would have little interest for anyone else, such as my clothes, shoes, books, notes, bedding, glasses, teeth, comb, and so on. Because they are personal and indispensable to me and of no value to anyone else, they must be inalienable to me, for there is great danger if they fall into the hands of another. The bully on the block who grabs another boy's glasses can get him to do almost anything to get them back, because he *must* have them, and the bully knows it. The mill-owner who threatened to withhold lunch from the workers could always get them to work on his terms, claiming their lunches as his private property to dispose of as he chose.

These two totally different views of private property are sharply contrasted in a case often brought to mind by Brigham Young in telling of the good Latter-day Saint businessman who buys a widow's only cow from her for five dollars "and then [goes] down on his knees and thank[s] God for his peculiar blessings to him."[21] The widow's cow was truly her private property and by the law of Moses could not be taken from her. But Old Bessy was something wholly different to the man who saw in her only an addition to his profits. He had no more personal interest, that "tenderness and affection" for one's own, than a dealer has for a thousand acres of canyon land (set aside by God as the proper sphere and element for his other creatures) that he bought last month, hoping to sell it next month to a Chicago syndicate or Arab oil emir for a neat profit. Such cannot be called private property at all.

But lunch is. In Israel every man received a plot of ground, assigned by lot, as his inalienable "inheritance" — it was his lunch and could never be taken from him, even because of debt. It was only as much land as he could "quicken" by his personal labor and loving attention, and no more. The same rule was observed in the settling of the Salt Lake Valley, where no man was allowed to buy and sell land or take more than he could cultivate. The small farm bestowed from tribal lands was also lunch and independence to the early Romans. But when the Conscript Fathers, claiming special privileges by divine decree for and by themselves, seized thousands of farms from the plebs to create their immense estates (the *latifundia*), as the English and Scottish lords did in the nineteenth-century Enclosure Movement, they forced the former owners either to stay on the land and go on working for them as serfs — for lunch only; or to move to the city, where the emperor, as God's vicar on earth, provided the famous "bread and circuses." The landlords, the industrialists of the time, did *not* contribute to the public lunch, the *annona*, which was a ritual and sacred affair, the food and lunch-tickets (*tesserae hospitales*) being actually showered from the skies by the emperor, acting as the kind and generous father of all. This should be noted here, because bread and circuses are routinely deplored as the cause of Rome's decline. What made them demoralizing was their secularization; in the later Rome, in which money was everything, nobody took the divine scheme of things seriously (see the Roman Satirists); lunch was lunch and nothing more. Rome's Zion passed away with Numa, the Roman Enoch. So once lunch was taken care of, the poor Roman had nothing to do but go to the shows and support the political candidates who spent the most on getting elected, while the rich enjoyed their notorious Roman banquets and the depraved pleasures that went with them. For without a sincere religious awareness, the free lunch corrupts rich and poor alike. It is the recognition of divine law that both sanctions and requires the free lunch for everybody.

The closing chapters of Deuteronomy describe point by point the calamities that will befall Israel if every item of the law is not scrupulously observed. It is the exact reverse of the list of blessings promised if the law is kept. And these terrible things are more than warnings; they are specific prophecies of just what is going to happen, and just what did happen to Israel, "because thou servedst not the Lord thy God with joyfulness, and with gladness of heart, for the abundance of all things" (Deuteronomy 28:47). The identical situation obtains in the Book of Mormon, to which we now turn.

King Benjamin and the Free Lunch

In the time of Lehi, to judge by the Lachish letters and other evidence, the ruling party in Jerusalem was sponsoring an enthusiastic revival of the law of Moses in its purity. The trend is signified by the large proportion of personal names ending in -*yahu* or -*iah*, referring to Jahweh, Jehovah the Lord, who gave the law. Five hundred years later there was another such revival among the Nephites, led by a pious and learned king, Benjamin, who was determined to preserve the same law in its purity. The name he gave his son Mosiah is clear indication of the survival of the tradition, of which King Benjamin by his dedicated studies was well aware. At the end of his reign he does exactly what Moses and later Joshua did: he summoned all the people together in the great annual assembly (they brought their firstlings with them) to hear a final exposition of the law from him as he handed over the rule and priesthood to his son. His great farewell address covers the same points as did that of Moses, yet it is highly original.

In both books, Deuteronomy and Mosiah, the great discourse on the law is divided into two parts. The first deals with the nature, importance, and purpose of the law. The history of Israel is traced from the beginning and the steps by which the people were brought to a knowledge of Jehovah, recounting their trials, tribulations, follies, punishments, and rewards. The holy nature of the covenant they have entered into is presented to them, and the glorious rewards and terrible punishments connected with it. In both books, the promised rewards are the same: You will prosper in the land the Lord has given you, heaven and earth will bring forth in abundance, you will never have to fear a foreign enemy — success and security should be yours, for "a thousand generations" (Deuteronomy 7:9). "That ye may prosper in the land according to the promises which the Lord made unto our fathers," says Benjamin, consciously appending his words to those of Moses (Mosiah 1:7). "Ye shall prosper in the land, and your enemies shall have no power over you" (Mosiah 2:31).

For his great farewell address, Benjamin summoned all the people to gather by families around the temple, bringing "the firstlings . . . that they might offer sacrifice and burnt offerings according to the law of Moses; . . . that they might rejoice and be filled with love towards God and all men" (Mosiah 2:2-4). There you have it in a nutshell. He begins his discourse on an economic note: "[I] have not sought gold nor silver, nor any manner of riches of you" (Mosiah 2:12). "I, myself, have labored with mine own hands. . . . I can answer a clear conscience before God this day. . . . Learn that when ye are in the service of your fellow beings ye are only in the service of your God" (Mosiah 2:14-15, 17). "I, whom ye call your king, am no better than ye yourselves are" (Mosiah 2:26). He is setting the keynote, which is absolute *equality*. And that follows naturally from the proposition that we owe everything to God, to whom we are perpetually and inescapably in debt beyond our means of repayment: "*In the first place*, . . . ye are indebted unto him . . . and will be forever and ever" (Mosiah 2:23-24). Let no one boast that he has earned or produced a thing: "Therefore, of what can ye boast? . . . Can ye say aught of yourselves? I answer you, Nay," right down to the dust of the earth, it all "belongeth to him who created you" (Mosiah 2:24-25). It is his property, not yours! What is more, no one can even pay his own way in the world, let alone claim a surplus: "If ye should serve him who . . . is preserving you from day to day . . . and even supporting you from one moment to another—I say if you should serve *him* with all your whole souls yet ye would be unprofitable servants," in other words, consuming more than you produce, unable even to support yourselves (Mosiah 2:21).

And what do we do, then, to qualify for his blessings? "Behold, all that he requires of you is to keep his commandments; and he has promised you that if ye would keep his commandments ye should prosper in the land" (Mosiah 2:22). It never fails, says Benjamin, "if ye do keep his commandments he doth bless and prosper you" (Mosiah 2:22) and in return, "ye are eternally indebted to your heavenly Father, to render to him all that you have and are" (Mosiah 2:34), which is simply the law of consecration.

In his preliminary address, Benjamin, like Moses, impresses upon the people at length the great importance of the instructions he is about to give them, their binding

obligation to keep them, and the great rewards that will
follow. He purposely gets them into a high state of anticipation by telling them (confidentially) that what he is
about to give them was made known to him personally
"by an angel from God," so that this is indeed a divine
restoration of the law that is being celebrated (Mosiah 3:2).
Furthermore, he assures them that it is all *good* news, "that
thou mayest rejoice [said the angel]; and that . . . thy
people . . . may also be filled with joy" (Mosiah 3:4), for
all this looks forward to the coming of the Lord. Eager as
they are, the people must again be cautioned before the
law itself is set before them, for though the law of Moses
is adapted to their weaker natures, these people, like those
taught by Moses, remain "a stiffnecked people" (Mosiah
3:14), and after all God did for them, "yet they hardened
their hearts" (Mosiah 3:15). "For the natural man is an
enemy to God . . . and will be forever and ever, unless
he . . . becometh as a child, submissive, meek, humble,
patient, full of love, willing to submit to all things" (Mosiah
3:19). At this point Benjamin again follows Moses' example
by declaring that the words "which the Lord thy God hath
commanded thee . . . shall stand as a bright testimony
against this people" (Mosiah 3:22, 24).

Thus ended the first address of King Benjamin, by
which the people were quite overcome, crying out for forgiveness and receiving a manifestation of the Spirit that
filled them with joy (Mosiah 4:2-3).

Benjamin now recognized that they were ready to
"hear and understand the remainder of [his] words," because at last they were "awakened . . . to a sense of [their]
nothingness, and [their] worthless and fallen state" (Mosiah 4:4-5), aware that they could only put their "trust in
the Lord, . . . keeping his commandments. . . . Believe in
God; . . . believe that ye must repent; . . . always retain
in remembrance, the greatness of God, and your own nothingness, and his goodness and longsuffering. . . . If ye do

this ye will always rejoice, and be filled with the love of God" (Mosiah 4:9-13). That being so, "ye will not have a mind to injure one another, but to live peaceably, and to render to every man according to that which is his due" (Mosiah 4:13). And who decides what is due him? Not you! The Lord will tell you that: "And ye will not suffer your children that they go hungry, or naked, [or] . . . transgress the laws of God" (Mosiah 4:14). Lunch will be provided, and "ye will teach them to love one another, and to serve one another," with no fighting or quarreling among themselves—this was not to be a competitive society (Mosiah 4:15). And beyond your family, "ye yourselves will succor those that stand in need of your succor; ye will administer of your substance unto him." A beggar is one who asks, for some reason or other not having what he needs: "Ye will not suffer that the beggar putteth up his petition to you in vain, and turn him out to perish" (Mosiah 4:16). He begs because he is hungry, and we must all eat to stay alive—to turn any beggar down, for all you know, is to sentence him to death—it has happened (Mosiah 4:16). The usual pious appeal to the work-ethic—there is no free lunch—will not do: "Perhaps thou shalt say: The man has brought upon himself his misery; therefore I . . . will not give unto him of my food, nor impart unto him of my substance that he may not suffer, for his punishments are just"—I worked for mine! (Mosiah 4:17). Indolent and unworthy the beggar may be—but that is not your concern: It is better, said Joseph Smith, to feed ten impostors than to run the risk of turning away one honest petition. Anyone who explains why he denies help to another who needs it, says Benjamin, "hath great cause to repent . . . and hath no interest in the kingdom of God" (Mosiah 4:18), which kingdom is built up on the law of consecration. "For behold, are we not all beggars?" That is no mere rhetoric—it is literally true: we are all praying for what we have not earned. No one is independent: "Do we not all depend upon the same Being, even God, for . . . food and raiment, and for gold, and for silver and for all the riches which we have? . . . You are *dependent* for your lives and for all that ye have and are" (Mosiah 4:19-20). And that is just what you must consecrate to the building up of the kingdom: "O then, how ye ought to impart of the substance that ye have one to another" (Mosiah 4:21-22). We all give and we all receive, and never ask who is worthy and who is not, for the simple reason that *none* of us is worthy, all being "unprofitable servants" (Mosiah 2:21). "And if ye judge the man" who asks for your "substance that he perish not," and find him unworthy, "how much more just will be *your* condemnation for withholding your substance, *which doth not belong to you* but to God," who wants you to hand it on and is testing you to see just how willing you are to hand it back to him when he asks for it—not at some comfortably unspecified date, but right now (Mosiah 4:22). Benjamin says he is speaking here to the rich, but the poor may not hold back either, for everyone should have enough but not wish for more; hence the poor who want to be rich, who "covet that which [they] have not received," are also guilty (Mosiah 4:24-25). In giving, the poor may keep what is sufficient for their needs, and food, clothing, and shelter covers it (Mosiah 4:26), for the rule is summed up simply, that every man "should impart of [his] substance to the poor, every man according to that which he hath"—which is also the wording of Deuteronomy, for all have a right to food, clothing, shelter and medical care, "both spiritually and temporally *according to their wants*" (Mosiah 4:26; 18:29).

Benjamin ends with the wise remark that no list of prohibitions would be sufficient to keep the people from sin: "Finally, I cannot tell you all the things whereby ye may commit sin; for there are divers ways and means, even so many that I cannot number them" (Mosiah 4:29). Instead of telling them what they should not do, he has told them what they absolutely must do, the minimum if they would expect God's blessings. If one who has more than he really needs (and without what he truly needs, he would, in fact, be one of the "truly needy") withholds it from those who do not have enough, he is stealing, holding on to that "which doth not belong to you, but to God" (Mosiah 4:22), who wants to see it distributed equally.

And that ends King Benjamin's discourse, devoted not to pious and high-sounding generalities but to the rule that whoever has more than he can eat must share to the limit of his resources with those who do not have enough. Two things are stressed in the address — *need* and the feeling of *dependence*. As to need, not a word is said from first to last about hard work, thrift, enterprise, farsightedness, and so on, the usual preludes to the No-Free-Lunch lecture, and wo to the man who questions another's qualifications for lunch, for "the same hath great cause to repent" (Mosiah 4:18).

The second issue is independence. Charged with a special emotional impact for Americans, the word has become a fetish for the Latter-day Saints and led them into endless speculations and plans. "They that will be rich fall into temptation and a snare," says Paul — all of which the Lord has strictly forbidden (1 Timothy 6:9). In the scriptures the word *independent* occurs only once, describing the church with no reference to any individual: "The church may stand *independent* above all *other* creatures" because it is entirely dependent on "*my* providence" (D&C 78:14). It is dependence that is important for Benjamin, total dependence on God; and if you serve him with your *whole* heart and with your *whole* soul, you are free from dependence on any other being. In the law of Moses, the Lord's release cancels all indebtedness of man, while God transfers his claims on our indebtedness to the poor; it is through them that he asks us to pay our debt to him. Let us refer back for the moment to Satan's promise of independence. When, following Satan's instructions, Cain murdered "his brother Abel, for the sake of getting gain" (Moses 5:50), he declared his independence: "And Cain gloried in that which he had done, saying: I am *free*; surely the flocks of my brother falleth into my hands!" (Moses 5:33). Recently this gospel was proclaimed by one of the richest Americans addressing the student body of Ohio State University (on TV): "There is nothing that gives freedom," he said, "like bucks in the bank." This seems to be the policy we are following today, and there is no doubt whose policy it is.

Feeding the Multitudes

With the coming of the Lord in the meridian of time, the feasts of thanksgiving and supplication continued, yet without the shedding of blood, except at Easter, when the paschal lamb, like the earlier blood offerings of the temple, remained a similitude of the great atoning sacrifice. The Lord's Supper and the *agape* (love, charity) were meals of real food, shared whenever the Saints came together for a meeting; and when the Lord visited them after the resurrection, he routinely shared a real meal with them, in which he provided the food, looking forward to the time when they would all share in the new wine of the world to come.

The Lord gave lunch to the people in the first place simply because they were hungry, they needed it, and he "was moved with compassion" (Matthew 14:14, 15:32). He both fed them and taught them, but the knowledge was worth far more than the food—he told them not to labor for that (John 6:27). When he miraculously produced the lunch, they wanted to accept him as their prophet and king (John 6:14-15), even as the Nephites, who when they had eaten and were filled all burst out in one joyful chorus of praise and thanksgiving (3 Nephi 20:9). Why the excitement? Hadn't they ever eaten dinner before? That had nothing to do with it; what thrilled them was seeing clearly and unmistakably the hand of the giver, and knowing for themselves exactly where it all comes from and that it can never fail. Now if we ask, Who at these love-feasts got the biggest share or ate the most? we at once betray the poverty and absurdity of our own precious work-ethic. Such questions would be nothing short of blasphemous to all present, as if one were to interrupt the ordinances and stop the feast by announcing: "Hold it right there, you people! Don't you know that there is *no free lunch*?"

The free lunch looms large in the Sermon on the Mount. First the Lord's Prayer: "*Give* us this day our *daily* bread" (Matthew 6:11); this comes with the understanding, expressed in the same sentence, that in return we are to show the same free and liberal spirit toward each other that he does to all of us: "And forgive our debts as *we* forgive our debtors." Next comes fasting, a most effective reminder of God's generosity to us and also of our complete dependence on him, a thing to be joyfully acknowledged (Matthew 6:16-18). Then an all-important principle; you cannot have it both ways, you cannot work for both employers, you cannot lay up treasures both on earth and in heaven—you cannot divide your heart between them; for to one master or the other you must give your *whole* and *undivided* devotion—both employers demand that, but only one of them can have it (Matthew 6:19-20). You must go one way or the other, there can be no compromise. "No man *can* serve two masters": love and hate cannot be divided up between them, "ye *cannot* serve God and Mammon," *mammon* being to this day the regular Hebrew word for business, particularly money and banking (Matthew 6:22-24). You must not yield to the enticings of that other master, nor let his threat of "no lunch if you leave my employ" intimidate you—you must ignore him and his arguments completely: "*Take no thought* for your life, what ye shall eat, or what ye shall drink; nor yet . . . what ye shall put on" (Matthew 6:25). All such things are taken

care of for God's creatures: "Behold the fowls of the
air, . . . your heavenly Father feeds them. Are ye not much
better than they?" (Matthew 6:26). It was the practice in
Sodom and Gomorrah, we are told, to rob all strangers of
their money and then let them starve to death because they
could not buy food; and the cities' inhabitants would put
nets over their trees so that the birds would have no free
lunch on *their* fruit. For Abraham, such meanness, as we
have seen, was the last straw, and "he cursed them in the
name of his God."[22]

On the subject of dress and appearance the same rule
holds as for lunch—sufficient covering is necessary, but
don't go beyond that. If you cannot add a cubit to your
stature, don't try to add other splendors to your person
that it does not possess: forget the obsession with an impressive appearance that goes with aspiring to the executive lunch ("dressing for success"); simply appear as what
you are, and don't fuss so much about it (Matthew 6:27-
30). "Therefore," he says again, "*take no thought*, saying,
What shall we eat? or, What shall we drink? or Wherewithal
shall we be clothed?" (Matthew 6:31). The Gentiles spend
their time going after these things—but you are not Gentiles.

Now comes a most enlightening explanation of the
economics of the gospel, the answer to the natural question, How shall we get on in the world if we don't even
think about such things? The injunction "take no thought"
must be taken seriously, since it is one of the most oft-
repeated in the scriptures, occurring in all the Gospels, in
the Book of Mormon, and the Doctrine and Covenants.
Here the formula "all these things" applies specifically to
what we must eat, drink, and wear—food and covering
(Matthew 6:32). It occurs three times as an objective clause,
and the key word is *seek*. In the same breath we are told
that the Gentiles *seek* after all these things, but *we* are
definitely *not* to seek after them. We are to be busy *seeking*

after something else, "the kingdom of God, and his [its] righteousness" (Matthew 6:33). But what about the other things, won't we need food and clothing too? Of course, they are very important, and you can rest assured that "your heavenly Father knoweth that ye have need of all these things" (Matthew 6:32), and he will provide them. If you have enough faith to trust him (Matthew 6:30) and spend your days seeking what *he* wants you to seek, he will provide "all these things" as you need them (*prostethesetai*).

"But seek ye first (*proton*) the kingdom of God and his righteousness, and all these things will be added" (Matthew 6:33). It has become customary to interpret this as meaning that one should *first* go on a mission or get a testimony some other way, and *then* turn to the business of getting ahead in the world. But the word for first, *proton*, means first in every sense— first and foremost, before all else, in preference to all else, and so on. It usually refers to time, but not in this passage. We are not told to seek first the kingdom and *then* seek "all these things"; nothing whatever is said about seeking them except the explicit command *not* to seek them. There is no idea of a time sequence here: Does one ever stop seeking the kingdom of God and his righteousness in this life, or was there ever a time before, during, or after a mission when one did *not* need food and clothing? We are not to seek them *ever*, for God supplies them *ever*.

The same teachings of the Lord are summarized in Luke 12, where he makes it quite clear that the command to "take no thought" applies not only to the apostles but to the entire church (Luke 12:22). He illustrates the principle of taking no thought for the morrow by the story of a man big in agribusiness (though it is only fair to note that it was a particularly fertile piece of ground and not the owner that "brought forth plentifully" and that the man himself did not, of course, do any work in the field). When with foresight and planning he had completed his arrangements for a splendid retirement, he congratulated himself, saying, "My soul, take thine ease, eat, drink, and be merry" — the deluxe lunch assured complete independence forever, with no humiliating necessity of praying for daily bread. "But God said unto him, Thou *fool!* This night thy soul shall be required of thee" (Luke 12:16, 19-20). Shouldn't he have worked for lunch at all, then? Answer: He should neither have made it the goal of his labors nor got it by manipulating others.

God is not pleased with those who rebuff his offer of free lunch with pious sermons about the work ethic: "A certain king . . . made a marriage for his son, and sent forth his servants to call them that were bidden to the wedding: and they would not come. Again he sent forth, . . . saying, . . . I have prepared my dinner, . . . and all things are ready. . . . But they made light of it, and went their ways, one to his farm, another to his merchandise" (Matthew 22:2-5). Back to the office and the farm as they virtuously called attention to solid work to be done and "made light" of mere partying. Yet it was a gross insult to their generous host. "Deny not the gifts of God!" is the final plea of the Book of Mormon (Moroni 10:8). Who would despise such gifts? We do, by not asking for them: "Yea, I know that God will give liberally to him that asketh" (2 Nephi 4:35), and they receive not because they ask not (2 Nephi 32:4). Moroni enumerates the spiritual gifts in the last chapter of the Book of Mormon, yet we rarely ask for these gifts today—they don't particularly interest us. There is only one that we do ask for in all sincerity, and duly receive, and that, for obvious reasons, is the gift of healing. But the other gifts? Who cares for them? We make light of them and prefer the real world of everyday life. We do not even ask for the *temporal* gifts, because we don't want them either—as gifts.

"Ye are cursed because of your riches," says Samuel

to the people of Zarahemla, "and also are your riches cursed." Why? For two reasons: (1) "because you have set your hearts upon them," and (2) you "have not hearkened unto the words of him who *gave* them unto you. Ye do not remember the Lord your God in the things with which he hath blessed you, but ye *do* always remember your riches, not to thank the Lord your God for them" (Helaman 13:21-22). They wanted the riches desperately, worked for them diligently, and were obsessed with them once they had them; but they simply would not accept them *as gifts*, but only as earnings. Today we have gone so far as to drop the idea of "unearned increment" and insist on labeling all income, even that of which the recipient is totally unaware, as "earnings." Nobody is going to make *us* accept welfare!

Enough Is Enough

"Having food and raiment," says Paul to Timothy, "let us be therewith content" (1 Timothy 6:8). We must have sufficient for our needs in life's journey, but to go after more is forbidden, though you have your God-given free agency to do so. "Our real wants are very limited," says Brigham; "When you have what you wish to eat and sufficient clothing to make you comfortable you have all that you need; I have all that I need."[23] How many people need to eat two lunches a day? We all eat too much, wear too much, and work too much. Brigham says if we all "work less, wear less, eat less, . . . we shall be a great deal wiser, healthier, and wealthier people than by taking the course we now do."[24]

It should not take too much hard work to assure anyone of the makings of a lunch; but what is one to do after that? That is the question. Aristotle's famous dictum in the *Nichomachean Ethics I,* that our proper function on earth is not just to live but to live well, to live as we can and should, reminds us that there should be no serious economic problems at the human level: after all, mice, cockroaches, elephants, butterflies, and dolphins have all solved the economic problem—their mere existence on earth after thousands of years of vicissitudes is adequate proof that they have found the secret of survival. Can we do no better than to dedicate all our time and energy to solving just that one problem, as if our whole object in life were simply lunch? "What is a man," asks Shakespeare, "if his chief good and market of his time be but to sleep and feed? A beast, no more. Sure he that made us with such large discourse, looking before and after, gave us not that capability and god-like reason to fust in us unused."[25] And what is it to be used for? Those very popular how-to-get-rich books, which are the guides to the perplexed of the present generation, say we should keep our minds fixed at all times on just one objective; the person who lets his thoughts wander away from anything but business even for a moment does not deserve the wealth he seeks. Such is the high ethic of the youth today. And such an ethic places us not on the level of the beast but below it.

For today many a TV documentary will show you the beasts of the field not spending their days perpetually seeking out and consuming each other for lunch, as we have been taught, but in pleasant relaxation, play, family fun, bathing, exploring (for many of them have lively curiosity), grooming, sparring, and much happy napping, and so on. Even the most efficient killers hunt only every few days when they are really hungry, kill only weaker members of the herds (thus strengthening the stock), and never take more than they need, usually sharing it with others. We see leopards, lions, and tigers between meals calmly loping through herds of exotic ungulates, who hardly bother to look up from their grazing at the passing visitors. It is only the human predator who keeps a twenty-four-hour lookout for victims in the manner prescribed in the flourishing contemporary success literature.

"No free lunch" easily directs our concern to "nothing but lunch." The Adversary keeps us to that principle, making lunch our full-time concern either by paying workers so little that they must toil day and night just to afford lunch (his favorite trick), or by expanding the lunch-need to include all the luxury and splendor that goes with the super-executive Marriott lunch, about which Paul's letter to Timothy is most instructive. Let us return to it, considering the passage in the "original": "Having adequate nourishment (*diatrophas*) and decent covering (*skepasmata*) we shall with these suffice ourselves (*arkesthēsometha*). But those who want to be rich (*ploutein*) fall into temptation (*peirasmon*, a test) and a snare (*pagida*, a trap, noose, decoy), and into hankering for many things (*epithumias*, a passionate desire to possess) which are silly (*anoētous*, mindless, senseless) and harmful (*blaberas*), and which drag (*buthizousi*, plunge) human beings down to ruin (*olethron*, deadly danger) and utter destruction (*apōleian*). For the root (*rhiza*) of all evil doings (*pantōn tōn kakōn*) is the desire for money (*philargyria*, cash-loving), being driven by which people have gone astray, got lost (*apeplanēthēsan;* Hebrew, *abad*, stray from the path) from the faith and become hopelessly involved (*peripeiran*, spitted, entangled) in agonizing situations (*odunais*, rapids, pangs). But thou, O man of God, keep away from these things" (1 Timothy 6:8-11). The Lord teaches the same lesson when he tells how members of the church fall away because of "the cares of this world, and the deceitfulness of riches, and the lusts of other things entering in, [which] choke the word (*logos*), and it becometh unfruitful (*akarpos*, fruitless, barren) (Mark 4:19; Matthew 13:22).

The parables of the Lord are particularly rich in matters relevant to the free lunch, and in them Jesus appeals before all things against meanness of spirit. What could be more abominable than to "offend one of these little ones," taking advantage of the helpless? What shall we say of one who uses the gifts that God has given him to take from others, no matter how legally, the gifts God intends to give them? "The kingdom of heaven is like a certain king. . . . One was brought unto him which owed him 10,000 talents. . . . The servant fell down, . . . saying, Lord, have patience with me and I will pay thee all. Then the Lord of that servant was moved with compassion, . . . and forgave him the debt. But the same servant went out and found one of his fellow-servants, which owed him an hundred pence: and he laid hands on him and took him by the throat, saying, Pay me that thou owest," and had him taken to prison (Matthew 18:28). It was all perfectly legal — we cannot legislate pity and compassion; altruism, argued Ayn Rand, is the greatest weakness in our society and the greatest obstacle to the unhindered operation of free enterprise.[26] But the kingdom of heaven, of which the Lord is here speaking, does not operate on that principle: "O, thou wicked servant, I forgave thee all that debt, because thou desiredst me," said the Lord. "Shouldest not thou also have had compassion on thy fellowservant, even as I had pity on thee?" (Matthew 18:23-35). Then the king "delivered him to the tormentors, till he should pay all that was due to him. So likewise shall my heavenly Father do also unto you, if ye from your hearts forgive not every one his brother their trespasses [or debts, the word is *aphete*, cancel a debt]" (Matthew 18:34-35).

And You Are to Be Equal

For the last days everyone has been invited to work for the kingdom with singleness of purpose and to enjoy the free lunch of the Saints. The first words of the Lord to the youthful Joseph after he had introduced himself in the grove were, "Behold the world lieth in sin at this time and none doeth good no not one. . . . And mine anger is kindling against the inhabitants of the earth to visit them acording [sic] to this ungodliness."[27] That being the present situation, we may well ask just what it is that renders the present world so depraved. The answer is loud and clear: "Behold, the beasts of the field and the fowls of the air, and that which cometh of the earth, is ordained for the use of man for food and for raiment, and that he might have in abundance" (D&C 49:19). Malthus was wrong; there is no need for grabbing, "for the earth is full, and there is enough and to spare" (D&C 104:17). And what is wrong just now? But it is not given that one man should possess that which is above another, *wherefore the world lieth in sin*" (D&C 49:20). So that is where the offense lies; some are taking more than they should and using the power it gives them over others to make them do their bidding. But how much is too much? "And wo be unto man that sheddeth blood or that wasteth flesh *and hath no need*" (D&C 49:21). The one criterion for taking is *need*, specifically "for food and raiment," not for sport or display.

We begin, as in the other scriptures, with the basic principle that everything we have is a free gift from God: "The earth [is] my very handiwork, and all things therein are mine; . . . and behold this is the way that I, the Lord, have decreed to provide for my saints" (D&C 104:14, 16). That does not mince matters but gets right down to business. He wants us all equal, "that the poor shall be exalted, in that the rich are made low" (D&C 104:16). And he wants to make us co-workers in the project, which is all for our benefit: "It is expedient that I, the Lord, should make every man accountable, as a steward over earthly blessings, which I have made and prepared for my creatures" (D&C 104:13). He wants all his creatures to enjoy his bounty, with never a mention of who is worthy or deserving— as ever, the only principle of distribution is that of need: "You are to be equal, or in other words, you are to have equal claims on the properties for . . . your stewardships, every man according to his wants and his needs, inasmuch as his wants are just" (D&C 82:17). That limitation on wants is important, since one often wants what one should not have; a want is "justified" only when it is a true need, and as we have seen, our real needs are few — "food and raiment," mansions and yachts not included. In introducing this particular revelation, the Lord repeats for the third time what he has said in the grove: "The anger of God kindleth against the inhabitants of the earth; and none doeth good, for all have gone out of the way" (D&C 82:6). And always the same reason is given for that anger, that men withhold God's gifts from each other in a power-game, and that this is the prevailing evil of the age.

How do we distribute it then? "I have given unto the children of men to be agents unto themselves" (D&C 104:17). You are perfectly free to make all the money you can; just as you are perfectly free to break any one of the Ten Commandments, as millions do every day, though God has forbidden it, as he has forbidden seeking for riches. But your behavior once you have entered a covenant with God will be judged by the standards *he* sets: "Therefore, if any man shall take of the abundance which I have made and impart not his portion, according to the law of my gospel, unto the poor and the needy, he shall, with the wicked, lift up his eyes in hell, being in torment" (D&C 104:18). A clear reference to the rich man who fed Lazarus the beggar with crumbs (Luke 16:23).

Modern revelation has some interesting things to say about idlers: "Let every man be diligent in all things. And the idler shall not have place in the church" (D&C 75:29). We are all to work in the kingdom and *for* the kingdom. "And the inhabitants of Zion also shall remember their labors, inasmuch as they are *appointed* to labor, . . . for the idler shall be had in remembrance before the Lord" (D&C 68:30). Note that it is not the withholding of lunch but the observant eye of the Lord that admonishes the idler. This refers to all of us as laborers in Zion, and "the laborer in Zion shall labor for Zion; for if they labor for money they shall perish" (2 Nephi 26:31). That is the theme here: "Now, I, the Lord, am not well pleased with the inhabitants of Zion, for there are idlers among them; . . . they also seek not earnestly the riches of eternity, but their eyes *are* full of greediness" (D&C 68:31). An idler in the Lord's book is one who is not working for the building up of the kingdom of God on earth and the establishment of Zion, no matter how hard he may be working to satisfy his own greed. Latter-day Saints prefer to ignore that distinction as they repeat a favorite maxim of their own invention, that the idler shall not eat the bread or wear the clothing of the laborer. And what an ingenious argument they make of it! The director of a Latter-day Saint Institute was recently astounded when this writer pointed out to him that the ancient teaching that the idler shall not eat the bread of the laborer has always meant that the idle rich shall not eat the bread of the laboring poor, as they always have. "To serve the classes that are living on them," Brigham Young reports from England, "the poor, the laboring men and women are toiling, working their lives out to earn that which will keep a little life in them [lunch is what they get out of it, and no more]. Is this equality? No! What is going to be done? The Latter-day Saints will never accomplish their mission until this inequality shall cease on the earth."[28] But the institute director was amazed, because he had always been taught that the idle *poor* should not eat the bread of the laboring *rich*, because it is perfectly obvious that a poor man has not worked as hard as a rich man. With the same lucid logic my Latter-day Saint students tell me that there were no poor in the Zion of Enoch because only the well-to-do were admitted to the city.

But quite apart from who works hardest, how can the meager and insufficient lunch of a poor child possibly deprive a rich man's dinner table of the vital proteins and calories he needs? It can only be the other way around. The extra food on the rich man's table does not belong to him, says King Benjamin, but to God, and *he* wants the poor man to have it (Mosiah 4:22). The moral imperative of the work-ethic is by no means the eternal law we assume it to be, for it rests on a completely artificial and cunningly contrived theory of property. Few seem to be aware today that less than fifty years ago it was considered among the upper classes of England to be a disgrace to *work* for a living, and the landed gentry refused intimate contact with families who were (sniff) "in trade," in other words, business. It is custom alone and not an eternal law of nature that gives us our attitude toward these things.

A common objection to the economic equality on which the scriptures insist is that it would produce a drab, monotonous sameness among us. But that sameness already exists—we all have about the same number of eyes, ears, arms, and legs. Few people are twice as tall or twice as short as the average, and Binet was unable to come up with an IQ double the average. Also, few of us need two lunches a day. We might as well face it, we are all very much alike in such things, though the thought mortally offends some people. It is in the endless reaches of the mind, expanding forever in all directions, that infinite variety invites us, with endless space for all so that none need be jealous of another. It is those who seek distinction in costly apparel, living quarters, diversions, meals, cars, and estates who become the slaves of fashion and the most stereotyped people on earth. And it is because communism is a "dialectical *materialism*" that it is the drabbest show of all, though our rival establishment is not far behind. "You may say," says Brigham, " 'If we live, we must eat, drink, and wear clothing'; and 'He that provideth not for his own household, has denied the faith, and is worse than an infidel'; [by 'providing' the same writer means 'food and raiment . . . and therewith content'] numberless arguments of this kind will present themselves to the minds of the people, *to call them away from the line of their duty.*"[29]

It is Satan's clever decoy to that fervid consumerism (Veblen's "conspicuous consumption") that is a confession of mental, moral, and spiritual bankruptcy.

Brigham Young also noted, however, that if the wealth were equally distributed one fine day, it would not be long before it would be as unequal as ever, the lion's share going to the most dedicated and competent seekers for it. True enough. But wealth is not lunch, and to make it such is an offense against nature. Let us say the lunch is equally distributed one day, and soon one man because of his hustle is sitting daily on seventy thousand lunches while many people are going without. He generously offers them the chance to work for him and get their lunches back— but they must work all day, just for him and just for lunch. Lunch and the satisfaction of helping their generous employer to get hold of yet more lunches (for that is the object of their work) are all they get out of it. Is this an exaggeration? Come with me to the mines of Scotland in which my grandparents toiled, as described by them and by Her Majesty's Commission on the Labour of Women and Children in Mines, 1842:

> Children are taken into these mines to work as early as four years of age, . . . often from seven to eight, while from eight to nine is the ordinary age. . . . Female Children begin to work in these mines at the same early ages as the males. . . . Parish apprentices, who are bound to serve their masters until twenty-one years of age, . . . shall receive *only* food and clothing. [Lunch is what they *live* for.] The employment . . . assigned to the youngest Children . . . requires that they should be in the pit as soon as the work of the day commences, and . . . not leave the pit before the work of the day is at an end. . . . Children engaged in it are commonly excluded from light and are *always* without companions. . . . In some districts they remain in solitude and darkness during the whole time they are in the pit. . . . *Many* of them

never see the light of day for weeks together. . . . From
six years old and upwards, the hard work . . . begins,
. . . [requiring] the unremitting exertion of all the physical power which the young workers possess. . . . Both
sexes are employed together in precisely the same kind
of labour. . . . [All] commonly work almost naked. . . . In the East of Scotland [where the Nibleys were
so employed], a much larger proportion of Children and
Young Persons are employed, . . . and . . . the chief
part of their labour consists in carrying the coals on their
backs up steep ladders. . . . The regular hours of work
for Children . . . are *rarely* less than eleven; more often
they are twelve; in some districts they are thirteen; and
in one district they are generally fourteen and *upwards*. . . . In the great majority of these mines night-
work is part of the ordinary system of labour. . . . The
labour . . . is . . . generally uninterrupted by any regular time set apart for rest and refreshment; what *food*
is taken in the pit being eaten as best it may while the
labour continues. [Why not? If there is no free lunch,
why should there be a free lunch *hour?*] In many mines
the conduct of the adult colliers to the Children . . . is
harsh and cruel; the persons in authority in these mines,
who must be cognizant of this ill-usage, never interfere
to prevent it. . . . Little interest is taken by the coal owners in the Children. . . . In *all* the coal-fields accidents
of a fearful nature are extremely frequent. . . . *No* money
appears to be expended with a view to secure the safety,
much less the comfort, of the workpeople. . . . Very
generally in the East of Scotland, the food is poor in
quality, and insufficient in quantity; the Children themselves say that they have not enough to eat; and the
Sub-Commissioners describe them as covered with
rags, . . . confining themselves to their homes on the
Sundays [because] . . . they have no clothes to go
in. . . . Notwithstanding the intense labour performed
by these Children, they do not procure even sufficient
food and raiment. . . . The employment in these mines
commonly produces . . . stunted growth of the

body. . . . The long hours of work, [etc.], in *all* the districts, deteriorates the physical constitution. . . . The limbs become crippled and the body distorted. . . . Muscular powers give way. . . . This class of the population is commonly extinct soon after fifty.[30]

One thinks of the infamous Roman mines, the ultimate in human horror stories; yet the workers there were all condemned criminals and enemies captured as slaves— these in Great Britain were innocent little children. No free lunch to undermine *their* characters! The pious mine-owners even waived the sacred imperative of the Sabbath in their case—even that yielded to the sanctity of the work-ethic: "A custom bearing with extreme hardship upon Children and Young Persons [is] . . . that of continuing the work without any interruption whatever during the Sunday," when "the labour . . . is continued for twenty-four hours in succession"[31]—a twenty-four-hour shift to make up for the every other Sunday they have off! When some proprietors tried doing away with the system, it was found that it was "without disadvantage to their works"—they lost nothing; yet even after it was shown unprofitable, the "custom . . . still prevails."[32] Better break the Sabbath than lose the honest day's work these kids owe you. The triumph of the Work Ethic is complete.

Of course the mine-owners and their lawyers responded with moral fervor to the charges in the report. They freely admitted that the condition in the mines "in regard both to ventilation and drainage is lamentably defective."[33] But what can they do about that? "To render them . . . safe does not appear to be practicable by any means yet known"[34]—so don't hold *them* responsible! Again, if "persons in authority in these mines . . . never [interfere] to prevent . . . harsh and cruel [treatment]," it is because, as they "distinctly [state], that they do not conceive that they have any *right* to do so";[35] let us keep this on a high moral plain: it is the owner's own business

what they do with their property. If no money at all is
"expended with a view to secure . . . safety"[36]—remember, that would be confiscatory—need we be reminded
that in 1982 a very devout senator from Utah labored to
cut federal mine inspection in half to save money for the
mining companies? If the kids work in "passages . . . so
small, that even the youngest Children cannot move along
them without crawling on their hands and feet, in which
unnatural and constrained posture they drag the loaded
carriages after them,"[37] again I ask you—is anyone to blame
for that? Did the owners create those thin seams of coal?
To quote the report: "As it is impossible, by any outlay
compatible with a profitable return, to render such coal
mines . . . fit for human beings to work in, they never will
be placed in such a condition [of fitness], and consequently
they never can be worked without inflicting great and ir-
reparable injury on the health of the Children."[38] So you
see there is just no way around it; the work must go on,
since the coal is "a main source of our national wealth and
greatness,"[39] which makes the mine owners benefactors
of the human race. Also bear in mind that if "notwithstanding the intense labour performed by these Children,
they do not procure even sufficient food and raiment," it
is "in general" because of their "idle and dissolute parents,
who spend the hard-earned wages of their offspring at the
public house."[40] Though nearly all of the parents worked
in the mines too, very many of them were too crippled by
sickness or injury to continue, but that is no excuse for
getting drunk.

Of course we must not overlook the *fun* side of working
in the mines. "The coal mine, when properly ventilated
and drained, . . . and the side passages . . . of tolerable
height, is not only not unhealthy, but . . . is considered
as a place of work, more salubrious and even agreeable
than that in which many kinds of labour are carried on
above ground"[41]—an eloquent commentary on those other

kinds of labor. And the excitement of it: where "seams of coal are so thick that horses go direct to the workings, or in which the side passages from the workings to the horse-ways are not of any great length, the lights in the main ways render the situation of these Children comparatively less cheerless, dull, and stupefying."[42] Here the little nippers could pop out of the side passages and take a look at the magnificent sight of a feeble line of lights burning in the damp and murky main passage—and when you hear a horse-car actually go by, what a thrill! And rest and relaxation? "From the nature of the employment, intervals of a few minutes necessarily occur during which the muscles are not in active exertion,"[43] so it is not necessary after all to "interrupt" the work "by any regular time set apart for rest and refreshment; what food is taken in the pit being eaten as best it may while the labour continues."[44] And that labor builds strong bodies: "The labour in which Children . . . are chiefly employed, . . . namely, in pushing the loaded carriages of coals, . . . is a description of exercise which, while it greatly develops the muscles of the arms, shoulders, chest, back, and legs, without confining any part of the body, . . . afford[s] an equally healthful excitement to all the other organs."[45] So who are they to complain if they are crippled at the ages of thirty and forty, and "extinct soon after fifty"?[46]

The story of the mines has been told not to harrow up our souls, but as a gentle reminder that the principles and practices of the nineteenth-century industrialists are still wholly and enthusiastically endorsed by the people of our own society, in proof of which we could cite present-day instances almost if not quite as horrendous as Grandpa's stories of bonny Scotland. The reason things have not changed lies in the basic nature of those principles, of necessity stern and inflexible. A thing is either free or it is not; a free lunch would have to be for everybody, and that would never do in the "real world" in which we live. The communists are even more insistent than we are on having a world in which everybody must work, work, work for lunch, with no other expectation in time or eternity than a booming economy here and now. Their periodic slumps and collapses are as predictable as our own, but that will not correct their fanatical obsession with a single way of doing things. We are wasting our time talking about free lunch in the world as we know it.

But the world as we know it is the very antithesis of Zion, in which we should all be living at this very moment. I have cited a few passages from the Pearl of Great Price, Old Testament, New Testament, Book of Mormon, and Doctrine and Covenants to show that whether we like it or not, in all those five dispensations of the gospel the free lunch was prescribed for all living under the covenant, and at the same time very special kinds of work were assigned to each and all of them, the object of which was not lunch but the building up of the kingdom and the establishment of Zion. Our real temporal wants, we have been told repeatedly, are few, and they are taken care of by the law of consecration. And in every dispensation, failure to act on principles that they promised and covenanted to observe, the most important being the law of love, has brought to an end the felicity of God's people and covered them with confusion as their enemies prevailed against them. No one is more completely "of the world" than one who lives by the world's economy, whatever his display of open piety.

Thus Moses sums it up: "See, I have set before thee this day life and good, and death and evil, . . . blessing and cursing" (Deuteronomy 30:15-19). We have already seen what is required of us to merit the blessing, and to these things Moses adds a useful list of the worst crimes that Israel is likely to commit, the most certain to incur the cursing. There are eleven sins in the list (Deuteronomy 27:15-26); all of them are of a secret and underhanded nature, and at least eight of them consist in taking advantage of weaker parties. The essence of evil being thus clearly exposed, the rationalizing, theorizing, and legalizing of the dialectical materialists on either side of the Iron Curtain is irrelevant to the issue—which is, that anyone who can argue that it is permissible to deny food to the hungry when we have food "shall with the wicked lift up his eyes in hell."

This started out to be an exhilarating study of the pleasures and advantages of the free lunch. But as it progressed it became more and more depressing as the relevant scriptures accumulated and the gulf steadily widened between the Zion of God and those Babylonian institutions in our midst that brazenly bear the fair name of Zion as a gimmick to promote local business.

We are being asked even at this moment to choose between the peculiar economy that God has prescribed for us and what we have always considered the more realistic, convenient, and expedient economy by which the world lives and in which at the moment it is convulsively gasping and struggling to survive. The difference between the two orders is never more apparent than at lunchtime, in the homely perennial ordinance that was meant to unite us all for a happy hour but which instead divides God's children with the awful authority and finality of the last judgment— in which, by the way, the Lord assures us that the seating order is going to be completely reversed.

Notes

1. Quoted by John C. Whitcomb, *The Genesis Flood* (Philadelphia: Presbyterian and Reformed, 1964), 443.

2. Omar Khayyam, *Rubaiyat of Omar Khayyam*, tr. Edward Fitzgerald (New York: Avon, n.d.), LII.

3. Hoimar von Ditfurth, *Children of the Universe* (New York: Atheneum, 1976), 10.

4. Lewis Thomas, "On the Uncertainty of Science," *Key Reporter* 46 (Autumn 1980): 2.

5. Albert Szent-Györgyi, "What Is Life?" in *Biology Today* (Del Mar, CA: Painter, 1972), xxix-xxxi.

6. R. Buckminster Fuller, *Intuition* (New York: Doubleday, 1972), 135.

7. Ibid., 138, 142.

8. Ibid., 110.

9. Ibid., 112.

10. Von Ditfurth, *Children of the Universe*, 13.

11. Fred Hoyle, "The Universe: Past and Present Reflections," *Engineering and Science* (November 1981): 10, 12.

12. Ibid., 12.

13. John K. Galbraith, *The Age of Uncertainty* (Boston: Houghton Mifflin, 1977), 48.

14. *JD* 3:323.

15. Dean C. Jesse, ed., *Letters of Brigham Young to His Sons* (Salt Lake: Deseret Book, 1974), 199.

16. *JD* 11:115.

17. Ibid., 8:134.

18. Ibid., 3:257.

19. Hugh W. Nibley, "Sparsiones," *Classical Journal* 40 (June 1945): 515-43.

20. Gerald Friedlander, *Pirkê de Rabbi Eliezer* (New York: Hermon Press, 1965), 176; cf. Lewis Ginsberg, *Legends of the Jews*, 7 vols. (Philadelphia: Jewish Publication Society of America, 1968), 1:245-50; cf. Nathan Ausubel, *A Treasury of Jewish Folklore* (New York: Crown, 1948), 124.

21. *JD* 6:46.

22. Friedlander, *Pirkê de Rabbi Eliezer*, 176; cf. Ginsberg, *Legends of the Jews*, 1:245-50; cf. Ausubel, *A Treasury of Jewish Folklore*, 124.

23. *JD* 13:302.

24. Ibid., 12:122.

25. Shakespeare, *Hamlet*, act IV, scene iv, line 38.

26. Ayn Rand, *The Virtue of Selfishness* (New York: Signet, 1961), vii-xi.

27. The 1832 recital of the First Vision as dictated by Joseph Smith to Frederick G. Williams. See Milton V. Backman, *Joseph Smith's First Vision* (Salt Lake City: Bookcraft, 1971), appendix A; cf. Dean C. Jessee, ed., "The Early Accounts of Joseph Smith's First Vision," *BYU Studies* 9 (1969): 280.

28. *JD* 19:47.

29. Ibid., 1:200.

30. "First Report of the Commissioners: Mines," in *British Par-*

liamentary Papers, 11 vols. (London: Clowes and Sons, 1842; reprinted Shannon, Ireland: Irish University Press, 1968), 6:255-58 (emphasis added).

31. Ibid., 259.
32. Ibid.
33. Ibid., 255.
34. Ibid.
35. Ibid., 257 (emphasis added).
36. Ibid.
37. Ibid., 259.
38. Ibid.
39. Ibid., 258.
40. Ibid.
41. Ibid.
42. Ibid., 256.
43. Ibid.
44. Ibid.
45. Ibid., 258-59.
46. Ibid., 258.

9

But What Kind of Work?

The last time I spoke to this august group it was on the subject of the free lunch. Of course I knew that there is no free lunch, but I wished to point out that the price varies. I cited the case of my great-grandparents, who toiled their lives away in the mines of Scotland just for lunch and nothing else; they were not even allowed to take off the time to eat it, lest they infringe on the rightful claims of the mine-owners to their time and labor. On the other hand, I learn from the leading article in the current issue of the *Scientific American* (May 1987) that "the top 2% of the population . . . have 28% of the total net worth," while the top 10% own 57% of it. On the other hand, "the bottom 50% have 4.5% of the total net worth. About half of the country's top wealth holders got there by inheriting their holdings."[1] Would it seem irreverent to suggest that some of those fortunate people enjoy something remotely akin to a free lunch? Somebody always pays for the lunch, and it is obvious that some people eat a lot of lunches they don't pay for, while a lot of others pay for a lot of lunches they never eat.

Naturally if you don't want to spend your life in shallows and in miseries, the thing to do is to get into the upper brackets—no matter how, just so you get there.[2] Ivan Boesky visited various college campuses preaching to

This talk was given May 19, 1987, as a sequel to Nibley's lecture entitled "Work We Must, But the Lunch is Free," given on April 20, 1982, both at the Cannon-Hinkley Club in Salt Lake City.

the youth on the merits of what he called cultivating a "healthy greed."[3] But it is before all else the terrifying assurance implicit in the smug free-lunch maxim that without money you are dead, while with it you can have anything in this world, that has turned everyone *en masse* almost overnight from whatever ideals and goals may have lingered from previous generations to one thing only. From interviews with the Class of '87, Haynes Johnson discovered that security is what they want, "Not some fuzzy notion of security, either—[but] . . . financial security." There is a mass shifting of majors from liberal arts to business. The reaction of the students to the insider trading scandals was a quick reply "in a tone of dismissal: 'Most of us just want a piece of the action' "! "As they spoke, their conversation took on a chilling quality and was filled with [a] string of spontaneous rationalizations. The end justifies the means. They all do it. Dog eat dog. Those who can't make it, don't deserve to. Whiners. Losers versus winners. It's not what you know, but who you know. Get out of my way. I'm No. 1. Crush 'em. Law of the jungle." "And this," concludes the interviewer, "from an era that was supposed to produce a rekindling of American values."[4]

A few weeks ago, the TV show "60 Minutes" showed the inability of a group of typical California college students to answer the most elementary questions on geography, history, literature, politics, and so on, in other words, the world we live in. Were the students ashamed of their ignorance of the fundamentals? On the contrary, they were indignant or indifferent when challenged. Why should we learn that stuff? they asked. Why should we know anything about faraway times and places? They could see no point in being concerned with anything that is not right at hand and in the hand. "We want it all, and we want it now!" is the slogan. Intelligence, said William James, is the ability to react to absent stimuli.[5] The cockroach and

the mouse act to what is immediately around them and
no more: "Still thou art blest compar'd wi' me!" says the
poet to the field mouse, "The present only toucheth thee."
Knowing that, Burns can expect to be concerned as "But,
och! I backward cast my e'e, on prospects drear! an' forward, tho' I canna see, I guess an' fear."[6] Our present-day
grads want none of that. The more intelligent animals
know that it pays to heed the rumble of a distant drum,
like flood waters advancing from far up in the canyon—
survival depends on it. That is why the new generation
are letting themselves be dangerously exposed. The great
tragedy, perhaps, is that no one, including their teachers,
has ever told them why they should be interested in anything but money. In teaching classes in a College of Education in California, I never heard a hint of any reason
but one for being in the business—salary was the name of
the game.

Just last Sunday [May 17, 1987], an Eastern professor
noted on the PBS about the Mormon Missionary Program
that Mormonism and Americanism are converging. To
what point? An ad from *Mademoiselle* shows a young
woman proclaiming a major achievement in life: "Kiss him
goodbye, Maggie. It was easy . . . taking him away from
you was a breeze. I deserve him. I have the best things in
life; cars, boats and now *him*. He's so *hot*. But he'll have
to cool off . . . for now. Go find yourself another guy,
Maggie, he's *mine* now."[7] The speaker is a damsel by the
name of Sandy, and the immediate secret of her success
is the sporting of the proper designer jeans.

This state of mind has been building up for a number
of years with steady encouragement of the youth of Zion
to become financially independent as their first project in
life; to be financially dependent after thirty has become as
reprehensible as being unwed. President Kimball exposed
the root of that evil in an inspired address to the Church
and the nation on the occasion of the national bicentennial.

He said he was "appalled and frightened" by what he saw around him. He singled out three primary objects: (1) contempt for the environment, (2) the quest for affluence, and (3) the trust in deadly weapons.[8] In all three of these vices, Utah leads the nation. I will not harrow up your minds by reading the long list of appalling statistics about Utah. Suffice it to say that what was designed to be Zion has turned out to be the purlieus of Babylon. For us (1) environment and ecology are dirty words, blocking access to the wealth of the land, which is meant for corporate developers. (2) "Working in the service of a self-image that includes sufficient money, stocks, bonds, investment portfolios, property, credit cards, furnishings, automobiles, and the like to *guarantee* carnal security throughout, it is hoped, a long and happy life,"[9] President Kimball continues, has given us a mindset that is firmly grounded in Satan's first article of faith, "You can have anything in this world for money." (3) Implicit trust in military hardware gives us the means of keeping the whole thing going — worldwide markets with mounting production and consumption, continuing to spread the gospel of virtuous violence "until the consumption decreed hath made a full end of all nations" (D&C 87:6).

The price we pay for these three items is staggering. The price we pay for the first is the loss of this earth, "most glorious and beautiful," designed from the foundations as a place of variety and beauty. The price we pay for the second, setting our hearts on riches, is truth and virtue. Who is not aware of this today? A recent issue of *U.S. News and World Report* devoted its cover story to the theme of "An Alarming Decline in Basic Honesty" and asks in bold headlines, are we "A Nation of Liars?"[10] And here is next month's issue of *Nation's Business* with another bold cover story: "Are Your Employees Stealing You Blind?"[11] Here is a brochure from Tom Harward, which promises to sell you a maverick lawyer's (Charles Abbott's) "Money-

Making Secrets of His Millionaire Clients." He zealously admonishes us, "You need to know how the most suc-cessful people in the world operate their *well-oiled money-machines* in acquiring enormous wealth at an incredibly fast rate."[12] Virtue goes down the drain with truth. And the author and pitchman of this plan "for making large amounts of money on a regular basis," which "doesn't require any special background or qualifications" (the new Law of the Harvest), is the bishop of a BYU ward.[13] The price we pay for the third obsession with the evil ways of other nations is life itself. Here we see the Mahan principle at work in all its glory: "Truly I am Mahan, the master of this great secret, that I may murder and get gain" (Moses 5:31). From the international drug and arms traffic to the sneaky chemical additions in the supermarket, the principle applies: life in exchange for profits. One example should suffice. This month a headline announces that "Radiation Dump Could Bring Cash to County."[14] Some counties actually clamor to convert the land Bountiful into the land Desolation for a quick buck. Here is an idealistic appeal for BYU students to get interested in a new Master of Public Administration program, involving themselves in selfless and dedicated public service [at this point the bemused informant holds aloft a small placard], "Bring in your brain for big bucks."

The cure for all such ills is, of course, the gospel, but nobody has explained that even to our BYU students. Why is this so? Dr. James R. Kearl, the Dean of Honors and General Education, and Professor of Economics and Law at the BYU, reports the situation in *BYU Today*: "It's pretty clear that we have a student body who come here *only* for job training. They're bright, they're capable, but they're not interested in liberal arts. I visit high schools in an effort to help recruit good students . . . : 'Tell me about your dreams and aspirations and hopes.' It's *always* 'money and a job.' None of them dream of becoming educated people.

That just never comes up; . . . institutionally, it appears, we are committed to a different model than our new students seem to be."[15] Just yesterday [May 18, 1987], it was announced on KUTV that Utah has more teenagers working outside of school than any other state. Earlier it was reported that Utah pays less for a child's education than any other state in the Union. That is great for employers who pay the lowest wages and taxes possible; but, as the report noted, it tends to produce young people who are poorly educated and materialistic—qualities that I have found over many years of teaching large Sunday School classes to be conspicuous among their elders.

Last semester, to find out whether an honors class of remarkably devout students (their unusual final examination papers showed that) made any connection between the gospel and their careers, I asked them, as a midterm assignment, to assume that they had been guaranteed a thousand uninterrupted years of life here on earth, with all their wants and needs adequately funded: How would you plan to spend the rest of your lives here? I explained that this is not a hypothetical proposition, since this is the very situation the gospel puts us in. Whether we want to or not, we are doomed to live forever—even the wicked—for "they cannot die" (Alma 12:18). In accepting the gospel, we are already launched into our eternal program. We can take covenants and receive ordinances for those who are on the other side because they are the identical covenants and ordinances we make on this side. When Elijah announced the establishment of the work among us with the ringing words "The time has fully come!" (D&C 10:14), we no longer ask when, but only what. We are taught to think of ourselves here and now as living in eternity, and how can it be otherwise, since the contracts we make and the rules we live by are expressly "for time and eternity"? So I asked them, How are you going to get started on that thousand-year introduction to a timeless existence? After reading Professor Kearl's report, I should have known what to expect. Here are some typical answers:

Overwhelmed by the proposition . . . [I] would have to refuse it ["Deny not the gifts of God!" (Moroni 10:8). And the greatest of these gifts is the gift of eternal life (D&C 14:7).]

First I would go crazy, . . . then I would be bored after 100 years. I would be like John and the three Nephites.

I would not want to live here that long. I would make long-term investments in the money markets, . . . would complete my education in business, get an MBA, would find a part-time job and teach my children the value of work. [All this is precluded, of course, by the premise, yet these students have been so brainwashed that they fail completely to see the point.]

It would be a dubious honor to prolong this probationary existence. [And when are we ever to be off probation, if even the angels (fell) "who kept not their first estate" (2 Peter 2:4; Jude 6; Abraham 3:26).]

It's not a nice question, the pressure would be too great from people who would like money from me. How should I pay tithing on it? How would I use all that money? [For this person the whole question is an economic one.]

I would spend my time in recreation with some serious moments. For a sense of success I might build or write something.

I don't know if I would want a thousand years. . . . Travel, study, and teach. [You have signed up for the duration and now you want out?]

Could be a blessing or a cursing; I would excel in athletics and general education, would procrastinate a good deal, live in the style of the well-to-do, . . . shopping, camping, dancing.

First I would pay tithing! I would stay out of debt. How to use the funding money is the problem.

I could do nearly everything there was to do several times over. Perform service and drive a Porsche 911.

I can't imagine changing things much; I am content with the path I am following.

I would turn it down. This life is okay, but I am anxious to get on with my progression in the hereafter. [Doing what? This *is* your progression into the hereafter!]

And so it goes. No wonder Hamlet finds a world of such people "weary, stale, flat, and unprofitable."[16] "What is a man" he asks, "if his chief good and market of his time be but to sleep and feed? A beast, no more. Sure he that made us with such large discourse, looking before and after, gave us not that capability and god-like reason to fust in us unused."[17] In the TV documentary on missionaries last Sunday, a General Authority declared that "more is expected of us than any generation," yet nothing could be further from the minds of these young people than the teaching of the Prophet Joseph: "The things of God are of deep import; and time, and experience, and careful and ponderous and solemn thoughts can only find them out. Thy mind, O man, . . . must stretch as high as the utmost heavens."[18] They don't seem to realize that we need such knowledge even for survival: "The Saints ought to lay hold of every door . . . to obtain foothold on the earth, and be making all the preparation that is within their power for the terrible storms that are now gathering in the heavens. . . . Any among you who aspire after their own aggrandizement, and seek their own opulence, while their brethren are groaning in poverty . . . cannot be benefited by the intercession of the Holy Spirit."[19] Students today greet such statements as alien and hostile.

What do people do in an eternal society? A recent news item, a typical one these days, tells us of a once flourishing

but now decaying mill town in which the population find
themselves with all the time in the world on their hands.
And what do they do? They spend their days watching
video tapes. Instead of exploiting an opportunity for the
"plain living and high thinking" that led to the intellectual
flowering of New England long ago, they fall back on the
paralyzing *theatromania,*[20] which was the final comfort of
the last days of Rome. President Harold B. Lee once addressed a group of religion teachers at Brigham Young
University; he had just attended a stake conference, and
he told us how at a meeting of the high council the question
of the hereafter came up. One of the group, an undertaker,
humorously noted that he would have to change his profession. Upon this, a dentist chimed in and confessed that
he was in the same case; next an insurance man (there are
always insurance men in such groups) admitted that there
would not be much call for his talents, and then a used-
car salesman saw only limited prospects for his own business, as did the never-failing real estate pusher in the
group, and so it went. If these men were not to dedicate
themselves to making money, what would they do? A
thousand years of guaranteed livelihood rule out the necessity of almost all the professions, businesses, and in-
dustries that thrive on the defects of our bodies and the
insecurity of our minds.

Needless to say, my students were quick to put me on
the spot. All right, wise guy, what would you do? Fortunately I had the whole corpus of scripture and ordinance
of the restored gospel to fall back on. In the scriptures we
are told that the Son does just what the Father does, and
in time it will be our calling to do the same works of the
Father (John 14:1–17:26). And how do we go about it? Last
Saturday I left the temple loaded with instructions, specific
instructions—I found it all laid out for me, because I was
looking for it. That is always the case when you are going
to the temple. I had had the question put to me point blank

and wondered if I could get some hints from the scriptures and in the temple. What I found was practically nothing else but things to do.

1. First of all, in the teachings in all the scriptures and in the House of God we are given to understand that there are certain things we must do and certain other things we must not do. The alternative to doing what God commands us to do, especially after our expressly agreeing to do such, is to be in Satan's power, for he is granted the authority to "deceive and to blind men, and to lead them captive at his will, even as many as would not hearken unto my voice" (Moses 4:4). There can be no compromise here; there is no third way.

2. At the outset of our endeavors, we are given the satisfaction of knowing what this is all going to lead to— exaltation in the celestial kingdom of God. Since that is a vast distance away, everything we do between now and then is *preparatory* in nature. This rules out dedication to a career on this earth. A *carrière* is one complete turn of the race course; you have not had a career, as Oedipus discovered, until it is over, until the thing is completed— the climb, the peak, and the decline "to second childishness and mere oblivion."[21] A more forlorn ambition than a career cannot be imagined, and years ago President Stephen L Richards made some scathing remarks in the old Smith Fieldhouse about the futility of aspiring to careers— a sentiment I have rarely heard since then.[22] (We now give courses in career planning at the BYU.)

3. Also from the beginning we can expect to be tried and tempted. Satan's calling and appointment is to try to break us—to see at what point we will give in, to see how far we can be trusted to be true and faithful in all things, in keeping the promises and covenants that cover the entire range of behavior.

4. We can be assured we are going to receive instructions all along. When we have shown our capacity and

willingness to keep one, we will be given the next, which is somewhat harder. The first, of course, is to agree to do things God's way instead of ours—to follow the law of God. This conditions our whole way of life and is expressed more specifically in what follows, the law of obedience to specific commands that we receive through revelation both in the scriptures and in the temple.

5. This means that we will be called upon to make some sacrifices; indeed, to please God we must be willing to sacrifice all the way, taking Abraham for our model, for a proper eternal life is not to be cheaply bought (D&C 132). Eternity is absolute. It must be all or nothing with us, and the law of sacrifice requires us to give up this world at a moment's notice. Again, "success" is not what we are after, for it's painfully obvious to us all what that word has come to mean to us today. It is not here that your ultimate goals are to be set or accomplished.

6. A moral life with proper deportment and conduct at all times and uncompromising insistence on chastity is a positive charge and command which theoretically is supposed to be followed by all Christians, and, of course by all who accept the restored gospel. It determines not only how we shall act in our general conduct, but specifically what course we shall steer through the waters of a wicked and adulterous generation, in which the mores and customs are no more, if they ever were, those of the celestial kingdom: "For I give not unto you that ye shall live after the manner of the world. . . . Zion . . . [must live by] the law of the celestial kingdom; otherwise I cannot receive her unto myself" (D&C 95:13).

I have written somewhat on the theme that "without the temple, civilization is a hollow shell," a world of convenience and expedience only, where a totally different set of beliefs prescribes all our activities.[23] From the outside, the temple is anything but a practical structure, and the activity within is a great inconvenience and time-consumer, with nothing to recommend it to our economy. Inversely, from inside the temple the shenanigans of the outside world look restless and absurd — everything the exact opposite from what is in the temple. But both worlds have one thing in common: neither is a permanent dwelling; they are both places of passage and of testing. You get your one time on earth and your one chance at endowment or approbation, and then you move on.

7. As the Lord's Prayer tells us, what we want here and now is for God's kingdom to come here below, so that his will may be done here on earth exactly as it is in heaven. That is not the state of things today; it is the law of Moses, the law of consecration, which was never changed because the people never really kept it, and which is carried on right into the New Testament and the restored gospel. The Lord's Prayer is a call to the law of consecration.

8. We can be sure that we will go on seeking instructions as we need them, perhaps forever, for we follow the example of Adam and Abraham, ever seeking *more* light and knowledge, and we leave the temple as we close the scriptures with that commitment. We are guaranteed instruction and guidance at every step and are advised to ask for it and to follow it.

It is all preparation, but preparatory for what? "As God is, so man may become";[24] specifically John tells us that the Lord was "worthy to take out . . . of every kindred, and tongue, and people, and nation; And hast made us unto our God kings and priests: and we shall reign on the earth" (Revelation 5:9-10). Rule, *malakh*, that is, to be a king, is to establish and follow the *regulum*, to keep things on the track, constantly prompting and instructing and acting with grace (D&C 121:34-46). To reign is from the same root but gives us *regnare*, to be righteous and truthful: *rex erit qui recte faciet, qui non faciet, non erit*, was the ancient Roman formula.[25] You are king only to the degree to which you are just and true, and if you do not do what is right and honest, you are no king. In the kingdom, the *rex* must be truth itself, in short, like "mine Only Begotten Son who is full of grace and truth" (Moses 6:52). There is no need for anyone in this life to feel lost for a lack of problems to work on!

Finally, the point of it all is summed up in the culminating words of every great ordinance and performance, the mandatory "Forever!" That is what we want to know more than anything else. The infinitely poignant question that is asked and implied on every side today is, Is that all there is? Must it all end so soon? In other words, must we renounce the countless accomplishments within the known scope of our present gifts and talents before we have even begun to realize the tiniest fraction of our potential? "I advise all," said the prophet, "to go on to perfection and search deeper and deeper into the mysteries of Godliness. . . . [As for myself] it has always been my province to dig up hidden mysteries, new things, for my hearers."[26] How we shy off from those things today! There is to be no discussion in the temple. When we leave the edifice, we leave one world, usually with a sigh of relief, feeling quite satisfied with ourselves, to return to the other, where we feel more at home. *Which is the real world?* That is the question.

There is a fascinating and much-neglected branch of early Jewish and Christian literature dealing with the debates in the Council in Heaven at the creation of the world.[27] Two main issues are discussed solemnly but with passion. (1) Is it worth the risk? In view of what the earth will have to suffer, is it really best to go ahead and let the human race do its worst—for they are not to be denied free agency? (2) The second question is the one that interests us here. If we create the world and the spirits go down there and take on bodies, *just what will they do* to fill the span of their earthly lifetime? Eating and drinking will not be enough, though in the present order the lunch ethic pretty well covers everything. Deprived of their former glory, what can interest them or profit them? There won't be time, it was argued, for really serious labors. Do they just hang on?

A definitive clue to what we should be doing here is provided in those ancient catalogues of the organs and faculties of mankind, listing and describing the things human beings are best equipped to do. The subject is impressively treated in the Egyptian Shabako Stone inscription, preserving what is thought to be the oldest connected text in the world, and in what is believed to be the oldest Hebrew book, the *Sefer Yetzirah*, commonly attributed to none other than Abraham. Both are accounts of the creation, and they are temple texts.[28] The subject is also treated in many resurrection texts, in particular the Egyptian initiatory rite of the Opening of the Mouth. In funeral ceremonies and in the Adam literature, we see the inflicting of the "Blows of Death," to put the members of the body on hold, or on ice as it were, until resurrection time.[29] Finally, a most interesting literature on the Demotion of Satan in both Jewish and Early Christian sources, and a large corpus of Egyptian texts on the overthrowing of Seth or Apophis, tells how the discredited angel is deprived of his supernal powers member by member.[30]

These are the gifts and talents that prescribe our proper activities on this earth (there are usually seven or twelve, the cosmic numbers):

1. First of all, before anything can happen, one must be aware of being in the world. A measure of awareness is apparently possessed by all living things, and the greater the awareness, the greater the intelligence. If our time here is to have any meaning at all, our brain and intellect must be clear and active; otherwise we might as well send bags of sand through the endowment while running up the most satisfying statistics on our computers. This is, of course, the most exhilarating aspect of the whole thing — our life

here, a constant mental exercise, the purest form of fun, with a minimum of mechanization.

2. In this life we have too many options. There are thousands of good things any of us could be doing at this moment but will never be allowed to do, because of the shortness of time and the peculiar need we have to focus on just one thing at a time. As I lie in my bed and gaze at the shelf-lined wall of my room, I suffer pangs of frustration, seeing there a wondrous array of books which I have spent many years preparing to read and gleefully collecting in dusty bookstores of Europe and America. But now, just as I am able to handle the stuff, I must forego the temptation and the delight because there is other work at hand — it's the Egyptian stuff that will keep me going me the rest of my days. What can any of us do in such a predicament? We can only "hear the word of the Lord," and to hear is to obey; that is why the Egyptian Opening of the Mouth actually begins with the ears.[31] From the very first amid a million possible paths we are lost and bumbling without God's instructions; and in fact both his works and his words are for our benefit (Moses 1:38-39), the words always going along with the works to put us into the picture: "My works are without end, and also my words, for they never cease" (Moses 1:4).

3. Next is the eye, a positive obsession with the Egyptians and the Hebrews (they called Abraham "the Eye of the World"), who believed that it commands the data necessary for a comprehension of the structure of the cosmos itself. "The eye cannot choose but see," and what it sees is the big picture — it gauges and measures, perceiving ratios and proportions and noting those that are pleasing and those that are not, and it compares and structures all by the awareness of light, the constant and the measure of all things. The word intelligence is from *inter-legere*, meaning to make a selection between things, to put a number of things together and to classify, to view the situation

and to make a decision; and to make a decision is to discern — the brain and intellect must have something to work
with, data that comes mostly by sight.[32]

4. Being aware, instructed, and informed does not
complete a fullness of joy, we are told, which can come
only when spirit is united with the body. The enjoyment
of the senses, says Brigham Young, is one of our greatest
privileges upon this earth. The most primitive and primary
of senses, we are told, and the one in which the Egyptians
find the liveliest earthly sensations and delights, is the
sense of smell, being most closely tied to emotion and
memory, as well as to the delights of taste and touch. If
an important aspect of our sojourn here is the release of
tension, monotony, and drabness by those sensual delights
best represented by the nose, it is the *disciplined* taste, smell,
and touch as well as hearing and seeing that have, as
Brigham Young again informs us, the greatest capacity for
enjoyment; and discipline means control.[33] Appetites, desires, and passions can give us the best of what they have
to offer only if they are kept within the bounds the Lord
has set. Beyond those bounds they become surfeit and
corruption, and the source of almost every *unpleasant* sensation. By a clear and definitive statement, we are saved
from wandering everlastingly amid moral quandaries and
probabilistic exercises such as the endless debates of the
doctors and schoolmen on just how naughty is naughty.

5. We are never alone; we share a universe of discourse
through the miracle of the *word*. Again we quote a favorite
passage: "There is no end to my works, neither to my
words" (Moses 1:4). "Behold, this is my work and my
glory," namely, to share with others what he has, "to bring
to pass the immortality and eternal life of man" (Moses
1:38-39). There is nothing mysterious about the endlessly
debated *logos* — it is communication. God does not choose
to live in a vacuum. Nothing is said about the mouth as
eating, and indeed the Lord says that what goes into the

mouth is not the important thing but what comes out of it; for it is that which puts us into touch with each other.

Back to the Egyptians and the Hebrews. Those two oldest books in the world which we mentioned, both contain the same peculiar doctrine of the Word. According to this, we have "the seven gates of the head,"[34] the openings—eyes, ears, nostrils, and mouth, which are the receptors by which we take in all the data that come to us in various energy packages from the outer world. In the mind, the brain, and the heart, so goes the doctrine, this data is processed, sorted, interpreted, and given form and meaning; but though we have seven receptors, there is only one projector, and that is the mouth. By word of mouth alone do we communicate with others to discover how closely our idea of the world matches theirs, thereby assuring ourselves that our world must indeed have an objective basis in reality. You must take my word for it that I see and hear what I *say* I see and hear, and therefore if I wish, I can so easily confuse you by spreading false reports that all values and relationships become confounded. Satan is the Author of Confusion, the Father of Lies, the Deceiver, "the fiend who lies like truth," and he does all of his work by distortion of the word, the systematic study of the ambitious rhetorician, lawyer, salesman, and politician. What God asks of the mouth and lips, therefore, is not that they eat the proper food—they have means of sensing that—but that they *never speak guile!*

6. It is essential while we are moving among the properties and characters of our earthly drama that we deport ourselves properly and keep our physical plant in top form, upright and alert. They used to make a big thing of the Posture Parade at the BYU, and I always used to wonder why my grade-school teachers made such a fetish of "holding your head up." The ancients considered the neck as the tower, a sort of control on the rest of the body, the index of confidence and courage. It is the characteristic

mark of the alert and healthy animal. All the basic signs for vitality in Egyptian depict the neck and esophagus. Let us not underestimate, as I long did, the importance of the neck in keeping the whole body properly in line.

7. You can expect to have trials and burdens not a few, for that is part of the game; and for that your shoulders and back should be strong—those burdens are necessary to the plan and are meant to be borne. Best of all, they will not hurt you! The kings of old did not disdain to represent themselves carrying loads of brick on their backs for the building of the temple.

8. Along with that, you are to be valiant; mere innocence is not enough, as Brother Brigham said, if you are to realize your potential. The ancient formula blesses the arms to be strong in wielding the symbolic sword of righteousness. At any rate, passivity is not for you; you must expect and prepare to face opposition, stiff opposition, head-on. And the Saints have always had more than their share of that.

9. Besides the brain, the *phrenos*, the ancients considered the *thumos*, the breast, the main receptacle and processor of our feelings and emotions. It is there that the surges of passion or fear are felt, and it is there that our prevailing attitude to things is engendered. If it is important for our words, our rational and objective intercourse, to be absolutely guileless, it is equally important that our feelings be pure and virtuous, for any other feelings are necessarily false and pernicious—what possible use or excuse can there be for them?

10. As to our reins (kidneys) and liver, you leave your innards alone; they should perform their proper function on their own, and the less they attract our attention, or anyone else's, the better! It is interesting that the less people are doing in the building of the kingdom or in seeking light and knowledge, the more they worry about their bodily functions, as our TV commercials amply attest.

11. The Hebrew and Egyptian rites place one goal and one delight above all others, the joy in one's posterity, in patriarchal succession. Everywhere, both people give us to understand that the ultimate delight is to be in the company of one's own flesh and blood. As Wilhelm Busch in one of the best-known lines in German literature informs us, it is not difficult to become a father, it may even be pleasant, but it is the result that is the wonder and glory and burden of our existence. Another quality we share with God.

12. Lastly comes our means of getting around in the world, feet and legs. The Egyptians place great emphasis on this; the resurrection is finally achieved only when the legs are set in motion on the path of eternity. As to Abraham, the official title of his biography, whether in the Bible or the Apocrypha, is *lech lecha*, "Get up and get going!" and so he did, a wanderer and a stranger until the end of his life. The Saints are the most mobile of mortals, *das wandernde Gottesvolk* (God's wandering people), like Abraham, strangers and pilgrims, but missionaries in the world, meant to circulate abroad, to get around and broadcast the good news and spread the stakes of Zion.

The Mystery of Creation

The scriptures tell us that God has a work to do, that the Son does the works of his Father (John 5:17, 19), and that he promises all those who believe on him in time to do the works that he does, and yet greater works (John 14:12). And what does God do? He creates: "Millions of earths like this . . . would not be a beginning" (Moses 7:30). There is no end to his creations, and he wants us to go with him, be where he is, and do what he does. The ultimate damnation is to be banished, "cut off," from his presence, just as the supreme blessing is to "enter into my joy and sit down on my throne."[35] He enjoys his work.

What is creation? An endless procession of worlds rolling off the assembly line? No, creation never duplicates; it is never mere production after a set mold. Creation begins where everything else, everything that has been done so far, has reached its utmost limit of accomplishment. Again, to refer to our two archaic sources, creation begins in the mind, with the intelligence, what the scientists call a singularity, a thing that cannot be described or explained or understood but that yet cannot be denied — it is real. According to our sources, God first conceived in his mind and then by his word explained his plan to the Council. They hailed the proposal with cries of inexpressible joy, the great Creation Hymn, "when the morning stars sang together and all the sons of God shouted for joy" (Job 38:7).[36]

But to expand the frontier of invention, one must first reach it, and to reach it one must pass through the whole vast realm of what has already been discovered. Must you learn everything? Yes, for if you leave anything out, how will you know that it is not the most important of all, "the stone which the builders rejected" (Matthew 21:42)? This journey may last for ages, and it holds forth the anticipation of wonders and delights that grow as ever-increasing knowledge heightens our capacity to comprehend what we are experiencing. This has nothing to do with the learning of the schools. The tradition of Western education is rhetorical, success oriented, and concerned wholly with appearances; it cost Socrates his life to show the Sophists just how superficial and dishonest their system was. The basic formula of creativity is $C = 1/M$, that is, the creative act is in inverse proportion to the material required, which could be illustrated in the case of the military. The creative act, as Sir John Eccles, Buckminster Fuller, Karl Popper, and others have described it, is the product of weightless and immaterial mind, pure and simple; that alone does all the creating.[37] All creative work is art, and none know that better than the great creative scientists, as John M. Keynes points out in his study on Newton.[38] All creative power is "genius," for all genius is by definition creative, an inborn capacity that cannot be traced back farther or derived from any other source than the mind of some individual. This, of course, is a mystery, but it is real.

But with that are we not asking for the impossible? We are talking here about ourselves and the rest of the Latter-day Saints. Geniuses are few and far between, and there is no known method of producing them. You can't ask miracles of people. But if that is the answer, then let us forget all that talk about men becoming as gods, "As God is, man may become," ruling and reigning forever. Just last Sunday Brother Ballard told the world what prodigies are expected of the Latter-day Saints, and he declared that "we believe that as spiritual children of our Father in Heaven we have that capacity."[39]

What Kind of Progress?

There are two stock objections to any proposal of living forever, namely, (1) the desperate monotony of the standard hymn-singing, harp-playing, Christian heaven, the endless boredom of it all. Related to that is (2) the non-progressive, stagnant, everlasting sameness of existence. Science fiction writers like Robert Heinlein have written about the Old Ones[40] in some imaginable future world who have lived on for untold ages, seen it all, are bored beyond endurance, yet who cannot die, doomed to the same terrible fate to which Alma consigns the wicked ones who are not fit for eternal life yet must suffer it (Alma 12:25-26).

And so we get to what we consider an improvement on the picture, what we call a dynamic society as opposed to a stable one. Let us consider briefly the case of the progressive, competitive, acquisitive society, which must always be expanding. This, as Brigham Young and John Kenneth Galbraith have shown, is a physical impossibility;[41] for not only is the supply of raw materials limited by nature (we do not go to the moon for them, said Brigham), but as Paul tells us, it is only good for people to consume what they need. To want more is a "temptation and a snare" (1 Timothy 6:8-10). We have contrived a way to keep things going by destroying our natural resources at an accelerating pace as long as there are any left, while assuring an expanding market by ever more extravagant excesses of Madison Avenue unreality, inventing outrageous needs for pernicious products. To keep producing what we do not need, not only high-powered advertising but deliberate obsolescence is necessary: the greatest buildings are designed to be pulled down in thirty years; mighty dams fill up in twenty to fifty years; oil fields and mines play out; the great woods vanish; and what is the end product of modern civilization? Quite literally and actually, the *garbage dump*.

In the winding-down phase of World War II, I was at Sixth Army Group headquarters in Heidelberg making out the daily intelligence reports. Just outside the city in the Rhine Plain was an enormous dump. I had never seen anything remotely resembling a city dump in Germany during my mission; such a thing was simply inconceivable. But in every European town the sign of American military occupation was sure to be a huge *tel*, smoldering amid miasmic vapors while the hungry natives busily salvaged among its foul deposits. Every civilization is destined at best to become rubble. What does an expanding, predatory civilization leave behind for posterity? Junk. Even the ruins are hideous.

Well, what do stable cultures leave behind? Themselves. By virtue of staying themselves, they survive indefinitely—five thousand years is quite possible. For they are not brittle as the wholly competitive orders are, easily shattered, as the Book of Mormon shows us, by envy and strife when the pressure is on. The well-known prehistoric ways of the "primitives" and the manners and customs of "the unchanging East" leave much to be desired, to be sure, for their vices and cruelties are often as much a part of the package as the appealing quaintness and sometimes haunting beauty of ancient things. But an *eternal* society, an everlasting Zion, worlds without end — that is quite another thing. It can no more carry on forever laden with defects and imperfections than a bridge or tower can stand forever weakened by even minor flaws in construction.

But there have been some almost-stable structures in which life is far more enjoyable than in the restless and acquisitive "progressive" order of things — that is precisely why they are so enduring — because everybody likes them. I saw the clearest contrast between these two ways of life when I was in Hotevilla some years ago. The Peabody Corporation, eager to grab tribal coal lands, had pitted what it called the "progressive" members of the tribal council against the "traditionalist" party led by John Lansa. The company's plan was highly progressive; it was to move the entire tribe to Los Angeles and establish them in mobile homes at the company's expense. This would supplant that nonprogressive, tradition-bound society that had found a secure and peaceful way of life (the word *Hopi* means "peaceful") for at least a thousand years in a land where none of us could survive for *one* year: Sister Teresa Harvey's house at Walpi was tested by the tree-ring method and found to be eight hundred to eleven hundred years old. Strangely enough, life in these stable societies is anything but boring, as my frequent visits to the Hopis showed me, for each new generation coming along has to learn about the mystery of the world as it is, "so various, so beautiful, so new"; and each individual, young or old, spends his whole lifetime familiarizing himself with ever-new and exciting wonders of the Creation, the world of nature, which, as President Joseph F. Smith said, exactly resembles heaven, after which it was patterned, as it came from the hand of God.[42]

On the other hand, for excitement in our dynamic, restless, ambitious society, we have virtually given the monopoly to the world of prime-time TV, glorifying the four things Mormon says will destroy a civilization—the lust for power, riches, popularity, and the desires of the flesh (3 Nephi 6:15): the whole scenario of our idealized lifestyle comes night after night to one ordained solution, the definitive quietus of the mandatory explosion, vaporizing all the bad guys in an instant and promising vistas of indefinable and ineffable future bliss to all the good guys. Even the "lifestyles of the rich and famous" have become a dismal bore in short order, a supersaturation of routines and postures. An issue of *Mademoiselle*—296 pages long—is nearly all advertising, scores and scores of ads all striving to be outrageously, impudently far-out and sophisticated, and all desperately and pathetically alike.

The smoldering dump, the frantic disinformation that keeps it going, the ghastly inner cities, and finally the terror of the age, the nondisposable mountains of radioactive garbage which only Utah welcomes, are all necessary to maintain the capacity to consume on a par with the capacity to produce. It is the stable cultures that are really progressive. We are only to stay here for a limited time in the brief testing situation; there is no need to replace the props by ever-new and improved models, because the props are new to every generation, and the test is a standard one. By neglecting to consult the writings of the ancients, we miss the fact that in their trials and triumphs, individually and collectively, they had to undergo exactly the same trials that we do: the props of the plays, the technology and the fashions, wear out and are constantly being replaced, but the issues and the plot always remain the same. Today, some scientists are observing with wonder that amidst all the vast, uncontrollable destructive powers that are on the loose in the universe, enlisted in the service of remorseless and irreversible entropy, here on this perilously exposed little planet, battered by solar winds from one side and cosmic rays from the other, while seething inwardly with unimaginable heat and pressure, we somehow find ourselves in an ambience peculiarly congenial to our comfort and convenience, as if somebody actually had us in mind. Why should we seek to alter the order of life in such a world at the ultimate risk of destroying it utterly.[43]

Few seem to realize that by the injunctions of our religion we are committed to a stable economy. Adam was told that he could eat freely of anything in the Garden, but that he was not to despoil it but was charged expressly to "take good care of it." We are no longer in the Garden, but we are striving to return to it: "We believe . . . that Zion (the New Jerusalem) will be built upon the American continent [in fact, by the law of consecration we are working on that right now]; . . . and that the earth will be renewed and receive its paradisiacal glory" — the earth again as it should be (Article of Faith 10).

With Adam we are invited to take freely of whatever we need of "the beasts of the field and the fowls of the air, and that which cometh of the earth" (D&C 49:19). That is the rule; taking what we need is not murder to get gain, not the Mahan principle; that is another economy entirely, which pretends to justify itself on the grounds of necessity. "That great secret" of converting life into property (Moses 5:31), we see it at work from the professional hit man and the impartial arms merchant down to the profit-boosting, life-shortening additives in the supermarket.

A far commoner objection to eternal constancy than lack of progress is the fear of a monotonous sameness in a stable society, where fashions of dress and diet stay the same for ages. It is even objected that as people become more perfect, they will become more alike. Well, in some things we should be alike. As people develop more perfect bodies, they do come to be alike in that aspect. As far as we know, the angels all dress alike, in basic white. How monotonous! But that is not where we seek variety and originality — no one had more boundless contempt for "the nasty and pernicious fashions" of the ladies than Brigham Young.[44] Yet it is precisely to the externals that decadent societies turn for inspiration. Doctors and trainers often see perfectly developed bodies, but nobody can even begin to imagine what a perfect *mind* would be like; that is where the whole range of progress and growth must take place.

Let us take the case of the three B's. After the marvelously inventive music of the Renaissance and early Baroque, there was little more to be said. And then along came Bach, who in all modesty opened up new worlds. That pretty well finished it, until along came Beethoven, and he opened up new worlds, leaving nothing else to do, that is, until Brahms came along and opened up yet new worlds. What each of these men did was unique; none of them ever produced a "school," none gave rise to generations of imitators — each was himself and himself alone. As the works of the masters progress, they tend to become ever more alike in their attributes of greatness, the loftiness of spirit, the total honesty and confident mastery of their idiom, their reverential awe in the presence of their own shortcomings and the genius of others. They resemble each other as the peaks of the Himalayas resemble each other. But at the same time, as each one grows, his works become less and less like those of anyone else, until the great masters are completely beyond imitation; no one would even want to imitate them. Minor composers by the hundreds flourished in the days of all three B's, and they all sound just alike. It is the inferior who lack variety, and they strive for it by frantic imitation of the most far-out type, which of course becomes the most stereotyped; or else they seek for recognition in titles, offices, and awards.

Philip of Macedon in a writing called the *Pseudo-*

Callistenes explains the peculiar greatness of his son, Alexander, by noting that he was *homoios te phusei*, of the same natural makeup as anyone else, but was of an *anomoios* character, that is, absolutely unique in character, that quality which "was not created or made, neither indeed can be" (D&C 93:29). Alexander, in turn, declared that there was only one man whom he would prefer to be "if I were not Alexander," and that was, of all people, Diogenes, who lived in a tub and went about like the prophets of Israel, advertising a "mystery" by waving his lamp in search for an honest man. For Alexander the Great, Diogenes was the greatest because he never felt obliged to be like anyone else.

Whenever a creator creates, it is something that has never been done before. "Lord, how is it done?" Admittedly we are launched into a daring enterprise of fearful commitment. "I saw the father work out a kingdom with fear & trembling, & I can do the same."[45] The creative moment is entirely one's own, or it is not creative; one must find oneself in a new and unprecedented situation and all alone, with nothing to sustain one but faith. Yet, strangely, the reality of one's existence is sufficient guarantee to keep one going; if we can seek no further, neither do we need to: "Through faith we understand that the worlds were formed by the word of God" (Hebrew 11:3). Faith suggests something like the four elemental forces: we know that they exist by observing their effects, and we can profit by respecting the rules they seem to prefer. But no one has even an inkling of an idea of what they are.

Vates malorum

There is a strange thing in the land. That tendency to suicidal suspension of reason and conscience which the Greeks called *atē* seems to have seized the whole world. Life on earth has suddenly taken on an apocalyptic aspect. There is much debate and uncertainty about the dating of the biblical plagues, but there can be no question about the timing of those set forth in our modern scriptures: "With the sword and by bloodshed the inhabitants of the earth shall mourn; . . . and with famine, and plague, and earthquake" (D&C 87:6). And just a few years ago we thought we had famine and plague licked. We have been taught to expect what we now see around us, "secret combinations and the works of darkness, . . . fires, and tempests, and vapors of smoke in foreign lands, . . . wars, rumors of wars, and earthquakes in divers places. . . . There shall be great pollutions upon the face of the earth; there shall be murders, and robbing, and lying, and deceivings, and whoredoms" (Mormon 8:27-31). You get it all on prime time: "For behold, ye do love money, and your substance, and your fine apparel, and the adorning of your churches. . . . Why do ye . . . suffer the hungry, and the needy, and the naked, and the sick and the afflicted to pass by you and notice them not" (Mormon 8:37, 29), and so on. "Behold, the sword of vengeance hangeth over you; and the time soon cometh that he avengeth the blood of the saints upon you" (Mormon 8:41). We could go on and on, but what about the other side of the picture? That too is prophesied.

"Israel, Israel, God is calling," we often sing, "Babylon the great is falling." But we have taken our stand between them; Brigham Young speaks of Latter-day Saints who want to take Babylon by one hand and Zion by the other — it won't work. Since World War II, it seems that we have been steadily converging with Babylon while diverging from some of the old teachings. Latter-day Saint children of the rising generation have never heard of their Guardian Angel, or of the recording of our every deed in a book in heaven; they were never told as we were as children that "it is a sin to kill a fly," and have never heard that satirical little verse which General Authorities used to quote in stake conference: "Money, O Money, thy praises I'll sing! Thou

art my Savior, my God and my King!" That would be quite
unthinkable today, a kind of sacrilege. Because some of
the old teachings are still preserved in the temple, certain
anomalies appear to the younger generation. A bishop told
me this month that people coming to renew their recommends when they are asked whether they keep all their
covenants frequently answer no, explaining that they do
not keep the law of consecration. A General Authority
recently told me that the important thing is to observe the
law of consecration "spiritually." Yes indeed, say I, and
the law of tithing also—how much better to observe *it*
spiritually than in a gross, material way—a great comfort
to the rich. And yet the express purpose of both those laws
is to test the degree of our attachment to material things,
not to provide an exercise in "spiritual" semantics.

Well, it has all been foreseen and prophesied. "Wherefore, fear and tremble, O ye people, for what I the Lord
have decreed . . . shall be fulfilled" (D&C 1:7). I find it
highly significant that *all* the prophecies of the Millennium
specify that it must be immediately preceded by tremendous destructions, a royal house-cleaning, with the vapors
of smoke covering the earth and all the tribes of the earth,
no matter how far removed, in mourning.

The best answer to our questions about what to do for
a thousand years and how one goes about creating is to
be found in what is perhaps the most portentous message
delivered to the modern world, the letter from Liberty Jail.
The whole thing deals with the perilous condition of the
Saints caught between the vision of Zion and the American
Dream. Their fixation on Zion put them terribly at odds
with the world around them: "Every species of wickedness
and cruelty practiced upon us will only tend to bind our
hearts together and seal them together in love."[46] "The
inhumanity and murderous disposition of this people! It
shocks all nature; it beggars and defies all description;
. . . it cannot be found among the heathens . . . among

the savages of the wilderness."[47] But even more dangerous was the threat of that other dream to their own integrity.

Was it expecting too much of ordinary people to turn from one world to another? They had a hard time making it: "How vain and trifling have been our spirits, our conferences, our councils, our meetings, our private as well as public conversations—too low, too mean, too vulgar, too condescending for the dignified characters of the called and chosen of God . . . from before the foundation of the world!"[48] They never completely broke contact with the world, and after the death of Brigham Young they were pulled irresistibly into its orbit. We say, The Prophet! The Prophet! We have got us a Prophet! But when he speaks on the most solemn occasion, the bicentennial of the nation, with the deepest fervor and conviction about the conditions of the time and the course we must take, we give his remarks the instant deep-freeze.

The supreme revelation on authority and guidance is the letter from Liberty Jail (D&C 121). We are everlastingly talking about being "spiritual"; what does that mean? The highest state of spirituality is to be filled with the spirit of God, the Holy Ghost, which has "no other effect," says the Prophet, than that of releasing our intelligence, "expanding the mind, enlightening the understanding, and storing the intellect with present knowledge."[49] I say "releasing" because "intelligence . . . was not created . . . neither indeed can be," for "man also was in the beginning with God" (D&C 93:29). Like other latent forces, intelligence is there and waiting to be released. Note the key words in this statement on the high estate of spirituality. It is peculiarly "powerful in expanding [1] the *mind*, enlightening [2] the *understanding*, and storing [3] the *intellect* with present [4] *knowledge*, of a man who is the literal seed of Abraham."[50] And if you do not happen to be that, "the pure [5] *spirit of intelligence*," if one cultivates it, "will make him actually of the seed of Abraham."[51] It is "[6] the *spirit of revelation* . . . when you feel *pure intelligence* flowing into you, it will give you sudden strokes of [7] *ideas.*"[52] It is the merit of the seed of Abraham, with all their stubbornness and backsliding, that above all people they treasure the things of the mind. The first commandment given to the Church in modern times was "seek not for riches but for wisdom, and behold, the mysteries of God shall be unfolded unto you" (D&C 6:7). It would be hard to imagine a program more repugnant to the present course the world is taking.

And what is the good news about those creative powers? How can they be approached even in this life? By faith, to be sure: "Let thy bowels also be full of charity towards all men . . . and let virtue garnish thy thoughts unceasingly; then shall thy confidence wax strong in the presence of God; and the doctrine of the priesthood shall distil upon thy soul as the dews from heaven" (D&C 121:45). We have, of all people, Sigmund Freud to thank for showing us how our sins, even if we don't think of them as sins and cover them up by protestations of noble and selfless motivation, nevertheless abide hidden in the subconscious, to undermine our *confidence,* paralyze action, and lead to all sorts of frustrations, ulcers, rashes, and nervous disorders; only with virtuous thoughts can we proceed with that total confidence which creative work requires. "The Holy Ghost shall be thy constant companion [that is the inspiration for which we are eligible here below], . . . and thy dominion [the scope of influence and control] shall be an everlasting dominion, and *without compulsory means,* it shall flow unto thee forever and ever" (D&C 121:45-46). What a timely message in a world that is unable to conceive of achieving anything at all except by compulsory means.

Question Period

Sister Camilla Kimball, with characteristic directness and insight, asked, "After all, just what specifically are we to do on our thousand-year vacation?" Others intoned Amen to that, and so further clarification was in order. This is how I would answer:

The solution is at hand in the very first step of our initiation into the kingdom—an active brain. We can think of the brain as Sir John Eccles and others do, as supplying the substance of thought to the mind.

Q. What does the mind do with the stuff?

A. That is up to the mind. It is up to you. Spengler thought the ultimate disaster for any civilization or individual was to end up in a condition of *Problemlosigkeit*—having completely run out of problems.

Q. What do we do then?

A. Not to worry. The mind itself is the problem and must, as Shakespeare tells us, minister to itself.

Q. But there is still the question, "Men and Brethren, what shall we do?"

A. Anything you want to!

Q. But that is no answer!

A. You will not get the answer until you get over your present hangup.

Q. How do we do that?

A. Do what Peter tells us to do: Have faith that there is more than you know; repent of all your present shallowness and silliness; wash off everything of this world in the waters of baptism, and be reborn, not in the self-congratulatory one-shot manner of pop religion, but to a course of action requiring perpetual, progressive repentance. Then "ye shall receive the gift of the Holy Ghost" and get the guidance you need (Acts 2:37-38).

Q. Perpetual repentance?

A. At least until you are full of grace and truth, which is nowhere within the foreseeable future. Meanwhile, "an unexamined life is not worth living," as Socrates said.

Q. And what do you examine?

A. The scope of things we can do and should be doing; the order of their priority is the domain of philosophy.

Q. Then why haven't the philosophers answered the question of what we should be doing?

A. Because they are required by their profession to disagree. They have answers, but altogether too many of them!

Q. Then where do we turn?

A. Always to the gospel. Let us review our rambling discourse. We began by noting that wherever we turn today we find frank admission of dire delinquency in the American way of life. That is why I asked the question What should we be doing? Then I noted that we are endowed at birth with capacities which in the Endowment proper we are challenged to put to use here and in eternity. We are expected to observe, listen, communicate, beget, construct, and so on. And the materials to work with are all at hand. What more could you ask?

Q. What indeed. You said what more when you pointed out that we have altogether too much potential and too much material to deal with ever to be sure of choosing the most profitable course of action. So we do need some more.

A. Meaning that we will always need the gospel.

Q. But we are also told that it is an unprofitable servant who must be commanded in all things; that men must do much good of themselves, and so on. Isn't that a contradiction?

A. No. Suppose you present the hypothetical Gentle Savage with a flute or a guitar. He asks you, What shall I do with it? If you are wise you will not answer him but let him find out for himself as others have, and that is best for all concerned, for he may come back to you for lessons and know how to appreciate them.

Q. And how does that apply to us?

A. The present generation of students are given the aptitude and the instrument, but they take no action.

Q. Why not?

A. They are simply not interested. They are too busy thinking about lunch, cooked on a jim-cracked philosophy that has been pushed on them as the epitome of wisdom, the credo of business civilization: "There is no free lunch!" They are paralyzed; Satan has won this round.

Q. What do you mean.

A. He has us all believing that if we stop working for him we will starve, that if we do not play his game we must become the victim; "he that departeth from evil maketh himself a prey" (Isaiah 59:15). The treasures of the earth — the precious metals, oil, coal, uranium, and so on — have indeed enabled the prophesied "secret combinations for power and gain" to buy up kings and presidents, armies and navies, popes and priests (the military-industrial-ecclesiastical complex, if you will) as a rule of blood and horror even now spreads over the entire earth.

Q. What has that to do with the subject at hand?

A. In such a condition I can think of no more timely or wholesome subject of study than what awaits us beyond all this feverish, depraved, and demented activity. If we could do what we really wanted to do, what would it be? We must at least think about it if we would ever start in that direction — in which, incidentally, we are supposed to have been moving ever since 1830.

Q. But weren't Brothers Joseph, Brigham, Taylor, Woodruff, Snow, and so on, looking beyond the mark? Aren't such things out of range of our feeble vision and even more beyond our capacity, best left for the present out of sight and out of mind? Shouldn't we keep within the safe and familiar boundaries of the world as we know it, the real world?

A. That, dear brethren, is the condition known as being damned. Do you want to settle for that?

Notes

1. Lester C. Thurow, "A Surge in Inequality," *Scientific American* 256 (May 1987): 30.

2. Cf. Horace, *Epistles* I, 1, 65-66: "Does he advise you better, who bids you 'make money, money by fair means if you can, if not by any means money.' " For English translation, see T. E. Page, ed. *Satires, Epistles and Ars Poetica* (London: Heinemann, 1966), 257. See also Alexander Pope, *Epistle* I, 1, 103: "Get place and wealth, if possible with grace; if not by any means get wealth and place."

3. Ivan Boesky, in an article by Mariann Caprino, "Healthy Greed Was Boesky's Undoing," *Salt Lake Tribune* (20 November 1986): D9.

4. Haynes Johnson, "Student Values? Peace, Love Give Way to Money, Power," *Salt Lake Tribune* (24 April 1987): A22.

5. William James, *Essays in Philosophy* (Cambridge: Harvard University Press, 1978), 19-20; cf. William James, *Essays in Radical Empiricism* (Cambridge: Harvard University Press, 1976), 45, where James differentiates between the "brain which functions so as to insure survival" and the "reflective intellect" which operates beyond experience.

6. Robert Burns, "To a Mouse," *Poetical Works of Robert Burns* (Philadelphia: Lippincott, n.d.), 134-35.

7. Advertisement in *Mademoiselle* (April 1987): 30.

8. Spencer W. Kimball, "The False Gods We Worship," *Ensign* 6 (June 1976): 3-6.

9. Ibid., 4.

10. Merrill McLoughlin, "A Nation of Liars?" *U.S. News and World Report* 102 (23 February 1987): 54.

11. *Nation's Business* 75 (June 1987): 1; Harry Bacas, "To Stop a Thief," *Nation's Business* 75 (June 1987): 16-22.

12. The brochure from Tom Harward begins in large bold letters: "The startling confessions of a Maverick Lawyer (Mr. Charles Abbott) who is willing to reveal the money-making secrets of his millionaire clients."

13. Ibid.

14. Jim Woolf, "Tooele Site Proposed as N-Waste Facility," *Salt Lake Tribune* (8 May 1987): B1.

15. James R. Kearl's report in Sue Bergin, "5 Views," *BYU Today* 41 (April 1987): 47.

16. William Shakespeare, *Hamlet*, act I, scene ii, line 133.

17. Ibid., act IV, scene iv, lines 33-39.

18. *TPJS* 137.

19. Ibid., 141.

20. Regarding *theatromania,* see Hugh W. Nibley, "Victoriosa Lo-quacitas: The Rise of Rhetoric and the Decline of Everything Else," *Western Speech,* 20 (Spring 1956): 57-82; "Sparsiones," *Classical Journal* 40/9 (June 1945): 515-43; *The Roman Games as a Survival of an Archaic Year-cult* (Ph.D. diss., University of California at Berkeley, 1939).

21. Sophocles, *Oedipus the King,* 1528-30; cf. F. Storr, *Sophocles,* 2 vols. (Cambridge, MA: Harvard University Press, 1968), 1:139.

22. Stephen L Richards, *Where Is Wisdom* (Salt Lake City: Deseret Book, 1955), 400; cf. Stephen L Richards, "Counsel," *Speeches of the Year* (Provo: Brigham Young University, 1957), 1-8.

23. See "Meaning of the Temple," (Provo: F.A.R.M.S., 1975); cf. Hugh W. Nibley, "The Idea of the Temple in History," *MS* 120 (August 1958): 228-37, 246-49; reprinted as "What Is a Temple," in *CWHN* 4:355-90.

24. Lorenzo Snow, in LeRoi C. Snow, *Improvement Era* 22 (June 1919): 655-56; cf. *TPJS* 345.

25. Horace, *Epistle* I, 1, 59-60.

26. Andrew F. Ehat and Lyndon W. Cook, eds., *The Words of Joseph Smith* (Provo: Religious Studies Center, 1980), 366.

27. Haggadah in Willis Barnstone, *The Other Bible* (San Francisco: Harper and Row, 1984), 15; cf. Angelo S. Rappoport, *Myth and Legend of Ancient Israel,* 3 vols. (London: Gresham, 1928), 1:139-40; cf. Rabbi H. Freeman and Maurice Simon, *Midrash Rabbah,* 9 vols. (London: Soncino Press, 1961), 1:56-59; cf. E. A. Wallis Budge, "Discourse on Abbatôn," in *The Dialect of Upper Egypt,* 6 vols. (London: Oxford University Press, 1914), 4:480-82.

28. Regarding the Shabako Stone, see *Das "Denkmal Memphi-tischer Theologie" der Schabakostein des Britischen Museums,* part I of *Dramatische Texte zu altaegyptischen Mysterienspielen* in Kurt Sethe, *Untersuchungen zur Geschichte und Altertumskunde Ägyptens* (Leipzig: Hinrichs, 1928), 10:20-80; for an English translation, see James B. Pritchard, ed., "Egyptian Myths, Tales and Mortuary Texts," *Ancient Near Eastern Texts,* tr. John A. Wilson, 3rd ed. (Princeton, NJ: Princeton University Press, 1969), 4-6; cf. Miriam Lichtheim, "The Memphite Theology," in *Ancient Egyptian Literature, a Book of Readings,* 3 vols. (Berkeley, CA: University of California, 1943), 1:51-57; James H. Breasted, "The Philosophy of a Memphite Priest," *Zeitschrift für Ägyptische Sprache und Altertumskunde* 99 (1901): 39-54, pls. I-II; Rabbi Akiba ben Joseph, *The Book of Formation (Sepher Yetzirah)* (London: Rider and Son, 1923), 247; cf. Papus (Gérard Encausse), *Qabalah* (Wellingborough, Northamptonshire: Thorson, 1977), 203-48.

29. On the initiatory rite of the opening of the mouth, see Hugh W. Nibley, *Message of the Joseph Smith Papyri: An Egyptian Endowment* (Salt Lake City: Deseret Book, 1975), 106-13; R. H. Charles, "The Books of Adam and Eve," *Apocrypha and Pseudepigrapha of the Old Testament,* 2 vols. (Oxford: Clarendon Press, 1973), 1:142; regarding "Blows of Death," see E. A. W. Budge, "Discourse on Abbatôn," 4:483-84; cf. Nibley, *Message of the Joseph Smith Papyri,* 106-13; 1 Enoch 69:6-7; E. I. Abrahams and C. G. Montefire, "The Pre-Talmudic Haggada," *Jewish Quarterly Review* 7 (October 1984-July 1985): 590-91.

30. S. Krauss, "Note sur le nom divin de vingt-deux lettres et sur le Démon de l'oubli," *Revue des Études Juives* 54 (1908): 254; on the "Demotion of Satan" see Budge, "Discourse on Abbatôn," 4:483-84; cf. Nibley, *Message of the Joseph Smith Papyri,* 106-13.

31. Regarding the opening of the mouth, see Nibley, *Message of the Joseph Smith Papyri,* 106-13.

32. Niger Calder, *The Mind of Man* (London: British Broadcasting, 1970), 14, 32-33.

33. JD 25:52-56; cf. JD 8:139.

34. For information regarding the Shabako stone, see above, note 28; cf. "Book of the Secrets of Enoch," 30:9, in R. H. Charles, *Apocrypha and Pseudepigrapha of the Old Testament,* 2 vols. (Oxford: Clarendon, 1973), 2:449.

35. "Come Let Us Anew," in *Hymns of the Church of Jesus Christ of Latter-day Saints* (Salt Lake City: Church of Jesus Christ of Latter-day Saints, 1985), no. 217.

36. Regarding Shabako Stone, see above, note 28; Joseph, *Book of Formation,* 7; and Papus, *Qabalah,* 226-27; cf. John Boslough, *Stephen Hawking's Universe* (New York: Morrow, 1985), 49-58.

37. John Eccles and Karl Popper, *The Brain and Its Self* (New York: Springer, 1981), 15-16; R. Buckminster Fuller, *Intuition* (New York: Doubleday, 1972), 15-16.

38. Royal Economic Society, ed., *Collected Writings of John Maynard Keynes,* 29 vols. (London: Macmillan, 1972), 10:364.

39. Elder Ballard's talk of May 12, 1987; Edward L. Kimball, *Teachings of Prophet Spencer W. Kimball* (Salt Lake City: Bookcraft, 1982), 393; Boyd K. Packer, "The Arts and the Spirit of the Lord," *Devotionals and Firesides* (Provo: Brigham Young University, 1976), 268.

40. Robert Heinlein, *Methuselah's Children* (New York: Signet, 1958).

41. John Kenneth Galbraith, *The Affluent Society,* 4th ed. (Boston: Houghton Mifflin, 1984); cf. JD 12:160; 17:41; 16:65; MS 39:119.

42. Joseph F. Smith, "The World of Nature Resembles Heaven," *Gospel Doctrine*, 8th ed. (Salt Lake City: Deseret Book, 1949), 21; cf. *JD* 23:169-75.

43. Nigel Calder, *The Violent Universe* (London: BBC, 1976); John D. Barrow and Frank J. Tipler, *The Anthropic Cosmological Principle* (Oxford: Clarendon, 1986).

44. *JD* 13:4.

45. *WJS* 6:358.

46. *TPJS* 130.

47. Ibid., 131.

48. Ibid., 137.

49. Ibid., 149.

50. Ibid.

51. Ibid., 150.

52. *TPJS* 151.

10

Funeral Address

Brethren and Sisters, after World War II, I taught a small Greek class. Don Decker was in it. He had grown up in the toughest part of Los Angeles, then had been a marine all his life; he was only twenty-one at this time when he came to Brigham Young University, and what on earth was he doing taking Greek? I soon discovered it was his own idea. If ever there was an independent young man, it was Don; he knew exactly what he was after. You ask, "But why? Why was he always running around looking everywhere for what he wanted?" He was looking for something. He was determined to follow Paul's injunction to prove all things, and he wasn't going to leave any stone unturned if he could help it. On the second day of class, it became immediately apparent that Don Decker was a person of all fire and intelligence. The keenness, the intensity, was consuming. I said to myself, "This is something! He can't keep this up." But after more than thirty-five years, it was the same old Don. He hadn't weakened. It was not a put-on.

When I was young, we used to use the word *genius* a lot. The word was thrown around and finally went out of use (a good thing, because it was being abused terribly). You rarely saw a genius, but Don was one. I've never known another person who comes closer to the true definition.

This talk was given at the funeral of Donald M. Decker on August 11, 1982, in Rexburg, Idaho, and is printed with permission of the family.

Don and Jere got married in the Salt Lake Temple; and Don, Jere, Phyllis, and I rode in the trolley car to Saltair to celebrate after the wedding. In the days of trolley cars, it was a very different world. Amazingly, this phenomenon, Don Decker, had a wife whose talents and strength of mind equaled his own. It was a case, as the ancients would have said, of the wise forces of the earth countering the mad force of the sun: "When the hot sun of the morning comes, all the little kids go out looking for things, turning over rocks, exploring everything. But when evening comes, you bring back the little goat and the sheep, and you bring the little boy back to his mother and to reason."[1] Don and Jere were an amazing, improbable combination, the happy combination you find in their children — all imaginative, idealistic, and quite sensible. That may sound like an oxymoron, an Irish bull, like soundless music or odorless perfume — sensible geniuses. But that's the way it worked.

Don was the most *sensitive* man in the world. Sensitive, yes, but not the most *sensible* man in the world. I don't think you ever find those going together. Don was something infinitely better than that and far more rare. He was a man determined to find out how things really are. That is where he directed his energies, and if he thought it might lie in this direction he looked here, and if in another direction then he looked there. He didn't exhaust any one direction because he thought he might be missing something somewhere else; he went remarkably far in more directions than any of the rest of us have risked. You see, one person wants him to go into biology, another into medicine; one wants him to go into literature, poetry, language, or into everything under the sun. Don got a good start in every one of them. He was looking for himself all the time. He was determined to devote his life, not to the momentary dictates of expediency or advantage, but to whatever schedule or scenario had been set for the eternal human family to live by. These he wanted to know. He was always studying the wider scenes. It sometimes made him impatient and daring, and restless.

When we first met, Don and I started going out to the Uintas together, often. Don was all for taking risks. You have to do that to be a Don Decker. But it is far better to take risks than not to move at all. You can always tone down; you can always, to some degree at least, redirect and control that volcanic energy. But if it isn't there, there is nothing you can do about it. In the case of all the rest of us, I'm afraid, very little is there.

Sometimes he was impatient, impulsive. He didn't want to be "cabin-cooped," confined, bound in by saucy doubts and fears, by little things. And I am pleased to say that as a result, Donald Decker had no career. Years ago, Stephen L Richards, at a devotional at BYU, spoke on the evils of "careerism."[2] He damned the idea of living for a career or having a career. Of course, we now give courses in careerism — how to make a career, how to do such and such for a career, and so forth. But this wasn't for Don.

Why don't we also climb the ladder? The degrees of glory? You're welcome to the corporate ladder, or to the military ladder, or to the academic ladder, which all go in terms of promotions. That is the all-important thing — to get the promotion. But in the end (and you very soon come to an end), as soon as you get where you think you're the best, you're cut off in any field. It ends with a whimper or a bang, depending upon whether it is retirement or suicide, and many of my friends have gone into both calamities. You certainly go nowhere after that. Don wouldn't have any of that.

Here was an inconceivable man. He never stopped doing what he was doing and was always doing something very different: "Without compulsory means it shall flow unto thee forever and ever" (D&C 121:46). Don did not worry about degrees and rank and who's better than who.

These have nothing to do with progress. Don wanted to find out things for himself. Don had the making of a great poet. These marvelously sympathetic lines say what Don would have said: "He speaks for everybody and to everybody." This line does not lack any of the qualities that make a poem great, and you rarely find them all combined in one immortal verse.

In terms of eternal progression, where are you going if you are not thinking of promotion? Paul said, "Eye hath not seen, nor ear heard, neither have entered into the heart of man, the things which God hath prepared" (1 Corinthians 2:9). We shouldn't try to guess what it will be like. But what is education for, then? Every time Don came around, I would heave a sigh: "Here we go. We're going to be talking all night long and Don will have the last word." But you don't let such opportunities go; you relentlessly follow an idea, the particular thing you are after—and Don was after it. He would search your brains for everything you had, and he knew how to do it.

A modest passage from Brigham Young answers the question What is education for? "Will education feed and clothe you, keep you warm on a cold day, or enable you to build a house? Not at all. Should we cry down education on this account? No. What is it for? The improvement of the mind; to instruct us in all arts and sciences, in the history of the world, in the laws of nations; to enable us to understand the laws and principles of life and how to be useful, while we live."[3] It all works together. It is the things of the mind that are really useful. Truth, wisdom, power, glory, light, and intelligence exist upon their own qualities. They do not, neither can they, exist on any other principle. Truth is congenial with itself. "Light cleaveth unto light" (D&C 88:40). It is the same with knowledge and virtue and all the eternal attributes. They follow after each other. Truth cleaves unto truth because it is truth. It

APPROACHING ZION

is to be adorned because it is an attribute of God, excellence for itself.

This picture describes Don—always after something, but not for any ulterior motive. There was no bread-and-butter motive behind his quest. One might think the guy crazy, wasting all that talent—always only searching. "Knowledge is power" is the slogan of a rascally world. Why else love truth? Is it because you can discover beauty in it, because it is congenial to you, or because you think it will make you a ruler or a lord? "If you conceive that you will attain to power, upon such a motive, you are much mistaken," says Brigham. "It is a trick of the unseen power that is abroad amongst the inhabitants of the earth, that leads them astray, binds their minds, and subverts their understanding." Then he goes all out: "Suppose that our Father in heaven, our elder brother, the risen Redeemer, the Saviour of the world, or any of the Gods of eternity should act on this principle, to love truth, knowledge, and wisdom, because they are all powerful. . . . They would cease to be Gods, . . . the extension of their kingdom would cease, and their God-head come to an end."[4] Yet this is the realm we seek and the direction we work forward: Leave the motives out and let the purpose in. Especially there are some things we should never look for— power and gain.

Donald was quick and intuitive; he had a positive genius for seeing connections. He loved to build structures, seeing dimensions of the gospel that Joseph Smith and Brigham Young and others saw, but that very few notice today. We would say he used the right side of his brain for much of his thinking, and that made him alien to much of our thinking, because we use only the left side. A great deal is being written and said about right- and left-brain processes today.[5] Don had the peculiar advantage of using both. He was profoundly intellectual but was at the same time a poet. There is supposed to be conflict between the right and left side of the brain. He worked them together, and as a result he was sort of a nine-days-wonder, a freak, a thing you never expect to meet on the street. Yet that's what he was. Also, his thinking, in which he pursued ideas with relentless persistence, was in directions alien to present-day scholarship, which uses only the left side of the brain. He enjoyed the great intellectual advantage of using both, which made him a man of two worlds with an impulsive, somewhat wildly youthful passion. Because of that, he was always jumping into places, exploring this, that, and the other, even some places he shouldn't have been. He was gaining experience, "finding out" (which is what we're supposed to be doing here).

How did he come to immerse himself in literature, particularly ancient literature, of all things? His passion for the Greeks grew increasingly, because he knew—he had seen as soon as he began to read—that the answers to the important questions may lie there, not at the shop or in the office. Today we ignore the documents. What do we have that Joseph gave us? Only books. The ordinances in the temple, as well as everything else, are all contained in the books he left behind. Although these were books written by men, God considers them of great value, and the angels do too. When the angel Gabriel came to Zacharias or to Mary, or when the angel Moroni came to Joseph Smith, what did they do? The margin of the New Testament will tell you that all the angel did was quote ancient scripture. Moroni came four times to Joseph Smith, quoting scriptures so well that Joseph knew them all by heart. He said some were different from what we find in our scriptures, and some were very much alike, but Moroni came four times, so that Joseph knew the message exactly. Still, he just quoted the words of ancient prophets who had lived before.

When the Lord himself came, what did he do after the resurrection? We read at the end of Luke 24, "Beginning at Moses and all the prophets, he laid out all the scriptures to them and their eyes were opened" (Luke 24:27). What did he do to the Nephites? He came to them; they didn't understand him. He read the scriptures to them. He insisted on going through the books, while also seeing to it that the books were all there. When the prophecy of Samuel the Lamanite came up missing, he said, "We've got to have this. Why didn't you write it down?" Nephi's face got very red, and he said, "Yes, we did forget to put that in, didn't we?" The Lord responded, "Well, see that you do put it in" (cf. 3 Nephi 23:8-14).

The Lord and the angels are concerned with the books written by the ancients. As Joseph said, "The immediate will of heaven is contained in the scriptures."[6] We are very much concerned with these things, very close to the books. This gives the books a timeless position. The Lord has said he will not reveal to us again what is already to be found in the books. We must read with great care, to make sure it isn't there already, before we ask for any more revelation.

It is not just the scriptures. We are commanded in D&C 109:14-16 (given at the dedication of the first temple, the great temple of Kirtland, which was to become a house of learning, a house of prayer, and President John Taylor tried to make it those things) to build a house of study. There people were to "seek . . . out of the best books words of wisdom" (D&C 88:118). A list of the best books had not yet been supplied. We must find these ourselves by diligently searching. If the scriptures bind the worlds together, the writings of man bind together the generations and the dispensations.

For Don Decker, the value of books was not academic. He did not seek the wisdom of the race, nor did he particularly note the skill of the writing (though you cannot avoid them), and he invariably gravitated to what was the greatest and best. What the books do contain is the experience of the race. In them you can see what men have learned and what they have gone through. For Don, reading this stuff was a profound experience. He could lose himself completely, identifying himself with a character from Shakespeare or Aeschylus or another author. It is not the author's intent we seek for at all. A wonderful passage at the end of Mormon reads: "The reason you will find this record valuable is not because we were wise men, but because we were damn fools. Thank the Lord that he has shown you our imperfections that you may learn to be a lot wiser than we have been" (cf. Mormon 9:31). These are books written by fools, and therefore they will help us. It is not just wisdom we are looking for, it is the experience that men have had, and we can find this in the record. We shouldn't expect new messages. Let us go to the books we have.

If this were somebody else's funeral, Don and I would go hence and discuss certain subjects until morning. These are subjects that constantly concerned him, because he did not linger on trivial things. Of course, he was after knowledge in my particular fields, which I myself know nothing about. He was as good in those fields as he was in his own, which was not bad at all. As I have mentioned today, many subjects concerned him. He was an astonishing man. He did what President Kimball tells us to do a great deal more of—to ponder.

Don's concern was with inexhaustible themes. He had nothing to do with mysticism. You see, *zen* implies there is nothing there. Nothing is real. It is all your own invention. The wisdom of the East is "Don't expect anything and you won't be disappointed." But that is not so. The new physics turns that notion right around. It used to be said, "Nothing is real. It is just all your own invention after all, isn't it?" And you have to admit, "Yes, it is." The new physics tells us, "If you can think of it, it is real. It must have come from somewhere. There is a real experience behind it. You wouldn't have invented it out of nothing."[7]

The idea of dispensations and episodes is very important here, because these notions are understood in limited context. Don always saw them in their historical context; without a limited, closed context, you cannot get anywhere. You will try to understand everything all at once. Doctrine and Covenants 93:30 says that everything must be understood in the sphere in which it exists. "Otherwise, there is no existence." If you wait until you get the ultimate answer, saying, "Take away all the boundaries; I want to know about everything now," you will never get anything. There is no existence unless you can see it in a closed system, which is, of course, what Einstein or anyone else gives us. We realize that now; all we will ever get is a closed system. That is why the episodes.[8]

The Christian world and the sciences alike believe that it is all just a one-act play. The Christians say it all began with the creation of Adam—there was nothing before; and it will end hereafter with the beatific vision, when we just look at the Lord or sing hymns forever. It came out of nothing (creatio ex nihilo), and it goes, as St. Jerome says, "back into the nothing, from which it came."[9] Science says it ends here. Wherever it began, it ends here.[10] In either case, it ends in a static heaven. But we say, "No, no, no." The play goes on forever, but in distinct episodes. Let us not mistake the episodes for the play, saying that is all there is. There was an episode that began with Adam, clearly marked, representing a particular age. The notion is very clearly defined in the temple. It is the transition from the Cretaceous to the Quaternary, where everything happens according to rule. (This is the sort of thing Don and I discussed. We would argue about the details of it.)

But let us never say that these episodes are all there is. Even in this short life, we pass through a number of distinct episodes, a number of distinct existences. You could refer to the "lives" of Don Decker, because he had very different lives, as we all have, our own seven stages. Biologically, I am assuredly a very different person from what I was a long time ago. These transitions, these rites of passage, are rites that take us from one state of existence to another; the process is an obsession with the human family, going back to the Stone Age (Don refers to them in a poem of his); and the rites of passage obsess us here and now. Quite literally, too. A cultural shock occurs when you pass from one state to the other. And the transitions are usually quite abrupt. You are born all of a sudden; you die all of a sudden. Each time you get a new name, a new rank, a new identity, a new function, a new office of priesthood or whatever it may be, you get new duties, new privileges; you become a different person. On many of these occasions, you change your name. You go not into another existence (the Egyptians would say *kheper*). That implies changing form without changing identity. The classic example with the Egyptians was the butterfly or the frog. A cocoon is not a caterpillar, nor is it a butterfly. The two states are the same creature, but what resemblance would you ever recognize?

Even while we are here, we must give up lives. *Lech lecha*, which means "get up and keep going," is the title of Abraham's life in the chapters of Genesis that describe him. The book of Abraham begins, "At the residence of my fathers, . . . I saw that it was needful for me to obtain another place of residence" (Abraham 1:1). Abraham had to get up and go, and he never settled until the end of his life. He had to buy a grave for his wife and himself from strangers in a strange land. His life was one continual going from one phase to another, moving from one existence to another all the time.

So it is with us here: *Lech lecha*. Sometimes it seems cruel. Shakespeare's sonnets are devoted very much to that theme. He treats the passing of youth as a form of

death, something you'll never get back again: you are another kind of person; it was another phase of life. Looking
back is very romantic. It was hell when you were in it, but
as you reflect back, it looks quite nice. We make that common mistake about youth; Shakespeare says it is death.
This is a profound tragedy, because as far as Shakespeare
was concerned, there is nothing to it. It is the "baseless
fabric of this vision, . . . it . . . shall dissolve; . . . and,
like the insubstantial pageant faded, leave not a rack behind."[11] That was Shakespeare's last word in the *Tempest*.
There is nothing more. It is the end of the show. We are
all going home. That is what makes the play so very sad:
to have to pass from one phase to another.

But not with us—not with us at all. Passing from one
phase is the normal thing; it makes existence more exciting.
That is the central theme of the temple—the subject to
which my and Don's discussions invariably tended. In each
state, the creature must pass through; there is something
we couldn't get anywhere else.

But how can a few brief years spent here, born to
trouble as we are, have a significant impact on eternal
existence? Eternity is a long time; earth life is just a second—a fantastic disproportion. This life, Lehi tells us, is
only a probation, only a test (1 Nephi 10:21; 2 Nephi 2:21;
Alma 34:32). A test, to be searching and definitive, need
last only a few seconds. You can test a person's knowledge
of a language in but two minutes, even one minute. Say
something to that person, and if he answers in the idiom,
you will know how well he knows the language. If you
are testing for acids or bases, you don't have to work all
day with a ten-thousand gallon vat, only a few minutes
with three drops.

The test for this life is not for knowledge; it is not for
intelligence, or for courage, or for anything like that. That
would be a huge joke. None of us knows very much, none
of us is very brave, none of us is very strong, none of us

is very smart. We would flunk those tests terribly. As Alma said, we are only to be tested on one thing—the desires of our heart (Alma 41:3); that is what we are really after. And in that way we betray ourselves completely. Anyone who knows the signs, who knows what to look for—not just our Heavenly Father, but even a good psychiatrist (another subject that interested Don immensely)—can spot it just like that. You yourself can see your own life; you can test yourself. Thus we don't need to go on forever suffering the same nonsense in order to see the things we can be tested for, namely the two things and the only two things we are good at: we can forgive and we can repent. These are the two things the angels envy us for, as the church fathers said. Repentance was a great subject with Don. For years Don had an obsession with his favorite character, Lear, the great example of repentance.

Of course, that is the whole thing in the gospel. "Wherefore [the first word to Adam], . . . thou shalt repent and call upon God in the name of the Son forevermore" (Moses 5:8). When the Lord came to the Nephites, among his first words to them were these: "This is the gospel, that the Father commandeth all men, everywhere, to repent" (3 Nephi 11:32). This is not a popular doctrine. In my thirty-five years at BYU, I have heard only one sermon (given by Stephen L Richards, incidentally) on repentance. And it was not well received. "Don't tell us to repent. Repentance is for the bad guys." But Don knew that it was called the gospel of repentance. All must repent constantly, each for himself. You can't repent another person.

Ezekiel 38:18-19 defines a righteous man. Who is righteous? Anyone who is repenting. No matter how bad he has been, if he is repenting he is a righteous man. There is hope for him. And no matter how good he has been all his life, if he is not repenting, he is a wicked man. The difference is which way you are facing. The man on the top of the stairs facing down is much worse off than the man on the bottom step who is facing up. The direction we are facing, that is repentance; and that is what determines whether we are good or bad.

Don always pondered the problem of repentance. He was aware of it; and how few are. We are expected to commit all kinds of sins here, and also discover them. We are supposed to dig the nitty-gritty out of the rug, so to speak. We are sent here, going on for eternity (and eternity is a long time), but we can't go on as defective vessels. If there is anything seriously wrong with our character, we want to find it out and get rid of it before we get launched on that tremendous project we are after. This is the place to find out all the dirty, nasty, little sides of our nature; it is the only place we can, because we are not in the presence of God and angels here, and it is possible for us to sin. So when God says to Adam, "We shall leave you now, but we shall visit you again" — as soon as he turns, who pops up? Satan. He says, "Aha! Here I am. Now we can really put Adam to the test." Satan is there to try him and to tempt him and us, but only if we are left here. We are supposed to find out all the dirtiness, the weakness, the sinfulness of our nature; and that is what keeps us repenting all the time until we reach the state of perfect grace and truth. Let us remember, the Only Begotten is full of grace and truth. When we reach that state, it will be just dandy. We can stop repenting, I suppose. But do we realize what that means? What grace, love, complete love for everything, and truth are? (Notice how that recurs in Don's poems. We mustn't spoof, we mustn't kid, and that is what makes a good poet as against the newspaper poet, the faker. Deep sincerity is not fakery; it is not a poetic device; it is not a gadget. There is nothing sentimental or mawkish. Probably the Church magazines would never accept it, because it is not sentimental enough. It is deep, and it is real.)

So it is here that we repent. I remember some of my former lives—my childhood and youth. I was bungling, bemused, wandering in a daze, getting pushed around, trying to push back, and not knowing what was going on. It was not the happy, carefree time we think. But it is profitable to me now. Our lives here will be profitable to us, of tremendous value, at some future time. We are told that spirits enter the other world somewhat in a daze (from the experience of many people—some of whom I know, including myself). The fact is, we are in a daze right here. I go around in a daze most of the time. Don owned a book of cartoons that very much expressed that common idea, "What am I doing here?" In the world we find ourselves in, the theme that comes to us first is, "What am I doing here?"—the dilemma of the person in the stews of New York, in the vileness of the ghettos, and so on.

It reminds me of my first day in Normandy. I woke up, saw beautiful red poppies waving in the breeze, and remembered, "In Flanders Field the poppies grow" from my grammar school days. I said, "Great guns! What am I doing here? This is where I came in." But one thing I have learned in the passage from one phase of existence to another is that nothing is lost in the process. If you had told me just a week or two ago, for example, that on August 11, 1982, I would be in Rexburg, Idaho, I would say, "You are absolutely crazy. This sort of thing doesn't happen. You're not a prophet. You don't know the future. What on earth would I be doing in Rexburg? I have too much to do in Provo." But here I am. That is the way things go. Did Don think he would be here, either? I am not at all disappointed. I am not at all shocked—now. In a strange way, it seems so natural and proper. This is one of the two miracles of the brain, a subject of almost furious investigation at the present time, namely consciousness: the fact that the brain can shut off completely and then turn on again; yet it is still all there.[12] Many scientific writings in various fields (and I just read the popular ones) are zeroing in on the idea of consciousness — the last mystery, a complete mystery. There are all sorts of switching centers in the head, but no locale for consciousness. It is not in the body (see Popper and Eccles' big book on the subject).[13] Popper is a strict evolutionist, a strict biologist, and the greatest authority on scientific method. Eccles is the best and foremost authority on the biology of the brain. Eccles came to the conclusion that the consciousness has nothing to do with the body. It is not in the body. Popper agrees, but he cannot accept the idea that it can exist independently of the body. Then how? asks Eccles (a very interesting dialogue in the book). Eccles concludes that it is inescapable that consciousness exists outside of and independent of the body. Popper will not go so far but knows no alternative.

Where is Donald Decker now? The answer has to do with time and place and dimensions. Today people are talking in terms of dimensions that are real but absolutely inconceivable. Remember, we begin with a *singularity* — we call it a singularity because we cannot describe it, we cannot imagine it, but it is absolutely real; that is the concentration of all that matters — and it ends with a black hole, which you cannot imagine, you cannot conceive, you cannot describe. But be assured, it really exists.[14] So if we talk about a universe that is full of things we cannot imagine but are real,[15] what a change things have taken in the past few years. The doors are wide open to all sorts of possibilities.

There are ties between the body and the mind. (This is a subject Don and I used to like to talk about.) There should be, for a physical resurrection does exist. We believe in it. We will need it. The body does play a definite role in the mind and the spirit. We came here to get a body for a definite purpose. But it is not a one-to-one relationship, certainly not here; for the time being only a temporary and wobbly relationship, I'm finding it to be, with consciousness going its own way. It blacks out completely sometimes, or at least partially. It fights the body or loses interest in it sometimes. Sometimes it makes me sick or well in spite of myself. Good old consciousness — overcoming the limitations of hunger and weakness, which it would impose; defying healthy revulsion for painful exposure, like holding our finger in a flame, or something like that. "We must eat in order to think. But how many thoughts will we get out of one crust of bread?" There is no proportion between the two, though there is a necessary connection. We must eat the bread in order to have the thought; if we get too weak, we can't think. We will be in a daze, and so we have to eat the bread. What is that proportion? How many thoughts are we going to get out of one piece of bread? That immediately makes us laugh, because the spirit is clearly independent.

The sessions would always end; Don would always win by wearing me out. That man had indefatigable energy. "Age could not wither nor custom stale"[16] Don's infinite variety, could it? But for once, you could say, I have the last word. No, I don't think I do have the last word here, brothers and sisters. May the Lord open the minds of all of us to understanding and becoming aware of these great blessings which we have been neglecting all this time and take the case of Donald Decker as an example to be followed, I pray in the name of Jesus Christ. Amen.

Notes

1. Sappho, Epithalamian Fragment 104a; see Denys Page, *Sappho and Alcaeus* (Oxford: Clarendon, 1955), 121.

2. Stephen L Richards, *Where Is Wisdom* (Salt Lake City: Deseret Book, 1955), 400.

3. *JD* 14:83.

4. Ibid., 1:117.

5. For example, Jan Ehsenwald, *The Anatomy of a Genius* (New York: Human Sciences Press, 1984), 3-19.

6. *TPJS* 54.

7. Heinz R. Pagels, *The Cosmic Code* (New York: Simon and Schuster, 1984), 153-65; cf. Harold Morowitz quoted in Paul Davies, *God and the New Physics* (New York: Simon and Schuster, 1983), 8, "Physicists, faced with compelling experimental evidence, have been moving away from strictly mechanical models of the universe to a view that sees the mind as playing an integral role in all physical events."

8. Karl Popper, *Logic of Scientific Discovery* (New York: Harper, 1965).

9. St. Jerome, *Apologia contra Rufinum* II, 5, 17 in *Corpus Christianorum*, series Latina, 74:37.

10. C. P. Snow, *Chronicles of Cambridge University*, cited in Hugh W. Nibley, "Science Fiction and the Gospel," *Latter-day Science Fiction*, ed. Benjamin Urrutia (Ludlow, MA: Parables, 1985), 2:6-7, says: "The tone of science at Cambridge in 1932 was the tone of Rutherford. [They had discovered the planetary structure of the atom.] Magniloquently boastful, creatively confident, generous, argumentative, and full of hope. [What more could he ask?] . . . He enjoyed a life of miraculous success." "But I am sure that even late in life he felt stabs of sickening insecurity." The author goes on to talk about the other giants at Cambridge: "Does anyone really imagine that Bertrand Russell, G. H. Hardy, Rutherford, Blackett and the rest were bemused by cheerfulness as they faced their own individual state? In the crowd, they were leaders; they were worshipped. But by themselves they believed with the same certainty that they believed in Rutherford's atom that they were going after this life into annihilation. Against this, they only had to offer the nature of scientific activity; its complete success on its own terms. It itself was a source of happiness. But it is whistling in the dark when they are alone."

11. William Shakespeare, *The Tempest*, act IV, scene i.

12. Nigel Calder, *The Mind of Man* (London: British Broadcasting, 1970), 25.

13. Karl R. Popper and John C. Eccles, *The Self and Its Brain* (New York: Springer-Verlag, 1981), 555-58.

14. Davies, *God and the New Physics*, 18, "The first instance of the big bang, where space was infinitely shrunken, represents a boundary or edge in time at which space ceases to exist. Physicists call such a boundary a *singularity*"; cf. John Boslough, *Stephen Hawking's Universe* (New York: William Morrow, 1985), 60, 101.

15. J. B. S. Haldane quoted in Arthur C. Clarke, *Profiles of the*

Future (New York: Holt, Rinehart, and Winston, 1984), 153, "The universe is not only queerer than we imagine—it is queerer than we *can* imagine."

16. William Shakespeare, *Anthony and Cleopatra,* act II, scene ii, line 240.

11

Three Degrees of Righteousness from the Old Testament

I was told that there were supposed to be three talks, and naturally I immediately thought of everything falling into three in the gospel and tradition. In the Old Testament there is the idea of the three degrees, which may rightly be designated as telestial, terrestrial, and celestial. For example, the ancient Gnostics, the early Christians, always talked about the *pneumatic*, the *psychic*, and the *hylic* types of human beings. The *pneumatic* is the spiritual, the *psychic* is the mixture of the two (body and spirit), and the *hylic* are those that are grossly and purely physical.[1] But this actually reflects the early Jewish teachings of the *neshamah*, which is the highest of the spirit; the *ruakh*, which is in between; and the *nefesh*, which is the lower spirit in this world.[2] We are taught in the Kabbalah a great deal about the three Adams. There is the celestial Adam, who was Michael before he came here; the terrestrial Adam, who was in Eden; and the telestial Adam, after he had fallen, who was down low.[3] The Kabbalah also tells about Jacob's ladder.[4] Joseph Smith taught that it represented the three stages of initiation in the temple, the three degrees of glory, which are designated as telestial, that is, the lowest order; and then astronomical, or dealing with the physical world, which is higher up still; and then finally the world which is beyond.[5] Particularly interesting is the designation in

---

This address was given in November 1982.

some of the newly discovered apocalyptic writings about the upper or hidden world, the Eden, and the lowest world.[6] The only way you can translate it is to use Joseph Smith's word, which is *telestial* (from the Greek *telos*), which means farthest removed, as distant as you can get, what the Arabs call the *aqsa*. Joseph Smith coined that word, and he couldn't have used a better one—the *telestial*, the farthest away of all the worlds. I will talk on the economies of the church in the Old Testament and elsewhere.

In every dispensation, the restoration of the gospel has brought with it a special way of life, not just an economy in the old sense. *Oikonomia* is the whole administration of everything we do, the way we do everything.[7] And it is made very clear in every dispensation: "I give not unto you that ye shall live after the manner of the world" (D&C 95:13). Whenever the gospel has been on earth, a peculiar order of things has been prescribed, and it has always been the same. This is because it is the celestial order—the order of Enoch, the eternal, the only order that God has found acceptable. So when we say that we believe in the same organization that existed in the primitive church (half of our Articles of Faith deal with the physical things of this world, with the church as an institution—and those are the only Articles of Faith that ever offended anybody; if you go through all the anti-Mormon literature [and years ago I did], the church's enemies don't object to doctrinal teaching but to those things that deal with the affairs of the world), namely apostles, prophets, teachers, and so on, what do we believe those offices did? What was their function? These titles are used by all other churches: the apostolic, bishops, and evangelists. But what did these people do? What was their function? How did the organization work: That is the subject of my remarks, first from the New Testament point of view. I take the New Testament before the Old Testament, because the New leads to the Old.

In Acts 2 and 4, we read what made the early organization of the church peculiar. Acts 2:42-43 reads, "They paid diligent heed to the teachings of the apostles and constantly and in common interest, in the breaking of bread and in prayers. And fear came upon many souls: and many wonders and signs were done by the apostles." There is the clue. If this was a marvelous system, why don't we have it today? Brothers and sisters, it will never work on any practical basis, and no economic expediency will ever put it over. You could argue until the cows came home that this is the only system that will ever work, that has ever been accepted by God or ever will be, and it's true; but it will work only in the celestial and eternal setting, where we are aware of these things. Notice what the motivation has to be. The people had to be scared stiff to begin with: "Fear came upon every soul: and many wonders and signs" (Acts 2:43). They lived in an element of supernatural manifestations. The system involved certain practices, but just try to make it work without the motivation of supernatural inspiration. Of course we are supposed to have it, but would you like a system in which fear came upon everybody? And signs and wonders were done by the apostles? Wouldn't we feel more comfortable if we just forgot the signs and wonders? They make us nervous.

Whenever an angel appears, what is the first reaction? People are scared to death, sore afraid, whether it be the apostles on the Mount of Transfiguration, the shepherds in the field, Mary in her room, or Zacharias in the temple. When someone comes from that other world, people are scared stiff, so the first thing the angel has to say is, "Don't be afraid. I bring good news, not bad news." It is culture shock. If the Lord were to come here, what would we ask? We would ask the rocks to cover us—anything but such a visit. It is not hell that we are afraid of—we can take plenty of that—but the thought of heaven, the thought of joy, that simply frightens us. The scriptures use the strongest possible language whenever they describe a person's reaction: "sore afraid"; still the translation is weak. The original means that they were scared to the point of paralysis.[8] When the angel reassures them, they feel all right again. But the most important thing is the spirit in which all this is done. "And all that believed were together, and had all things common; and sold their possessions and goods, and distributed them to everybody according to the needs of each. And they did continue daily with one accord in the temple and breaking bread from house to house, did share their nourishment with rejoicing and without guile, with simplicity of heart and without affection" (cf. Acts 2:44-46). But the happy days of the primitive church didn't last very long, as we know.

In Acts 4 the church is threatened. Naturally the world persecutes the church, because it is a culture shock for the world, too. The Christians are a standing rebuke to the world around them, the sort of thing that just cannot be tolerated. "And now, Lord, behold their threatenings: and grant . . . that signs and wonders may be done by the name of thy holy [son] Jesus. And when they had prayed, the place was shaken" (Acts 4:29-31). This is no normal procedure, to hold a meeting and decide to organize. It must be forced on people. The Lord takes us by the scruff of our necks when we're ready and says, "You're going to do things this way" or "That's the way I'm going to have it." Otherwise, the alternative becomes something else (though the other two orders have virtues, too). "And they were all filled with the Holy Ghost, and they spake the word of [the Lord] with boldness" (Acts 4:31). They had to be bold; the place was shaking. When the cards are on the table, you have got to play the game. It is the state of hesitancy, the in-between state, that so paralyzes. So the church decided to go one way: "And the multitude of them that believed were of one heart and of one soul" (Acts 4:32).

As in the city of Enoch, God called his city Zion because the inhabitants were of one heart and one mind. "Neither said any of them that ought of the things which he possessed was his own; but they had all things common. . . . And with great power gave the apostles witness" (Acts 4:32-33). There is always a power, a drive — heaven intervening because the people are willing to accept it finally, and embrace it boldly. *Then* the Lord can carry it out. But there is no compromise, no working gradually to this sort of thing. It comes by revelation, like the gospel itself. The restoration of the gospel was one long series of surprises, which things we never had supposed. That was one of the marvelous things about it, beginning with the story of not just the angels in the field, but Zacharias in the temple. He was actually paralyzed. He came out shaken, white as a sheet, and dumb — he couldn't speak. That was the effect of seeing the first angel that had visited the earth in four hundred years. Nobody had conceived anything like it. And it happened to everybody who received these heavenly manifestations. This is the atmosphere in which we are dealing.

The disciples witnessed with great power the resurrection and the forty-day ministry of Christ. For forty days the Lord came and taught them, on and off, how to establish the church.[9] Thus they were equipped to do it, whereas they hadn't been before. At the time of the crucifixion, they were a pitiful lot — scattered, frightened, despairing. They certainly didn't expect to see the Lord. When Mary and John said they had seen him, the disciples said, "You are raving, you are crazy. You haven't seen any such thing." And when they first saw him, what does Mark tell us was their first impulse? To run away. Frightened, they scampered away as far as they could get (Mark 16:8). Thomas was the only one who really believed in the resurrection of the Lord Jesus.

"And great *grace* was upon them all" (Acts 4:33; em-

phasis added). The word used is *charis*, supernatural manifestation. The disciples had the gifts of the Spirit. "Neither
was there any among them that lacked: for as many as
were possessors of lands or houses sold them, and brought
the prices of the things that were sold, and laid them down
at the apostles' feet"; we are told, for example, of Joses, a
wealthy Cypriote who, having land, "sold it, and brought
the money, and laid it at the apostles' feet" (Acts 4:34-35,
37). Incidentally, a surprising number of rich men in the
church today have come to the General Authorities and
offered to give the church everything they have. There are
people ready to do that today. Imagine that!

This isn't all so fantastic as it sounds. It *is* a total commitment. The story of Ananias is relevant here. "A certain
man named Ananias, with Sapphira his wife, sold a possession, and kept back part of the price, his wife also being
privy to it, and brought a certain part, and laid it at the
apostles' feet" (Acts 5:1-2). But Peter didn't believe in doing
things by halves. It's the cheating we don't like: "But Peter
said, Ananias, why hath Satan filled thine heart to lie to
the Holy Ghost [it is Satan that holds these things back],
and to keep back part of the price of the land? . . . Thou
has not lied unto men, but unto God" (Acts 5:3-4). The
amount didn't make any difference, the sin was the lie.
As Peter said, "Silver and gold have I none" (Acts 3:6) —
"I never carry it. We have sufficient for our needs." Ananias, hearing these words, had a heart attack, which
shows that the church leaders weren't fooling; it was all
deadly earnest. He "fell down, and gave up the ghost: and
great fear came on all them that heard these things" (Acts
5:5) — again fear, the driving motivation. Then Ananias'
wife came along and tried the same trick, and Peter said
to her, "How is it ye have agreed together to tempt the
Spirit of the Lord? . . . Then fell she down straightway at
his feet, and yielded up the ghost." Again, "and great fear
came upon all the church" (Acts 5:9-11). Ananias and his

wife were to be an example: one is not to play around with these things — not to deal, not to hedge, not to bargain with the Lord. "Great fear came upon all the church, and upon as many as heard these things" (Acts 5:11).

In all the Gospels we see the foundation of this order being laid by the commandments given by the Lord. Paul says, "Silver or gold or apparel of no man have I desired. You yourselves know that mine own hands have administered to my needs, and to those who were with me. I have shown you everything. It is necessary for you to work hard and support the weak, keeping in mind the teaching of the Lord Jesus when he himself said, 'It is better to give than to receive' " (cf. Acts 20:33-35). Peter, the president of the church, in doing the first miracle after the departure of the Lord, heard a lame man in the temple court, asking for alms; Peter, spoke to the man, saying, "Silver and gold have I none" (Acts 3:6). What did Peter have? He had sufficient for his needs, and that's all. This was the policy that the disciples followed. According to the teachings of the Lord, "Lay not up for yourselves treasures upon earth, where moth and rust doth corrupt, and where thieves break through and steal: But lay up for yourselves treasures in heaven. . . . For where your treasure is, there will your heart be also" (Matthew 6:19-21). This was an important part of the gospel. "These twelve Jesus sent forth, and commanded them, saying, . . . freely ye have received, freely give. Provide neither gold, nor silver, nor brass in your purses" (Matthew 10:5, 8-9). That is why Peter says, "Silver and gold have I none"; the Lord had commanded that he shouldn't have any.

Then was the interesting case of the rich young man, to whom Jesus said, "If thou wilt be perfect, go and sell that thou hast, and give to the poor, and thou shalt have treasure in heaven" (Matthew 19:21). But the young man didn't want to do it. He was very rich, but he did love the Lord and he was a good young man. The Lord did not say, "Wait a minute, fellow. Perhaps we can work something out here." So the young man went away sorrowfully. And the Lord let him go sorrowfully, then turned to the apostles and said (this is the point), "I say unto you, It is easier for a camel to go through the eye of a needle, than for a rich man to enter into the kingdom of God" (Matthew 19:24).

We are told that the apostles were amazed beyond measure when he told them that. They didn't know about any postern gates through which a camel comes. That's an invention of modern-day criticism. There is no evidence anywhere at all that there was a gate called "The Eye of the Needle." No, Jesus really meant it: It's impossible. You've got to get rid of your treasures; you have to have the one way or the other. "No man can serve two masters" (Matthew 6:24); compromise is out of the question. That's just the way it is: "Either he will hate the one, and love the other; or else he will hold to the one, and despise the other. Ye *cannot* serve God and mammon" (Matthew 6:24; emphasis added). You've got to make the choice. "And he called unto him the twelve," says Mark, "and began to send them forth by two and two; and gave them power over unclean spirits; and commanded them that they should take nothing for their journey, save a staff only; no scrip, no bread, no money in their purse" (Mark 6:7-8).

We can summarize with Paul and Timothy. 1 Timothy talks about "men of corrupt minds, and destitute of the truth, supposing that gain is godliness" (1 Timothy 6:5). People were rationalizing then. "The reward of virtue is wealth"—this was the common teaching of that time. "From such withdraw thyself. But godliness with contentment is great gain. For we brought nothing into this world, and it is certain we carry nothing out. And having food and raiment let us be therewith content" (1 Timothy 6:5-8). "According to his needs." Those are the needs. "But they that will be rich fall into temptation and a snare, and into many foolish and hurtful lusts, which drown men in destruction and perdition. For the love of money is the root of all evil" (1 Timothy 6:9-10). Similar sentiments are expressed in several noncanonical writings.[10] (We know now that the Bible is full of quotations from such works, like the book of Enoch.[11] Enoch had disappeared but now has been found again. Joseph Smith's Enoch is the best book we have on this subject.) "Which while some coveted after, they have erred from the faith." (Joseph Smith said that because of covetousness in the church the heavens were often sealed up.[12]) "But thou, O man of God, flee these things" (1 Timothy 6:10-11).

In all of this, the early Christians conscientiously followed the ancient order of Enoch. The order was constantly on their lips. And it, in turn, went back to the order of Adam. (We find many references to these things now that we didn't even know twenty years ago. The only person who knew was Joseph Smith.) The order was not invented by the apostles; the Dead Sea Scrolls show us that. The sectaries of the desert — the people out in the desert trying to live the old law of Israel — always followed these rules and always identified themselves with the order of Zion or Enoch (see Moses 7:18).[13] (Joseph Smith is called Enoch [D&C 78:1].[14]) The pious sectaries of the desert thought of themselves as living after the order of Enoch. The Old Testament tells us little about Enoch, just four verses in Genesis (Genesis 5:21-24). But the Apocrypha tell us a great deal, and especially the books of Enoch, which were always a part of the scripture until the fourth century, when they were thrown out. Now we know they were the most sacred parts, esteemed as number one by both the Christians and the Jews.[15] The doctors of the Christian Jews didn't like them at all and couldn't get rid of them fast enough. The new apocryphal writings tell us a great deal about Enoch, but it's Joseph Smith who tells us most of all.

With the loss of the temple in A.D. 70, an entirely new

social and economic order was imposed on Judah—the doctors went to Jamnia and founded the academy, the beginning of rabbinical Judaism—rabbinical halakhic normative Judaism. It was violently opposed to the older order, of which Enoch is the idealized leader, and which goes by the code name of *Zion*. The Jewish doctors were as zealous as the Christians in getting rid of every trace of this tradition. So the Enoch literature disappeared, and the relevant passages were deleted from the Bible.[16] We find now that Enoch is quoted at least 128 times in the New Testament and also by the Church Fathers, who never realized it was Enoch they were quoting;[17] and you find in the Book of Mormon some beautiful quotations from the old, lost book of Enoch.[18]

Passages about the order of Enoch and the city of Zion are emerging with great clarity. Let us say a few things about Zion, generalizing from the Old Testament. *Zion* is a code word that denotes a very real thing: Any community in which the celestial order prevails. Specifically in the Old Testament, all the prophets speak of Zion as the place that can receive the Lord, to which he will be willing to come and in which he is willing to dwell. Not every place can receive the Lord as his habitation—only Zion, a place fit to receive God himself. We ask when we are going to have the millennium; it will be when the pure in heart are able to receive the Lord. But it is also a real city, or any number of real cities. It is constant, it is unchanging. There are Zions among all the worlds, and there are Zions that come and go. Zion is a constant in time and place. It belongs to the order of the eternities. We are not making Zion here; we are preparing the ground for the upbuilding of the kingdom of God and the establishment of Zion. As the Lord says, "My people must be tried in all things, that they may be prepared to receive the glory that I have for them, even the glory of Zion; and he that will not bear chastisement is not worthy of my kingdom" (D&C 136:31).

We must be prepared to receive the glory. We don't produce it ourselves, but we must be ready so that we won't die of shock when it comes, the same shock the early Christians had to sustain.

In every dispensation, there has been a Zion on the earth. The first was in the time of Adam. Doctrine and Covenants 78 tells us of "the Holy One of Zion, who hath established the foundations of Adam-ondi-Ahman" (D&C 78:15). "And . . . [Enoch] built a city that was called the City of Holiness, even Zion" (Moses 7:19). But then "it came to pass that Zion was not, for God received it up into his own bosom; and from thence went forth the saying, ZION IS FLED" (Moses 7:69). Zion comes and goes. When the earth can't receive Zion, Zion doesn't become corrupt and decline. It is taken away: "Zion is fled." Enoch says, "Thou hast taken Zion to thine own bosom, from all thy creations" (Moses 7:31). When the world is qualified to receive Zion, the Lord says, "there shall be mine abode, and it shall be Zion, which shall come forth out of all the creations which I have made" (Moses 7:64). (There are Zions elsewhere.)[19]

Accordingly, the ancient prophets of Israel yearned for the time when Zion would be restored again. Jeremiah and Isaiah hoped to see Zion restored in their time. (They certainly knew it would come in a later day.) Typical is the prophecy of the Psalmist: "My days are like a shadow that declineth; and I am withered like grass. But thou, O Lord, . . . shalt arise, and have mercy upon Zion: for the time to favour her, yea, the set time, is come" (Psalm 102:11-13). There is a set time when these things are to happen. It all happens according to schedule: when the earth is ready to receive it, then it will come and nothing can stop it. "When the Lord shall build up Zion, he shall appear in his glory. . . . This shall be written for the generation to come" (Psalm 102:16, 18). And after all the calamities, says Jeremiah, "there shall be a day, that the watchmen upon the mount Ephraim shall cry, Arise ye, and let us go up to Zion unto the Lord, our God" (Jeremiah 31:6). Of course we all know the prophecy of Micah that "in the last days . . . the mountain of the house of the Lord shall be established in the top of the mountains" and "the law shall go forth of Zion, and the word of the Lord from Jerusalem" (Micah 4:1-2; cf. Isaiah 2:2-3). This was the hope of the prophets. It was also anticipated in the days of the ancient apostles. "Ye are come unto mount Sion," Paul says to the Hebrews, "and unto the city of the living God, the heavenly Jerusalem" (Hebrews 12:22). It's the "heavenly Jerusalem," the eternal order; if we are to go on forever, there has to be a perfect order. It can't be defective. Any building, any structure, will be destroyed by time if there is any defect in it at all. Time will work on that. And in our human relationships in the order that exists here, a perfect order is practically impossible. Human order is a day-to-day, makeshift sort of thing, not the sort of thing that can go from eternity to eternity. The freeways will use up all our oil and gasoline in the next seventy-seven thousand years, but we are talking about eternity. It is inconceivable that we should make idiots of ourselves by driving around like mad for the next one hundred thousand years or so. That's not the order of eternity. Yet there is such a concept—there is an eternity. People upon this earth have enjoyed a society of such nature that could go on forever and ever without anybody getting bored, or worn out, or tired. What is that ideal Zion like?

In the first place, we are told, it will be a place of refuge in a doomed world, "and it shall be called the New Jerusalem, a land of peace, a city of refuge, a place of safety for the saints of the Most High God; . . . and the terror of the Lord also shall be there, . . . and it shall be called Zion" (D&C 45:66-67). At that time, "every man that will not take his sword against his neighbor must needs flee unto Zion for safety. . . . And it shall be said among the wicked: . . .

the inhabitants of Zion are terrible" (D&C 45:68, 70). Terrible because it is indestructible. Her invulnerability makes
her an object of awe and terror. As Enoch says, "Surely
Zion shall dwell in safety forever." And the Lord count-
ered, No, not on this earth. You can't keep it here. "But
the Lord said unto Enoch: Zion have I blessed, but the
residue of the people have I cursed. . . . And lo, Zion, in
the process of time, was taken up into heaven" (Moses
7:20-21). So Zion was taken away and the rest destroyed.
Zion itself is never in danger. On the contrary, it alone
offers safety to the world. The Doctrine and Covenants
says, "The gathering together upon the land of Zion, and
upon her stakes, may be for a defense, and for a refuge
from the storm, and from wrath when it shall be poured
out without mixture upon the whole earth" (D&C 115:6).
It would seem that Zion enjoys the complete security of
the celestial world, and nothing can touch it as long as it
retains that character. But celestial it must be. We have
seen that "Zion cannot be built up unless it is by the principles of the law of the celestial kingdom; otherwise I cannot receive her unto myself" (D&C 105:5). It must at all
times be holy enough to receive the Lord himself, "for the
Lord hath chosen Zion; he hath desired it for his habitation" (Psalm 132:13). There is no place for those who promote themselves "to honor and glory by deceitful practices,
who misapply and misinterpret straightforward statements, who have given a new twist to the everlasting
covenant and then produce arguments to prove that you
are without guilt." That is from the very valuable Greek
Enoch, discovered in 1930.[20] Enoch explains that all this
self-deception is really quite stupid; it leads to self-destruc-
tion (D&C 99:5). Specifically, it operates through the manipulations of written documents, for the evil one has
"taught the children of men the bitter and the sweet"[21]
(which they learned through the Fall). "And he instructed
mankind in writing with ink and paper, and thereby many

sinned . . . until this day. For men were not created for such a purpose, to give confirmation to their good faith with pen and ink. For men were created exactly like the angels,"[22] thus they could trust each other, who live necessarily in a condition of perfect trust and understanding. So here come the lawyers with their legal jargon and fine print, and this, according to Enoch, has thrown everything into a state of confusion. "And Satan taught men how to make knives, weapons, shields, and breastplates, the trade secrets, and showed them the various metals and how to work them, and bracelets, jewelry, makeup, and eyepaint, and all kind of precious stones and hairdos."[23] Manuscript E, another one of the Giza fragments, adds,

> . . . and all the treasures of the earth. And there were great wickedness and whoredoms, and they all became perverted and lost in all their ways. And he taught them spells, drugs and quackery. And Araqil taught them astrology, the interpretation of signs, the observations of signs, and the series of the moon. They maliciously brought them gold and silver and copper and all manner of metals; and this was what finally completed their ruin, and established their perennial earthly order of human society, which persists to this day.[24]

This is from a recently discovered Coptic Testament of John, which refers to the time of Enoch.

Abraham was preeminently a fair dealer. The Abraham literature includes the Old Testament, which also makes it clear that the people he dealt with were scoundrels — mean and inhospitable. The nature of their economy is fully set forth: their one guiding principle was the maximizing of profits. After the flood, the Jewish writings explain, the people were haunted by an understandable feeling of insecurity. To overcome it, they undertook tremendous engineering projects and became very knowledgeable in fire, flood, earthquake, and other potential disasters. A great economic boom and commercial expansion enabled them to undertake all kinds of engineering projects for controlling a dangerous nature.[25] But the Lord fooled them by altering the course of nature and creation. And the Nimrod legends are full of the great scientific understanding of Abraham's day of which a good deal is made in the time of Enoch.[26] The people had a great deal of sophistication and know-how. It was a world of unrest and insecurity, and the people were mean and short-tempered. But Abraham's Canaan didn't offer escape for long. The fabulous prosperity of the cities of the plain turned them into little Babylons. The record describes their ways of doing things, how they dealt with all strangers, taking away possessions by force; then the wrath of the Lord came upon them.[27]

The Testament of Levi, speaking of Abraham, says that he found the same hostility elsewhere. There was worldwide cruelty, inhospitality, insecurity, suspicion wherever he went.[28] The Bible tells us that the Jordan depression was a veritable paradise when Abraham first visited it, before the Lord destroyed Sodom and Gomorrah (Genesis 13:10). It was not surprising that "the men of Sodom were the wealthy men of prosperity, on account of the good and fruitful land whereon they dwelt. For every need which the world requires, they obtained therefrom. . . . But they did not trust in the shadow of their Creator, but [they trusted] in the multitude of their wealth, for wealth thrusts aside its owners from the fear of Heaven."[29] Rabbi Eliezer seems to be quoting the same source as Samuel the Lamanite. "The men of Sodom had no consideration for the honour of their Owner by (not) distributing food to the wayfarer and the stranger."[30] The same thing is described in Deuteronomy and the Book of Mormon. "They [even] fenced in all their trees on top above their fruit so that they should not be seized; [not] even by the bird of heaven."[31] The law of Moses forbade doing these mean things to the olives, the wheat, and other crops, but they did them.

These were the crimes of Sodom and Gomorrah. At the time of Abraham, the people elected leaders "of falsehood and wickedness, who mocked justice and equity and committed evil deeds."[32] This isn't something invented by a Jewish doctor of the thirteenth century. These are contemporary records that tell us that the wicked oppressed the weak and gave power to the strong. Inside the city was tyranny and the receiving of bribes. Everyday, without fail, they plundered each others' goods. The son cursed his father in the streets, the slave his master. They put an end to the offerings and entered into conspiracy.[33] This sounds like the Book of Mormon, though it was discovered long after the Book of Mormon. All manner of wickedness is described. But we don't need to go into this sad story here.

It's not surprising, the records tell, that travelers and birds alike learned to avoid the rich cities of the plain, while the poor emigrated to other parts.[34] "If a stranger merchant passed through their territory, he was besieged by them all, big and little alike, and robbed of whatever he possessed."[35] As the Amarna letters show us, this was a world in which every man was for himself.[36] What a terrible state of things. Being grossly materialistic, they rated the hardware high above the software.[37]

A famous quotation recurs a numbers of times: "If a man was killed working on the tower, he was ignored. But if a brick fell they sat down and wept. Abraham, seeing them, cursed them in the name of his God" for doing this sort of thing:[38] "Behold, this was the iniquity of thy sister Sodom" (Ezekiel 16:49).

Satan's concern with Moses was not to turn him against religion but to enlist his devotions. In Moses 1, a most marvelous piece of epic and dramatic literature, Satan confronts Moses, and Moses doesn't yield. But Aaron does — he falls for Satan's golden calf. The prophets through the Old Testament designate this world by the code name of

Babylon. It was Babylon where Abraham dwelt, the Ur of the Chaldees. Then he went north.

Babylon is a state of mind, just like Zion. Like Zion, Babylon is a city: "Babylon is fallen, is fallen, that great city" (Revelation 14:8). It's a world center of commerce and business. Isaiah has a lot to say about it: "O virgin daughter of Babylon, . . . thou hast laboured, even thy merchants, from thy youth" (Isaiah 47:1, 15). She dominates the world. Her king is equated with Lucifer, who says, "I will be like the most High" (Isaiah 14:14). Satan said to Moses, "I am the Only Begotten, worship me" (Moses 1:19). Babylon dominates the world, and the king of Babylon is who? Satan, who says, "I will be like the Most High" (Isaiah 14:14). "How art thou cut down to the ground, which didst weaken the nations! (Isaiah 14:12). He was "the man that made the earth to tremble, that did shake kingdoms, that made the world as a wilderness" (Isaiah 14:16-17). "The lady of kingdoms" (Isaiah 47:5), who ruled over polluted lands, says, "I shall be a lady forever" (Isaiah 47:7). "I am, and none else beside me" (Isaiah 47:10). She leads the world, and nations have drunk of her wine." Here Jeremiah talks (not John the Revelator yet): "The nations have drunken of her wine; therefore the nations are mad. Babylon is suddenly fallen and destroyed" (Jeremiah 51:7-8). All the world is involved. At the noise of the taking of Babylon, the earth is moved, and a cry is heard among the nations. "So at Babylon shall fall the slain of all the earth" (Jeremiah 51:49). Her clever, experienced, unscrupulous men will be helpless. She thinks that she can get away with anything, so she says, "None seeth me. Thy wisdom and thy knowledge, it hath perverted thee" (Isaiah 47:10). "I will make drunk her princes, and her wise men, her captains, and her rulers, and her mighty men: and they shall sleep a perpetual sleep" (Jeremiah 51:57). The notion that an establishment of this majesty and power is a permanent institution fools them every time. But don't worry, they'll fall asleep too. It's happened before. "Her military might is helpless," says Jeremiah. "A sound of battle is in the land, and of great destruction. How is the hammer of the whole earth cut asunder and broken" (Jeremiah 50:22-23). The king of Babylon is then equated to Lucifer: "How art thou fallen from heaven, O Lucifer, son of the morning! How art thou cut down to the ground which didst weaken the nations!" (Isaiah 14:12).

In calling attention to the beauties of Adam's Zion, after the Fall, Satan hastens to point out that it all belongs to him. He makes a well-known agreement by which he will take possession of the treasures of the earth. Babylon is firm in the conviction that her system is a permanent one. She says in her heart, "I am, and none else beside me" (Isaiah 47:10). In such possession of power, she can get away with anything and keep power indefinitely by crooked means, concealing her acts. Her place is the place of the merchants, "a golden cup in the Lord's hand . . . [from which] the nations have drunken of her wine; therefore the nations are mad" (Jeremiah 51:7). Nebuchadnezzar, who was then the king of Babylon, calls it Great Babylon, "that I have built for the house of the kingdom by the might of my power, and for the honour of my majesty" (Daniel 4:30).

The Book of Mormon describes pointedly a quick transition from the celestial. Fourth Nephi describes the celestial order. When the Nephites decided to give up that order, they went the other way. They didn't slowly subside into the more relaxed economy of Israel. They went right to the other extreme, in a quick transition to the telestial. Israel's economy has a strong appeal. (If you don't believe it, spend a few nights before the telestial economy of television fare.) "Now, in this two hundred and first year there began to be among them those who were lifted up in pride" (4 Nephi 1:24) (the Nephites had to work all the time to preserve the order—eating, fasting, praying, and doing all the other things). They couldn't tolerate the righteous pace, so they were lifted up in pride, such things as wearing costly apparel and seeking the fine things of the world. "And from that time forth they did have their goods and their substance no more common among them. And they began to be divided into classes" (4 Nephi 1:25-26). They did not dwindle in unbelief but willfully rebelled against the gospel of Christ. They didn't just subside imperceptibly into a more relaxed way of life. Not at all. They didn't dwindle. "They did wilfully rebel against the gospel of Christ" (4 Nephi 1:38). Even as it was in the beginning, they went back to their old vices: "As a dog returneth to his vomit, so a fool returneth to his folly" (Proverbs 26:11). They actually taught their children to hate the children of God, even as the Lamanites were taught to hate the children of Nephi from the beginning. It was the old order — the same old hatreds and tribal warfare — and they actively promoted it. The teaching was deliberate: "And also the people . . . of Nephi began to be proud in their hearts [fighting fire with fire], because of their exceeding riches, and become vain like unto their brethren, the Lamanites. And from this time the disciples began to sorrow for the sins of the world. And . . . both the people of Nephi and the Lamanites had become exceedingly wicked one like unto another" (4 Nephi 1:43-45). In a few verses and a few decades, they had deliberately pushed themselves all the way from a celestial order (there couldn't be a happier people ever created by the hand of the Lord on the earth; 4 Nephi 1:16) to the other extreme; the prophets mourned and withdrew, for the people of Nephi and the Lamanites had become equally wicked (4 Nephi 1:45). This is the state described by Samuel the Lamanite: "Ye are cursed because of your riches, . . . because ye have set your hearts upon them, and have not hearkened unto the words of him who gave them unto you. Ye do not remember the Lord your God, . . . but ye do always remember your riches"

(Helaman 13:21-22). Always the economy, the economy —
as if that were the solution to anything. "For this cause
hath the Lord God caused that a curse should come
upon . . . your riches. . . . Yea, wo unto this people.
. . . And behold, the time cometh that he curseth your
riches, that they become slippery, that ye cannot hold
them" (Helaman 13:23-24, 31). Here is the passage from
the Chester Beatty Papyrus of the book of Enoch, which
was just discovered: "Wo, wo to ye rich, for you have
trusted your riches and from your riches. . . . You and
your riches shall depart because you have not remembered
the Most High in the days of your riches."[39] In Samuel's
words, "the one who gave them to you, you have not
remembered." "Wo unto you who have accumulated gold
and silver by dishonest means and say, We have acquired
wealth and procured properties, have been successful, and
are in a position to do whatever we please because we
have silver laid up in the treasuries [in the banks]. And
our buildings are filled with valuable things to overflowing
like water."[40]

This is interesting, because the book of Enoch is quoted
so many times in the New Testament. The Lord tells the
story about the man who built his barns and expanded his
business, then said, Now, heart, be content. You can retire
now and live off the fat of the land. The Lord replied that
he had done just the wrong thing: "Thou art filled with
valuable things to overflowing like water [this man's barns
were full], and you are very much mistaken." "That night
the voice of God came to him and said, 'Thou fool, this
night thy soul shall be required of thee' " (Luke 12:20).
The Book of Mormon uses the word *slippery*. We don't
understand how, but the Dow Jones is now up, yet after
the past two years' experience, how can we have trust in
anything?

The word *slippery* is a good one, and it's the word used
in the old Enoch book. "It will slip away from you because

you got it all dishonestly and have come under a great
curse."[41] Notice the last words, "come under a great curse";
and Samuel says, "For this cause hath the Lord God caused
that a curse should come upon . . . your riches" (Helaman
13:23). The passages are the very same.

If it's obvious that the Lord is referring to this parable
of the rich man (Luke 12:20-21), the parable of Samuel's
sermon is even more convincing. And in Enoch 29:2, the
ambience of corruption is characteristically that of wealth
and power. The Greek version: "For men shall get themselves up as if they were women and outdo young girls
with their pretty appearance while acting like the kings in
their lofty pretense of authority. And they shall feed upon
gold and silver poured out like water in their houses.
Therefore, you shall perish along with your possessions."[42]
"Their hearts are upon their treasures; wherefore, . . .
their treasure shall perish with them also" (2 Nephi 9:30).
And the last verse of the Greek Enoch: "Therefore shall
they perish along with all their property."[43]

Satan's great confrontation with Jesus, after forty days
of fasting, repeats his confrontation with Moses (Moses
1:12-22) and his proposed deal with Adam, with Abraham,
with Job, and with Isaiah. There are all sorts of stories of
Satan coming with his propositions, of the kind he converted Cain to.[44] The devil said to the Lord himself, who
had fasted and was susceptible (otherwise he wouldn't
have been), "If thou be the Son of God, command this
stone that it be made bread" (Luke 4:3). You serve me or
you starve. And Jesus said, "Man shall not live by bread
alone [that's the point], but by every word of God. And
the devil, taking him up into an high mountain, shewed
unto him all the kingdoms of the world in a moment of
time. And the devil said unto him, All this power will I
give thee, and the glory of them: for that is delivered unto
me" (Luke 4:4-6). Note, Satan claims to have the power
and the glory of this world. It's delivered unto me, he says.

I have the authority. I am authorized to offer you all this glory and power in the world, if you will serve me. "For that is delivered unto me; and to whomsoever I will I give it" (Luke 4:6). Note that: it is all mine. This is my greatness and my kingdom. He claims it, and the Lord so allows him that for that purpose. "If thou therefore wilt worship me, all shall be thine" (Luke 4:7). That's the famous pact that Satan makes. He promises you anything for this world, and that is what people go for. And Jesus' answer to him was, "Get thee behind me, Satan: for it is written, Thou shalt worship the Lord thy God, and him only shalt thou serve" (Luke 4:8). And Satan said to him, on the pinnacle of the temple, All right, if you are the son of God, cast yourself down from thence and the angels shall save you. And Jesus said, Don't try to tempt me that way, Satan (Luke 4:9-12).

Why did he say, "It is written," "It is said"? He meant, you yourself should know this, Satan. It's well known. I am not making something up you haven't heard before. The church at the time of the apostles referred to their surroundings as Babylon, the same code name as used by the prophets. Peter writes, "The church that is at Babylon . . . saluteth you" (1 Peter 5:13). In Revelation 14:8, another angel is saying, "Babylon is fallen, is fallen, that great city, because she made all nations drink of the wine of the wrath of her fornication." "Great Babylon came in remembrance before God, to give unto her the cup of the wine of the fierceness of his wrath" (Revelation 16:19) — "MYSTERY, BABYLON THE GREAT, THE MOTHER OF HARLOTS" (Revelation 17:5), and so forth. And then finally, "Babylon the great is fallen" (Revelation 18:2). The classic description of Babylon in Revelation is a Jewish apocalyptic writing considered now to be the most Jewish work of the whole Bible, let alone the New Testament. Babylon is rich, luxurious, immoral, full of fornication; there are merchants, riches, delicacies, sins, and "the mer-

chandise of gold, and silver, and precious stones, and of
pearls, and fine linen, and purple, and silk, and scarlet,
and all thyine wood, and all manner vessels of ivory, and
all manner vessels of most precious wood, and of brass,
and iron, and marble" (Revelation 18:12).

This is the ground floor, a giant delicatessen with its
"wine, and oil, and fine flour, and wheat, and beasts, and
sheep" (Revelation 18:13), a perfumed counter with its
cinnamon, odors, ointments, and frankincense. It reads
like a savings stamp catalog, a guide to a modern supermarket, or something similar. It goes on: elegant transportation, horses, chariots, all manner of services available,
slaves, and the souls of men (Revelation 18:13). It is all for
sale. These are "the fruits that thy soul lusted after, . . . all
things which were dainty and goodly" (Revelation 18:14).
Dainty and goodly in themselves, but when your soul lusts
after them, there is the mistake. That is the point of emphasis. This mighty city was the center of commerce with
its ships, its sailors, its trade by sea, full of busy shops and
factories, craftsmen (a world of business and world leaders), millstones working away; and lots of fun, too: musicians, harpers, pipers, and great sexual life (Revelation
18:17, 22). As for business, "the kings of the earth have
committed fornication with her, and the merchants of the
earth are waxed rich through the abundance of her delicacies" (Revelation 18:3). "For thy merchants were the
great men of the earth; for by thy sorceries were all nations
deceived" (see Revelation 18:23).

John, like the early Hebrew prophets, liked the particular emphasis on the fact that Babylon has built up great
power by deception. The word that Brigham Young likes
to use is *decoy*: These things "decoy . . . [our] minds" away
from the real values of things.[45] They are irresistible. The
merchants do research: they know what we'll take and
what we'll not. They know what will sell, and they know
the line that nobody can resist. This is the very real thing

we are being tempted by. By these deceptions—through public relations, the skill of advertising, and people who devote their lives to nothing else than trying to entice— the devil tries to entice and tempt us, "by sorceries and witchcraft that deceive the nations" (cf. Revelation 18:23).

The Doctrine and Covenants opens with a vivid description of this world that is totally dominant in the modern world: "They who will not hear the voice of the Lord, neither the voice of his servants, . . . seek not the Lord to establish his righteousness, but every man walketh in his own way, and after the image of his own god, whose image is in the likeness of the world, and whose substance is that of an idol, which waxeth old and shall perish in Babylon, even Babylon the great" (D&C 1:14, 16). And then, "There is none which doeth good" (D&C 33:4). No, not one. "They seek not the Lord to establish his righteousness, but every man walketh in his own way" (D&C 1:16). This is part of the picture, the dominant order of things, and there is no one who is not following that way today. The Lord insists that the whole history of the world is about to turn on its hinges. It will change; this is not an order with which he is pleased. Brigham Young and Joseph often warned the Saints about subsiding into this telestial order. Even though the Lord said that Zion could not be built up unless it is in the principle of the law (otherwise I cannot receive her unto myself), the Latter-day Saints still wanted to compromise and say, "We will not go up unto Zion, and will keep our moneys" (D&C 105:8). But as long as that was their plan, there could be no Zion, they were told.

This is the most effective weapon that Satan has, among his many weapons. There are many ways in which you can sin; he has more than one arrow in his quiver. But this is the one, after all, none of us can resist. In its first capacity, it has a powerful soporific and paralyzing effect. Asks Brigham, "Are not the sordid things of this life before our eyes? Have they not thrown a mist before them so that we cannot see? What do we know of heavenly things when we are in this situation?"[46] These tabernacles are dull, subject to sin and temptation, and to stray from the kingdom of God, and the ordinances of his house, to lust after riches, the pride of life and the vanities of the world, and these things are prone to be uppermost in the minds of all; old and young, even Latter-day Saints."[47] We are not immune, because when the Lord said, "We will allow Satan, our common enemy, to try and to tempt," he meant that this was the main trial and temptation, not an easy one. Naturally, he'd use the strongest, the most powerful pitch he could use, the most irresistible weapon in his arsenal, the one that is tried and true. And "I know that there is no man on this earth who can call around him property, be he a merchant, tradesman, farmer, with his mind continually occupied with: 'How shall I get this or that; how rich can I get'; . . . no such man ever can magnify the priesthood nor enter the celestial kingdom."[48] Now remember, "They will not enter into the kingdom" (cf. Matthew 18:3).

Recently I wrote a letter to a very dear friend of mine, an exceedingly wealthy man in Arizona who has made fortunes and has given every cent of it away, time and again, just as Brigham Young did. He has a marvelous knack for accumulating stuff, but he has never kept it for himself. He is now right down to nothing again and feeling very happy, as if greatly relieved of all sorts of burdens. The things that he has given away are fabulous. There are such people; it can be done. "If the Lord ever revealed anything to me, he has shown me that the Elders of Israel must let speculation alone, . . . otherwise they will have little or no power in their missions or upon their return."[49] The Latter-day Saints have a weakness for speculation. My father could never free himself from it. Once you get into mining, you are gone. There couldn't be a better decoy, a more fatal allurement away from the things of the kingdom. "The Latter-day Saints who turn their attention to

money-making soon become cold in their feelings toward
the ordinances of the house of God. They neglect their
prayers, become unwilling to pay any donations. . . . The
providences of heaven seem to shut out from them — all in
consequence of this lust after the things of this world."[50]
When you see the Latter-day Saints greedy and covetous
in the things of this world, do you think their minds are
in a fit condition to be written upon by the pen of revelation?" Joseph Smith said, "God had often sealed up the
heavens because of covetousness in the Church."[51]

At the dedication of the Manti Temple, the Prophet
Brigham Young offered this prayer: "We ask Thee that
Thou would hide up the treasures of the earth, . . .
preserve thy people from the inducements which these
perishable things offer, which are liable to decoy the minds
of Thy saints." We don't want to discover the gold around
here, he insisted, and this just after George Albert Smith
had reported discovery of a great gold vein. "And cause
that these things may not come in their path to tempt
them." The wealth of the earth is a clever decoy;[52] "it is a
fearful deception which all the world labors under, and
many of its people, too."[53]

This is one of the last speeches Brigham Young gave:
"Many professing to be saints seem to have no knowledge,
no light to see anything beyond a dollar or a pleasant time,
or a comfortable house, or a fine farm." These have their
place, but what do we enjoy? "O fools, and slow of heart
to understand the purposes of God and his handiwork
among his people."[54]

> Go to the child, and what does its joy consist in?
> Toys, we may call them, . . . and so it is with our youth,
> our young boys and girls; they are thinking too much
> of this world; and the middle-aged are striving and strug-
> gling to obtain the good things of this life, and their
> hearts are too much upon them. So it is with the aged.
> Is not this the condition of the Latter-day Saints? It is.

What is the general expression through out our community? It is that the Latter-day Saints are drifting as fast as they can into idolatry.[55]

This was all Brigham Young could preach in his last year: "fast into idolatry, drifting into the spirit of the world and into pride and vanity."[56] "We wish the wealth of things of the world; we think about them morning, noon and night; they are first in our minds when we awake in the morning, and the last thing before we go to sleep at night."[57] "We have gone just as far as we can be permitted to go in the road on which we are now traveling. One man has his eye on a gold mine, another is for a silver mine, another is for marketing his flour or his wheat, another for selling his cattle, another to raise cattle, another to get a farm, or building here and there, and trading and trafficking with each other, just like Babylon. . . . Babylon is here, and we are following in the footsteps of the inhabitants of the earth, who are in a perfect sea of confusion. Do you know this? You ought to, for there are none of you but what see it daily. . . . The Latter-day Saints [are] trying to take advantage of their brethren. There are Elders in this Church who would take the widow's last cow, for five dollars, and then kneel down and thank God for the fine bargain they had made."[58] This is the great voice of the economy of Babylon. It does not renounce its religious pretensions for a minute. Many in it think they are identical with a pious life.

Now to Brigham's final word—his last speech, as a matter of fact:

> Now those that can see the spiritual atmosphere can see that many of the Saints are still glued to this earth and lusting and longing after the things of this world, in which there is no profit. . . . According to the present feelings of many of our brethren, they would arrogate to themselves this world and all that pertains to it. . . . Where are the eyes and the hearts of this

people? . . . All the angels in heaven are looking at this little handfull of people, and stimulating them to the salvation of the human family. So also are the devils in hell looking at this people, too, and trying to overthrow us, and the people are still shaking hands with the servants of the devil, instead of sanctifying themselves, [given a choice between the two].[59]

We are being pulled in two directions, he says; all the powers of heaven are looking to us, waiting for us to perform our mission; the devils are looking at us to fail in it, and we are shaking hands with them, instead of the other way around. "When I think upon this subject, I want the tongues of seven thunders to wake up the people."[60]

We see clearly the three economies. There is such a thing as a celestial economy. After all, Mormons believe in cosmism. Some churches still say that the greatest vice of the Mormons is that they look upon the physical universe as having some relationship to the gospel. We say it's all physical—there are universes we know nothing about; there is matter of a nature that we can't perceive at all. It's all real—what's on the other side of the black holes, or wherever it may be. This is part of the celestial order, and we have been given the great honor. The Lord has flattered us to the point of revealing to us this particular order. This is what has worked in ancient times, he explains. In the time of Adam I did it; in the time of Noah I had it. In the time of Moses I tried to introduce the people, but they wouldn't take it. In the time of apostles, I restored it. The Nephites had it for two hundred years, and you could have it too. I want you to have it. It's the only thing I will accept from you. And meanwhile, you will live by these rules and work your way toward it, but for heaven's sake, don't let yourself be decoyed and sucked into this third order, which becomes dominant. This picture of Babylon is so very striking, it's overpowering. It meets us everywhere. Today's newspaper is like a commentary on the whole scriptures. You could find in it a hundred items that are completely relevant on this subject, which makes us wonder how far along the way we are, and what the Lord is doing in these things otherwise.

I certainly pray that we may fill our hearts with the desire to fulfill the Lord's purposes on the earth. Some of us are good at administering the things of the earth. "Some of us"—I use that very flatteringly, because there never was a worse one than myself for bungling with things like that, so I can very well talk sour grapes. But notice the spirit in which it's to be done. Brigham, the greatest and certainly the most able economist and administrator and businessman this nation has ever seen, didn't give a hoot for earthly things: "I have never walked across the streets to make a trade."[61] He didn't mean that literally. You always do have to handle things. But in what spirit do we do it? Not in the Krishna way, by renunciation, for example. I have never visited Calcutta, but the reports are utterly heartbreaking. If you refuse to be concerned with these things at all, and say, "I'm above all that," that's as great a fault. The things of the world have got to be administered; they must be taken care of, they are to be considered. We have to keep things clean, and in order. That's required of us. This is a test by which we are being proven. This is the way by which we prepare, always showing that these things will never captivate our hearts, that they will never become our principal concern. That takes a bit of doing, and that is why we have the formula "with an eye single to his glory" (Mormon 8:15). Keep first your eye on the star, then on all the other considerations of the ship. You will have all sorts of problems on the ship, but unless you steer by the star, forget the ship. Sink it. You won't go anywhere.

This is the important thing: we must keep our eye on the principles of the gospel that have been given us. The Lord has given us great blessings in these things, and great promises; and because the spirit of the Lord is stirring in the church today, I am sure we all feel it in various ways. The interesting thing is how we all operate in different areas. I don't suspect for a minute either the burdens, or the trials, or the troubles, or the privileges of the capacities of any other person in the world. I am sure that if I were to start to analyze and describe them, I would be completely wrong, so I just forget it. Here we are, all relating to our Heavenly Father, and as such, related to each other as brothers and sisters. He's the one we go to; he's the one we keep in mind. So we are not concerned to lay down the law to each other, saying, "This is the way you have to do it. That is the kosher way." Let us each go to the Lord, who will reveal these things to us. May he inspire each one of us with understanding and the good sense and the faith and devotion that we need in order to live by the laws of the kingdom, I pray in the name of Jesus Christ. Amen.

Notes

1. Andrew K. Helmbold, *The Nag Hammadi Gnostic Texts and the Bible* (Grand Rapids, MI: Baker, 1967), 37; James M. Robinson, tr., *Nag Hammadi Library* (New York: Harper and Row, 1977), 54, 89; Gilles Quispel, *Gnostic Studies*, 2 vols. (Intanbul, Nederlands: Historisch-Archaeologisch Instituut in het Nabije Oosten, 1974), 1:15; cf. G. R. S. Mead, *Pistis Sophia* (London: John M. Watkins, 1921), L-LI. In his introduction Mead outlines the gnostic idea of the three degrees of glory in heaven as presented in the Pistis Sophia. See also Robert M. Grant, *Gnosticism* (New York: Harper and Brothers, 1961), 61; Testament of Levi 3:1-10; Hugo Odeberg, *3 Enoch or The Hebrew Book of Enoch* (New York: KTAV, 1973), 176.

2. Harry Sperling and Maurice Simon, trs. *The Zohar*, 5 vols. (London: Soncino Press, 1984), 1:278; cf. A. E. Waite, *The Holy Kabbalah* (London: Williams and Norgate, 1929), 619.

3. Isidore Singer, ed., *Jewish Encyclopedia*, 12 vols. (New York: Funk and Wagnalls, 1901), 1:176-77, 181.

4. Z'eu ben Shimon Halevi, *Adam and the Kabbalistic Tree* (London: Rider, 1974), 34.

5. *TPJS* 12-13, 305.

6. Testament of Levi 3:1-10.

7. Regarding *oikonomia*, see James Strong, *Strong's Exhaustive Concordance of the Bible* (Nashville, TN: Abingdon, 1986), see *Greek Dictionary*, p. 68, ref. 3622: "*oikonomia*, administration (of a household or estate); spec. a (religious) *economy*: dispensation, stewardship."

8. The context implies the greatest distress. See Strong, *Strong's Exhaustive Concordance of the Bible*, reference numbers 3173 and 5399 on pages 61 and 103, respectively, of the book's Greek Dictionary.

9. See Hugh W. Nibley, "The Forty-Day Mission of Christ—The Forgotten Heritage," in *When the Lights Went Out* (Salt Lake City: Deseret Book, 1970), 33-54; reprinted in *CWHN* 4:10-44.

10. Testament of Judah 18-19; cf. Sibylline Oracles 2:109-18; Pseudo-Phocylides 42. For English translations, see James H. Charlesworth, ed., *The Old Testament Pseudepigrapha*, 2 vols. (Garden City, NY: Doubleday, 1983), 1:800; 1:348; 2:575, respectively.

11. R. H. Charles, *The Book of Enoch* (London: Oxford, 1913), xcv-ciii; cf. Richard Laurence, *The Book of Enoch the Prophet* (London: Kegan, Paul, Trench, 1883; reprinted San Diego, CA: Wizards Bookshelf, 1977), xxv-xxxiii; Elizabeth C. Prophet, *Forbidden Mysteries of Enoch* (Livingston, MO: Summit University Press, 1983), 231-62.

12. *TPJS* 9.

13. Theodor H. Gaster, *The Dead Sea Scriptures*, 3rd ed. (Garden City, NY: Anchor, 1976), 10-12, 44: "All who declare their willingness to serve God's truth must bring all of their mind, all of their strength, and all of their wealth into the community of God, so that their minds may be purified by truth of His precepts, their strength controlled by His perfect ways, and their wealth disposed in accordance with His just design." Cf. A. R. C. Leaney, *The Rule of Qumran and Its Meaning* (London: SCM, 1966), 66-69; and Millar Burrows, *More Light on the Dead Sea Scrolls* (New York: Viking, 1958), 71-72.

14. See editions of the Doctrine and Covenants previous to the 1981 version.

15. Hugh W. Nibley, "A Strange Thing in the Land," *Ensign* 5 (October 1975): 80-82; reprinted in *CWHN* 2:95-99.

16. Ibid.

17. Charles, *The Book of Enoch*, xcv-ciii.

18. E.g., 1 Enoch 97:10 (cf. Helaman 13:31); 1 Enoch 94:8 (cf. Helaman 13:33).

19. *JD* 17:331-32.

20. Campbell Bonner, *The Last Chapters of Enoch in Greek* (Darmstadt: Wissenschaftliche Buchgesellschaft, 1968), 41; for English translation, see 89-90.

21. R. H. Charles, *The Apocrypha and Pseudepigrapha of the Old Testament*, 2 vols. (Oxford: Clarendon Press, 1913), 2:233; cf. E. A. Wallis Budge, "Discourse on Abbatôn," *Coptic Martyrdoms*, 6 vols. (London: Oxford University Press, 1914), 4:485.

22. 1 Enoch 69:9-11.

23. Ibid., 8:1-2.

24. Charles, *The Book of Enoch*, 279-80.

25. H. Freedman and Maurice Simon, *Midrash Rabbah*, 10 vols. (London: Soncino Press, 1939), 1:302-3; cf. Angelos S. Rappoport, *Myth and Legend of Ancient Israel*, 3 vols. (London: Gresham, 1928), 1:234.

26. Zohar, *Bereshith* 56a, in Sperling and Simon, *The Zohar*, 1:178-80; cf. Louis Ginzberg, *Legends of the Jews*, 7 vols. (Philadephia: Jewish Publication Society of America, 1909), 1:173-74.

27. *MS* 37:674; cf. Ginzberg, *Legends of the Jews*, 1:245-50; Book of Jasher 18:16-43.

28. Testament of Levi 6:9; cf. M. H. Segal, "The Religion of Israel before Sinai," *Jewish Quarterly Review* 52 (1961): 44-45.

29. Gerald Friedlander, *Pirkê de Rabbi Eliezer* (New York: Hermon, 1965), 181.

30. Ibid., 181-82.

31. Ibid.

32. Rappoport, *Myth and Legend of Ancient Israel*, 1:264.

33. Ibid.

34. Sperling and Simon, *The Zohar*, 1:339-40; Ginzberg, *Legends of the Jews*, 1:247.

35. Ginzberg, *Legends of the Jews*, 1:245.

36. Ibid., 245-50.

37. Friedlander, *Pirkê de Rabbi Eliezer*, 176; Rappoport, *Myth and Legend of Ancient Israel*, 1:237.

38. Friedlander, *Pirkê de Rabbi Eliezer*, 176; Book of Jasher IX, 28.

39. 1 Enoch 93:7; for English translation, see Michael A. Knibb, *The Ethiopic Book of Enoch*, 2 vols. (Oxford: Clarendon, 1978), 2:227.

40. Ibid., 97:8-9.

41. Ibid., 97:10.

42. Ibid., 98:2-3; see Bonner, *Last Chapters of Enoch in Greek*, 88.

43. Ibid.

44. Apocalypse of Abraham 13:1-14; Testament of Job 6:1-6 in Charlesworth, *The Old Testament Pseudepigrapha*, 1:695; 1:841-42; Rutherford H. Platt, ed., "The First Book of Adam and Eve" and "Second Book of Adam and Eve," in *The Lost Books of the Bible and the Forgotten Books of Eden* (Canada: Collins World, 1977), 60:1-29, 70:1-17, 76:10-12; and 3:1-15, respectively.

45. *MS* 39:372.
46. *JD* 15:3.
47. Ibid., 18:238.
48. Ibid., 11:297.
49. Ibid., 8:179.
50. Ibid., 18:213.
51. *TPJS* 9.
52. *MS* 39:372.
53. *JD* 10:271.
54. Ibid., 8:63.
55. Ibid., 18:237, 39.
56. Ibid., 18:239.
57. Ibid., 18:238-39.
58. Ibid., 17:41.
59. *MS* 39:118-19.
60. Ibid., 39:119.
61. *JD* 12:219.

12

We Will Still Weep for Zion

A new Lamentation Literature is born. Here is the standard scenario: "I am a young, hard-working Latter-day Saint; six months ago I was well on the way to financial independence, following the admonitions of my elders. Today I am broke, and my children lack necessities. What went wrong?" Maybe the following can explain some things.

Breaking Away

In every dispensation of the gospel, the Lord has insisted on segregating his covenant people from the rest of the world: if they were not ready to "come out of her, [O] my people" (Revelation 18:4) willingly, he saw to it that the world was more than willing to persecute and expel them.

Two ways were placed before Adam, to see which one he would follow. Cain followed the one; Abel, and after him, Seth, the other. But soon Seth's posterity drifted over to the camp of Cain. Things being very bad, Enoch, the supermissionary, was sent out and was able "in [the] process of time" (Moses 7:21) to draw many after him into his city of Zion, which was then totally segregated from the rest of the world, pending the world's destruction.

After the Flood, things went bad again, so that the call to Abraham was *lech lecha* — get out of here! And he kept

---

A revised transcript of a talk given in 1984.

moving all his days, forming his own society as he went, initiating all his followers into a special covenant with God.

The law of Moses insists before all else that the Chosen People preserve their aloofness from the world by constant purification and instruction: the people must be *qadosh,* "sanctified," both words having the basic meaning of "cut off," "separated." God has always given his people the same choice of either living up to the covenants made with him or being in Satan's power; there is no middle ground (Moses 4:4). True, we spend this time of probation in a no-man's-land between the two camps of salvation and damnation, but at every moment of the day and night we must be moving toward the one or the other. Progressive testing takes place along the way in either direction; the same tests in every dispensation and generation mark the progress of the people of God.

(1) Do you, first of all, agree to do things *his* way rather than *your* way—to follow the law of God? (2) If so, will you be *obedient* to him, no matter what he asks of you? (3) Will you, specifically, be willing to *sacrifice* anything he asks you for? (4) Will you at all times behave morally and soberly? (5) Finally, if God asks you to part with your worldly possessions by *consecrating* them all to his work, will you give his own back to him to be distributed as *he* sees fit, not as *you* think wise?

That last test has been by far the hardest of all, and few indeed have chosen that strait and narrow way. The rich young man was careful and correct in observing every point of the law—up to that one; but that was too much for him, and the Savior, who refused to compromise or make a deal, could only send him off sorrowing, observing to the apostles that passing that test was so difficult to those possessing the things of the world that only a special dispensation from God could get them by.

Like the people of Lehi and the primitive Christians, the Latter-day Saints were asked and forced to make a clean break with the world—"the world" meaning explicitly the world's economy.

The first commandment given to the Saints in this last dispensation, delivered at Harmony, Pennsylvania, in April of 1829, before the formal incorporation of the Church, was an ominous warning: "Seek not for riches but for wisdom" (D&C 6:7)—all in one brief mandate that does not allow compromise. Why start out on such a negative note? The Lord knew well that the great obstacle to the work would be what it always had been in the past. The warning is repeated throughout the Doctrine and Covenants and the Book of Mormon again and again. The positive and negative are here side by side and back to back, making it clear, as the scriptures often do, that the two quests are mutually exclusive—you cannot go after both, you cannot serve both God and Mammon, even if you should be foolish enough to try.

The Reluctant Saints

A year later the Saints were in Kirtland, and being warned again: "They also seek not earnestly the riches of eternity, but their eyes are full of greediness" (D&C 68:31). Those who seek not the eternal riches but are greedy for the other riches are here called "idlers" in the Lord's vineyard; the laborers are those who "labor for Zion; for if they labor for money they shall perish"! (2 Nephi 26:31).

At the next General Conference (1831), the law of consecration was laid down clearly and explicitly (D&C 82), with some anticipation of strong resistance (D&C 82:21). The Lord gave them his own special plan for his own people, by which "the church may stand independent above all other creatures beneath the celestial world" (D&C 78:14). The whole thing, in fact, was to be under celestial supervision, alien to the ways of the world: "And Zion cannot be built up unless it is by the principles of the law of the celestial kingdom; otherwise I cannot receive her unto myself" (D&C 105:5). The Saints were warned at length against interpreting the invitation to *independence* as a franchise to individuals for seeking private gain and thereby endowing the church with independence (D&C 78), a bit of sophistry that soon became and ever remained very popular.

In the October Conference of 1831, before the Church was a year old, the Prophet had to remind them "that God had often sealed up the heavens because of covetousness in the Church, . . . and except the Church receive the fulness of the Scriptures . . . they would yet fail." Covetousness, the desire to be rich, was the one thing that could wreck the whole program.[1] Properly impressed, "the conference voted that they prize the revelations to be worth to the Church the riches of the whole earth, speaking temporally."[2]

They were warned by the example of the saints of old: "Christ . . . proposed to make a covenant with them (the Jews), but they rejected Him and His proposals. . . . The Gentiles received the covenant, . . . but the Gentiles have not continued . . . but have departed from the faith. . . . [They] have become high-minded, and have not feared; therefore, but few of them will be gathered."[3] And now it was their turn, for they were in the same danger: "Repent, repent, is the voice of God to Zion; and strange as it may appear, yet it is true, mankind will persist in self-justification until all their iniquity is exposed, and their character past being redeemed. . . . Hear the warning voice of God, lest Zion fall, and the Lord swear in His wrath the inhabitants of Zion shall not enter into His rest."[4] Self-justification, that was the danger—the exhilarating exercise of explaining why my ways are God's ways after all. "Intemperance, immorality, extravagance, pride, blindness of heart, idolatry, the loss of natural affection; the love of this world, and indifference toward the things of eternity [are] increasing among those [Latter-day Saints] who profess a belief in the religion of heaven."[5] Even the Elders in high positions gave the prophet a bad time: "He said he had been trampled under foot by aspiring Elders, for all were infected with that spirit."[6] What spirit? That of a business-boom in Kirtland. By 1834 the plan was given up (D&C 104:47), "the covenants being broken through transgression, by covetousness and feigned words" (D&C 104:52) — that is, greed and hypocrisy, that pious self-justification in which the covetous are so adept.

The Way of the World

The opening of frontier lands offered fierce temptation. Joseph Smith wrote,

> The spirit of speculation in lands and property of all kinds, which was so prevalent throughout the whole nation, was taking deep root in the Church. As the fruits of this spirit, evil surmisings, fault finding, disunion, dissension, and apostasy followed in quick succession, and it seemed as though all the powers of earth and hell were combining their influence in an especial manner to overthrow the Church at once, and make a final end. . . . The enemy abroad, and apostates in our midst, united in their schemes, flour and provisions were turned towards other markets, and many became disaffected toward me as though I were the sole cause of those very evils I was most strenuously striving against.[7]

In Kirtland,

> many of the leading brethren had given their time and talent to speculation and were absorbed in schemes detrimental to their religious standing, and quite contrary to the counsel of the Prophet. Speculations brought on jealousies and hatreds, and those evil attributes manifested themselves toward Joseph who sought so diligently to suppress them. Prominent men — men who had shown the highest degree of loyalty to the Prophet — became disaffected. Their financial speculations brought

on a spirit of self-sufficiency, and that spirit made them wise in their own conceit. The affairs of the Church were put to the test of "wisdom" — wisdom as they understood it. Such wisdom, however, was undermining their integrity to the Church.[8]

As Brigham Young often noted, men who considered themselves sound, practical businessmen did not approve of the Prophet's unwise fiscal policies. "Joseph . . . mourned because of unbelief and treachery among many who had embraced the gospel. He feared lest few in Kirtland should remain worthy to receive an inheritance."[9]

"Warren Parrish . . . was what is termed a smart man [businessman], and through his smartness, which was distorted by ambition, envy, and bitterness, he turned against Joseph and the Church. . . . Apostasy and rebellion were rampant at Kirtland. . . . A scurrilous letter sent by Warren Parrish to the postmaster at Vinal Haven aroused a strong opposition."[10]

Heber C. Kimball tells how, returning from his mission to the East,

> we were very much grieved on our arrival in Kirtland, to see the spirit of speculation that was prevailing in the Church. Trade and traffic seemed to engross the time and attention of the Saints. When we left Kirtland a city lot was worth about $150; but on our return, to our astonishment, the same lot was said to be worth from $500 to $1000. . . . In fact everything in the place seemed to be moving in great prosperity, and all seemed determined to become rich. . . . This appearance of prosperity led many of the Saints to believe that the time had arrived for the Lord to enrich them with the treasures of the earth, and believing so, it stimulated them to great exertions.[11]

This was the very self-justification against which they had been warned in the beginning: it was time to realize a cash return on hard work and tithing.

Then came the crash of 1837, brought on by those same shrewd, hardheaded businessmen. "During this time," President Kimball recalled, "I had many days of sorrow and mourning, for my heart sickened to see the awful extent that things were getting to."[12] Many apostatized and "also entered into combinations to obtain wealth by fraud and every means that was evil."[13] Later, Kimball returned to Kirtland again after a mission to England: "The Church had suffered terribly from the ravages of apostasy." Looking back over many years, he recalled that "the Ohio mobbings, the Missouri persecutions, the martyrdom, the exodus, nor all that Zion's cause has suffered since, have imperiled it half so much as when mammon and the love of God strove for supremacy in the hearts of His people."[14] Note that they were torn between God and Mammon, and "no man can serve both!"

At the Center Stake

So Kirtland ended in disaster, and the Saints moved on, chastened and repentant, to Jackson County, where they sought "a counterpart of the Zion of Enoch."[15] As the Prophet viewed the exodus, he rejoiced in a new hope: "See the church of the LDS, selling all that they have, and gathering themselves together . . . that they may be together and bear each other's afflictions in the day of calamity." In the famous rescue mission, "some of the brethren had considerable and others had little or none, yet all became equal." This was the Prophet's desire, and so it was "in the day of calamity." But in the day of prosperity? As the new boomtown of Far West was building, the Prophet stood on the framework of a schoolhouse under construction and made some significant observations and a disturbing prophecy:

> Brethren, we are gathering to this buitiful land, to build up "Zion." . . . But since I have been here I perseive the spirit of selfishness, Covetousness, exists in

the hearts of the Saints. . . . Here are those who begin
to spread out buying up all the land they are able to do,
to the exclusion of the poorer ones who are not so much
blessed with this worlds goods, thinking to ley foundation for themselves only, looking to their own individual familys and those who are to follow them. . . .
Now I want to tell you that Zion cannot be built up in
eny such way. . . . I see signs put out, Beer signs, speculative schemes are being introduced this is the ways of
the world — Babylon indeed, and I tell you in the name
of the God of Israel, if thare is not repentance . . . and
a turning from such ungodlyness, covetousness, and self
will [in other words, "independence"] you will be broken up and scattered from this choice land to the four
winds of Heaven [sic].[16]

Did the people hearken to that voice? As ever, the
financial independence "of their own individual families"
came first. Brigham Young can tell us how it was:

Said the Lord to Joseph, "See if they will give their
farms to me." What was the result? *They would not do it,*
though it was one of the plainest things in the world.
No revelation that was ever given is more easy of comprehension
than that on the law of consecration. . . . Yet, when the
Lord spoke to Joseph, instructing him to counsel the
people to consecrate their possessions, and deed them
over to the Church in a covenant that cannot be broken,
would the people listen to it? No, but they began to find
out that they were mistaken, and had only acknowledged with their mouths that the things which they
possessed were the Lord's. [Feigned words were still
covering up their covetousness.] I wish to see the people
acknowledge the principle of consecration in their
works, as well as in their prayers. The Lord makes them
well by His power, through the ordinances of His house,
but will they consecrate? No. They say, "It is mine, and I
will have it myself." There is the treasure, and the heart
is with it.[17]

The thing to note here especially is that no one can evade the law of consecration on the grounds that it is not clear; still less are we free to give it our own "clarification," identifying consecration with tithing, gifts to the Church, and so on. We should all know by now that there is no limit to the plasticity, adaptability, contrivance, and manipulation of economic theory; as Tertullian says, "Oh, what a powerful argumentatrix is human ignorance!"[18]

> There is another revelation, . . . stating that it is the duty of all people who go to Zion to consecrate all their property to the Church of Jesus Christ of Latter-day Saints. . . . It was one of the first commandments or revelations given to this people after they had the privilege of organizing themselves as a Church, as a body, as the kingdom of God on the earth. I observed then, and I now think, that it will be one of the last revelations which the people will receive into their hearts and understandings, of their own free will and choice, and esteem it as a pleasure, a privilege, and a blessing unto them to observe and keep most holy.[19]

President Young explains how they got around ignoring the highest and clearest of revelations:

> When the revelation which I have read was given in 1838, I was present. . . . The brethren wished me to go among the Churches, and find out what surplus property the people had, with which to forward the building of the Temple we were commencing at Far West. I accordingly went from place to place through the country. Before I started, I asked brother Joseph, "Who shall be the judge of what is surplus property?" Said he, "Let them be the judges themselves, for I care not if they do not give a single dime."[20]

(As in Israel, the amount of the free-will offering was left entirely up to the giver, since it was he who was being tested. The offering was required but the amount was up to him.) The results, Brigham Young reports of his journey, were laughable—nobody had any surplus property! One "would say, 'I have got so many hundred acres of land, and I have got so many boys, and I want each one of them to have eighty acres, therefore this is not surplus property.' . . . I would go on to the next one, and he would have more land and cattle than he could make use of to advantage" and he would say, "We have no children, but our prospects are good, and we think we shall have a family of children, and if we do, we want to give them eighty acres of land each; we have no surplus property." No matter how well-to-do, the Saints would insist, "I have use for everything I have got," therefore no surplus. There were exceptions,

> and once in a while you would find a man who had a cow which he considered surplus, but generally she was of the class that would kick a person's hat off, or eyes out, or the wolves had eaten off her teats. [Or] you would once in a while find a man who had a horse that he considered surplus, but . . . he had the ringbone, was broken-winded, spavined in both legs, had the pole evil at one end of the neck and a fistula at the other, and both knees sprung. . . . They would come to me and say, "Brother Brigham, . . . I want to raise fifty dollars on this horse [today it would be a car], and the balance I am willing to turn in on tithing. If you will pay me twenty dollars in money, ten in store pay, and so much on another man's tithing, and so much on my own, you shall have the horse for eighty dollars;" when I could get as good a one for forty.[21]

In the law of Moses the giving of an offering in such meanness of spirit is called "an abomination unto the Lord" (Deuteronomy 25:16).

Some rejected the commandment outright: "At Far West, in April, 1838, Presidents Oliver Cowdery and David Whitmer were excommunicated from the Church." This was "for urging vexatious law-suits against the breth-

ren, . . . [each] leaving his calling in which God had appointed him by revelation, for the sake of filthy lucre, and
turning to the practice of law, disgracing the Church by
being connected in the bogus business, . . . forsaking the
cause of God, and returning to the beggarly elements of
the world."[22] Business and law were the world's keys to
success. In 1838 at Far West, "when these troops surrounded us, . . . the first persons that I knew were men
who had once professed to be beloved brethren, and they
were the men who piloted these mobs into our city, namely
William M'Lellin & Lyman E. Johnson, two of the twelve;
John Whitmer, and David Whitmer, . . . William W.
Phelps and scores of others."[23] And it was all for business.

And so the prophecy of the schoolhouse was fulfilled
quickly and thoroughly, as the Saints were driven from
their exciting new boomtown in the worst persecution in
their history. "Could our brethren stay in Jackson County,
Missouri?" Brigham Young asked a later conference. "No,
No. Why? They had not learned 'a' concerning Zion; and
we have been traveling now forty-two years, and have we
learned our a, b, c? . . . I will say, scarcely. Have we seen
it as a people?"[24]

Nauvoo the Bonanza

And so we move on to Nauvoo, where the prophet
began by changing the town's name of Commerce to "Nauvoo the Beautiful"—a significant shift of emphasis—and
followed up by warning the Saints more strenuously than
ever against seeking personal financial independence as a
milestone on the Way of Salvation. He laid the strongest
emphasis on the importance of distinguishing the two
kinds of independence: "If there are any among you who
aspire after their own aggrandizement, and seek their own
opulence, while their brethren are groaning in poverty, . . . they cannot be benefited by the intercession of
the Holy Spirit."[25] (The reader is referred to such recent

gems by Mormon authors as *How to Prosper during the Coming Bad Years* and *Survive and Win in the Inflationary Eighties*.) "Organization of large bodies upon common stock principles . . . opens such a dreadful field for the avaricious, the indolent, and the corrupt hearted to prey upon the innocent and virtuous and honest. . . . [They are] aspiring men . . . who had not the substance of godliness about them."[26] But they do make money, and there is prophetic portent for the future in those ominous words: "Every man who is afraid, covetous &c. will be taken in a snare,"[27] for fear and covetousness are the twin offspring of insecurity. To be ambitious and competitive have been the natural tendencies in the New World: "Now, in this world, man-kind are naturally selfish, ambitious and striving to excel one above another. . . . Some seek to excel. And this was the case with Lucifer when he fell."[28] To counter that, the Prophet assures us that "the greatest temporal and spiritual blessings which always come from faithfulness and concerted effort, *never attended individual exertion or enterprise*,"[29] and that "the advancement of the cause of God and the building up of Zion is as much one man's business as another's. . . . Party feelings, separate interests, exclusive designs should be lost sight of in the one common cause, in the interest of the whole."[30] The Saints had entered an order in which even the idealism of Free Masonry

> was superseded by a more perfect fraternity found in the vows and covenants which the endowment in the House of God afforded members of the Church. Besides, the Saints learned that they must surrender worldly affiliations, since the world was opposed to the mission of Joseph Smith and his followers. . . . The Church, however, rests upon the rock of revelation and must follow divine guidance rather than precedence [and the laws of the marketplace.]"[31]

The sanctity of their calling became a franchise for she-

nanigans among those brethren in Nauvoo who quickly
caught on to the now familiar trick of promoting private
business (and later political) interests, with promises of
apocalyptic profits, by identifying them with the Church:
"Thus we find that there have been frauds and secret abominations and evil works of darkness going on, leading the
minds of the weak and unwary [most Latter-day Saints
have always been unsuspecting and naive] into confusion
and distraction, and all the time palming it off upon the
Presidency."[32] It was Far West all over again. On June 18,
1842, in a grove near the Nauvoo Temple,

> Elder Woodruff says, "Joseph, the prophet, arose
> and spoke in great plainness upon the corruption and
> wickedness of John C. Bennett. He also prophesied that
> if the merchants of the city and the rich did not open
> their hearts and contribute to the poor they would be
> cursed by the hand of God and cut off from the land of
> the living." . . . All efforts to stand upon a common
> ground with the citizens generally of Nauvoo were, how-
> ever, unavailing."[33] Why? Because, wrote Wilfred Wood-
> ruff, who lived through it all, "The people in those
> days, . . . like Israel of old associated certain worldly
> successes with their ideas of right, and misfortunes with
> their ideas of wrong."[34] That, of course, would make
> them morally obligated to get rich—which is what Pres-
> ident Woodruff calls sophistry when he notes that "the
> fear of the enemy was less trying to him [Joseph Smith]
> than the folly of many of his brethren who were swayed
> by the spirit of the age and the peculiar sophistries of
> those times.[35]

That was the greater danger: "There were those who
were ready to listen to the sophistries and cunning arguments of the hypocrite and the Pharisee in their midst
[Nauvoo],"[36] and this they had often done elsewhere in
the history of the Church. Sophistry again: Under God's
plan there could be no compromise. "Any person who is

exalted to the highest mansion has to abide a celestial law, and the whole law too. But there has been a great difficulty in getting anything into the heads of this generation. . . . Even the Saints are slow to understand."[37]

On the eve of the expulsion from Nauvoo, Brigham Young wrote that "the Saints were becoming slothful and covetous, and would spend their means upon fine houses for themselves before they would put it into a House of the Lord."[38] The result we all know, though we tend to overlook the cause: "Through the selfishness of some, which is idolatry, through their covetousness, which is the same, and the lustful desire of their minds, they were cast out and driven from their homes."[39]

Stout Resistance

The next settlement was on the plains, and Brigham Young recalled:

> While we were in Winter Quarters, the Lord gave to me a revelation. . . . I talked it to my brethren; I would throw out a few words here, and a few words there, to my first counselor, to my second counselor, and the Twelve Apostles, but with the exception of one or two of the Twelve, it would not touch a man. . . . I would have given it if the people had been prepared. . . . But I could not touch them. One would say, "I am for California," and another one, "I am for gold," and I am for this and I am for that.[40]

The good old frontier spirit of independence.

And a New Beginning

Crossing the Plains to Utah brought the Saints to their senses, and the famine that afflicted them in 1848 was averted only "by the exercise of the highest wisdom and the broadest charity, and the partial observance of the principle of the United Order, which the Saints had before sought to introduce, and still have it in their mission to establish. The people were put upon rations, all sharing the same, like members of one great family."[41] To the hungry Pawnees, they gave freely of their scarce grain. "The spirit begotten by such an act of generosity opened the hearts of the Saints for the enjoyment of their conference, and fitted them more perfectly for the worship of God."[42]

When the crickets and drought struck in 1855, Heber C. Kimball wrote in his journal, "Perhaps many feel a little sober because our bread is cut off, but I am glad of it, because it will be a warning to us. . . . The earth is determined to rest, and it is right that it should."[43] The next year he wrote:

> Money will not buy flour or meal. . . . I sell none for money but let it go where people are truly destitute. Dollars and cents do not count now. . . . Some of the people drop many big tears, but if they cannot learn wisdom by precept, nor by example, they must learn it by what they suffer. . . . I wish to God this people would all listen to counsel . . . and move as one man and be one. If this were the case, our enemies would never have any more power over us, our granaries never would be empty, nor would we see sorrow.[44]

> The design of President Young was that no speculation in lands by the brethren should be allowed whereby the first comers should enrich themselves at the expense of their brethren who should follow. . . . This arrangement prevented any one man from holding a large tract [of land] near the city, and by so doing prevented speculation by the individual to the detriment of the whole community. . . . In other words, the interest of the whole was to be uppermost in the mind of each man, and the spirit of greed and avarice seldom asserted itself on the part of those noble founders of Utah's great commonwealth.[45]

By present-day standards, Jesse W. Fox, the official

surveyor, was woefully deficient in vision, enterprising spirit, and business know-how: "If anyone asked him to select one [tract] for him he promptly refused, saying that those who owned the land should be builders on it and that no one by his assistance should ever speculate at the expense of the poor Saints coming to the valley."[46]

Speaking on that subject, "the question of consecration was presented [in Conference of April 1854]. President Kimball said, 'I want all I have to be secured in the Kingdom of God.' They knew the dangers and temptations of wealth, the selfishness which it begets, as well as the destruction of brotherly love."[47] The main thing Brother Brigham insisted on in their new home was that they get over the illusion of personal economic independence.

> As I have already observed, the people are ignorant. . . . We are here on the earth . . . and it seems as though we, as individuals, were perfectly independent of every creature or being throughout the immensity of space. . . . We do not fully realize from whence we have received anything we now have in our possession. This is in consequence of our shortsightedness.[48]

"Some of the Saints are almost persuaded to think that the Lord has called upon them to consecrate, to give up something which they consider their own, but in reality is not, to somebody that never did own it. . . . It is a vain and foolish thought for men to think they own anything of themselves."[49] "If men are faithful, the time will come when they [can] . . . obtain, organize, bring into existence, and own. 'What, of themselves, independent of their Creator?' No."[50] "He has called upon the people to consecrate their property, to see whether they could understand so simple a thing as this."[51] Their reaction to the command was the usual. With the Christian world, the Latter-day Saints acknowledged in their meetings that the earth was the Lord's. In their weekly meetings, they have told how the Lord has blessed them. Did they mean it?

Relapse to Normalcy

How did they take these teachings? Brigham Young in 1851 was sick at the sight of so many of the Saints running to California chiefly after the God of this world, and he was unable to address them.[52] Two years later, he deplored the rise of juvenile crime, but even more the pious men who inspired it: Who are the real delinquents? he asks.

> I have not the least hesitation in saying that the loose conduct, and calculations, and manner of doing business, which have characterized men who have had property in their hands, have laid the foundation to bring our boys into the spirit of stealing. You have caused them to do it, you have laid before them every inducement possible, to learn their hands and train their minds to take that which is not their own.[53]

"Why not . . . day by day watch and chasten your-selves?" he asks the Saints, but instead of that, everyone "becomes so absorbed in their improvement and increase, that he forgets why he came here, [and] that the hands upon the Public Works need food to sustain life, that after all he is only a steward at most. . . . While another, still more culpable in that he produces nothing, strives to amass wealth, and build up a name by becoming a mere trader, and far too often a *shaving* trader, and of course he too is soon fully imbued with the ruling passion of selfishness."[54] He is not speaking of isolated cases: "The grand difficulty with this community is simply this, their interest is not one. When you will have your interests concentrated in one, then you will work jointly, and we shall not have to scold and find fault, as much as we are now required to."[55]

> The man, or the woman, that mainly looks after the fruit, after the luxuries of life, good food, fine apparel, and at the same time professes to be a Latter-day Saint, if he does not get that spirit out of his heart, it will obtain a perfect victory over him; . . . and if he does not get

rid of that spirit, the quicker he starts east for the States,
or west for California, the better.[56]

Heber C. Kimball, preaching "against pride and covetousness," expressed his "fear of riches. . . . Said he: 'If
the Saints will repent, the Lord's wrath will be turned
away, but they will not repent until it is too late.' " And
as before, it *was* too late — within the year Johnston's army
struck.[57] As it approached, in 1857, Brigham Young made
an oft-quoted statement:

> I am more afraid of covetousness in our Elders than
> I am of the hordes of hell. Have we men out now of that
> class? I believe so. I am afraid of such spirits; for they
> are more powerful and injurious to this people than all
> hell outside of our borders. All our enemies in the United
> States or in the world, and all hell with them marshalled
> against us, could not do us the injury that covetousness
> in the hearts of this people could do us; for it is idolatry.[58]

And in the next year: "Whether you can see it or not,
I know that this people are more or less prone to idolatry;
for I see that spirit manifested every day, and hear of it
from nearly every quarter."[59] And so the enemy moved in
and the Mormons moved out: "The roads are lined with
men, women, children, teams, and wagons — all moving
south," wrote Wilford Woodruff.[60] In this crisis, "speculators thought they saw an opportunity to make money
from the Saints by purchasing their homes in these the
hours of their distress,"[61] thus anticipating those far-
sighted Saints of a later day who would write best-selling
books on *How to Profit by the Coming Hard Times*. In the
first year, "the city seemed to be over-run by speculators
and adventurers,"[62] such as "Wardle, Russel, and
Miller, . . . a firm of speculators who were making money
out of the conditions incident to the presence of the United
States Army." In 1858, the Chamber of Commerce was
organized "for the purpose of protecting the citizens

against the exorbitant prices demanded by those merchants who were taking advantage of the times" — price control, no less.[63]

Business not only followed the flag, setting an example for years to follow, but it also showed the way, "for it is the conduct of traders who have fattened in our midst that has brought an army into our Territory. I would rather see every building and fence laid in ashes than to see a trader come in here with his goods."[64] "Instead of reflecting upon and searching for hidden things of the greatest value to them, they rather wish to learn how to secure their way through the world as easily and as comfortably as possible. The reflections what they are here for, who produced them, and where they are from, far too seldom enter their minds" (compromise).[65]

I Got Mine!

After all their suffering, had the Saints learned? In 1860, President Young asked that question: "Are those who have been in the Church twenty, twenty-five, or thirty years prepared to have the visions of eternity opened to them? No."[66]

> Instead of being united in our feelings to build up all, each one takes his own course; whereas, if we were united, we would get rich ten times faster than we do now. How are you going to bring a people to that point when they will all be united in the things of this life? By no other means than prevailing upon them to live their religion that they all may possess the Holy Ghost, the spirit of revelation, the light of Christ, which will enable them to see eye to eye.[67]

Did they fail to see the light? "Do you think you will have your farm and your substance by yourself, and live in the gratification of your selfish propensities as you now do? 'O, no, we expect to be made pure and holy.' Where will you begin to be pure and holy? If you do not begin here, I do not know where you will begin."[68] But there was always that insistence on having things both ways:

I will ensure that there are scores, and perhaps hundreds, looking at me while I am speaking, who think, "Brother Brigham, you are a fool; we have as good a right to trade with one man as another; and we will go to what store we please, and do what we please with our means, and we will trade with those who will do the best by us." Yet there are hundreds who, and in fact the most of the people, understand the folly of this course, as the experience of the past six-months has proved.[69]

They did see it, but still, "We have to become more like a single family, and be one, that we may be the Lord's; and not every one have his own individual interest."[70] He repeated the admonition of 1858:

[There is] too much love of the things of the world. There is more danger to be apprehended from this source than all the mobs that could be organized and brought in opposition. Lust after the things of the world had ruined the most powerful nations. . . . Wherever there existed a hunger for ease and wealth in place of a hunger for righteousness, sooner or later the parties thus inclined would lose the Spirit of God, and go into darkness. After the lust for women, this greed for gain was next in order in its corrupting tendencies.[71]

To be specific,

Take a man, for instance, who has got a five acre lot. He wants his team, he must have his horses, harness, wagon, plow, harrow and farming utensils to cultivate that five acres, just as though he was farming a hundred acres. And when harvest comes, he is not accommodated by his neighbors with a reaping machine, and he says — "Another year, I will buy one," and this to harvest five acres of grain. Take the article of wagons among this people, we have five where we should not have more

than two. . . . Again, take mowing and reaping machines, and we have probably twice or three times as
many in this Territory as the people need. . . . If this
community would be united, and work cattle instead of
horses, they might save themselves from two to five
hundred thousand dollars yearly.[72]

Having It Both Ways

In Brigham Young's last year, the course of things
caused him great concern: The Saints wanted it both ways:
"Now those that can see the spiritual atmosphere can see
that many of the Saints are still glued to this earth and
lusting and longing after the things of this world, in which
there is no profit. . . . According to the present feeling of
many of our brethren, they would arrogate to themselves
this world and all that pertains to it. . . . Where are the
eyes and the hearts of this people?"[73]

> If we do not wake up and cease to long after the
> things of this earth, we will find that we as individuals
> will go down to hell, although the Lord will preserve a
> people unto himself. . . . Well, now, some of the Elders
> are running after these holes in the ground, and I see
> men before me, in this house [the St. George Temple]
> that have no right to be here. They are as corrupt in their
> hearts as they can be, and we take them by the hand
> and call them brother.[74]

> You may think this is plain talk, it is not as plain as
> you will find by and by. If you should ever go to the
> gates of heaven, Jesus will say he never knew you. While
> you have been saying your prayers and going to your
> meetings and are as corrupt in your hearts as men can
> be. . . . Not but what there are a great majority of the
> people as good as they know how to be, . . . but show
> some of the Elders of Israel according to their present
> conduct a dollar on one side and eternal life on the other,
> and I fear they would choose the dollar.[75]

> Some of the Latter day Saints had an idea that they

could take the follies of the world in one hand and the
Savior in the other, and expect to get into the presence
of the Lord Jesus.[76]

We need not refer to the traditions of the fathers
with regard to the manifestations of covetousness we
see so much of. Observe the customs and hab-
its . . . of . . . our brethren and sisters here. We see men
from twenty years up to old age who are entirely overcome by their desire to obtain gold. . . . We exhort the
people not to be such fools as to run after the golden
image; and sometimes we tell them that we will cut them
off from the Church, if they do. This has caused this
great outcry.[77]

At a conference Brigham Young "advised men not to
work so hard that they had to get half drunk in order to
keep it up."[78]

After the Utah Reformation and the Crisis of 1856-58,
things went back to normal, with the usual drift in the
usual direction. Brigham Young in 1867: "The Latter-day
Saints, in their conduct and acts with regard to financial
matters, are like the rest of the world. The course pursued
by men of business in the world has a tendency to make
a few rich, and to sink the masses of the people in poverty
and degradation. Too many of the Elders of Israel take this
course. No matter what comes they are for gain—for gathering around them riches."[79]

In the Gilded Age of the 1870s, Brigham Young never
ceased to plead and explain: "Will he ever grant power to
his Saints on the earth? Yes, . . . but in the capacity they
are now, in the condition that they now present themselves
before God, before the world and before each other? Never,
Never!"[80] And next year: "Do the people understand it?
Scarcely! scarcely! . . . How is it? Are not the sordid things
of this life before our eyes, and have they not thrown a
mist before them so that we can not see?"[81] "How long
shall we travel, how long shall we live, how long shall

God wait for us to sanctify ourselves and become one in the Lord, in our actions and in our ways for building up of the kingdom of God, that he can bless us?"[82] "The Lord is merciful to us, that he still remembers us, that he is still feeling after us, and that he is sending forth his voice — the voice of his Spirit, into the hearts of his people, crying unto them—'Stop! Stop your course! Cease to bring in and build up Babylon in your midst.' "[83] But alas, "What is the general expression through our community? It is that the Latter-day Saints are drifting as fast as they can into idolatry, drifting into the spirit of the world and into pride and vanity."[84]

Babylon Rejected (Again?)

Things had gone so far by 1875 that another Reformation was in order. President Young at conference spoke on

> the great duty that rested upon the Saints to put in operation God's purposes with regard to the United Order, by the consecration of the private wealth to the common good of the people. The underlying principle of the United Order was that there should be no rich and no poor, that men's talents should be used for the common good, and that selfish interests should make way for a more benevolent and generous spirit among the Saints.[85]

In response, "The whole assembly [of the priesthood] voted to renew their covenants, and later the Presidency, the Twelve, the Seventies, and the Presiding Bishop were baptized and entered into a special covenant to observe the rules of the United Order. . . . This movement became general throughout the Church."[86]

John Taylor, Wilford Woodruff, and Lorenzo Snow, who were to be Brigham Young's successors, all became enthusiastic leaders in the movement. They fervently sang the hymn "Adam Ondi Ahman":

This earth was once a garden place, with all her
glories common,
And men did live a holy race, and walk with Jesus
face to face
In Adam-ondi-Ahman.
We read that Enoch walked with God, above the
rule of Mammon . . .

Wilford Woodruff in 1879 reported from Arizona,

The people of these settlements all live in the United
Order. . . . There seemed to be universal satisfaction . . . with this order of things. . . . All fared alike,
the president, priest, and people. . . . I could see many
advantages they had above those who were living, each
man for himself. . . . They are daily getting rich, . . . all
is theirs, . . . as though one man owned the whole. . . .
Until I can learn a better way, I feel to say with every
sentiment of my heart to . . . every . . . settlement living in the Order, go ahead and God bless you; . . . and
as President Taylor and the Apostles advocate the same
principle, I hope that all the priesthood will sustain
[it]. . . . It appears to me that the further we withdraw
from this union into individuality of gardens, lots, orchards, cows, pigs, and chickens, the further we withdraw from the United Order, and the more we open the
door for selfishness, temptation, and fault-finding with
each other, the same as before [when] we . . . would
open a door to give each man an excuse to spend his
time attending to his individual affairs, instead of laboring for the general good of all.[87]

Lorenzo Snow's enterprise in Brigham City was perhaps the most successful one. The first five presidents of
the Church all knew the United Order would work, and
yet but five years after the death of Brigham Young, in
1882, President Taylor hesitantly permitted "some of our
brethren to branch out into business on their own." That
the idea was not his own, and that he had serious reservations, is clear from the official letter:

Babylon Delivered (Again!)

> A feeling had been manifested by some of our breth-
> ren [it was *their* idea] to branch out into the mercantile
> business on their own account [independence at last],
> and his [John Taylor's] idea, as to that, was, if people
> would be governed by correct principles, laying aside
> covetousness and eschewing chicanery and fraud, deal-
> ing honestly and conscientiously with others as they
> would like others to deal with them, that there would
> be no objection on our part for our brethren to do these
> things; that it was certainly much better for them to
> embark in such enterprises than our enemies.[88]

Far from being a commandment, the change was only
permitted with uneasy reservations; the reluctance of the
"no objection" concession is apparent in the argument that
free enterprise would be even less desirable if it was the
prerogative of the enemies in our midst. Would the new
enterprises be "laying aside covetousness"? What was
their purpose if not to acquire wealth? As to "eschewing
fraud and chicanery," which is still the plea to this day,
has not the experience of the past shown that such appeals
are as futile as giving a small boy a drum with the sober
admonition to play it softly forever after?

What had happened to sidetrack the United Order? A
recent in-depth economic history of the 1870s explains:

> During this period, astute businessmen gradually
> gained control of the cooperatives and replaced the co-
> operative methods of retailing with methods closer to
> pure private enterprise. In the process these new owners
> completely changed the character of the companies;
> though they often kept the company name the same, in
> order to take advantage of the local appeal the cooper-
> atives still held.[89]

Retaining the name might be considered a stroke of
genius were it not so very obvious; the religious note had

to be retained in the territory, and few will protest today that the stately emblem of ZCMI breathes neither the unworldly aroma of Zion nor the tainted breath of a true cooperative.

"By the mid-eighties, most of the stock of the cooperatives [which needed large sums of money to buy machinery made only in the east and abroad] had been sold to a few businessmen who now controlled the entire operation, . . . making them corporations run by the major stockholders whose main concern became profit-making."[90]

Square One

If we ask what improvement has been made up to the present, there is no better standard to judge by than that given by President Spencer W. Kimball in a solemn and inspired message to the church on the occasion of the 200th anniversary of the nation.[91] The address gives us a picture of the Church, the nation, and indeed the world that is a miracle of clarity and condensation, placing the physician's finger with unerring accuracy on the really important issues. First, by way of introduction, a general observation: "When I review the performance of this people in comparison with what is expected, I am appalled and frightened." Not a particularly cheerful or even optimistic message. What is it that so frightens and appalls the prophet? Three things in particular:

1. *The abuse of the environment:* "When I . . . fly over the vast and beautiful expanses of our globe, . . . I have the feeling that the good earth can hardly bear our presence upon it. . . . The Brethren constantly cry out against . . . pollution of mind, body, and our surroundings. . . . That such a cry should be necessary among a people so blessed is amazing to me."

2. *The pursuit of personal affluence:* "Carnal man has tended to transfer his trust in God to material things. . . .

When men have fallen under the power of Satan and lost the faith, they have put in its place a hope in the 'arm of flesh' and in 'gods of silver, and gold, of brass,' . . . that is, in idols. . . . Many people spend most of their time working in the service of a self-image that includes sufficient money, stocks, bonds, investment portfolios, property, credit cards, furnishing, automobiles and the like to *guarantee* carnal security throughout, it is hoped, a long and happy life."

3. *Trust in military security:* "We commit vast resources to the fabrication of gods of stone and steel — ships, planes, missiles, fortifications — and depend on them for protection and deliverance. When threatened, we become anti-enemy instead of pro-kingdom of God; we train a man in the art of war and call him a patriot, thus, in the manner of Satan's counterfeit of true patriotism, perverting the Savior's teaching. . . . What are we to fear when the Lord is with us? Can we not take the Lord at his word and exercise a particle of faith in him? . . . We must leave off the worship of modern-day idols and a reliance on the 'arm of flesh,' for the Lord has said to all the world in our day, 'I will not spare any that remain in Babylon' [D&C 64:24]."

And how did the Saints, who never tire of saying, "The Prophet! The Prophet! We have a prophet!" receive his words? As might be expected, reaction has ranged from careful indifference to embarrassed silence and instant deep freeze. As to the three things against which they were warned, it can be shown with cruel documentation that Utah leads the nation, at least through its representatives, in outspoken contempt for the environment, unabashed reverence for wealth, and ardent advocacy of military expansion.

On various occasions, Brigham Young made it perfectly clear that no possible grounds remain for evading or postponing the law of consecration; there is nothing to argue or temporize about; the clarifying and explaining have all been done. It has been repeatedly presented to the people in the most clear and unequivocal terms — and flatly rejected by them. Not by a show of hands — that would have been perfectly permissible — but by proclaiming by word and deed after leaving the meetings that they had no intention of keeping certain parts of the law. Notice how Israel and the Saints of every age, when called to keep the law, are reminded that unless they live up to every point of the agreement the whole covenant will be nullified — it is the whole law or nothing. The Saints covenanted and promised to observe it with the clear understanding that God is not to be mocked in these things, and that the only alternative to living up to every item of covenants made with him is to be in Satan's power (cf. Moses 4:4). Which is where we are today, along with the rest of the world. It is the stubborn insistence on having it both ways, keeping parts of the law that content them while putting the rest on hold, that generates those crippling contradictions that mark our present condition.

If Brigham Young could say in 1877 that "the Latter-day Saints present a strange spectacle to those that enjoy the spirit of revelation," today the spectacle is unfolding to all the world. Economists, journalists, political analysts, sociologists, historians, psychologists, and not least of all General Authorities have all had occasion in the present year to offer explanations for the paradoxical phenomenon of "Utah, the Fraud Capital of the World." If you have followed our little history, there is nothing paradoxical about it. Almost all of the experts agree that the cause of the thing lies in a strange combination of goodness, gullibility, and greed among the people who have always, "like Israel of old," to quote President Woodruff, "associated certain worldly successes with their ideas of right, and misfortune with their ideas of wrong." Since the beginning, the Saints have been under the necessity of frequent routine warnings against "the hard-sell techniques

of men not interested in truth, who insist that the acquisition of wealth is a state of blessedness" (1 Timothy 6:5).
The King James translators, innocent of the economic jargon of a decadent society, gave the passage a more phil-
osophic turn, but just as damning: "Perverse disputings
of men of corrupt minds, and destitute of the truth, supposing that gain is godliness: from such withdraw thyself"
(1 Timothy 6:5). The urgent warning, indeed the whole
epistle, shows that such men were influential and dangerous in the church; and all Paul could do about it was
to advise his hearers to steer clear of them.

What can we look forward to now? "Happy is the man
whom God correcteth!" If the Lord still loves the Saints,
he will treat them as before and give them some very rough
times indeed to bring them to their senses. Meanwhile the
constant cry of their great leader Brigham Young still reverberates in the hearts of the faithful: How long, O Lord?
How long will it be? "We may travel for many years before
the sunshine appears. It does not yet appear to this people,
they are merely in the twilight."[92] "Could we expect them
to become prepared to be the disciples of the Lord Jesus
in one, in five, in ten, in twenty, or in thirty years?"[93] On
the eve of the Civil War, he asked them: "Are the Latter-
day Saints preparing themselves for the calamities that are
coming upon the earth? or are they *covetous?*"[94] And when
the war is over: "We look forward to the day . . . when
we will be prepared to build up Zion. Are we prepared
now? No, we are not. We are only professedly Latter-day
Saints."[95] The feigned words of the profession covered an
ever-growing covetousness that blossomed into spectacular flower in the Gilded Age of the nation's history: "We
are constantly receiving communications from the elders
laboring in the States. . . . There is a coldness in the minds
of the people, a total indifference to the gospel and its
glorious truths and the whole sum of their inquiries [is]
how and where we can make the most money."[96] And two

years later: "How long shall we travel, how long shall we live, how long shall God wait for us to sanctify ourselves and become one in the Lord, in our actions and in our ways for building up of the kingdom of God, that he can bless us?"[97] The question still awaits an answer.

In the face of all this, students still cling to the belief that it is all right to get rich if you intend to help the Church. Let us hear the wise, experienced, and inspired Brigham Young on the subject:

> When the people arrive here, many of them come to me and say, "Brother Brigham, can we go here, or there, to get us farms? Shall we enter into this or that speculation? We have been very poor, and we want to make some money. . . . We want to go where we can have plenty of range for our stock, where we can mount our horses, and ride over the prairies, and say, I am Lord of all I survey. We do not wish to be disturbed, in any way, nor to be asked to pay tithing, to work upon the roads, nor pay territorial tax, but we wish all the time to ourselves, to appropriate to our own use."[98]

Here, if ever, was the culmination of the American Dream on the wildest of the frontiers. But with it they wanted the rewards of faith:

> If you ask them if they are ready to build up the kingdom of God, their answer is prompt—"Why, to be sure we are, with our whole souls; but we want first to get so much gold, speculate and get rich, and then we can help the Church considerably. We will go to California and get gold, go and buy goods and get rich, trade with the emigrants, build a mill, make a farm, get a large herd of cattle, and *then* we can do a great deal for Israel." When will you be ready to do it? "In a few years, brother Brigham, if you do not disturb us. We do not believe in the necessity of doing military duty, in giving over our surplus property for tithing; we never could see into it; but we want to go and get rich, to accumulate and amass

wealth, by securing all the land adjoining us, and all we have a knowledge of." If that is not the spirit of this people, then I do not know what the truth is concerning the matter.[99]

Here the prophet shows us what today is glorified as the spirit that won the West, that made America great, and so on, in direct conflict with the spirit by which the kingdom must be built up, and he rebukes those Saints who insisted that they could sustain the one in the spirit of the other. It is time to give up that pious sophistry. So here is the answer to our question, What has gone wrong? The Lord has not let you down after all your plans and exertions. You have let him down by all your plans and exertions.

A Note on Being Independent

God has announced that he has a plan to prepare for himself special people and to make his church "independent above all other creatures beneath the celestial world" (D&C 78:14). We get as far as the word "independent" and, without reading another syllable farther, declare our resolution to get rich and thereby achieve the independence God wants us all to have.

But if God has a plan, why not let *him* tell us what it is, instead of cutting him off in the middle of a sentence the way Cain did when he saw that God's plan would interfere with his own plans for getting rich (Moses 5:23-33)?

The Lord speaks of the *Church's* being independent— nothing about the individual; and of independence, but only of the powers here below "beneath the celestial world," not of orders from above. He makes it all very clear: It is *my* plan—not yours! (D&C 78:14). "It is *my* purpose to provide for my saints, for all things are mine. But it must needs be done *in mine own way,* . . . that I, the Lord, have decreed to provide for *my* saints" (D&C 104:15-

16). The plan is a heavenly one, given as a special blessing to the elect, God's own people, to set them apart from the rest of the world – there is no human invention about it. But that one word, "independent," is enough to set us off after the way of the world, interposing our own plan right in the middle of the sentence, so that it will look like his, not even bothering to consider what the Lord has in mind. And what do we come up with? Nothing in the world but the old familiar run-of-the-mill capitalism – the world's way after all. Is *this* what the Lord has been holding in reserve for his people?

"It must needs be done in mine own way," says the Lord, and in the very same sentence gives us as the essence of that plan, "that the poor shall be exalted, in that the rich are made low" (D&C 104:16) – all brought to the same economic level – so that we all have "sufficient for our needs," which is quite enough for anyone. The idea is "that you may be *equal* in the bonds of heavenly things, yea, and earthly things also. . . . For if ye are not *equal* in earthly things ye cannot be equal in obtaining heavenly things" (D&C 78:5-6). It is nothing more nor less than a redistribution of the wealth, for "it is not given that one man should possess that which is above another" (D&C 49:20). As Brigham Young put it, "the underlying principle . . . was that there should be no rich and no poor."[100]

Now Joseph Smith knew as well as anyone that "if we were eaquel in property at present in six months we would be worse [off] than Ever [sic]." And he tells us exactly why – *not* because the more industrious, far-sighted, dedicated, and enterprising members of society would quickly acquire most of the wealth, but because "there [are] too many *dishonest* men amongst us who [have] more injenity [ingenuity] to threat the Rest [of us]."[101] The inevitable inequality comes from dishonest men with ingenious plans, who endanger "the Rest" by forcing all to play the game their way to avoid becoming their victims: "Yea, truth faileth; and he that departeth from evil maketh himself a prey" (Isaiah 59:15). It is Satan's master stroke—all must set their hearts on riches or become the servants of those who do.

Consecration and the United Order begin with the observance of civic duty. "I prophecy [sic]," said Joseph Smith in 1841, "that the day will come when you will say Oh that we had given heed but look now upon our public works the store schoolhouse for instance the Simoon of the Desert has passed over it." The people had neglected the common interest for the private: "The people will not hearken nor hear and bondage Death and destruction are close at our heels." With this dire prophecy (and there never was a truer) goes another, most reassuring to us all: "The Kingdom will not be broken up"! What then, can we relax? Now comes one of the most enlightening and reassuring of prophecies. In view of what has happened, one cannot help but ask, How will it all turn out, and how can the Lord go on tolerating such behavior? Here is the answer: "The Kingdom will not be broken up *but we shall be scattererd and driven* gathered again & then dispersed reestablished & driven abroad *and so on* until the Ancient of days shall sit and the kingdom and power thereof shall then be given to the Saints and they shall possess it forever and ever, which may God hasten for Christs sake Amen."[102] Now this is exactly the process we have been describing. The discouraging thing is that we never learn; the encouraging thing is that when we see the dismal cycle repeating itself again, we are beholding the fulfillment of prophecy—all is going forth as foretold, and, best of all, the kingdom still hangs on; it will never be too late for the faithful to work for the building up of the kingdom. Each individual is being tested every hour of the day: "The devil has no power over us only as we permit him; the moment we revolt at *anything* which comes from God the Devil takes power."[103] One or the other—we will never be allowed the luxury of compromise.

A most enlightening account of how one gets rich to help the Church is the story of F. A. Hammond, a man who landed in San Francisco in 1848, joined the Church there, and by great industry and sound common sense acquired considerable wealth—Sam Brannan begged him to become his business partner. Involved in the Gold Rush from the first, he recalls, "I was so full of the spirit of the gathering that I did not regard gold at all." He got rich selling food and supplies to the miners, and then he set out on advice of Brigham Young to join the struggling Saints in the Valley. Passing through the gold country "opposite Mormon Island" on the Sacramento River, he found that "the goods loaded on his splendid wagon were in such great demand that he could easily make from 200 to 500 percent profit on them, . . . and prices were increasing every day." "It fairly made my head swim, and Satan whispered in my ears, 'Why not remain another year, and trade and speculate and get rich; and *then* you can assist the poor Saints, the widow and the orphan, and take them up to Zion. . . . The people already there are hard put to it to sustain themselves.' In this manner I was tried, and sorely too."[104] Note who was reasoning so piously and wisely, like Judas protesting his lively concern for the poor (John 12:4-6)—it was Satan. This reasoning caused Brother Hammond "great perplexity of mind"[105]—what was he to do? A vision that came to him on three successive nights solved the problem. In it, he was shown a terrible threat that hung over all those so diligently seeking gold on the river, and after the third revelation, "When I awoke . . . my mind was perfectly clear, and I felt to thank the Lord . . . that He had thus warned me . . . to flee from that land and gather with His people . . . and learn to be obedient to *His* commands."[106] The Lord had made clear that he is not pleased with the familiar sophistry of getting-rich-to-help-the-church.

Notes

1. *TPJS* 9.
2. Ibid., 8.
3. Ibid., 14-15.
4. Ibid., 18-19.
5. Ibid., 47.
6. Ibid., 225.
7. *HC* 2:487-88.
8. Matthias Cowley, *The Life of Wilford Woodruff* (Salt Lake City: Bookcraft, 1964), 67.
9. Ibid., 68.
10. Ibid., 88.
11. Orson F. Whitney, *Life of Heber C. Kimball* (Salt Lake City: Bookcraft, 1945), 99.
12. Ibid., 101.
13. Ibid.
14. Ibid., 181.
15. Ibid., 36.
16. Edward Stevenson, *The Life and History of Elder Edward Stevenson* (n.d.), 40-41.
17. *JD* 2:305-6.
18. Tertullian, *De Spectaculis* II, 89-90.
19. *JD* 2:299.
20. Ibid., 2:306.
21. Ibid., 2:306-7.
22. Whitney, *Life of Heber C. Kimball*, 185.
23. Ibid., 217-18.
24. *JD* 15:4.
25. *TPJS* 141.
26. *HC* 3:301.
27. *WJS* 11.
28. *TPJS* 297.
29. Ibid., 183.
30. Ibid., 231.
31. Cowley, *Life of Wilford Woodruff*, 160.
32. *TPJS* 127-28.
33. Cowley, *Life of Wilford Woodruff*, 166.
34. Ibid., 169.
35. Ibid., 167.

36. Ibid., 170.
37. *TPJS* 331.
38. Cowley, *Life of Wilford Woodruff*, 320.
39. *JD* 13:1.
40. Ibid., 18:244.
41. Whitney, *Life of Heber C. Kimball*, 389.
42. Cowley, *Life of Wilford Woodruff*, 328- 29.
43. Whitney, *Life of Heber C. Kimball*, 400.
44. Ibid., 405-6.
45. Cowley, *Life of Wilford Woodruff*, 317.
46. Ibid.
47. Ibid., 356.
48. *JD* 2:300.
49. Ibid., 2:303.
50. Ibid., 2:304.
51. Ibid., 2:305.
52. From the *Manuscript History of Brigham Young* (Church Historical Archives).
53. *JD* 1:255.
54. *MS* 17:120.
55. *JD* 4:30.
56. Ibid., 4:52.
57. Whitney, *Life of Heber C. Kimball*, 446.
58. *JD* 5:353.
59. Ibid., 6:197.
60. Cowley, *Life of Wilford Woodruff*, 400.
61. Ibid.
62. Ibid., 406.
63. Ibid., 409.
64. *JD* 7:47.
65. Ibid., 7:282.
66. Ibid., 8:164.
67. Ibid., 11:349.
68. Ibid., 13:2.
69. Ibid., 13:31-32.
70. Ibid., 13:314.
71. *MS* 35:691.
72. *JD* 17:57-58.
73. *MS* 39:118.
74. *MS* 39:119.
75. Ibid.
76. Ibid., 35:275.

77. Ibid., 22:737-38.

78. Ibid., 21:825.

79. *JD* 11:348.

80. Ibid., 15:2.

81. Ibid., 15:3.

82. Ibid., 15:4.

83. Ibid., 17:37.

84. Ibid., 18:239.

85. From the *Manuscript History of Brigham Young* (Church Historical Archives).

86. Cowley, *Life of Wilford Woodruff,* 487-88.

87. Ibid., 517-18.

88. Leonard J. Arrington, *Great Basin Kingdom* (Cambridge: Harvard University, 1958), 314.

89. M. E. Christensen, "The Making of a Leader," (Ph.D. diss., University of Utah, 1980), 128.

90. Ibid.

91. Spencer W. Kimball, "The False Gods We Worship," *Ensign* 6 (June 1976), 3-4.

92. *JD* 3:191.

93. Ibid., 5:167.

94. Ibid., 8:344 (emphasis added).

95. Ibid., 12:310.

96. Dean C. Jessee, ed., *Letters of Brigham Young to His Sons* (Salt Lake City: Deseret, 1974), 138 (February 16, 1870).

97. *JD* 15:4.

98. Ibid., 1:164.

99. Ibid.

100. From the *Manuscript History of Brigham Young* (Church Historical Archives).

101. *WJS* 68.

102. Ibid., 67.

103. Ibid., 60.

104. N. B. Lundwall, *Faith Like the Ancients,* 2 vols. (Manti: Mountain Valley, 1968), 2:121.

105. Ibid.

106. Ibid., 2:123.

13

Breakthroughs I Would Like to See

Though I did not assign the topic, I like it: "Breakthroughs I Would Like to See." Not that I *expect* to see any, or that anyone *else* would like to see any, yet I am grateful for this opportunity to discuss an unpopular subject that I would otherwise have avoided but that cannot be much longer overlooked.

Anything I discuss with anybody from this time on must be within the framework of the scriptures. Why? Isn't that rather narrow? Arbitrary? Confining? Authoritarian? No, the scriptures have immense breadth—the world is not aware of that, because the clergy have always had their favorite themes and passages, about 5 percent of the total, necessarily taken out of context, since the other 95 percent which is overlooked *is* the context. The scriptures, with modern revelations added, are far more explicit and detailed than people realize. There are places where they are silent, but how can we know what is missing and what we are missing in them unless we read them all? Within that framework we are free to ponder, speculate, discuss, criticize, check, and control from other sources—it is all perfectly legitimate. Above all, we are not only justified in falling back on the scriptures, but we are obliged to—because there is *no other* framework available to appeal to.

This talk was given November 8, 1984, in the Varsity Theater at Brigham Young University as part of Breakthrough 1984 in the Spheres of Influence series.

378

For one thing, that is the framework within which all the productive scientists, artists, composers, and scholars have done their work right up until the early twentieth century. The world greeted one other framework with reverence, awe, and unbounded enthusiasm because at last in Darwinism they thought they had found something to supplant the old one. However, like all scientific structures, this one was tentative and contrived, and Darwin in the end always rested his case on anticipation of possible future breakthroughs, putting it indefinitely on hold. The scriptures really give us something to work with.

All real breakthroughs in the history of the race follow the same pattern. There is only one kind of breakthrough; that is to say, they all come from above. Some interesting studies were made after World War II on the great, inspired scientists and artists of the past to account for whatever it was that made them peculiarly productive, or, as we say, "creative." In almost every case they reported that their great moments came to them by inspiration, in sudden flashes of insight for which they could not account. Arthur C. Clarke has written a book in which he discusses two kinds of inventions: the routine ones; and the real breakthroughs — inventions that no one could have anticipated and only the writers of science fiction dared to invent.[1] In my lifetime I have seen the radio (I well remember scratching a crystal with a tiny wire to pick up a station a hundred miles away), and then Alamogordo, New Mexico, the atomic breakthrough, which staggered even its inventors; and there is the laser, and the jet engine. At an army investigation into whether the Germans had planes that could fly without propellers, Jimmy Doolittle testified against all the experts that he could take them to five hundred graves that would tell them of planes that could fly without propellers. There is the whole field of subatomic physics; the unpredictable and uncontrolled nature of such things obliges us to classify them as the unexplained or the miraculous. Of course, for us the important break-throughs are the dispensations of the gospel, which can come only by the opening of the heavens, only by reve-lation, not by the counsels of men seeking to *restore* what was lost by our own efforts. Twenty years ago the words *restoration, revelation,* and *dispensation* were fired at Joseph Smith like missiles; they epitomized all his crimes and offenses against humanity. Today journals and confer-ences speak endlessly of *restoration, revelation,* and *dispen-sation* — such were the subjects of a Jewish and Christian conference I attended in Washington, D.C., a year ago, where the three portentous words were used constantly together, because you can't have one without the other.

The Latter-day Saints have always believed that the breakthroughs in science that have bettered the condition of man by bringing light and truth are an organic part of the restoration of the gospel. For us that is the great break-through: "The morning breaks, the shadows flee,"[2] "Now a glorious morn is breaking,"[3] "The veil o'er the earth is beginning to burst,"[4] "An angel from on high the long, long silence broke."[5] For us the whole thing was a break-through. And it was just one surprise after another, noth-ing expected, contrived, or anticipated. The testimony of Oliver Cowdery appended to the Pearl of Great Price catches the spirit of the event: "What joy! what wonder! what amazement! While the world was racked and dis-tracted — while millions were groping as the blind for the wall, and while all men were resting upon uncertainty, as a general mass, our eyes beheld, our ears heard. . . . 'Twas the voice of an angel, from glory, 'twas a message from the Most High! . . . Man may deceive his fellow-men, de-ception may follow deception, and the children of the wicked one may have power to seduce the foolish and untaught, till naught but fiction feeds the many [we just saw that on Tuesday, Nov. 6, 1984 — Election Day], . . . but . . . one ray of glory from the upper world, or one word from the mouth of the Savior, from the bosom of eternity, strikes it all into insignificance, and blots it forever from the mind!"[6] Every breakthrough is also a breakout, liberating mankind from restraints and repressions of various kinds.

This is illustrated all through the Book of Mormon, beginning with the case of Lehi, depressed and frustrated by conditions in Jerusalem. Traveling in the desert, he saw a spectacle like Moses' burning bush, "a pillar of fire . . . upon a rock before him; and he saw and heard much," which sent him scurrying back to Jerusalem, where he threw himself on his bed and had a vision in which "he saw the heavens open," and so on (1 Nephi 1:6-8). Here, then, was a breakthrough presently leading to a breakout, as Lehi fled in the night from the land of Jerusalem into the desert; and then another breakthrough when he left the Old World behind. Arriving in the New, Nephi suffered oppression under his brethren until he received a revelation and broke with them, leading his own following into a place apart, where they were able to live "after the manner of happiness" (2 Nephi 5:27). Other such breakthroughs followed in the Book of Mormon — those of Mosiah, and of Alma at the waters of Mormon. This is all in the old Rekhabite tradition; it is stated as a general principle by Nephi: "He raiseth up a righteous nation, and destroyeth the nations of the wicked. And he leadeth away the righteous into precious lands" (1 Nephi 17:37-38). What he meant by "the manner of happiness" is illustrated in the model society of 4 Nephi: "And they had all things common among them; therefore there were not rich and poor, bond and free, but they were all made free" (4 Nephi 1:3); "and it came to pass that there was no contention among all the people, in all the land" (4 Nephi 1:13); "and how blessed were they! . . . The first generation from Christ had passed away, and there was no contention in all the land" (4 Nephi 1:18). It was a noncompetitive society, which is the breakthrough I would ask you to envisage.

Every breakout has been quickly confronted with a barrier as the adversary has made frantic efforts to contain it. These efforts have always been successful—that is why there is more than one dispensation. Adam, cast out into the dark, dreary world, was presently visited by heavenly messengers, who proceeded to instruct him in how he was to get out of his present difficult situation as quickly as possible; they put him on the road that would return him to the presence of the Father. Satan counterattacked at once and converted Cain to his cause; and before long all of Adam's posterity began to apostatize. For it was time for another breakthrough, and a "crash program" was undertaken as "the Gospel began to be preached, from the beginning, being declared by holy angels sent forth from the presence of God" (Moses 5:58).

The leader of the dispensation was Enoch, whose city of Zion was a tremendous breakthrough and also a "breaking out," the mass evacuation of a polluted planet, due for a thorough purging. "From Noah to Abraham, ten generations" goes the saying, and the world was in darkness again, for Noah's posterity had also gone astray; it was time for God to speak with Abraham face to face, restore the covenants, and organize the church, beginning with his 318 servants.

Again the oppression and flesh pots of Egypt, with the world in darkness until Moses saw the burning bush (it was not his idea), then upon the mountains talked with God as one man to another. The display on the mountain was overwhelming, but as we know from the story of the golden calf, Satan wasted no time in getting back; and Moses in his farewell speech said that if the people would not obey him while he was with them, what hope could there be thereafter?

The prophets deplored the condition of Israel until the

coming of the Lord, and if there was ever a dazzling series of breakthroughs, it is that recounted with clinical accuracy by Luke. Angels appeared for the first time in four hundred years, scaring Zacharias and Mary and the shepherds half to death: "Fear not!" Peter, James, and John were "sore afraid" when on the Mount of Transfiguration they saw the Lord as he really was and heard the voice of the Father speaking from behind the cloud (Matthew 17:6). But "the prince of this world cometh, who hath nothing in me" (John 14:30), and Satan took over again in what we know as the Great Apostasy, which lasted until the time was ripe for the visions and blessings of old to return and angels to come and visit the earth. What need we say about the ferocity with which the moral majority reacted the instant that news got out? I once had two ministers in a Greek class who were always protesting that once God had delivered his "once for all" message to the saints, there was no need for a further breakthrough. The few instances we have reviewed should answer that question; in the Latter-day Saint philosophy there should never be an end to breakthroughs.

Since I have been asked to tell what breakthrough I would like to see, I will state it quite frankly. It is the same one the prophets, seers, and revelators of modern times have yearned and worked for: namely, the observation by the Latter-day Saints of the law of consecration. I'm only expressing a personal wish, but that is what was asked for. I would like to see it happen in the first place because I have covenanted to keep it, and I would like to be able to do so. Even with that I cannot avoid it, as we are told in the Doctrine and Covenants, which we shall take as our guide from here on out, since it contains the definitive statement of the law of consecration.

One thing that gives top priority to the law of consecration is that no one is excused from observing it: "This is what the Lord requires of every man in his stewardship. . . . And behold, none are exempt from this law who belong to the church of the living God" (D&C 70:9-10); "for according to the law every man that cometh up to Zion must lay all things before the bishop in Zion" (D&C 72:15). "Every elder . . . must give an account of his stewardship unto the bishop" (D&C 72:16), to qualify for an "inheritance, and to be received as a wise steward and as a faithful laborer" (D&C 72:17); "let every elder . . . give an account unto the bishop" and receive a recommend recording his labors to qualify him in acceptance (D&C 72:19).

Another reason for acceptance of the law of consecration without delay is that such a treasure should no longer lie unclaimed. The Lord has been good enough to give us the answer to a question that no mortal has ever been able to decide for himself, namely, what one should be doing in one brief spell on earth. I recently read an article on NASA that said the scientists have developed magnificent equipment but haven't the vaguest idea what to do with it. Out of a million things I could be doing, how can I possibly know what is best? "We look before and after and pine for what is not."[7] Here the Doctrine and Covenants helps us out; recall how many of the early revelations are addressed to individuals telling them what is best for them to do in the present circumstances. It would be a folly and shame to deny such a gift. Remember the closing lines of the Book of Mormon: "Deny not the gifts of God" (Moroni 10:8).

Most pressing of all is the disturbing awareness that God is not mocked. He has been good enough to reveal these things to us from heaven, and there is only one alternative to living up to every covenant—that is to be in the power of Satan, whose purpose is "to deceive and to blind men, and to lead them captive at *his* will, even as many as would not hearken to *my* voice" (Moses 4:4). "Except thou shalt hearken unto *my* commandments, I will deliver thee up, and it shall be unto thee according to *his desire*" (Moses 5:23). By which am I to be governed, God's commands or Satan's desire? Are we in Satan's power? The world is; it is being ruled with blood and horror and controlled by him who holds the treasures of the earth — the gold and silver, oil and coal. Speaking to those who paid lip service to the law of consecration while seeking personal gain, the Lord reminds us, "For I, the Lord, am not to be mocked in these things" (D&C 104:6). If "any man belonging to the order . . . shall break the covenant with which ye are bound, he shall be cursed in his life, and shall be trodden down by whom I will" (D&C 104:5). Don't think you can get away with it: "Inasmuch as you are found transgressors, you cannot escape my wrath in your lives," and being "cut off for transgression, ye cannot escape the buffetings of Satan until the day of redemption" (D&C 104:8-9). There is no other penalty, for the contract is between the individual and his Heavenly Father alone. As Heber C. Kimball reminded the saints, there are no covenants made between individuals in the church. All promises and agreements are between the individual and our Father in Heaven; all other parties, including the angels, are present only as witnesses. Therefore whether anybody else observes and keeps the promise is not my concern, but if I do not do what I have promised, what blessings can I expect?

Another disturbing thing is that I cannot put off fulfilling my part of the agreement. "The time has come, and is now at hand; and behold, and lo, it must needs be that there be an organization of my people, in regulating and establishing the affairs of the storehouse for the poor of my people . . . in the land of Zion [or in other words, the city of Enoch] — for a permanent and everlasting establishment and order unto my church" (D&C 78:3-4). It must begin *now* and from here on must continue. This is essential, we are told, if the church is to fulfill its purpose: "To

advance the cause, which ye have espoused, to the salvation of man, and to the glory of the Father who is in
heaven" (D&C 78:4). This is the way he wants it; the law
of consecration is inseparable from the law of God, the law
of obedience, and the law of sacrifice which the saints have
already accepted.

Can it for any reason be postponed? No! Those who
have failed to keep it here and now are denounced: "Inasmuch as some of my servants have not kept the commandment, but have broken the covenant, . . . I have
cursed them with a very sore and grievous curse" (D&C
104:4). Why on earth would anyone want to disregard it
after accepting the gospel and bidding farewell to the ways
of the world? The answer: "by covetousness and feigned
words" (D&C 104:52)—unable to give up their habits of
greed, they pretended to accept what they did not accept.
Of course, they argued that the thing wasn't practical or
convenient just then. When will it be? Thirty years after
the above revelation, Brigham Young, along with John
Taylor, Wilford Woodruff, and Lorenzo Snow, were still
vigorously appealing to the saints to wake up:

> Some of our Elders, and, in fact, some of the Twelve
> will tell you, "yes, yes, the Order is a splendid principle
> and will bring happiness, etc., but it is not hardly time
> to enter into it, wait a little while until the people un-
> derstand it a little better." Why, they are fools! They
> don't know what they talk about. They have ears to hear
> and will not hearken, and have eyes to see and will not
> understand. . . . When our conduct hedges up the way
> of angels how can they bless us? . . . How can they help
> us work out our salvation? When Joseph Smith was alive
> I can say that I never heard him lay one plan out for the
> people but would have been a success if it had been
> carried out as he directed. And I have seen the same
> thing in myself. I don't care how the world goes, what
> the President [of the U.S.] or his emissaries do. It matters

nothing to me. What I am thinking of and interested about is how do the Latter-day Saints do? The devil is in the community and he has not been turned out. . . . Well, I still have hope in Israel.[8]

So spoke Brigham Young at St. George on June 1, 1876, commenting on the purposes of the temple there.

The program is an urgent one, and since the world is steadily getting worse, the chances of carrying it out in a sympathetic environment have not been improving. If ever a breakthrough was announced, it is in section 1 of the Doctrine and Covenants, where two diametrically opposed ways of life are held up side by side. Likewise, in section 33: "Ye are called to . . . declare my gospel unto a crooked and perverse generation. . . . And my vineyard has become corrupted every whit; and there is none which doeth good save it be a few; and they err in many instances because of priestcrafts, all having corrupt minds" (D&C 33:2-4). There is much in the same vein: "For the veil of darkness shall soon be rent [another breakthrough!], and he that is not purified shall not abide the day, . . . for all flesh is corrupted before me; and the powers of darkness prevail upon the earth, among the children of men, . . . which causeth silence to reign, and all eternity is pained, and the angels are waiting, . . . and, behold, the enemy is combined" (D&C 38:8, 11-12). Do such statements mean nothing to us? "Lift up your voice . . . and cry repentance unto a crooked and perverse generation. . . . And it shall be a great day at the time of my coming, for all nations shall tremble" (D&C 34:6, 8). "There shall be a great work in the land, even among the Gentiles, for their folly and their abominations shall be made manifest in the eyes of all people" (D&C 35:7). "But without faith shall not anything be shown forth except desolations upon Babylon" (D&C 35:11).

This is an interesting thing—the saints need faith to follow the prophets and discern how things are going in these latter days, except for one thing: the desolations and destruction are going to be obvious to everybody; and now that they are beginning to become plain enough even to the most skeptical of the world, the Latter-day Saints, like the Christians of the third and fourth centuries, prefer not to take them too seriously.

And consider this: I am not free to lay out my own plans or justify special routines as the equivalent of keeping the law of consecration. Every attempt at rationalization fails. The plain fact is that I have promised to keep a law, and to keep it now. I know exactly *what* I am supposed to consecrate, exactly *how*, exactly *why*, exactly *when*, and exactly *where*. Consecration is the whole of the covenant of Israel. The chosen people themselves are consecrated, *qadosh* meaning "cut off, set apart," the same meaning as saints — *sanc-ti*, sancti-fied (cf. *sanctum*, "a place set apart"). They are called *sigillim*, which is translated "peculiar" in our King James Bible, but which means "sealed, reserved." What is *con-secrated* is then made sacred, withdrawn from the ordinary economy, dedicated to a particular purpose and to that purpose only. It can never be recalled or used for any other purpose without being *de-secrated*. A striking passage in Helaman brings this out while providing a powerful bit of evidence for the bona fides of the Book of Mormon. Samuel the Lamanite tells the people that their riches will be cursed because they have set their hearts upon them; and that when they flee before their enemies and bury their treasures, if they bury them not unto the Lord, they will become slippery and can never be found again. In the Copper Scroll of the Dead Sea Scrolls we learn that when the Jews fled from Jerusalem before their enemies, they also buried their treasures; and they also buried them up unto the Lord so that they could never again be used in profane negotiations. All such buried treasures had to be used for the temple and nothing else.[9] It would be hard to find a more convincing parallel. It is a reminder that when I consecrate, it cannot be with limitations or qualifications. The ancients, including the Hebrews and other nations, consecrated by "heaving"; that is, they would throw the gift over a barrier into an area to which they had no access—they could never claim it again.

So I can take or leave consecration, but I cannot temporize or dissemble.

> Said the Lord to Joseph, "See if they will give their farms to me." What was the result? *They would not do it,* though it was one of the plainest things in the world. No revelation that was ever given is more easy of comprehension than that on the law of consecration. . . . Yet, when the Lord spoke to Joseph, instructing him to counsel the people to consecrate their possessions, and deed them over to the Church in a covenant that cannot be broken, would the people listen to it? *No,* but they began to find out they were mistaken, and had only acknowledged with their mouths that the things which they possessed were the Lord's ["covetousness and feigned words"—D&C 104:52].[10]

"The Lord makes them well by His power, through the ordinances of His house [where the agreement was made], but will they consecrate? *No.* They say, 'it is mine, and I will have it myself.' There is the treasure, and the heart is with it."[11] So spoke Brigham Young soon after the exodus from Nauvoo.

The world is as ready for the system now as it ever will be; there is nothing the least bit negative about it. This is the way God means to provide for his people: it is "this commandment I give unto my servants for their benefit . . . and for a reward of their diligence and for their security [security has become our obsession—the answer, because it takes care of everybody]; for food and for raiment; for an inheritance; for houses and for lands" (D&C 70:15-16). Yes, the conditions were different then, but here the Lord tells us that it will work "in whatsoever circumstances I, the Lord, shall place them, and whithersoever I, the Lord, shall send them" (D&C 70:16). "Behold, I, the Lord, am merciful and shall bless them, and they shall enter into the joy of these things" (D&C 70:18).

The express purpose of the law of consecration is the building up of Zion; it is God's plan, and his alone, for doing that. We do not wait until Zion is here to observe it; it is rather the means of bringing us nearer to Zion. "Hear my voice and follow me, and you shall be a free people, and ye shall have no laws but my laws when I come" (D&C 38:22), "If thou lovest me thou shalt serve me and keep all my commandments. And behold, thou wilt remember the poor, and consecrate of thy properties for their support . . . with a covenant and a deed which cannot be broken" (D&C 42:29-30). What I most like about the law of consecration is that it has nothing to do with economics. It belongs to the celestial order of things. There are no graphs, curves, figures, rising and falling prices, no Dow Jones, booms and slumps. Such things are quite unthinkable in the order that the Lord has said is to be observed for all eternity. "Adam, we have created for you this earth and 'planted a garden eastward. . . . Of every tree of the garden thou mayest freely eat' " (Moses 3:8, 16). Everything was all ready and waiting for him—trees bearing fruit of every kind; all Adam had to do was to help himself. Taking good care of the place was part of his privilege; he was to enjoy himself at it and be happy; and since he regularly conversed with the Lord and spent his time in the company of the most marvelous of women—we can be sure that gardening was not his only activity—would that we had minds and intellects as clear and active! Being ageless and immortal, he was not gardening for a living—he was working for no one and no one was working for him. In their letters from the Valley, the brethren reminded people back East that the great advantage of their present life was the beauty of a noncompetitive society in which they were free to cultivate their minds. To the present generation the most terrifying aspect of living in such a manner is the dullness of a world without the fiercely competitive doings of prime-time TV. They would have to spend their days engaged in other things than "the management of the creature" (Alma 30:17).

What could they possibly find to do? Like the barons of the Middle Ages who, when the Bishop of Rheims rebuked them for slaughtering each other, could only answer, "What else can noblemen possibly be doing?" On what other terms can human beings possibly exist together? Any change would be a disturbing culture shock, and they didn't like it at all. President Harold B. Lee once talked to a group of us after he visited a stake conference; at a meeting of a high council, an undertaker lamented that he would have no work to do in the next world. At this a banker, a dentist, a real estate promoter, a policeman, and various businessmen all chimed in with the same complaint.

What *will* we be doing in the next world? Farmers and musicians, remembering Adam and the heavenly choirs, need not be overly concerned, but the question really is important, because it is that very life in the eternities for which we are supposed to be rehearsing right now. That is what the Church is for with its law of consecration: to build up the kingdom and establish Zion, "that it may be prepared for the celestial glory" (D&C 88:18). The Lord has told us that there is no other course of action for us, and why should there be? "Zion cannot be built up unless it is by the principles of the law of the celestial kingdom; otherwise I cannot receive her unto myself" (D&C 105:5). "For I give not unto you that ye shall live after the manner of the world" (D&C 95:13). The conditions are emphatic: "If you will that I give unto you a place in the celestial world, you must prepare yourselves by doing the things which I have commanded you and required of you" (D&C

78:7). The saints must learn to do by doing, and however impractical it may seem they must follow instructions — "Neither are your ways my ways, saith the Lord" (Isaiah 55:8). "Verily thus saith the Lord, it is expedient that all things be done unto my glory, by you who are joined together in this order" (D&C 78:8). This is a "counsel, and a commandment, concerning . . . [the] united order, . . . an everlasting order" — not for some future time, but to save the church now — "for the benefit of my church, and for the salvation of men until I come" (D&C 104:1). Again, not waiting until he does come. We are assured that it will always work, and the people "should be blessed with a multiplicity of blessings" (D&C 104:2).

I am not free to observe the law of consecration partially or to subordinate to other interests. All of our how-to-get-rich books, including those by Latter-day Saints, insist that the only way to succeed in any enterprise is to give it undivided, dedicated attention. A prosperous member of a ward in which my son was in the bishopric was wont to say that what he liked best about the gospel was that it was just like a cafeteria, where you could take what you want and leave what you want. Some maintain that by making a substantial contribution they are keeping the law of consecration. But if I keep only *some* of the Ten Commandments, I am not keeping the Ten Commandments; if I pay *some* of my tithing I am not paying tithing; if I keep the law of obedience, doing things God's way, when I find it convenient, I am not keeping that law; a person who is chaste some of the time is not keeping the law of chastity; if I part with odds and ends from time to time, I am not observing the law of sacrifice; a minifast of say twenty minutes or so between meals is not fasting.

Yet that is the condition we are all in, since no one is perfect in keeping any law; but now things have reached a critical point, and we have been told to repent. A young man asked the Lord what he must do to have eternal life.

Did he keep all the commandments? The Lord went through the list. Yes, said the young man, "What lack I yet?" What he lacked was the last and hardest to keep of all the commandments—had he consecrated his goods to the poor? No. "He went away sorrowful; for he had great possessions" (Matthew 19:20-22). The Lord could make no concessions or exceptions and had to let him go. The disciples were "exceedingly amazed" (Matthew 19:25) when the Lord explained to them that wealth is an almost insuperable barrier to entering the kingdom. It is plain that the apostles themselves had kept the law of consecration, for Peter said, "Behold, we have forsaken all and followed thee" (Matthew 19:27). How hard the ministry have worked to rationalize themselves out of that one!

So it would seem that I could find no practical objections. Is the law of consecration "unworldly"? Of course it is! I have accepted the law of God and the law of obedience, accepting "this commandment, that ye bind yourselves by this covenant, and it shall be done according to the laws of the Lord" (D&C 82:15); it is "for your good" (D&C 82:16), though you may want to do it your way. "That's all very well for the next world," I may say, "but in this world there is a lot of dirty work that must be done; we can think of the ivory tower later on." I have noticed that the people who say that are never the people who do the dirty work but have others do it for them through the exercise of useful legal fictions. "Your sins . . . are not pardoned, because you seek to counsel in *your own ways*. And your hearts are not satisfied. And ye obey not the truth, but have pleasure in unrighteousness. Wo unto you rich men, that will not give your substance to the poor, for your riches will canker your souls. . . . Wo unto you poor men . . . whose hands are not stayed from laying hold upon other men's goods, whose eyes are full of greediness, and who will not labor with your own hands!" (D&C

56:14-17). What do the two have in common? Both want riches; "ye are cursed because of your riches, and also are your riches cursed because ye have set your hearts upon them" (Helaman 13:21). The same requirements are made of rich and poor, namely a broken heart and contrite spirit, contentment with sufficiency (1 Timothy 6:5-8), no envy of another's possessions, no preoccupation of getting more, not acquiring by the labor of others. God rejects all our rationalizations, our fervid moral tone and glorification of those traits of character that lead to success. These are often held up by the youth as peculiar to the tycoon, over-looking the fact that the same qualities of persistence, courage, dedication, enterprise, ingenuity, and so on, are in far greater demand for success in almost any other field of activity—science, athletics, music, literature, scholarship, crime, politics, and so on—than in business: the existence of over six hundred thousand millionaires in the land over against a mere handful of truly productive scientists and artists should make that clear. Forget your systems and methods; "It must needs be done in my own way"— not yours! "And behold this is the way that I, the Lord, have decreed to provide for my saints, that the poor shall be exalted, in that the rich are made low" (D&C 104:16).

Why the working of the law of consecration remains still only something I would like to see is that the individual cannot keep it alone. The essence of the law is sharing. "The greatest temporal and spiritual blessings which always come from faithfulness and concerted effort," said the Prophet Joseph Smith, "never attended individual exertion or enterprise."[12] The first rule is to "remember in all things the poor and the needy, the sick and the afflicted" (D&C 52:40). "And behold, thou wilt remember the poor, and consecrate of thy properties for their support that which thou hast to impart unto them, with a covenant and a deed which cannot be broken" (D&C 42:30). This is frankly a redistribution of wealth, "for I will consecrate of the riches of those who embrace my gospel among the

Gentiles unto the poor of my people who are of the house of Israel" (D&C 42:39). "And if thou obtainest more than that which would be for thy support, thou shalt give it into my storehouse" (D&C 42:55). All distribution is on the basis of *need*; the question of who is deserving never arises. Writing from Liberty Jail, Joseph tells how the enemies of the church have twisted the law of consecration to include a community of wives, and so he explains, "Now for a man to consecrate his property and his wife & children to the Lord, is nothing more nor less than to feed the hungry, clothe the naked, visit the widow and the fatherless, the sick, and the afflicted, and do all he can to administer to their relief in their afflictions, and for him and his house to serve the Lord"; then he explains the basis for distribution: "When we consecrate our property to the Lord it is to administer to the wants of the poor and needy, for this is the law of God; it is not for the purpose of the rich, those who have no *need*."[13]

In the matter of deserving there are two schools of thought. There is the Good Samaritan or King Benjamin school, which does not ask whether a poor man is deserving or whether he has "brought [it] upon himself" (Mosiah 4:17-18) but only considers his need. The other school is that which punches the computer to find out exactly who deserves what. More interesting are the two schools of the deserving rich. One is the school of Andrew Carnegie, whose motto was "the man who dies thus rich dies disgraced," following the doctrine that there is only one legitimate reason for seeking wealth, and that is to get rid of it.[14] The other is the Malcom Forbes school of thought, which teaches that possession of wealth is itself sufficient proof of virtue, and that the rich are deserving of all the fun, glamor, prestige, admiration, envy, and emulation that only wealth can bring; this is the prevailing school of thought among us.[15]

But more than enough is more than enough: "Every

man shall be made accountable unto me, a steward over his own property, or that which he has received by consecration, as much as is *sufficient* for himself and family" (D&C 42:32). It is from this that one pays tithing. Tithing is not consecration and does not supersede it. To pay a tithe of what is sufficient and no more is to pay a real tithe, given out of one's own necessities, something of a test and a sacrifice, as tithing is meant to be. Ten percent taken out of a surplus that one will never miss or need is indeed a strange "offering."

I do have private property under the law of consecration, but it is the terms *private* and *property* in the private and proper sense, of something intimately and personally necessary to one's functioning in the world. "Thou shalt not take thy brother's garment; thou shalt pay for that which thou shalt receive of thy brother" (D&C 42:54). This is what is meant by *private* and *property:* something intimate, personal, and indispensable, like a person's garment, the sort of thing everyone must have for his own under any economic system. One may not accumulate property, for then it ceases to be property and falls into the forbidden category of "power and gain." Oil under arctic seas or mahogany in unexplored jungles can be neither private nor property, save by a theory of possession cultivated in another quarter.

The conditions of sharing demanded by the Lord can only be satisfied by complete *equality*, a point that is ceaselessly repeated. The purpose and intent in the order is "that you may be equal in the bonds of heavenly things, yea, and earthly things also, for the obtaining of heavenly things. For if you are not equal in earthly things ye cannot be equal in obtaining heavenly things" (D&C 78:5-6). "Nevertheless, in your temporal things you shall be equal" (D&C 70:14). "And let every man esteem his brother as himself. . . . For what man . . . saith unto the one [son]: Be thou clothed in robes and sit thou here; and to the other:

Be thou clothed in rags and sit thou there—and looketh upon his sons and saith I am just?" (D&C 38:24-26). You must follow my instructions, saith the Lord, and "I am no respecter of persons" (D&C 1:35). He explains that he made the earth and made it rich and there is no excuse for poverty; everything we have is a free gift from him, "and I hold forth and deign to give unto you greater riches, . . . a land of promise, . . . flowing with milk and honey, upon which there shall be no curse when the Lord cometh" (D&C 38:18). Why should there be a curse on the land? In the first vision the Lord declared, "behold, the world lieth in sin," and the reason for that is given in D&C 49:20: "But it is not given that one man should possess that which is above another, wherefore the world lieth in sin."

Substance is shared on the basis of need alone. "And you are to be equal, . . . to have equal claims on the properties, for the benefit of managing the concerns of your stewardships, every man according to his *wants* and his *needs* [that is, the things he happens to lack that everyone should have], inasmuch as his wants are just" (D&C 82:17). Note that the question of the deserving poor never arises. Who decides what is necessary for your support? You do; you are accountable for that decision; that is your stewardship (D&C 42:32-33, 55). The presiding bishop "also should travel round about and among all the churches, searching after the poor to administer to their wants by humbling the rich and the proud" (D&C 84:112). We cannot be equal, as the Lord commands, and live on different levels of affluence. True, some are stronger than others, some are smarter than others, but our gifts and talents were given us to be put at the disposal of our fellowman, not to be put at our disposal in the manner of Nimrod. "This is my work and my glory" to see to it that others get a full share of the glory and the work—to bring about eternal life and exaltation (Moses 1:39). The Lord descended below all things that he might raise all the others up. The bishop is assisted by agents "to do his secular business" (D&C 84:113), which is also spiritual in nature in this context: Ye cannot be one in spiritual things if ye are not one in temporal things (D&C 70:12-13). "And . . . more than is necessary for their [his family's] support . . . is a residue to be consecrated unto the bishop . . . to administer to those who have not, from time to time, that every man who has need may be amply supplied and receive according to his wants" (D&C 42:33). The most concise statement of the law is that of King Benjamin: "Render to every man according to that which is his due" (Mosiah 4:13). Something is due *to* every human being, and something is due *from* every human being. What is it? "I would that ye should impart of your substance to the poor, every man *according to that which he hath* . . . to their relief, both spiritually and temporally, *according to their wants*" (Mosiah 4:26). Everything depends, of course, on the spirit in which this is carried out. "You shall be equal, and this not grudgingly, otherwise the abundance of . . . the Spirit shall be withheld" (D&C 70:14). "God had often sealed up the heavens [and no revelation given] because of covetousness in the Church."[16]

The title of this series being what it is, "Breakthroughs 1984," we should be remiss in our duty not to mention George Orwell's book that has made 1984 a year to conjure by.[17] Consulting convenient collections of reviews of Orwell's novel at the time it appeared in 1949, one is impressed today by the optimism of the critics, who often take the position that Orwell has gone too far in depicting total mind-control in such a near future; surely, they say, the people of the free world can never be so easily manipulated.

Alas, how innocent we were in those days! Who could have guessed that in the *real* 1984 it would not be necessary for "The Party" to go to great pains to "control the past" by systematically removing from old news files and libraries whatever records refuted the Party's prophecies, replacing them by a more favorable rewriting of the past. In the real 1984, it made no difference whatever what had been said and done in the past—people would take anything they were told here and now without question if the presentation pleased them. Who could have known that in the real 1984, 97 percent of the students at a university, a shrine of free and unhampered thought, would all vote exactly alike, unwilling to consider the issues that their candidate simply refused to discuss? Or who would have thought that all those laborious and ingenious ways of controlling the press in Orwell's *Nineteen Eighty-Four* would only be wasted effort in the real 1984, when a candidate could cheerfully ignore the press and win by a landslide?

Control of people's behavior is achieved in the novel by what Mr. Orwell calls the telescreen (a word of his invention),[18] a TV screen that also monitors everything that goes on in every house and cannot be switched off. How much simpler it has proven in our own day to control their acts by controlling their minds, debauching them with TV fare that they want and ask for, so that they are psychologically unable to turn it off or to resist following its cunningly crafted instructions, disguised as entertainment and good cheer?

What we have in Orwell's book is, Sir Harold Nicolson notes, "an awful twilight of the mind"[19]—a thing we are being warned against even now in the schools of 1984. Paralysis of thought is assured in the Orwellian world by the cultivation of "Newspeak" or "Doublespeak," in which words mean whatever the father figure, called Big Brother, wants them to mean. Thucydides notes the phenomenon in his day when "words lost their meaning," so that no one could be sure of anyone else. With mental and moral decline went "a new kind of prudery, disgusting in its unctuousness and hypocrisy."[20] Where could one find this more in evidence than in the local election of 1984? In the

novel, everything is run by "The Party." Which party? It
makes no difference, most of the reviewers agree. As an
eminent German scholar wrote, Orwell warns against
"dangers that are typical of our age anywhere [in the
world], . . . danger that lies within ourselves and in all
political systems of our time."[21]

To retain loyalty and enthusiasm, Orwell's Party has
everybody "bursting with energy all the time, . . .
marching up and down cheering and waving flags."[22] It
is possible to keep up the pressure thanks to a condition
of constant war, hot and cold, between two or three great
Super Powers that divide the world, each constantly reminding its citizens that the other is an Empire of Evil.
The object of all this is power; "power is not a means,"
says one of the characters; "it is an end. . . . The object of
power is power"—a phrase right out of Nixon's and Kis-
singer's writings.[23] Most reviewers are repelled by the sa-
distic cruelty of the Party in the person of O'Brien: "Mr.
Orwell has conceived the inconceivable,"[24] wrote one re-
viewer; but what is inconceivable in the real 1984 when
the leader of a state solemnly declares, "Against Marxism
nothing is wrong." If *nothing* is wrong, what cruelty remains inconceivable?

The book ends in "smells of death, decay, dirt, diabolism and despair."[25] Diabolism indeed—it is Satan's dominion (D&C 1:35). Some see in this the end of the world,
not a physical end but something much worse. The worst
thing about hell, as Alma has made clear, is to be at home
there; and in the famous last sentence of *Nineteen Eighty-
Four*, "He loved Big Brother,"[26] the hero ends up totally
in Satan's power. Is this then the alternative to keeping
the law of God? It is if we would listen to a Harvard so-
ciologist who, viewing Orwell's world and modern society
as a whole, concludes that no other kind of a system is
imaginable for the future—he can think of no alternative.

Neither can we unless it is the law of consecration, which turns out after all to be the only workable solution.

So what is our present condition? Can you imagine a more horrendous paradox than "Zion, the Fraud Capital of the World"? Saith the Lord, "You have many things to do and to repent of; . . . your sins . . . are not pardoned, because you seek to counsel in your own ways. . . . Your hearts are not satisfied. And ye obey not the truth, but have pleasure in unrighteousness" (D&C 56:14-15). What unrighteousness? The explanation follows: "Wo unto you rich men, that will not give your substance to the poor, for your riches will canker your souls [the scriptures call wealth a cancer, a pernicious, malignant growth]; and this shall be your lamentation. . . . The harvest is past, the summer is ended, and my soul is not saved!" (D&C 56:16). This time of probation is to be taken seriously, for the poor as well if they too seek riches (D&C 56:17). What the Lord insists on is that all who qualify must be "pure in heart" (D&C 56:18).

Adam was cast out of the garden into an alien world where he had to work his head off just to stay alive, and this is our excuse today for total absorption in the economy. But Adam was not only given protection and told what to do until help arrived, but also "after many days" an angel came and began to teach him what he must do to reverse his condition at once and begin his return to the presence of the Father. For this he took the same covenants that we take today. Satan had already introduced his order of things on the earth, where money was the name of the game, and the treasures of the earth could get you anything you wanted. Adam refused his propositions and the devil took his business elsewhere, to Cain, who learned from him how to get gain by becoming a predator and whose master's thesis was an exercise in getting possession of his brother's flocks. He said it was all perfectly legal in the name of free competition; he was not responsible for Abel.

According to the best and oldest account, as soon as the Lord introduced himself to the Prophet Joseph in the first vision, he declared, "Behold the world lieth in sin at this time and none doeth good no not one. . . . And mine anger is kindling against the inhabitants of the earth to visit them acording [sic] to this ungodliness."[27] "The world lieth in sin" — what is the cause of that? It is explained in D&C 49:19-20: "That which cometh of the earth, is ordained for the use of man for food and for raiment, and that he might have in abundance. But it is not given that one man should possess that which is above another, wherefore *the world lieth in sin*." For those who wonder how the Nephites could turn so quickly from righteousness to wickedness the prophet explains, "Now the cause of this iniquity of the people was this — Satan had great power, unto the stirring up of the people to do all manner of iniquity, . . . tempting them to seek for power, and authority, and riches, and the vain things of the world" (3 Nephi 6:15). Let us recall that it was Satan's assignment to try man and to tempt him, and after considering all other approaches, this is the one he would find most effective. His business, as Brigham Young says, is to decoy us from our proper callings to seeking after those things. The wealth of the earth is to provide a means of subsistence during our time of probation here below; all have to take the test, and lunch is provided for all of them, "for the earth is full, and there is enough and to spare; yea, I prepared all things, and have given unto the children of men to be agents unto themselves. Therefore, if any man shall take of the abundance which I have made, and impart not his portion, according to the law of my gospel, unto the poor and the needy, he shall, with the wicked, lift up his eyes in hell, being in torment" (D&C 104:17-18). Who can be "agents unto themselves" if they are in bondage to others and have to accept their terms? The abundance of supplies is not placed here as the reward for which we are all striving—that is Satan's decoy trick, that is what he promises those who serve him—the famous "pact with the devil," by which Mephisto supplies you with all the wealth and power you could dream of as long as you are here, but as soon as it is time to leave he presents his bill and you belong to him. This is not the place of judgment, but there will be a judgment hereafter. To take the test we must all stay alive, but we have made staying alive the test itself, as if we had come to this earth to spend our days of probation grabbing more and more stuff or sweating to get enough lunch. Like medicine, the stuff of this earth is to preserve life; too much of it is unnecessary and dangerous and so is not enough. Without the law of consecration men have set themselves up as judges of who is worthy to live and have joy on the earth. If an "ergometer" could be designed to tell exactly how much work everyone did, that would be a great eye-opener and put an instant end to the "work ethic." Lacking such a device, we equate wealth with work, saying that each is the measurement of the other. Mozart died young and in poverty, a lazy bum. Mr. Mughiba, with his hundred and fifty billion petro dollars, must certainly be the hardest worker who ever lived.

The greatest of the breakthroughs have occurred when the Lord has come in person to deliver the message, which has ever been "in the days of wickedness and vengeance" (Moses 7:46). When the Lord came to Enoch he told him, "Among all the workmanship of mine hands there has not been so great wickedness as among thy brethren" (Moses 7:36), and he declared, "The fire of mine indignation is kindled against them" (Moses 7:34). When Enoch asked the Lord if the world would have another chance, if he would come again, "the Lord said: It shall be in the meridian of time, in the days of wickedness and vengeance" (Moses 7:46). When Enoch saw the horrors that would follow that, he again asked, "I ask thee if thou wilt not come again on the earth. And the Lord said unto Enoch:

As I live, even so will I come in the last days, in the days
of wickedness and vengeance" (Moses 7:59-60). And so
when the Lord repeated those words to Joseph Smith in
the grove, "the world lieth in sin at this time, none doeth
good . . . and mine anger is kindling against the inhabitants of the earth,"[28] we are all in it together, and there is
no Zion here.

Brigham Young as governor once addressed the state
legislature in terms that show us his idea of Zion, a Zion
as far removed as the remotest galaxy from what we have
today: "You are now assembled in a legislative capacity,
are so remote from the highwrought excitement and con-
sequent entangling questions common to the populous
marts of national and international commerce, are so little
prone to deem mere property, rank, titles and office the
highest prizes for human effort, . . . that your duties [are
far from] . . . that varied, perplexing and intricate description so characteristic of the legislation of most if not all
other communities. . . . These pursuits . . . are tame and
uninteresting to those who dwell amid the whirl of mental
and physical energies constantly taxed to their utmost tension in the selfish, unsatisfying and frenzied quest of
worldly emolument, fame, power, and maddening
draughts from the syren [sic] cup of pleasure."[29] This is
the world of the prime-time super soaps, which, with all
their crime, violence, and sex, a recent study has shown,
have become immensely popular not as an escape from
reality but as a vision of the world of affluence for which
we yearn and to which we aspire.

I started out by saying that I would stick to the scriptures, and I must. I would not dare to describe our times
in such words as these, but they were written to be quoted,
and they promise yet another breakthrough: "For the veil
of darkness shall soon be rent, and he that is not purified
shall not abide the day. . . . For all flesh is corrupted before
me; and the powers of darkness prevail upon the earth,

among the children of men. . . . Which causeth silence to reign, and all eternity is pained, and the angels are waiting; . . . and, behold, the enemy is combined" (D&C 38:8, 11-12). May you yet live to see that great breakthrough.

Notes

1. Arthur C. Clarke, *Profiles of the Future* (New York: Holt, Rinehart and Winston, 1962).

2. "The Morning Breaks," in *Hymns of The Church of Jesus Christ of Latter-day Saints* (Salt Lake City: The Church of Jesus Christ of Latter-day Saints, 1985), hymn 1.

3. "Israel, Israel, God Is Calling," ibid., hymn 7.

4. "The Spirit of God," ibid., hymn 2.

5. "An Angel from on High," ibid., hymn 13.

6. *The Pearl of Great Price* (Liverpool: Richards, 1851), 47.

7. Percy B. Shelley, "To a Skylark," *The Complete Works of Percy Bysshe Shelley*, ed. Roger Ingpen and Walter E. Peck, 10 vols. (New York: Gordian, 1965), 2:305.

8. Elden J. Watson, *Brigham Young Addresses 1870-1877*, 6 vols. (unpublished), 6 (1 June 1876).

9. John M. Allegro, *The Treasure of the Copper Scroll* (Garden City, NY: Doubleday, 1960), 61-62.

10. *JD* 2:305-6 (emphasis added).

11. Ibid., 2:306 (emphasis added).

12. *TPJS* 183.

13. Dean C. Jessee, ed., *The Personal Writings of Joseph Smith* (Salt Lake City: Deseret Book, 1984), 379 (emphasis added).

14. Andrew Carnegie, *The Gospel of Wealth* (New York: Century, 1900), 19.

15. Any issue of *Forbes* magazine.

16. *TPJS* 9.

17. George Orwell, *Nineteen Eighty-Four* (New York: Harcourt, Brace, and World, 1949).

18. Ibid., 7.

19. Harold Nicolson, "Review of Nineteen Eighty-Four," *Observer* (12 June 1949): 7.

20. Philip Rahv, "Review of Nineteen Eighty-Four," *Partisan Review* (July 1949): 743-49.

21. Golo Mann, "Review of Nineteen Eighty-Four," *Frankfurter Rundshau* (5 November 1949): 6.

22. Orwell, *Nineteen Eighty-Four*, 134.

23. Ibid., 266-67.

24. Diana Trilling, "Review of Nineteen Eighty-Four," *Nation* (25 June 1949): 716-17.

25. Fredric Warburg, "Publisher's Report," *All Authors Are Equal* (London: Hutchinson, 1973), 103-4.

26. Orwell, *Nineteen Eighty-Four*, 300.

27. The 1832 recital of the First Vision as dictated by Joseph Smith to Frederick G. Williams. See Milton V. Backman, *Joseph Smith's First Vision* (Salt Lake City: Bookcraft, 1971), appendix A; cf. Dean C. Jessee, ed., "The Early Accounts of Joseph Smith's First Vision," *BYU Studies* 9 (1969): 280.

28. Ibid.

29. Excerpted from the governor's message given to the legislative assembly of the territory of Utah on December 15, 1857; reported in the *Deseret News* 7 (23 December 1857): 330.

14

Change out of Control

Last year, if you can bear to remember, I spoke on the assigned subject "Breakthroughs I Would Like to See." This year I was given two minutes to decide on a title, and being in a panic I could only think of "Change Out of Control."

What can we say about change except that it is inevitable? What can we do about it? Direct it or control it? One thinks of those signs at the airport, "Low-Flying Planes"— what can you do about it except duck and drive on? They fly low anyway. We can always assume that we want change to be for the better, and since we can't avoid it we should do something to assure that it won't be retrograde or even disastrous. But in so doing, we should be aware that some things should change as much as possible and some things as little as possible. While you can't avoid alterations in your person—appearance, size, voice, gait, and so forth—as you progress through the infamous seven ages of man as stipulated by the insight of a Solon[1] or a Shakespeare, you would like your better qualities to hang on for a while and defy time. Actually they do: steadiness and durability are the marks of the highest and best qualities of character, as in God himself, who exhibits no "variableness neither shadow of changing" (Mormon 9:9). Your visible attributes, on the other hand, will change inevitably, but those are not the qualities that concern us. As civili-

This lecture was given in the Spheres of Influence lecture series on November 7, 1985, at Brigham Young University.

zation declines and "seeming" becomes more important than "being" (to use the Greek formula and the Roman example from the Satirists), we do everything we can in a forlorn effort to keep our appearance from changing, which means making all manner of concessions to truth and integrity as we become increasingly vain, giddy, shallow, and superficial, ever more dependent on exquisitely commercialized products. We are told by Madison Avenue that without advertising something terrible happens, which is *nothing*. Well, is that bad? What the ad-men really mean, of course, is that nothing happens to make money for them, but whether we advertise or not, things are always going to change.

If we can't stop it, can't we at least speed it up or slow it down? Can't we direct it? One would like optimum conditions to be permanent, for from the best of possible worlds any change must be away from the best. Must it be so? Can optimum conditions in one situation be different from optimum conditions in another, so that we can have a whole string of optimums, each leading to a better? Believe it or not, that is what they used to teach us in school. We were taught that change is inevitable and that it is evolutionary, which in the 1920s made an ever-progressive and unbroken march of ever-advancing optimum conditions. No evidence for this was required—it was axiomatic, so we naturally assumed that the evidence for it must lie all around us; if the medium is the message, any change is in itself progress. Noise and bustle, smoke-darkened skies, and arrogant billboards were all signs of progress. If one objected to the foul stench of a paper mill, one was immediately challenged and rebuked: Are you against progress? What a happy world that was where change was the first law of nature, and all change was good!

We are told in 2 Nephi 5:27 that the people "lived after the manner of happiness." Does that mean in a world without change? Times and seasons, conveniences and techniques inevitably change, but there is something that does not need to change, and that is that state of mind we call happiness. Nephi's people made adjustments and did not depend on the adamantly immovable euphoria of such jubilant spirits as Pippi and Pollyanna; those moppets had a point—the irrepressible sprites made their own happiness. This point was not lost among the well-to-do who advised the unemployed and the hungry to rejoice in their adventurous situation and examples of life on the brink. The torch was taken up by Little Orphan Annie, whose temperament and juvenile image, along with her rigid philosophy, have defied change for fifty-five years.

The unchanging, standard, permanent ideal of a safe, secure environment cannot possibly exist if we are going to have the one quality that adds interest and beauty to the scene, and that is variety. Mountains and hills, great rivers and small streams, just as surely as they impart that variety and beauty to the scene, are going to effect changes. Some students have complained that having to live on a Urim and Thummim, a sea of glass, no less, must be infinitely boring. How wrong they are! The face of the Urim and Thummim is no featureless flatland; rather, as Abraham found out, it can give you more dimensions than you can even imagine. It is true, you have to exercise your mind in that environment, but where would you not wish to do that? If you want scented breezes over purple seas, the Urim and Thummim will gladly oblige; if it's towering mountains you want, you can have them, too. Whatever it is you yearn to experience, that marvelous instrument can put you into the picture, if you only know how to operate it. This is not entirely facetious; after all, we have already anticipated the miracle in the device to which almost all Americans resort daily and nightly in order to retreat into other worlds, and the ease with which they can shift from one station to another is a bedizening pageant of high and low living that bids fair to make change—

mindless, restless, ceaseless, frantic change—in very truth the dominant feature of our existence.

Mormon doctrine presents the Latter-day Saints with a challenge: What will they be doing in eternity? Many find themselves stuck in a strange predicament. They imagine the eternal family as the typical young household with a number of little children that can never grow up. Yet many a patriarch had sons and grandsons whose ages surpassed his own; are they always to remain daddy's little men? So what will we do forever? The movie studio imagines something like an eternal family reunion held in the city park with everybody sitting or standing around in old-fashioned nightgowns in an exchange of insipid smiles and small talk. After twenty minutes of that, anyone would settle for inferno.

If the question of what we will be doing in eternity stumps us, it should. That's the whole point: if we knew the answer we'd have little enough to look forward to. The only way to know what fun lies ahead on the other side is to experience it, because, as Paul tells us, as long as we are here we can't even begin to imagine what any of it is like: "Eye hath not seen, nor ear heard, neither have entered into the heart of man" (1 Corinthians 2:9). No use trying to figure it out; you will just have to wait and see. And the gospel invites us to move toward the unknown.

If I cannot guide or direct an activity that I cannot even imagine, how can I have any control over change? I must have some in order to prepare for what is to come. And sure enough, there is a means of taking charge of change. It is the same way in which one can control a jet plane or a violin: by following instructions. As you practice an instrument, you begin to make your own adjustments, important changes, but only to the degree to which you have learned from your teacher; he requires you to make certain often awkward and uncomfortable changes as you learn the new positions on an instrument, but after that you make your own.

But why do we make so little progress in this life? Because, of course, we all peak and then decline and depart as a new class comes along to go through the same frustrating process, "and so from hour to hour we ripe and ripe, and then from hour to hour we rot and rot." That is certainly change.

C. S. Forester wrote a novel about a general whose whole ambition in life was to end up in a bath-chair in Bournemouth,[2] because that is what respected and tolerably wounded British generals have done for generations. Faust won all the honors and credentials there were in the learned world and concluded that the next logical step for him was suicide.[3] How long can one continue to be upwardly mobile in the corporation? What comes after the lifestyles of the rich and famous? All the generations seem to go through the same routine, for all are taking the same test and all have been given the same standard orders, which do not change: "I gave unto them their knowledge in the day I created them; and in the Garden of Eden," says the Lord to Enoch, "gave I unto man his agency" (Moses 7:32). Agency to act, and knowledge to act by. What more do you need? Either supernatural wisdom or higher instruction. And that we also have — "and I also gave unto him commandments" (see Abraham 3:25). That takes care of everything, and these are the things we don't change, because one generation is much like another and must be tested by the same standards, "to prove them herewith, whether they will be true and faithful in all things."

Next in the lamentable but unlamented address of November 7 last came a brief review of major changes in the past over which men have had no control. First of all the Big Bang, which brought total and instantaneous change from a condition of utter singularity to another condition of utter singularity, that is, moving from an everything-

and-nothing to a world furnace of photons in a matter of
less than nanoseconds. This was followed by a whole series
of impossible instantaneous or infinitely drawn out
changes from photons to hadrons to leptons to galaxies to
stars to more explosions to planets and so, by this declen-
sion, to this present veil of tears we all mourn for.[4] Neo-
catastrophism in geology continues the parade of calamitous changes, geological crises in which many forms of life
were suddenly extinguished as others just as suddenly
popped up on the scene.[5] At this point we held up a chart
in the current *National Geographic* that marked the mass
extinctions taking place at circa 650,000,000 and 230,000,000
and 65,000,000 years ago and finally in the present age,
marked as "man-induced extinction." If you want change,
there is change! Findings in caves show a continuing story
of periodic crisis fatal to some forms of life and favorable
to others. Such ambitious studies as those of Claude
Schaeffer and Samuel Noah Kramer carry the data into
human history when the whole race has been shaken up
and shifted all over the globe as in the great crises of circa
3000, 1700, 1200 B.C. or the third to fifth centuries A.D.
Usually such worldwide human overthrows are correlated
by the ancient writers with descriptions of the upheavals
of nature and the phenomenal depravity and violence of
man. It is an interesting coincidence that the great geological and biological changes of the past were affected by
two things—dust and smoke in the atmosphere occasioned
by the impact of great meteorites, and radioactivity from
outer space, also caused by the impact of the meteorites,
which played strange tricks with the possibilities of DNA.
Interesting because those are exactly the agents we are
now enlisting to bring the curtain down on the present
age of man.

America has ever been dedicated to the cult of change,
esteeming it a sign of great vitality, exuberance, and hope.
I remember in the 1930s when Paxman and others discov-

ered the frontier as a topic for scholarly inquiry. What excitement there was in Berkeley about the prodigal possibilities of the thesis: America from first to last had been frontier! But what we always find on the frontier has ever been a set of rascals, outlaws, con men, and gangs. What do you expect where everything is up for grabs? That is the picture I got from my grandparents. In record time the face of the continent was completely changed. But the finished product was not "America the Beautiful" (you should live so long). Incidentally, Miss Katherine Lee Bates, who wrote "America the Beautiful," was a sister of my second-grade school teacher, so we sang a lot about the alabaster cities where nobody ever cries, but that is not what came out of the frontier.

When the West had been liberated and the Winchester had removed the last dangerous antelope and won the West and the bad guys were all six feet under, then came Carl Sandburg and John Dewey. Sandburg wrote of an exciting, vigorous, explosive, progressive America.[6] It wasn't the real America. The greatest vigor displayed in his Chicago was by the mobs in their wars with each other. Dewey was the great apostle of change in education.[7] He was going to change everything and make it dynamic, progressive, exciting, and all that, and of course it turns out that in education as in everything else it was just what the fashion designers call running up and down stairs — wearing them short this year and long the next.

Since ancient times, the educationalists have been coming up periodically with the New Education — enlightened, free, emancipated, unhampered — only to be followed inevitably in a few years by the new reform movement calling for more discipline, more basics, more solid study, until the time comes again to discover the new vibrant unshackled order, and so on. I am reminded of a great work by one Karl Joel called *Die Wandlungen der Weltanschauung*,[8] or *The Pendulum of the World View*. In a massively documented work, he divided world history into two phases that run roughly through the centuries. A century of *Bindung* or binding together, strict rule, discipline, a time of collecting, cataloging, ordering, regimenting, classifying, and so on, makes it possible to digest the accumulations of the preceding century, which was a century of *Lösung*, which means loosening, letting go — the creative, romantic, free, and spontaneous spirit in which the arts and sciences alike flourish and bring forth new harvest. We are now in a time of extreme *Bindung*, so tight that it can probably only be released by something like a big bang.

Attempts to direct and control more serious change can only mean *havoc*. That is an interesting word. The word *havoc* can be traced everywhere and is one of the most widespread words in the languages of the world. Furthermore, it always has the same basic meaning. Havoc is something you start which then carries on beyond your control. Mark Anthony shouts, "Cry 'havoc!' "[9] and then remarks with satisfaction, "Now let it work. Mischief, thou art afoot. Take thou what course thou wilt!"[10] He knows big changes are at hand, and he doesn't particularly care what they are, for havoc is what he wants. And so if I launch something without knowing for sure what is going to follow — and who does? — I am wreaking havoc. We live in a world in which men are capable of little more than havoc, since everything is so complicated that the outcome of any project is unpredictable. The nuclear genie is the ultimate and, I believe, inevitable conclusion to this apocalyptic folly.

When I consider the changes I have seen, I recall how often my grandmother used to say (and we firmly believed it as children), "It is a sin to kill a fly; much more to harm a greater thing." Who would buy that today? Back then the first rule was that life as such was sacred. Today, of course, we don't think it's a sin to kill anything at all except the good guys, the ones we happen to like. We get little credit for that, for, as the Lord says, the publicans and sinners like their friends. What merit can we claim in that? Today we accept half of the Ten Commandments: You should not kill your friends, but you get medals for the others. You should not lie, at least not to those you like; the others are fair game. Such a shift in morals gives an idea of how far the ship has drifted in our own day; and now it is caught up in the full current and is racing for the falls with nothing to stop it.

In ancient times when everything was completely out of control, the world turned to special effects to achieve the direction of change or reverse the trend. Constantine used this trick to great effect,[11] borrowing the idea from Diocletian, who got it from the East. That is, you got the kind of world you wanted by canvas and paint, parades and shows, and a vast display of ceremonial patriotism. The Roman emperors, to get and stay in office, all had to be very skillful managers. Each one would set the course of empire and promptly lose it, usually by assassination, because it was always up for sale. The real power was money, and so the story then was the quintessential stuff of prime-time TV today. It's no surprise that one of the best shows from *Masterpiece Theater* was Robert Graves's story of the Emperor Claudius.

In the great and irresistible rush of lemmings to the sea, change both unavoidable and uncontrollable, what is the individual to do? What difference can one person make? We are told that the only control in our time must come through repentance, but what difference will it make if one person repents and nobody else does? Well, that's the story of Jerusalem and the prophets, of the Book of Mormon, and the book of Abraham, and the book of Moses, and the New Testament, and the Joseph Smith story. Each one is the predicament of the one righteous repentant person against the stream. The Book of Mormon is a long list of men who stood almost wholly alone, from

Ether to Moroni. The early Christians paid the price, but then, as Duchesne and other church historians observe, Christianity gave up its integrity as the price of survival. "Woe to thee, tide of human custom," cried St. Augustine, "who can resist thee?"[12] He decided it was best and safest not to try, and he took the church along with him, or rather went along with it. But, according to the scriptures, there is security in repentance even if you are the only one, for God will pay attention to you whether anybody else does or not. True, you will seem to pay a high price, but "who loses his life . . . shall save it" (Mark 8:35). If you actually keep the commandments, you will get no lack of attention from both sides, standing out like a sore thumb.

There is a very special pattern of change established for the promised land, and it is set forth in the Book of Mormon. You may easily observe how civilizations in the Old World go on and on and suffer; they are the rafts that can't sink. Egypt, Greece, India, China, the unchanging East have all paid the price of survival with endless suffering, yet their civilizations are still in place. But it is a different story in the New World, where great civilizations have arisen and collapsed for reasons that students are still wholly at a loss to explain. They just disappeared, and nobody knows why. And I think that is a warning. Recently when I was in New York City, a guide pointed out a new hundred-million-dollar skyscraper, which had just been built with the intention that it would be torn down after another thirty years. Does that suggest a stable civilization? We are proud of not standing still. Joseph Smith noticed that wherever he looked, he seemed to see the word *destruction* written on everything in capital letters. On the eve of the French revolution, *ca ira* was the theme—"That's going to go!" Today the new and improved product is always assumed, and we are constantly bidding farewell to the best that we have now. Good-bye to all that.

Prophecy tells us that things are going to change and

that there is nothing we can do to stop it. Certain things are certainly going to happen. Must we therefore resign ourselves to fate? Not at all. There is a vital rule that leaves the door wide open to effective individual repentance and escape. We have Professor Heisenberg to thank for that. He found that though you can predict with absolute certainty how masses of particles are going to act, you can never predict how any *one* particle is going to behave. That is the Heisenberg Uncertainty Principle, which used to be called "the free will of the atom." The single particle is unpredictable; only the mass is absolutely bound to behave according to the unimpeachable laws of physics.[13] In the same way one can prophesy with absolute certainty what a nation or people or society is going to do: you can talk about aggregates and predict the behavior of masses, but you can never deny any individual the freedom to repent and go the other way. "Thou shalt not follow a multitude to do evil." The prophets and Professor Heisenberg show us the way out. You do not have to wait for the group to change, for the society to repent, nor do you have to change your ways to comply with theirs; the individual is free to ignore the multitude, and only he is free. Only an individual can repent. *Repent* is a reflexive verb—you can't repent somebody else or force somebody else; you just repent. The clear rule for assuring desirable change is set forth in 2 Nephi: "As many of the Gentiles as will repent are the covenant people of the Lord; and as many of the Jews who will not repent shall be cast off; for the Lord covenanteth with none save it be with them that repent and believe in his Son" (2 Nephi 30:2).

On the other hand, Satan has his plan for initiating and controlling change in the world, and it is a very effective one. It rests on his manipulation of the treasures of the earth, the economy. In a single thundering speech, Shakespeare shows us how money is the great lord of change, the great change artist. Timon of Athens was the richest man in the city and very lavish in his hospitality and kind to everyone, always willing to help out a friend in need. As a result, everyone took advantage of him and he went bankrupt. When he tried to get loans and help from his friends, they were never at home and could not recognize him in the street. He was dead because he didn't have any money. So he became a misanthrope and went out into the sticks to dig for roots to keep himself alive. (Incidentally, this is based on the true story of Herodes Atticus.[14]) As he was digging one day, he struck gold, an enormously rich buried treasure, and so Shakespeare gives us the scene. "Earth, yield me roots! Who seeks for better of thee, sauce his palate with thy most operant poison!" At that moment he strikes the treasure, "What is here?" he says. "Gold! Yellow, glittering, precious gold! No, gods, I am no idle votarist." He doesn't want it. "Roots, you clear heavens!" As the treasure emerges he picks up a coin and says,

> Thus much of this will make black white, foul fair, wrong right, base noble, old young, coward valiant. Ha! you gods why this? What this, you gods? Why, this will lug your priests and servants from your sides, pluck stout men's pillows from below their heads: This yellow slave will knit and break religions; bless the accursed; make the hoar leprosy adored; place thieves, and give them title, knee, and approbation, with senators on the bench; this it is that makes the wappen'd widow wed again; she, whom the spital-house and ulcerous sores would cast the gorge at, this embalms and spices to the April day again. Come, damned earth, thou common whore of mankind, that putt'st odds among the rout of nations, I will make thee do thy right nature.[15]

At that point he hears a drum and says, "Thou 'rt quick, but yet I'll bury thee: Thou'lt go, strong thief, when gouty keepers of thee cannot stand."[16] He has no sooner found it than everybody, including his former friends, are after it, and fawning on him to get a clue.

Now just consider what a magnificent effector of change Satan possesses in an instrument that will get you anything in this world. It can change the most obvious realities, all moral values—black to white, making foul fair and wrong right; it can reverse priestly devotion and personal loyalty to their opposites; it can turn one's bodyguards into one's murderers, as it often did in Rome; it can sanctify the damned and damn the sacred; it can reverse the impulses of natural revulsion to all that is filthy and foul. It is what is now pitting the great powers against each other; and everybody is out to get all of it they can. All this Shakespeare has told us, and, alas, there is not the least bit of exaggeration in it. You can all illustrate each of his points by many examples. The miraculous power of money lies above all in the faith that it can stop the ravages of time. As the vigor of youth wanes, accumulating fortune can guarantee that time's effects will be minimized. The scriptures also speak of money as the most irresistible of all agencies of change in one direction. They call it a deadly cancer which once started cannot be stopped (James 5:3; Mormon 8:38). It is called filthy and nasty in the letter to Titus (Titus 1:7, 11). In 1 Timothy it is called the great deceiver whose deceptions lead always to ruin (1 Timothy 5:6). Repeatedly in the Book of Mormon we are told that when people "set their hearts upon riches," their doom is sealed. When the obsession for power and gain overcomes everything else in its final stages, it preempts the whole program of change.

Change out of control? We often hear the quotation from Yeats, "Things fall apart; the centre cannot hold; mere anarchy is loosed upon the world."[17] Things reach a point where only one more change is possible. "The earth also was corrupt before God, and the earth was filled with violence, and God looked upon the earth, and, behold, it was corrupt; for all flesh had corrupted his way upon the earth, and God said unto Noah, The end of all flesh is come before me; for the earth is filled with violence through them" (Genesis 6:12-13). If men leave room in those great conflicts that rage about the economy for nothing but violence, God will take over, and they will have the ultimate solution to their problems.

I just spent a week with my wife in the Islands. One looks at the palms that have been waving timelessly in tropical breezes, and here at last it seems we have a world that does not change and does not need to change. The natives like it that way, too. And everybody says, Why should it change? Everyone goes there to see the kind of world they would like to live in. Some people we visited were very upset because the last beach where the young people can enjoy themselves and have their church parties is to be sold by the bank. Some considered that progress. The last time I was there years ago, the same thing was happening; they sold two patches for highrises. The highrises went up, and the beaches were lost forever; and now it turns out that if those shrewd men had waited just a little longer, they could have gotten ten times as much for the property as they did. So they lost the money, the beach, the island paradise, and everything else. They thought they were in charge and were improving things by what turned out to be a foolish and ruinous business deal.

May God bring about his own changes while there is still something left to change.

Notes

1. See, for example, Ivan M. Linforth, *Solon the Athenian* (Berkeley: University of California, 1919).

2. C. S. Forester, *Hornblower Saga: Mr. Midshipman Hornblower* (Los Angeles: Pinnacle, 1950).

3. Johann Wolfgang von Goethe, *Faust I and II*, ed. and tr. Stuart Atkins (Cambridge, MA: Suhrkamp/Insel, 1984).

4. Nigel Calder, *Violent Universe* (New York: Viking, 1969), 133-39; John Boslough, *Stephen Hawking's Universe* (New York: Quill/Morrow, 1985), 45-58.

5. Von Otto H. Schindwolf, "Neokatastrophismus," *Zeitschrift der deutschen geologischen Gesellschaft* 114 (1963): 430-31.

6. See Hazel Curnell, *The America of Carl Sandburg* (Washington, D.C.: University Press of Washington, D.C., 1965); cf. Carl Sandburg, *The Chicago Race Riots* (New York: Harcourt, Brace and Howe, 1919).

7. John Dewey, *On Education*, ed. Reginold D. Archambault (New York: Modern Library, 1964).

8. Karl Joel, *Die Wandlungen der Weltanschauung*, 2 vols. (Mohr: Tübingen, 1928).

9. William Shakespeare, *Julius Caesar*, act III, scene i, line 276.

10. Ibid., act III, scene ii, lines 253-54.

11. Eusebius, "Concerning the Life of the Most Blessed Emperor Constantine," chapter X in *PG* 20:1063-66; for English translation, see Eusebius, *Life of Constantine*, chapter X in *Nicene and Post-Nicene Fathers*, 14 vols. (Grand Rapids, MI: Eerdmans, 1978), 1:522.

12. St. Augustine, *Confessions* I, 16, 25.

13. Heinz R. Pagels, *The Cosmic Code* (New York: Bantam, 1984), 68-75.

14. Regarding the life of Herodes Atticus, see Philostratus, *Lives of the Sophists*, 2:546-48; for English translation, see E. H. Warmington, ed., *Philostratus and Eunapius* (Cambridge, MA: Harvard University Press, 1968), 138-251.

15. William Shakespeare, *Timon of Athens*, act III, scene iii.

16. Ibid.

17. Joseph Hone, *W. B. Yeats, 1865-1939* (New York: Macmillan, 1943), 351.

15

Law of Consecration

The "Old Law" — the Only Law

As there was only one law given to Israel, so there is only one law given to the human race, the law by which the sons and daughters of God are supposed to live in this world. All are capable of observing it, otherwise it would not be required of them. It is a minimum requirement; anyone can be expected to keep it (Zechariah 14:17-18). All the families of the earth that don't come up to Jerusalem to make their offerings, for them there will be no rain. Untold millions have accepted the law, but only a handful of people at brief and scattered intervals have lived up to it. It was given complete to Moses, but the people would not receive it, so he could give them only a part of it (Exodus 32:19; cf. JST Exodus 34:1-2). Moses smashed the tablets, which was as he prophesied.

The partial law was in the province of the Aaronic Priesthood; the bishop administered it. In his farewell speech, Moses concluded by declaring, "I know what a stiffnecked people you are. If you were rebellious while I am still alive with you, how will you behave when I am gone? Bring the elders together so that I can speak a final word to them and call heaven and earth to record against them. For I know that after my death you will be utterly corrupt and turn aside from the way I commanded" (see Deuteronomy 31:27-29). Israel never heard the law, not

---

This talk was given February 6, 1986, in the LDS Church Office Building in Salt Lake City, Utah.

even the lesser law. Repeatedly on that occasion, Moses reminded them, "Behold I set before you this day a blessing and a curse" (Deuteronomy 11:26). "If thou wilt not hearken, . . . these curses are for you." Then he repeated a list of promised blessings in reverse (Deuteronomy 28:15-68). "See, I have set before thee this day life and good, and death and evil. . . . I call heaven and earth to record this day against you, that I have set before you life and death, blessing and cursing: therefore choose life" (Deuteronomy 30:15, 19).

The children of Israel were not being put to an unfair test; as Nephi says, anyone who is righteous will qualify. "If the former inhabitants of the land had been righteous, they would have qualified too" (cf. 1 Nephi 17:33-38). For the people accepted the condition wholeheartedly, after each cursing. Moses went down the list and said: "All the people cried with a loud voice, Amen!" for they were accepting the curse along with the blessing (Deuteronomy 27:14-26); the same pattern occurs in the opening lines of the Dead Sea Scrolls, the Serekh Scroll.[1] Everyone comes together. The law is put before them point by point. "Do you accept it?" "Yes." "Do you accept the *berakhah*," the blessing? "Yes." "Do you accept the curse?" "Yes." "Amen." They must accept it all before they can continue with their endowment.

Those who have accepted the covenant are expected not to follow the world but to be set apart from it—to be completely sanctified. "Ye stand this day all of you before Jehovah, [before] your God, . . . that he may establish thee today for a people unto himself" (Deuteronomy 29:10, 13). Let there be none with mental reservations as to what he has sworn to. That would be gall and wormwood (Deuteronomy 29:18), for God will not be mocked; if anyone thinks that the words apply to him only in a limited sense and says to himself, "This won't bother me, I'll just go my way," the Lord will not spare him. All the curses written in this book will fall upon him (Deuteronomy 29:18-19). Because you are something different from the world—holy, set apart, chosen, special, peculiar (*am segullah*—sealed), not like any other people on the face of the earth (Deuteronomy 7:6), God will keep faith with you all the way. He wants to bless you for a thousand generations (Deuteronomy 7:9). To reject such an offer is to incur the judgment of God; despised love turns to hate: despise not the gifts of God!

The Book of Mormon ends on that theme. "Deny not the gifts of God!" says Moroni (Moroni 10:8; Mormon 9:26-27). God intends to bless you above all other people; he will be a veritable Zion of eternal increase without sickness (Deuteronomy 7:14-15). And this law will remain the law until God himself sees fit to change it (Deuteronomy 4:2). But you must not consider it as a mere heritage, something for the ancients, nothing but a venerable tradition; it is given explicitly to "those living right now and right here" (cf. Deuteronomy 5:3). It was always to apply in the present, and it will never be rescinded. It is a standing law.

One does not enter lightly into such a covenant. To organize a race of priests in ancient as in modern days, God processed all volunteers by a series of preparatory steps. First, there is an initiatory stage in which one is physically set apart from the world: actually washed, anointed, given a protective garment, and clothed in sanctified robes.[2] This is merely preliminary and qualifies one to proceed, in earnest not of what one has become, but of what one may and wishes to become.

After the initiatory, the candidates are assembled and asked (and this we find in the Dead Sea Scrolls as well as in many other ancient works): "Do you agree and are you resolved to do things his way rather than your way—to follow the law of God?" The candidate is not told at this time what the law of God requires, only whether he is willing to trust God's judgment and accept it no matter what it is. After that, all argument is out of the question.

Next the candidate is asked, "If so, will you be obedient to him no matter what he asks of you?"—a commitment to obedience before demand is made.

The next step is more specific and more serious: "Will you willingly sacrifice anything he asks for, including your own life?"

Whoever accepts this in the solemnity of the occasion may easily relax his resolve in days that follow, and so the next question is, "Will you at all times behave morally and soberly?"—that is, take all this very seriously, not just now but every day throughout your life. Thus a pattern of life is set to implement this. Your determination must be confirmed by your deportment at all times. This is the law of the gospel.

Finally God says, "Very well, this is what I want you to do" (see Deuteronomy 5:6). The next verse begins to describe the Ten Commandments, implemented by a strict and specific regime. It begins with general orders, to be observed all the times. The Ten Commandments are standing orders. What follows are the necessary steps to implement the law and put it into operation. The book of Moses is the law, the Torah. The prophets that follow don't add to the law; they but appeal to the people to observe it, to return to it, because the people, again and again, haven't been observing it. Whether Isaiah, Jeremiah, or the minor prophets, they decry the conditions of the people. They promise destruction. Why? Because the people have not kept the law. All the prophets promised that things would be wonderful if the people would only keep the law. That's the message of the prophets: Keep the law. It will be wonderful if you do, and terrible if you don't. This is the message. This is the one law that Moses gave.

First of all, the community are to establish a center,

that they may be united, a "place which Jehovah your God has chosen out of all your tribes to put his name there for his dwelling; ye shall seek that place out and go there. That is where ye shall bring your sacrifices, burnt offerings, heave offerings, tithes, freewill offerings, firstlings. There you shall hold your feasts before the Lord joyfully with your families" (cf. Deuteronomy 12:5-7). The first thing every individual will do in the New Land when the holy place is established is personally offer his firstfruits in a basket. Note that this is a personal law. The individual acts with the multitude. Each is to set the first-fruits before the altar and recite this speech: "A Syrian ready to perish was my father, and he went down into Egypt . . . and became there a nation, . . . and the Egyptians treated us badly. The Lord brought us forth, . . . and brought us to this place and has given us this land" (Deuteronomy 26:5-9). What the King James Version renders "Syrian" is an Aramaean; Abraham was the first Hebrew, meaning a displaced person, a tramp, an outcast. He was always homeless, always wandering.

The theme is sacrifice, which was also the theme of Abraham's life. That is what you do in the ordinance. The ordinance, from beginning to end, up and down the whole scale, Aaronic to Melchizedek, is the offering, and so is the theme of Abraham's own life. The test is whether one will cheat the Lord: "A tribute of a freewill offering of thine hand [always the singular] is required at the feast of the weeks" (i.e., Pentecost; cf. Deuteronomy 16:10). The offering, the tribute, is required; but the amount you determine yourself, by your free will; a helpful hint is the basis "how much the Lord has given you" (the Septuagint *kathoti hē chier sou ichyei* — to the limit of your ability): "According to that which he has given you, even that with which your God hath blessed you." He requires you to take the test, which is whether you will try to short change him (Deuteronomy 16:10).

Three times a year (at the feasts of the unleavened bread, weeks, and tabernacles), all males come together, and "every man shall give as he is able, according to the blessing of the Lord thy God which he hath given thee" (Deuteronomy 16:16-17). And how much is one able to give? Exactly as much as the Lord has given him—all that with which the Lord has blessed you, or with which he may bless you. We don't realize how close our temple is to the ancient one or how near the ancient one is to ours. The new temple documents coming forth confirm this, and the Jewish scholars recognize it. All such dealings are between the individual and the Lord; men do not make deals with one another in this economy. That is an abomination (Deuteronomy 16:19). You must never get the idea "when you have eaten and are full and your silver and gold has piled up along with everything else" that you have earned it, "and say to yourself, 'my ability and hard work have made for me this fortune' " (cf. Deuteronomy 8:12-13, 17). Bear in mind that God has given you the capacity to get what you have only for the sake of confirming the covenant which he made with your fathers—it is their merit, not yours, that has deserved it (Deuteronomy 8:18). If you forget that in any degree, you will be destroyed, just like other nations, because you would not obey the voice of Jehovah your God (Deuteronomy 8:19-20). This is not being done because of your righteousness: "Speak not thou in thine heart . . . saying, For my righteousness the Lord hath brought me in to possess this land: but for the wickedness of these nations the Lord doth drive them out" (Deuteronomy 9:4). Because you are not righteous, but wicked, "Jehovah has given you this good land not as a reward of righteousness, because in fact you are a stiffnecked people" (cf. Deuteronomy 9:5-6). In these chapters, the Lord calls Israel down just as they are entering the covenant, saying, "I've changed my mind. I think I'll give it to someone else." Moses pleads with him passionately to spare Israel.

And this special pleading by Moses to the Lord is all that saves the people from destruction.

There is to be no dickering or cheating: "Thou shalt not sacrifice unto the Lord . . . any bullock, or sheep, wherein is blemish or any evil-favoredness: for that is an abomination unto the Lord thy God" (Deuteronomy 17:1). Trying to put one over on God — he won't mind — is a cheap trick, and a mean one. In all these doings it is you who are being tested.

Every generation was to observe the covenants exactly as agreed: "Thou shalt teach them diligently unto thy children." How? By the most effective teaching, not by precept only, not by attending a class. The *yeshiva* ("a school for advanced Talmudic study") comes later. "Talk of them when you are sitting at home, talk of them whenever you are on the move, about town or on a journey, talk of them going to bed and getting up" (cf. Deuteronomy 6:7). In other words, they overhear what you are talking about; it becomes just natural for them to assume that that is the way things are. It is not to be left in the hands of professional teachers: "Bind them for a sign on your hand, . . . between the eyes; . . . write them on the doorposts of your houses [but always individually] and gateways" (cf. Deuteronomy 6:8-9). You have it individually, not just the priests — that is, to make children ask questions, and you answer their questions by telling them the story of Moses, the deliverance from Egypt, what our obligation is, how grateful we should be, and about the giving of the law (Deuteronomy 6:20).

At the same time, the law tests us in our dealings with each other. The cornerstone of the whole economy is "the Lord's release." At the end of every seven years, every creditor must cancel all debts (Deuteronomy 15:1-2). Because you get into the whirlpool of debt, this policy puts things on a new basis. It wipes the slate clean, the only way you can possibly break out, by an absolute law that cuts debts right off. With all men, either debtors or creditors, this is not a convenient arrangement; yet it is the only way. Only God can draw the line and say, "Here the business of exploiting each other must stop." The Lord guarantees to make up any losses to those who keep the law, "for the Lord will greatly bless you" if, but only if, you "carefully hearken to observe and do these commandments" (cf. Deuteronomy 15:4-5).

Now comes the important part of the business, which is the *spirit* in which it is all done: "If there be a poor man of your brethren living anywhere within your knowledge, . . . thou shalt not harden thy heart nor shut thy hand from thy poor brother. But thou shalt open thy hand wide unto him and shall surely lend him sufficient for his need, of whatever he is in want" (cf. Deuteronomy 15:7-8). Since it is a loan, "beware that there be not a thought in thy wicked heart, saying, the seventh year, the year of release, is at hand; if I give anything to him now, he will not have to repay it, and I will never get it back; and thine eye be evil against thy poor brother, and thou givest him nought, and he cry unto the Lord, . . . and it be sin unto thee" (cf. Deuteronomy 15:9). This is not to be regarded as a business operation: "Thou shalt surely give him, and thine heart shall not be grieved when thou givest unto him" (Deuteronomy 15:10). (I hate to do this, but it is the law! — however fiscally unsound. You shouldn't give if that is the way you feel about it.) If you give in the spirit God requires, you will not be without your reward, "because . . . for this thing the Lord thy God shall bless thee [no amount specified] in all thy works" (Deuteronomy 8:10). And now comes that famous verse quoted by the Lord: "For the poor shall never cease out of the land" (Deuteronomy 15:11; cf. Matthew 26:8-11). This is taken by many as welcome proof of the hopelessness of trying to end poverty and the futility of giving; in the Bible it means just the opposite. In the New Testament, Judas had protested that the costly ointment used to anoint Jesus' feet could better have been sold for the benefit of the poor, but Jesus reminded him that if he was so eager to help the poor, he would always have excellent opportunities, while the Son of Man was to be with them only for a day or two. But the poor you have always with you; you have plenty of time to bless them. That is not an excuse to help them; it's an obligation to help them all the more. Likewise in Deuteronomy the presence of the poor is presented as offering an opportunity to please God: "Therefore, I command thee, saying, thou shalt open thine hand wide unto thy brother, to thy poor, and to thy needy in thy land" (Deuteronomy 15:11). After six years of service, any and all servants must go absolutely free, no matter what was paid for them; "and . . . thou shalt not let him go away empty: Thou shalt furnish him liberally out of thy flock, . . . out of thy winepress: of that wherewith the Lord thy God has blessed thee thou shalt give unto him" (Deuteronomy 15:13-14). Why? "Thou shalt remember that thou wast a bondman in the land of Egypt and the Lord thy God redeemed ·thee [bought you free; paid the price]. Therefore I command thee this thing to day" (Deuteronomy 15:15). Inasmuch as the Lord has given his life for you, we should be willing to give everything. That is what Deuteronomy 15 says. Again the important point: "It shall not *seem hard* unto thee, when thou sendest him away free" (Deuteronomy 15:18). "Thou shalt not deliver unto his master the servant which is escaped from his master unto thee" (Deuteronomy 23:15)—human rights supersede property rights. Not only shall the refugee "dwell with thee . . . in that place which *he* shall choose, . . . but while he is with you thou shalt not *tonennu* [grumble, mutter about it under your breath] about him" (cf. Deuteronomy 23:16)—a neat psychological touch. Passing through a neighbor's vineyard, help yourself to what you can eat; if he denies you that, he is greedy. But you may not carry off any in a container—if you do that, then *you* are greedy (Deuteronomy 23:24). The idea is that we have sufficient for our needs. Everyone is to have that much if he is to take the test that life puts before us. To play a game, you must have the minimum of equipment; you can't spend all day trying to save up enough for gym shoes or a helmet.

Everyone is under a sacred obligation to get involved — and this is important in the ancient lot. Everything concerns you; you are your brother's keeper. "If you see a stray ox or sheep and recognize it, you must absolutely return it to your brother" (cf. Deuteronomy 22:1). If you don't recognize it, you keep nothing you find for yourself; you must hold it until an owner shows up (Deuteronomy 22:2-3). If you see someone's ox or ass fall down, you cannot pretend not to notice or make yourself scarce, like the priest or Levite passing by on the other side (Deuteronomy 22:4; Luke 10:30-32). Remember Moroni: "Why do ye . . . suffer the hungry, and the needy, and the naked, and the sick and the afflicted to pass by you, and notice them not?" (Mormon 8:39). If someone falls from the roof of your house because you have failed to put a railing around it, you may not plead contributory negligence (Deuteronomy 22:8). "You cannot take for a pledge a millstone or anything else upon which a man's livelihood depends" (see Deuteronomy 24:6). You may not go to the house of a creditor to take something as security, but stand at a distance and let him bring it out to you—his house is sacred (Deuteronomy 24:10-11). If the security is something he needs, you must return it to him by sundown (Deuteronomy 24:13). You shall not appeal to the iron law of wages, paying a worker as little as you can because he is desperate for work, and this applies to strangers, the wetbacks, as well as to Israelites (Deuteronomy 24:14). You must pay a worker every day before sundown, "for he is poor, and setteth his heart upon it"; everyone has a right to his daily bread (see Deuteronomy 24:15). Well-known is the law of the gleaning: "When thou cuttest down thine harvest in thy field, and hast forgot a sheaf in the field, thou shalt not go again to fetch it: it shall be for the stranger, for the fatherless, and for the widow" (Deuteronomy 24:19). In beating the olive trees, thou shalt not glean them afterward (Deuteronomy 24:20). Best known of all is the law "Thou shalt not muzzle the ox when he treadeth out the corn" (Deuteronomy 25:4; 1 Corinthians 9:9; 1 Timothy 5:18)—he is working for you; give him a break. Do the decent thing, but you won't make money that way. The vilest criminal may be punished with a beating but never to the point where he is robbed of his human dignity, lest "thy brother . . . seem vile to thee" (Deuteronomy 25:3).

In other words, the whole law is validated only when carried out in the right *spirit:* "And now, Israel, what doth the Lord thy God require of thee, but to fear the Lord thy God, to walk in all his ways, and to love him, and to serve the Lord thy God with all thy heart and with all thy soul" (Deuteronomy 10:12). Behold, "everything in heaven and earth belongs to him" (cf. Deuteronomy 10:14), and "all mortals are his children, all living things his creatures; he does right by the orphan and the widow, and he loves the stranger and wants him provided with food and clothing" (cf. Deuteronomy 10:18). These reflect God's attributes, which must be ours also: "Therefore *you* must do the same: love the stranger, remembering that you were strangers in the land of Egypt" (cf. Deuteronomy 10:19). This is repeated over and over again; it is empathy—remember how *you* felt when you were down and out, put yourself in their place, and do something about it! If they fail to act on this principle, "heaven will be brass over thy head and the earth will be iron beneath thy feet" (cf. Deuteronomy 28:23). "The Lord himself will cause you to be smitten before your enemies" (cf. Deuteronomy 23:25). Promised disasters go on and on, matching every promised blessing with a curse, "till thou be destroyed" (Deuteronomy 28:45).

And all this "because thou servedst not the Lord thy God with joyfulness, and with gladness of heart, for the abundance of all things" (Deuteronomy 28:47). In short, "as the Lord rejoiced . . . to do you good, and to multiply you; so the Lord will rejoice . . . to destroy you, and reduce you to nothing" (cf. Deuteronomy 28:63). You will have no security at all; thou "shalt have none assurance of thy life" (Deuteronomy 28:66). Therefore, "rejoice in every good thing which the Lord thy God hath given unto thee, and unto thine house, and the Levite, and the stranger that is among you" (Deuteronomy 26:11). All shall share equally, "the Levite, the stranger, the fatherless, and the widow, that they may eat within thy gates and be filled" (Deuteronomy 26:12). The Lord insists that you do and observe these things with all your heart and soul (that is the first of the two commandments—all your heart, might, mind, and soul). And you have promised and covenanted this day that you would do that; while he has accepted you this day as a special people, set apart, the wonder of other nations, that you may be a holy people, as he said (cf. Deuteronomy 26:16-19). The first two commandments cover everything, to "love the Lord thy God . . . with all thy might, and these words, which I command thee this day, shall be in thine heart" (Deuteronomy 6:5-6). So the law was established and abides to this day, whether anyone keeps it or not, for Moses knew perfectly well that it would not be kept: "Ye have been rebellious against the Lord ever since the day I first became acquainted with you" (cf. Deuteronomy 9:24).

The Law Carries On Despite the Opposition

We have said that there is only one law, the law given to Adam, Enoch, Abraham, Moses, the ancient apostles, the Nephites; all those who have the law also appeal to all the rest of the world to enter the covenant and accept that law. All of them were missionaries. Its rejection has

APPROACHING ZION

been almost total, though millions have done lip service to it. How much more kind, just, humane, and edifying is the strict law of Moses we just reviewed than the laws of the land we live today. To cover our delinquency in the attempt to distance ourselves from it and its responsibilities, we have downgraded the old law even to the point of contempt. It was the theological schools and seminaries of the nineteenth and twentieth centuries (Protestant seminaries) who invented the savage, vengeful, primitive, tribal God of the Old Testament, who fitted so well into the pattern of evolution. But already in ancient times, we know the Jews denatured and diluted the law with legalistic trivia, and the Christians went along with that and evaded Moses's commandments by holding in abomination every aspect of Jewish culture (as we read in the *Merchant of Venice*), making the whole thing alien and repulsive.

In giving his children the law, God repeatedly specifies that he is placing before them two ways, the ways of life and death, light and darkness. For parallel to the one law runs another. It is part of the plan that Satan should be allowed to try us and to tempt us to see whether we would prove faithful in all things: Who does not live up to every covenant made with the Lord will be in his power (cf. Moses 4:4, 5:23). So we find ourselves drawn in two directions (Moroni 7:11-13). Thus this life becomes a special test of probation set before us in this world—it is an economic one. If the law of consecration is the supreme test of virtue—the final one—money is to be the supreme temptation to vice; sex runs a poor second, but on both counts, this is the time and place for us to meet the challenge of the flesh. It is the weakness of the flesh in both cases to prove our spirits stronger than the pull of matter, to assert our command over the new medium of physical bodies before proceeding onward to another state of existence. As Brigham Young often repeats, "God has given us the things of this world to see what we will do with them." The test will be whether we will set our hearts on the four things that lead to destruction. Whoever seeks for (1) wealth, (2) power, (3) popularity, and (4) the pleasures of the flesh — anyone who seeks those will be destroyed, says the Book of Mormon (1 Nephi 22:23; 3 Nephi 6:15). Need we point out that those four things compose the whole substance of success in the present-day world. They are the things that money will get you.

Satan's power is over the flesh, over which he intended to take direct control. "Well, we'll just take control of their bodies directly." "No, you don't," said the Lord, and he set up a formidable barrier. "I will place enmity between thy seed and the serpent." It is the first line of defense, a natural revulsion one feels at the sight of a deadly serpent. You jump a mile high, whether it is poisonous or not. You don't take a chance; you move when you first see the snake. That is your first line of defense. Though a good one, it can be broken down; and just as you can do an end-run around that defense, you can also do it around the law of consecration. How can that obstacle be broken down? Satan boldly announced his clever plan to use that very enmity to his advantage and set men against each other by it in a rule of blood and horror. How? By offering men "anything in this world for money" and so making men competitive — competitive in a big way. He would, with the natural wealth of the earth (precious metals, coal, oil, timber, real estate), as exploited by financiers (manipulation of the money market), buy up armies and navies (they cost the most — the military-industrial complex), and the leaders of nations and churches (who embody power), and rule the earth with terror (a world at war is Satan's own dominion) (cf. D&C 1:35).

Failing to enlist Adam in this project, Satan approached Cain and taught him the basic principles of business: he took his fee, made him swear confidentiality, taught him how to get rich, and gave him the degree of Master Mahan, making him privy to the "great secret" of how to get the stuff. Cain wanted his brother's flocks (*pecus, Vieh, fee, ghani, qinyan,* etc. — all the oldest words for *money* simply mean flocks; our words *fee* and *pecuniary* mean flocks). So he murdered his brother Abel to get gain (Moses 5:50). An important part of the course was to overcome moral scruples; the real master of the game is necessarily a sociopath; he feels no qualms, admits no guilt, and easily defeats the polygraph. Cain, in fact, "gloried in that which he had done" (Moses 5:33). (It is not enough to just live with it, you have to glory in it. Then you feel all right. This was the big obstacle, and he gloried in it. And what gives him the moral right to glory? The greatest of all appeals — freedom. Freedom sanctifies all.) So Cain says, Now "I am free; surely the flocks of my brother fall into my hands" (Moses 5:33). He was free now, so he gloried in what he had done. His murder didn't bother him in the least. Thus when the Lord asked him, "Where is your brother Abel?" Cain said, "That is none of my business; he can take care of himself. If not, that is just too bad for him — he deserves what he gets" (cf. Moses 5:34). It's a dog-eat-dog world, says the entrepreneur who comforts his ruined investors with the magnanimous submission that life is unfair after all.

The "Mahan principle" is a frank recognition that the world's economy is based on the exchange of life for property. This is most apparent, of course, in time of war — a Catch-22. Today the biggest business in the world is the selling of deadly weapons by all to all, with the advantage going to the most efficient killing machines. Not long ago it was drugs, but it is all the same in a descending scale of accountability, where none is free from guilt: the hit man, soldier of fortune, weapons dealer, manufacturer, plundering whole species for raw materials, destroying life in both processing them and getting them (by pollution, dangerous work conditions, and so on), and by distributing them (additives, preservatives). The fearful processes of industry shorten and impoverish life at every level, from forced labor to poisonous air and water. This is the world's economy, for Satan is "the prince of this world" (John 12:31; 14:30; 16:11; D&C 127:11; cf. 2 Corinthians 4:4). The old law is carried on in the Book of Mormon. The Lachish Letters reflect the proper names, a movement restoring the law of Moses in Israel in the time of Lehi. (The Lachish Letters put us right in the picture, and *Mosiah* is a perfect name come down from Lehi's time to depict that movement, the restoration of the old Mosiac Law.) Did the Nephites accept the law of consecration? They did indeed, and so did the Lamanites. It achieved its purity and perfection when the Lord himself laid down the rules; they dropped all race distinctions and enjoyed a righteous society for two centuries. "They did not walk any more after the performances and ordinances of the law of Moses" (4 Nephi 1:12). Notice the terms *performances* and *ordinances*. They were rebuked because their whole law had become a law of ordinances and performances; they had left the spirit out. Now they walked no more by performances and ordinances, which had been considered adequate by the legalistic movement of the rabbis that took over. We know how they lived and had all their things in common. Fourth Nephi presents us with the law of consecration in its purity; it also describes the forces that broke it down.

Again and again we read in the Book of Mormon how "Satan had great power [over the people], . . . tempting them to seek for power, and authority, and riches" (3 Nephi 6:15). Well, that is his job. We will allow Satan, our common enemy, to try them and tempt them, and he uses the most efficient way. He says, "I'll try one way," and the Lord says, "No. I've checked you there." And he says, "I know another way that will really work." And the Lord lets him do that. Of course, and that is the way we are being tested—tempted to see if we'll seek wealth, popularity, power, and the pleasures of the flesh. We need not repeat the sophisticated arguments of Korihor (Alma 30), which are still in full force today, save to note that in the Book of Mormon we always hear the bells of Hades ringing whenever that fateful formula is intoned: "They began to set their hearts on riches."

During the Lord's earthly ministry, the rich young man who wished to enter the order of the disciples answered in the affirmative all preliminary questions as to his keeping of the commandments: "Not to murder, commit adultery, steal, bear false witness" (Matthew 19:16-18). He had honored his father and mother and loved his neighbor as himself, so he thought; what else was there to do? (Matthew 19:19-20). One thing more, said the Savior, to be perfect. The word *perfect* (*teleios*) does not mean perfect digestion, perfect eyesight, perfect memory, and so on; it is a special word meaning keeping the *whole* law. What remained for the young man, before he could be really serious (*teleios*), was keeping the law of consecration. If he did not keep that, he could not be perfect in keeping the others either, in other words, the *whole* law, for he could not become one of the Lord's disciples. So there was nothing but for Jesus to dismiss him—and a very sad occasion it was when they parted.

The Lord observed to the apostles that the rich just can't take it; nevertheless, any alternative plan, any proposal of compromise, easier payments, or tax write-offs, was out of the question. The Lord did not say, "Come back; perhaps we could make a deal." No, he had to let the young rich man go. One does not compromise on holy things. Unless we observe every promise we make in the endowment, we put ourselves in Satan's power. Christ's disciples were already observing the law, for Peter on that same occasion declared, "Behold, we have forsaken all, and followed thee; what shall we have therefore?" (Matthew 19:27). In reply he was given the most satisfying answer possible, being assured by the Lord that he was on the high road to salvation.

When Peter spoke to Adam, which Peter was it? The Peter of Adam's day? No, the timeless Peter. Satan had just introduced the question of money, asking Peter, "How much money do you have?" "We have enough," Peter replied—the apostles were observing the law of consecration. Enough was enough; more than enough was more than enough. No more was necessary. It is all right to have enough money to meet your needs. Satan had different ideas: "Oh, no, that is not enough. Everything in this world has a price, and with money you can buy it. You can have it all." It is the big money that traps people. That is why the law was rejected.

Incidentally, if the young rich man had earned his wealth, what had he *done* to earn it? Thousands of struggling students at Brigham Young University work harder than anyone would have to work under the law of consecration to make ends meet. Why do we pass them by and notice them not? Is it because of the chilling thought of being like them, or the equally chilling thought of being less rich than we really are? This is the question. Ah, yes, but if you gave these students much more than they have, they would be less spiritual. Is that really so? As long as that condition continues, why should there be a school for the sole purpose of students preparing themselves? It is becoming the only purpose for which anyone attends school anymore. This is a new trend of just the past few years. They go not to get an education but to learn to acquire wealth, to earn more money. Students think there is something idealistic about that because they sacrifice for a time.

The Law Rejected

We need not go into detail to define the law of consecration (as contained in the Doctrine and Covenants) and its implementation. "No revelation that was ever given is more easy of comprehension than that on the law of consecration," said Brigham Young; and he tells us what it is:

> When the Lord spoke to Joseph, instructing him to counsel the people to consecrate their possessions, and deed them over to the Church in a covenant that cannot be broken, would the people listen to it? No, but they began to find out that they were mistaken, and had only acknowledged with their mouths that the things which they possessed were the Lord's.[3]

> It was one of the first commandments or revelations given to this people after they had the privilege of organizing themselves as a Church, as a body, as the kingdom of God on earth. I observed then, and I now think, [as Moses says] that it will be one of the last revelations which the people will receive into their hearts and understandings, of their own free will and choice and esteem it as a pleasure, a privilege, and a blessing unto them to observe and keep most holy.[4]

Notice that these things are the minimum requirements of the law of Moses, namely, to observe it with all the heart and soul, and to rejoice and be glad in doing so. But it is the last thing the Saints will observe, as Brigham Young said, "as a privilege and a pleasure."[5] Twenty years later, President Young said before the Saints at conference:

> The great duty that rested upon the saints is to put in operation God's purposes with regard to the United Order, by the consecration of the private wealth to the common good of the people. The underlying principle of the United Order is that there should be no rich and no poor, that men's talents should be used for the common good, and that selfish interests should make way for a more benevolent and generous spirit among the saints.[6]

The spirit is all that counts. In response, "The whole

assembly [of the Priesthood] voted to renew their covenants, and later the Presidency, the Twelve, the Seventies, and the Presiding Bishopric were baptized and entered into a special covenant to observe the rules of the United Order. . . . This movement became general throughout the Church."[7]

It was nothing else but the old law that had been given long ago to Moses, but it did not last any more than it lasted in Israel. So today, we accept it or reject it as we want, but we cannot temporize or dissemble it. "Said the Lord to Joseph, 'See if they will give their farms to me.' What was the result? *They would not do it.* . . . The Lord makes them [the people] well by His power, through the ordinances of His house [the temple where the agreement was made], but will they consecrate? No. They say, 'It is mine and I will have it myself.' There is the treasure, and the heart is with it."[8] So spoke Brigham Young soon after the exodus from Nauvoo.

Arguments and Objections

Brigham Young was perfectly familiar with all the economic arguments and protestations. But for him they were all forestalled by the knowledge that after accepting the law of sacrifice, any further objections were out of the question. We have noted that the covenants of the endowment are progressively more binding, in the sense of allowing less and less latitude for personal interpretation as one advances. Thus (1) the law of God is general and mentions no specifics; (2) the law of obedience states that specific orders are to be given and observed; (3) the law of sacrifice still allows a margin of interpretation (this is as far as the old law goes—the Aaronic Priesthood carries out the law of sacrifice and no farther; and it specifies that while sacrifice is a solemn obligation on all, it is up to the individual to decide just how much he will give); (4) the law of chastity, on the other hand, is something else; here

442   APPROACHING ZION

at last we have an absolute, bound by a solemn sign; (5) finally the law of consecration is equally uncompromising—*everything* the Lord has given one is to be consecrated. This law is bound by the firmest token of all.

The first objection to the law of consecration is that it runs counter to the spirit of the times. Our people are so conditioned as to view any substantive sharing of the wealth with great suspicion. When Scott Nearing bought a farm in Vermont for $2,200 and the opening of a ski resort nearby raised the value to $6,000,000, the Nearings, opposed to any form of exploitation or unearned income, gave the property to the town of Winhall for a town forest or park. The town meeting expressed not a single word of gratitude for the gift, though they accepted it; and many accused Mr. Nearing of being a Communist for dealing so lightly with natural property.[9] Yet in our society today, people can deed everything they have to anything or anybody, from a cat to an asylum or orchestra, and nobody raises any objection.

One of the most common objections to the law of consecration is that it imposes a sameness on the members of our society, the uniformity of the ant-heap. Uniformity, sameness. The drive to Salt Lake City used to be a pleasant ride to a fascinating city. Now it could be any ugly urban sprawl in the world except that it has more billboards than any other area (Orrin Hatch being the great backer of the billboards). We used to enjoy the fields and the mountains, but now when we come to Salt Lake City (which I rarely do now), we are staggered by the absolute uniformity—the city is absolutely blocked in by buildings, all the same style, all from the same drawing board, with the Church Office Building in the lead. Brigham Young said that he never built two houses alike, but here uniformity is the law, because it's economical and convenient. Every prophet of the Church down to Spencer W. Kimball pleaded for the Saints to make Zion beautiful, but it becomes uglier every time you make the drive.

Recently on a visit to Heber City, I was amazed to see that the town had the appearance of a multinational sales convention. Like the other Utah towns that once had such color and personality, the marks of the old pioneer culture—the stake houses, chapels, bishop's storehouses—have nearly all been torn down, to be replaced by more efficient, mass-produced structures. As you travel you see only the same multinational brand names, the same Texaco, Holiday Inn, K-Mart. And if you go in the store, you see exactly the same things being sold, the same brands in all the stores; in the cities throughout the world, the same high rises, airports, traffic-glutted smoggy sameness. One city is like another, whether it's a Nairobi or an Ogden. Even in our yearning to escape to nature, business takes over, as at Bear Lake and Park City—condominiums bumper to bumper, the wilderness partitioned into small, expensive tracts so that each can have his private wilderness surrounded by a high Cyclone Fence for his own security. One citizen (Roselie Sorrells) notes, "I think there's a giant conspiracy on the part of—who? ITT or them?—the rich, the powerful, the manipulators, to make us all the same. Make sure that we watch a lot of television. Make sure that we all have credit cards and cars and houses that are all kind of sleazy."[10] Does sameness depress you? The heavenly hosts, so we are told, all wear the same simple white garment—how monotonous! We all dress alike in the temple. Are you depressed to be there? No, the difference is in the person himself. It shines through as the individual spirit. The Father and the Son glowed exactly alike. Why doesn't one wear black and the other wear green or something like that? No. It is the outward sameness that allows inward sameness, the spirit, to shine through. Such monotony is put to shame by the multi-billion-dollar fashion industry of our times. The difference is that in heaven it is the individual spirit that shines through. What do we see in the temple, when we are all dressed alike? We must go out to the parking lot to assert our individuality in Mercedes, Cadillacs, and so forth. And which is the more depressing picture? The gaudy display of vanity fair is an attempt to cover up the spiritual and intellectual barrenness of the present world we live in.

Another objection is that the law of consecration would not deal fairly in rewarding each according to his needs and no more. No fairness? "Why does it always come," asks Senator Abourzek, "that two hundred million people sacrifice and fifty-thousand at the top are never called upon to sacrifice?"[11] Karl Hess, the busiest Republican speech writer of our time, and the principal formulator of the National Party Platform of 1960, has protested: "I don't know why in the world West Virginia miners should put up with people in Palm Beach owning the stuff they work on. Why? It doesn't make sense. I understand that it's legal, but legal does not necessarily mean right." It is not fair. In any sacrament meeting, you can hear young people get up and tell what a struggle they are having living on practically nothing, and yet the Lord has seen them through, and they are joyful and happy in it. That is a good thing. We say, Well, we can't give up anything or we'll have to suffer. Could we suffer any more, or even that much under the law of consecration? We see it happening: the Lord does give the blessings.

These statements touch on another point, the sacred work ethic — "There is no free lunch," and so on. Will the law of consecration leave us with nothing to do? It's a funny thing. We think there is something heroic about working our way through college. Actually the work that students do there isn't a tenth as hard as work they would do if they really studied. It's hard work. College is practically a handout. Is money or things money can buy the only thing one can work for? That's the new code at

Brigham Young University — why do you study? Because it's going to make you more money. It was the whole teaching of Brigham Young that the law was adorable because there are so many other and better things to do than simply accumulate goods.

"The cares of the world" (D&C 40:12), said the Lord, have taken many away from the real path, the real work, for the cares of the world quickly become our sole concern. Brigham's favorite word for Satan's trick was "decoy"[12] — the work ethic decoys us away from the work we *should* be doing. Mammon is a jealous god and will not tolerate a competitor. But we get the idea that the only virtues are business virtues. Consider the qualities you need to be a successful businessman. You should have persistence, reliability, a measure of courage, hard work, and all the rest of it, but those qualities are the same required in any other profession; to be an athlete or musician, a scientist, or an international jewel thief, you need those same qualities in far higher degrees than you do to succeed in business. We are told now there are almost a million millionaires in the country. Does it take a genius to become rich? How many first-class artists are there? You can count them. How many Nobel Laureates and so forth? You can count them on the fingers of your hand. Yet the country swarms with millionaires. The virtue is the virtue of getting ahead. Of course that's the virtue in any field. We make it seem as if that fact obliges a person to go into business — because this is where it counts, because then you possess these qualities. Anyone knows that cheating pays off very well in this country.

But the solid businessman will of course protest that the law of consecration is impractical. After all, men are not really created equal. But why did God give some superior advantages? Answer: to put their time, talents, and so on at the disposal of their less fortunate brethren, as God himself does when he makes it his work and his glory to exalt us lowly creatures (Moses 1:38-39). If the law of consecration is impractical, so is tithing, and so are the time and inconvenience of meetings and endowment sessions. But is it impractical? Which of the two makes the real mischief? One often hears the argument "If all the wealth in the world were divided up equally, nobody would have very much." True, but the average person would be much richer than today, and no one would be hard up. Ah, but there would be no big capital to invest, no giant industry to supply the wants of the world. This is a cultural argument: if the present order of things passed away, what would happen? It was the plea of the medieval barons that if the lord of the manor didn't own everything and keep all in strict subjection, there would be no great lords to fight the other great lords who were trying to subject their people. When God says, "I have a plan," it is pointless to speculate on whether it is practical or whether it will work or not, for in agreeing to abide by it, we have voted to accept his judgment. The decision is closed—this quite apart from the fact that practical economists are the most completely certain of all leaders and the most often completely wrong.

Perhaps the most common excuse for holding us back is that the plan is premature. It was restored by Elijah, who brought the temple ordinances, declaring in his opening words to the Prophet Joseph: "The time has fully come!" (D&C 110:14). Brigham Young, speaking at St. George in 1876 on the purposes of the temple, said:

> Some of our Elders, and, in fact, some of the Twelve will tell you, "Yes, yes, the Order is a splendid principle and will bring happiness, etc., but it is not hardly time to enter into it, wait a little while until the people understand it a little better." Why, they are fools! They don't know what they talk about. They have ears to hear and will not hearken, and have eyes to see and will not understand. . . . When our conduct hedges up the way

of angels how can they bless us? How can they help us to work out our salvation? . . . When Joseph Smith was alive I can say that I never heard him lay one plan out for the people but [that] would have been a success if it had been carried out as he directed. And I have seen the same in myself. I don't care how the world goes, what the President (of the U.S.) or his emissaries do. It matters nothing to me. What I am thinking of and interested about is how do the Latter-day Saints do? . . . The devil is in the community and he has not been turned out. Well, I still have hope in Israel.[13]

Today we suggest *compromises*. We are perfectly willing to put the law of consecration into practice just as soon as the rest of the world is ready to receive it—otherwise the world might not approve of our action. But the law was not designed for the world; compromise is out of the question: "Zion cannot be built up unless it is by the principles of the law of the celestial kingdom; otherwise I cannot receive her unto myself" (D&C 105:5). "I give not unto you that ye shall live after the manner of the world" (D&C 95:13). However praiseworthy, giving through a foundation is not a device to implement the law of consecration, but a contrivance to evade it. I knew well a bishop, Charles W. Nibley, my grandfather, who had a standard appeal for tithing. I was sort of his favorite grandson, the only one that ever stayed at his house. We had long talks together, and of course, he was quite successful in his day. We talked a lot about all these things. What he said stayed with me, believe me. His argument—and he was using it throughout the Church in conferences and I remember it well—was that after you had paid the Lord 10 percent, you still have 90 percent for yourself, all yours to do with as you pleased. That can never be tithed; the Lord can't touch it. He gets only 10 percent and leaves you with all the rest.

There is quite a difference between consecrating 10

percent of your net gain to the building up of the kingdom and consecrating your time, talents, and everything you have been blessed with up to this time to the building up of the kingdom of God. Tithing is no part of consecration, though it is an eternal law. There is no conflict here; the law of consecration demands everything you have, but at the same times it fills your every physical need; and it is from that sustaining income, from that substance, that you pay your tithes. This makes it a genuine sacrifice and not a mere token offering skimmed off from a net increase that you will never miss.

The Two Cultures

Our difficulty with the law of consecration is a cultural one; since the days of Cain and Abel men have been pulled in two opposite directions, given a choice between two ways, representing what some have called "the mad force of the sun and the wise force of the earth." The two contrasting cultures may be characterized as stable or stationary on the one hand, and acquisitive or expansive on the other hand—eternal vs. temporary, agrarian vs. hunting, cooperative vs. competitive, contemplative vs. execrated, seeking either wisdom or riches, and so on (D&C 6:7). The law of consecration is that of a stable society; the law of the marketplace is that of an expansive, acquisitive, brittle, untrustworthy, predatory society.

Today we are treated in many TV documentaries to the natural operation of the primal or predatory culture. Everything in the jungle is on the prowl, to eat or escape being eaten. Half the human race has been permanently engaged in such activities—nomadic, predatory, military. Cain went off to the land of Nod, which means he became a Nomad; and his great descendant, Nimrod, established that order in which man lives by conquest. The drive behind such activities is a perfectly natural one, justified as a tendency to growth. The doctrine as we hear it on every side is that if we do not grow, we must perish. It is not enough for the economy to hold its own, the Gross National Product must constantly increase, which means manufacturing must expand and consumption increase, demand must increase, nothing must relax lest everything contract and collapse. Says the president of a large American corporation (Rock of Ages):

> Let's face it, if we don't grow and get more profit, there isn't any more money for raises, there aren't promotions for people. If you don't grow, you don't buy more products from your suppliers. You don't have new machines, you don't give more and better products to your customers. . . . I can make a case for hurting God because there isn't more money for the collection plate. The American dream is to be better off than you are. How much money is "enough money"? "Enough money" is always a little bit more than you have. There is never enough of anything. This is why people go on. If there was enough everybody would stop. . . . You must go for more — for faster, for better. If you are not getting better and faster, you are getting worse.[14]

The mandatory state of mind for success is that of Mr. Wallace Rasmussen, president of none other than Beatrice, a corporate supergiant that has contributed so much to our diet in the way of additives and preservatives: "I never wanted to be a loser. I always wanted to be the first one off the airplane. . . . People would say they saw me on the street and I didn't say hello. I was thinking about something else. It isn't my nature to be friendly. . . . It comes down to — who's gonna be the survivor? . . . Trust everybody with reservations. . . . I was reading about people who were successful and how they did it. That was basically all my reading."[15] In closing, the interviewer adds that Rasmussen "doesn't allow anybody to do to Wallace Rasmussen what he has done to others."[16] In a more pleasant vein, but no less clearly, does Mr. Arnold Schwarzenegger proclaim the doctrine: "I learned English and then started taking business courses, because that's what America is best known for: business. Turning one dollar into a million dollars in a short period of time. . . . I have emotions. But what you do, you keep them cold or you store them away for a time. . . . This is sometimes called selfish. It's the only way you can be if you want to achieve something."[17] "California . . . is the absolute combination of everything I was always looking for. It has all the money in the world there. . . . You have beautiful-looking people there. They all have a tan. . . . I am a strong believer in Western philosophy, the philosophy of success, of progress, of getting rich."[18] For better or for worse, such is indeed the philosophy of acquisition, expansion, exploitation — energetic and competitive, and admirable in ways as Homeric heroes are admirable, but inevitably ending as Homeric heroes end, doomed, as we shall see later.

The stable society is equally ancient, and of course no community is completely the one or the other. The glorious Old Kingdom of Egypt, which saw the peak of its civilization, leaves no evidence whatever of military aggression or expansion, whereas the New Kingdom (Asiatic Kings) was explosively acquisitive. I had welcome opportunity to study a stable civilization in my frequent visits to the Hopis in the 1940s and 1950s. During the Great Depression there was a federal project to pipe and pump up the water from the springs below to the top of the First Mesa. The Indians emphatically rejected the proposal. The carrying of water by the women from the spring to their houses was a time-honored ritual, an important social function, an integral part of the way things were done and had always been done. But that way, the agent protested, they would never progress. Progress to what? The great industrial civilization that offered to show them how things were to be done at that time was on the verge of collapse (it was the Works Progress Administration that wanted to build the pump), seized with wild disarray and hysteria. Yet during those same years the Hopis were as well off as ever; they had carried on there for at least a thousand years, and now they were expected to give all that up? Carrying water, putting corn in the ground, weaving blankets or baskets, making pottery, grinding corn at the matate, making piki or dyes, seeking herbs, nuts, feathers, rare clays in the washes — all was part of a single organized activity, thoughtfully and prayerfully pursued, but not without much fun and laughter on the side. And of course everyone had to be at the dances. "What a bore!" we would say. But it was not. I always looked forward to going down there because everybody had such a good time. And I never saw people work so hard — but not for money. "If one of us has corn," they said, "we all have corn"; and they worked very, very hard, for we had left them nothing to live on but dry sand. What impressed me more than anything else was that their weekly dances and ceremonies to which everyone looked forward with eager anticipation followed most exactly, even to astonishing details, the doings of the Greeks, and the Egyptians, yes, and the Israelites, the most stable and the most productive societies, those that have given us our history, our culture to this day, those to which we owe our civilization, those that have given us our history (Chinese and Indian religions), and the one to which we owe our whole civilization. This thing goes on and on for thousands of years, apparently without "progress." Sister Maria Harvey's house was the first one they ever tried out the tree-ring dating on. That's at Walpi, beyond the first Mesa, and her house is eight hundred to eleven hundred years old. It's been standing there, and the Hopis have been doing the same things, for eleven hundred years. It goes on, it at least survives. With nothing to live on, you say. All we see on the mesa is rock and dry sand.

But where among the Hopis is the progress, then? Do

they progress? It is exciting and marvelous to see progress in the learning experience of each generation. As an unceasing stream of children enter the scene, they must learn it all from the beginning, and for them it is as fresh and new as the world in the creation, and nothing is more delightful to their elders than to teach them and watch them learn and grow while the teachers themselves discover wonder upon wonder, more than a lifetime can contain, both in the world around them and in the contemplative depths of their own minds. For these people, who seem to us to be stuck in a rut, the world is always changing, for they move with the miracle of the year and the revolutions of the heavens from one ambience to another. And beauty swallows them up all the time. They revel in it. They have to express themselves in prayer as they go out to their fields or come back. And this is common to all the great civilizations of the past. To endure long enough to make a contribution, a culture had to be stable. In bad times of world crisis caused by major climatic changes, many were forced to become marauding nomads, the hordes of the steppes, the expansive warriors who made their final camp the capital of the world and sought to spread their empires over all people as their divine calling. Of course, that is the Roman heritage, and our heritage too.

We have the two cultures, and between them mortal enmity. You can't compromise between them. For the hordes of the steppes feel it their sacred obligation to extend their domination over all who have not yet been subdued, for such, of course, are potential enemies who, having rebuffed the invitation to surrender, are now in a state of open rebellion and must be made to do the will of God. So it's the world, divided into the two camps, each trying to swallow up the other. That was the Roman dictum. The whole world was either *ager pacatus,* pacified and broken to the will of Rome, or *ager hosticus,* that is, unsubmissive and rebellious, and therefore the mandatory object of conquest. God wants the world to live in peace, so we cannot live with those people on our borders. "The calling of Rome was to rule from the rivers [the natural boundaries] to the ends of the earth—*imperium Oceano, famam qui termine astris*"; this was the formula that makes sure that the lands from the ends of the earth *qui terminet* ("which end") and the renowned Rome will end only with the stars, and the *imperium* will end only where the land ends. *Pax Romana* ("Roman peace") assured that none would molest or make afraid, in other words, threaten Roman holdings.[19] This is the formula followed in the world since.

This is not a mere indifference to or distaste for each other that separates the two cultures, but a vivid antipathy. There is a powerful enmity between them, and this again can best be expressed in what goes on with the Hopis. The president of a firm that supplies equipment for coal and oil companies wrote a letter in January (less than a year ago [1985]) to the Navajo Tribal Council, protesting preferential treatment in the hiring of their own people to work on their own reservation: "Given the historical facts, we consider ourselves to be members of the conquering and superior race and you to be members of the vanquished and inferior race. . . . [The law of Moses strictly forbade the Jews to engage in such activities (Deuteronomy 2:4-5).] Through the generosity of our people, you have been given a reservation where you may prance and dance as you please, obeying your kings and worshipping your false gods." There was no public outcry when the statement was published, and the writer, Ronald Vetrees, said he had no regrets about sending the letter.[20] The Mormons learned, especially in 1906, at Moencopi that "it was government policy to aid missionaries [of other churches] in converting the Indians to one or another of the Christian denominations," using, among other things, the well-known "Religious Crimes Codes" that curtailed the Indi-

an's freedom of religion. Albert W. Fall, the Secretary of
the Interior in 1921, enacted a regulation that "although
aimed particularly at the Sun Dance, concluded that 'all
similar dances and so-called religious ceremonies, shall be
considered "Indian offenses," ' punishable by 'incarcera-
tion in the agency prison.' "[21] As we all know, Secretary
Fall went to prison for high crimes committed in office. In
1923, Commissioner Charles H. Burke softened the sentence in an edict to all Indians: "I could issue an order
against these useless and harmful performances, but I
would much rather have you give them up of your own
free will. . . . I urge you . . . to hold no gatherings in the
months when the seedtime, cultivation and harvest need
your attention [as did Israel], and at other times to meet
for only a short period and to have . . . no dancing that
the superintendent does not approve. If at the end of one
year the reports . . . show that you reject this plea, then
some other course will have to be taken."[22] But these gatherings have been precisely the way the Indians survived.
They have kept them going, kept their spirits up, kept the
economics permanent. It's heartbreaking to go to the reservations now.

    When uranium, oil, and coal were discovered on these
reservations, originally given to the Indians as their last
holding since the land was considered absolutely worthless, the heat was on. In 1985 lawyers of the coal companies
severely rebuked the Navajos for wishing to raise the roy-
alties they were getting for their coal to more than fifteen
cents a ton; in righteous wrath the lawyers lectured the
natives on the sacredness of a contract and the need to
keep one's word under all circumstances and not be carried
away by barbaric greed—and that for not being satisfied
with fifteen cents a ton for coal by plundering from their
land amid scenes of appalling ruin and destruction, mer-
ciless strip-mining with machines ten stories high. The *New*

York Times went out of its way to point out that the lawyers in question were *Mormons*. There is which side we're on.

Today, Hopis and Navajos alike are being driven from Navajo Mountain (this is going on right now), the most sacred place of all for those people, for it has turned out to contain rich coal deposits. For some years the lawyers have stirred up such a tangle of legal complications for claims to the land that they can now declare that the Indians are incapable of managing their own affairs, and both tribes must leave it. Recently, I heard Barry Goldwater declare over PBC that as commander of the Arizona National Guard, he would come in with his helicopter gunships, running interference for the coal companies or Peabody, to make sure the Indians put up no resistance in being removed from their ancient lands which they held by sacred treaties with the United States. There is a prophecy that if and when the white man seizes Navajo Mountain, from that moment his fortunes will turn forever downward. As the Book of Mormon puts it, "From this time forth did the Nephites gain no power over the Lamanites, but began to be swept off by them, even as the dew before the sun" (Mormon 4:18). Rome died not with a bang, but with a whisper. All such civilizations do. They just sort of fade out, when the Lord has withdrawn his spirit. It doesn't take great wars, calamities, or anything else. Rostovzeff wrote a very good economic history of Rome, and interest fell on the same thing. Everybody in the empire suddenly lost their balance. A fatty degeneration *in drag*. Nobody did anything right. Nobody could rely on anything. The whole thing just fell apart. It wasn't the barbarian invasion.

I was present some years ago when one of the giant multinationals offered to move the whole Hopi population to Los Angeles and provide them all with mobile homes. Isn't that better, they argued, than all this primitive, toilsome planting and chanting, dancing, and prancing? Before that I also traveled with an apostle who fervidly argued with Indians the advantages of TV and washing machines over the age-old rounds of ceremonial dancing and visits to the sacred spring: Give up all that out-of-date stuff, he pleaded, and accept the blessings of the modern world. For the one thing that makes the acquisitive culture appeal to the ordinary mortal is the promise of *convenience*. With the best intentions in the world, we think we are relieving those who live under a sort of ancient consecration of all sorts of inconveniences. It's not convenient to go the temple. Lots of things aren't convenient, though it's very interesting that at the same time, we praise the importance of the work ethic, of work for its own sake—talk about inconvenient. Think of banging away with a hammer all day just to straighten nails that will be of no use whatever for building. Is that inconvenient? Is that saving effort? Oh! That's the work ethic. That's an example of hard work we should hold up to our children and so forth. But is that convenient, I ask? Which program is the more convenient? In all sincerity we have tried to appeal to the Indians on that basis, which shows how completely committed we are to the one culture alone.

Incidentally, we need not decide to join either Peabody Enterprise, on the one hand, or the snake dance on the other. The Hopis have always classified the Mormons as a special culture of their own: there are the Hopi, and *Bahami* or white man, and the *Momona*, Mormons, who are neither the one or the other but contain some of the qualities of both, with strong leanings to the Hopi way, but with strong tendency to offend the Indian agents. The Hopis readily embraced the gospel at first hearing it; they maintain that they will join us in Zion as soon as we start living the gospel. And many of them did join, as you know. In the days when the Mormons joined hands with the Indians, and the government agents and sectarian ministers went all out to break it up, "a woman from the LDS knocks on my door," says an Indian woman. "I'm gracious and I invite her in, because that's our way. She says: 'Oh, look at all your pretty children. Oh, what a nice family. I see that your roof leaks and your house is a little cold and you don't have sanitation. By the looks of your kitchen, you don't have much food, and I notice that you have very little furniture. You don't have running water, and you have an outdoor toilet. And the nearest school is sixty miles away. Wouldn't you like your children to go and live in a nice house, where they'll have their own bedrooms, wonderful people who care about them, lots of money to buy food, indoor plumbing, posturepedic mattresses and Cannon sheets, and wonderful television sets, and well-landscaped yards? Etc., etc. . . . And then she says, 'If you reeeeally, reeeeally love your children, you wouldn't want them to live like this. You would want them to have all the good things they need.' And that mother thinks: [Oh], I love my children and what a monster I am! How can I possibly keep them from this paradise?"[23]

This is a fair picture. What is wrong with it? The LDS woman has nothing to offer but *conveniences,* what the scriptures call "the world" in its strictest sense. The work is commendable here. At least here are some people willing to inconvenience themselves in the interest of others, while sincerely believing that it's in the best interest of the others. But they are at the same time condescending and patronizing, giving no thought to the idea that the Indians may have something just as good as we have or better.

The cultural confrontation is fundamental to understanding the law of consecration. Which of the two cultures is nearer to the law of consecration? There can be no doubt: Do temple ordinances change from year to year? Do we all wear individual and fashionably changing styles of clothes there? What gave Egypt its matchless stability was Pharaoh's "seeking earnestly to imitate that order established by the fathers in the first generations, in the days of the first patriarchal reign [the *Paat*], even in the reign of Adam" (Abraham 1:26). They always sought that, and it produced a tremendous stability, centering around the temple. The genius of stable societies is that they achieve stability without stagnation, repetition without monotony, conformity with originality, obedience with liberty. The Egyptian civilization reached its peak at the very beginning when it was thought to be a faithful and unchanging imitation of heaven; on the other hand, each of the rulers of the New Kingdom (in the eighteenth dynasty), seized by Asiatic invaders, boasts that he expands the boundaries of Egypt and excels all his predecessors in their building operations, war roads and everything else, and so the bubble grows and grows and inevitably bursts. What makes one hesitate before conversion to consecration is the absolute and uncompromising nature of the decision. Must it be one or the other all the way? I am afraid it must. Countless books on how to succeed in the world all come down to one basic principle, that total dedication to making money is the secret and the only secret. Mammon is a jealous god, and so is the true God; he is unwilling to let you decide your allegiance to him, as the real God is; and there is a distinctly religious note in his cult with its company hymns, prayers, breakfasts, sermons, and homilies. We should have respect for such piety, were it not for the assurance that absolute lifelong loyalty to the company can be canceled in an instant by a better offer from another company.

A Rock of Offense

As to the uncompromising nature of the choice we must make, it is a stumbling block indeed. Brigham Young says:

> The man or woman who enjoys the spirit of our religion has no trials; but the man or woman who tries to live according to the gospel of the Son of God, *and at the same time* clings to the spirit of the world, has trials and sorrows acute and keen, and that too, continually. This is the deciding point, the dividing line. They who

love and serve God with all their hearts rejoice evermore, pray without ceasing, and in everything give thanks; but they who try to serve God and still cling to the spirit of the world have got on two yokes — the yoke of Jesus and the yoke of the devil, and they will have plenty to do. They will have a warfare inside and outside, and the labor will be very galling, for they are directly in opposition one to the other.[24]

Speaking to the Mormon Battalion in 1848, he warned them, "If we were to go to San Francisco and dig up chunks of gold or find it here in the valley, it would ruin us. Many wanted to unite Babylon and Zion; it is the love of money that hurts them."[25] "Shall we now seek to make ourselves wealthy in gold and silver and the possessions which the wicked love and worship, or shall we, with all of our might, mind, and strength, seek diligently first to build up the Kingdom of God? Let us decide on this, and *do one thing or the other.*"[26]

From the outset the choice was clear: "Seek not for riches but for wisdom, and behold [mutually exclusive] the mysteries of God shall be unfolded unto you, and then you shall be made rich. Behold, he that hath eternal life is rich" (D&C 6:7). The two are mutually exclusive, but to satisfy our desire for riches, we are told that we may indeed seek them, but only the true riches of eternal life. Who would want anything else? A young man of my acquaintance who has majored in business, and at an early age made a good deal of money, recently decided to study something else for a change, the things he had really been yearning for all his life. When he announced his intention to his stake president, the man was furious: "Do you mean to tell me that you are going to be spinning your wheels reading books instead of making money?" Here was enmity indeed: anyone who was making money was fulfilling the measure of his existence; he who has made money has already fulfilled his calling and has no further obligation —

in fact, the whole virtue of money is that it frees one from any feeling of obligation to anyone, so says Malcolm Forbes. So he gets a magazine out on the subject. Competitiveness always rests on the assumption of a life-and-death struggle: "There is no free lunch" is the clarion cry. The name of the game is survival — a dirty word; we hear it a lot. It means to still be on the scene after everyone else has been wiped out. John Chrysostom tells how in his city of Antioch just before the great earthquake a common joke went around the town, with everybody saying, "I wish there would be an earthquake and kill everybody in Antioch but me, and then I would be the richest man in the city." Well, they got their earthquake, and Antioch was never rebuilt. The chairman of the board of one of the biggest banks in the nation, Gaylord Freeman, says, "Business is so *#!$ competitive! The head of a business is really competing . . . with your friends in other businesses, your dearest friends."[27] "My good friend Milton Friedman [whose word is gospel at the BYU] says the worst thing is for a businessman to feel responsible to society. He says that's a lot of baloney, and it's contrary to the businessman's assignment."[28] As the head of Beatrice has said, "If you're going to be successful, you can't let any person stand in the way."[29]

There is a Jewish legend of how when the waters of the flood began to rise, the people took their children into their arms to protect them. As the water rose higher, they placed their little ones on their shoulders above the water level. When it rose still higher, they held them on their heads; but when the water level continued to rise, they placed them under their feet to save themselves.[30]

In the end you are competing with everyone, or as everyone was saying when I was young, "Self-preservation is the first law of nature," a doctrine that justifies the commission of any possible crime in the name of survival. Nobody loves the rat race, but nobody can think of anything else—Satan has us just where he wants us. Also when I was young it was assumed that anyone seeking knowledge was willing to pay the highest price and go without the luxuries of life, and for years without even the necessities (that isn't so anymore), out of his pure love of learning. How the scene has shifted. People were horrified when General Barrows, at the time president of the University of California at Berkeley, bluntly proclaimed at a commencement exercise, "The only reason anyone goes to college is to increase his earning power." I was petrified by the statement, little realizing that the time would come that it would be treated by everyone as a universally accepted truism and even an idealistic proclamation.

You say, well, if you're not in business, then what are you supposed to be doing? It is, as usual, Brigham Young who puts things into perspective: "Will education feed and clothe you, keep you warm on a cold day, or enable you to build a house? Not at all. Should we cry down education on this account? No. What is it for? The improvement of the *mind;* to instruct us in all the arts and sciences, in the history of the world, in the laws of . . . how to be useful while we live."[31] Useful here and fulfilling hereafter. "Truth, wisdom, power, glory, light and intelligence exist upon their own qualities; they do not, neither can they, exist upon any other principle. Truth is congenial with itself, and light cleaves unto light." (Brigham is a marvelous man. Here's a man who went to school eleven days, yet he's the best master of English prose we have, and he saw the light on every side.) "It is the same with knowledge, and virtue, and all eternal attributes; they follow after each other. . . . Truth cleaves unto truth *because* it is truth; and it is to be adored, because it is an *attribute* of *God,* for its *excellence,* for *itself.*"[32] There can be no ulterior motive in the study of heavenly things: "Knowledge Is Power" is the slogan of a rascally world. "What do you love truth for? Is it . . . because you think it will make you a ruler,

or a Lord? If you conceive that you will attain to power
upon such a motive, you are much mistaken. It is a trick
of the unseen power, that is abroad amongst the inhabitants of the earth, that leads them astray, binds their
minds, and subverts their understanding."[33]

"Men and brethren, what shall we do?" (Acts 2:37).
That is the question. I asked my students, "If you were
granted one thousands years of life with whatever worldly
means you might request, what would you plan to do?"
This is precisely the situation in which the Latter-day Saint
finds himself; the answer would be the same if the grant
were for only a hundred or fifty years. The opening chapters of the Doctrine and Covenants are taken up with an-
swering that question for various new members of the
Church, telling each brother what he is to do at the moment. Our patriarchal blessings assume that we are looking
farther afield. It is certain that in this world, especially in
the acquisitive and expanding world, we are not going
anywhere, but throwing our lives away. "Be wise in the
days of your probation" (Mormon 9:28). A highly successful corporation president said,

> One of the great tragedies of American business life
> is what happens to talented executives who dedicate
> their lives to the company, who are successful and part
> of a system that is so bad. I didn't take the company
> from a million-dollar loss to a million-dollar profit with-
> out hurting a lot of people. . . . You do to others, and
> then it is done unto you. . . . One morning, I found my
> own resignation on my desk. Absolutely no reason was
> given. I didn't know what to think. . . . I left immedi-
> ately. That was part of the deal. They used the same
> formula I had used. You do to others, and then it's done
> unto you. . . . You begin to wonder about this capitalism
> you preached, the profit motive. I used to tell young
> executives the name of the game is profit. You wonder
> whose game it really is. . . . Our profit system, the one

we all live by, is presented as a fun game for young people training to be managers. If you can reduce the time it takes to do something, you increase the profit. Growth and investors' happiness are based on this. You can expand your facilities . . . that's why America is the land of *plenty* [a bitter note]. I'm so *proud* of the system, . . . that we all have television sets and cars and pollution and everything. There's no place like it.[34]

He found himself out of work. He had gone nowhere.

Historical

Historical commentary has been suggested on the subject. The first thing to notice is that the law of consecration has no historical development; the issues are perennial. We like to think that we are living under special conditions today—our economy, the product of the Industrial Revolution, and its philosophy formulated by the Scottish economists. But in every age the same lines are drawn. I recently made a study of some of the great Utopians of the past; all faced exactly the same situation that we face today. In the prehistoric days for Lycurgus, "There was," Plutarch tells us, "an intolerable inequality, with swarms of impoverished and helpless people burdening the city while all the wealth had been concentrated in the hands of the few; arrogance, and envy and crime, and luxury prevailed, and the fundamental cause of this chronic social disease was the wide gap between wealth and poverty."[35] Solon, the great contemporary of Lehi and the father of democracy, described the Athens of his day: "The ruin of our state will never come by the doom of Zeus. . . . It is the townsfolk themselves and their false-hearted leaders who would fain destroy our great city through wantonness and love of money. . . . They are rich because they yield to the temptation of dishonest courses. . . . They spare neither the treasure of the gods nor the property of the state, and steal like brigands one from another."[36] The root of the matter, he says, is that "no visible limit is set to wealth among men. Even now those among us who have the largest fortune are striving with redoubled energy."[37] Plato sees in this situation the doctrine of the Two Ways: "Perhaps you have seen wicked men growing old and leaving their children's children in high office, and their success shakes your faith. You have seen crooks become heads of state, hailed as the great men of their time, and that leads you to conclude that the gods are not particularly interested in what goes on here."[38] In the end he says it all comes down to "that immortal conflict which is going on within us."[39] No system will procure happiness unless "the soul is perfectly qualified to be carried to a higher and better place which is perfect in holiness."[40] The monastic movement was started by St. Anthony, who, as the scion of the rich family in Alexandria, had heard the constant denunciation of the fickle Alexandrian mob, and looked into the situation: "It is we, on the contrary, who own all the wealth, who are the plunderers of the poor. . . . Truth does not exist anymore, it is mendacity that rules in the land."[41] The most famous of Utopians, Sir Thomas More (the greatest economist of his time), puts his criticism into the mouth of an honest sailor:

> It seems beyond doubt to me, my dear More, if I would speak frankly, that where private property rules, where money is the measure of all things for everyone, it is virtually impossible for society to flourish under righteous administration. That is, unless one thinks it right and proper that every good thing be owned by immoral people, or that prosperity consists of a few owning everything, albeit the favorite few themselves are not at all happy, while all the others live in abject misery. . . . How much better and nobler the arrangements of the Utopians seem to me where everyone has more than enough although nobody has more than another. . . . Compare with that the nations of the world

which must be constantly inventing new legislation and yet never have good laws; where every individual thinks to own for himself alone what he has earned and the daily accumulation of countless laws is adequate to keep people safe in their possessions. One must admit that Plato is right. . . . He realized that the only way to cure the evil was by economic equality, which is simply not possible as long as property is privately owned. . . . Granted there are ways of improving the situation without abolishing private property, there remains no other cure for the evil.[42]

He points out that laws limiting ownership, sumptuary laws, laws against corruption in government, and so on, none of these will cure the fatal disease as long as we have private property, which indeed *is* the disease. Thomas More insists that *philargyria,* the desire for more money, is the root of all evil: "Greed, theft, and envy are all caused by fear of not having enough. But Utopia always has a super abundance and people's time belongs not to the economy but to the free development of the mind, for in that they find the blessings of life."[43] "Such," says Raphael, "is not only the best, but the *only* constitution of society worthy of the name. Elsewhere people speak of the common good but actually work for the private good, for every man knows that he must go hungry if he does not work for himself, no matter how flourishing the society may be or how booming the economy; he must always consider his own well-being before that of others."[44] In Utopia, on the other hand, everyone knows that none will ever be in need as long as the common barns are full. "With everything equally divided among them, no one is poor. . . . Thus all are rich [cf. Jacob 2:17]. What greater wealth can there be than a healthy and secure life?"[45] They live after the manner of happiness.

Then More, in the manner of the prophets, reverts to the dark world in which we live:

What kind of justice is it when the nobleman, the banker (goldsmith), the money lender, in short, those who do nothing productive, glory in riches while day laborers, teamsters, blacksmiths, carpenters and field workers, whose work can not be dispensed with for a year can sweat out a miserable existence at a level below that of beasts of burden? Our animals do not work so long, are better fed and have better security than they do, for our workers are pressed down by the hopelessness of the situation and the expectation of beggary in old age. What they are paid does not cover their daily needs, and to save anything for old age is out of the question. So we find shocking waste, luxury, triviality and vanity [the lives of the rich and famous] on the one side and utter abject misery on the other.[46]

So as things are, we get the worst of both worlds.

As God loves me, when I consider this, then every modern society seems to me to be nothing but a conspiracy of the rich, who while protesting their interest in the common good pursue their own interests and stop at no trick and deception to secure their ill-gotten possessions, to pay as little as possible for the labor that produces their wealth and so force its makers to accept the nearest thing to nothing. They contrive rules for securing and assuring these tidy profits for the rich in the name of the common good, including of course the poor, and call them laws![47]

"But after they have divided among themselves in their insatiable greed all that should go to the society as a whole, they still are not happy."[48] The law can avenge but never hinder the deceptions, thievery, riots, panics, murders, assassinations, poisonings, and so on, all of which spring from one source — money. That is Thomas More writing — and it cost him his life.

It has been the same story all along, only suddenly we have reached a new level. For the first time selfishness goes by its own name: "The virtue of selfishness" is the testament of Ayn Rand, the guru of Milton Friedman, Alan Greenspan, and James Watt, long the favorite reading of BYU students. "No other civilization has permitted the calculus of self-interest so to dominate its culture," writes R. L. Heilbroner; "it has transmogrified greed and philistinism into social virtues, and subordinated all values to commercial values."[49] This is exactly what Thomas More said: "What has heretofore passed as unjust, . . . they have turned upside down, and in fact proclaimed it publicly and by law to be nothing less than justice itself."[50] Mr. Ivan Boesky, in a college convocation, commended "healthy greed" as a virtue to be cultivated by the young.[51] That's a virtue! A frenzy of privatization now insists that the only public institution with a reason for existence is the military, to defend us against societies more committed to sharing, and to root out those among us who doubt the sacredness of property.

How would such a world take the law of consecration? If *we* have objections, surely the world must have much stronger objections. Yet that is not the case, as Gaylord Freeman in reply to his "good friend" Milton Friedman observes: "There's nothing sacred about a profit-oriented society. There's no guarantee in the Bible or the Constitution that you can have private property. If we're going to continue to have these opportunities, it's only because this is acceptable to a high enough proportion of our people that they don't change the laws to prevent it."[52] What many Latter-day Saints are saying is that they are perfectly willing to put the law of consecration into practice just as soon as the rest of the world is ready to receive it. We will have to wait and see. When we ask others what wonderful plan the Lord has reserved for his chosen people, people tell us it is, of course, nothing more nor less than the conventional and accepted economy.

"How will the world take it?" How strange this sounds

coming from Mormons, of all people, who for a century
went ahead and did what the Lord told them to, while the
world screamed bloody murder. Like the Word of Wisdom,
the time has fully come for the law of consecration, and it
is "adapted to the capacity of the saints or the least that
may be called saints" (D&C 89:3), for the Lord, as Nephi
says, does not give us commandments which he knows
we cannot fulfill (1 Nephi 3:7).

But the covenant is made by the individual to the Father
in the name of the Son, a private and a personal thing, a
covenant with the Lord. He intends it specifically to implement a *social* order—to save his people as a people, to
unite them and make them of one heart and one mind,
independent of any power on earth. If I as an individual
offer all I have to the bishop and ask him to meet all my
needs in return, he must consult higher authority before
he can accept; the plan is so designed that we must all be
in it together. Back to Brigham Young:

> The doctrine of uniting together in our temporal la-
> bors, and all working for the good of all is from the
> beginning, from everlasting, and it will be for ever and
> ever. No one supposes for one moment that in heaven
> the angels are speculating, that they are building rail-
> roads and factories, taking advantage one of another,
> gathering up the substance there is in heaven to ag-
> grandize themselves, and that they live on the same
> principle that we are in the habit of doing. No Christian,
> no sectarian Christian, in the world believes this; they
> believe that the inhabitants of heaven live as a family
> [Deuteronomy 31:12 and 12:6-7 say that offerings should
> always be made in a family group—the individual is the
> one responsible, but he must always bring his family],
> that their faith, interests, and pursuits have one end in
> view—the glory of God and their own salvation, they
> may receive more and more. . . . We all believe this, and
> suppose we go to work and imitate them as far as we
> can.[53]

Are we wasting our time talking about the law of consecration? From the days of Joseph to the present, there has been one insuperable obstacle to the plan, and that is the invincible reluctance of most of the Brethren. When Brigham Young proposed it to the Brethren at Winter Quarters, he could not move them; only one or two of the apostles would listen to him. The rest announced their intention to follow their own plans and get rich.[54]

The dilemma the Saints found themselves in is nowhere better illustrated than in the experience of my grandfather, with whom I have become closely acquainted at first and second hand. The poverty and toil of Scottish miners, which his family experienced, filled him with a strong dedication to the idea of justice and at the same time an absolute horror of poverty. For some years he managed the United Order sheep and lumber companies in Cache County. Then almost overnight, to judge by the newspaper reports, the best timber was gone. So Charles W. Nibley cast his eyes toward Oregon, where he saw the most magnificent forests in the world; he simply could not stand the sight, he has told me; there was all that timber neglected, unclaimed, simply rotting, going to waste. Somebody had to take it. It was a condition not to be borne.

With his partner, David Eccles, he tore into the woods, wiping out miles of unsurveyed forest, acquiring vast stretches of it through manipulation of the Homestead Act, easily paying off government agents who came from the East to ask what was going on. I can tell you the tricks, because he told them to me and laughed about it. It was not until 1910 that the scandal broke and a Senate investigation took place. He moved into sugar, and again Oregon promised rich pickings. But there was a child labor law in Oregon, which made beet thinning expensive, and the unions also wanted a share in the take. Nibley frankly made his fortune on stolen timber and child labor. The moral issue? Obviously, the enemy was the government and the unions; it was they who put restraints (which he interpreted as crippling) on his boundless free enterprise, denying men their God-given free agency. It became a standard doctrine among the Latter-day Saints. They pushed this by the conciliation of bishops and well-to-do stake presidents. In his journal he writes, "It has become the custom in the church to give the high seats in the synagogue to men who have made 'money.' "

But all along there was compromise with principle; actually Charles W. Nibley was one of the most liberal industrialists of his time. But he had to compromise. Thus to finish the Hotel Utah, it was necessary to borrow $2,000,000, so President Smith sent Brother Nibley to Barney Baruch in New York to raise the money. He succeeded, and President Smith was delighted; but he was also alarmed when he heard the terms: it would all have to be paid back in two years. "Charley, what have you done? How in the world will we ever pay it back in that time?" Not to worry, they would have the whole thing paid off in two years. How? "I'm going to build the largest and finest bar in the West in the basement of the Hotel, and will see that we will pay off every penny of that debt." President Smith went through the ceiling; which was it to be, the Word of Wisdom or fiscal soundness? The dollar won.

The Backlash

Attempts to compromise on the law of God put one, as Brigham Young said, in an intolerable situation, a state of perpetual tension; one becomes defensive and self-justifying, and to clear his conscience all the way one assumes an aggressive posture. The result is that the Latter-day Saints are perhaps the most rigidly opposed to the principles of sharing of any people in the world. Consider some of those things in which Utah today ranks *number one*. We can go through the newspaper headlines of the last year or two at random, but first let me note two items that have appeared in the news this week:

2/4/87   The Senate . . . advanced a measure that would make Utah the *most* difficult state in the union in which to successfully sue corporate officials for irresponsible actions. [Everything is always in favor of money, in Utah more than any other state, making it hard to sue a rich crook.]

2/4/87   House Votes to Let Students Out [of school] at Age 16

Environment

2/4/87   Load of California Hazard Waste Bound for Tooele

5/9/87   Nevada Town Welcomes Idea of Nuclear Dump [San Juan County Fights for It]

9/1/85   Research Groups Flunk Utah's Nielsen for Votes of Clean-up of Waste Sites

1/14/87   Time Bandits [southern Utahns claim freedom to loot Indian ruins as sacred right of free agency]

1/18/87   Group Says Forest Service, Developers Are in Cahoots

1/23/87   Kennecott Cited for Gas Leak That Injured 43

1/23/87   Criminal Investigation into UP&L and Emery Mining

5/7/86   Thiokol Guilty of 5 Serious Safety Violations

7/17/86   Mountain Fuel Sued in Hazardous Waste Disposal

12/1/75   Utah Valley Leads the Nation in Air Pollution [before closing Geneva]

12/1/85   15 Year Clean Up of Military Toxic Waste Brought to Utah from Rocky Mountain Arsenal

9/12/86   Nielsen Tells Caucus He'll Try to Kill Acid-Rain Bill

1/7/87   Nader Group Gives Nielsen an 'O' Rating on Environment

9/19/86   Hatch Opts for Road Funding over Billboard Protections

1/24/86   Beaver Ranchers [two corporations] Face Cruelty Charges [starving the beavers]

Distribution of Wealth

9/11/85   Utah Ranks 48th in Per Capita Income

5/6/86   Utah Neck-and-Neck with West Virginia and Mississippi for Lowest Annual Income

7/15/86   Utah Still Ranked 48th in Per Capita Income

3/12/85   Utah in Top 5 Proportion of Millionaires. [West Virginia has the fewest millionaires, but the same per capita as Utah, making Utah the most unequal state in the nation.]

7/26/86   America's Ultra Rich Are Richer Than Ever
           1/2 of one percent of the nation's population
           now control more than 35% of America's
           wealth [Note: USA, by far the richest land in
           the world, is only seventh in per capita income;
           and within the USA by far the most unequal
           distribution of the fifty states is in Utah. Con-
           clusion: No Democratic society in the world
           has greater inequality of wealth than Utah.]

1/14/86   Utah Makes "Terrible 10" Tax Listing [greatest
           inequality of taxing]

2/18/86   In Utah an income of $9,750 a year is in the
           same tax bracket as $50,000 per year

1/26/87   Plan to Shift Tax Burden from Income to Sales

9/6/85   Officials Hail Rejection of Comparable Worth
           Ruling

10/27/85   AFL-CIO Study Says Right-to-Work Law Cut-
           ting Earnings in Utah

4/10/85   Utah Ranks Last in Per-Pupil Funds . . .
           says NEA

1/15/86   Three Southeast Idaho Counties Make "Hun-
           griest List"

8/28/85   Utah's Farmers Losing Ground — 2% a Year

1/11/87   More Folks Are Leaving Utah Than Arriving

Morals in Zion

4/31/85,   Satan Worship in Zion, Provoan Finds Satan-
8/31/85,   ism, Fantasy, "Thing of Escape," etc.
8/1/86,
7/31/85

3/26/86   Utah Students Admit Drug Use

1/21/87   Divorce, Prescription Drugs, Suicide, Three
             Factors Contributing to Teenage Drug Use

10/23/85   Student Survey [Cedar City] Says Many Use
             Drugs, Alcohol

9/17/86   Ex-Users Claim Drugs Readily Available
             throughout Utah County

7/28/85   Salt Lake Has High Crime Rate, FBI Says Worst
             of Rocky Mountain Cities

7/27/86   Utah Crime Is above U.S. Average

8/21/86   Ex-Dealer Scolds LDS Youth about Drug Use

5/30/86   Utah Major Crime Rate Up Nearly 10%

White Collar Division

             "SLC, the Fraud Capital of the world" [Well-
             known Front Page Box in *Wallstreet Journal*]

5/29/85   Utahns Likely to Fall for Scams

6/15/86   Haddow Hired Utahns for Dubious Founda-
             tion

6/15/86   Utahns Caught in Swirl of "T. Bear" Suspicions

12/3/85   Utah Senators Expected to Oppose PAC Contribution Limits

12/28/85   Hatch Puts False Claims Act on Hold

10/28/82   Hatch Gets 3rd Largest Handout From Oil, Gas PAC's

1/22/87   Charter Thrift and Loan Sued 68 Million for Racketeering and Fraud

11/30/81   Naive Utahns Pay More for Scams than State Tax

11/24/86   Utah County Leads in Investment Fraud [Wilkinson]

9/1/82   Law Agencies Launch Fraud Ads Blitz

1/8/82   374 Land Violations Boggle [Utah] County

8/24/82   White Collar Criminals Are Like Your Neighbors

12/30/86   Leading Article in *Wallstreet Journal:* Wizards Fall, Loss of Midas Touch Leads to Bankruptcy, Law Suits and Murder [J. Gary Sheets]

6/17/86   Hansen Loses Bid for Shorter Sentence [Hatch and Garn went to Idaho to campaign for him]

Our Freedoms

10/21/85   Lawyers Overrun Salt Lake City [more per capita than New York, Philadelphia, Chicago, Los Angeles, etc. That's great, isn't it?]

4/10/85   Hatch Helps Draft Ideology Tests for Judges

9/11/85   Hatch Gives Guarded Support to South African Sanctions

9/7/85   Hatch Denies Calling President of National Organization for Women a Communist and Pinko [in so many words]

6/1/86   Exposé Ties Both Utah Senators to World Anti-Communist League

5/3/85   Utahns in Congress Rate Extreme Right

5/26/86   Utah Delegates [in Washington] Are Among the Most "Right"

6/5/85   Hatch to Present Prayer Amendment

8/5/86   Hatch Wants Inquiry on Manion Critic

11/7/86   Artist Asked to Remove Maeser's Beard in Painting on cover of Student Directory [at BYU]

11/7/86   Censorship Long Standing Question [at BYU]

11/19/85   BYU Officials Threaten ELWC Roach Revealers

7/17/86   Deseret Closes Book on Racy Novels

3/27/86   Pupils Protest Attack on Libya: 40 Are Sus-
            pended, 3 Arrested [at Bonneville Jr. High]

8/23/85   Constitution Panel Bars Public from Salt Lake
            Meeting

The Militants

10/27/85   75% of Utahns Favor Star Wars Plan

4/10/86   Utah Lawmakers Reject Gun Control [unani-
            mously]

11/8/85   Former Lawmaker Rebukes Governor on Mis-
            sile Issue [feeble resistance to 6 missile sites in
            Utah]

3/13/85   Spanish Fork Marine Helps Train Wyoming
            Youth, in trench-knife techniques basis of
            hand-to-hand combat [Rambo photo]

Where Your Treasure Is, There Will Your Heart Be Also

8/20/82   Richer, Faster Attitude in Utah Valley Attracts
            Scams ["Dr. Steven D. Nadauld . . . started
            his speech at BYU's Management Society Con-
            ference Monday with the audience chanting
            'Richer, faster, richer, faster' "]

7/7/86   Utah County May Have the Nation's Largest
            Number of Entrepreneurs

9/7/86   Hatch Defends President of Teamsters

APPROACHING ZION

1/13/85   Bangerter Cuts Funds for Mental Health

6/9/86   Official Charges City-Hired Managers to Side-
           step Unions

2/14/86   Dress for Success Conference at BYU, Spon-
           sored by Skaggs Institute of Retail Manage-
           ment

3/1/86   BYU Poster for Public Administration Schol-
           arships: "Bring in Your Brain for Big Bucks"

3/5/86   Wirthlin Outlines American Values: Economic
           Security, Personal Security, Family, Neighbors
           and Patriotism

           Financial Entrepreneur Defends Controversial
           Ad: "The price of my integrity if converted into
           dollars is in the tens of millions." [Now there's
           a man with integrity. Sir Simon's famous joke:
           We know now what you are, now the only
           question is how much.]

This is only a modest sampling. It is money we love
and respect. This week it was announced that judges must
have higher pay if lawyers are to respect them, the corollary
being that no one respects anyone who has less money
than he has. Not that they need it — these old duffers who
are tapering off spend all their days in closets, so why do
they need more than $125,000 a year? Oh, to make them
more respected by the lawyers. You can't respect a man
who is making less than you, can you? That is the sentiment
expressed by the late great lawman John Mitchell. The
Latter-day Saints reverenced Howard Hughes and resented any criticism of the sickly and unbalanced billion-
aire; his money sanctified him. On a single day in the

newspaper in 1972 the president declared drugs the nation's number-one problem; along with this is a statement that alcohol is the most dangerous of all drugs, and on the same page United Airlines is announced as the world's largest purveyor of alcohol by the drink, with W. Marriott in second place.

This week a finance writer is proud to boast the Utah connections of Daniel K. Ludwig, perhaps the world's richest man, and glowingly praises the purity and simplicity of his way of life—like Mr. Walton's bringing his lunch to work in a brown bag. We forget that the arrogance of wealth is not in the spending, which is merely foolish, as Veblen showed, but in the acquiring of it. This man by his penurious personal habits simply shows, as did Scrooge, that nothing in the world counts for him but money. The word *miser* describes one who lives a miserable existence out of reluctance to spend a penny of his ever-growing and zealously watched wealth. It is as if we were to pronounce blessed a man who keeps a thousand expensive suits locked in his closet and proves his humility and modesty by never wearing one of them—or letting anyone else wear one.

This sentiment is marked by an undisguised contempt for anyone without money. My own experience from talking with many transients has shown that nowhere in the nation are tramps more evilly treated than in Utah. So much for the stranger within thy gates.

Let us make a list of the offenses that are darkening the skies of our time. Crime of all sorts—street crime, muggings, rape, white collar crime (the worst in our nation, and worst of all since it is committed against those who trust us), corporate fraud, drug traffic, steroids, corrupt athletes, pornography, prostitution (and the resulting AIDS), wars great and small, brush-fire wars, paramilitary organizations, soldiers of fortune, hit men, terrorism, arson, kidnapping, illegal aliens, armaments sold by all to all—including germ warfare, gas and nuclear weapons, pollution of water and air, poisonous spills, dangerous and inferior products, destruction of the environment, extermination of species, urban decay, educational neglect and fraud, racism, religious fraud, and on and on. Carry on the list for yourself, and ask yourself at each label in the cumulation of horrors, What is the prime motive behind it? Can we deny that money really *is* the "root of all evil?" Has not Satan carried out the work he threatened to do? You can see it all on the TV.

The best possible summary of the situation is the inspired First Presidency message given by President Kimball on the solemn occasion of the bicentennial of the nation. When he viewed the condition of the Church and the country, his reaction was not one of glowing admiration and praise. On the contrary: "The Lord gave us a choice world and expects righteousness and obedience to his commandments in return." This is the principle stated a hundred times in the scriptures: Notice the old law of Moses: "I have given you this land and I expect obedience." President Kimball continued, "But when I review the performance of this people in comparison of what is expected, I am *appalled and frightened.*"[55] What appalls and frightens him? He views the prime evils of the time under three headings: (1) deterioration of the environment, (2) quest for affluence, and (3) trust in force of arms. Massive documentation will show that in the enjoyment of each of these three vices, the people of Utah are second to none. At the first meeting of Congress under the present administration, it was declared that the delegation from Utah were the most anti-environmentalist in the nation. Ecology and environment are dirty words in Utah. As we have seen, more people are dedicated to the quest for wealth and none more trusting in military solutions to all problems.

And whatever became of President Kimball's remark-

able address to the Church? It was given the instant deep-
freeze, the most effective of censorship, a resounding silence. In 1969 an even more painful silence greeted another
voice, that of the Lord Jesus Christ. In that year was re-
produced in the pages of the *BYU Studies* the earliest known
and fullest account of Joseph Smith's First Vision, written
in the hand of Warren Parrish in the winter of 1831-32 at
the dictation of the Prophet. When I heard the news, which
was just before general conference, I declared that there
would be dancing in the streets when this document came
out. Instead I have heard not a mention of it from that day
to this. How is that possible that we should censor the
words of the Lord himself? Well, those words began with
unflattering picture of all us of: "Behold the world at this
time lieth in sin, and there is none that doeth good, no
not one, and mine anger is kindling against the inhabitants
of the world to visit them according to their ungodliness."

"The world lieth in sin." Why? we ask. The answer is
loud and clear in Doctrine and Covenants 49: "For behold,
the beasts of the field and the fowls of the air, and that
which cometh of the earth, is ordained for the use of man
for food and for raiment, and that he might have in abundance. But it is not given that one man should possess that
which is above another, *wherefore the world lieth in sin*. And
wo be unto man that sheddeth blood or that wasteth flesh
and hath no need" (D&C 49:19-21). That need does not
include killing for pleasure, or to provide a pleasurable
spectacle for the public, activities that seem to have become
the national avocation in our time.

The End of It All

And where is it all leading? The prophetic Book of
Mormon and prophetic Doctrine and Covenants and the
Bible all tell us where. Read section 1: "Wherefore the voice
of the Lord is unto the ends of the earth, that all that will
hear may hear. . . . The anger of the Lord is kindled, and

APPROACHING ZION

his sword is bathed in heaven, and it shall fall upon the inhabitants of the earth, . . . for they have strayed from mine ordinances, and have broken mine everlasting covenant" (D&C 1:11, 13, 15). "They seek not the Lord to establish his righteousness, but every man walketh in his own way, and after the image of his own god, whose image is in the likeness of the world, and whose *substance* is that of an *idol,* which waxeth old and shall perish in Babylon, even Babylon the great, which shall fall" (D&C 1:16). Let us note that the issue is an *economic* one. The people of Zarahemla were not denounced for having the wrong ideas about the economy, but for thinking of nothing else all the time: "Behold ye do always remember your treasures, therefore ye are cursed and your treasures are cursed *because* ye have set your hearts upon them" (see Helaman 13:22-23). The prophecy continues: "Wherefore, I the Lord, knowing the *calamity* which should come upon the inhabitants of the earth, called upon my servant Joseph Smith, Jun., and spake unto him from heaven, and gave him commandments" (D&C 1:17). Strange that there should be no distinction between the good and bad inhabitants of the earth. (He's talking to all the world.) Why doesn't he mention those awful Soviets? On the contrary, they are to be lumped together. "Verily I say unto you, O inhabitants of the earth: I the Lord am willing to make these things known unto all flesh; for I am no respecter of persons [he does not take sides], and will that all men shall know that the day speedily cometh; the hour is not yet, but is nigh at hand, when peace shall be taken from the earth, and the devil shall have power over his own dominion" (D&C 1:34- 35). So it all goes back to Satan's dominions, power applied by buying the armies' supporters with the treasures of the earth, a thoroughly practical approach to the world where you can have anything for money. There is a bright side to the picture: "And also the Lord shall have power over his saints, and shall reign in their midst" (D&C 1:36). But not until they decide to do things his way.

I have spent a lot of time speaking here. It's insolent for me to speak after the Lord has spoken. We should just go read the written word. What does every civilization leave behind? What is going to be the net product of our civilization? It's garbage, it's junk. You can see that, and it's mounting. It sounds rhetorical: we have to produce things (expand in producing); then we have to increase consumption, so we have to increase desire for things with advertising flim-flam; then we have to consume very fast and discard a great deal, because there is available a new and improved version. So discarding goes on, as Congressman Wright pointed out recently: "The principal exports of the United States today are used packages and scraps." We are impatient of the slow ways of nature. We have to go faster and faster, and the biggest question has become the dumps.

In the last phase of World War II, I was in Heidelberg in the Sixth Army Group, writing up the daily intelligences. I had been there on my mission, and nobody had ever heard of such a thing as a garbage dump in Europe; yet here was a huge garbage dump. You knew the Americans had arrived—the Army. And everywhere the Americans were in occupation were the giant garbage dumps. Since then there have been garbage dumps everywhere; what our civilization leaves behind is garbage. Which is what happens everywhere. Rubble is all we have of any ancient civilization, as far as that goes; it's more sanitary now because it's been oxidized.

But it has also become the main problem of the world. What can we do with this stuff? We've now got a new kind of garbage, which is eternal; waste disposal has become one of the biggest headaches of the day. We put the garbage where we don't notice—out of sight, out of mind; but it's getting bigger and bigger, and now Utah is being eyed,

APPROACHING ZION

more than any other place, as the great place to dump deadly garbage, which is the only thing our civilization will leave behind unless it's the written word, the documents, the one thing that binds civilization together.

What do the other civilizations leave behind, the ones I call the stable ones? The ones after the manner of the old people. They leave themselves behind. Their next generation takes over and carries on. Time means nothing to them. It's an eternal order of the law. The law of consecration is an eternal order. We will just leave ourselves, the culture, behind, without any loss of product. People will have plenty to do and plenty to think of.

Quite literally, the net contribution of our present society to the history of the world will be a pile of garbage—and that very ugly garbage. Great civilizations like the Egyptian or Greek left magnificent garbage, sometimes great stuff to look at. When Salt Lake City is leveled by a nuclear bomb, what will be left behind? What will future civilizations dig up? What will be worth even looking at or digging up? What will survive? The Lord says, "There is no end to my works or my words" (Moses 1:4). The civilization survives only on its words. That's what we have from the Greeks, the Egyptians, and the Hebrews. We have the scriptures. We have the Testaments. We have the Book of Mormon. What has survived is a voice from the dust speaking to us; that's all that has survived. We wouldn't even know that that civilization ever existed without the voice from the dust. That which survived is the word. At least we will leave that behind. But the nice thing about the order the Lord wishes to establish here is that it is eternally perpetrated, not only in the heavens but here, as long as it needs to be anywhere. We can carry on and have a wonderful time.

And it is my prayer that we may be awakened to the glorious promises the Lord has given to Zion through the temple, which I ask in the name of Jesus Christ, Amen.

Notes

1. *The Manual of Discipline* I, 13-15; see Theodor H. Gaster, ed., *The Dead Sea Scriptures* (New York: Anchor, 1976), 45-46.

2. This subject is treated at length in Hugh W. Nibley, *The Message of the Joseph Smith Papyri: An Egyptian Endowment* (Salt Lake City: Deseret Book, 1975).

3. *JD* 2:305.

4. Ibid., 2:299.

5. Ibid.

6. From the *Manuscript History of Brigham Young* (Church Historical Archives).

7. Matthias F. Cowley, *Wilford Woodruff* (Salt Lake City: Deseret, 1909), 487-88.

8. *JD* 2:305-6 (emphasis added).

9. Studs Terkel, *The American Dreams: Lost and Found* (New York: Pantheon, 1980), 326.

10. Ibid., 43.

11. Ibid., 338.

12. Cf. *MS* 39:372.

13. Eldin J. Watson, *Brigham Young Addresses 1870-1877,* 6 vols. (1984), vol. 6, June 1, 1876.

14. Terkel, *American Dreams,* 338.

15. Ibid., 14-15.

16. Ibid., 17.

17. Ibid., 127-28.

18. Ibid., 128.

19. Vergil, *Aeneid* I, 287.

20. "Racial Navajo Letter Prompts Removal of Subcontractor," *Salt Lake City Tribune,* 17 January 1986.

21. Harry C. James, *Pages from Hopi History* (Tucson: University of Arizona Press, 1974), 185-86.

22. Ibid., 188.

23. Terkel, *American Dreams,* 176.

24. *JD* 16:123 (emphasis added).

25. *Journal History of the Church* (October 1, 1848).

26. *JD* 10:268 (emphasis added).

27. Terkel, *American Dreams,* 21.

28. Ibid., 19.

29. Ibid.

30. Variations on this story may be found in Louis Ginzberg, *Legends of the Jews,* 7 vols. (Philadelphia: Jewish Publication Society of America, 1968), 1:159.

31. *JD* 14:83 (emphasis added).

32. Ibid., 1:117 (emphasis added).

33. Ibid.

34. Terkel, *American Dreams,* 30-32.

35. Plutarch, *Lycurgus* VIII, 1.

36. Solon fragment 12 in Ivan M. Linforth, *Solon the Athenian* (Berkeley: University of California Press, 1919), 140-41; cf. Demosthenes, *Defalsa legatione,* 254-70.

37. Ibid., fragment 40, page 169.

38. Plato, *Laws* 899D-900A.

39. Ibid., 906A.

40. Ibid., 904D-E.

41. Anthony, *Sermo de Vanitute Mundi et de Resurrectione Mortuorum,* in *PG* 40:962, 986.

42. Thomas More, *Utopia,* tr. Robert M. Adams, 2 vols. (London: Yale University Press, 1964), 1:29.

43. Ibid., 2:146-49.

44. Ibid., 2:146.

45. Ibid., 2:88.

46. Ibid., 2:88-89.

47. Ibid., 2:89.

48. Ibid.

49. See Leonard Silk, "The End of the Road?" *New York Times Book Review,* a review of Robert L. Heilbroner, *Business Civilization in Decline* (New York: Nolton, 1976).

50. More, *Utopia,* 1:25.

51. Mariann Caprino, "Healthy Greed Was Boesky's Undoing," *Salt Lake Tribune,* 20 November 1986, D9.

52. Terkel, *American Dreams,* 19.

53. *JD* 17:117-18.

54. Ibid., 18:244.

55. Spencer W. Kimball, "The False Gods We Worship," *Ensign* 6 (June 1976): 3-4.

16

The Utopians

I was asked to talk about "Breakthroughs I Would Like to See" and "Changes I Would Like to See." I changed the title to "Change out of Control," then to "Utopias I Would Like to See," and I have changed the title again — but not the subject. I define *utopia* in the generic sense as simply the ideal society, the best imaginable. The task of describing my utopia has been both simplified and complicated by the fact that the breakthroughs, changes, and utopias I would like to see are all the same, and that my idea of utopia happens to be the same as that of the score of other utopians I am about to mention, all of whom see eye to eye on all essentials.

The surprise of finding consensus among men living so many years and miles apart is a reminder that there is one aspect of the gospel that we all tend to ignore, and that is the credit and recognition belonging to the righteous of other ages, for their zeal and dedication to the cause of Zion. We could call this paper "Holy Men Ye Know Not Of," referring in particular to the utopian writers who invoked the tradition of man's past glory (as John Taylor does in his hymn "Adam-ondi-Ahman"), as well as the prophecies of the millennial future, as ample evidence of man's ability to achieve a better order than the one in which we live.

All ancient civilizations of record were dedicated to the

This transcript is taken from the Sphere of Influence Lecture Series address on November 6, 1986, at Brigham Young University.

proposition that the earthly order is or should be a faithful reflection of the heavenly. The centers of action were the great ceremonial complexes that dominate the scene throughout antiquity. The ruins and the texts setting forth the rituals and the hymns make it clear that the people had a pretty good idea of what heaven was like and did their best to imitate it. The idea was, we would say, utopian.

Of course reality fell short. But more idealistic souls did not give up. They followed what can be called the "Rekhabite principle," that is, when the real world became too corrupt for them to endure, the truly pious ones banded together and emigrated, like the Jaredites, to a pure place, "into the wilderness, yea, into that quarter where there never had man been" (Ether 2:5). The motive for emigrating into the wilderness is made clear in many "Rekhabite" writings, such as the Dead Sea Scrolls and the Book of Mormon, where resounding statements of discontent with the way the world has gone are followed by a program for establishing or awaiting a better order of things. Thus spake Enoch, the super-utopian, to his contemporaries: "[The righteous] have . . . met with much evil . . . and have become few and small . . . and have not found any to help [us] even with a word. . . . Sinners have laid their yoke heavily upon us. They have had dominion over us that hated us and smote us; and to those who hated us we have bowed our necks."[1] To the oppressors he says: "You have got by through juggling the books and falsifying reports; that is how you got your power, influence, and wealth."[2] "For these many generations, . . . have they gone astray," said the Lord to Enoch, "and have denied me, and have sought their own counsels in the dark; and in their own abominations have they devised murder, and have not kept the commandments, which I gave unto their father, Adam" (Moses 6:28). So Enoch went up to found his city of Zion, the first and greatest utopia, where all "were of one heart and one mind, and dwelt in righteousness; and there was no poor among them" (Moses 7:18).

Among the most ancient of all records is the corpus of lamentation literature, both Egyptian and Mesopotamian, proclaiming the calamities of the times, lamenting lost glories and looking forward to a return of the same under a messianic king.[3] Abraham was the first "Hebrew," or outcast person, in a world of desperate wickedness, a refugee driven from place to place, "looking for a city builded without hands," as Paul says, "whose ruler and maker was God" (Hebrews 9:11; 11:10).

The great world economic collapses that sent the nations migrating in search of new promised lands from time to time left people everywhere with dim memories of better times—a Golden Age, far away and long ago. It seems to have been particularly strong among those incurable idealists the Greeks. Pindar, the greatest of lyric poets, sees in the great *panegyris* of the sacred games the attempt to achieve and preserve something of the celestial order of the lost age of the gods, the time from which Hesiod traces the sad decline of mankind into successive ages of silver, bronze, and iron.

Plutarch's *Lycurgus* stands at the head of most recommended reading lists on utopia; this is the utopia that serves as a pilot study for all the others, ancient and modern, who follow it in form and substance. Plutarch tells us that later utopians followed his lead, including Plato, the most influential of them all. Lycurgus begins his work in a state on the verge of total collapse: "For there was an intolerable inequality, with swarms of impoverished and helpless people burdening the city while all the wealth had been concentrated in the hands of the few; arrogance, and envy, and crime, and luxury prevailed, and the fundamental cause of this chronic social disease was *plutos kai penia*, the conjunction of wealth and poverty."[4] Lycurgus, who on the death of his brother became the guardian of his brother's young son and hence became the strongest man in the state, resorted to drastic remedies, beginning with redistribution of all the land into equal plots, each producing enough to feed a man and his family adequately—and no more! Even more daring was the equalizing of personal property, but Lycurgus was able to do it quickly and effectively simply by abolishing money. He did that very simply by replacing gold and silver with cast iron as a medium of exchange, which he was free to do, since money is only a token. The new money was so inconvenient that people quickly gave it up. This discouraged foreign trade and corruption;[5] it meant that luxury items practically vanished, while indispensable commodities were all homemade, and Sparta became renowned for the high quality of the things it produced for use, and the high technical ingenuity displayed in them.[6]

 To counter wealth and luxury, common dining-halls and dormitories were provided, the unfailing mark of every true utopia. The meals were delightful affairs, with fifteen friends at each table exchanging wit and wisdom,[7] for friendship and fun are the theme of this utopia.[8] The whole society was a school, with no distinction between male and female; dress was uniform, simple and light weight.[9] There was a public stigma on bachelors,[10] and adultery was unknown.[11] For all their vigorous physical regime, "To be a Spartan was to love philosophy more than gymnastics";[12] since "the busy and demanding activity of amassing money had no place at all, there being nothing admirable (azelon) or honorable in wealth," they had more leisure than any other people. "Dances and songfests, parties, games, and athletics, hunting, and conversation took up their time when they were not on military duty."[13] The conversation, if one knows the Greeks, was no idle chatter, but the discussion of serious things in a lively and often humorous way—and it was never boring. The ideal, Plutarch tells us, was that of a hive of busy and happy bees—a little Zion.[14]

For their leaders they chose not the swift or the strong, but the wise.[15] The well-known grim Spartan military state, says Plutarch, took over only after an earthquake in 464 B.C. and the campaign of Lysander, which for the first time poured gold and silver money into the city.[16] Satisfied to remain a city and a people with few wants, they had no ambitions abroad except to secure their way of life at home, which sometimes meant discouraging imperialism in others; but in that their policy was never to bring undue military pressure to bear on a foreign power, which would only make trouble for Sparta by forcing the offending state to feel threatened and to arm itself. When Agesilaeus was wounded in Thebes, a fellow general told him, "This is what you deserve for making the reluctant Thebans go to war and at the same time teaching them how to do it."[17] They refused to strike an enemy when he was down or pursue one who had fled the field, which looks like real nonaggression. Finally, Lycurgus wrote nothing down and would not even allow the laws to be written: Like the laws of Moses, practice should write them on the hearts of the people.[18]

The wisest of the Greeks was always held to be Solon, the father of democracy. Before Solon, the idea of a democratic state with the people ruling themselves was considered wildly utopian (for example, in the *Fürstenspiegel* literature), so that Solon as the true father of democracy can be considered the most successful of utopians. He calls his great work the *Eunomia*, "the proper order of things," or the way things should be—a better name than utopia for the ideal society. Like the prophets of Israel with whom he was contemporary, Solon begins by describing the world as it is, a dismal picture.

> The ruin of our state will never come by the doom of Zeus; . . . it is the townsfolk themselves and their false-hearted leaders who would feign destroy our city through wantonness and love of money; . . . they are

rich because they yield to the temptation of dishonest courses. . . . They spare neither the treasures of the gods nor the property of the state, and steal like brigands one from another. They pay no heed to the Unshaken rock of holy Justice; . . . our beloved city is rapidly wasted and consumed in those secret deals which are the delight of dishonest men.[19]

It is the perennial story: "Ye yourselves raised these men to power over you, and have reduced yourselves by this course to a wretched state of servitude. Individually, you are a lot of sly foxes, but collectively, you are a set of simpletons. For ye look to the tongue and the play of a man's speech and ignore the deed which is done before your very eyes."[20] The trouble is that "no visible limit is set to wealth among men. Even now those among us who have the largest fortune are striving with redoubled energy." Then Solon, a contemporary of the equally idealistic Lehi, strikes a familiar note: "Wealth comes to mortals by the gifts of the gods. But out of it comes madness, which leads to destruction when Zeus sends this madness as a punishment to men."[21]

By way of explaining Solon's *eunomia*, we may point out that the greatest of all idealists, Pythagoras, taught that "by the *nomos* we help each other, and by *anomia* we make war." *Anomia*, the opposite of *eunomia*, we should note, is the normal scriptural word for *unrighteousness* or *sin*. Pythagoras was the most influential of all utopians. Plato quotes him as saying, "The ancients were abler (*kreittones*) than we and lived nearer to the gods."[22] By a law of natural decline, an entropy from light to dark, birth to death, gods to demons, and heroes to ordinary men, the world has come to its present state. Nevertheless, we are under obligation to realize on earth a copy of that higher order in which all men are brothers. Pythagoras himself went all out to realize such a community. "Friends have all things in common," he taught, "for friendship *is* equality."[23] He claimed to have derived his doctrine from Delphi, in other words, by revelation. He organized communities throughout southern Italy, having visited such sacred conventicles throughout the world. All followed austere rules of living, with perfect equality among all members, male and female. All wore white, observed a strict diet and strict chastity, and so on. The communities were super think-tanks, Pythagoras himself being a mental giant without peer whose scientific discoveries and inventions have made him immortal. As might be expected, he and his followers suffered violent persecution and extermination by fire.

Solon's plan for democratic government also met with fierce resistance: "I was like a wolf at bay between two packs of dogs,"[24] he wrote, for the rich denounced his sweeping economic reforms as vehemently as the leaders of the *demos* resented his moderation. Lehi, Solon's contemporary, faced with similar greed and corruption, in the end had to take the Rekhabite way and flee from the society that had become dangerous to him and odious to God. Throughout the Book of Mormon, inspired leaders often break off from corrupt states to go out and found their own utopias, living, as Nephi says, "after the manner of happiness" (2 Nephi 5:27). Such separatists were Lehi, Nephi, Mosiah, Alma, and the brother of Jared. The standard text that all but the last were following was that of the great Isaiah.

The three major prophets speak with a single voice when they hold up to us the three pictures on which all utopian enterprises are based: Israel's blessed past, its glorious future, and the evil present. Isaiah is a master of the art, in which ecstatically lyrical passages describing the world as it could be and some day shall be again alternate with the most harrowing and horrifying pictures of the world as it is. Again and again he shifts from the one to the other to make his point, the powerful emphasis, of course, being on the present state of things: "None calleth for justice, nor any pleadeth for truth: they trust in vanity, and speak lies" (Isaiah 59:4). "Yea, truth faileth; and he that departeth from evil maketh himself a prey" (Isaiah 59:15). He might as well be paraphrasing Solon. And the cause of it? Money: "Woe unto them . . . which justify the wicked for reward, and take away the righteousness of the righteous from him!" (Isaiah 5:22-23). The princes "have eaten up the vineyard; the spoil of the poor is in your houses" (Isaiah 3:14), "that widows may be their prey, and that they may rob the fatherless" (Isaiah 10:2). "Every one loveth gifts, and followeth after rewards: they judge not the fatherless, neither doth the cause of the widow come unto them" (Isaiah 1:23). But every denunciation is followed by an abrupt shift to a time when the celestial order will be restored to earth, when the lion lies down with the lamb, when beauty and holiness fill the earth and "the earth shall be full of the knowledge of the Lord, as the waters cover the sea" (Isaiah 11:9), and when man and animal shall live without enmity and in perfect harmony (see Isaiah 11:6-9; 14:7-16; 35:1-10; 65:25).

We all know Plato's utopian *Republic*. In his *Laws*, when he failed to find the true philosopher-prince in Dionysius of Syracuse, his final solution was that reached by all the others, namely that the great plan has worked in the past and could work now; but for the present it is out of the question. Perhaps, says the Athenian in Plato's last dialogue, you have seen wicked men growing old and leaving their children's children in high office, and their success shakes your faith. You have seen crooks become heads of the state, hailed as the great men of their time, and that leads you to conclude that the gods are not responsible for that sort of thing.[25] "We must realize," he says in reply, "that an immortal conflict is going on within us with the gods as our allies";[26] we may not settle for a merely pleasant and moral life or a serene country-club existence. No system or environment will procure happiness unless "the soul is properly qualified to be carried along a holy road to a better place."²⁷ The realistic appraisal of the present world is what induces the usual encyclopedia articles on utopia to refer us to *Messianism* and leave us there — no utopia for the present.

It was because the memory of the Golden Age lingered on that the ancients, faced with the immorality and meanness of their own times, resorted to bitter satire. Recall that it was the technique of the prophets to contrast the world as it is and as it should be in passages that are often distinctly satirical. The hopes of Athenian democracy went down the drain with Aristophanes' *Plutus*. As he had spoofed Plato's utopia in the *Birds*, so in the *Plutus* he tells it to the Athenians as it is, which is simply that *ploutôs* (money) is the only power to be reckoned with in the world any more; Zeus himself, since people have deserted religion and morality, goes to find himself a job working for Plutus — the universe has become a vast money market.

The Roman Empire was introduced on a utopian note by Vergil's fourth *Eclogue* and Horace's *Carmen Saeculare*, but one thing spoiled it all: Horace's fellow satirists — Persius, Martial, Juvenal — lacking his sweet nature, have given us the one great original contribution of Roman letters, its satire, the damning indictment of a society corrupt from the beginning in its cruel inequalities. The Julians were still in power when Petronius, a close friend of the Emperor and master of his revels, penned the most devastating attack ever written on the obscene excesses of the rich and famous, and the power of money to corrupt and destroy everything it touches. There is no shortage of documents describing the end of classical civilization. Salvian traveled all over the Empire in the fourth century and described city by city what he found there — nothing but greed and violence.

But the worldwide social unrest and corruption that Salvian found produced one genuine utopian reaction in his century. In the rich and licentious city of Alexandria lived the scion of a wealthy family who did not like what he saw around him. While the rulers feared the famous and fickle Alexandrian mob, the youthful Anthony saw that the real danger came not from them: "It is we, on the contrary, who own all the wealth, who are the plunderers of the poor; . . . truth does not exist any more, it is mendacity that rules in the land." He goes on to picture the most cultivated and wealthy city in the world as nothing but a "den of thieves."[28]

So what does he do? He takes the Rekhabite way and goes out into the desert by himself as a hermit; but he soon attracted hosts of followers, and the movement of holy men into the desert was skillfully organized by Anthony's great contemporary, Pachomius, into well-ordered monasteries, whose profession was to follow Jesus' instruction to the letter: "If thou wilt be perfect, go and sell that thou hast, and give to the poor, and thou shalt have treasure in heaven: and come and follow me" (Matthew 19:21). "You are the children of Israel," Anthony told his monks.[29] In particular they were to think of themselves as following Abraham's example in fleeing from the wicked world; his quest for the perfect city was to be their quest.[30] Nay, even before Abraham they find their example by "transferring" themselves back "to that primeval condition . . . obtained before the Fall [disobedience] (inobedientiam),"[31] and even before that to the realms of the angels: "We are acting as hosts to God and all his angels and saints, . . . sharing the company and the great joy of their ministries."[32]

It was back to utopia. The pattern had already been laid down in Qumran and in the predecessors of Qumran in Egypt, where priestly colleges had flourished from the beginning. The Essenes form a common bond, much discussed and much debated, between such societies in Africa, Asia, and Greece. The resemblances and relationships of such societies lead also to the rich variety of Gnostic sects, which mingled Jewish and Christian elements with those of every other persuasion. Thus the Carpocratians claimed to be following the secret teachings of both Christ and Plato and fell into the common practice of sharing wives as well as property. The Montanist striving for the purity and unworldliness of the early church attracted an enormous following, including even such illustrious names as Tertullian and Augustine. Duchesne has shown how the church became a world church only at the price at giving up its old idealism. But droves of members objected, for the scriptures remained in spite of all; and there never was a time when Christians could not point to them and remind the world that Christ and the apostles had been poor men. The life of Anthony caused a sensation in the West, where Jerome and Ambrose, western saints who had lived in the East, vigorously promoted the new monasticism.

We need not go down the list of utopias that flourished from the fourth century to the present. They were utopian in varying degrees, but all were animated by what they considered the example of Christ and the apostles, and all denounced the horrible injustice and inequality of the world in which they lived. Since the monastic movement began with hermits (monk = *monachos,* one living alone), and the land was soon swarming with individuals acting on their own, for it was easy for any down-and-outer in the city to put on a robe and take to the road (and who would challenge a holy man?), soon the countryside, villages, and cities were swarming with vagabonds and tramps, *gyrovagi,* making the rounds of the monasteries and sponging off the hospitality of each in turn. Inevitably, such vagrants ganged up and took what they wanted. To curtail the abuse, Benedict of Nursia composed his famous Benedictine rule, around A.D. 530, and put it into operation at Monte Cassino, which became a real utopia.

The rule required *stabilitas loco* (one had to stay put),

conversatio morum (vows of poverty and chastity), *obedientia* (obligation to perform useful labors of all kinds), strict rules of admission, but a surprisingly mild ascetic discipline. As an institution, the monastery was bound to universal hospitality, care for the poor, and an educational program for the *pueri oblati* ("candidates for the priesthood" or "prospective priests").

Naturally, the ideal order of things declined, and at the beginning of the tenth century, the Cluniac reform aimed at restoring it, particularly to get the monasteries out of the clutches of greedy nobility and bishops. This was followed by another decline, until the clouth of Agnes of Poitou and her husband, the Emperor Henry III, made Cluny independent even of the Pope (Council of Sutri, A.D. 1064).

St. Bernard (A.D. 1095), preaching the first Crusade, began with a lurid and detailed description of the evils into which the search for power and gain had plunged all of Europe, and he not only called for a crusade but insisted that its purpose was the purification of the participants by the trials and dangers of pilgrimage. A product of the movement was the chivalric orders: Templars, Hospitalers, Knights of St. John, Knights of Malta, and so on, which were all secret monastic societies dedicated to the compassionate and idealistic work of protecting and aiding pilgrims to Jerusalem, while living in model communities in strict and saintly brotherhood. As we all know, they soon became very rich and very corrupt.

The next response to the evils of the time was in the great mendicant orders, the Franciscans, Dominicans, and Carmelites, who strove to stay within the obedience of the church but often found it difficult to do so in the ever-renewed insistence of literal-minded brethren on returning to the justice and simplicity of Christianity. The *gyrovagi* of the early centuries now took advantage of the new wandering life as Fratres Barbati, Laici, Conversi, the Begards, the Tisserands, Humiliati or Artisans of Milan, Pauperes Lombardi, the Guilds, the Mysteries, and so on, all of whom claimed the much publicized poverty of Christ and the apostles as a franchise for their own freebooting gangs and camps of free-love and other such shenanigans. More established societies, sometimes with roots deep in the past, such as the Catharians or New Manichaeans, Paulicians, Bogomils, Albigensians, and Waldensians, continued to preach the one unfailing first article of faith common to all, that Christ and the apostles had no property. There were real saints as well as real rascals among them, but all such irregular persuasions met with the same quick and violent suppression from the rulers; and to counteract their teachings, Pope Gregory IX went to the other extreme and in 1232 introduced the Inquisition.

The most renowned utopian of the Middle Ages was Joachim of Fiore, who became Cistercian Abbot of Corazzo of Sicily in 1177 but later retired to the mountains and was permitted by the Pope to found an order of his own. He taught that there were three ages or stations — of the Father, Son, and Holy Ghost; the third stage to be reached only after Israel had toiled in the desert and reached in the Millennium the Age of the Spirit, which would dawn in the year 1260. He drew a ground plan for the New Jerusalem and was hailed far and wide, even by some Franciscans and Dominicans, not only as the true prophet of "the Spiritual Men," but as a true Messiah. We must not forget that such men as Joachim and his followers, sincere seekers after righteousness, are never wholly missing from the stage of history, and they have deserved far more respect and attention than they have received. For they have been downgraded as heretics by Catholic writers and as Catholic by Protestants. The recent best-selling novel *The Name of the Rose*, by Umberto Eco, created a sensation by resurrecting this forgotten world, to which it provides an excellent introduction.

John Wycliffe, born in 1328 of illustrious birth but of even more remarkable mental powers, quickly became famous as a scholar, but he spoiled everything by declaring in 1374 that all church property should be nationalized. The Peasant Uprising of 1381 lost him the support of the nobility, but he was protected by the rising citizens of London. In 1383 he attacked the Mendicant orders, which had become altogether too rich and powerful, announcing that the present church was no less than anti-Christ. His followers, the Lollards, preaching that righteousness and materialism simply cannot coexist, would have been completely burnt out of existence had they not gone underground after 1401. The year before the Peasant Uprising, Gerhard Degroot had organized the Brethren of the Common Life, the original Lollards, at Deventer. Youthful members of the Czech nobility studying at Oxford took Wycliffe's ideas to Bohemia. In the next century, Savonarola led the religious democracy of Florence for three years and ended up at the stake. Luther was caught between two ideals, and his denunciation of the Peasant revolt lost him popular support in 1525.

This takes us in time to the three classic utopians, beginning with Sir Thomas More. His father was a judge in the king's bench, and, like Wycliffe, Sir Thomas early achieved renown as a prodigy in letters. At his father's request, he became a successful lawyer, but for all his great acumen and early recognition, he felt the urge to become a Franciscan monk. He gave up the idea only when he saw what wealth and power had done to the order. As an advocate, he became the chief counsel for the merchants of London, who represented the liberal movement of the day, and proved himself a skillful business manager and attorney. In 1504 he was elected to Parliament, and he is recognized as the first man to combine in eminent degree the qualifications of lawyer, businessman, and philosopher—for he was among the great lights of the sixteenth-

century Renaissance. But when he opposed a tax demanded by Henry VII, he had to flee the country and went
to Flanders. It was there in 1515, at the age of thirty-seven,
that he wrote his *Utopia*.[33] It was a smash hit throughout
Europe (printed in Louvain in 1516, Basel in 1518, and
Paris in 1520). More's immense ability brought him to the
highest offices in the state, but in 1529 he resigned as Lord
Chancellor, refusing to bow to the autocratic will of Henry
VIII; he was condemned to be tortured and burned, but
the sentence was mercifully commuted by his dear friend
and patron Henry, to beheading.

More's *Utopia* is divided into two parts, the first a vivid
account of the present state of the world, followed by the
second part, which gives us a better way of doing things.
The word *utopia*, "the place that is not," has been interpreted by the opposition as synonymous with Never-
Never-Land, Cloud-Cuckoo-Land, or any unworkable and
crackpot social order. But we must bear in mind that More
was a preeminently hard-headed, practical, experienced,
common-sense Englishman; and that his work had great
appeal among the most influential magnates, merchants,
and artisans in the Netherlands, Germany, France, England, and Italy. The thing was really meant to work.

He deals first with general principles to establish guide-
lines for his utopia. The work takes the form of a dialogue,
which begins when More in Antwerp (Lollard country)
meets Raphael the sailor, who has spent five years on the
Island of Utopia near Brazil. "It seems beyond doubt to
me, my dear More," the sailor Raphael Hytholdaeus begins,

> if I would speak frankly, that where private property rules,
> where money is the measure of all things for everyone,
> it is virtually impossible for society to flourish under
> righteous administration. That is, unless one thinks it
> right and proper that every good thing be owned by
> immoral people, or that prosperity consists of a few own-

ing everything, albeit the favorite few themselves are
not at all happy, while all the others live in abject misery. . . . How much better and nobler the arrangements
of the utopians seem to me where everyone has more
than enough although nobody has more than another; . . . compare with that the nations of the world
which must be constantly inventing new legislation and
yet never have good laws; where every individual thinks
to own for himself alone what he has earned and the
daily accumulation of countless laws is inadequate to
keep people safe in their possessions. One must admit
that Plato is right; . . . he realized that the only way to
cure the evil was by economic equality, which is simply
not possible as long as property is privately owned; . . .
granted there are ways of improving the situation without abolishing private property, there remains no other
cure for the evil.[34]

He points out that laws limiting ownership, sumptuary
laws, laws against corruption in government, and so on —
none of these will cure the fatal disease as long as we have
private property, which indeed *is* the disease.

In defending the status quo for the sake of argument,
More replies that with things as they are, we must have
laws protecting people and their possessions or else live
in a state of constant insecurity. Raphael's reply is that
things do not have to be as they are: "If you had ever lived
in utopia, you would know that," he says. Briefly, the
utopian order makes the family the center of everything
in the twenty-four cities of utopia, the nearest relatives
forming groups of about thirty persons. A portion of each
family does a pleasant two-year stint of duty on the farm
as the family members rotate their activities. For the harvest, everybody goes out to the fields, and the job is done
in a single day. Because all work, no one lives a life of
drudgery. Everyone has a trade, but the working day is
only six hours, relieved by a two-hour break in the middle
of the day. No one has the silly idea that unless people

work for money, they will not work at all; in fact "money is unknown in utopia." Everyone producing over-abundance is the rule; but production is carefully controlled at the national level. Every city sends delegates every year to a congress at the capital, so that the whole island op-erates as one big family.

Throughout the nation, the old-fashioned discipline prevails; "wives serve husbands, children serve elders, and the younger serve the older." On the farms, each family lives for itself. Religion is a private affair. Government officials are called Father, and every city consists of fam-ilies, which are as far as possible interrelated. Like Paul, Thomas More insists that *philargyria*, the desire for more money, is the root of all evil: "Greed, theft, and envy are all caused by fear of not having enough. But utopia always has a super abundance, and people's time belongs not to the economy but to the free development of the mind, for in that they find the blessings of life." "Such," says Ra-phael, "is not only the best, but the *only* constitution of society worthy of the name. Elsewhere people speak of the common good but actually work for the private good, for every man knows that he must go hungry if he does not work for himself, no matter how flourishing the society may be or how booming the economy; he must always consider his own well-being before that of others." In uto-pia, on the other hand, everyone knows that none will ever be in need as long as the common barns are full. "With everything equally divided among them, no one is poor, . . . thus all are rich."[35] "What greater wealth can there be than a healthy and secure life?" They live after the manner of happiness.

Then More, in the manner of the prophets, reverts to the dark world in which we live:

> What kind of justice is it when the nobleman, the banker [goldsmith], the money lender, in short, those

who do nothing productive, glory in riches while day
laborers, teamsters, blacksmiths, carpenters and field
workers, whose work can not be dispensed with for a
year, can sweat out a miserable existence at a level below
that of beasts of burden? Our animals do not work so
long, are better fed and have better security than they
do, for our workers are pressed down by the hopelessness of the situation and the expectation of beggary in
old age. What they are paid does not cover their daily
needs, and to save anything for old age is out of the
question. So we find shocking waste, luxury, triviality
and vanity [the lives of the rich and famous] on the one
side and utter abject misery on the other.[36]

So as things are, we get the worst of both worlds.

As God loves me, when I consider this, then every
modern society seems to me to be nothing but a conspiracy of the rich, who while protesting their interest
in the common good pursue their own interests and stop
at no trick and deception to secure their ill-gotten possessions, to pay as little as possible for the labor that
produces their wealth and so force its makers to accept
the nearest thing to nothing. They contrive rules for
securing and assuring these tidy profits for the rich in
the name of the common good, including of course the
poor, and call them laws![37]

"But after they have divided among themselves in their
insatiable greed all that should go to the society as a whole,
they still are not happy."[38] The law can avenge but never
hinder the deceptions, thievery, riots, panics, murders,
assassinations, poisonings, and so on, all of which spring
from one source — money.

The next most famous utopia is Thomas Campanella's
City of the Sun (1602).[39] Again we have a youthful prodigy
brought up in the highest society of the Renaissance,
whose fame at an early age spread far and wide. At fifteen
he became a Dominican at Cossenza and was sent all over

the country to display his genius in competitive disputation at monasteries and schools, relentlessly attacking Aristotle and earning the implacable hatred of the Jesuits. Medieval heresy was closely tied to social and political reform, and Spanish rule lay heavy on Calabria. Campanella led the monks of his cloister in one of the plots to free his land from the Spanish and set up a theocratic republic. By an interesting coincidence, this was the very Calabria in which Pythagoras' communities flourished and were cruelly suppressed.

Campanella said that God had chosen him for the task, and such important people as Father Dionysius Ponzio of Nicastro hailed Campanella as an emissary of God, to free the people of the misdeeds of the Minister of the King of Spain, who turned blood to gold as he trod on the poor and weak.[40] The monks of the area, more than three hundred Dominicans, Augustinians, and Franciscans, championed Campanella's project; but two insiders betrayed the whole scheme, and the troops were brought in from Naples for mass arrests and public hangings and burnings. Campanella hid in a shepherd's hut but was imprisoned in Naples in the following year, 1600, the same year that Giordano Bruno was burned at Rome. When he made a break from the prison, a common boatman refused to lend him his vessel to escape in—meanness was not limited to the rich; Campanella wrote a philosophical poem on the subject, entitled *The People*:

> The People are a capricious and stupid beast that doesn't know its own strength and bears burdens and blows with patience; . . . it knows not what fear it inspires, or that its masters have prepared a magic potion to stupefy it. What a fantastic situation! The People beating and tying itself up with its own hands; fighting and dying for a few pennies from the King, . . . totally unaware that everything between heaven and earth really belongs to it and stoning to death anyone who would remind it of its rights.[41]

In addition, Campanella bitterly wrote that he had been incarcerated in fifteen different prisons and been tortured seven times, the last time for forty hours. But he never yielded, and they never got one word out of him. Miraculously healed after six months of sickness, he was thrown into a pit. Fifteen times he was brought to trial. They would ask him, "Where did you learn all these things? Have you got a demon to serve you?" He answered: "To learn what I know I have burned more midnight oil than you have drunk wine."[42]

From his dungeon, Campanella became renowned throughout Europe: James I of England and the Popes sought his counsel, especially in astrology, and he corresponded with Gassendi and Caspar Scioppius; his manuscripts were printed in Germany, France, and Italy. When liberal Popes like Paul V and Urban VIII took his part, the Jesuits resorted to stirring up the people to riot against Campanella as a godless heretic and enemy of the church. But so great was his reputation that Richelieu called him to Paris, where the king greeted him with kisses on both cheeks. "I was born to fight three evils," he wrote, "tyranny, sophistry, and hypocrisy."

He classified his *City of the Sun* as *philosophia realis*, practical philosophy. Like Thomas More, he was convinced that it could really work, and it became very popular with the utopians of the 1840s in America. Like More and the prophets, he holds up the two pictures before us, showing us on one hand the world of dispossessed farmers and ragged beggars, kept in place by savage measures to protect the sacredness of property and the power of money. His ideal city was a fortress on a hill with seven walls. It was "neither a republic nor a monarchy," but one big family divided into groups by generations, with an annual great assembly to coordinate affairs. Campanella constantly refers to monastic orders as his model. There was total equality of sexes and uniformity of dress. Science was the ruling influence; the city was a gigantic museum, with didactic materials posted on all the walls for the instruction of young and old; everywhere one looked one was faced with geometric theorems, star charts, geological and biological specimens, and so on. Astrology was not mystical, but the recognition of the power of numbers to instruct and animate — the cosmic numbers 3, 7, and 12 dominate the structure of the society. The fundamentals of existence are power, wisdom, and love.

In a famous passage he tells how "the Solarians laugh heartily at us with our concern for breeding dogs and horses and our total neglect of the human stock."[43] Education must have the quality of play. Teaching is peripatetic, as all study science on continual fieldtrips. Everybody goes bareheaded and barefooted (as in John Locke's model school), and all are constantly exercised through games. Everyone must know several trades, and all work is treated as exhilarating exercise: "They make fun of our contempt for working people." Hopelessly backward people work in the fields, and the lame and the halt are made useful as the managers. No one needs to work more than four hours a day (a Brigham Young idea), and earning one's lunch is not the beginning and ending of existence as it is, Campanella observes, in his own society, which keeps people slaving sixteen to eighteen hours a day merely to get enough to eat. Agricultural work is one prolonged festival. The people sleep in great dormitories and eat in splendid refectories while being edified with reading or music in the monastic fashion. Food is prescribed by dietitians, and extreme cleanliness with frequent baths is mandatory. There is great concern for personal hygiene, and everybody chews fennel every morning. Men and women dress alike, all in white. No one worries about tomorrow, for all things are held in common and distributed according to need by a council (cf. the law of consecration). There is no need for money or commerce, yet full advantage is taken of technology—the Solarians have ships that move without sails or oars. In conclusion, Campanella invites all to enter his City and "to return to the Golden Age."

The third great utopian classic is Francis Bacon's *Nova Atlantis* (1638).[44] Of all our utopians, none was of more illustrious birth than Bacon, nor more justly famed for his brilliance—as we know, he is even credited with having written the works of Shakespeare. At this point it can hardly come as a surprise to learn that he barely escaped ending his life on the scaffold. Again we find an author enjoying a vast reputation in his own time and holding the highest position of power in the state, and yet not being willing to settle for his own comfort and convenience.

Bacon's New Atlantis is of course an island, a society seeking to avoid contamination from the outer world. The visitors are quarantined and disinfected before being admitted to the city, where they are put up in a hospice like a monastery. When they offer gold to their guide, he indignantly asks, "Do you want me to serve two masters?" Their instructor is a Christian priest whose only desire is brotherly love and the salvation of their souls. "We have come to a land of Angels," say the visitors, "who appear to us daily and shower us with comforts such as we never dreamed of."[45] Though Bacon was a man of the world if there ever was one, the spirit of his New Atlantis is strongly religious. The guide, delighted that the first question of the visitors is about the kingdom of God, tells them "how a pillar of light appeared over the sea topped by a cross and none could approach it but a boat containing a member of the house of Solomon";[46] the pillar suddenly turned into the starry heavens, and then a small cedar box appeared on the water, containing the Old and the New Testaments and a letter of explanation from Bartholomew, who writes that an angel had commanded him to put the book in the box with the blessing of the Father and the Lord Jesus. There had been other and earlier visitations, bringing the wisdom of Egypt and Athens. The house of Solomon, which was called "the Eye of the Realm," set the tone for the whole society, which was devoted to "studying and observing the works of the creations of God." Every twelve years a ship was sent to the outer world to bring back the latest in scientific technological invention and artistic production. The one object of all is "Seeking the Light."

As in the other utopias, the nation is organized in families. Families of thirty have their yearly family feasts, where the charter is read and the patriarch prays and blesses them all. Naturally there is a general conference of the whole island every year. The ultimate laws of Bensalem (for such the city is called) come from the Cabbala of Moses. God, religion, and marriage are the three great social controls, and the Atlantians, as the most chaste people on earth, are shocked by European morals and customs. The combination of religion and science, which reached such a happy fruition in the seventeenth century, is in full view here, for this religious world is a land of laboratories, observatories, arboriums, elaborate arrangements for experiments in heat, light, air pressure, acoustics, and so on. Science, technology, and general principles are what they are seeking, and the city is adorned by statues of Columbus, Friar Bacon, and every other great discoverer.

The list of utopian writings inspired by the above is a long one, the most important contributions being Hobbes' *Leviathan*, Harrington's *Oceana*, and Fenelon's *Telemaque*. But theorizing about utopia always seems to suggest doing something about it, and the Western world was never without stirrings of utopian movements. Lilburne and the Levellers were rebuffed by Cromwell, even as the German peasants were by Luther; and Lilburne ended up as a Quaker. And that gives us an excuse for jumping over to the New World, to the Ephrata community in Pennsylvania in 1732. The Mennonites, like the Quakers, did better on this side of the water than on the other. George Rapp's project in New Harmony, Pennsylvania, moved to Indiana, where Robert Owen took it over and founded New Harmony in 1828. His work brought forth lasting results in the first kindergarten, the first trade school, the first free library, and the first public schools in America, all of which have endured until the present administration. The Shakers flourished in eighteen villages in eight states, and Charles Fourier's Brooke Farm experiment spread to twenty-eight colonies in the 1840s. John Humphrey Noyes made a lasting contribution at Oneida, New York, in the same decade, and when the Mormons left Nauvoo, the place was taken over by Etienne Cabet and his Icarians. Historians have often observed that of all the utopian projects that swarmed in nineteenth-century America, only Mormonism, which they all ridicule as the craziest of all, has flourished.

Parley P. Pratt paints a picture of utopian bliss in a letter to his brother written from Salt Lake City just a year after the arrival of the pioneers: "All is quiet—stillness. No elections, no police reports, no murders, no wars in our little world. . . . No policeman . . . have been on duty to guard us from external or internal dangers."[47] That would get nowhere in the Nielson ratings—what on earth would the people do if they would not die of boredom? Answer: "Here we can cultivate the mind, renew the spirits, invigorate the body, . . . or polish and adorn our race. And here we can receive and extend that pure intelligence which is unmingled with the jargon of mystic Babylon."[48] This qualifies Brother Pratt as a full-blown utopian, and indeed the revelations to the Church back him up: "and all this . . . that every man may improve upon his talent, that every man may gain other talents, yea, even an hundred fold" (D&C 82:18). The "all this" is the law of consecration, by which all is "to be cast into the Lord's storehouse, to become the common property of the whole church—every man seeking the interest of his neighbor, and doing all things with an eye single to the glory of God" (D&C 82:18-19). This is no pilot study or tentative arrangement: "This order I have appointed to be an everlasting order unto you, and unto your successors, inasmuch as you sin not" (D&C 82:20).

Is it surprising that the words of the revelations and the leaders of the Church should sound so utopian? It is unavoidable. We have seen that the three great utopians were deeply religious and in the end took their teachings from the Bible; and the religious devotion they expressed is surprisingly the same, whether they are Christian or heathen. The constantly emerging utopian movements from the desert sectaries to the present day were all attempts to return to the true order of Israel. I remember the efforts of my friend Clendenning, who took his idealistic order of Aaron out into the deserts of Western Utah, where earlier in the century a society of utopian Jews had founded the Clarion Community. If all such efforts have failed, what of Israel? Moses and the prophets clearly and vividly describe the order God wanted established among men and just as clearly and vividly declare Israel's total failure to live up to it.

Brother Pratt's "Mystic Babylon" has ever been the reverse image of utopia. As Satan carefully parodies everything that God does, so he has always offered men a utopia in which "you can have anything in this world" for the one thing the other utopians said turned heaven into hell and made it possible for the world to groan in blood and horror as Satan has wielded "great dominion among men" (Moses 6:15).

I mentioned monasticism as a response to the question, Where is the true Christian society? An answer was imperative back then because the great orating Bishops of the fourth century were promising the world that the victory of the church would bring the Golden Age: church and empire, born together in the time of Caesar Augustus, fused into one would surely bring in the Millennium. Constantine exploited the proposition and zealously performed his part: "The great scaffoldings, acres of painted canvas, firmaments of tapers and torches, fabulous displays of jewels and lavish applications of gilt paint left no one in doubt that the glory of the Lord was round about. Heaven in our Time was not something to be worked for but something to be accepted; not a hope, but a fulfillment, a stupendous miracle." The great display was no longer mere form but "a reality on a newer and higher level of existence."[49]

None endorsed the doctrine more ardently than Augustine, until in the end of his life reality caught up with him and he had to explain that the city of God was after all only spiritual. Let us hark back to Vergil's fourth *Eclogue*. It made him a saint in the Middle Ages; for its picture of the coming of the Messianic age, foretold from the beginning, unites the Christian and the pagan world in the shared oracle of the Sibyl—glorified alike in Vergil's poem and Michelangelo's Sistine Chapel. More than that, it was picked up by the Founding Fathers and placed on the Great Seal of the new nation; Vergil's *magnus ab integro saeclorum nascitur ordo* ("the great line of the centuries begins anew")[50] is indeed the *novus ordo seclorum* ("the new order of the ages") of the Great Seal of the United States. In both documents, the heavy emphasis is on the bold new beginning and the return to primal purity. Lycurgus's first step, says Plutarch, was to recognize that his great society would have to be a whole new system from the ground up; all utopias are brand-new heavens. Vergil's theme was *iam nova progenies caelo demittitur alto*,[51] a new generation descended from heaven"; and now *toto surget gens aurea mundo*[52]—"a new golden race has taken over the world." If you will look at the back of a dollar bill, you will see added to the picture of the Great Seal, with the words *novus ordo seclorum*, the upbeat announcement *annuit coeptis* ("he approves what we have begun")—with the all-seeing

eye on the capstone of an Egyptian pyramid—the ancient
hope fulfilled, another new age, another utopia, and all
ironically announced on a dollar bill! We proclaim it from
the housetops: "Thine alabaster cities gleam undimmed
by human tears"—but when? "Beyond the years,"[53] to be
sure, but for the present it is hail and farewell. Utopia is
already past—and it was the dollar that killed it.

Everybody knows about false utopias, here-and-now
utopias. The famous Potemkin Village was rigged to last
only long enough to pass a quick inspection. Disneyland
is more solid, but still only for visitors, and so we must
advance to Las Vegas and Hollywood for the more permanent delights and splendors. Finally, with the "Lifestyles of the Rich and Famous," we reach that enduring
state of blessedness insured by unlimited wealth. The celestial glories of Old World nobility at Versailles or Blen-
heim were made available at the turn of the century to
anyone who had the character, gumption, and vision to
make lots of money in the palaces of Newport and the
imperial ranches of the West. The American dream was
right back on square one. As More put it, the one insuperable obstacle to utopia had become the one indispensable condition to achieving it.

When I was in high school, the most effective rebuttal
to *Erewhon* and *Looking Backwards* was the all-conquering
philosophy of evolution. By an unimpeachable law of nature, the present order is the crowning achievement of a
long process of natural selection, and therefore the best of
possible worlds. (The doctrine has been revived with renewed fervor in a run of pretentious TV documentaries,
by Bronowski, Sagan, and Burke.) I was brought up on
the Great Pageant of Progress, the Ascent of Man from the
primordial ooze through the beast, the savage, the Egyptians, the Greeks, the Romans, the Middle Ages, the Ren-
naisance, the modern Enlightened Age, and finally the
wonderful World of Tomorrow, where science and tech-

nology have removed the inconvenience of anything not made to our specifications — utopia at last! It made a wonderful subject for murals in libraries and schools, but even H. G. Wells saw his dream world turn into a nightmare, a dehumanized hell, a phony utopia. The problem is to popularize such a dream, and now we are assured that it has been done.

"There is nothing wrong with America," cries the leader, and he proves it by showing us Currier and Ives prints, and especially the heart-warming calendars and magazine covers of Mr. Norman Rockwell. There we find our utopia, as Mr. Wright Morris points out:

> In soaring into the past rather than the future, Mr. Rockwell is true to himself and his public, since that is where the true Territory Ahead actually lies. In knowing this he illustrates, with admirable fidelity, the American Land of Heart's Desire. . . . It was in the past — just yesterday — that there were giants in the earth, dreams in our hearts, love in our homes, religion in our churches, honor in our markets, and a future of such promise that the very thought of it brings an ache to the throat and eyes grow dim.[54]

This is the art and the world that meets us on the covers and pages of our lesson manuals and in the sentimental talks at conference that take us back to a life on the farm which few of us today have ever known.[55]

In my youth I heard of nothing but "unlimited opportunities" and "inexhaustible resources"; ours was a Manchester utopia with smoke-blackened skies and a labor market willing to settle for starvation wages in return for employment. Some still call pre-Depression America "the Greatest Civilization the world has ever seen."

But to claim the prize prematurely is to lose it forever. The economist Daniel Yergin writes of the present situation,

There is an increasing doubt [among economists] that anything at all can be done about anything; . . . if that wisdom is correct, then any "solutions" to poverty become far more difficult and painful; they cannot be financed out of a growth dividend, but only by redistributing what others already have, in turn creating massive social unrest [most utopians did that merely by suggesting such a move]. Before the 1974-1975 minidepression, all financial poverty could have been eliminated at a modest shift of $10-15 billion to the poor from the rest of the community. 15 billion is less than 1.5% of the GNP, about the size of one of the cheaper weapons systems.

Our society has gone out of the way *not* to do what could be done to solve the problem. Why? A community which can at tolerable expense eliminate human distress but refrains from doing so either must believe that it benefits from unemployment or poverty, or that the poor and unemployed are bad people, or that other more important values will be impaired by attempts to help the lower orders—or all of these statements.

"No other civilization has permitted the calculus of self-interest so to dominate its culture," writes the eminent economist and historian Robert L. Heilbroner. "It has transmogrified greed and philistinism into social virtues, and subordinated all values to commercial values."[56] This is exactly what Thomas More said: "What has heretofore passed as unjust, . . . they have turned upside down, and in fact proclaimed it publicly and by law to be nothing less than justice itself."[57] And that is exactly what Ivan Boesky proclaimed when he recently commended "healthy greed" as a high virtue to a college audience.[58] The complete inversion of the utopian ideal is reached when success itself becomes synonymous with money. And what is the end result? The old familiar pictures. A citizen of New York writes,

You have to be on the alert constantly to sense when somebody nearby is out of place, waiting, looking, ready to pounce. You have to clutch your handbag up close, ready to fight for it should that become necessary. You have to put three locks on your door, plus a burglarproof chain. You have to avoid the subways, night or day, and don't smile at strangers on the bus.[59]

Still the writer is determined to hang on: "I can't accept a life-style that makes us wary of community or civility, where human beings have to take on the attributes of jungle animals in order to protect themselves, in order to live." Foreigners coming to this same city from Eastern Europe hail it as an earthly paradise, a utopia; which only goes to show that anyone can adjust to anything. But our writer objects: "Something inside of me says that I will die if I accommodate to this way of living."

Is this an exaggeration? Every day walking to school I pass a number of signs on the south side of the campus that read, "For your safety do not walk in this area alone after dark." This is the Zion to which we have become accustomed for the sake of the economy. It is the same fantastic situation as that confronting all the utopians.

The trouble is that it is all too convenient. Its great power is that it enables you to cheat. Let us with Shakespeare's Timon cast a backwards glance at Athens: "Let me look back upon thee. O thou wall, that girdest in those wolves! . . . Bankrupts, hold fast; rather than render back, out with your knives, and cut your trusters' throats! Bound servants, steal! Large-handed robbers your grave masters are, and pill [steal] by law!"[60]

Timon harks back to his lost utopian Athens: "Religion to the gods, peace, justice, truth, domestic awe, night-rest, and neighbourhood, instruction, manners, mysteries, and trades, degrees, observances, customs and laws"; only to have it swept away by greed: "Decline to your confounding contraries, and yet confusion live! Plagues, incident to men, your potent and infectious fevers heap on Athens, ripe for stroke!"[61] So spoke the prophets to other cities, "ripe in iniquity" and ready to be swept away (see 1 Nephi 17:35). Timon's whole argument is that money creates values that do not exist, "confounded contraries," and thus gives us a completely phony world.

The most unique and concise utopian text we have is 4 Nephi in the Book of Mormon. We should all know the familiar passages, some of which were read at the last general conference; what is interesting is how and why such a highly desirable state of affairs should have been abandoned and come to an end. The process is put before us with vivid clarity in the Book of Mormon itself, as I summed it up in a recent talk in Salt Lake City.[62]

We begin with a society in which "they had all things common among them; therefore there were not rich and poor" (4 Nephi 1:3), "and surely there could not be a happier people" (4 Nephi 1:16), in other words, utopia. (1) The first step in the decline came when things were privatized, and "they did have their goods and their substance no more common among them" (4 Nephi 1:25). (2) Next they became ethnicized, as the Lamanite children "were taught to hate the children of Nephi" and vice versa (4 Nephi 1:39). (3) Next they gloried in "their exceeding riches" and made them the measure of success—the old pride was back (4 Nephi 1:43). As a result, (4) they became "divided into classes" (4 Nephi 1:26) and next (5) formed clubs, combinations, consortiums, and secret societies to promote their interests, as (6) a fever of business activity and acquisition seized everyone (4 Nephi 1:46). Fourth Nephi ends at this point, but Mormon and Moroni carry on. (7) Thinking was nationalized as each side faced the old traditional enemy, but then (8) the central government and its controls were eliminated, and the society became regionalized and tribalized; (9) in all the confusion and insecurity that followed, the world became terrorized by robber bands, and the people regretted their hasty action in abolishing the federal government. Fear of the Lamanites brought on by their own guilt forced them to become (10) militarized on the national level again and to put destruction on a more efficient footing as the entire population became (11) polarized along traditional lines, each side with but one objective, to exterminate the enemy, the sole cause of all evil in the world. When ignorant armies clashed in all-out battles and campaigns, both were (12) pulverized, the one obliterated, the other completely shattered.

This is all repeated (as we are reminded again and again) specifically for our benefit, and we are also told the manner in which we may participate in the final step when the wicked are swept from the land, consumed as stubble, and become extinct—that is, (13) vaporized.

The great question with which all utopians deal is, Can the mere convenience that makes money such a useful device continue indefinitely to outweigh the horrendous and growing burden of evil that it imposes on the human race and that ultimately brings its dependents to ruin? Plato is right, wrote More; all systems fail because of private property. Christians try to dodge the teachings of Christ, unwilling to adapt themselves to them.[63] And he pronounces the common dictum of the other devout utopians: "Christ recommended a communal way of life, which is still practiced among the communities of the true Christians."[64] More concludes his great work with his strongest argument: "The rational recognition of one's own best interests or else the example of our Redeemer, Jesus Christ, who in his great wisdom must well have known what is best, and in his grace would only counsel what he knew was best, [should assure that] the world would long ere now have readily embraced the laws of that state were they not opposed by a single monster, the parent and original of all pestilence—*superbia*,"[65] the pride of the world.

Here is what all the great utopians have in common:

1. They were not losers with axes to grind but the most successful and respected men of their times.

2. They were preeminently practical men of the world, with far more experience in leadership and organization than their critics.

3. All attempted to implement the setting up of societies that they believed had existed among men in the past and would again in the future.

4. Whether Jew, heathen, or Christian, all thought of their utopias as religious societies, and they preached both religious tolerance and the cultivation of faith.

5. Yet all, in spite of all the great esteem in which they and their works were held, were persecuted by the powers that be, and few escaped violent death.

6. All suffered disillusionment in their own day; their communities were either violently destroyed or went underground.

7. They taught that the object of life was joy, and none of them either displayed or recommended stern puritanical judgments. Their utopias were liberal and easygoing.

8. The advantage of technology and its possibilities for bettering the human condition were first fully realized by the utopians.

9. They all realized that joy is to be found only in the active *mind* — the glory of man is intelligence, and knowledge is the stuff on which the mind feeds.

10. Science, art, scholarship, philosophy, literature were all cultivated together as the principal activity of the citizens. There is quite enough there to keep us all busy even without the urgent imperative of getting lunch. It is because of this that what appears to us as a disturbing uniformity in dress, housing, and so on, presents no problem but rather removes obstacles to the proper studies of mankind.

11. The joy derived from the senses — beautiful sur-

roundings and impressions — and from the vigorous exercise of our physical as well as our mental faculties is never neglected.

12. Goods of "secondary intent" (Campanella uses the expression) — clothing, housing, food, medicaments, transportation, etc. — are essential to assist in carrying on the more serious work of the mind and body, but they never become primary, in other words, their own excuse for being, as is the case with us, where to make and market such goods fulfills the measure of one's existence.

13. Money and private property are the insuperable obstacles to the achievement of utopia. The two are inseparable because the idea that there is no limit to what money can represent is necessary to implement the equally outrageous idea that there is no limit to what an individual can own. The relationship is succinctly stated in a formula propounded by one of awesome authority in the very beginning, in the first utopia, where he cast the long, dark shadow ahead with those ominous words: "You can have anything in this world for money."

Were all of these shrewd, experienced, and concerned observers being simplistic in unanimously tracing the root of all evil to money? Well, make a list of some of those evils that today as never before threaten the whole world with dissolution — drugs; pornography; terrorism; nuclear armaments; fraud; corruption; soldiers of fortune; corporate outrages; opportunistic preachers; pollution of air, water, food, and information; acid rain; extinction of species; and so on. Which of these does not have big money as the driving force behind it? The drive for power and gain is the soil in which they all flourish.

Enoch, Abraham, and Moses all sought against frightful opposition to restore the order that alone offers happiness to earth's inhabitants. Their program is renewed in full force in the law of consecration. To consecrate is to set aside, to dedicate to a particular purpose; what has been dedicated is no longer at the donor's disposal.[66] Happily, the Latter-day Saints have agreed to consecrate here and now everything with which they have been blessed in order to establish on earth Zion, which is the perfect utopia. For those who have enlisted in the project there can be no turning back, hedging, or rationalizing, for God is not mocked, and to rewrite the contract after accepting it is to put one's self into the power of Satan. What they are seeking is to be "equal in the bonds of heavenly things, yea, and earthly things also" (D&C 78:5), to "stand independent above all other creatures beneath the celestial world . . . under the council and direction of the Holy One" (D&C 78:14, 16). That is the utopia to which we now are committed.

Notes

1. Hugh W. Nibley, *Enoch the Prophet* (Provo: BYU, 1976), 76-85, first appearing in a Pearl of Great Price Symposium; reprinted in *CWHN* 2:209-10.
2. Ibid.; in *CWHN* 2:215.
3. For a general treatment, see August Freiherrn Von Gall, *Basileia tou Theou* (Heidelberg: Winter, 1926).
4. Plutarch, *Lycurgus* VIII, 1.
5. Ibid., IX, 1-3.
6. Ibid., IX, 4.
7. Ibid., XII, 2.
8. Ibid., XII, 1.
9. Ibid., XIV, 2, 4.
10. Ibid., XV, 1.
11. Ibid., XV, 9.
12. Ibid., XX.
13. Ibid., XIV, 2, 4.
14. Ibid., XXV, 3.
15. Ibid., XVI, 5.
16. Ibid., XXX, 1.
17. Ibid., XIII, 5-6.
18. Ibid., XIII, 1, 3.
19. Ivan M. Linforth, *Solon the Athenian* (Berkeley: University of California Press, 1919), 140-45. This is a collection of all known texts attributable to Solon; Nibley translation, in part.

20. Ibid., 145.

21. Ibid., 169.

22. Plato, *Philebus* 16C.

23. Diogenes Laertius, *Pythagoras* VIII, 10.

24. Linforth, *Solon the Athenian*, 139.

25. Plato, *Laws* 899D-900A.

26. Ibid., 906A.

27. Ibid., 904D-904E.

28. Anthony, *Sermo de Vanitate Mundi et de Resurrectione Mortuorum*, in *PG* 40:962, 986.

29. Anthony, *Epistolae* VII, 5-7, and *Epistolae Viginti* I, in *PG* 40:994-1001.

30. Anthony, *Epistolae Viginti* I, in *PG* 40:999-1000, and *Epistolae* VII, 6, in *PG* 40:977.

31. Anthony, *Epistolae Viginti* I, in *PG* 40:1001.

32. Ibid., 5, in *PG* 40:1010.

33. Thomas More, *Utopia*, tr. Robert M. Adams, 2 vols. (London, Yale University Press, 1964).

34. Ibid., 2:88.

35. Ibid.; cf. Jacob 2:17.

36. Ibid., 2:88-89.

37. Ibid., 2:89.

38. Ibid.

39. Translations of More, Campanella, and Bacon are easy to find. A Scolar Press Facsimile of the first edition of *Utopia* (Louvain, 1516) has been reprinted (Menston, England: Scolar Press, 1971), with a title page in the utopian language and script.

40. Cf. Luigi Firpo, ed., sonnet 123 in *Tutte le opere de Tommaso Campanella*, 2 vols. (Italy: Mondadori, 1954), 1:252, lxvi (preface); cf. Nino Valeri, *Tommaso Campanella*, profili no. 115 (Rome: Formiggini, 1931).

41. Ibid., see "Della Plebe," no. 33, 1:97.

42. Cf. Ibid., xxiii-iv, lxxii-v (preface); "Al carcere," no. 60, 1:129; and "Lamentevole orazione profetale dal profondo della fossa dova stava incarcerato," no. 72, 1:141. Cf. Romano Amerio, *Campanella: I maestri del pensiero* (Brescia, Italy: La Scuola, 1947).

43. Thomae Campanellae, "Appendix Political," *Civitas Solis, Idea Republicae Philosophicae* (Francofurti: Emmelli, 1623); cf. original Italian version, in Tommaso Campanella, *La città del sole: dialogo poetico*, tr. Daniel J. Donno (Berkeley: University of California Press, 1981), 36-37.

44. *Nova Atlantis Fragmentorum alterum* per Franciscum Baconum baronum de Verulano (London: Haviland, 1638).

45. Cf. Basil Montagu, *The Works of Lord Bacon*, 16 vols. (London: Pickering, 1825), 2:334.

46. Ibid., 335-37.

47. Brigham Young Manuscript History (August 23, 1848): 57; *MS* 11:24.

48. Ibid.

49. Hugh Nibley, "The Unsolved Loyalty Problem," *WPQ* 6 (December 1953): 641-43.

50. Vergil, *Eclogue* IV, 5.

51. Ibid., IV, line 7.

52. Ibid., line 9.

53. Katherine Lee Bates, "America the Beautiful," Hymns of The Church of Jesus Christ of Latter-day Saints (Salt Lake City: The Church of Jesus Christ of Latter-day Saints, 1985), no. 338.

54. Wright Morris, "Norman Rockwell's America," *Atlantic Monthly* (December 1957): 136, 138.

55. Ibid., 136: "We might say that Mr. Rockwell's special triumph is in the conviction his countrymen share that the mythical world he evokes actually exists. This cloudland of nostalgia seems to loom higher and higher on the horizon, as the horizon itself, the world of actual experience, disappears from view, . . . leaving the drab world of commonplace facts and sensations behind."

56. See Leonard Silk's *New York Times* book review of Robert L. Heilbroner, *Business Civilization in Decline* (New York: Norton, 1976).

57. More, *Utopia*, 1:25.

58. Mariann Caprino, "Healthy Greed Was Boesky's Undoing," reported in *Salt Lake Tribune* (20 November 1986): D9.

59. Carolyn Lewis, "The Beasts in the Jungle," *Newsweek* (19 January 1981): 8.

60. William Shakespeare, *Timon of Athens*, act IV, scene 1, much like the real Athens of Aristophanes' *Plutus*.

61. Ibid.

62. See above, "Law of Consecration," pages 422-86.

63. More, *Utopia*, 1:29.

64. Ibid., 2:79.

65. Ibid., 2:90.

66. *TPJS* 127: "When we consecrate our property to the Lord it is to administer to the wants of the poor and needy, for this is the law of God; it is not for the benefit of the rich, those who have no need; . . . now for a man to consecrate his property . . . to the Lord, is nothing more nor less than to feed the hungry, clothe the naked, visit the widow and fatherless, the sick and afflicted, and do all he can to administer to their relief."

17

Goods of First and Second Intent

In this morning's paper we have a headline, "The American Intellect Is Dying," and a month or so ago, somebody gave me Allan Bloom's book *The Closing of the American Mind*.[1] There seems to be general agreement that we are not doing what we should here. So I am going to talk about that. Remember, it is the goods of first and second intent.

If you look up *intendo* in the *Oxford Latin Dictionary*, it says it means "to strain, to exert [one's strength], etc." (I like that "etc.") After all these definitions, it continues: "to concentrate [the mind or attention], to exert oneself, to direct [the eyes, sight, hearing, etc.], to aim at; to direct one's course, steps, to set out for, to direct one's efforts or activities, turn [to], apply oneself, set about, to be bent on." If that doesn't satisfy you, we have the nominal form *intentio*: "concentrated attention [of the eyes, etc.], mental effort, etc., aim, purpose, intention"; and the adjective, *intentus*, means "having the mind keenly occupied, intent [of the eyes, ears], closely attentive; intensely serious, earnest [of actions or conduct], strict, rigorous, earnest," and so on. The Greek equivalent is *spoudaios*: "quick, energetic, earnest, serious, active, zealous, wholly committed"; it also characterizes virtuous qualities in general—what is "good,

This talk was given to the Retired Teacher's Association on October 9, 1987, at the Salt Palace in Salt Lake City.

excellent, moral, worth attention, and weighty." This suggests that all real intent is in itself good.

When is a person really intent on something? How
many times in your life have you asked this, or do you
feel it yourself? If we don't have much of it, its rarity alone
should give it the value of pearls and rubies among a youth
whose highest *desideratum* is to be "cool," slurring his
words with a "man" and a "you know" every third word,
and whose highest pitch of excitement and ecstasy is reserved for rock bands. So one asks, contemplating the
antics of the young, Is it all right just to be intent in any
way? What difference does it make what the object is, as
long as one becomes committed and involved?

Obviously all objects of our attention are not equally
worthy of our devotion. How can we grade or classify
them? Aristotle, speaking as a teacher, says that the school
is a *schole*, which means leisure, and *ludus*, a place where
you play, where the serious work of the world is not done.
It is where you get a liberal education, where you are freed
from all other ties of the moment, where you are at liberty
to choose and decide what you want to do without any
pressing bread-and-butter concerns. That is what *schole* and
ludus mean. Before the words force choices on us in this
sanctum, we should ask ourselves, what is the best thing
we could possibly be doing now, and forever after, for that
matter? How can we rate or classify our choices? Very
simply.

Aristotle, in Book XII of the *Metaphysics*, gives us just
two choices — two items to choose from in every situation:
(1) "that which is good in itself and is to be chosen for its
own sake"; that is, a good of first intent (*to kalon kai to di'
hauto haireton*). This quality necessarily makes an object
also *to ariston*, the best of all possible choices, in any combination the one thing to be chosen. That is an important
clue to the thing. But there are other things necessary to
obtaining it — there are also goods of second intent, also to

be earnestly pursued: (2) *to . . . hou heneka . . [kai] tinos,* "that which is good for the sake of getting something else."[2] Watches and shoes and string and houses and roads and horses are all good, but they are good for doing something useful in attaining something else. They aren't good in themselves; they are a means of getting something else. So Aristotle would call them goods of second intent. They are also earnestly pursued; we have to have them, yet they are not the ultimate good. But what is? Thinking, says Aristotle, is the big thing—merely to be thinking; awareness in its highest state is the most exhilarating of all experiences. It is "that object which is in itself best, . . . in the highest sense that which is best; thought itself becomes an object of thought, by the act of apprehending and thinking";[3] and so we get to the standard scholastic definition of God as pure intellect—awareness is the greatest blessing, the awareness of being alive. But that is oversimplification, and it certainly leads to endless debate. God is the pure act of thinking, say the scholastic philosophers; and what does he think about? He thinks about Thought.

But goods of first intent actually can be very solid in content. As we all know, the good, the true, and the beautiful are desirable for their own sake. Yet there is certainly that which is good, true, and beautiful in the workmanship of goods of second intent; a well-made knife is a beautiful object in itself and therefore of first intent. Socrates in Xenophon gives us an extreme case when he tells us that a dung basket can be as beautiful as a golden shield can be ugly.[4] And what makes it beautiful? How can that be? What makes a dung basket beautiful? Its functional perfection. This is a paradox: it is beautiful because it fulfills its secondary function, and its beauty gives it primary value. What, on the other hand, would make an ornate golden bowl ugly? To be sure, its meaningless embellishments and especially its lack of proportion—its lack of a particular proportion. Measurements have been made of thousands of Greek vessels in museums and were found to present in the overwhelming majority of cases the famous "golden proportion" or "golden section." That is an exact measure, an exact number—2.618 to one.[5] It's an unreal number, not a round number; it goes on forever, but that is the number. In 99 percent of cases, you say that a vase is beautiful because it follows that proportion.

This is a very interesting thing: we have an internal control that provides an objective measure of beauty, dictated not by the strict mathematical rule which it follows, but by the eye alone, which approves it as a good object of undebatable first intent. Its precise proportion establishes a bridge between the objective world and our minds, and that remains a mystery to mathematicians to this day, as it was in the very beginning. All the mysteries of Pythagoreans are still the same mysteries, such as why a particular mathematical organizational structure of things is inevitable; it is, and nobody knows why. We cannot say that the highest good is merely relative, because we have an absolute scale of value built in, so to speak. For example, golf is a good of first intent to many people. This is true. My grandfather, Charles W. Nibley, built Nibley Park because he loved golf. He discovered golf in his old age; he was Scotch and knew all about it. But it was a good of first intent as far as he was concerned; it was marvelous relief and relaxation. It didn't need any medical prescription; golf was its only excuse for being. It was primarily therapeutic in his case. It prolonged his life, and isn't life to be placed first in the order of good things to choose from? Increasingly, sports are becoming the climax of civilization. Take the America Cup, for example. Millions of dollars and years of studying, planning, and designing are spent to win a boat race by fifty feet. Men will do a thing like that. Well, is that a good of first intent? Are they worth all that trouble?

Plato says that *theoria* (our word "theory" comes from

that) is the inspection or study of symbols in the mysteries as they are presented in a regular order for purpose of instruction.[6] *Theoria* is contemplation of the symbols of the mysteries. But alas, *theoria* became *theatromania*, the rage for spectator sports and shows. The ancient experience ended as does the modern, as announced in this article which I herewith display: "Football lunacy shows how the American intellect is dying." It has become *theatromania*, even as the ancient world went completely overboard for *theatromania*.[7] You know about *panem et circenses* ("bread and circuses"),[8] how the people had nothing to do but go to games and watch spectator sports. They were every bit as obsessed with them as we are with TV.

Who then is to judge what is good, true, and beautiful? You are. Plato says it is the soul: the proper dimensions and proportions are already stored in our minds, and when we recognize the good, true, and beautiful—how is it that we do it? It is by *anamnesis*, the act of recalling what we have seen somewhere before. You must have received an impression of what is right somewhere else, because you recognize it instantly; you don't have to have it analyzed; you don't have to say, "That is beautiful," or "That is ugly"; you welcome it as an old acquaintance. We recognize what is lovely because we have seen it somewhere else, and as we walk through the world, we are constantly on the watch for it with a kind of nostalgia, so that when we see an object or a person that pleases us, it is like recognizing an old friend; it hits us in the solar plexus, and we need no measuring or lecturing to tell us that it is indeed quite perfect. It is something we have long been looking for, something we have seen in another world, memories of how things should be. That is the basic principle of Plato's idealism: you know when a thing is good and what the ideal proportion is because you have seen it somewhere, and you recognize it.[9]

One test for goods of first intent is that you cannot get

enough of them: "The eye—it cannot choose but see; we cannot bid the ear be still."[10] There are certain things of which we never tire, with which we never become bored. Those are the things of eternity. Yet strangely enough it is these which we easily dismiss and neglect as if they were highly expendable. Arthur Clarke compares our mental state to the condition of a man who, having inherited a magnificent palace, prefers to spend his days holed up in a broom closet in the basement. That is the popular mentality. On the first day of school in the only course I ever took at Brigham Young University, the professor, having only a month before taken his final examinations and received his Ph.D., reported with delight how his major professor had told him at the conclusion of the test: "Congratulations, my boy, now you will never have to take another examination as long as you live!" And he really believed it. Such is the terminal degree, the well-appointed broom closet (for the rest of his life), a world of second intent.

A test of the goods of second intent for which we all strive is that far from being infinitely gratifying, they are strictly limited in value. As Paul tells us, "Having food and raiment, let us be therewith content"; if you want too much more, you are in real trouble: "They that will be rich fall into temptation and a snare [or *a trap*], and into many foolish and hurtful lusts [*epithumias*, meaning desiring things you don't really need and shouldn't have], which drown men in destruction and perdition" (1 Timothy 6:8-9). The eager seeker gets himself into a trap, caught in the rapids, hankering all the days of his life for things that can only do him harm—yet in acquiring goods of this category, as the great Solon said, no man ever thinks he can get enough, though the results are always frustrating and disappointing.[11] There can be too much of our goods of second intent—but never enough of the first.

We nevertheless constantly reverse the order. The secondary need is necessarily first in action, though it leads to the other; yet the primary must be first in thought to get the second going. But once we get immersed in that auxiliary activity, there is great danger of never emerging from it, for it is concerned with what is immediately urgent and has priority over everything else. There is no free lunch, we say; you get yourself financially fixed, and then you might consider some of the other things. Of course acquisition soon becomes the measure of existence; we become hooked on the idea of "success" and everything goes into it. Yet once you have "succeeded," what else is there? Only retirement. I know of a number of men who looked forward to retirement, only to find when they had reached it that it was too late for the things they knew in their heart all along were the most important. Like the young man with a fine singing voice who worked in a boiler factory to get enough money for music lessons. By the time he had enough, he was stone deaf.

The purpose of education, of course, is to bring the two goods together in proper balance: *Mens sana in corpore sano* ("a sound mind in a sound body")[12] — the two must go together. We all stand in need of constant nourishment for both body and spirit. The trouble is that we are not allowed to forget the hunger of the body; it will always remind you that you are in need of nourishment. But what about the other? We think the hunger of the mind can wait, but if we separate the mind and body, we nourish neither. Both are susceptible to junk food and anorexia: TV supplies the junk food, the school the other. But it is always the mind that stands to lose the most.

If there are no goods of first intent, then there are no goods of second intent, which by definition are the necessary approach to the former. Besides goods of first and second intent, is there a third category? There is not. Nothing is better known today than the division of the brain into right and left halves, the yin and the yang, the polarized particles, parity, the coincidence of opposites, male and female, and so on, in which neither one is expendable—there is no third choice. And they should pull together; that is the way of goods of primary intent, which are good and everlasting in themselves; the goods of secondary intent are the goods that lead to them.

And so when limited secondary intent steals the show, we are left with a phenomenon we find all through literature: you devote your whole life to the second thing, and "the summer has come and gone, and our souls are not saved; *vita brevis est, ars longa* ("life is short, art long");[13] *gaudeamus igitur iuvenes dum sumus,* and so on—the most famous of all school songs which goes back to the fourth century: "Let us rejoice while we are young because after miserable old age, *nos habebit humus,* the dirt is waiting to receive us."[14] It is the realization too late that there has been nothing for us beyond the business of day-to-day, and that we are not going anywhere. The humanist stands proudly with William James "on the firm foundation of unyielding despair."

How can we escape that nihilism that attends total attachment to the things of this world, and rejoice in goods of first intent without trespassing on religion, and how can we go that far without jeopardizing our religious freedom? The best education of the past has found an easy solution to that one, and it is to study whatever you study with real *intent,* Aristotle's *spoudaiotes,* "high seriousness."[15] If you approach any study in a spirit of high seriousness, if you take it as a thing of first intent, your study, whether of science, literature, art, or philosophy, is necessarily a spiritual and a devout study.

When we graduate we wear, if only for a moment, the sober caps and gowns of our mystery. Apparently this is quite a solemn business in which we are engaged, and if that is so, how can we avoid thinking of things suspiciously bordering on religion? In my high school days, in first year, everyone in the school system was required to read Milton—"L'Allegro," parts of *Paradise Lost*, and, notably, "Il Penseroso," all of a strong religious and holy resonance. We read and memorized extensively *Julius Caesar* (which was often dramatized in class, as you will recall), *Ivanhoe*, *Pilgrim's Progress*, and even such heavy stuff as *Macbeth*— all in the freshman year of high school. All these were serious reading in which it was quite impossible to escape an occasional mention of God. But that was in the 1920s, which was also the great day of the smart alecks and debunkers; we all remember the Scopes Trial, so badly bungled by both celebrated lawyers. We recited the "Rubaiyat" of Omar Khayyam to each other and devoured H. L. Mencken and Robert Ingersol and the Haldeman-Julius Little Blue Books.

But the interesting thing to me was that the debunkers themselves simply could not get God off their minds. They were always talking about him as if they had a personal vendetta with him. Why not "take the cash and let the credit go," as Omar said;[16] if people were silly enough to worry about God, that was their business. But they could not leave it there. The subject bugged them, and aside from that, the religious issue was the only way any of them could get an audience.

But as soon as I try to promote God in a public school, I feel uncomfortable. Evangelism is salesmanship: if you are going to sell your product, you cannot avoid preaching; and nothing is more essential than a sign on the school door that says, "No Peddlers or Agents Allowed," no peddlers or agents of *anything*. Today the school has become the salesman's happy hunting ground, a vanity fair for peddlers of goods of second intent to the exclusion of all else. A fair overall definition of a good of second intent is anything that can be exchanged for money—"at the devil's booth are all things sold, . . . bubbles we buy with a whole soul's tasking, . . . 'Tis only God may be had for the asking."[17] We all recall these lines of James Russell Lowell that we learned in the eighth grade. You have to work hard for goods of second intent, or else you can inherit them without turning a hand. For goods of first intent, you must *ask, search, knock*. It is another state of mind. How can we avoid the dross and seek the sacred without going sectarian? For one thing, the classics cover the vast sweep and scope of human experience and emotions, mostly tragic. In reading them, one cannot escape the problems of life and death and eternity. The best example of sound education is that which contemplates the possibility of things beyond, that sense of infinite possibilities, which, according to Alfred North Whitehead, gives to the Bible and Plato a transcendant importance and recommends them to all mankind.[18] It is that forthright education that does not evade the issues enjoyed by the Founding Fathers, a club including men of every religious persuasion. An official religion was one thing they were determined to avoid, because each had his own ideas on the subject, and no two were alike. Education invites the young to join that club, and at an early age. The Founding Fathers were brought up on the Bible, Plutarch, Cicero, and the philosophers of the Enlightenment, steeped in sacred and profane poetry, alert to every new science, given to discussion and philosophy.

Then along came John Dewey and his army of "New Education" peddlers.[19] For them the education of the past was nothing but hoary, outdated, antiquated, authoritarian, narrow-minded rote-learning. He is the pragmatist and the father of our modern educational society. Forget the musty books and take the class on field trips to the farm, the store, the factory, or the bank, to learn how things are done in the real world. How is cheese made, how do you board a bus? How do you discuss traffic problems, dress, and the cafeteria? Why are whales interesting? Why, to be sure, because that is where we get soap from! That is typical of Deweyism. We explore the nature of the universe by having each child tell the class what his opinion of it is; so then we know. When I was at Claremont teaching in the school of education, the instructors had a lot of farm kids in Corona chewing up paper to make papier-mâché to construct a cow in order to show children how milk was made. There were a couple of decades when students learned to write only in block letters because they could learn faster that way. For years I had hundreds of students who could neither read nor write cursive script, which was regarded as an elitist, antiquated, old-fashioned, nonprogressive, and ornamental device. In the 1940s, on the eve of entering the war, there was a great demand for mechanical drawing, so urgent that in the Pasadena School District some classes were devoted entirely to drawing horizontal lines, while in others, students drew only vertical; they never found out what they were drawing—it was all second intent simply perverted, because there was no first intent. At the same time it was proposed in the same school district that the teaching of history be supplanted by the more pragmatic discipline of dry-cleaning. They were going to have all the useless ornamental history classes converted to the study of dry-cleaning; and you can see where that would leave us today with its eternal values, because it is not a high technique any more. Such was the real Deweyesque "preparation for life."

I was on a curriculum committee for a couple of years with Asael Woodruff, who championed the New Education—progressive, exciting, throbbing, ever-changing, experimental, and therefore "scientific." My two oldest boys were experimented with, and after the experimental school was dropped, the experimenters went happily on to new fields and new fads. But the boys were left in limbo; they would never get another chance. Fortunately we never had a television in the house, and they both read a great deal, though the educationists protested that parents should not interfere—"we have our methods," they said, and we should not interfere by having our boys read anything. Dr. Woodruff went on to the University of Utah, where he wrote a book on the New Education that opened with the ringing words, "We do not go to school to learn, but to live"—none of your pie-in-the sky; the pie in the bakery is all you will ever see.

Dewey's ideal has achieved complete fulfillment in the shopping-mall. An article in the *Wall Street Journal* (which understandably has become the spiritual guidelight to the nation) gives us the cheering news: "Shopping is arguably the nation's favorite pastime, next to watching TV." There are "shocking statistics—shopping has taken on a life of its own. It . . . has spawned such bumper stickers as: 'I shop, therefore I am.' " Remember, Aristotle said the highest possible good was thinking, and it was Descartes that said, "I think, therefore I am." That is the ultimate good. Now shopping has taken the place of thinking, the ultimate good of first intent. "There is a kind of mindless character to it," says the article; "the shopping epidemic . . . has infected everybody." There are 347 shopping centers in Atlanta. It is "an ever-spiraling and hopeless search for happiness through the acquisition of things." They are goods of second intent.

One would hope that our shopping-mall someday might become the equivalent of the ancient *sūq*, the *agora* of the Greeks, or *forum* of the Romans, with their lively exchange not only of goods but of business news and ideas and valuable information. The *sūq* and the *agora* were where philosophers preached, and in the *forum* was where the great orations were delivered—the marketplace was an educational place. Will the mall ever become anything like that? Alas, the possibility of that is completely canceled by the imperative of the TV. Here we reach a state of total nihilism; all day long, and half the night, a procession of plots, murders, bedrooms, fights, and lethal explosions passes before the bemused spectator, sharing time with cunningly calculated interruptions by lavishly contrived commercial sideshows, thus combining the overlapping images of utter depravity with total triviality; and the thundering *Hauptmotif* that runs through it all is *money*. The inversion of the values is complete, for the less important an object is, as the ancient rhetoricians taught, the more fervidly and persistently it must be brought to the public's attention, so that what the new generation gets is a world turned upside down, with the froth as the substance and foundation of reality. They get that all the time, while the perennial base of intelligent thought and action is at best tolerated as a picturesque, elitist, old-fashioned frill of education. We have a complete switch of values: "All is dross that is not Madison Avenue."

I bluntly tell my students today that they are not in my class to prepare for life but to prepare for eternal life. That sounds like a shocker. It surprises me when I say anything as radical as that, because it is perfectly true. Incidentally, Allan Bloom argues, "The real motive of education [is] the search for a good life."[20] Oh, no, it isn't. See, he is limited to this world, and that makes the whole thing very sad. When we wear those caps and gowns improperly, we also receive a certificate that testifies not that we know anything, or have learned anything, but that we have completed a course, a *cursus*, meaning one turn around the race track. This we think of as preparation for a *career*, which is actually the same word, *carrière*; and again, if you consult the *Oxford English Dictionary*, you will find that it also means "one complete circling of the track." In both cases it means a circular course, as the word plainly states — you are really going nowhere. Once around and that is the end. The word *term* is equally emphatic: "I shall not pass this way again" — the closing line of the *Oedipus Rex*: "Don't call any man happy until he has finally passed the term and finished it all without suffering terrible things."[21] Then he can say he is happy, but everyone is going to suffer before that. Every student looks forward to graduation when he can forever shrug off all that encumbered his time and patience at school; and every successful career ends up in retirement, a full stop. The moral of this is that our so-called "preparation for life" is a good of secondary intent only. You have arrived nowhere *unless* there is more to come. The final reckoning of a thousand poets, artists, philosophers, and scientists is but a wailing chorus.

But let me interrupt my chronology and turn to some of the wisdom of the past, the cry of the tragic Muse: Oedipus, Catullus, Dover Beach. Does it have to be that way? There are two possibilities in graduation. *Graduation* means to take a step up, either in the secular *gradus honorum*, which was the scale of promotion of upward mobility in the Roman state and military and business career and was a source of infinite mischief among the Romans, as its counterpart is in the world today. On the other hand, we have the *gradus ad Parnassum* ("steps to Parnassus") (best known as the progress of the piano-student in the European Conservatories), the step-by-step ascent of the mountain of the Muses that goes right on up and up to that perfection of the arts that no one achieves but to which all great souls aspire — a pure good of first intent.

Preparation is necessarily secondary, since it is always preparing for something else to come. And what is that? Just more of the same? asks Dr. Faustus with a cry of despair — a *bemooster Herr* (Dewey would love that) *auch ein gelehrter Mann studiert sofort weil er nichts anders kann;*[22] the most learned "moss-covered" man goes right on studying because he cannot think of anything else to do. Strange as it sounds, *everything short of eternal life* is gall and wormwood, not only to Faust, but to the most successful men of our time. C. P. Snow in his *Chronicles of Cambridge University* explains the point: "The tone of science at Cambridge in 1932 was the tone of Rutherford." They had discovered the planetary structure of the atom. "Magniloquently boastful, creatively confident, generous, argumentative, and full of hope." What more could he ask? "He enjoyed a life of miraculous success." But then something strange follows: "But I am sure that even late in life he felt stabs of sickening insecurity." The author goes on to talk about the other giants at Cambridge:

> Does anyone really imagine that Bertrand Russell, G. H. Hardy, Rutherford, Blackett and the rest were bemused by cheerfulness as they faced their own individual state? In the crowd, they were leaders; they were worshipped. But by themselves they believed with the same certainty that they believed in Rutherford's atom that they were going after this life into annihilation. Against this, they only had to offer the nature of scientific activity; its complete success on its own terms. It itself was a source of happiness. But it is whistling in the dark when they are alone.[23]

Was their success, then, a thing of first intent? It certainly was not of second intent, since it led nowhere. Must the intent be a choice between life eternal or annihilation? Shakespeare's Claudio in *Measure for Measure*, after suggesting all the alternatives, laments: "Ay, but to die, and go we know not where; to lie in cold obstruction and to rot. . . . And the delighted spirit to bathe in fiery floods, or to reside in thrilling region of thick-ribbed ice—to be imprison'd in the viewless winds, and blown with restless violence round about the pendent world; or to be worse than worst, of those that lawless and incertain thoughts imagine howling—Tis too horrible!"[24] He finds the new doctrine of purgatory even less comforting than the other and concludes that "the weariest and most loathed worldly life that age, ache, penury, and imprisonment can lay on nature is a paradise to what we fear of death."[25] The eternity he imagines is horrible, but the idea of death is even worse.

Granted that eternal life is something devoutly to be wished, one cannot simply wish for the Happy Land and then believe in it, any more than we can bring God into existence by wishing for him, as St. Augustine recognizes at the beginning of the *Confessions*. We must remember, on the other hand, that a thing devoutly to be wished is not necessarily nonexistent just because we would like it to exist. You cannot deny that some kind of eternity is there (though some quantum physicists like John Wheeler would deny it); the only question is What fills it? There is not much use in debating about that, but you can certainly recognize that you are already in it.

This takes us back to *carpe diem quam minimum credula postero* ("seize the day, put no trust in the morrow") — live for the moment.[26] This was the favorite doctrine of John Dewey and his final word of advice to the human race and to students: Get all the fun you can out of the present moment, for that is all there is. Can you find fulfillment in that? Can it be a good of first intent? It is the bleak advice of Catullus in his most famous ode: "Let us live it up" — *vivamus atque amemus*[27] — the sun goes down and rises again, but once our brief candle has gone out, there is nothing but a black night of everlasting sleep. Therefore, let us have sex unlimited. The cheeriest view to be taken of this is the Epicurean: *Nil admirari*, says Horace, don't get too involved in anything; just come to the party and join me as a *Epicuri de grege porcum*,[28] one of the happy pigs in the sty of Epicurus. Solon too tells us to stop worrying and enjoy the banquet while we can. But the admonitions of the most genial Greek (Solon) and Latin (Horace) poets are, after all, nothing but grim reminders that the end is on the way. There is Catullus's *carpe diem*, reworded for us by the even more cheerful Omar, but in a mathematician's chilling reality, "One moment in annihilation's waste, One moment of the wine of life to taste. The stars are setting and the caravan starts for the dawn of nothing—O make haste!"[29] There is your *carpe diem!* All end on a sour note.

Solon's second most famous line is that no mortal ever enjoys complete happiness; "wretched are all on whom the sun looks down."[30] It is a sentiment endlessly repeated in literature and familiar to all from Greek tragedy, where the chorus cries its eyes out, "O poor human race, I can only reckon you equal to exactly nothing."[31] This philosophy of the moment is really the most poignant of all, akin to "the hollow laugh of the libertine." We, alas, cannot be innocently frightened field mice: "But, Mousie, thou art no thy lane, In proving foresight may be vain: the best-laid schemes o' Mice an' Men gang aft a-gley, an' lea'e us nought but grief an' pain, for promis'd joy! Still thou are blest compar'd wi' me! The present only toucheth thee: But Och! I backward cast my e'e on prospects drear! and forward tho' I canna see, I guess an' fear!"[32] That's the best we could hope for in this world. Even great literature is cold comfort—it especially loves to harp on that theme: Hamlet's advice for living it up and fighting the calendar says, "Now get you to my lady's chamber, and tell her, let her paint an inch thick, to this favour she must come"[33]— pointing to the skull of Yorick.

Education is *Paideia*. I studied with Professor Jaeger at the time he was writing his three-volume work by that title, and we had long discussions together at his apartment in Berkeley and again at Watertown when he was at Harvard. *Paideia* was the forming of the type of man a certain culture or society looks upon as its ideal.[34] Egon Friedell has written on the subject.[35] There is, for example, the English Gentleman, the French *Homme du monde*, the *Hidalgo* in Spain, in Germany, the *petite philosophe comme tous les Allemands* (the Little Philosopher like all the Germans, as Voltaire puts it), the stern, competent but literate and

urbane Roman *patrician*, and, best-known of all, the So-
cratic ideal displaying the four Platonic virtues, the *kalos-
kagathos* — all that is right and proper. These were the qualities that formed the ideal citizen in each state. But as Pindar
teaches, this training but prepares the candidate; it remains
for the individual winner to bring down celestial beams
from above;[36] you have a type here, but from there is where
you take off.

The idea of education as the training up of the new
generation to established and accepted ("not progressive")
standards of a society or culture is by no means the fruit
of civilization alone. TV documentaries will show you the
elaborate training through which the youth of so-called
"primitive societies" must pass before they can receive the
full initiation of acceptable and proper men — membership
in the tribe. As we know, it was not only the Greeks but
the Egyptians and Babylonians who considered themselves
the only real men and the rest of the human race babbling
barbarians. Yet we need not smile; there were none of
these people among whom adoption into the tribe was not
possible — even (or especially) the Jews; but you had to
have the accepted education and initiation to qualify. The
routines practiced have all proven their survival value for
the Egyptians, Chinese, Greeks, and Pueblo Indians — their
education is thousands of years old, but the survival to
which they *all* look was that in the higher and better world,
to be reached by unity with the stars, by joining in the
heavenly ring-dance of the seasons. This is always a basic
part of this training.

But these periods of training and often elaborate, fright-
ening, and even painful rites of initiation were no mere
fraternity hazing. A recent study by Herbert Schutz, called
The Prehistory of Germanic Europe, is very enlightening. It
surveys in some detail the entire field of European prehistory between the upper Paleolithic and the Iron Age.[37]
The conclusion of the whole study is very significant —

they have studied all of primitive society and all its remains in Europe. They conclude, "From the material evidence surveyed, culture appears to be a collective attempt at providing answers to the questions posed by man *about his position in this life and the next.*"[38] It is not the economic man at all that keeps the culture going, but his questions about his position in this life as well as the next. As long as a distinct set of answers are satisfactory, the distinctive aspects of a culture remained constant and offered that degree of continuity which made for stability. It appears, on the other hand, that experiment, innovation, and change are response to inadequacy or outright failure in some sector of a culture's general view of the world. Note that it is the good of first intent that keeps a culture going, not the tools and gadgets to which anthropologists are fond of attributing the evolution of thought. The implements are secondary; if people cannot answer the big questions, the whole show runs down.

This is consistent with the interesting situation found in the ancient schools from the Greegree school of the Australian aborigines to Aristotle's Academy and the *Stoa.* All of them are devoted to the problem of the eternity and of their place in the cosmos. We might say that if God did not exist, we would have to invent him. But that is not necessary, for there is such a vast sea of possibility and probability, as Whitehead pointed out, that we should be willing to settle for that. All these schools indulged before all else in speculation—in speculation on "higher" things.

Since archaic times the *Museum,* the place of the Muses, could be found on the hilltops and groves of Greece, "far from the town," Plutarch specifies; there had to be an altar there, and in some cases a regular temple—Delphi itself was a home of the Muses, as was the inaccessible height of Helicon. Even in the groves where there were no buildings, there stood images of great poets, artists, and scientists. Solon in the first democratic constitution around

600 B.C. included an annual school festival, the *Mouseia* in the official calendar. The Muses could not very well be separated from the schools, since *mousike* (the art of the Muses, which is our word for music) is simply the Greek word for education or culture.[39] The museum was not a shrine; the teachers were elected in a general public assembly, which, however, began with prayer. The term *museum* became synonymous with *didaskaleion* and *paideuterion*, public schools. Athens was called both the *Paideusis* of Greece and the *Mouseion* of Greece. There was always something holy about the blessed Muses: When you are that serious about a thing, you cannot separate the sacred and profane—it is all sacred. For the ancients, the goods of first intent par excellence were the gifts of the Muses. If goods of second intent are anything that can be had for money, the goods of Muses are gifts to the gifted, and rewards to the faithful. They are of purest first intent, infinitely satisfying in themselves, ever fresh and delightful both because they offer infinite variety and demand a perfection that woos us on forever. In the pursuit of the Muses, one can engage forever, with suitable rest, in moving freely among the nine delightful disciplines they represent.

It is apparent from the lists of the literary occurrences of their names and callings compiled by Professor H. Kees that the original Muses cannot be separated.[40] They are all very ancient and have to do with prophecy, divination, mourning, choral dances, bacchic celebrations, psaltery, the ring-dance of the stars and the celestial globe, the masks of the dancers, the flute players, and so on—in short, all that touches human life most closely and puts it into tune or phase with all nature, including the heavens above. It may sound paradoxical to say that we have a gut reaction to the cosmos, but it is not. I am sure that we all have a feeling like that when we listen to the music of the spheres in the planetarium. Thus Polyhymnia, the ninth of the nine, bears the barbitone (the most primitive of the stringed instruments), leads the dance and the pantomime, and, of all things, teaches geometry. There is a gut feeling between you and the stars. It is not as abstruse as you think. There is no paradox there, for even the most primitive celebrations of life followed the motions of the heavens and the seasons of the earth with meticulous calculation. The "primitives" are very careful about it. I have spent much time with the Hopis, and their observance, especially of the stars, is constant and careful. Theirs is a cosmic dedication. Professor Kees duly notes that Plato found the model for his style in Pythagoras, who called his school a *museum*.[41] The famous museum of Alexandria, the most celebrated university in history, was a continuation of an age-old tradition in Egypt, where priestly colleges had pondered the things of time and eternity since prehistoric times: word for word, passages from their schools echo those of the classical world, as well as the scriptures—a fact being fully appreciated for the first time today. Just within the last ten years, we realized that their writings are full of the same scripture we use. For ages wise men, *sophoi*, traveled from holy center to holy center, observing, teaching, and exchanging wisdom of the brethren, as Santillana says, a vast archaic world together in one great concept.[42] They had a word of wisdom far excelling anything we could imagine. It had a great survival value, being much more sophisticated than anything the evolutionary pattern has given us.

The Muses are archaic, "primitive," and universal. For those who knew them all, life was a school; the whole society sat at a Greek drama, a seasonal religious presentation, as critics and connoisseurs. Havelock Ellis in his book the *Dance of Life* notes how in such societies "life becomes all play."[43] Also life becomes all school. Loren Eiseley observes that in such societies, goods of first and second intent become completely fused; but of the few such communities he finds existing in the world today, he cites only the Hopis.[44] Our pragmatic society, coveting first the Hopis' uranium and now their coal, has fought with determination to obliterate that culture—it is so totally alien to what we are doing. It is actually a clash between goods of first and second intent, for we all know what the big corporations are after.

Alas, in the showdown between goods of first intent and second, the *second* will always win. The supreme Delphic wisdom of our day, "there is no free lunch," excludes all but acquisitive activity as trivial, egghead, effete, what in the Utah school system is called frills, such as music and drama. Of course, since it seems that in some branches of the barbaric arts such as hard rock and TV commercials there is big money, we are willing to accept them as goods of any intent you please.

The Muses, as we all know, patronize both the arts and the sciences, and they, as inseparable sisters, join together in an eternal choral dance in which harmony, rhythm, number, ratio, pitch, proportion, and structure are all united. And what is most wonderful, we do not react to their gifts by instruction alone, nor does their efficacy have to be demonstrated; we react to them spontaneously and directly; we are swept along. The sixth muse, Terpsichore, the Bacchic muse, bids us join the fun with abandon. No special plea needs to be made for goods of first intent, for, as Aristotle says, they *are* the ultimate good, whatever *we* may find it to be. Go ahead and try anything and everything, and you will always come back to them, for they are holy.

In my first year in high school, Ms. Gunning's English class labeled themselves the *Mnemosyneians*, dedicated to Mnemosyne, the Mother of the Muses—her name means, simply, "memory." The object of the society was to memorize as many notable passages of literature as possible, and indeed if one is to be serious in seeking goods of first intent, one must make some effort to take them to heart.

I am astonished to think that by far the best teacher I ever had was an old maid in the first year of high school, but I find that most people report a like phenomenon.

It was not until late Roman times that the muses were given their final assignments: Calliope of heroic epic (immortalized in the circus parade), Cleo of history, Euterpe of hymns, Melpomene of tragedy, Thalia of comedy, Polyhymnia of the mimic art, and Eurania of astronomy.

In the oldest Egyptian writing, the concept is fully at home in the person of Dame Seshat, the secretary of the gods and the keeper of all wisdom. Her activity is represented by a pair of inverted horns signifying the opening of the heavens, from which a seven-pointed star sends down a laser beam to earth, where seven books are neatly ordered between the outstretched fingers of the Seshat. They represent the seven departments of learning in the library of which she had charge and showed her possessing and dispensing all wisdom at will.

I may be pardoned here for quoting Brigham Young, for no one ever made a sharper distinction between goods of first and second intent: "Will education feed and clothe you, keep you warm on a cold day, or enable you to build a house?" Let us remember that no one knew the necessity of those more than Brigham Young in the conditions under which he led the people. "Will education . . . keep you warm on a cold day, or enable you to build a house? Not at all. Should we cry down education on this account? No. What is it for? The improvement of the mind; to instruct us in all arts and sciences, in the history of the world, in the laws of nations; to enable us to understand the laws and principles of life, and how to be useful while we live."[45] This is the knowledge that makes us really useful. In Utah today we cry down this education as "frills," which we cut from the program.

The mind craves knowledge as the body craves food. Experiments at the University of Utah have shown that when people are deprived of all information in a state of isolation, they start creating their own information by hallucinating—they *must* have it; even though they can do without cigarettes or coffee, the one thing they *must* have is information.[46] To repeat, paradoxically, things of primary intent are actually the most useful of goods—the only useful ones in the long run. We can and do get along without many goods of second intent and never really miss them; life without them may be inconvenient, as the Pioneers found and as we learn during shortages, but it is still possible and even enjoyable. Without goods of primary intent, on the other hand, we wither and die; we go crazy and become lost and ill-at-ease, unsure of ourselves, haunted by a sense of doom and futility; life becomes pointless. The world becomes "weary, stale, flat, and unprofitable, . . . an unweeded garden, that grows to seed; things rank and gross in nature possess it merely."[47] Hamlet was indeed the intellectual par excellence, but the good of primary intent keeps escaping him, as he complains throughout the play, because he is never sure of any life beyond this one. He had listened to the philosophers too long at Wittenberg.

Today we have given up entirely on goods of first intent. The most eminent universities for the first time are now places where one goes primarily to buy MBA and law degrees. The full measure of the success of their graduates is the avoidance of criminal prosecution. I believe there should be more to education than that. Remember General Barrows, the president at Berkeley long ago? He used to say that the only reason anyone goes to school is to increase his earning power.

We have followed the course of the Middle Ages when educators reversed the values to the *trivium*, consisting of grammar, rhetoric, and logic, all training in skills in communication and persuasion. Though called the "liberal arts," they were strictly the business of getting along in the world. "Liberal" arts are supposed to be goods of first intent only, "liberal" because they are not devoted in any way to making a living but are the study of free and liberal souls. On the other hand, the four liberal arts of *quadrivium* came to be viewed as secondary, grist for the operations of the *trivium*; yet the *quadrivium* is the real catalogue of goods of first intent: arithmetic, music, geometry, and astronomy—such were the studies of the ancient priestly colleges who sought through them to contemplate the *pleroma*; each one deals with things that are eternally valid and true—they are all cosmic.

What am I trying to say? I know that some goods are more valuable than others; but that is not what the ancients had in mind—it is something far beyond that. Where can I find firm footing in my own pursuit of it? Well, I can begin with one indisputable proposition: If there is anything good in life, the thought of its total abolition, along with our own annihilation, is an absolute evil—there can be nothing good in the removal of what is good. And this is an evil that faces us all constantly, deny it though we will: "But men at whiles are sober and think by fits and starts, and if they think, they fasten their hands upon their hearts!"[48] We can't be drunk all the time, you see. The Epicurean banquet comes to an end, and we conclude again with Claudio (in *Measure for Measure*), after listing the various theories regarding the hereafter, that "the weariest and most loathed worldly life that age, ache, penury and imprisonment can lay on nature is a paradise to what we fear of death!"[49]

And so we have a sort of equation. If we have an infinite and undeniable, though horrible, reality on one side, it must be balanced on the other by something equally real. The ancients felt this keenly. For each particle there *must* be a counter-particle. Though T. S. Eliot's "Eternal Footman," with his chilling snicker, haunted the ancients as much as it does us ("Oh, do not ask what it is!" Eliot says),[50] they could not rid themselves at the same time of other intimations; it is akin to Plato's *anamnesis*, the feeling that what is really good is eternally good (how could it stop being good?), and that good things belong together and reinforce each other—"Light cleaveth unto light" (D&C 88:40); and accordingly, there must be a condition that is *all good*, of which this world is the reverse image— a black hole. They saw the conviction in that. Some physicists can prove definitely that a particle exists because its anti-particle exists. If the one exists, the other must exist. That is physics today. So if we have this absolutely evil world that is very flat, stale, and unprofitable (and the Greeks really excel in this one and really tear loose in telling you how bad the world is—the great Solon says that none is happy upon whom the sun shines;[51] and Goethe says, all that Homer proves to us is that this world is hell[52]); if that is the case and to every particle there is an anti-particle, there must be a condition that is all good, a reverse image of our present black hole.[53] Aristotle uses the figure of the reflection of the mountain in the lake: the higher up one goes on the real mountain, the lower one descends in the reflected false mountain. The higher you get in heaven, the lower you get in this world. The Psalmist says, "I would rather be a doorkeeper in the house of God, than dwell in the pavilions of the princes of the wicked" (Psalm 84:10). Better the lowest position in the best of worlds than the highest position in the lowest of worlds, which is what Satan wanted, remember? "Hail, horrors, hail! . . . Better to reign in hell, than serve in heaven."[54] If Satan could only be top man, he would accept that position in the worst possible world. Whereas the Psalmist says, Even if it means I must be the lowest man, give me the best possible world. So it is the complete reversal. Plato, as we all know, uses the figure of the world as a cave full of shadows.[55] If the one world is real, the other must be real, the Greeks felt, because they are images of each other, and each depends on the other—and the one is only too real.

If this sounds like the reasoning of quantum physicists, it is no mere syllogism but was deeply felt by men of old and was confirmed by all they saw around them. It is absolutely certain that we are missing out on something, that we have barely had a sniff or taste of what is really good and is really there, only to have it snatched away from us: "The caravan starts for the dawn of nothing—O make haste!"[56] That is what we used to sing in high school when we were being cynical, but we knew that there was something very wrong with this. It is your neglected capacity. You haven't used it at all. Of all the things you could be doing—and the list of them is a mile long—you could only do one or only get started on one in a short lifetime. But a taste is not enough; we rightfully feel cheated of what is ours by right. All belongs to us that we are capable of conceiving, and containing, and enjoying. But what happens? We go and spoil everything, and then in our feelings of guilt, we petulantly slam the door on faith and repentance, and we doggedly pretend to find fulfillment after the "vision splendid" of our immortality has faded into the light of common day, which we smugly call "the real world."

In the dialogue with his friend Gorgias, who was bringing the exciting "New Education" to Athens, Socrates admits that his teaching has no more chance of competing with Gorgias' easy, business-oriented courses than a competent pediatrician would in competition for juvenile patients with a pastry-cook who prescribed nothing but dessert.[57] Goods of the second intent will always win out with the public, bringing with them sickness and debility. Let us hope it does not prove fatal this time, as it did in Athens, and at many other times in the past.

Notes

1. Allan Bloom, *The Closing of the American Mind* (New York: Simon and Schuster, 1987).

2. Aristotle, *Metaphysics* XII, 7, 3-4.

3. Ibid., XII, 9, 4-5.

4. Xenophon, *Memorabilia* III, 8, 6.

5. Joe Mislan, *The Golden Mean* (New Jersey: Princeton University, 1977); cf. Lyall Watson, *Supernature* (New York: Anchor, 1973), 107.

6. Plato, *Symposium* 210A-212E; see comments of Gunther Bornkamm, in Gerhard Kittel, ed., "Mysterion," *Theological Dictionary of the New Testament*, tr. Geoffrey W. Bromiley, 9 vols. (Grand Rapids, MI: Eerdmans, 1967), 4:808.

7. Regarding *theatromania*, see Hugh W. Nibley, "Victoriosa Loquacitas: The Rise of Rhetoric and the Decline of Everything Else," *Western Speech* 20/2 (Spring 1956): 57-82; "Sparsiones," *Classical Journal* 40/9 (June 1945): 515-43; "The Roman Games as a Survival of an Archaic Year-cult," (Ph.D. diss., University of California, Berkeley, 1939).

8. Juvenal, *Satires* X, 79.

9. Plato, *Phaedrus* 249B-250A.

10. William Wordsworth, "Expostulation and Reply," lines 17-18; see John O. Hayden, ed., *William Wordsworth: The Poems*, 2 vols. (New Haven: Yale University Press, 1977), 355-56.

11. See poem 12 in Kathleen Freeman, *The Work and Life of Solon* (London: Milford, 1926), 211.

12. Juvenal, *Satires* X, 356.

13. Seneca, *De Brevitate Vitae* I, 1.

14. The Student song (circa 1267) begins with "Let us live then and be glad while young life is before us." For English translation, see John Bartlett, *Familiar Quotations* (Boston: Little, Brown, 1980), 134.

15. Aristotle, *Rhetoric* II, 1, 7.

16. Omar Khayyam, *Rubaiyat* XIII, tr. Edward Fitzgerald (New York: Avon, n.d.).

17. James Russell Lowell, *The Vision of Sir Launfal* IV, lines 25, 28, and 30.

18. Paul Weiss, "Alfred North Whitehead 1861-1947," *Atlantic Monthly* 181 (May 1948): 105-7.

19. See Neil G. McCluskey, *Public Schools and Moral Education: The Influence of Horace Mann, William Torrey Harris and John Dewey* (New York: Columbia University Press, 1958); Arthur G. Wirth, *John Dewey as Educator* (New York: Wiley and Son, 1966); Anthony Flew, "Democracy and Education," and "John Dewey's Philosophy of Education," in R. S. Peters, ed., *John Dewey Reconsidered* (London: Routledge and Kegan Paul, 1977).

20. Bloom, *The Closing of the American Mind*, 34.
21. Sophocles, *Oedipus Rex*, lines 1528-30.
22. Goethe, *Faust*, lines 355-68.
23. C. P. Snow, *Chronicles of Cambridge University*, cited in Hugh W. Nibley, "Science Fiction and the Gospel," in Benjamin Urrutia, ed., *Latter-day Science Fiction* (Ludlow, MA: Parables, 1985), 2:6-7.
24. William Shakespeare, *Measure for Measure*, act III, scene i.
25. Ibid.
26. Horace, *Odes* I, 11.
27. Catullus, *The Poems of Catullus* V, 1-2.
28. Horace, *Epistle* I, 4, 16.
29. Omar Khayyam, *Rubaiyat*, XXXVII.
30. Ivan M. Linforth, *Solon the Athenian* (Berkeley: University of California, 1919), 171.
31. For example, see *Oedipus the King*, lines 1188-90, "Races of Mortal Man / Whose life is but a span / I count ye but the shadow of a shade."
32. Robert Burns, *To a Mouse*, stanza 7.
33. William Shakespeare, *Hamlet*, act V, scene i.
34. Werner Jaegar, *Paidea: The Ideals of Greek Culture*, tr. Gilbert Highet, 3 vols. (New York: Oxford University Press, 1944).
35. Egon Friedell, *A Cultural History of the Modern Age*, tr. Charles F. Atkinson, 3 vols. (New York: Knopf, 1930-31), 1:11-12.
36. Pindar, *Olympian Odes* III, 42-44.
37. Herbert Schutz, *The Prehistoric Germanic Europe* (New Haven: Yale University Press, 1983).
38. Ibid., 353 (emphasis added).
39. Regarding Solon, see Müller-Graupa, "Museion," *Paulys Real-Encyclopädie der Classischen Altertumswissenschaft* (Stuttgart: Metzler, 1933), 16:1:798.
40. Hermann Kees, "Musai," in ibid., 16:1:680-757.
41. Müller-Graupa, "Museion," 799-801.
42. Giorgio Santillana, *Hamlet's Mill* (Boston: Godine, 1977), 1-11, 332-43.
43. Quoted in Havelock Ellis, *Dance of Life* (Boston: Houghton Mifflin, 1929), 21.
44. Cf. Loren Eiseley, *The Star Throwers* (New York: Harcourt Brace Jovanovich, 1979).
45. *JD* 14:83.
46. For information, see Niger Calder, *The Mind of Man* (London: British Broadcasting, 1970), 33.
47. Shakespeare, *Hamlet*, act I, scene ii.

48. "Last Poems X" in *Complete Poems: A. E. Houseman* (New York: Holt, 1959), 109.

49. Shakespeare, *Measure for Measure*, act III, scene i.

50. T. S. Eliot, "The Love Song of J. Alfred Prufrock," in *The Complete Poems and Plays* (New York: Harcourt and Brace, 1952), 2, 6.

51. Linforth, *Solon the Athenian*, 171.

52. Regarding Goethe, see Johann Goethe's correspondence with Friedrich Schiller, 3 December 1803, in *Goethes Sämtliche Werke*, 46 vols. (Munich: Müller, n.d.), 15:83.

53. Regarding the scientist Dirac, who discovered the anti-particle in 1928, see P. T. Matthews, *Nuclear Apple* (London: Chatto and Windus: 1971), 17.

54. Milton, *Paradise Lost*, ed. A. W. Verity, 2 vols. (New York: Cambridge, 1934), 1:16-17, lines 250, 263.

55. Plato, *Republic* VII, 1.

56. Omar Khayyam, *Rubaiyat*, XXXVII.

57. Plato, *Gorgias* 521E-522A; cf. 464A-E, 501A-C; cf. Hugh W. Nibley, "Victoriosa Loquacitas," *Western Speech* 20 (1956): 57-82; and "Rhetoric and Revelation," *The World and the Prophets* (Salt Lake City: Deseret Book, 1954), 98-106; reprinted in *CWHN* 3:110-16.

18

The Meaning of the Atonement

The Good News

The last talk, on the Terrible Questions[1], leads us directly and unerringly to the subject of the Atonement. For the Atonement is nothing less than the answer to the Terrible Question: "Is this all there is?" If you are a saint, you know that this is a wicked world; if you are the most cynical and worldly unbeliever, you still know by experience that it is a vicious one. It seems that everything we want here is either destructive or trivial. I am going to bypass the tempting list of quotations on the subject—Shakespeare, Sophocles, Matthew Arnold, William James, and so on— and turn directly to the scriptures, where Peter is not philosophizing or theologizing but stating the facts of life: "Go about (*anastraphete,* conduct yourselves) in fear during your transient stay (*paroikias chronon*), knowing that perishables like silver and gold cannot free you from the futile way of life of your fathers" (1 Peter 1:17-18). Thus he concludes his comment: "For all flesh is grass, and all the glory of man as wild flowers; the grass withers and the flowers crumble. But the word of the Lord endures forever" (1 Peter 1:24-25). Between these two statements of the problem Peter gives us another choice; there is an order of things that goes back "before the foundation of the world" and

---

This talk, given November 10, 1988, in Riverton, Utah, was the second in the "Hugh Nibley Lecture Series," sponsored by Deseret Book and F.A.R.M.S.

is now emerging again to our advantage—"manifest in these last times for you" (1 Peter 1:20). It is the carrying out of the Atonement, for which the law of Moses was a preparation.

Jacob, in the Book of Mormon, goes right to the point. The problem is "that our flesh must waste away and die; . . . death hath passed upon all men" (2 Nephi 9:4, 6); and without the resurrection, entropy—the good old Second Law of Thermodynamics[2]—must take over, "and if so, this flesh must have laid down to rot and to crumble to its mother earth, to rise no more" (2 Nephi 9:7). That is entropy, and what is to stop it? Jacob grasps the situation: "There must needs be a *power*," he says, "of resurrection," and such a power has indeed been provided, "to fulfill the merciful plan of the great Creator" (2 Nephi 9:6). What a comfort to know that things are under control after all. The Fall has put us into a state of corruption in which it would be disastrous to remain if man should "put forth his hand and partake also of the tree of life, and eat and live forever [in his sins]" (Moses 4:28). Nobody wants to live forever in a sewer, yet according to Shakespeare even that is preferable to the alternative: "The weariest and most loathed worldly life that age, ache, penury, and imprisonment can lay on nature is a paradise to what we fear of death."[3]

But it doesn't have to be that way. That is just the point.

The Atonement makes available the only kind of lasting life worth having. The great Christian tract on the Atonement, Paul's epistle to the Hebrews, begins with an exhilarating prospect: "God . . . hath in these last days spoken unto us by his Son, whom he hath appointed heir of all things, by whom also he made the worlds [note the plural]. Who being the brightness of his glory, and the express image of his person, and upholding all things by the word of his power, when he had by himself purged our sins, sat down on the right hand of the Majesty on high" (Hebrews 1:1-3).

The Word and the Deed

People are usually surprised to learn that *atonement,* an accepted theological term, is neither from a Greek nor a Latin word, but is good old English and really does mean, when we write it out, at-*one*-ment, denoting both a state of being "at one" with another and the process by which that end is achieved. The word *atonement* appears only once in the New Testament (Romans 5:11 in the King James Version), and in the Revised Standard Version it does not appear at all, since the new translation prefers the more familiar word "reconciliation." Paul has just told us that the Lord "sat down at the right hand of the Majesty on High," so reconciliation is a very good word for atonement there, since it means literally to be seated again with someone (*re-con-silio*) — so that atonement is to be reunited with God.

The Greek word translated as "reconciliation" is *katallagein.* That is a business term which the *Greek-English Lexicon* tells us means "*exchange, esp. of money; . . . change from enmity to friendship, reconciliation; . . . reconciliation* of sinners *with God.*"[4] It is the return to the status *ante quo,* whether as a making of peace or a settlement of debt. The monetary metaphor is by far the commonest, being the simplest and easiest to understand. Hence, frequently the word *redemption* literally means to buy back, that is, to reacquire something you owned previously. Thus Moses: "But because the Lord loved you, and because he would keep the oath which he had sworn unto your fathers, hath the Lord brought you out with a mighty hand, and redeemed you out of the house of bondmen, from the hand of Pharaoh" (Deuteronomy 7:8). Redemption, or atonement, restores one to a former, happier condition. "And what one nation in the earth is like thy people, even like

Israel, whom God went to redeem for a people to himself, and to make him a name, and to do for you great things and terrible, for thy land, before thy people, which thou redeemest to thee from Egypt, from the nations and their gods?" (2 Samuel 7:23).

By redemption, someone has paid a price to get you off, but the frequent use of the commercial analogy is not out of reverence for trade and commerce but the opposite. The redeemed are bought to clear them of all worldly obligation by paying off the world in its own currency, after which it has no further claim on the redeemed: "And the child of eight days shall be circumcised for you, every male through your generations, born of a house or a purchase of silver of any outsider who is not of thy seed. He must certainly be circumcised, born of your house, or bought with your silver; and it shall be my covenant in [among or with] thy flesh for an everlasting covenant" (Genesis 17:12-13). All the newborn are taken into the family, which is united by an eternal covenant by the token shedding of blood (circumcision) to become the seed of Abraham—this is a real at-*one*-ment. The Greek equivalent is *lytrōsis*, a ransoming. Paul tells the saints to prepare for the salvation that has been made available by disengaging from this world—"denying ungodliness and worldly lusts, we should live soberly, righteously, and godly, in this present world"—so that God "might redeem us from all iniquity, and purify unto himself a peculiar people" (Titus 2:12, 14). Salvation is likewise rescue (*sōtēria*), also rendered deliverance. Another expression is "for a price," the word being *timē*, "that which is paid in token or worth of value." He paid for us what he thought we were worth so he could join us with him. In his letter to the Ephesians, the proposition reads like a business agreement, not binding but releasing: "In whom we have bail (*apolytrōsin*—our release pending the judgment) through his blood, the pardoning (*aphesin*, setting-aside) of misdemeanors (*paraptōmatōn*, blunder, trespass) on consideration of the riches (*ploutos*) of his generosity (*charitos*), which he has bestowed upon us in all wisdom and understanding (*phronēsei*) (Ephesians 1:7-8). Next Paul tells us that it was all the Savior's idea, "that in the economy (*oikonomia*) of the fullness of times the whole thing might be brought together again in Christ (*anakephalaiōsasthai*) — things in the heavens and things on earth" (Ephesians 1:9-10). A great at-*one*-ment indeed! Meanwhile Paul counsels the saints, "Grieve not the holy Spirit of God, whereby ye are *sealed* unto the day of re-demption (bought free, *apolytrōseōs*)," and to be united in love, "forgiving one another, even as God for Christ's sake hath forgiven you" (Ephesians 4:30, 32). So when the scrip-tures speak of atonement, it is always re-conciliation, re-demption, re-surrection, re-lease, salvation, and so on. All refer to a return to a former state. This is even more vividly and concretely expressed in the Hebrew terminology.

In Semitic languages, where one root can have many meanings, the first rule is always to look for the basic or literal meaning of the word, which in Hebrew, Aramaic, and Arabic usually takes us back to early days and simple homely affairs of life in the desert or the countryside. One simple physical act often triggers a long line of derivatives, meanings that are perfectly reasonable if one takes the most obvious steps from one to the next, but which can end up miles from the starting place. The basic word for atonement is *kaphar*, which has the same basic meaning in Hebrew, Aramaic, and Arabic, that being "to bend, arch over, cover; . . . to deny, . . . to forgive, . . . to be expiated, . . . renounce."[5] The Arabic *kafara* puts the emphasis on a tight squeeze, such as tucking in the skirts, drawing a thing close to one's self. Closely related are Aramaic[6] and Arabic *kafat*,[7] meaning a close embrace, which are certainly related to the Egyptian *hpet*,[8] the common ritual embrace written with the ideogram of embracing arms. It may be cognate with the Latin *capto*,[9] and from it comes the Persian *kaftan*,[10] a monk's robe and hood completely embracing the body. Most interesting is the Arabic *kafata*,[11] as it is the key to a dramatic situation.

It was the custom for one fleeing for his life in the desert to seek protection in the tent of a great sheik, crying out, *"Ana dakhīluka,"* meaning "I am thy suppliant," whereupon the Lord would place the hem of his robe over the guest's shoulder and declare him under his protection. In the Book of Mormon, we see this world as a plain, a dark and dreary waste, a desert. We see Nephi fleeing from an evil thing that is pursuing him. In great danger, he prays the Lord to give him an open road in the low way, to block his pursuers, and to make them stumble. He comes to the tent of the Lord and enters as a suppliant; and in reply, the Master, as was the ancient custom, puts the hem of his robe protectively over the kneeling man's shoulder (*katafa*). This puts him under the Lord's protection from all enemies. They embrace in a close hug, as Arab chiefs still do; the Lord makes a place for him and invites him to sit down beside him — they are at-*one* (2 Nephi 4:33; Alma 5:24).

This is the imagery of the Atonement, the embrace: "The Lord hath redeemed my soul from hell; I have beheld his glory, and I am encircled about eternally in the arms of his love" (2 Nephi 1:15). "O Lord, wilt thou encircle me around in the robe of thy righteousness! O Lord, wilt thou make a way for mine escape before mine enemies!" (2 Nephi 4:33). "Behold, he sendeth an invitation unto all men, for the arms of mercy are extended towards them, and he saith: Repent, and I will receive you" (Alma 5:33).

This is the *hpet*, the ritual embrace that consummates the final escape from death in the Egyptian funerary texts and reliefs, where the son Horus is received into the arms of his father Osiris. There is a story confirmed by the recently discovered Apocryphon of John in which Jesus and John the Baptist meet as little children, rush into each other's arms and fuse into one person, becoming perfectly "at-*one*."[12]

In Israel when the sacrifices and sin offerings were completed on the Day of Atonement, the High Priest went to the door of the *kapporeth* to receive assurance from the Lord within that he had accepted the offerings and repentance of the people and forgiven them their sins: "At the door of the tabernacle of the congregation before the Lord: where I will meet you, to speak there unto thee" (Exodus 29:42). The *kapporeth* is usually assumed to be the lid of the Ark, yet it fits much better with the front, since one stands before it.[13] The Septuagint, a much older text, tells us more: I will meet you at the "door of the tent of the testimony in the presence of the Lord, on which occasion I shall make myself known to you that I might converse with you" (Exodus 29:42).

We get the situation in Luke when Zacharias, a direct descendent of Aaron (as was also his wife), entered behind the veil into the Holy of Holies (*naon tou kuriou*, the *skēnē* or tent of the Old Testament) while people waited on the outside (Luke 1:9-10). He did not meet the Lord but his personal representative, a messenger of the Lord standing beside the altar (Luke 1:11), who identified himself as "Gabriel, who stands in the presence of God, sent down to converse with thee and to tell thee the good news" (Luke 1:19). The news was about a great at-*one*-ment about to take place in which the children would "turn to the Lord their God" while the hearts of the fathers would be "turned again (*epistrepsai*) to the children, the disobedient to the wisdom of the just; to make ready a people prepared for the Lord" (Luke 1:16-17). It is all a preparation for a great bringing together *again* through the office of baptism after they had been separated by the Fall. "I will sanctify the tabernacle of the congregation and . . . Aaron and his sons, . . . and I will dwell among the children of Israel, and be their God" (Exodus 29:44-45). They will all be one happy *family* forever. It is understandable that the *kapporeth* should be called the mercy seat, where man is reconciled at-*one* with God on the Day of Atonement: "And after the second veil, the tabernacle [succoth, booth, tent] which is called the Holiest . . . [contained] the cherubims of glory shadowing the mercyseat; of which we cannot now speak particularly." Thus Paul to the Hebrews (Hebrews 9:3, 5).

Commenting on the ancient synagogue at Beth Alpha in Palestine, Goodenough notes, "The scene as designed shows the curtains drawn back at either side to disclose the objects behind them." The custom has persisted: "In a synagogue the Torah shrine is still properly concealed by a curtain, but these curtains in the mosaic are not especially connected with the shrine: they serve when drawn to open up a whole stage, a whole world. . . . So the curtains have taken the place of the old carved screen which seems to us to separate the world of man from heaven. . . . Only the few were allowed to penetrate to the adyton behind. . . . The sense of distinction between the earthly and heavenly [was] still kept." Even more important than the idea that the veil introduces us into another realm is that "the curtains have also the value of suggesting the curtain in the Temple which separated the sanctuary from the world of ordinary life."[14]

And where does the Atonement motif come in? In a stock presentation found in early Jewish synagogues as well as on very early Christian murals, "the hand of God is represented, but could not be called that explicitly, and instead of the heavenly utterance, the *bath kol* [echo, distant voice, whisper] is given."[15] From the hand "radiate beams of light."[16] "To show the hand and light thus emerging from central darkness," writes Goodenough, "is as near as one could come in conservative Judaism to depicting God himself."[17] In early Christian representations the hand of God reaching through the veil is grasped by the initiate or human spirit who is being caught up into the presence of the Lord.[18]

Philo of Alexandria, who for all his philosophizing had a thorough knowledge of Jewish customs, compares all the hangings of the tabernacle with the main veil: "But in a sense the curtains also are veils, not only because they cover the roof and walls but also because they are woven of the same kinds of material. . . . And what [Moses] calls the 'covering' [kalumma] was also made with the same materials as the veil, . . . placed . . . so that no unconsecrated person should get even a distant view of the holy precincts."[19] The material makes it the cosmic veil, the four colors being "equal in number to the elements . . . out of which the earth was made, and with a definite relation to those elements. . . . For it was necessary that in framing the temple of man's making, dedicated to the Father and Ruler of All, he should take substances like those with which that Ruler made the All. The tabernacle, then, was constructed to resemble a sacred temple in the way described."[20]

Ordinances

This yearly rite of atonement included the *teshuvah*, a "return to God, repentance."[21] The prophets repeatedly invite Israel to return to God, who is waiting with open arms to receive them if only they will repent (Jeremiah 3:14; Leviticus 16:30). They not only return and are welcomed in, but they also sit down, and that is the *yeshivah*, " 1) *sitting, rest*, 2) *settlement, dwelling*, . . . 3) . . . session, council, . . . court";[22] the meanings all combine in the *Yeshivah shel macalah* or *Metivta de-Rakiᶜa* ("The Academy on High" or "Academy of the Sky," respectively): "Heaven (where the angels and the souls of the righteous are believed to dwell), a place of divine justice to which all will be summoned";[23] the root *yashav* has the basic meaning of sitting or settling down to live in a place, *yashub* "seated, . . .

[a] sitting."[24] You have a place because you have returned home.

All this we find in the Book of Mormon. Along with the embrace already mentioned, we find the formula "have place" used in exactly the same sense (Alma 5:25; cf. Mosiah 26:23-24, "a place at my right hand"; Enos 1:27, "there is a place prepared for you, in the mansions of my father," and so on). Thus Nephi promises Zoram that if he goes down to his father's tent, "if thou wilt go down into the wilderness to my father, thou shalt have place with us" (1 Nephi 4:34). This is the metaphor that Alma uses, combining the *yashuv* and *yeshivah* in proper order: "Do ye suppose that such an one can have a place to sit down in the kingdom of God, with Abraham, with Isaac, and with Jacob, and also all the holy prophets, whose garments are cleansed and are spotless, pure and white?" (Alma 5:24). Need we recall that it was on the Day of Atonement that the priest entered the tent and that the people's garments were all made white by the atoning sacrifice of the Lamb? Alma continues, "Ye cannot suppose that such can have place in the kingdom of heaven" (Alma 5:25), and in the next verse he adds a most significant thing: "And now behold, I say unto you, my brethren, if ye have experienced a change of heart, and if ye have felt to sing the song of redeeming love, I would ask, can ye feel so now?" (Alma 5:26). In the next verse he asks again if their garments "have been cleansed and made white through the blood of Christ, who will come to redeem his people from their sins?" (Alma 5:27).

The Song of Redeeming Love

Of particular interest here is the song of redeeming love, which we hear resounding in the oldest known synagogue, the ruin of Dura Europos, discovered in 1932 and well preserved by the sands since its destruction in A.D. 256. The focal point of the assembly hall was the niche

thought to contain the Torah Roll, the synagogue equivalent of the Holy of Holies. Immediately above the niche
was painted "a great tree, rising nearly to the ceiling, . . . without grapes (and thus called a 'tree-vine')."
According to the Jewish scholars, "the tree led to the great
throne above" under the high ceiling. On the panel immediately above the niche on one side of the tree trunk is
depicted the sacrifice of Isaac, the *akedah* for the Day of
Atonement. On the other side we see "Jacob . . . blessing
his twelve sons." Some lions had been painted over to
accommodate this picture. Another panel shows Jacob
"bless[ing] Ephraim and Manasseh in the presence of Joseph."[25]

Along with the Old Testament figures we see felines
and masks of Dionysus and fertility symbols of Demeter.[26]
In the midst of the tree are mingled various birds and
animals, and there above them sits Orpheus playing his
harp. His music brings all things into love and harmony,
and Jewish scholars suggest that here he may represent
David, "who saved Israel through his music."[27] Music is
certainly the theme. Every figure in the elaborate display
is facing the viewer full-face, and they seem to have their
mouths open as if they are all singing together. The Orphic
motifs are found in other synagogues as well.[28] But how
does this pagan theme relate to the Day of Atonement?
The connection is found in the New Testament word for
the *kapporeth*, or mercy seat of the Day of Atonement. In
the Greek, both of the Old Testament (Septuagint) and the
New, the *kapporeth* is called the *hilastērion*, literally the place
of the *hilaria*. *Hilaria* is the same word in Greek and Latin,
from which we get our *hilarious*. *Hilastērion* is the word
used by Paul for "atonement" in his address to the Romans
(Romans 3:25), since the Romans would understand it. The
Roman writer Macrobius tells us that the *hilaria* was held
at the Spring Equinox to celebrate the revival of life with
the new vegetation year. The Mater Dea and Attis preside,

he says, the very figures we find at Dura as Dionysus and Demeter, and the latter is drawn by her lions.[29] Another Roman tells us that on that occasion Orpheus was regarded as the king of the *primum regnum*, the primal god and creator.[30]

The *hilaria* was the occasion on which all the world joined in the great creation hymn, as they burst into a spontaneous song of praise recalling the first creation "when the morning stars sang together, and all the sons of God shouted for joy" (Job 38:7). That song of creation has left its mark throughout the literature of the ancient world.[31]

The mingling of pagan with Jewish and Christian symbols in the early art of the synagogue and the church (Marucci's Manual) was long discounted as "purely decorative," an explanation that was soon discredited by the evidence.[32] As Goodenough sees it, "Dura presented its Old Testament scenes clustered about a great vine over the Torah shrine, a vine in which Orpheus played his lyre to the animals, while numerous other pagan symbols appeared in various parts of the room. The two, the pagan symbols and the Old Testament illustrations, could not be separated."[33]

The *Apostolic Constitutions*, one of the earliest Christian writings, mingles early Jewish and Christian formulas with strong predominance of the former. Here the bishop leads the congregation in the litany, praising the "Creator and Savior, rich in love, long-suffering; who leads the chorus of mercy; always mindful of the salvation of thy creatures. . . . The rolling sea . . . sustaining countless forms of life . . . instructs all thy creatures to shout: 'How exalted are thy works, O Lord!' All things hast thou created in wisdom, . . . the holy Seraphin along with the Cherubim; . . . with unwearied voices cry, Holy, Holy, Holy is the Lord of hosts.' " It is the old Hebrew *qadosh, qadosh, qadosh* (cf. Greek *trishagion*, "thrice holy"), found in Isaiah

6:3, as all Israel and the Church unite their voices, "and the power below heaven sing," as the stars join in "this Hymn of the cosmos to God's bounty and love."[34] "Israel thy earthly church, . . . gather together in one [*hamillomēnē*] by the powers under heaven by day and night with a full heart and willing spirit sings the hymn." The four elements join in, "The creatures praise Him who gave them the breath of life, and the trees Him who caused them to spring up. Whatsoever things exist by thy word testify to the might of thy power. Hence it behooves every man to feel in his heart to send up a song to thee through Christ for the sake of all; for thou art kind in thy benefactions and generous in thy compassion."[35] As Alma puts it: "My brethren, . . . if ye have felt to sing the song of redeeming love, I would ask, can ye feel so now?" (Alma 5:26). And John tells us that "they sung as it were a new song before the throne, . . . and no man could learn that song but the hundred and forty and four thousand, which were redeemed from the earth" (Revelation 14:3). The theme was renewal and liberation, which was also the theme of the *hilaria* at the time of the Saturnalia. The 144,000 are another striking example of at-*one*-ment.

Temple and Atonement

The word *atonement* appears only once in the New Testament, but 127 times in the Old Testament. The reason for this is apparent when we note that of the 127 times, all but 5 occur in the books of Exodus, Leviticus, and Numbers, where they explicitly describe the original rites of the tabernacle or temple on the Day of Atonement; moreover the sole appearance of the word in the New Testament is in the epistle to the Hebrews, explaining how those very rites are to be interpreted since the coming of Christ. In the other Standard Works of the Church, atonement (including related terms atone, atoned, atoneth, atoning) appears 44 times, but only 3 times in the Doctrine and Covenants, and twice in the Pearl of Great Price. The other 39 times are all in the Book of Mormon. This puts the Book of Mormon in the milieu of the old Hebrew rites before the destruction of Solomon's Temple, for after that the Ark and the covering (*kapporeth*) no longer existed, but the Holy of Holies was still called the *bait ha-kapporeth*. The loss of the old ceremonies occurred shortly after Lehi left Jerusalem. "As long as the Temple stood," we read in the Talmud, "the altar atoned for Israel, but now a man's table atones for him."[36] Thus the ordinances of atonement were, after Lehi's day, supplanted by allegory. Let us recall that Lehi and his people who left Jerusalem in the very last days of Solomon's temple were zealous in erecting altars of sacrifice and building temples of their own. It has often been claimed that the Book of Mormon cannot contain the "fullness of the gospel," since it does not have temple ordinances. As a matter of fact they are everywhere in the book if we know where to look for them, and the dozen or so discourses on the Atonement in the Book of Mormon are replete with temple imagery.

From all the meanings of *kaphar* and *kippurim*, we concluded that the literal meaning of *kaphar* and *kippurim* is a close and intimate embrace, which took place at the *kapporeth* or the front cover or flap of the tabernacle or tent. The Book of Mormon instances are quite clear, for example, "Behold, he sendeth an invitation unto all men, for the arms of mercy are extended towards them, and he saith: Repent, and I will receive you" (Alma 5:33). "But behold, the Lord hath redeemed my soul from hell; I have beheld his glory, and I am encircled about eternally in the arms of his love" (2 Nephi 1:15). To be redeemed is to be atoned. From this it should be clear what kind of *oneness* is meant by the Atonement—it is being received in a close embrace of the prodigal son, expressing not only forgiveness but oneness of heart and mind that amounts to identity, like a literal family identity as John sets it forth so vividly in chapters 14 through 17 of his Gospel (see below).

Borrowed Ordinances

Mention of the Egyptian endowment raises the question of whether the Hebrew rites are original. In the late nineteenth and early twentieth centuries wide-ranging comparative studies in philology and religion made it look as if the Hebrew ceremonies of atonement were just one among many rites found throughout the ancient world by which societies, primitive or civilized, would practice purification and expiation, individual and collective, to enter the New Year with a clean slate, their collective and individual sins having been transferred to and carried by a *pharmakon*, scape-goat, *rex saturnalicus*, Lord of Misrule, Year-King, and so on.[37] Some of these are attested in pre-Hebraic times, and it was assumed that the Mosaic rites were not original but derivative. It must be admitted that other societies seem to share the tradition; the most notable is the grasp of the situation by the Greek dramatists, whose plays in fact were religious presentations, the main theme of the tragedies being the purging of guilt. No one ever stated the problem of man's condition more clearly than the great Greek dramatists. They show us what life is without the Atonement, for their view of life, like that of all the ancients, is a profoundly tragic one.

The standard tragedy begins with something gone very wrong in the city. After all, that is the way the Book of Mormon and Doctrine and Covenants also begin – in the one case, that "great city Jerusalem [about to] be destroyed" (1 Nephi 1:4); in the other, "peace [is about to] be taken from the earth, and the devil shall have power over his own dominion" (D&C 1:35). Things are not as they should be in the world; nothing short of immediate destruction is in the offing. Someone must be responsible. Why? Because things don't just happen; appeal must be made to the oracle. Long before Aeschylus' *The Suppliant Maidens* (the earliest Greek tragedy), we find the same dramatic scene as Moses stands before the people and cries out, "Ye have sinned a great sin: and now I will go up unto the Lord; peradventure I shall make an atonement for your sin" (Exodus 32:30). For they had turned to the golden calf and were smitten with the plague.

But who is guilty? Not just one person, certainly; society makes us what we are and do, at least in part. Should all the society be punished, then? How do we apportion the blame when all share in it? We cannot. The law of Moses insists with great strictness that every individual man, woman, and child, rich and poor, shall pay "ransom for his soul" of exactly the same amount—one-half shekel, no more, no less (see Exodus 30:11-16). Just as sweeping is the other provision that God "commandeth all men, everywhere, to repent" (3 Nephi 11:32) and to keep repenting as long as our days are extended for that express purpose. We are all in it together.

To satisfy both offended justice and offended deity, something must be done. Appeasement, payment, settlement—call it what you will—it must restore the old unity of the heavenly and the human order, it must bring about at-*one*-ment of the two. And what payment or sacrifice is sufficient to do that? The usual practice throughout the ancient world was to sacrifice the king, who after all took credit for victory and prosperity and was answerable when they failed.[38] This is the Egyptian theme on which the book of Abraham starts out, but the Egyptians had no word for sin; even the Hebrew word *khata* properly means "to fail or miss, not to hit the mark," exactly like the Greek *hamartanein* (Genesis 20:6). The Egyptian idea of atonement appears in the regulation that if Pharaoh has knowingly or unknowingly taken life by the shedding of blood he must atone for it (*entsühnen*) by making a sacrifice, "by which sacrifice he is purified of the Serpent which has

defiled him before the Gods."³⁹ That is a long way from
the Hebrew atonement.

As to the resemblances that have beguiled the scholars,
one hundred years ago Joseph F. Smith gave the most
rational and still the most acceptable explanation for them,
since Frazer's theory of spontaneous generation of parallel
rituals is now widely discredited. To quote President
Smith: "Undoubtedly the knowledge of this law and of
other rites and ceremonies was carried by the posterity of
Adam into all lands, and continued with them, more or
less pure, to the flood, and through Noah, who was a
'preacher of righteousness,' to those who succeeded him,
spreading out into all nations and countries. . . . What
wonder, then, that we should find relics of Christianity,
so to speak, among the heathens and nations who know
not Christ, and whose histories date back beyond the days
of Moses, and even beyond the flood, independent of and
apart from the records of the Bible." The scholars of his
time, he notes, took the position that " 'Christianity'
sprang from the heathen, it being found that they have
many rites similar to those recorded in the Bible, &c." This
jumping to conclusions was premature to say the least,
"for if the heathen have doctrines and ceremonies resembling . . . those . . . in the Scriptures, it only proves . . .
that these are the traditions of the fathers handed
down, . . . and that they will cleave to the children to the
latest generation, though they may wander into darkness
and perversion, until but a slight resemblance to their origin, which was divine, can be seen." Which comes first,
the Pagan or the Hebrew version? As President Smith observes, "The Bible account, being the most rational and
indeed [the] only historical one, . . . we cannot but come
to the conclusion that this is *not* the work of chance."⁴⁰

The Competitors

Not a work of chance, to be sure, but were there others?
Is the Bible account indeed the only rational historical one?

These are questions that must be asked, and the vast amount of work on the subject that has almost all been done since Joseph F. Smith made his remarks over a hundred years ago calls for a word of comment. In the nineteenth century, a string of scholars with monosyllabic names—Jones, Bopp, Rask, Grimm, Pott, Diez, Zeuss—discovered unexpected relationships between all sorts of languages. In the early twentieth century their studies were followed up by grand, sweeping surveys of comparative literature, revealing a wealth of religious parallels that set the experts to their favorite game of arguing about where which rite or expression began, and who borrowed what when from whom. It was more than a matter of general resemblances between doctrines and cults: the Hellenistic mystery religions, the Gnostics, the Mandaeans, the Early Christians, the Cabbalists, and so on—all seemed to be speaking the same language. Looking back in time, the scholars saw the strong influence of Plato almost everywhere, but where did he get it from? From the first, the consensus was always for Egypt, but in the 1920s there was a strong swing to Iran, with emphasis on Plato's dependence on Zarathustra. The fad wore off, but still the argument goes on.

What were the teachings in question? The basic ideas (*Grundgedanken*) of all of them are the yearning for return to God and eternal life, which Eduard Meyer, the most learned of them all, maintained came from Moses to Philo.[41] With this went the conviction expressed by Plato that this world is a place of evil from which we are liberated to return to God, this world being in a state of decline toward inevitable catastrophe and ultimate restoration by God.[42] The escape of the individual to eternal bliss is anticipated by such things as baptism, sacred meals, prophecy, and visions or dreams of ascension to the Seventh Heaven. Eschatology and cosmology are conspicuous, and great importance is laid on the office and calling of the First Man.

With such things in common, it is not surprising that all the mystery religions recognized and copied each other;[43] but it is equally clear that human vanity requires that each religion claim for itself the right to be the one and only exclusive original, given to the first man. Indeed, in studying this stuff "one cannot avoid the feeling," as Reitzenstein puts it, "the speculative effort to view all religions as one great unity."[44] "The isolating of separate religions as we present them in our textbooks . . . breaks down completely if we trace the history of a religious idea or concept. . . . What may originally have been Babylonian can become Iranian or even Persian, just as we may trace a Persian doctrine in the end back to China."[45]

But the great Eduard Meyer sees an exception to this in Christianity as a revealed religion. Of course he was challenged; how was it possible for a religion resembling so many others to appear out of nothing? For proof of his point, Meyer produced the case of Joseph Smith and Mormonism. Though knowing nothing whatever of the immense background material brought forth long after his time, Joseph Smith nonetheless put together the most complete and comprehensible exposition of those same abundant motifs in eminently reasonable form. His nephew, Joseph F. Smith, was right.

The evidence that excited the debates of the early twentieth century was almost exclusively of a literary nature, so that the experts concluded that the cults themselves that came from Egypt, Greece, or the East confined their activities largely to the intellectual and literary exercises of individual practitioners and their followers. In either case the Atonement for them was a scenario in which all the biblical terms become lofty abstractions, spurning the childish simplicity of the vulgar. Most scholars attributed this to Philo. The *unio mystica* of the cults and mysteries was a form of atonement, indeed, but with that difference. To the devotee impatient of the promised glory, eager for the great experience, waiting until the Resurrection and the last judgment was out of the question. They were not kept waiting. From the first, theatrical effects were provided to meet the demand—lights, incense, processions, chants, mystifying formulas, even narcotics provided the experience of another world. Immediate seating, no waiting. The biblical terms do not apply here; being born again was a matter of a few days or hours. And then there was that irrestible appeal to the vanity of the average man, suddenly rid of all of his dull mediocrity to become an exalted spirit overnight, like the Marcosians, immune to the weaknesses and vices of the flesh, infinitely superior to all who had not received the enlightenment.

What is so different in Joseph Smith's religion from the others that sound so much like it? The difference is the literal Atonement. It was, of course, the easy application of the rhetorical tropes that made it possible for the Neo-Platonists, mystics, gnostics, and clergy to enjoy immediate fulfillment. It is significant that the Book of Mormon insists not only on willingness to believe but a firm and stable mind to qualify for atonement—no hysterical or ego-maniacal characters like Simon Magus need apply (Jacob 3:2; Alma 57:27; Moroni 7:30).

Another point that places the gospel of Jesus Christ and the ideas of others worlds apart is that concept of sin that I have already mentioned. It makes such a teaching as that of the Lord in 3 Nephi 11:32 ("And this is my doctrine . . . that the Father commandeth all men, everywhere, to repent and believe in me") simply unthinkable to them. In the three degrees of gnostic glory—the hylic, the psychic, and the pneumatic—those who had achieved the final degree were incapable of sin no matter what they did, just as a gold ring when plunged into filthy sewage in no wise becomes impure since it cannot possibly enter into reaction with such nasty stuff.[46]

Joseph Smith took the Atonement back even before

Abraham to Adam. There was a teaching that the sacrifice of Isaac was a great atoning sacrifice for Israel, and Isidore Levi has discussed "the offering of Isaac as an atonement for Israel";[47] Isaac offered himself as a free-will sacrifice on the Day of Atonement with Abraham functioning as the High Priest at the altar.[48] This was known among the Jews as the *akedah*, which means the binding, because Isaac submitted of his own free will to be bound and offered. (It was always a bad omen if the sacrificial victim, animal or human, went unwillingly to the altar.) It has been maintained by some that Isaac actually was put to death on the occasion and was then restored: "And Isaac received his spirit again, while the angels joined in a chorus of praise: 'Praised be the eternal, thou who hast given life to the dead.' "[49] Again, the chorus reminds us of Alma's "song of redeeming love." Though most of the Jewish doctors reject the instant resurrection of Isaac, according to Roy A. Rosenberg, still even for them "Isaac was 'the perfect sacrifice,' the atonement offering that brings forgiveness to the sins of Israel through the ages."[50] The trouble is that Isaac was *not* sacrificed, but another, a ram, a substitute or proxy, even said to bear his name, was offered in his stead, serving as a type of the great sacrifice to come;[51] for long after Isaac, the sacrifice was continued in the temple as a similitude of the great and last sacrifice until that actually took place, as Paul explains in his letter to the Hebrews (Hebrews 7:26-10:22).

Without the temple and its appointments for blood sacrifice, the Atonement becomes for the Jews a theological, philosophical, and especially psychological exercise.[52] What was it then for the Christians? "There is no single New Testament doctrine of the Atonement," writes William J. Wolf. "There is simply a collection of images and metaphors . . . from which subsequent tradition built its systematic doctrines and theories. . . . Tradition has tried to decide what parts of this picture should be taken literally and what parts metaphorically and has developed extended rationales."[53] That authority then lists the ransom metaphor, the buying free of a slave, and so on, in Mark 10:45; this is the commercial interpretation. There is the emphasis on the forgiveness of sins (Matthew 26:28). There is the image of the lamb developed by John 1:29, 36, and Revelation 13:8. The main issue, he says, is whether the Atonement is the completion of the Old Testament sacrifice or something independent and unique.

There are three main Christian interpretations today. First is the classical interpretation of the Greek Fathers, which integrates Incarnation, Atonement, and Resurrection, and uses the military context — the Christus Victor. Second is Anselm's interpretation, in which "satisfaction" must be paid for offense to God's honor, because a son or subject, by the Medieval code of fealty and honor, must vindicate any offense to his lord.[54] The Roman catechism defines sin as "any damage done to the glory of God." Also, Christ's death, being undeserved, has a superfluous virtue to cover all sins. Third is the Reformation theory of Calvin that Christ was a substitute who endured God's punishment for man or for the elect. H. Grotius and Jonathan Edwards propounded the rectorial or governmental theory of Christ's death having a deterrent effect on sinners in the public interest. More recently, emphasis has been put on the "moral-influence theories," that we "respond to Jesus' message and example of love" in our minds and hearts.[55] This is Abelard's "love answers love's appeal," which he intensifies by making the crucifixion an object of such pity as to stir all beholders to reform.[56] Albrecht Ritschl argues that Christ's example inspires "ethical response in history."[57] And so it goes. Vatican II and the Ecumenical Movement have turned back to the patristic writers and Anselm, restoring "sacrificial language," the "Christus Victor," and "moral-influence," with an inclination toward the theatrical, now moving toward "a reformation of sacrificial theory, which [is] fortified by the use of liturgy and . . . comparative history of religions."[58]

The Atonement and the Law

The Nephites lived by the law of Moses, as implemented, for example, by the laws of King Benjamin and Mosiah. Yet they are constantly being notified that salvation does *not* come by the law of Moses: "Notwithstanding we believe in Christ, we keep the law of Moses, and look forward with steadfastness unto Christ, until the law shall be fulfilled. For, for this end was the law given" (2 Nephi 25:24-25). "Wherefore, we speak concerning the law that our children may know the deadness of the law; . . . that they need not harden their hearts against him when the law ought to be done away" (2 Nephi 26:27). For the law is tailored to our weakness, beginning with the Word of Wisdom, "adapted to the capacity of the weak and the weakest of all saints, who are or can be called saints" (D&C 89:3). Merely keeping that, no matter how scrupulously, will not assure everlasting exaltation. Some of the Ten Commandments are for a barbaric people. Do you have to be reminded every morning not to kill anyone during the day, or to steal, or to bear false witness, or to commit adultery? Even so we observe even these commandments only halfway today, applying them only to our friends—it is now acceptable or even commendable to kill, lie, or steal, as long as the victims are the bad people. The Lord summed up "all the law and the prophets" in the two great commandments; if you keep them you can forget all about "the law," for would anyone who loves the Lord with all his heart, might, mind, and strength, and his neighbor as himself ever be capable of committing any of the awful things forbidden in the Decalogue?

Joseph Needham in his extensive research concludes that the idea of a law handed down from above is a cultural concept originating in empires and great kingdoms where the law is codified and enforced by the ruler. Normally, he maintains, people live not by written law but by established customs, as in China, where for ages the people have followed "that body of customs which the sage-kings and the people had always accepted, i.e., what Confucians called *li*,[59] . . . practices . . . which unnumbered generations of the Chinese people have instinctively felt to be right, . . . and we may equate it with natural law."[60] It is the difference between the *ethos* and the *nomos* of the Greeks, and actually the difference is small indeed, since both are sacred and binding. In Israel what begins as the written law handed down by revelation from Sinai must in the end be "written in their hearts" (Jeremiah 31:33; Romans 2:15). Needham quotes what he calls a Newtonian hymn: "Praise the Lord, for he hath spoken, worlds his mighty voice obeyed. Laws, which never shall be broken, for their guidance he hath made."[61]

Here *guidance* is the keyword, for *guidance* leads the way, and that is what the law is to most people. The image is nowhere more vividly presented than in Nephi's account. What could be more natural to a family wandering in the wilderness than constant concern for guidance? The Liahona and the Iron Rod were not the goal they sought but were simply the means of getting them there, like the Tree of Life in the Dura Synagogue,[62] which, as the scholars note, leads straight to the throne.[63] What better guide to life-giving waters in the desert than the sight of a tree? "And by the law," says Lehi, "no flesh is justified" (2 Nephi 2:5); merely keeping the law will not save you. If you cling to it and make it your whole concern, you will find the temporal law cut off, and even "the spiritual law" will leave you to perish, not because it fails of its purpose but because that purpose is limited to getting you to where you are going: "For, for this end was the law given; wherefore the law hath become dead unto us, and we are made alive in Christ because of our faith; yet we keep the law because of the commandments" (2 Nephi 25:25). The law leads us back home; the at-*one*-ment takes place when we get there. In other words, the law is all *preparation*. Everything we do here is to prepare for the Atonement: "Therefore this life became a probationary state; a time to prepare to meet God; a time to prepare for that endless state . . . which is after the resurrection of the dead" (Alma 12:24). The early Christians taught that as this life is a preparation for the next, so in the preexistence we had to prepare for this one.[64] To reach a stage where the test would be meaningful—the plan itself being "prepared from the foundation of the world," well ahead of time and well understood by those who accepted it here—angels were sent to remind men of that preparation (Alma 12:30; 13:2-5).

The Ordinances

Consider now how the rites of atonement were carried out under the law of Moses. Before approaching the tabernacle or tent covering the Ark, Aaron and his sons would be washed at the gate (Exodus 29:4); then they would be clothed with the ephod, apron, and sash (Exodus 29:5), and a mitre, a flat cap or pad that was meant to support the weight of a crown, was placed on his head (Exodus 29:6). The priests were also anointed (Exodus 29:1, 7) and consecrated or set apart (Exodus 29:9). Then they put their hands upon the head of a bullock (Exodus 29:10), transferring their guilt to the animal, which was slain, and its blood put upon the horns of the altar (the four corners of the world) (Exodus 29:12). The same thing was done with a ram (Exodus 29:15-16), and its blood was sprinkled as an atonement for all and placed upon the right ear and right thumb of Aaron, to represent his own blood as if he were the offering (Exodus 29:20). The blood was sprinkled over the garments of the priests (Exodus 29:21), who then ate parts of the ram with bread (Exodus 29:22-24), Aaron

and his sons "eat[ing] those things wherewith the atonement was made" (Exodus 29:33). For the rest of the year,
every day, a bullock was offered for atonement (Exodus
29:36). Then the Lord received the High Priest at the tent
door, the veil (in Leviticus 16:17-19, the High Priest alone
enters the tabernacle), and conversed with him (Exodus
29:42), accepting the sin offering, sanctifying the priests
and people, and receiving them into his company to "dwell
among the children of Israel, and [to] be their God" (Exodus 29:45). This order is clearly reflected in D&C 101:23:
"And prepare for the revelation which is to come, when
the veil of the covering of my temple, in my tabernacle,
which hideth the earth, shall be taken off, and all flesh
shall see me together." What an at-*one*-ment that will be!

In reading the full account, it becomes clear that there
were a number of blood sacrifices of different animals and
at different levels. There is perhaps much that escapes us.
The newly discovered Temple Scroll is important on this
score, describing some things that are quite different from
what we find in the Old Testament.[65] Such freedom of
action makes clear that the ordinances are indeed but a
type and a similitude, and Aaron must continue to make
atonement once a year "with the blood of the sin offering
of atonements" (Exodus 30:10), while every individual
must continue to pay ransom for his own soul of one-half
shekel, the atonement money going to "the service of the
tabernacle" (Exodus 30:16).

As understood by the rabbis today, though atonement
can only be granted by God (Leviticus 16:30), to have it
one must make a confession of guilt with an *asham* or guilt
offering. With the loss of the temple and its sacrifices,
teshuvah was interpreted as a "turning" or "returning" to
the way of righteousness, requiring both remorse and re-
paration for one's sinful ways.

"Judaism maintains that human beings have the capacity to extricate themselves from the causal nexus and

determine freely their conduct."[66] Though *teshuvah* is achieved by one's own effort, "divine mercy is necessary to heal or redeem man from the dire aftereffects of sin"; since sin "damages a person's relationship with the Creator, divine grace is required to achieve full atonement." But while prayer and suffering are required for atonement, Rabbi Yishma'el says for the "desecration of the divine name" only "death completes atonement."[67] The idea that one's death is an atonement is widespread, but since death is usually anything but a willing sacrifice, that leaves much to be required; also, the doctrine of "blood atonement" as understood by some is out of the question, since only one sacrifice was adequate to atone for our sins. You cannot clear yourself of the sin of suicide by committing suicide, and all sin is a form of suicide, "for the wages of sin is death" (Romans 6:23).

Particularly interesting is the teaching of the rabbis that "the dead require atonement,"[68] and since the dead cannot repent they must be helped by the living through charity, prayer, and Torah study. The prayer for the dead (the *Qaddusha* or *Kaddish*) goes directly back to the temple in the time of the Maccabbees.[69] "Significantly, vicarious expiatory significance is attributed to the death of the high priest or that of the righteous."[70] Here we have elements of the rites of atonement reflected in rabbinical teaching long after the temple and the priesthood had been taken away. It is interesting that the idea of "work for the dead" still lingers, if only on the level of good intentions.[71]

As to the Atonement as "the plan laid down before the foundation of the world" (Alma 12:30), that is, when it was approved at the Council in Heaven, this event is often mentioned in the earliest Christian and Jewish literature.[72] One of the most notable texts is the Discourse on Abbatōn by Timothy, Archbishop of Alexandria (circa A.D. 380).[73] When the plan was voted on, according to this account and others, it was turned down. For the earth herself complained, as in the book of Moses and other Enoch literature, of the defilement it would bring upon her, knowing the kind of inhabitants to come; and the heavenly hosts objected to a plan that would cause such a vast amount of sin and suffering — was all that necessary? The Only Begotten broke the deadlock by volunteering to go down and pay the price. This opened the way; the plan could go forward; the sons of God and the morning stars all shouted and sang for joy — that was the great creation hymn which left an indelible mark in ancient literature and ritual. The Lord had made it all possible, leaving men their agency, and obeying the Father in all things. Satan and his followers refused to accept the majority vote; for that, Satan was deprived of his glory in a reversal of the en-dowment and was cast out of heaven, which was the re-verse of at-*one*-ment.[74]

Only in such a context does the Atonement, otherwise so baffling, take on its full significance. There is not a word among those translated as "atonement" that does not plainly indicate the return to a former state or condition; one rejoins the family, returns to the Father, becomes united, reconciled, embracing and sitting down happily with others after a sad separation. We want to get back, but to do that we must resist the alternative, being taken into the community of "the prince of this world" (John 12:31).

Jacob, contemplating our possibilities here on earth both for dissolution and salvation, breaks out into an ec-static cry of wonder and awe: "O the wisdom of God, his mercy and grace!" (2 Nephi 9:8). The resurrection is the first step to a physical at-*one*-ment which has been pro-vided, a resurrection which is indispensable to saving our spirits as well — they too must be atoned, for when man yielded to the flesh at the Fall, it was the spirit that com-mitted an act of disobedience and independence and could not undo that which was done. In the next verse Jacob

gives a concise summary of the situation: "Our spirits must
have become like unto him, and we become devils, angels
to a devil, to be shut out from the presence of our God
[for no unclean thing can dwell in his presence, and being
shut out is the utter reverse of at-*one*-ment], and to remain
with the father of lies, in misery, like unto himself; yea,
to that being who . . . transformeth himself nigh unto an
angel of light, and stirreth up the children of men unto
secret combinations of murder and all manner of secret
works of darkness" (2 Nephi 9:9). Here we have a neat
chiasm, for "lies and misery" of the pretender are in every
sense the reverse of the "grace and truth" of the Son. The
part about the angel of light is important to let us know
that Satan is with us as a regular member of the group,
he does not show himself as a halloween horror; that point
is vital in establishing the reality of the scene.

What is the justification for Jacob's alarming statement
of total loss without atonement? For the answer, look
around you! In the next verse Jacob describes our condition
as Homer does that of his heroes, "all those noble spirits
caught like rats in a trap,"[75] doomed ahead of time, but
for the Atonement: "O how great the goodness of our God,
who prepareth a way for our escape [we *are* caught!] from
the grasp of this awful monster; yea, that monster, death
and hell, which I call the death of the body, and also the
death of the spirit" (2 Nephi 9:10); by this "the temporal,
shall deliver up its dead" (2 Nephi 9:11), i.e., from the
grave; but more important, "the spiritual death, shall deliver up its dead," and that is the death that really is hell—
"which spiritual death is hell." So now we have them both,
body and spirit, brought together, another at-*one*-ment,
"restored one to the other" (2 Nephi 9:12).

And how, pray, is this all done? Not by a syllogism or
an argument or an allegory or even a ceremony; "it is by
the power of the resurrection of the Holy One of Israel"

(2 Nephi 9:12). Another outburst from Jacob: "O how great [is] the *plan* of our God!" (2 Nephi 9:13).

The Plan

To know that everything is going according to *plan* is a vast relief. Yet the word *plan* is nowhere found in the English Bible! Why not? It was among the precious things removed, no doubt. We mentioned in the last lecture how eager the churchmen and the rabbis were to expunge from the record any doctrines of our premortal existence or the Council in Heaven at the creation, both teachings being corollaries to the idea of a *plan*.[76] What do the schoolmen have left in place of the *plan*? For premortal existence they exchanged predestination, St. Augustine's *praedestinatio ad damnationem* ("predestination to damnation") and *praedestinatio ad salvationem* ("predestination to salvation")—it is all the will of God and there is nothing we can do about it. For the original sin makes mankind a *massa perditionis*, incapable of doing good.

A lively debate in the ninth century ended an attempt to soften the doctrine with the victory of "predestination to life and to death"—a victory for Augustine. Luther and Melanchthon issued a joint statement declaring that "everything that happens occurs necessarily according to divine predestination, we have no freedom of will." Zwingli actually suggested a "universal plan" by which God predestined man to sin in order to display his own full glory and justice in forgiveness, but the Consensus of Geneva in 1552 was a victory for Calvin's rigorous pre-destinationism (*supralapsarismus*), according to which God predestined each individual to damnation or salvation from eternity. Rigorous predestination won another victory in the Arminian Controversy, at the Synod of Dordrecht (1618-19), which still reverberates in the unyielding sever-ity of the Afrikaners. It was the issue of predestination that divided Wesley and Whitefield in 1741 and emerged in the 1870s as the Walther Predestination Controversy.[77]

For over fifteen hundred years Christians have tried to mitigate or get rid of the bitter doctrine of predestination, but they have never been able to let it go, having nothing to put in its place. In particular, Augustine and his successors found the doctrine of infant damnation painful — no atonement for unbaptized babies stained by the original sin. But what could they do? The alternative to predestination is premortal existence, a firmly held tenet of the early church;[78] but Aristotle had declared that a no-no when he ruled out the existence of any other world than this or any other intelligent beings than ourselves.

Yet I hear preachers today using the word *plan* freely, and no wonder, for what is of greater comfort than the assurance that what we are going through is all as it was planned, as it should be. What! This dismal routine? *Planned* this way? What is the rationale of that? I shall explain presently. Meanwhile an essential part of life is that all things have their opposites — action and reaction are equal and opposite; and that is a good thing, as the early Christian writers observed, for if we couldn't be bad we couldn't really be good; and if nothing bad ever happened to us we could never know how blessed we are.[79]

Washed in the Blood

There is one expression connected with the ceremonies that seems strangely paradoxical. It is having one's garments washed white with the blood of the Lamb. It is the Book of Mormon that clarifies the apparent contradiction. Alma tells us that "there can no man be saved except his garments are washed white; yea, his garments must be purified until they are cleansed from all stain, through the blood of him of whom it has been spoken by our fathers, who should come to redeem his people from their sins. And now I ask of you, my brethren, how will any of you feel, if ye shall stand before the bar of God, having your garments stained with blood and all manner of filthiness? Behold, what will these things testify against you? Behold will they not testify that ye are murderers, . . . guilty of all manner of wickedness?" (Alma 5:21-23). Being guilty of the blood and sins of your generation, you may not "have a place to sit down in the kingdom of God, with Abraham, with Isaac, and with Jacob, and also all the holy prophets, whose garments are cleansed and are spotless, pure and white" (Alma 5:24). This is nothing less than the *yeshivah*, literally "sitting down" in the presence of God.[80]

Note there are two kinds of bloodstained garments here, the one showing the blood and sins of this world, the other attesting (for Alma expressly states that "these things *testify*") that Aaron and his sons have completed the sacrifice of the Lamb and thus cleansed the people of their defilements, and their garments are white. The blood that washes garments clean is not the blood that defiles them, just as the serpent that healed the people in the wilderness was not the serpent that killed (see Numbers 21:9).

It is on that principle of opposites that Satan's participation in our lives is to be explained. If we can be "encircled about eternally in the arms of [God's] love" (2 Nephi 1:15), we can also be "encircled about by the bands of death, and the chains of hell, and an everlasting destruction" (Alma 5:7); and if we can be perfectly united in the at-*one*-ment, we can also be "cast out" (Alma 5:25), separated and split off forever—"their names shall be blotted out; . . . the names of the wicked shall not be mingled with the names of my people" (Alma 5:57). When Satan claims you as his, there is indeed a horrible oneness; for he too will embrace you to get power over you: Do "not choose eternal death, according to the will of the flesh and the evil which is therein, which giveth the spirit of the devil power to captivate, to bring you down to hell, that he may reign over you in his own kingdom" (2 Nephi 2:29; cf. 1 Nephi 13:29; 2 Nephi 28:19; Alma 8:9). He will hold you in his strong embrace, having a great hold over you (Alma 10:25; 12:17; 27:12; Helaman 16:23). Joseph Smith felt that power, and it was not an imaginary power at all, a power many have felt since (JS–H 1:16). For he "get[s] possession" of you (3 Nephi 2:2), "for Satan desireth to have you" (3 Nephi 18:18), just as the Lord does. So while on the one hand, God "inviteth and enticeth to do good" and be one with him, so on the other hand Satan "inviteth and enticeth to sin" (Moroni 7:12-13).

Why don't we just get rid of Satan? Augustine lamented as an awful tragedy that God had not made us incapable of sinning—*o miseria necessitas, non posse non peccandi*. But as Irenaeus pointed out much earlier, without some kind of a test we could not prove ourselves good or bad, never being obliged to choose between the two.[81] If a probation on earth is to have meaning, then there "must needs be that there is an opposition in all things" (2 Nephi 2:11, 15). So, says Lehi, we must take a turn at resisting various enticements (2 Nephi 2:16, 21). Lehi knew the old literature: "That an angel . . . had fallen from heaven; wherefore, he became a devil, having sought that which was evil before God" and then proceeded to administer temptation, deception, and misery to the human race (2 Nephi 2:17-18).

Is there any evidence for that? Well, why is the world full of misery? Who wants it? And yet someone seems to be pushing it on us all the time. His system works beautifully, and so he rules to this day on this earth (1 Nephi 13:29; John 12:31; 14:30), but it is our privilege to rise above his viciousness and our own weakness by repentance; and now comes one of the most heartening and encouraging verses in the Book of Mormon: the way is wide open and God "commandeth all men, everywhere, to repent" (3 Nephi 11:32)—all men all the time. In fact, our lives have been prolonged beyond the age of procreation for the spe-

THE MEANING OF THE ATONEMENT

cific purpose of giving us more golden opportunities to repent: "The days of the children of men were prolonged, according to will of God, that they might repent while in the flesh," all living in "a state of probation, and their time was lengthened," to give them every possible chance, for otherwise "they were lost" (2 Nephi 2:21). So "all men must repent" and keep repenting as long as they live, for who would throw away that generous extension?

Lehi goes on to tell us that Adam interrupted an eternal existence to get himself into the predicament that we are in (2 Nephi 2:22). For this the Christians execrate his name, him who "brought death into the world and all our woes." But he brought something much better than that; verse 25 is perhaps the best known statement in the Book of Mormon: "Adam fell that men might be; and men are, that they might have joy" (2 Nephi 2:25). Humans, "redeemed from the fall, . . . have become free forever, knowing good from evil; to act for themselves and not to be acted upon, . . . free according to the flesh; . . . free to choose liberty and eternal life, . . . or to choose captivity and [eternal] death" in the power of one who "seeketh that all men might be miserable like unto himself" (2 Nephi 2:26-27). He has that "power to captivate" because we give it to him (2 Nephi 2:29). The purpose of the plan, it should be clear by now, is to get us all involved. We are "invited and enticed" from both sides.

But how can I withstand Satan's skillful ploys of temptation? King Benjamin tells us how to go about it, first warning us that there is no other salvation to look for and no other conditions for achieving it (Mosiah 4:8). First, "believe in God; believe that he is, and that he created all things." This does not require suspension of judgment, since honesty alone obliges us to "believe that man doth not comprehend all the things which the Lord can comprehend" (Mosiah 4:9). We can go farther than that: "Always retain in remembrance, the greatness of God, and your own nothingness, and his goodness and long-suffering towards you, unworthy creatures, and humble yourselves even in the depths of humility, calling on the name of the Lord daily" (Mosiah 4:11). Is that asking too much? On the contrary, says Benjamin, never was there such a bargain, for "if ye do this ye shall always rejoice" (Mosiah 4:12). If "nothingness" seems a rather low estimate of the human race, we have the overwhelming voice of the greatest viewers of the scene to confirm it. The most honest and enlightened ones do not hesitate to tell us that we are nothing; and the rebellious and wicked ones are the most cynical and despairing of all.

What are we to do? Lehi explains that if we approach the Lord with "a broken heart and contrite spirit," we have a case, "and unto none else can the ends of the law be answered" (2 Nephi 2:7). This puts an end to legalism and litigation. A broken heart and a contrite spirit cannot be faked or even calmly discussed, and that is a prime point: "How great the importance to make these things known unto the inhabitants of the earth" (2 Nephi 2:8). When all men stand in God's presence to be judged, punishment will be meted out in terms of legal penalties—the law by which we were bound, the preliminary trials and tests to get us to our final hearing, but that is not what the judgment is about. What we are expecting in this final judgment is that "happiness which is affixed" to the law and which is the final purpose or end "of the atonement" (2 Nephi 2:10).

So we also have our part in achieving in the Atonement. How is it all done? The explanation of the Predestination-ists, Neoplatonists, and Moslems is simply that God does it all because he can, which leaves us completely irresponsible nonentities. That is not what we want. We want to be one with the Father, which obviously is completely beyond our present capacity; it is only the Son who can help us: then "look to the great Mediator, and hearken unto his great commandments" (2 Nephi 2:28). He will tell us just what to do, for he is anxious to help us. "Be faithful unto his words, and choose eternal life, according to the will of his Holy Spirit" (2 Nephi 2:28). The Holy Ghost, that other Mediator, who comes to take over when the Lord is absent, seconds him in all things. "Redemption cometh in and through the Holy Messiah," Lehi tells his son, "for he is full of grace and truth" (2 Nephi 2:6). That says everything: to be full of grace is everything good that you can possibly conceive of; it is a combination of love, charity, and joy—*charis, gratia,* and "cheer." It is everything to be cheerful about and grateful for, and it is boundless love without a shadow of mental reservation, self-interest, or ulterior motive, in short, of anything false or untrue; it is all real, for he is full of grace and truth.

The Atonement and the Economy

It is interesting that in the Book of Mormon every teaching of the Atonement includes, as the principal condition of its fulfillment, the observance of certain economic practices. Why should anything as spiritual as the Atonement be so worldly? It is because of the nature of the sacrifice we must make.

If we would have God "apply the atoning blood of Christ" (Mosiah 4:2) to our case, we can also reject it. We can take advantage of it or we can refuse it. The Atonement is either dead to us or it is in full effect. It is the supreme sacrifice made for us, and to receive it we must live up to every promise and covenant related to it—the Day of Atonement was the day of covenants, and the place was the temple.

By very definition we cannot pay a partial tithe—but then tithing is not among the covenants, since it is only a partial sacrifice, or rather, as my grandfather used to say, no sacrifice at all but only a token contribution from our increase. And if we cannot pay a partial tithe, neither can we keep the law of chastity in a casual and convenient way, nor solemnly accept it as St. Augustine did, as to be operative at some future time ("God give me chastity and continency, only not yet!"[82]). We cannot enjoy optional obedience to the law of God, or place our own limits on the law of sacrifice, or mitigate the charges of righteous conduct connected with the law of the gospel. We cannot be willing to sacrifice only that which is convenient to part with, and then expect a reward. The Atonement is everything; it is not to be had "on the cheap." God is not mocked in these things; we do not make promises and covenants with mental reservations. Unless we live up to every covenant, we are literally in Satan's power — a condition easily recognized by the mist of fraud and deception that has enveloped our whole society.

The Real Test

What Benjamin was setting forth in his address to the nation was the only way by which we can have a claim on the atoning blood of Jesus Christ. "There is none other salvation, . . . neither are there any conditions" other than these (Mosiah 4:8). Since "God so loved the world, that he gave his only Begotten Son" (John 3:16), what must we do about it? Nothing short of a supreme sacrifice was demanded of Abraham, whom we are commanded to take as a model if we would have the rewards of Abraham (D&C 101:4-5). Of course, we cannot begin to comprehend the greatness of the supreme sacrifice, but we can make what for us is the supreme sacrifice, as Abraham did when he firmly intended to sacrifice first his own life, as shown in Abraham 1, and then the life of "his only son." Fortunately, it was not necessary for Abraham or Isaac to go so far, since another would pay the price. The Atonement makes it unnecessary, but as with Abraham, "the real intent" (Moroni 10:4), to use the Book of Mormon expression, must be there: "And God said, lay not thy hand upon the lad and do not do anything to him; for now I know that thou art one who fears Elohim, and hast not held back thy son, thy one son, from me" (Genesis 22:12). A ram was substituted, which in the rites of atonement became forever after the similitude of sacrifice of the Only Begotten. Fortunately for us the Lord has paid the price for us, too. Here let us repeat that no "blood atonement" is required of us, since the sacrifice of our own lives "if necessary" has nothing to do with atonement for our sins, for which only one sacrifice could pay, but is expressly required only if it should be necessary in the course of building up and defending the kingdom of God on the earth, which is another thing. The point of all this is that atonement requires of the beneficiary nothing less than willingness to part with his most precious possession.

Joined with the law of sacrifice is the law of consecration, which has no limiting "if necessary" clause; we agree to it unconditionally here and now. It represents our contribution to our salvation. The same rule applied in Israel. On the tenth day of the seventh month, the Day of Atonement, was held the great assembly of the entire nation, "an holy convocation . . . [to] afflict your souls" (Leviticus 23:27), for the purpose of bringing a special "sin offering of atonement" (Numbers 29:11). The trumpet of the Jubilee was sounded, "proclaiming liberty to all the inhabitants" and announcing the seven-times-seventh year (Leviticus 25:8-10), the Jubilee year when all debts were canceled and no profits were taken (Leviticus 25:14-17). This is the indispensable step to achieving Atonement for the people, since it is debt to each other that keeps men from being one: there can be no Zion of rich and poor. It is a depressing thought that the law of consecration should be the hardest sacrifice for us to make, instead of the easiest. But this is made perfectly clear to us in the story of the rich young man who zealously kept all the commandments but was stopped cold by that one: "But when the young man heard that saying, he went away sorrowful: for he had great possessions," and Jesus sorrowfully let him go—there was no deal, no mitigation of the terms (Matthew 19:22; Luke 18:18-30). "If ye are not *one* ye are not mine" (D&C 38:27), and you cannot be one in spiritual things unless ye are one in temporal things (D&C 70:14). Atonement is both individual and collective. That is what Zion is—"of one heart and one mind" (Moses 7:18), not only one with each other but with the Lord. So in 3 Nephi 11, after the Lord had contact with every member of the multitude personally, "one by one" (3 Nephi 11:14-15), "when they had all gone forth and had witnessed for themselves, they did cry out with one accord, saying: Hosannah! Blessed be the name of the Most High God! And they did fall down at the feet of Jesus, and did worship him" (3 Nephi 11:16-17). That was a true at-*one*-ment. Now, the law of consecration is expressly designed "for the establishment of Zion," where "they were of one heart and one mind, and dwelt in righteousness; and there was no poor among them" (Moses 7:18). For that we must consecrate everything we have to the whole, losing nothing, for we are all one. To consecrate means to set apart, sanctify, and relinquish our own personal interest in the manner designated in the Doctrine and Covenants. It is the final decisive law and covenant by which we formally accept the Atonement and merit a share in it.

It is at the climax of his great discourse on the Atonement that Jacob cries out, "But wo unto the rich, who are rich as to the things of the world. For because they are rich they despise the poor." This is a very important statement, setting down as a general principle that the rich as a matter of course despise the poor, for "their hearts are upon their treasures; wherefore, their treasure is their God. And behold, their treasure shall perish with them also" (2 Nephi 9:30). Why does Jacob make this number one in his explicit list of offenses against God? Because it is the number-one device among the enticings of "that cunning one" (2 Nephi 9:39), who knows that riches are his most effective weapon in leading men astray. You must choose between being at one with God or with Mammon, not both; the one promises everything in this world for money, the other a place in the kingdom after you have "endured the crosses of the world, and despised the shame of it," for only so can you "inherit the kingdom of God, which was prepared for them from the foundation of the world," and where your "joy shall be full forever" (2 Nephi 9:18). Need we point out that the main reason for having money is precisely to avoid "the crosses of the world, and . . . the shame of it"?

I once told as a joke the story of a student who wrote in an exam that when we are told that there were no poor in Zion, it meant that only the well-to-do were admitted. To my amazement this is no longer a joke; most students are surprised and sometimes offended to be told that that is not actually the meaning of the passage. The objection to the law of consecration is that it is hard to keep. We want eternal life in the presence of God and the angels, but that is too high a price to pay! God has commanded and we have accepted, but then we have added a proviso: "We will gladly observe and keep the law of consecration as soon as conditions make it less trying and more convenient for us to do so." And we expect Atonement for *that*?! We are clearly told in the Book of Mormon that when God commands us to do something, no matter how hard, he will open the way for us if we put our hearts into it: "For I know that the Lord giveth no commandments unto the children of men, save he shall prepare a way for them that they may accomplish the thing which he commandeth them" (1 Nephi 3:7). How fortunate for Nephi that the Lord did not ask him to observe the law of consecration! And perhaps he should have prudently waited until the coast was clear before going back to Jerusalem for the plates.

The key to keeping this commandment is, of course, faith, and faith is never without hope (anticipating and envisioning the results), and neither of these is of the slightest avail without charity (Moroni 7:41-44). So we pray with energy for "charity which seeketh not her own self-interest" (see 1 Corinthians 13:4-5). For "this love which . . . [God has] for the children of men is charity" (Ether 12:34); without it there is no "place . . . prepared in the mansions of my Father" (Ether 12:37)—that is to say there is no atonement. Charity alone should answer all our pious arguments for putting the law of consecration on hold: "Ye have procrastinated the day of your salvation until it is everlastingly too late . . . for ye have sought all the days of your lives for that which ye could not obtain" (Helaman 13:38). Even lots of money cannot guarantee you security.

But Is It Real?

Alma took up the scriptures "to explain things beyond" (Alma 12:1). Having come this far, I ask myself with Alma, "O then, is not this real?" (Alma 32:35). And I find the answer in Jacob, who faces the issue fairly and squarely by placing the two conflicting views of reality side by side. First he speaks of prophecy: "For the Spirit speaketh the truth and lieth not. Wherefore, it speaketh of things as they really are, and of things as they really will be; wherefore, these things are manifested unto us plainly, for the salvation of our souls" (Jacob 4:13). But most people will have none of this. "They despised the words of plainness," refusing to take the world literally. They are always missing the point "by looking beyond the mark." They want to explore "many things which they cannot understand," and God permits them to go their way, "that they may stumble" (Jacob 4:14), which they are bound to do if they insist on finding definitive final answers to the Terrible Questions in learned debate or even in the laboratory.

The first argument in favor of the reality that Jacob insists on is that it gives us a correct and incisive view of our present world. This is not a rigmarole or primitive mumbo-jumbo; it gets down to the basic facts of life and begins the argument on a solid premise. You do not have to be an inspired prophet to know that man's state is parlous, that life is more than we can handle, and that death is more than we can face. Nothing is more real in this life than the constant awareness that things could be better than they are. The Atonement does not take place in this world at all, and hereafter only when this world is made part of the celestial order. The unreality is all on this side of the great and awful gulf. If there is anything manifestly evident about the doings in the great and spacious building, it is the hollow laughter and silly pretensions of the people in it. Today the sense of unreality is beginning to haunt us all—life has become a TV spectacular to which we are beginning to adapt our own behavior. In this age of *theatromania*, where everything is a contrived spectacle, our lives reflect an endless procession of futility.[83]

Wishful Thinking?

For the Neo-Darwinist Korihor, the Atonement is nothing but wishful thinking, "the effect of a frenzied mind" (Alma 30:16). But as Lord Raglan has shown at length, such a doctrine is the last thing in the world that a seeker for an easy and blissful happy land would invent.[84] The rigorous terms of the Atonement, which demands the active participation of all its beneficiaries, and passes the bitter cup of sacrifice to all of them, has made it unpopular to the point of total rejection by the general public—hardly a product of wishful thinking or human invention! Science itself is more worthy of that description, as a recent statement by a Harvard professor of biology makes clear. Com-

menting on the remark of a political writer that "at least
in the sciences nature sets the terms," she writes: "I am a
materialist and firmly believe that nature exists out there,
not just in our heads [the Atonement requires this too].
So, no doubt it 'sets terms' but not 'the terms.' The nature
that the sciences—which means, scientists—tell us about
is a nature scientists invent so as to provide the kinds of
explanations of it, and uses of it, that the society requires.
Societal intentions toward nature are what shape scientific
descriptions of it, the descriptions, if you will, are inten-
tion-laden. . . . What I am getting at is that science and
the conceptualizations of nature that scientists explain by
means of it are no less cultural products and social pro-
ductions than are economics, political science and philosophy."[85] On the other hand, as C. S. Lewis points out, the
teachings of Jesus did anything but cater to wishful thinking, constantly baffling, bewildering, and antagonizing his
hearers and disciples. The fact that the Lord and his teachings were mocked is strong evidence that they were real
and he was real, for one does not mock a legend or a
figment of one's own imagination.

But is that other world any more real? It is the standard
by which we judge this one. It is hard to argue with the
voices that keep telling us that we are strangers here.
Charles Addams' famous cartoons entitled "What am I
doing here?" make clear both that this is not where he
wants to be and the implied corollary that there must be
some place better. Whence this nostalgia, the "intimations
of immortality," the yearning for the good, true, and beautiful, the ideal which we recognize in Plato's *anamnēsis*? It
is so vivid and compelling that we must actually fight to
suppress it; the whole massive, dismal routine of modern
life is a screen we have thrown up to protect ourselves
against the terrifying reality, too big for us to handle. Many
birds and animals have a powerful and mysterious homing
instinct that drives them for thousands of miles. This is

real. When we feel overpowering nostalgia, can it be ignored as utterly meaningless? With experience our growing revulsion to this mad world is matched by a growing
yearning for another that can become very real for us. Or
is it not rather the young, as Wordsworth tells us, who
feel most out of place and homesick here?[86]

But is there nothing more solid? There must be something up there, many scientists tell us, because there is
something down here. Whatever it was that produced this
astonishing theatre is perfectly capable of producing more
and better. Who will deny that what we have here is a
defective article, a broken off fragment of something
greater and handsomer? We can recognize the pieces, as
Joseph F. Smith said, of a more complete and perfect order
surviving in the wreckage around us. From all of this we
can easily reconstruct or imagine a more perfect antetype.
We would not come down here unless something was to
be done; the work is not finished, the story is not over.
What, say the theologians—could a perfect God have left
anything undone? Even the quantum physicists tell us that
everything that was going to happen should already have
happened long, long ago.[87] And so we have to fall back
with Professor George Wald by acknowledging that the
show is not over, things are still going on against all the
rules, and there is no explanation for it except that there
is something very powerful at work beyond our world and
our ken.[88]

How Much Pain?

Another question that the Atonement raises, which has
puzzled me for years, is that to achieve the Atonement the
Lord "suffereth the pains of all men, yea . . . of every
living creature . . . who belong[eth] to the family of
Adam" (2 Nephi 9:21; cf. D&C 18:11). There are two questions here. The first question is, How is such suffering
possible or conceivable? We are told that as a mortal, Christ

suffered "temptations, and pain of body, hunger, thirst, and fatigue, even more than man can suffer, except it be unto death" (Mosiah 3:7; cf. Alma 7:11). Here death seems to place a limit on suffering, but there is suffering that knows no limit. Anyone who has suffered the extreme of both physical and mental pain knows that there is no comparison between them. Our physical capacity for pain is quite limited — nature's defenses take over and we black out. But what about the reach of imagination, comprehension, or surmise — to such things there is no limit. However great the physical pain, it was not that which atoned for our sins, "for behold, blood cometh from every pore, so great shall be his anguish for the wickedness and the abominations of his people" (Mosiah 3:7; cf. D&C 19:18). This was the cause of a suffering of which we cannot conceive, but which is perfectly believable.

But how could a few hours on the cross be effective through infinite time? Even in our limited sphere of action, one can never know how one's actions affect the lives of others for good or ill. One deed can go on reverberating through the ages; such were certain actions of Adam, Abraham, or Cain. The Atonement was one such act, the greatest, performed only once, Paul tells us. The Catholics think they repeat it literally in the mass. We call it to remembrance in the sacrament. The Atonement is universal and eternal (2 Nephi 9:7). The fifth-century rhetorician Isocrates once observed that if every man in Greece could lift twice as much, run twice as fast, jump twice as far, and so on, the world would be little better off — animals and machinery do the fast and heavy work anyway. But if just *one* man could think twice as clearly as anyone does now, the whole world could be blessed forever after.[89] Here is a kind of action that has infinite leverage, and what gives it that leverage is faith.

Vicarious Suffering?

And this raises the second question: How is it possible that one person should suffer for another? How can anyone else suffer pain for me? Since we are speaking of mental anguish, we can safely say it happens all the time. One explanation of this miracle is that the sight of the crucifixion spurs one to a sense of pity or shame and hence to repentance and good deeds.[90]

The possibility of suffering for another becomes real by the principle of substitution, which is a central doctrine of the Atonement. The sacrifice itself is *vicarious*; as a ram was a vicarious sacrifice for Isaac, so Isaac himself was to be sacrificed for others — by the *akedah* ("binding") he expressed his own willingness to be offered up, and that was all God asked of him. But blood still had to be shed, hence the substitute. So also in that other arrested sacrifice — circumcision, with its real but token shedding of blood. The blood of the bullock, ram, or lamb is the blood of the officiator who lays his hands upon its head. The whole economy of the temple balances justice, which demands fulfillment of the law against the mercy that spares the life of the individual. Is this just a game of make-believe, then? Far from it; the "real intent" of the *akeda* is required of all who would profit by the great atoning sacrifice.

What makes the vicarious sacrifice valid? It is the intent of the ransomed: "For now I know" (Genesis 22:12). As the law of sacrifice teaches, those of whom the sacrifice is required may "if necessary" actually have to go through with it, so that the substitute sacrifice is entirely acceptable if it is made in good faith. That is why the law of consecration is so important. It is before all a test of our good faith. A sincere sacrifice is required of all:[91] "Redeem every firstling of an ass with a lamb [a substitute] . . . and all the firstborn of man among thy children shalt thou redeem. And none shall appear before me empty," all must sacrifice

(Exodus 34:20; 13:13). Finally, circumcision was a token sacrifice, a similitude, demanding the actual shedding of blood, and absolutely mandatory if one were to be united to the people of the covenant and to the God with whom the covenant was made (Genesis 17:10-14).

The Silent Treatment

And now we have another question. What good is a teaching or a teacher that nobody is going to be willing to accept or listen to? What a strange phenomenon! Why is the most important principle of our existence designed to be almost totally ignored? Moses and the prophets complained that Israel did not heed it; John the Baptist and the Savior were voices in the wilderness; people accepted the doctrine for only three generations in the Book of Mormon; the Doctrine and Covenants and the Pearl of Great Price are both addressed to reluctant audiences. And even where the message was accepted in each dispensation, righteousness was soon overtaken by self-righteousness. It is as if someone had died and left us a bequest in which we have no interest, since accepting it would entail a change in our life-style. Who is willing to accept Benjamin's invitation: "If the knowledge of the goodness of God . . . has awakened you to a sense of your nothingness, and your worthless and fallen state . . . and also, the atonement which has been prepared from the foundation of the world"? (Mosiah 4:5-6). Who wants to accept the atonement on such terms? Who would "always retain in remembrance the greatness of God, and your own nothingness, and his goodness and long-suffering towards you, unworthy creatures" (Mosiah 4:11), forsooth? So cool has been the reception of the message that through the centuries, while heated controversy and debate have raged over evolution, atheism, the sacraments, the Trinity, authority, predestination, faith and works, and so on, there has been no argument or discussion at all about the meaning of the Atonement. Why were there no debates or pronouncements in the synods? People either do not care enough or do not know enough even to argue about it. For the doctrine of the Atonement is far too complicated to have the appeal of a world religion.

Give Us Smooth Things!

A religion to be embraced by large segments of humanity must be before all else capable of simplification to the point of nullity. Indeed our word *silly* comes from the Old English *saelig*, blessed—to be blessed one must be simple-minded even to the point of near idiocy attained by the bumbling old saints in Russian folktale and fiction. By far the favorite Article of Faith of the Jews is the *shema*, which declares that God is One and that is all there is to it; a thousand times as a missionary I heard *nur Gnade*, and "God is love"—that's all anybody needed or wanted to know. When a poor Moslem has said *Allah akbar!* or a Hindu uttered *om*, they have said it all. Why the elaborate machinery of Christian doctrine? The Moslems ask, and Ireneaus asks the sectaries, Why can't we simply say that God did it and end the matter? The great Krister Stendahl took issue with your humble informant for approving Joseph Smith's saying that nobody was ever "damned for believing too much."[92] My answer is that if anyone was damned for believing too much then we are all damned, for everyone believes far more than he will ever be able to prove, and constantly shifts ground on his beliefs.

But those who are repelled by the plan of Atonement as too long and complicated—with the Fall, repentance, resurrection, judgment, and the rest—have their own creeds. Ask the Moslem for his: "I believe on God, and on his angels, and on his prophets, and his apostles, and on his books." Why not God alone? Why all the paraphernalia? And why does Irenaeus write volumes on the subject after dismissing the whole problem in a single sentence? Moslems, Christians, and Jews are all "the people of the Book" — a *big* book. Why big? The book must contain something more than epithets for God. One of the main weaknesses of Christian theology has been its simplistic heaven, with nothing but harps and hymns of praise. And predestination, while posing no end of problems, has the sole virtue of being supremely simple: *deus vult; insha'allah.*

The scriptures engage us in a very serious and thoughtful project, but the minimal involvement that makes for popular religion plainly shows that something had been removed which has caused the Gentiles to stumble. It was removed by the doctors with the loss of the temple, as I explained at the last lecture, and that makes it worth the trouble. It was known from the beginning that "the light shineth in darkness; and the darkness comprehend[eth] it not" (John 1:5). "He was in the world, and the world was made by him, and the world knew him not. He came unto his own, and his own received him not" (John 1:10-11). Why bother with this hopelessly unpopular doctrine? Because there are always some who do accept it, "but as many as received him, to them he gave the power to become the sons of God, even to them that believe on his name: Which were born, not of blood, nor of the will of the flesh, nor of the will of man, but of God" (John 1:12-13). That makes them the children of God before they lived in the flesh, and what more consummate at-*one*-ment than to resume their status as sons of God? For their sake it was all worth it. It was the same in Old Testament times. The house of Israel, as Jacob reminds us, "[is] a stiffnecked and a gainsaying people; but as many as will not harden their hearts shall be saved in the kingdom of God" (Jacob 6:4). As for the others, they must be given the benefit of the doubt in the days of their probation: "If I had not done among them the works which none other man did, they had not had sin: but now have they both seen and hated both me and my Father" (John 15:24).

The Power behind It

In its sweep and scope, atonement takes on the aspect of one of the grand constants in nature — omnipresent, unalterable, such as gravity or the speed of light. Like them it is always there, easily ignored, hard to explain, and hard to believe in without an explanation. Also, we are constantly exposed to its effects whether we are aware of them or not. Alma found that it engages the mind like a physical force, focusing thought with the intensity of a laser beam (see Alma 36:17-19). Like gravity, though we are rarely aware of it, it is at work every moment of our lives, and to ignore it can be fatal. It is waiting at our disposal to draw us on. When the multitude were overwhelmed by King Benjamin's speech, "and they had viewed themselves in their own carnal state, even less than the dust of the earth, . . . they all cried aloud with one voice, saying: O have mercy, and *apply* the atoning blood of Christ that we may receive forgiveness of our sins, . . . for we believe in Jesus Christ, the Son of God, who created heaven and earth, and all things; who shall come down among the children of men" (Mosiah 4:2). The blessing is there waiting all the time, needing only to be applied when the people are ready for it.

Reversing the laws of entropy (2 Nephi 9:7) requires knowledge that we do not possess; it is out of our league. But as many scientists have reminded us, whatever put us here is capable of doing the impossible.[93] In discoursing on the nature of the Atonement, the Book of Mormon writers constantly refer to power. "My soul delighteth in the covenants of the Lord . . . in his grace, and in his justice, and *power*, and mercy in the great and eternal plan of deliverance from death" (2 Nephi 11:5; cf. 9:12, 25; Mosiah 13:34). That would seem to be the final word by way of explaining things. The word *power* occurs no fewer than 365 times in the Book of Mormon and 276 times in the

APPROACHING ZION

Bible. The power of the devil is also referred to, but that is only the power we give him when we "choose eternal death, according to the will of the flesh and the evil which is therein, which giveth the spirit of the devil power to captivate, to bring you down to hell, that he may reign over you in his own kingdom" (2 Nephi 2:29).

We have what might be called an aliphatic chain, or rather something like a benzene ring, of power. Does it begin with love, faith, hope, or charity? Yes, for they all work together: "The Lord God prepareth the way that the residue of men may have faith in Christ, that the Holy Ghost may have place in their hearts according to the power thereof; and after this manner bringeth to pass the Father, the covenants which he hath made unto the children of men" (Moroni 7:32, 37-38). Moroni says it begins with love (Moroni 7:47-48), the desire to be *one* with the Beloved. The power source is faith: "By faith, they did lay hold upon every good thing" (Moroni 7:25). It is interesting that though we exercise faith and so can increase it, we have faith but we never read of receiving it; we ask for and receive health, wisdom, protection, the necessities of life, and life itself, but we do not ask for faith; it is a principle that we seem to generate in ourselves, being dependent on some auxiliary source, for it is stimulated by hope. We can "lay hold" of these things only if we are "meek and lowly" (Matthew 11:29), for we cannot create power by an act of will; if that were possible Satan would be all-powerful. "And [as] Christ hath said: If ye will have faith in me ye shall have power to do whatsoever thing is expedient in me" (Moroni 7:33).

If it appears to be begging the question to fall back on power, we are in good company—that is as far back as the scientists can take us too. A recent study, "Explanation and Gravity" by Gerd Buchdahl,[94] will illustrate the point. Descartes explained gravity as a phenomenon "in accordance with the properties of matter and motion." This is supposed to be an explanation of the cause, but by merely substituting the word *properties* for *cause* we have still explained nothing. For Newton, "matter . . . does not . . . 'act,' even on impact"; it cannot " 'act' independently of a non-material source." For him "gravitational action [is] a universal characteristic of matter," yet he "does not . . . claim . . . an understanding of 'the cause' of this attraction, or of its 'physical reason.' "[95] For Locke, it "cannot be explained or made 'conceivable by the bare Essence . . . of matter in general, *without something added* to that Essence *which we cannot conceive.*' "[96] In the end, Newton "contends that the existence of gravitational phenomena becomes rational [and thus real] only on the supposition that they are an expression of divine providence . . . an 'active principle' which . . . operates *continually* . . . 'in preserving and continuing the beings, powers, orders, dispositions and motions of all things.' "[97] In short, we know the cause is there only because we see its effects; and so it is with all the great forces in the universe, from gravity to the weak force.

Going to the Source

The standard guide to the Atonement is the Gospel of John. Four solid chapters, 14-17, are devoted to showing that the Atonement is literal; it is real. It is not surprising that John is the only New Testament character besides the Lord who is named in the Book of Mormon. The clergy have ever insisted that John is the most "spiritual" book in the Bible, instructing us in things that are true without being real. It is true that John is the most other-worldly of books, but it is also the most literal. John himself testifies to "that which was from the beginning, which we have heard, which we have seen with our eyes, which we have looked upon, and our hands have handled, of the Word of life" (1 John 1:1). And it is John who reports what the Lord said on the subject: "Verily, verily, I say unto thee,

We speak that we do know, and testify that we have seen; and ye receive not our witness" (John 3:11). "And what he hath seen and heard, that he testifieth; and no man receiveth his testimony" (John 3:32). How can those who would make ghostly abstractions of such passages claim that they are receiving the witness? We need only compare the technical and legalistic and sectarian language of some of the epistles of the Apostles with the simple straightforward statements of John to see why the doctors of the schools refused to take him at face value. In their world no one could be that naive; John can't possibly expect us to take literally what he says, no matter how strongly he seems to insist on it.

But in John there is no room left for ceremony or metaphysics; it is all real and it is all in the other world. "Jesus raised his eyes to the sky and said, Father, the hour has come. Glorify thy Son that the Son may glorify thee; . . . thou hast given him authority over all flesh so that everything thou gavest him, he can give to them, namely, eternal life" (John 17:1-2). "So now Father, glorify me in thy presence [or by your side] with the glory I had in your presence before the world existed" (John 17:5).

Where were we then? We were there: "They were thine, and thou hast given them to me; . . . now they know that all that thou hast given me comes from thee" (John 17:6-7). "I am asking for their sake: I do not plead for the world [that is the exclusion principle], but for those whom thou gavest me, because they are thine, and everything that is thine is also mine, and I am glorified in them" (John 17:9-10). "Holy Father, keep through thine own name those whom thou hast given me" (John 17:11), reads the King James Version; but in the Greek text there is no direct object "whom," and the word *tereo* can mean to "test by observation or trial."[98] Instead we have an instrumental dative, so we get, "test them on the name with which you endowed me, that they may be one even as we are one."

THE MEANING OF THE ATONEMENT 607

This takes us back to the *kapporeth*, for only the High Priest knew the name that he whispered for admission through the temple veil on the Day of Atonement.[99]

Here then is the sense in which we are one, the true at-*one*-ment. As to the ordinances on earth, "When I was with them I tested them in the name by which thou didst endow me, and they have kept the secret and not one of them has been destroyed except the son of perdition, that the scriptures may be fulfilled" (John 17:12). "I have given them thy word; and the world hath hated them, because they are not of [do not come out of] the world anymore than I am of the world" (John 17:14). "And the glory which thou gavest me I have given to them; that they may be one: even as we are one—I in them and thou in me" (John 17:22-23), that we may be endowed (initiated, completed) to make *one*, "so I have sent them into the world" (John 17:18). "I ask not only for them but also for those who believe on me through their teachings, "that they all may be one; as thou, Father, art in me, and I in thee, that they also may be one in us: that the world may believe that thou hast sent me" (John 17:20-21).

Was the world then to be converted? No, says John, but they have to be given a chance: "Who of you can charge me with being wrong (*hamartias*)? If I am speaking the truth, why won't you believe me? You cannot hear my teaching because you are from your father, the devil, and you want to engage in his lustful practices. He was a murderer from the beginning, and abode not in the truth" (John 8:44, 46). That goes back to the drama in the premortal existence: "If God was your Father you would love me. For I come from the Father and I am going back" (John 8:42). This constant reference to place and motion in John has ever been a perplexity to theologians, who maintain that God must be everywhere, but John will not allow that: "These things have I spoken unto you, being yet present with you. . . . Ye have heard how I said unto you, I go away and come again unto you. If ye loved me, ye would rejoice [they are sorrowing because they do not understand it], because I said, I go unto the Father: for my Father is greater than I. . . . Hereafter I will not talk much with you: for the prince of this world cometh, and hath nothing in me" (John 14:25, 28, 30). How are we to avoid seeing the whole atonement in the other world when we read, "Father, concerning what thou hast given me, what I want is that wherever I am they too might be with me that they might behold my glory which thou gavest me, because thou hast loved me before the foundation of the world" (John 17:24). They are going back to that premortal glory. "And I have made known to them thy name, and I shall make known that the love with which thou hast loved me may be in them as I also in them" (John 17:26).

There are more than a dozen enlightening discourses on the Atonement in the Book of Mormon.[100] None is more remarkable than the impressive epitome contained in a single verse, the conclusion of Enos's movingly personal story: "I soon go to the place of my rest, which is with my Redeemer; for I know that in him I shall rest. And I rejoice in the day when my mortal shall put on immortality; and shall stand before him; then shall I see his face with pleasure, and he will say unto me: Come unto me, ye blessed, there is a place prepared for you in the mansions of my Father. Amen" (Enos 1:27).

Notes

1. "The Terrible Questions" was a talk given September 8, 1988, in Riverton, Utah.

2. The Second Law of Thermodynamics states: "All physical or chemical changes tend to proceed in such a direction that useful energy undergoes irreversible degradation into a randomized form called *entropy*. They come to a stop at an equilibrium point, at which the entropy formed is the maximum possible under the existing conditions." Albert L. Lehninger, *Principles of Biochemistry* (New York: Worth, 1982), 362.

3. Shakespeare, *Measure for Measure*, act III, scene i, lines 129-32.

4. Regarding *katallagein*, see Henry G. Liddell and Robert Scott (revised by Henry S. Jones and Roderick McKenzie), *A Greek-English Lexicon* (Oxford: Clarendon, 1968), 899.

5. Regarding *kaphar*, see Marcus Jastrow, *A Dictionary of the Targumim, the Talmud Babli and Yerushalmi, and the Midrashic Literature*, 2 vols. (New York: Pardes, 1950), 1:661-62.

6. Regarding the Aramaic *kafat*, see William Gesenius, *Hebrew and English Lexicon of the Old Testament*, tr. Edward Robinson (Oxford: Clarendon, 1974), 1097; defined as "bind (. . . Syr. form knots, . . . twist into a knot, Ar. draw together. . . . II. bring together); . . . they were *bound . . . bind; . . .* bound."

7. Regarding the Arabic *kafat*, see Ed Stanley Lane-Poole, *Arabic-English Lexicon*, 2 vols. (London: Williams and Norgate, 1885), 1 (7): 2618-23, defined as "He drew the thing together to himself, . . . and contracted it, grasped it or took it. . . . It [a garment] was drawn up, or tucked up, and contracted. . . . He took the whole of the property to himself." (The general idea seems to be that of an embrace.)

8. Regarding *hëpet*, see Adolf Erman and Hermann Grapow *Wörterbuch der Aegyptischen Sprache* (Leipzig: Hinrichs, 1929), 71.

9. Regarding *captō*, see, P. G. W. Glare, ed., *Oxford Latin Dictionary* (Oxford: Clarendon, 1982), 273; defined as "To try to touch or take hold of, grasp at."

10. Regarding the Persian *kaftan* (*caftan*), see Philip B. Gove, ed., *Webster's Third New International Dictionary* (Springfield, MA: Merriam, 1971), 313, "caftan: An ankle-length coatlike garment, usu. of cotton or silk, often striped, with very long sleeves and a sash fastening [note the garment is drawn up around the body by the sash], common throughout the Levant." Cf. David B. Guralnik, *Webster's New World Dictionary* (New York: Collins and World, 1953), 198, "caftan [Turk. *kaftan*] a long-sleeved robe with a girdle, worn in eastern Mediterranean countries"; Jess Stein, ed., *Random House Dictionary* (New York: Random House, 1983), 208, "caftan. n. a long garment having long sleeves and tied at the waist by a girdle, worn under a coat in the Near East. Also. *kaftan* [⟨ Russ kaftan ⟨ Turk ⟨ Pers qaftan]."

11. Regarding the Arabic *kafata*, see Poole, *Arabic-English Lexicon*, 1 (7): 2618-19.

12. Aprocryphon of John (Papyrus Berolensis 8502 p. 19.6-22. 17; pp. 79-85 Till), in Edgar Hennecke, *New Testament Apocrypha,*

ed. Wilhelm Schneemelcher, 2 vols. (Philadelphia: Westminster, 1963), 1:322.

13. Regarding *kapporeth*, see Francis Brown, *The New Brown— Driver— Briggs— Gesenius Hebrew and English Lexicon* (Lafayette, IN: Assocated Publishers and Authors, 1978), 498; "It was a slab of gold 2 1/2 cubits by 1 1/2 cubits placed on top of the ark of testimony. On it, and a part of it, were two golden cherubim facing each other, whose outstretched wings came together above and constituted the throne of Yahweh." Cf. Miles Martindale, *Dictionary of the Holy Bible*, revised and corrected by Joseph Benson (New York: Bangs and Mason, 1823), 116; "The Hebrew word, rendered atonement, signifies covering; a proper atonement covering sin and the sinner from the avenging justice of God." Paul J. Achtemeier, ed., *Harper's Bible Dictionary* (San Francisco, CA: Harper and Row, 1985), 64; "Interest is focused on the gold 'mercy seat' or cover on top of it. This is now God's throne, where he appears in a cloud [Lev. 16:2] to communicate his will [Exod. 25:17-22]. As the Hebrew term *kapporeth* suggests, this was also the place where atonement was made, supremely by the sprinkling of blood on the Day of Atonement [Lev. 16:14-16]." This notes the contradiction between the idea of the lid or the roof. The original entrance to the most holy place was definitely a veil (Exodus 26:31-33). The earliest representations of synagogues show both the door to the Temple and to the Holy of Holies behind a heavy veil that has been partly drawn aside; Georgette Corcos, ed., *The Glory of the Old Testament* (Jerusalem: Jerusalem Publishing House, 1984), 45 (see caption of photo 64): "Such curtains conceal the doors of the ark in which the Scrolls of the Law are kept in the synagogue ('that you mayest bring in thither within the vail of the ark of testimony')." Illustrations on pages 45 (photo 64), 51 (photo 71).

14. Erwin R. Goodenough, *Jewish Symbols in the Greco-Roman Period*, 13 vols. (New York: Pantheon, 1953-68), 1:251.

15. Ibid., 246.

16. Ibid.

17. Ibid., 248.

18. Hugh W. Nibley, *The Message of the Joseph Smith Papyri: An Egyptian Endowment* (Salt Lake City: Deseret Book, 1975), 244-46, 253; cf. Fernand Cabrol, *Dictionnaire d'archéologie chrétienne et de liturgie* (Paris: Letouzey, 1907), 2929 (figure 988).

19. Philo, *On the Life of Moses* II, 17, 87; for English translation, see Philo, *On the Life of Moses*, 10 vols. (Cambridge, MA: Harvard University Press, 1966), 6:491, 493.

20. Philo, *On the Life of Moses* II, 17, 88-89; cf. Philo, *On the Life of Moses*, page 493.

21. In Jastrow, *A Dictionary of the Targumim*, 2:1703, the first meaning given by Jastrow is "return to God, repentance"; Walter S. Wurzburger, "Atonement," in Mircea Eliade, ed., *The Encyclopedia of Religion*, 16 vols. (New York: Macmillan, 1987), 1:494.

22. Jastrow, *A Dictionary of the Targumim*, 1:600.

23. *Encyclopedia Judaica*, 16 vols. (New York: Macmillan, 1971), 2:208-9; regarding the *Yeshivah shel malah* or *Metivta de-Rakia* ("The Academy on High" or "Academy of the Sky," respectively), "It is clear from the *Bava Mezia 86a* that the two terms are identical. . . . He [God] instructs young children who died before they could study (Avolah Zarah 3b). . . . On the Day of Atonement, . . . the permission of the Academy on High is invoked to hold the service together with 'transgressors.' It is also invoked in the prayer recited before changing the name of a sick person, see *Seder Berakhot* (Amsterdam, 1687), 299-301." "*Yeshivah shel malah* sitting, rest divine court. B. Metsia 86a, . . . has been summoned before divine justice (is dead)," Jastrow, *A Dictionary of the Targumim*, 1:600.

24. Philo, *On the Life of Moses* II, 87-88.

25. *Encyclopedia Judaica*, 16 vols. (New York: Macmillan, 1971), 6:294; cf. Corcos, *The Glory of the Old Testament*, 122 (picture number 185).

26. Ibid., 276.

27. Ibid., 294.

28. Goodenough, *Jewish Symbols*, vol. 9.

29. Macrobius, *Saturnalia* I, 21, 7, in Macrobius, *Saturnalia*, tr. Percival V. Davies (New York: Columbia University Press, 1969), 142.

30. Servius, *Nigidius*, fr. 29a.

31. Richard Reitzenstein, *Die hellenistischen Mysterien-religionen* (Stuttgart: Teubner, 1966), 50, and his other book *Studien zum antiken Synkretismus aus Iran und Griechenland* (Darmstadt: Wissenschaftliche Buchgesellschaft, 1965), 99, citing Macrobius, *Saturnalia* I, 20, 17.

32. Goodenough, *Jewish Symbols*, 1:31.

33. Ibid.; cf. 1:71.

34. *Apostolic Constitutions* VII, 35, in *PG* 1:1029.

35. Ibid.

36. Berakoth 55a in Seder Zera'im, *The Babylonian Talmud*, tr. Maurice Simon, 10 vols. (London: Soncino Press, 1948), part 5:334.

37. Regarding the "scape-goat," or "Azazel," see Yoma 67b; cf. "Noah," 10-11 in Louis Ginzberg, *The Legends of the Jews*, 7 vols.

(Philadelphia: Jewish Publication Society of America, 1983), 5:170-71; *Encyclopaedia Judaica*, 3:1001-2.

38. For an entertaining discussion, read Mary Renault, *The King Must Die* (New York: Pantheon, 1958).

39. Siegfried Schott, "Die Reinigung Pharaohs," in *Nachrichten der Akademie der Wissenschaften in Göttingen Philogisch historische Klasse* 3 (January 1957): 67.

40. *JD* 15:325-26.

41. Reitzenstein and Schaeder, *Studien zum antiken Synkretismus*, 23.

42. Plato, *Republic* X, 613-20.

43. Reitzenstein, *Die hellenistischen Mysterienreligionen*, 27.

44. Reitzenstein, *Studien zum antiken Synkretismus*, 112.

45. Ibid., 65.

46. Irenaeus, *Against Heresies* I, 6, 2 in *PG* 7:1:508; cf. Alexander Roberts and James Donaldson, eds. *Ante-Nicene Fathers*, 10 vols. (Grand Rapids: Eerdmans, 1950), 1:324.

47. Israel Lévi, "Le sacrifice d'Isaac et la mort de Jésus," *Revue des Études Juives* 64 (1912): 161-84; especially 168.

48. See Gerald Friedlander, tr., *Pirkê de Rabbi Eliezer* (New York: Hermon, 1965), 227, footnote 9.

49. B. Beer, *Das Leben Abrahams* (Leipzig: Leiner, 1859), 69.

50. Roy A. Rosenberg, "Jesus, Isaac, and the 'Suffering Servant,' " *Journal of Biblical Literature* 84 (December 1965): 388.

51. See Hugh W. Nibley, "The Sacrifice of Isaac," *Improvement Era* (March 1970): 84-94.

52. Wurzburger, *Encyclopedia of Religion*, 1:494.

53. William J. Wolf, in ibid., 1:496.

54. Regarding "Cur Deus Homo [circa 1097]," see Anselm of Canterbury, *Why God Became Man and the Virgin Conception and Original Sin*, tr. Joseph M. Colleran (Albany, NY: Magi, 1969).

55. Ibid., 498.

56. Ibid.

57. Ibid.

58. Ibid.

59. Joseph Needham, *The Grand Titration* (London: Allen and Unwin, 1956), 301.

60. Ibid., 312.

61. Ibid., 299.

62. Regarding the Dura Synagogue, see Erwin R. Goodenough, *Jewish Symbols in the Greco-Roman Period*, 13 vols. (New York: Pantheon, 1964), 9:78-123.

63. Ibid; cf. *Encyclopaedia Judaica*, 6:294.

64. Discussed in Hugh W. Nibley, "The Expanding Gospel," *BYU Studies* 7 (1965): 3-27.

65. Yigael Yadin, *The Temple Scroll* (New York: Random House, 1985).

66. Wurzburger, *Encyclopedia of Religion*, 1:494.

67. Ibid.

68. Ibid.

69. 2 Maccabees 12:45-46.

70. Wurzburger, *Encyclopedia of Religion*, 1:494. Also regarding *kaddish*, see Isaac Landman, ed., *The Universal Jewish Encyclopedia*, 10 vols. (New York: Universal Jewish Encyclopedia, 1941), 6:273-75.

71. Hugh W. Nibley, "The Idea of the Temple in History," *MS* 120 (August 1958): 228-49; also published as "What Is a Temple," *The Temple in Antiquity: Ancient Records and Modern Perspectives* (Provo: Religous Studies Center, 1984), 30-32; reprinted in *CWHN* 4:355-90.

72. Nibley, "The Expanding Gospel," 3-27.

73. E. A. Wallis Budge, tr., "Discourse on Abbatôn by Timothy, Archbishop of Alexandria," in *Coptic Martyrdoms*, 6 vols. (London: British Museum, 1914), 4:225-49 (English translation on 474-96).

74. Ibid., 480-84.

75. Homer, *Iliad*, I, line 3, *pollas d'iphthimous psychas Aidi proiapsen*. See Homer, *Iliad*, tr. A. T. Murray (Cambridge, MA: Harvard University Press, 1971), 2-3.

76. "The Terrible Questions" was a talk given by Hugh Nibley at the Riverton Stake Center on September 8, 1988.

77. For treatment of the issues and sources, Karl Heussi, *Kompendium der Kirchengeschichte* (Tübingen: Mohr, 1910), 64.

78. Nibley, "The Expanding Gospel," 11-12, 18-26.

79. Hugh W. Nibley, *The World and the Prophets* (Salt Lake City: Deseret Book, 1954), 167-69; reprinted in *CWHN* 3:182-83, "The Ancient Law of Liberty."

80. Jastrow, *A Dictionary of the Targumim*, 1:600, 603.

81. Nibley, *The World and the Prophets*, 166-68; in *CWHN* 3:182-84.

82. Augustine, *Confessions*, 8:17.

83. Regarding *theatromania*, see Hugh W. Nibley, "Victoriosa Loquacitas: The Rise of Rhetoric and the Decline of Everything Else," *Western Speech*, 20/2 (Spring 1956), 57-82; "Sparsiones," *Classical Journal*, 40/9 (June 1945), 515-43; "The Roman Games as a Survival of

an Archaic Year-cult," (Ph.D. diss., University of California at Berkeley, 1939).

84. Lord Raglan, *The Origins of Religion* (London: Wattson, 1949), 25.

85. Ruth Hubbard, "The Laws of Nature," *The Nation Since 1865* (October 24, 1988): 247:371.

86. W. Wordsworth, "Intimations of Immortality," *Poetical Works of Wordsworth* (London: Frederick Warne, 1854), 315.

87. P. T. Matthews, *The Nuclear Apple* (London: Chatto and Windus, 1971), 71.

88. George Wald, "The Origin of Life," *Scientific American* (August 1954): 46, 53.

89. See George Norlin, tr., *Isocrates*, 3 vols. (Cambridge, MA: Harvard University Press, 1968).

90. William J. Wolf, *No Cross No Crown: A Study of the Atonement* (Garden City, NY: Doubleday, 1957), 118; Wolf quotes Abelard's verse (from *The Hymnal*, Church Pension Fund, 1940): "Alone thou goest forth, O Lord, In sacrfice to die; Is this thy sorrow naught to us Who pass unheeding by? Our sins, not thine, thou bearest, Lord, Make us thy sorrow feel, Till through our pity and our shame Love answers love's appeal."

91. Joseph Smith, *Lectures on Faith*, compiled by N. B. Lundwall (Salt Lake City: Bookcraft, n.d.), 58, "A religion that does not require the sacrifice of all things never has power sufficient to produce the faith necessary unto life and salvation."

92. *TPJS* 374.

93. Lyall Watson, *Supernature* (Garden City, NY: Doubleday, 1973), 5, 8; Wald, *The Origin of Life*, 46; John D. Barrow and Frank J. Tipler, *The Arthropic Cosmological Principle* (Oxford: Oxford University Press, 1988).

94. Gerd Buchdahl, "Explanation and Gravity," in Mikuls Teich and Robert Young, eds., *Changing Perspectives in the History of Science*, (London: Heinemann, 1973), 173-74.

95. Ibid., 176.

96. Ibid., 177-78.

97. Ibid., 180.

98. Regarding *tēreo*, see Liddell and Scott, *A Greek-English Lexicon*, 1789.

99. See for a possible example in Gnosticism, 1 Jeu 38-40; for an English translation, see Carl Schmidt, ed., *The Books of Jeu and the Untitled Text in the Bruce Codex*, tr. Violet Macdermot (Leiden: Brill, 1978), 99-111.

100. For example, 2 Nephi 2; 9; Jacob 4; Mosiah 3-4; 12-16; Alma 5; 7:11-13; 34; 42; 3 Nephi 11:9-17; Ether 12; Moroni 7; and others.

Index

Aaronic Priesthood, 422
Abraham, 270, 299, 426;
  literature of, 321-23; separated
  himself from world, 341-42,
  489; dispensation of, 382
Adam: Zion established by, 4-5;
  work assigned to, 10-11, 105-
  6, 126-27, 145, 208; is placed
  in garden, 91, 390; desires
  knowledge after fall, 92-93;
  gifts given to, 126-27, and
  three degrees of righteousness, 308; covenants of, 401
Adam-ondi-Ahman, 5
Akish, 94
Alcohol, selling, 470, 479
Alexander the Great, 278
Amalek, 194, 219
Amalickiah, 97-99
Ananias, 169, 313-14
Ancient texts, 265-70; of Enoch,
  320-21; about Abraham, 321-
  23
Angels: scriptures quoted by, 86-
  87, 295; fearing, 310-12; New
  Testament appearances of,
  383, 560
Animals, salvation of, 13
Anthony, 496
Apostasy, 155; following
  speculation, 345-47; of Adam's
  posterity, 382; the Great, 383
Apostles, ancient: performed

signs and wonders, 310, 311;
  Christ's postresurrection
  ministry among, 312; kept law
  of consecration, 393, 439
Apostolic Constitutions, 565-66
Aquinas, Thomas, 122
Arab custom of seeking
  protection, 559
Aristophanes, 495
Aristotle, 68, 235, 525-26, 549,
  584
Astronomy, 120-21, 204-5
Atonement: answers life's most
  terrible question, 554-56; as
  reconciliation, 556, 560-61;
  etymology of term, 556-59;
  imagery of, 559-60; Day of,
  560, 562-63, 591; term used in
  scriptures, 566-67; rituals of,
  throughout world, 568-70;
  literal, taught in gospel, 573-
  74, 606; New Testament
  doctrine of, 574-75; law as
  preparation for, 577-78; rites
  of, in law of Moses, 578-83;
  economic aspects of, 589-94;
  sacrificing to have claim on,
  590; rigorous terms of, 595;
  suffering of, 597-99;
  complicated doctrine of, 600-
  602; power of, 603-5; guide to,
  in Gospel of John, 605-8
Augustine, 416, 512, 539, 583-84,
  586, 590

Meanness of spirit, 192-93, 218-19, 232, 350-51

Meetings, time wasted in, 67, 281

Metaphysics, 525-26

Meyer, Eduard, 571-72

Military hardware, 161-62, 255, 367

Millennium, perfect unity in, 13

Milton, John, 3, 532

Mind. *See* Conscious mind

Mining industry, 161, 243-47

Mitchell, John, 478

Monasticism, 496-98

Money. *See* Wealth

Monotony: in commercialism, 275; fear of, 276, 442-43; lack of, in perfection, 276-78, 443

Moral life, living, 262, 342, 425

More, Thomas, 464-66, 500-504, 515, 518

Moroni, Captain, 98-101

Moroni (son of Mormon), 85-86, 89, 295

Morris, Wright, 514

Morrison, A. B., 8

Mortality: as time of probation, 66, 586-87; likened to school, 104; joy as purpose of, 106, 587; preparatory nature of, 261, 263; debate concerning, in Council in Heaven, 264-65; activities of, described in ancient texts, 265-70; test of, is desires of heart, 301; economic test of, 434; man's questions about, 542; necessary end to, 554-55; recognizing, as incomplete state, 596-97

Moses: gives law to Israel, 178-85, 212-14; farewell prayer of, 196; warns of curses attending broken covenants, 197-98;

calls for Israel to choose, 199-200, 423; King Benjamin likened to, 224-25; dispensation of, 382

Moslems, 601

Mountains, plundering of, 159, 161

Multitudes, feeding, 146-47, 230-31

Muses, 542-46

Museums, 542-44

Music symbolizing redeeming love, 563-66

Mysteries of Godliness, searching out, 264

Nature: laws of, 206, 236; upheavals of, 412; cultural conceptualizations of, 596

Nauvoo, Illinois, 351-53

Navajo Indians, 453-55

Nearing, Scott, 442

Needham, Joseph, 576-77

Needs: supplying, getting sidetracked on, 106-7, 242; temporal, taking care of, 107-8; trusting Lord for, 115-16, 130, 132; taking in excess of, 139, 229, 233-34, 239, 273, 439; filled through consecration, 167-68, 248, 395; provision for, in law of Moses, 184, 216-17, 430-32; as sole criteria for receiving, 220-21, 227, 239-40, 397; limited, 235, 240

Nephites: competitive philosophy of, 18; decline of, 325-26, 517-18; law of consecration among, 437; recognized limits of law of Moses, 576

Newspaper headlines, 470-78

Newton, Isaac, 605

Nibley, Charles W., 447, 469-70, 527

of, 40-41, 236, 458; rhetoric of, 45-48, 253; equality in, 50, 225, 372, 396-97; seeking, for "righteous" reasons, 53, 370, 374-75; is greater danger than sex, 54-56, 434; power of, in depraved society, 58-59, 94; seeking, instead of knowledge, 76-78, 104, 211-12; Book of Mormon passages about, 95-101, 103-4; scriptures forbid seeking of, 130-34, 142, 315-16; conflicting philosophies of, 134-35, 395; concentration of, among few, 141, 252; cannot buy sacred things, 157-58; imparting, to one another, 228; desiring, as earnings, not gift, 234-35; as end justifying means, 252-53, 286 n. 2; as goal of education, 256-57, 439, 461; Nephites cursed by, 326-27; slippery, 327-28, 388; love of, as idolatry, 333-34; associating, with righteousness, 353, 368-69; consecrating, 388; redistribution of, 394-95, 446, 490; choosing, over eternal life, 403; as instrument of change, 417-19; problems of, throughout history, 463-66; "sanctifying" influence of, 478-79. *See also* Covetousness

Weeping for Zion, 25-26

Wells, H. G., 514

Whitmer, David, 350-51

Wisdom: seeking, instead of riches, 131, 282, 343, 459; seeking, from best books, 296-97

Wolf, William J., 574

Woodruff, Asael, 534-35

Woodruff, Wilford, 156, 353, 358, 364

Word, doctrine of, 267-68

Work: in Zion, 9-10, 79-80; assigned to Adam, 10, 11, 105-6, 126-27, 208; "ethic" of, 48, 236, 403; does not sanctify wealth, 49; true, gifts leave us free for, 101, 124, 143-44; for power and gain, 124; valuing, more than God's gifts, 137-38; appropriate kinds of, 145, 240-41; without profit motive, 168; eternal, 259-64; of mortality, ancient texts describe, 265-70

Workers, exploitation of, 207, 241, 243-47

World: all things in, have price, 17, 76, 93, 127-28, 209, 253, 255; man's, versus God's, 22; coming out of, 32, 164-65, 262, 341-42; hatred of, for Saints, 33-34; forced separation of Saints from, 34-35, 341; Satan's mastery in, 42-43, 80, 165-66, 209-10, 385; goals of, 102, 111; all choices of, are wrong, 112-14, 163-64; Israel called out of, 195-96, 213; temple as opposite of, 262-63; administering things of, 336; wickedness of, in Enoch's day, 403-4; limitations to progress in, 411; as opposite of heaven, 548-50

Written documents, manipulation of, 320-21

Wycliffe, John, 500

Yeats, William Butler, 419

Yergin, Daniel, 514-15

Young, Brigham, quotations from: on beauty, 12-13; on millennial unity, 13; on Babylon creeping into Zion, 17, 41, 334; on making Zion,

.